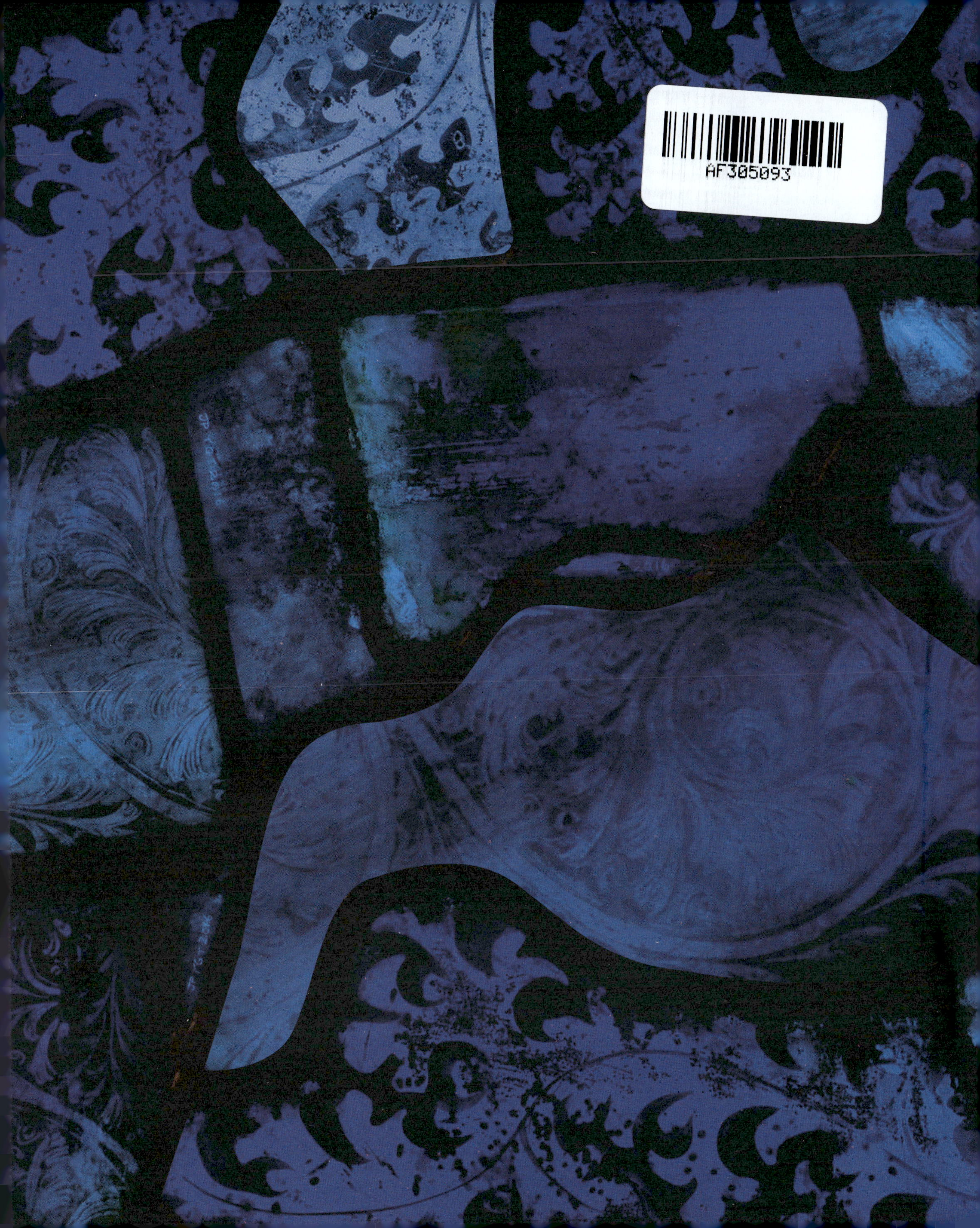

AF305093

The Great East Window of York Minster

An English Masterpiece

First published in Great Britain in 2018 by Third Millennium Publishing, an imprint of Profile Books Ltd

3 Holford Yard
Bevin Way
London WC1X 9HD
United Kingdom
www.tmbooks.com

A CIP catalogue record for this book is available from the British Library.

Hardback ISBN 978 1 78125 978 8
Paperback ISBN 978 1 78125 979 5

Project editor: Pamela Hartshorne
Design: Eleanor Ridsdale
Reproduction by Opero, Verona
Printed and bound in China by 1010 International Ltd

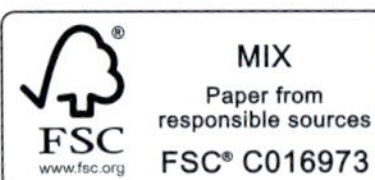

All photographs were taken by the York Glaziers Trust and are reproduced with the kind permission of the Chapter of York except for:

1.4 and **1.11** York Minster Archives
1.5 York City Art Gallery
1.12 The Francis Frith Collection
2.8 Museu d'Art de Girona
2.20 Edinburgh, National Gallery of Scotland
2.23 London, British Library
3.9 Los Angeles, J. Paul Getty Museum
3.10 Oxford, The Bodleian Library
4.1 The Chapter of York
5.2 English Heritage
5.3 Cambridge, Trinity College
5.4 Peter Albion

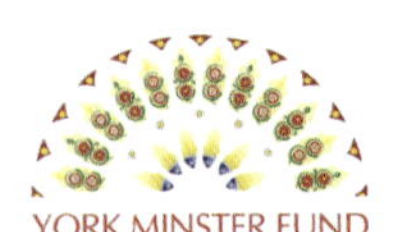

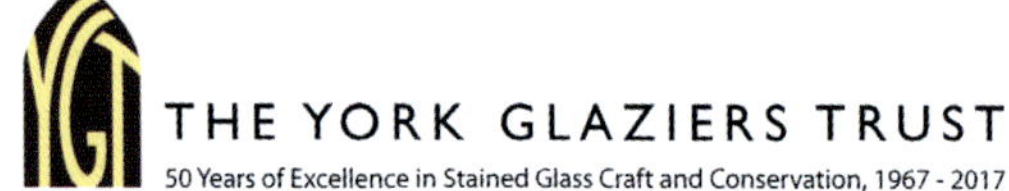

The Great East Window of York Minster

An English Masterpiece

Sarah Brown

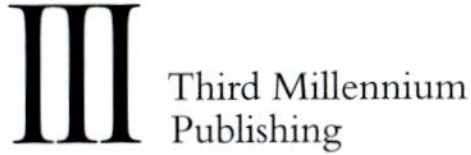

Third Millennium Publishing

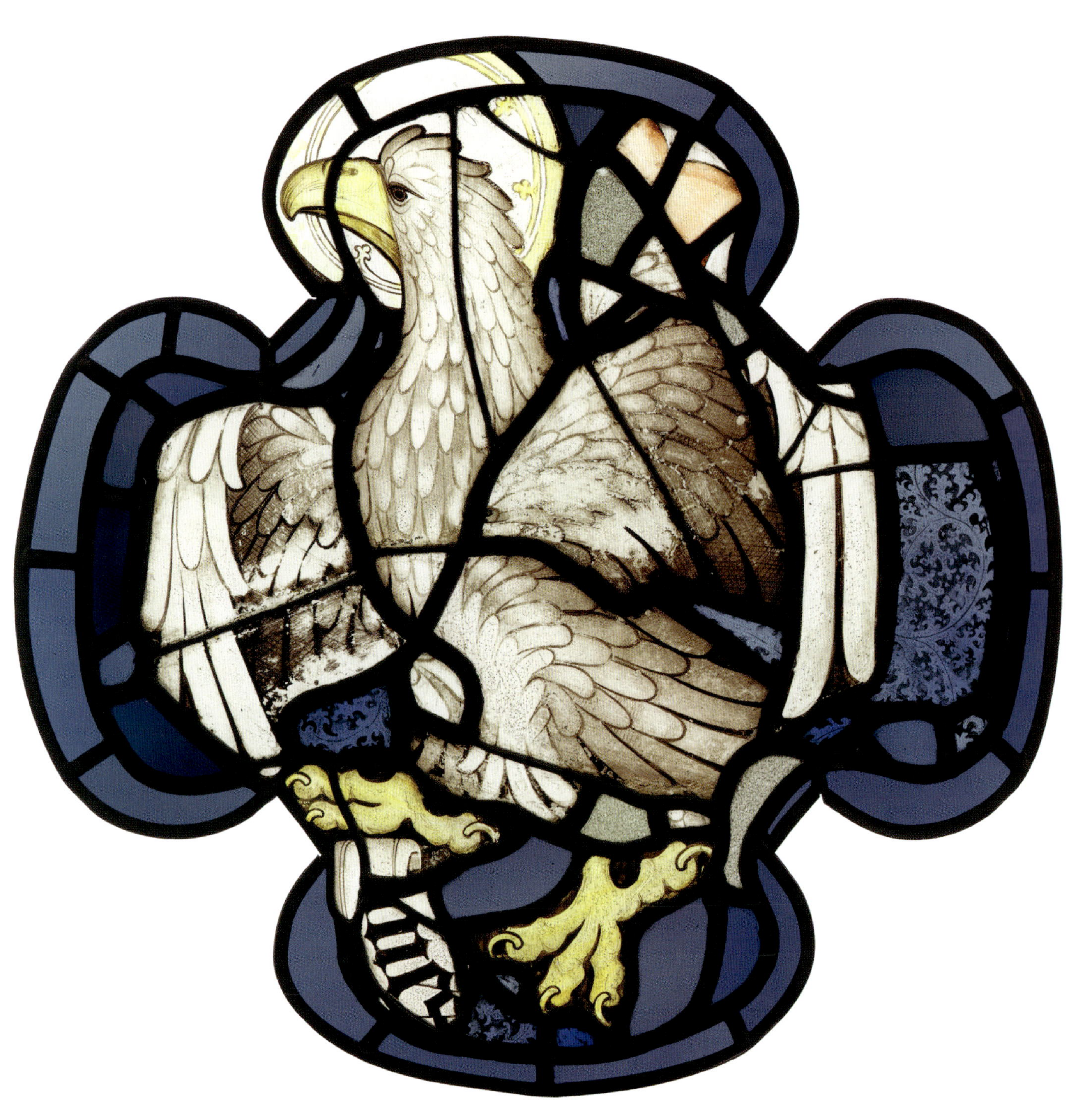

Contents

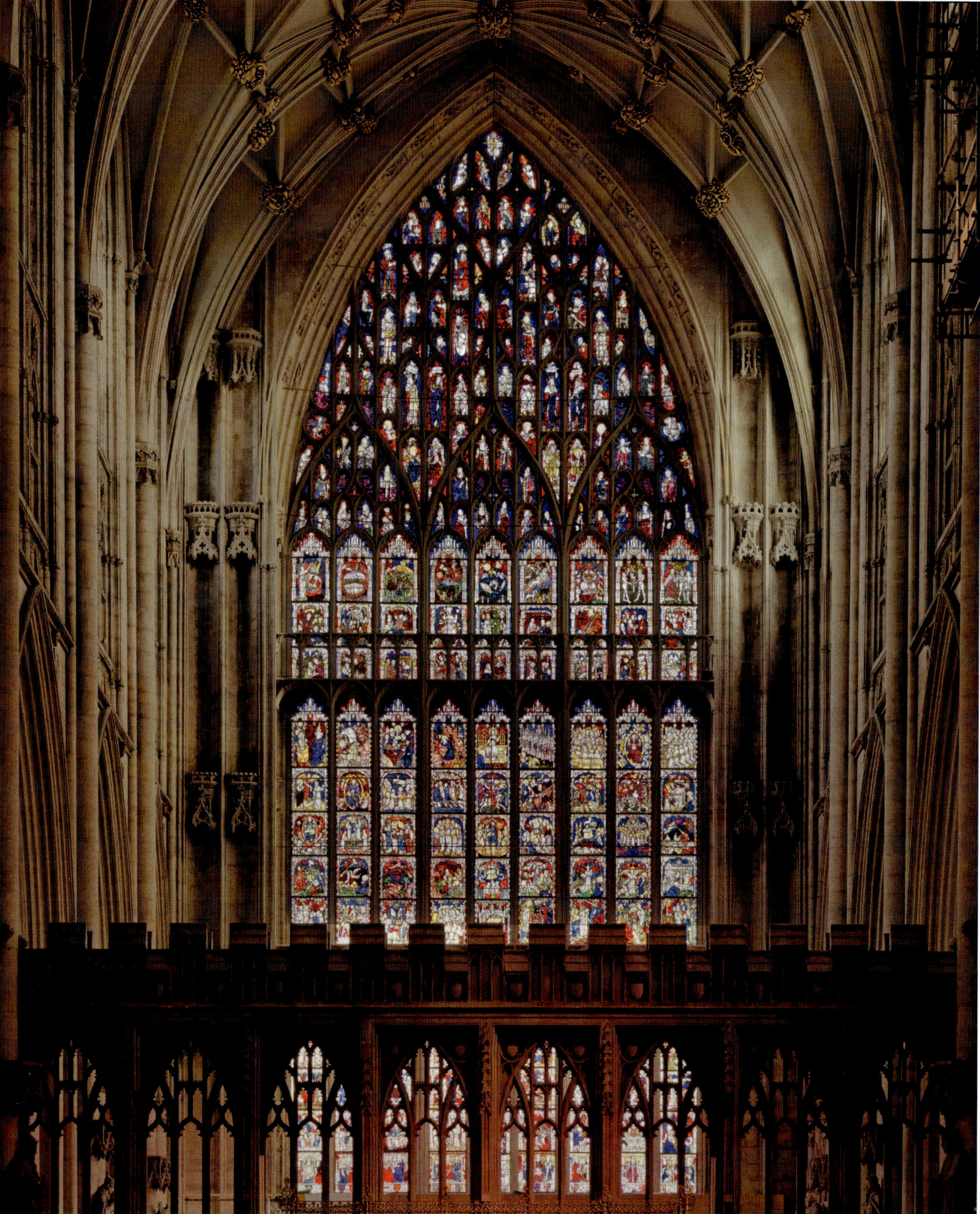

Chapter 1

A Miraculous Survivor
A Brief History of the Great East Window

Adorned with Uniform Beauty: Building the New Choir

On 30 July 1361 Archbishop John Thoresby (d.1373) laid the foundation stone for a new extension to the east end of York Minster. This new building would ensure that the Gothic cathedral was 'adorned with uniform beauty'. Thoresby was initiating a construction campaign that by 1420 had completely replaced the 12th-century choir of Archbishop Roger of Pont L'Évêque (1154–81). Thoresby's project substantially enlarged the eastern arm of the building, a majestic space lit by the Great East Window (Fig. 1.1), the subject of this book, the largest expanse of medieval stained glass in Britain and one of England's greatest medieval masterpieces.

In fact, it is clear that a new choir had already been in prospect in the 1340s, as the new nave neared completion. In 1348 Canon Thomas Sampson made provision in his will for £20 to be paid to the fabric fund, on the proviso that work on the new choir, a project that he had discussed with the keeper of the fabric and the master mason, was begun within a year. The fact that work on the new building did not begin as planned can probably be attributed to the arrival in York of the Black Death by Ascension Day 1349, just as Sampson's death released the promised funds. The Minster's master mason, Thomas Pacenham, may have been a casualty of the plague, which raged until high summer.

Only with the arrival in York of Archbishop Thoresby in 1354 did plans revive. Thoresby, a remarkable theologian and pastoral reformer, had enjoyed an illustrious and profitable career in the service of Edward III, but in 1356 he resigned as chancellor of England and thereafter devoted himself to his archdiocese, where he was in almost continuous residence. While his first priority was the restoration of the morale and strength of the depleted clergy of his province, and the education and spiritual renewal of the laity, he also diverted a huge proportion of his considerable wealth to the rebuilding of the Minster. Between 1361 and his death in 1373 he contributed £200 per year to the project, a third of the total annual cost. By 1371 work on the four eastern bays of the new building was well advanced. The building

Fig. 1.1
The Great East Window of 1405–8, Britain's largest expanse of medieval stained glass and one of the largest medieval windows ever made, dominates the eastern arm of York Minster.

had been roofed and the wooden vault could be raised. In 1373 Thoresby was buried immediately before the Lady Chapel altar, just underneath the Great East Window, accompanied by six of his illustrious archiepiscopal predecessors, relocated to join him in the new building, and each one provided with a new marble stone. We cannot know if Thoresby had planned the contents of the Great East Window that shone down on his place of burial, but it was certainly during his tenure that the decision was made to fill the new east façade with a cliff-like expanse of stained glass (Fig. 1.2). However, St John, Thoresby's name saint, plays a prominent role in the window, and the choice of the Apocalypse as a central subject in it may reflect his early decisions for the building. Thanks to the survival of the content of the medieval contract for the making of the window, discussed in Chapter Two, we know that the stained glass was only actually commissioned in 1405, but how – or indeed if – the window was glazed at all in the intervening 30 years we do not know.

Following Thoresby's death, work on the reconstruction of the east end of the cathedral came to a halt, as funds were in short supply and the project received little encouragement from his successor. For 20 years Thoresby's new four-bay extension butted up against Roger of Pont L'Évêque's 12th-century choir, the two structures either flooded by light from the plain glazing that temporarily filled the window opening, or else plunged into gloom as a consequence of it being boarded up. In December 1394 services transferred from the 12th-century choir to the new vestry on the south side of the Minster, signalling that work had resumed, and the old choir began to be dismantled to make way for the western bays of the choir we see today. This project was only completed in about 1420, and not without crisis and problems along the way, including the execution of an archbishop and the fall of the central tower, events that threatened the political, ecclesiastical and financial stability of the Minster.

In 1398, not long after the project restarted, Richard Scope (d.1405) was appointed archbishop. He was a member of an important local baronial family, the Scropes of Masham, and

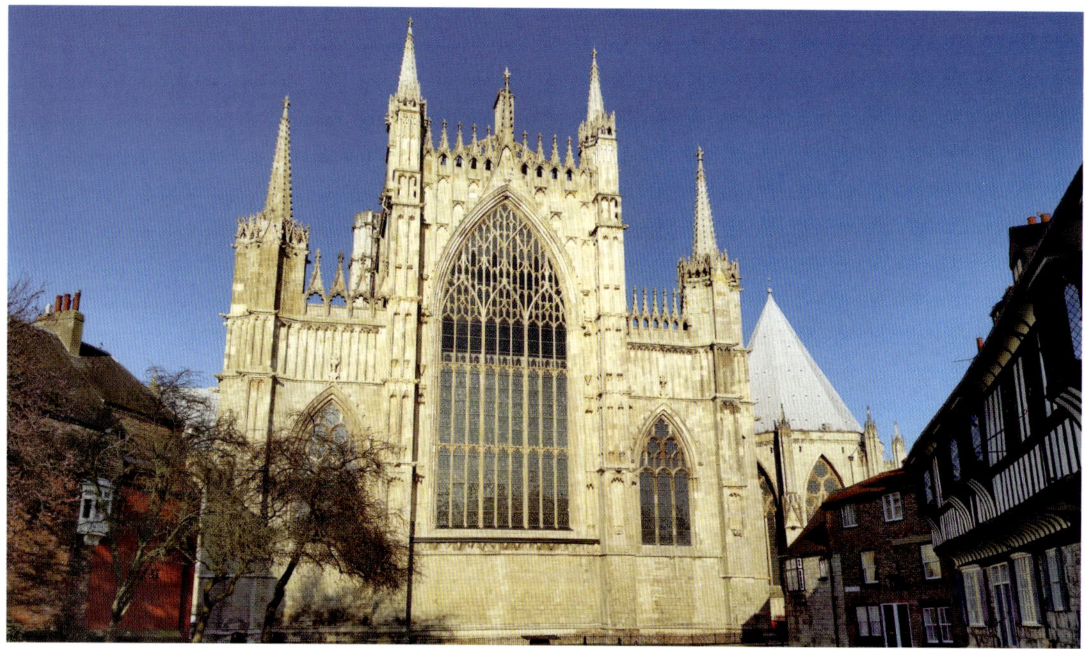

Fig. 1.2
The east façade of York Minster is dominated by a cliff-like expanse of glass, recalling the description of the Heavenly Jerusalem, 'the city itself, pure gold, like unto clear glass' (Revelation 21:18).

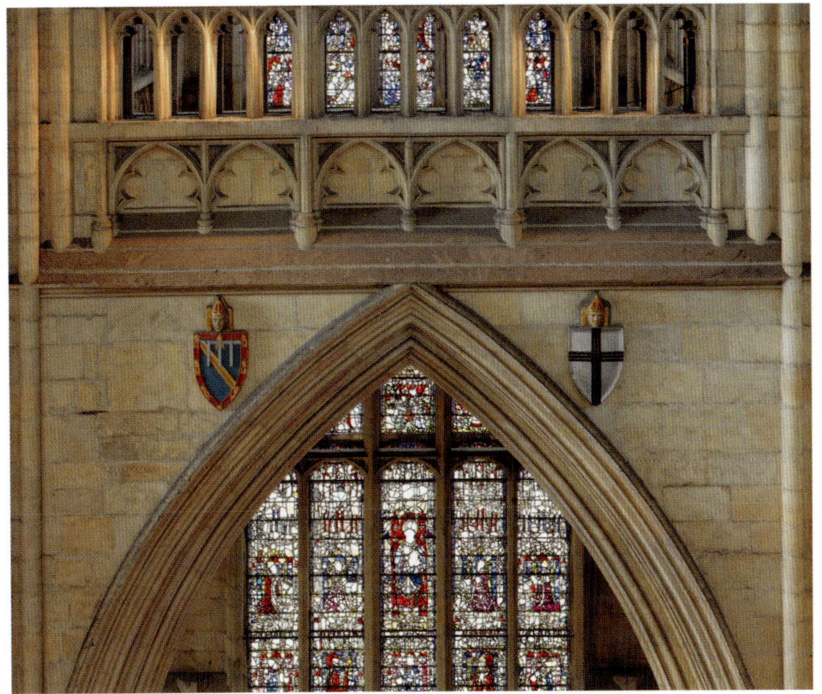

Fig. 1.3
Side by side, carved in stone, the arms of Archbishop Richard Scrope (d.1405) and Bishop Walter Skirlaw (d.1406) looked down on the medieval high altar.

members of the Archbishop's immediate family, who like Thoresby had also prospered through service to Edward III, were to become significant patrons of the Minster as a result of his elevation to the see. As a senior canon lawyer Scrope had contributed to the deposition process that in 1399 saw Richard II removed from the throne and Henry IV made king in his place. In the early years of the new reign, however, Archbishop Scrope focused his energy on his pastoral duties and there is evidence that he also involved himself actively in the promotion of the building project begun by Thoresby. He seems to have been supported in this endeavour by the senior bishop of the northern province, Bishop Walter Skirlaw of Durham (d.1406). Their personal coats of arms sit side by side in the spandrel of the south-east transept arcade, immediately overlooking the location of the medieval high altar (Fig. 1.3). From the monastic library at Durham where St Cuthbert was buried, Richard Scrope borrowed an illuminated manuscript of the life of the saint, the subject of the south-east transept window.

Even though the window was not made until many years after the Archbishop's death, and was eventually to be given by Bishop Thomas Langley of Durham (d.1437), the relationship between the window's narrative and that of the book borrowed by Scrope has long been recognised.

The Great Windows of the Choir

It is clear that by 1399 the task of filling the East Window with new stained glass was in sight. In that year an inventory of the cathedral's building stores records a large stockpile of white glass for the great windows of the choir, presumably the Great East Window, the St William and St Cuthbert windows, which far exceed the others in size. Late in 1405 the formal contract for the making of the Great East Window was made between the Dean and Chapter and the master glazier John Thornton, although its donor was actually Bishop Walter Skirlaw. So, while the majestic window opening was conceived as part of the first phase of construction which saw the complete remodelling of the eastern arm of York Minster, the provision of its stained glass was chronologically part of the second phase of work, achieved only 30 years or so after Thoresby's Lady Chapel was completed. The relationship between the creation of the window opening, its masonry framework and the stained glass provided in the period 1405–8 remains enigmatic and intriguing. It was normal medieval practice to infill the mullions and the tracery head of a window sometime after the creation of the opening in the wall. Close archaeological examination by Dr Alex Holton has identified the telling differences between the mouldings of the sill and outer jambs of the window and those of its internal mullions, which are evidence that this was indeed the practice adopted for the Minster's East Window. However, what remains unclear is how much time had elapsed between the creation of the window opening and the installation of the tracery, an issue that has a bearing on the relationship between the configuration of the stone tracery and the symbolism of the stained glass, discussed in greater detail in Chapter Three. The picture is further complicated by the clear evidence of a change in plan as the construction of the east wall progressed. This allowed the uppermost transom, which also provides a rather perilous walkway across the face of the window, to be positioned at a lower point than originally envisaged. This change altered the configuration of the stone tracery that supports the stained glass and created the critical division between the part of the window that depicts the Apocalypse imagery in the main section of the window and the 27 Old Testament scenes immediately above. As will be discussed later, this does not seem to have been an accidental alteration, but suggests that in this case the masonry was designed to be subservient to the window's iconographic content.

The presence of the date 1408 actually in the stained glass at the top of the window (in panels Z1 and Z2) shows that it was in place by the date required by the 1405 contract, a remarkable feat by any standards. The glazing of the East Window was the first major step to reglaze the new choir, and its subject matter is the key to our understanding of the scheme as a whole, the subject of Chapter Three. The Minster glaziers were kept very busy for the next 30 years. The north-east transept window, dedicated to St William, was commissioned *c*.1414. The choir aisle and clerestory windows had all been filled with glass by *c*.1420 and probably only in the 1440s was the St Cuthbert window finally installed in the south-east transept, ensuring that the lives of the two greatest saints of the northern province illuminated the high altar.

'The Wonder of the World': From 1408 to 1800

After 1408 the Great East Window almost disappears from the historical record, only to reappear in the later 17th century. By this time it had been witness to the dynastic struggles of Plantagenets, Lancastrians and Yorkists which had left their imprint on the Minster, but had left the Great East Window unscathed. The Lancastrian chapter faced the challenge of managing the burgeoning unofficial cult of the popular 'martyr' Archbishop Richard Scrope, executed in June 1405 for armed insurrection against Henry IV. Any plans Scrope may have had to glaze the St Cuthbert window died with him and the project was taken up by Lancastrian Bishop Thomas Langley of Durham, who is accompanied at the feet of St Cuthbert by John of Gaunt, Henry V, Henry VI and members of the Lancastrian episcopate. In *c*.1479 the Yorkist Archbishop Lawrence Booth ordered the removal of an image of the Lancastrian King Henry VI that was attracting inappropriate devotion from the citizens of York, and the scroll accompanying his figure in the St Cuthbert window shows signs of having been deliberately defaced. The upheavals of the Reformation of the 16th century saw the destruction of the shrines of St William and of many other saints' images at the Minster's altars, but there is little evidence of religiously inspired destruction of Minster windows. The English Civil War of the mid-17th century posed far more serious threats. When York was besieged by Parliamentary forces in the spring and summer of 1644, it is said that citizens took refuge in the Minster, praying for deliverance during the bombardment, with musket rounds apparently coming in through the windows. Minster antiquary James Torre (1649–99) attributed the loss of a nave aisle window to the 'late troubles' of the 1640s and thereafter many windows of the chapter house required repair. However, the period is far more remarkable for the preservation of the Minster's glass during the aftermath of the Parliamentary victory, thanks to the intervention of General Sir Thomas Fairfax (1612–71), a member of one of Yorkshire's most illustrious families.

Comparison of the testimony of the antiquaries Henry Johnston (1670) and James Torre (*c*.1690) reveals that two panels in the bottom row of the Great East Window had been

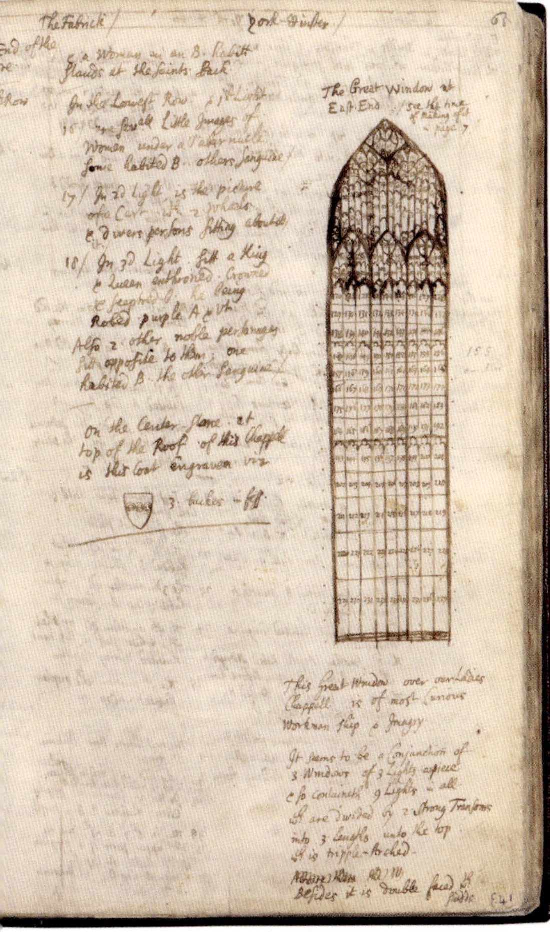

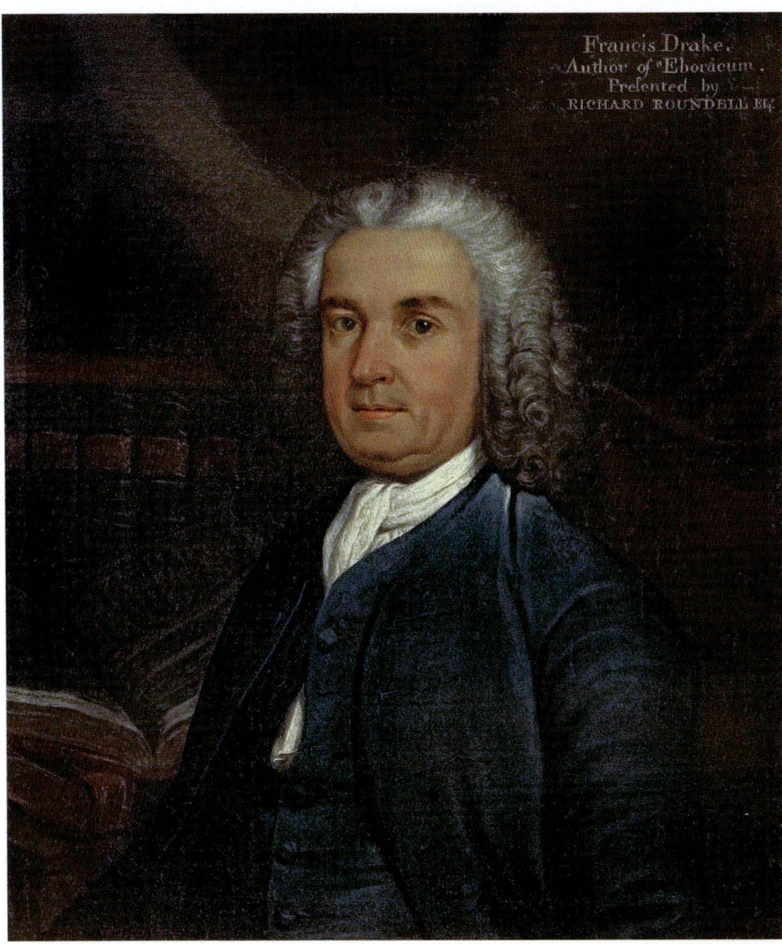

Fig. 1.4
The opening of James Torre's (1649–99) description of the Great East Window, each panel meticulously located on his drawing of the window tracery.

Fig. 1.5
York antiquary Francis Drake (1696–1771), whose 1736 volume *Eboracum* published the first illustration of the Great East Window.

moved, although how this had come about is not known. The bottom row was the most accessible row of panels, easily reached from the floor of the Lady Chapel, and so it is perhaps not surprising that some damage and disturbance had been sustained. On the other hand, Torre, compiling a meticulous panel-by-panel description of the whole window, recorded disturbances at a higher level of the window, in the Old Testament narrative immediately above the transom walkway. Perhaps access from the wall passages and onto the walkway had been achieved and the reference in the fabric rolls of 1581 to 19*s*. 2*d*. for 23 days of glazing work on 'the greete glasse window at the end of the quere' may pinpoint when this occurred. In the great Apocalypse cycle below this, in rows 2–11, Torre recorded only four scenes that were not in their correct biblical order. Once upon a time, this was interpreted as evidence of an undocumented intervention of the late 16th or early 17th century, and Dean Milner-White, writing of the window in the 1950s, explained this by asserting that it would have required releading by the early 16th century. Conservators and art historians now realise that medieval window lead had immense strength and so there is no reason to assume that the window would have required such substantial repair so early in its life. Recent research and examination of the window during conservation has offered an alternative explanation. We now realise that the panels in question have always been incorrectly positioned in terms of the biblical narrative and had been installed in the 'wrong' positions in the 15th century as a consequence of a production error in the medieval workshop (discussed in Chapter Two). It was for this reason that the Chapter of York decided that after the most recent conservation they should be returned to the window in the order recorded by James Torre, the order in which they had been installed by their creator, John Thornton.

It is a tragedy that James Torre's remarkable descriptions of the history, glass and stone of York Minster were never published (Fig. 1.4). However, his research has continued to be a rich source of information and insight for all subsequent students of the Minster's windows and monuments and was extensively mined for information by his 18th-century successors. It was in the 18th century that the window and its creator began to acquire celebrity status. In 1736 Francis Drake, city surgeon and antiquary (Fig. 1.5), published his monumental *Eboracum, or, The History and Antiquities of the City of York from its Origins to the Present, together with the History of the Cathedral Church and the Lives of the Archbishops*. This large and costly volume, priced at five guineas, was dedicated to the Earl of Burlington and was destined for the library tables of its gentlemanly subscribers, a list which included the Archbishop of Canterbury and Bishop of London, albeit not the Archbishop of York! Drake had commissioned a specially drawn and engraved full-page plate of the Great East Window, and arranged for the plate in the specially leather-bound copy presented to the Corporation of York to be coloured by hand (Fig. 1.6). In his text he declared:

Fig. 1.6
A detail from the hand-coloured plate of the Great East Window in the copy of *Eboracum* presented to the Lord Mayor of York.

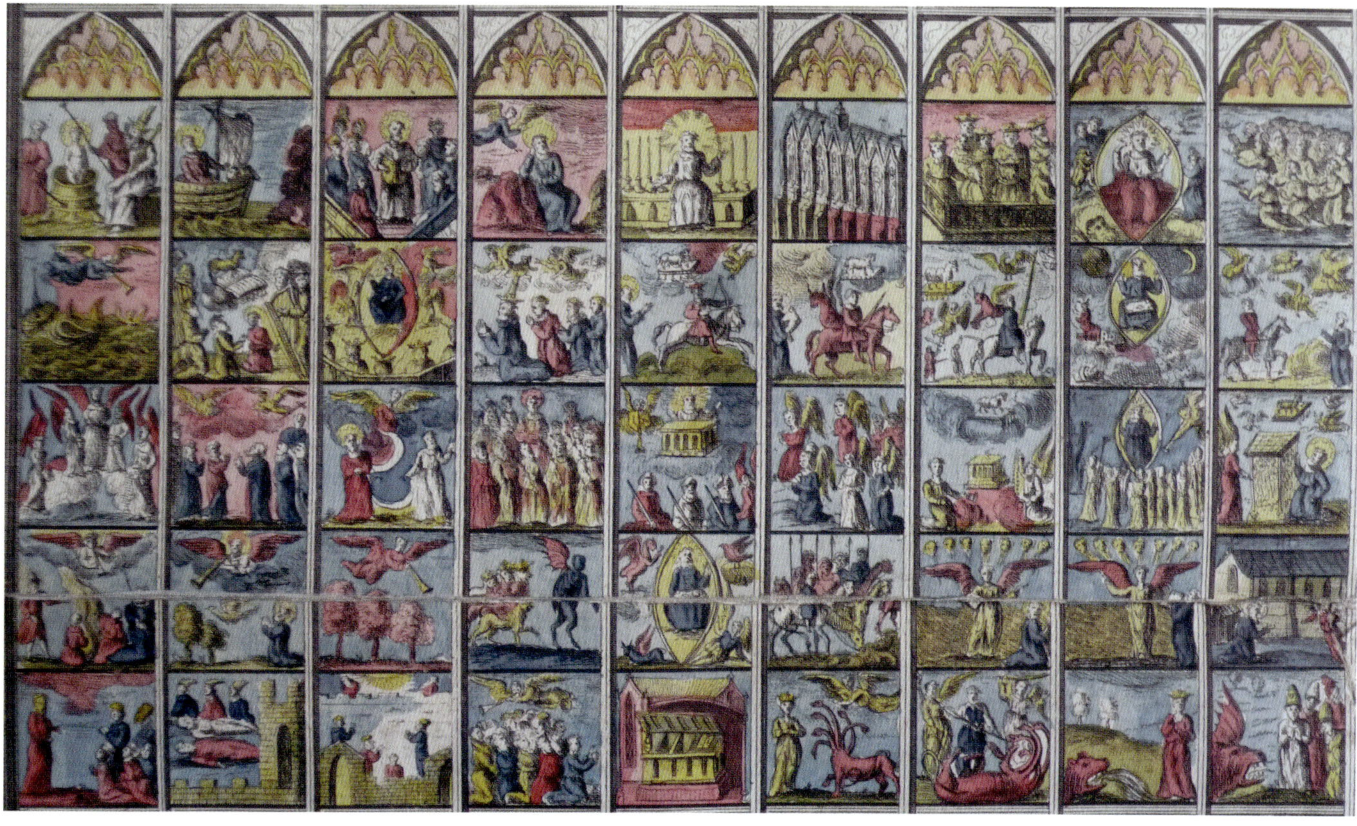

What may justly be called the wonder of the world, both for masonry and glasing, is the noble east window … This window was begun to be glazed, at the charge of the dean and chapter, anno 1405; who then contracted with John Thornton of Coventry glazier to execute it … We may suppose this man to have been the best artist in his time, for this kind of work, by their sending so far for him. And indeed the window shews it. I hope my drawer and engraver have done justice to his memory.

This is perhaps the first public acknowledgement in print of Thornton's role as creator of the window, a statement in which the role of the window's donor has no place. This is a fascinating reversal of the medieval concept of agency, as its donor, Bishop Walter Skirlaw, identified by his coat of arms, and depicted prominently at the base of the window (panel 1e), at the feet of Christ the Judge, receives no mention. The large plate of the window, first published in *Eboracum*, also circulated as an independent image. Perhaps for this reason, the imagery of the window was 'edited' in one important regard. Bishop Skirlaw does not kneel before a medieval stone altar draped in a frontal and adorned with a reredos depicting Christ and the saints, as he does in the stained glass, but before an unimpeachably Protestant, unadorned communion table (Fig. 1.7). While Thornton's artistry was of interest in the libraries of Georgian York, the 'popery' of its donor was not.

While Drake's work was edited and reissued in several editions, its unwieldy size (even in its half-size version) and relatively high cost meant that for many visitors to York Minster it remained

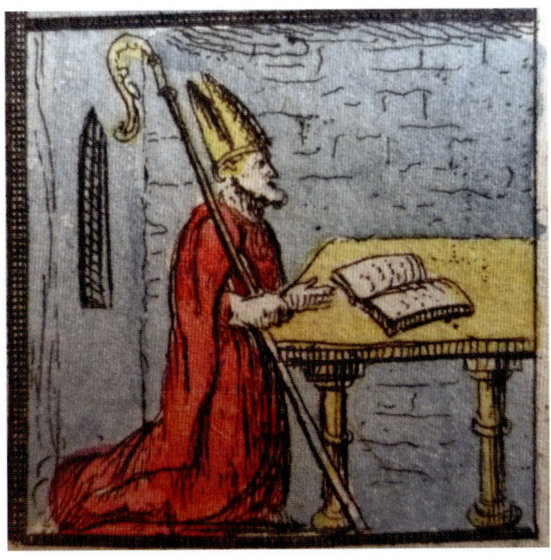

Fig. 1.7
Bishop Skirlaw as he appears in *Eboracum*, kneeling before a communion table rather than a medieval altar.

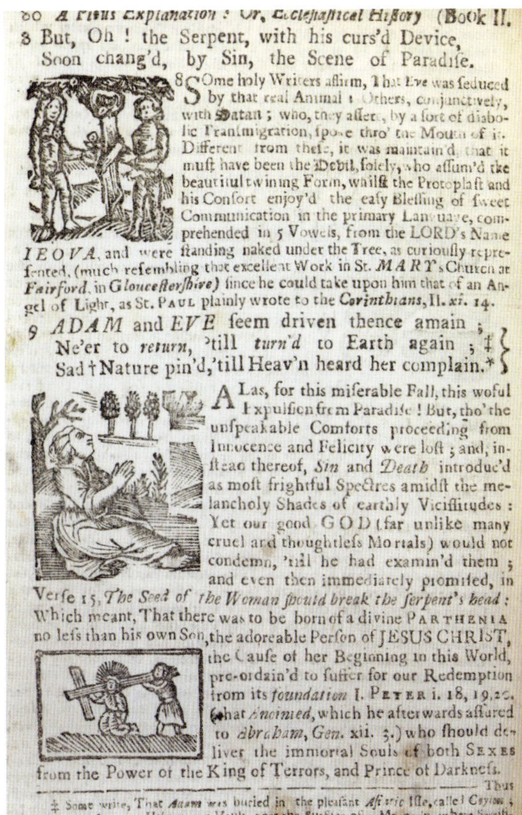

Fig. 1.8
A page from Thomas Gent's 1762 fanciful and poetic *Most Delectable, Scriptural and Pious History*.

a relatively inaccessible luxury item. The smaller, cheaper works of Thomas Gent (1693–1778), printer and bookseller, and from 1724 to 1741 publisher of York's only newspaper, provided a far more accessible and infinitely more portable guide to the Minster and its windows. His 1730 volume *The Ancient and Modern History of the Famous City of York* was printed in convenient octavo size, and 1,000 copies were circulated. The text was in many places indebted to Torre and attempted to list systematically all the Minster's monuments and windows. Gent, like Drake, acknowledged John Thornton as the window's author but overlooked Skirlaw's donation, and his figure at the window's base is identified as that of Archbishop 'Aldred'. The success of Gent's more affordable publication probably prompted Drake to make his own book of a conspicuously different style, aimed at a rather different readership. From the 1740s Gent was no longer the only printer in York and his business began to fail. In an attempt to capture the trade of the growing number of leisure visitors to the Minster, he produced what has been rather harshly called 'his least impressive topographical work', the idiosyncratic 1762 book devoted exclusively to the Great East Window. Entitled *The Most Delectable, Scriptural and Pious History of the Famous and Magnificent Great Eastern Window*, it described (in terrible verse!) every scene in the window, each one illustrated by a series of 'wretched woodcuts' that actually bear little resemblance to the appearance of the glass (Fig. 1.8). Torre's account of the window, meticulous and accurate though it is, provided an objective description of what he saw rather than an identification of the individual biblical scenes, so can have been of little use to the poetically inclined Gent. While *The Delectable, Scriptural and Pious History* did nothing to revive Gent's seriously declining fortunes, the book suggests that a commercial printer active in York for nearly 50 years believed that the Great East Window was of sufficient interest to warrant a dedicated guidebook, probably the first ever

devoted to English stained glass. Gent's text is also fascinating in that it presents the window as an illustrated Scripture lesson, thereby side-stepping Georgian Britain's continuing sensitivities to Catholic ideology and imagery.

Architect John Carr's 1770 survey of the building had fuelled concerns about the state of the Minster fabric, although only in the 1790s were the repairs he advocated to be undertaken. In 1793 the choir interior was scaffolded and cleaned and two artists, Joseph Halfpenny (1748–1811), who served as Carr's clerk of works, and William Fowler of Winterton in Lincolnshire (1761–1832), best known for his measured drawings of mosaic pavements, took advantage of high-level access to make drawings of panels 8f and 4c in the Great East Window. Some small repairs also seem to have been done at this time. The 15-year-old glazier's apprentice Thomas Clarke scratched his name and the year 1794 on a scorpion's rump in panel 8f, and his name and the year 1796 on a medieval head used to repair the figure of the Emperor Domitian in panel 11a.

'Henry Bewlay New Leaded This Light': Restoration 1824–1827

The first full-scale restoration of the window was conducted between 1824 and 1827, occasioned by the need to remove all the glass from the window tracery to allow for extensive masonry repairs supervised by Master Mason William Shout (d.1827). The exact nature of Shout's work on the east façade is far less well documented than his work on the west front, but thanks to the glaziers' graffiti, the progress of the restoration of the window can be charted with some confidence. The window was fully scaffolded in July 1824 to allow the stained glass to be removed, and the first names scratched onto the glass, on 17 July 1825, are those of Henry Bewlay, Thomas Jackson and Richard Snowdon, inscribed on a piece of plain glass inserted into the robe of God the Father at the window's apex (Fig. 1.9). The dates of subsequent

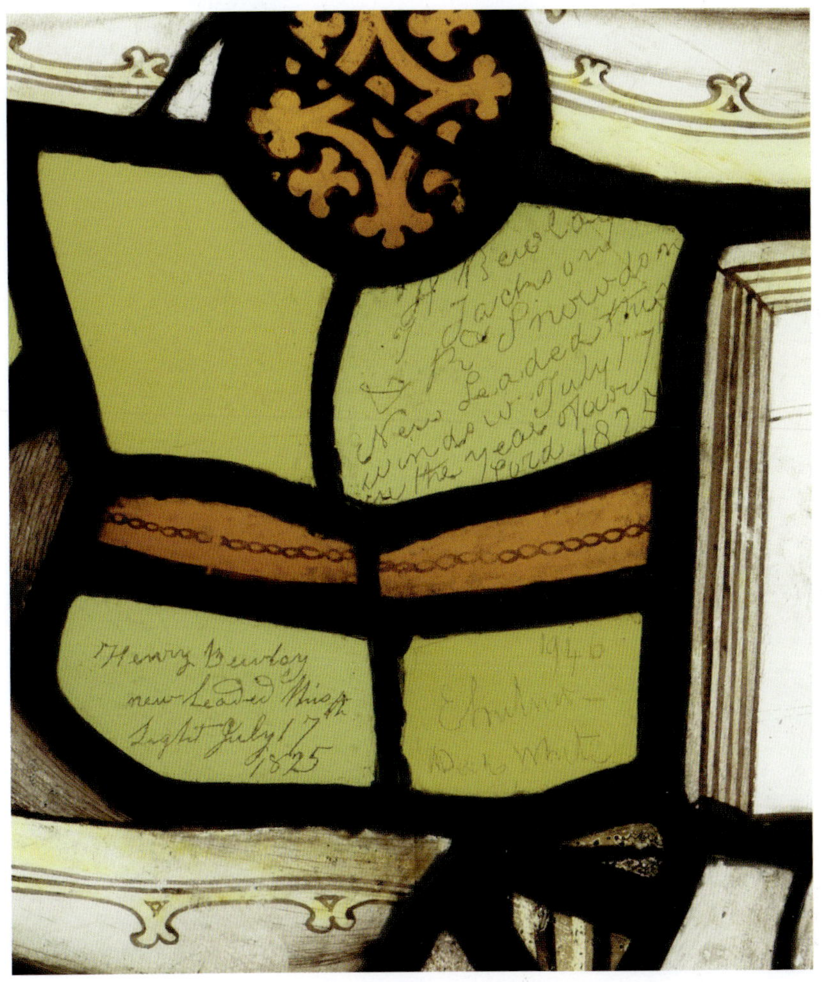

Fig. 1.9
The names of the glaziers who, in 1825, releaded the panel depicting God the Father (DD1) from the apex of the Great East Window. Glaziers' graffiti, scratched with a diamond, are found all over the window.

inscriptions make it clear that the glaziers worked in sequence from top to bottom. In addition to their names, which include those of H. Barlag, William Coverdale, Henry Stephenson, and John and Elisha Drinkel, the glaziers marked the panels (often more than once) with incised numbers which recorded the location of each one, and ensured that they returned to the place from which they had come. In fact, they did not always get this right and further alterations in panel order in the Old Testament section of the window can be attributed to this period. This was therefore a conservative programme of repair rather than an attempt to reorder the window. Some new glass was needed – particularly blue, purple and pale green – to patch holes or replace glass so corroded or opaque that the 19th-century glaziers could not save it. These are the same medieval colours that were found to be the most heavily corroded during the most recent conservation programme. In common with their predecessors, the 19th-century glaziers used scraps of old glass from the Minster stores with which to patch some of the holes. Conspicuous among these 'stopgaps' were pieces of glass of c.1340 closely related in style to the Great West Window of 1339. There are also a small number of newly painted heads (notably in panel 9e), carefully, if not always completely convincingly, emulating the style of the medieval originals (Fig. 1.10). This is a fascinating and hitherto unrecognised example of careful and sympathetic restoration in a period in which glass painting and glass technology were undergoing transformation under the influence of the promoters of the 'true principles' of the Gothic Revival.

The Fire of 1829

On the night of 1 February 1829 the Great East Window faced its most serious test – an ordeal by fire. Having attended evensong on that fateful Sunday evening, the millenarian 'ranter' Jonathan Martin (c.1782–1838) hid himself in the Minster. In the quiet of the locked building he set a fire, fuelled by the choir's crimson hangings and the service books laid against the medieval wooden stalls on both sides of the choir, and the archbishop's throne on the south side. Crying 'Glory to God' so loud that he feared being heard from outside the building, Martin lit his bonfire before cutting his way out through a window in the north transept. It was four hours before an early-bird choirboy spotted smoke coming out of the building. By 8 am the fire had consumed the south stalls and the organ, thereby making its way into the wooden vault of the choir, eventually bringing about the collapse of both vault and roof. The damage to the choir was extensive (Fig. 1.11) and in the windows of the choir clerestory,

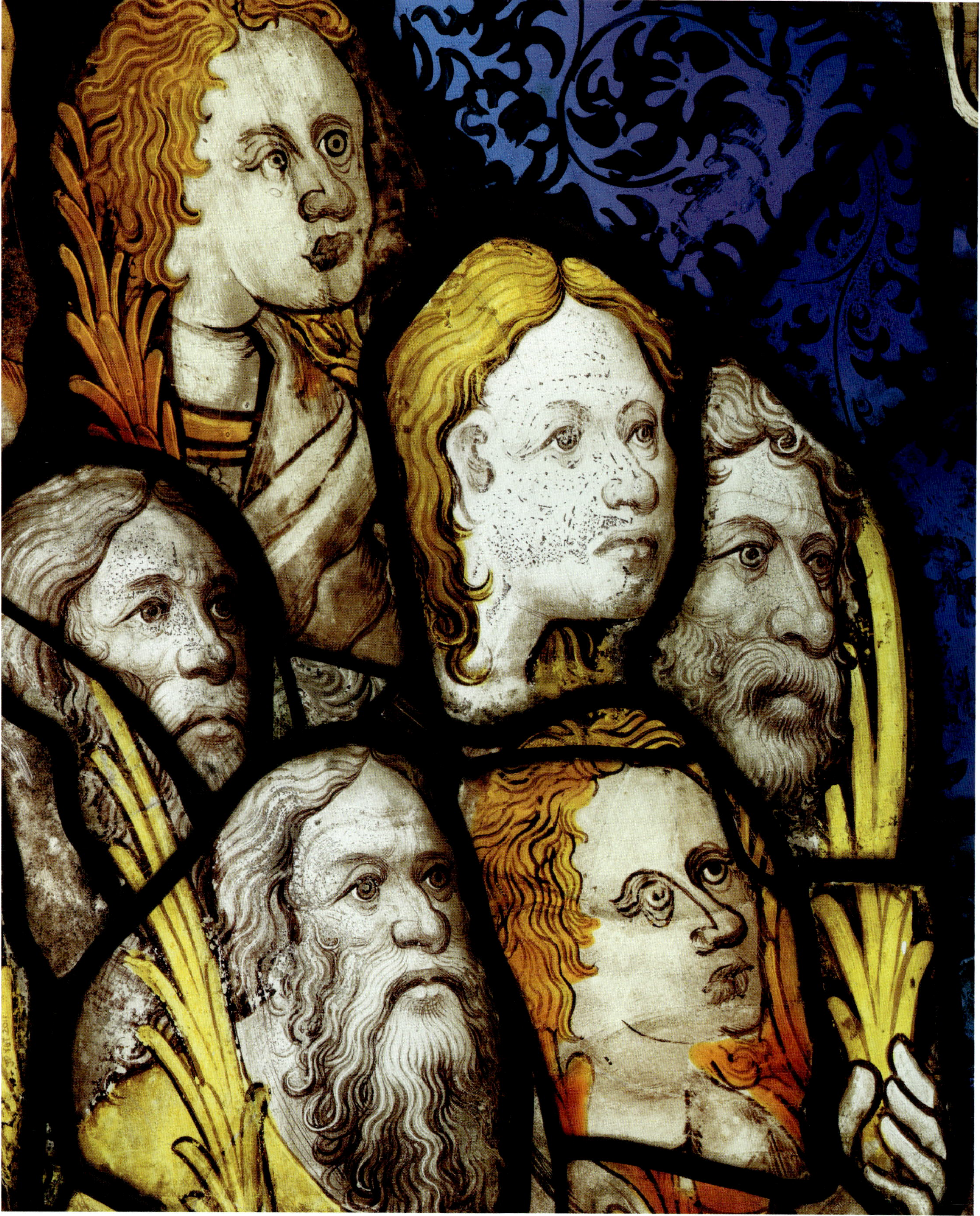

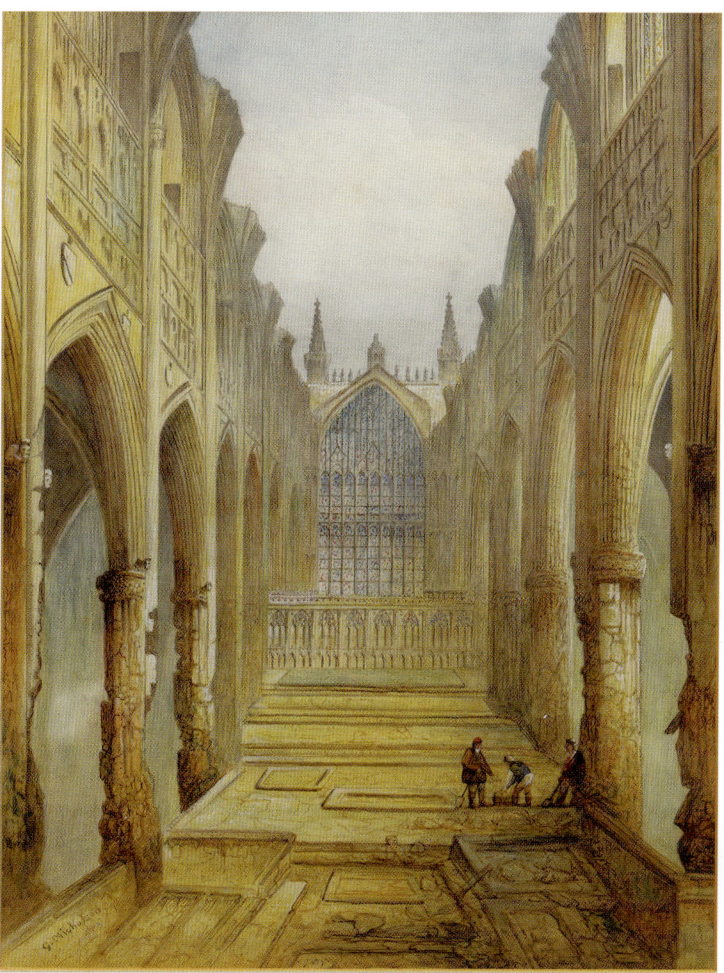

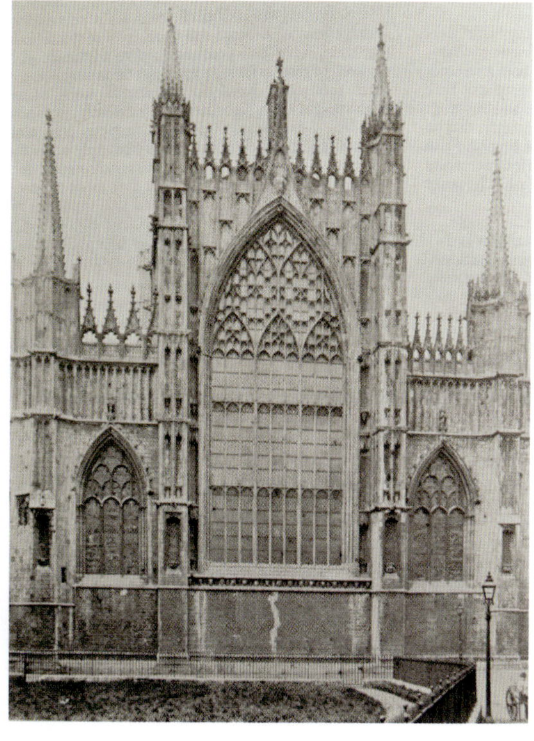

especially those of the south side, evidence of its destructive force can still be seen today in the crizzled and micro-cracked glass (Fig. 1.13).

The survival of the Great East Window was heralded as nothing short of miraculous. On 5 March 1829 the newly appointed cathedral architect, Robert Smirke, reported to Chapter that 'The Great East Window has suffered very little injury'. He was also sure that other windows could be repaired and the numerous dated graffiti of 1829 and 1830 in the north and south choir clerestory windows attest to this. The window was boarded up for safety while the choir was restored. At the very least it would have needed to be cleaned of smoke residue, but the complete absence of 1829–30 glaziers' graffiti suggests that little else needed to be done. The work of the glaziers of 1824–7 had probably saved the window from disaster, much as the 1970s restoration of the Rose Window is believed to have saved it from collapse during the south transept fire of 1984. The choir reopened in 1832, albeit only after an acrimonious dispute between the Chapter and the builders of the new organ, who were asked to design an instrument that in no way obstructed a view of the window. The organ builder sued the Dean and Chapter for the delays and extra costs that ensued, declaring 'Confound the east window. What a bother it is to us all!'

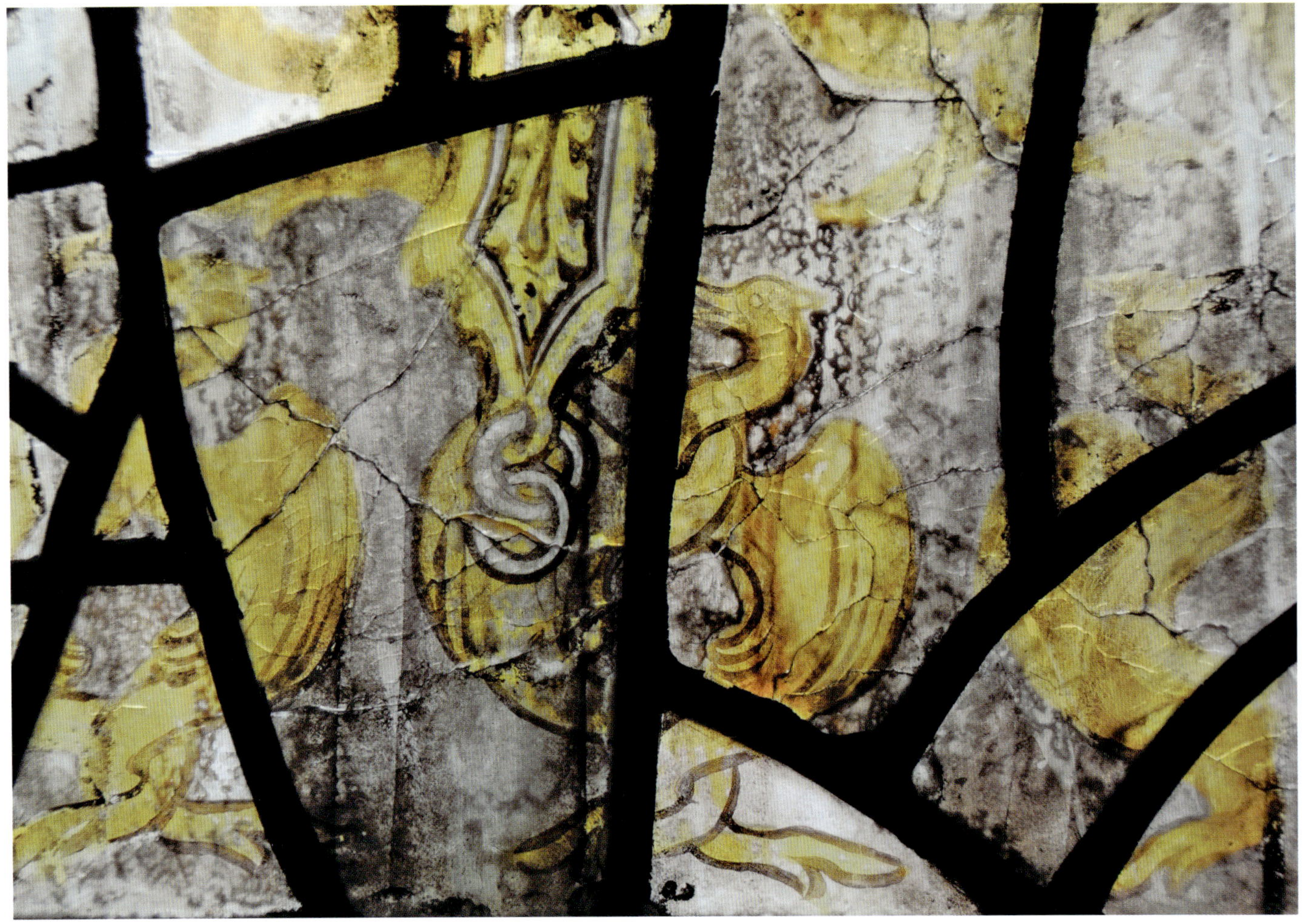

'The Glory of English Stained Glass'

The backdrop to the Gothic Revival was the Industrial Revolution. Industrialisation had significant implications for the environment, and the increased pollution generated by the huge increase in the burning of fossil fuels took its toll on stone and glass as well as on the health of a growing populace. Although York was far less industrialised than other cities like Manchester and Birmingham, the sulphurous emissions of coal-fired factories and coal-burning homes accelerated the deterioration of the Minster's windows. While some attributed the pitting of the windows' exterior surfaces to the pecking of birds, more serious observers realised that air quality was an issue and that external protection was the answer. The provision of effective protective glazing is now so integral to stained-glass conservation throughout Europe, that it is easy to overlook how prescient was the decision, early in 1861, to provide some of the Minster's most treasured windows, including the Five Sisters, the West Window and the Great East Window, with external protective glazing (Fig. 1.12). New glazing grooves were cut so that the window openings could accommodate the original medieval panels as well as the new exterior glazing. In the east wall this was first in the form of sheets of plate glass from Hartley's Sunderland glassworks,

Fig. 1.13
Extensive fire-crazing of glass in the southern-choir clerestory (window S8), caused by the intense heat generated by the burning medieval choir stalls immediately below.

Fig. 1.14
Dean Eric Milner-White
(dean 1941–63).

roundly criticised by the correspondent of the architectural journal *The Builder* for its impact on the cathedral's exterior which was 'as bad as it is dismal in the interior'. The combination of a poor aesthetic effect and the cracking of stone caused by the iron frames that held the glass plates led to their replacement in 1910 with more traditional diamond quarries. The quarries did not, however, assist in the illumination of the window. Writing in 1913, the Arts and Crafts stained-glass artist Hugh Arnold (1872–1915) described the window as 'the glory of English stained glass' but nonetheless regretted the impact of 'the dirty quarry glazing' which, in his view, robbed the window 'of quite a third of its beauty of light and colour'.

Two World Wars and the Arrival of Eric Milner-White

If it was industrial pollution that had posed the greatest threat to the Minster's windows in the 19th century, it was industrialised war that represented the greatest danger in the 20th. Aerial bombardment of the medieval city had first threatened the Minster in May 1916, when a bomb dropped from a Zeppelin had landed uncomfortably close to the building. A campaign to remove windows to safety was launched, but the war had ended with only 22 windows removed and before the Great East Window was reached. It was, however, the realisation that many windows were in very poor condition that had prompted the restoration campaign launched in 1920, which saw many of the windows cleaned and releaded. The restoration of a number of individual windows was sponsored as a memorial to the fallen of the war. The campaign of the 1920s was not without its controversies, but the protection of windows was gradually extended. The programme concluded in 1930, in the face of worldwide economic depression, with the restoration and reinstallation of the West Window. The three great windows of the choir, all restored in the 19th century,

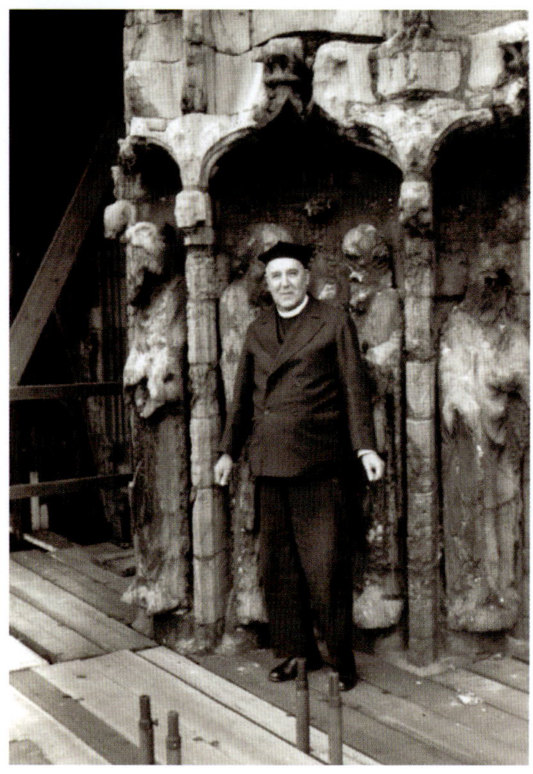

were excluded from this restoration campaign and apart from the alteration to its external protection, the Great East Window remained exactly as the restorers of the 1820s had left it.

At the outbreak of the Second World War in the summer of 1939 swift action to safeguard the glass was an immediate priority, strongly supported by Canon Chancellor Frederick Harrison, author of an important guide to the stained glass of the Minster and city churches published in 1927, who also sought funds to help the parish churches to safeguard their windows too. Eighty Minster windows, this time including the Great East Window, were removed into safe storage in locations around the county. The Great East Window retired to Thicket Priory at Thorganby, about seven miles outside the city. The removal of the window was also an opportunity to take photographs of it, images that have been of inestimable value during the most recent conservation. The wisdom of this campaign was borne out in the aftermath of the Baedecker raid on York in the early hours of 29 April 1941, during which the medieval Guildhall and the parish church of St Martin le Grand in Coney Street were badly damaged and precious stained glass was lost in both buildings. Slight damage was even sustained by the Minster when a bomb fell close to the west end and shook out some 19th-century stained glass in the west aisle of the north transept.

Perhaps the most momentous wartime event in terms of the fate of stained glass of York Minster in general and of the Great East Window in particular, was the arrival of Eric Milner-White (1884–1963), appointed dean in 1941 (Fig. 1.14). Milner-White came to York from King's College, Cambridge, where he had first developed a passionate interest in stained glass. After graduating from King's, he had trained for the priesthood and, after a distinguished career as an army chaplain during the First World War, returned there, first as chaplain and then as dean. Despite his many activities and responsibilities in the national Church, and his active career in the civic life of his adopted city, where he contributed greatly to the development of the Art Gallery and promoted the foundation of the University of York, Milner-White found the time and energy to direct a massive campaign of stained-glass conservation, as the 80 windows removed at the outbreak of the war were returned to the Minster. Work on the Great East Window, untouched since the 1820s, had already begun quietly in 1943 and by the time the Dean turned his attention to the project, over a third of the tracery had been releaded in the conservative 'as found' manner that had long characterised the work of the Minster glaziers. Under Milner-White a far more interventionist approach was adopted, as the Dean sought to recover meaning and legibility, undeterred by the size and complexity of the Great East Window, which had been reinstalled by 1953. He described his approach thus:

There is everything to be said for this if good knowledge of medieval mind and craftsmanship cannot be continuously present. But, if present, it becomes merely absurd to perpetuate the mistakes made by ignorant and careless glaziers … when all understanding of the older glass had vanished.

Over the next 20 years the Dean's little team of glaziers restored scores of windows in this way, although no new external protection was provided. The Dean's legacy has left an indelible mark on the Minster's stained glass and was the context in which the conservation programme of 2011–17 has unfolded, the subject of Chapter Four.

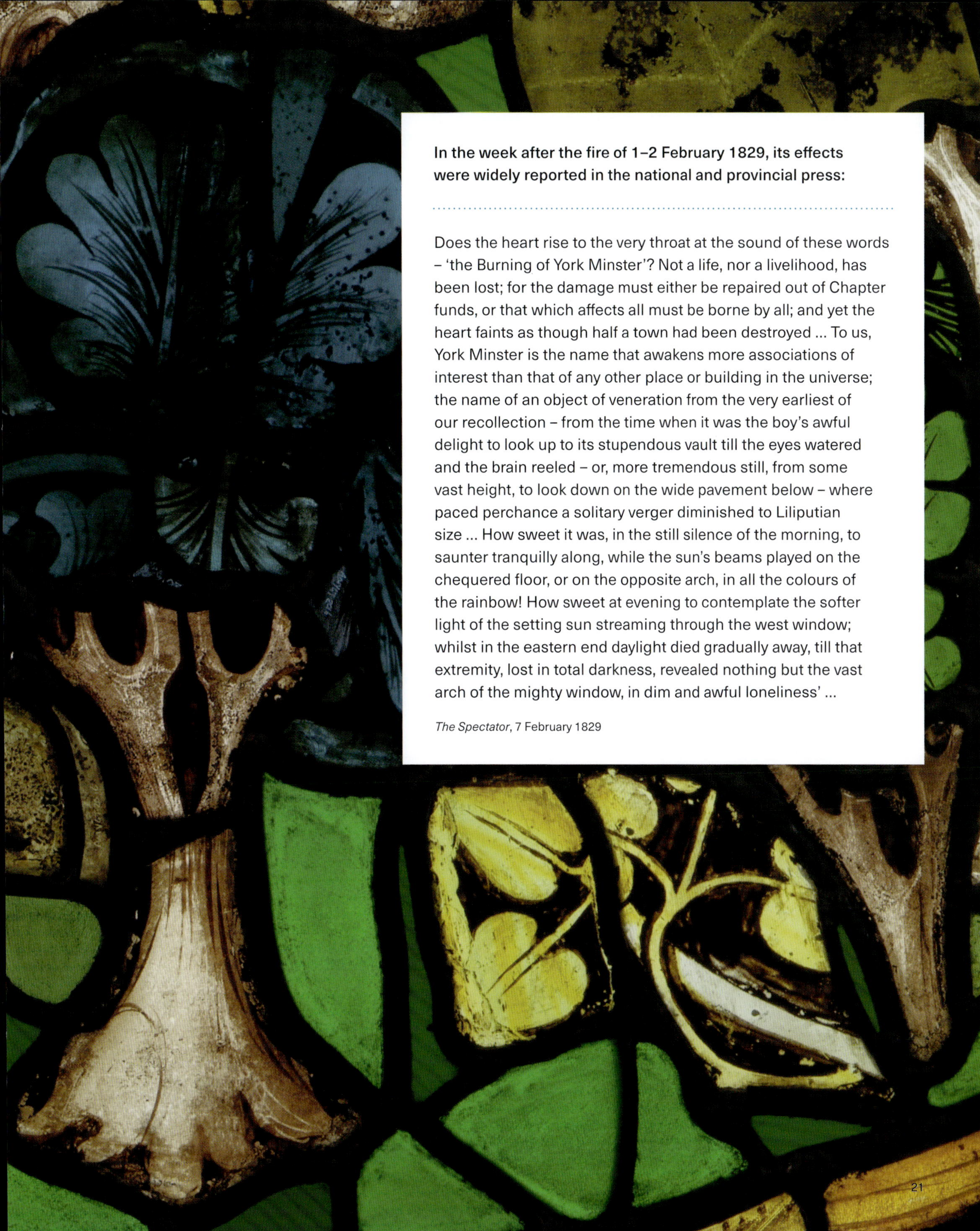

In the week after the fire of 1–2 February 1829, its effects were widely reported in the national and provincial press:

Does the heart rise to the very throat at the sound of these words – 'the Burning of York Minster'? Not a life, nor a livelihood, has been lost; for the damage must either be repaired out of Chapter funds, or that which affects all must be borne by all; and yet the heart faints as though half a town had been destroyed … To us, York Minster is the name that awakens more associations of interest than that of any other place or building in the universe; the name of an object of veneration from the very earliest of our recollection – from the time when it was the boy's awful delight to look up to its stupendous vault till the eyes watered and the brain reeled – or, more tremendous still, from some vast height, to look down on the wide pavement below – where paced perchance a solitary verger diminished to Liliputian size … How sweet it was, in the still silence of the morning, to saunter tranquilly along, while the sun's beams played on the chequered floor, or on the opposite arch, in all the colours of the rainbow! How sweet at evening to contemplate the softer light of the setting sun streaming through the west window; whilst in the eastern end daylight died gradually away, till that extremity, lost in total darkness, revealed nothing but the vast arch of the mighty window, in dim and awful loneliness' …

The Spectator, 7 February 1829

The Great
Window at the
E. End of the
Quire

On 10. Augᵗ. AᴰD 1405 : 6 H4)

An Indenture was made between
the Dean & Chapter on the one pᵗ
And John Thornton of Covintry glazier
on the other, whereby.
The ſᵈ John covenanted to make a Great
window at the E: End of the Quire, according
to the best of his Skill & Cunning
And undertook to glaze the same wᵗʰ
Glaſs, Lead, Sodder & other necessaries
requisite, & to find all sufficient
workmen, to be disposed at the Costs
of the ſᵈ Dean & Chapter.
And to finiſh the ſame wᵗʰin 3 years
from the date hereof. And obliging
himself, wᵗʰ his own hands to portraiture
the ſᵈ Window wᵗʰ Historicall Images
& other painted work, in the best
Manner & form that he poſsibly could
And likewiſe paynt the ſame where
need required, according to the Ordination
of the Dean & Chapter.
For all wᶜʰ the Dean & Chapter
should pay him 4ˢ ſterling pᵉʳ week
during the term aforeſd, that he
wrought in his Art.
And beſides that wᵒ. ſterling every
of theſe 3 years.
And if he performed his work well
& truly, & perfect it according to the
tenor of theſe Covenants, then he
should receive more of the Dean &
Chapter for his care therein, the ſum
of 10ᴸ in Silver.   Gᵐ 96)

Annᵒ D. 1464. temp. H 6

The Minſter of York was burnt dow[n]

Goodroy.
Dᶜ Præs.

On 11. July. AᴰD. 1465 / 6 E4)   The B[ells]

For the founding of 4 bells, there was
then delivered into the hands of Thomas
Innocent Bell founder, by John Knapton
Under Treaſurer, & Mʳ. John Sapton.
certain Metalls. all particularly named,
& ſhews the weight of each bell   (Lʸ 10)

On 7 Jun. AᴰD 1655 /

The 4 bells in the Lady Steeple of the
Minſter were taken down & hung wᵗʰ
the Great bells in the other Steeple
the Charge thereof being by Collection
through the City /   &c

John Thornton and his Patrons

The Appointment of John Thornton

Thanks to the survival into the 17th century of a summary of the medieval contract for the making of the Great East Window, the name of John Thornton, the glazier entrusted with this huge project in the winter of 1405, has been preserved, and Coventry identified as his city of origin (Fig. 2.1). As Thornton is a name not unknown in Yorkshire it is possible that this information was included to ensure that the incoming master glazier was differentiated from other craftsmen with a similar name. The reasons behind the decision to entrust this prestigious project to a 'foreign' artist deserves some comment. It was not unusual for 'outsiders' to be brought in to lead especially prestigious or challenging commissions, as happened in 1351–2 at the royal chapel of St Stephen at Westminster, when John de Chestre was put in charge. It was a strategy not without risk, however. In 1407, barely two years after the Great East Window contract had been signed, the Westminster architect William Colchester was given charge of the Minster stone yard at the instigation of King Henry IV. He and his assistant, William Waddeswyck, were set upon by the local masons and both were injured. Thankfully Thornton was apparently afforded a warmer welcome. Writing in the 1930s, J. A. Knowles suggested that the decision to bring in Thornton was explained by a shortage of skilled glaziers in York in the aftermath of the plague. In fact, the city's freemen's register shows that despite the losses of the Black Death, 15th-century York had plenty of glaziers and glass painters. Examination of the registers has shown that the numbers of glaziers admitted to the freedom of the city had increased in the plague's aftermath. Between 1307 and 1349 only seven had been admitted, while between 1350 and 1399 the names of 17 were enrolled. In reality, this number was probably even higher, as those admitted 'per patres' were not usually listed in the register, which also excludes the names of assistants and apprentices. Professor Barrie Dobson has suggested that in order to replenish the depleted ranks of craftsmen in the city, there may have been some relaxation of the regulation of apprenticeships, which normally lasted

Fig. 2.1
James Torre's English transcript of the chapter acts, recording John Thornton's contract for the making of the Great East Window (see also p. 48).

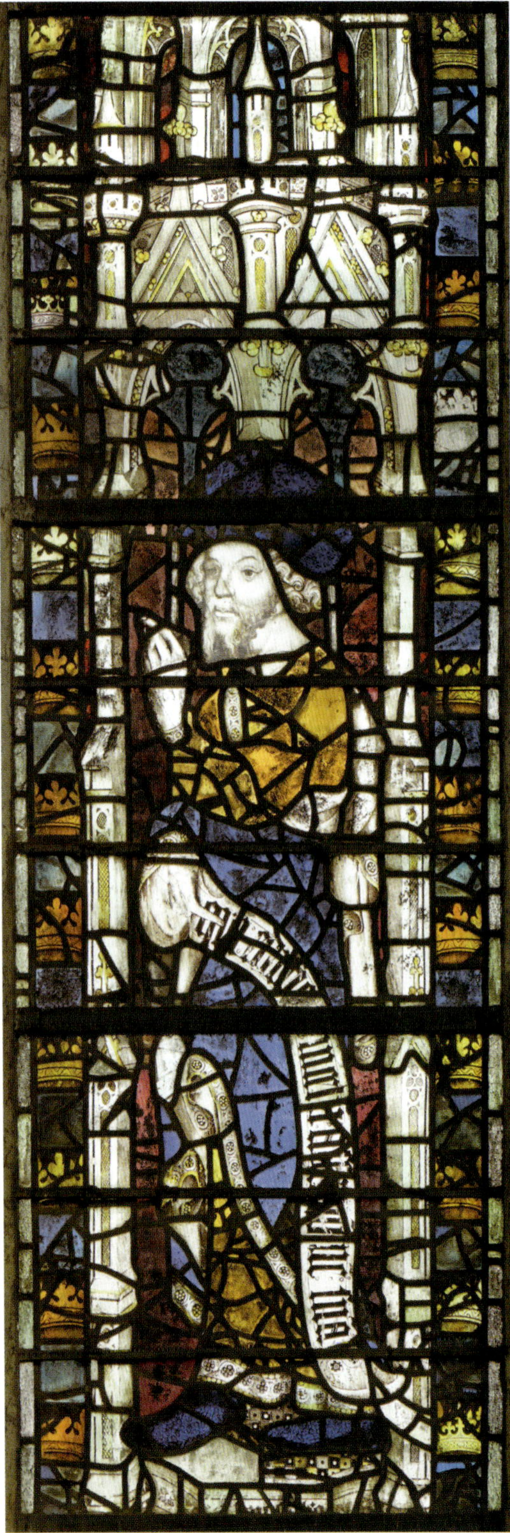

six or seven years for those who could not expect to succeed their father. Could this have impacted adversely on the quality of the craftsmanship in the city? Perhaps in the 1360s and 1370s, but the quality of the glazing installed in the Minster in the years immediately before the Great East Window, normally attributed to glazier John Burgh (Fig. 2.2), is high and compares favourably with other prestige projects of this date elsewhere in England. In fact, Burgh continued to be employed by the Minster throughout the period in which the Great East Window was being made and beyond, only relinquishing the role of retained glazier to John Chambre between 1419 and 1422. That John Thornton offered his patrons a very special set of skills not matched among native York glaziers is the inescapable conclusion, and is something to which we will return later.

The contract gave Thornton a free hand in recruiting the workforce he needed to make the window, and while we cannot know whether this team included other Coventry glaziers, who may have followed their master to York, we think that Thornton probably also continued to operate a business in his native city, which suggests that while for his new enterprise he may have been accompanied by some of his most trusted Coventry staff, he is also likely to have employed local collaborators already living and working in York. That Thornton must have worked with others in order to deliver this enormous project in the short time allotted in the contract cannot be doubted, but tantalisingly we do not know how many were employed in its manufacture, as the contract concerns only Thornton's responsibilities, and his rewards, which were considerable. He was to be paid 4*s.* a week for every week of the project's three-year duration. This was a far more attractive option than being paid a daily rate, as was common practice, as the large number of religious holidays in any week could make the craftsman's income vary considerably from week to week. In addition, he was to receive an annual bonus of 100*s.* (£5), and on successful completion of the project

Fig. 2.2
The prophet Amos in clerestory window N4, perhaps the work of glazier John Burgh, probably installed in the 1390s.

within the three-year timescale set out by the Dean and Chapter, a further payment of £10. As the date 1408 appears in medieval glass at the top of the window, we may safely assume that Thornton received a total of £56 for his service, although the total cost of the window must have been far in excess of this figure, as the cost of materials as well as the wages of the other glaziers were to be met by the Dean and Chapter.

Bishop Walter Skirlaw

The contract was drawn up between Thornton and the Dean and Chapter of York. It gives no insights into any negotiation that may have preceded the conclusion of the formal agreement, which must have been conducted by a far smaller group of individuals. Nor is any mention made of the source of the money that paid for the window. As we have seen, early accounts of the window either attempt no identification of the figure in the central panel at the window's base, or follow Gent's incorrect identification of an Anglo-Saxon archbishop. Even Frederick Harrison, who correctly identified the coat of arms accompanying the figure, was cautious in his 1927 attribution, asking if the episcopal figure could be Archbishop Henry Bowet (1406–23). The window itself proves incontrovertibly that the donor was Bishop Walter Skirlaw of Durham (d.1406). He kneels, dressed in his full mass vestments in the central panel (1e) at the base of the window, directly below the feet of Christ in Judgement. An inscription (in Latin), now damaged, probably once read, 'O God I offer to thee this noble work. Receive it graciously.' The donor panel is the only one in the row to contain a single figure rather than a trio, which gives Skirlaw additional visual prominence, and he is kneeling rather than enthroned, which stresses his humility before his maker and judge. His coat of arms, of entwined osier twigs in the form of a cross, displayed prominently on the altar frontal before which he kneels, has also been found in two other places in the window. In both cases

these are significant and honoured locations (in panels 8j and 7e), adorning the Temple of God (Fig. 2.3). We do not know when Skirlaw gave the money for the window and he did not live to see it completed. It is not mentioned in his will, first made in March 1404, with subsequent codicils. As the Chapter had purchased a great deal of glass for the choir windows by 1399, and was able to commit to Thornton's employment in 1405, it is likely that Bishop Walter had committed the funding during his lifetime, and probably well before he first drew up his will.

Skirlaw's association with York was of long standing. He had served as domestic chaplain and secretary to Archbishop Thoresby and in 1360 was appointed archdeacon of the East Riding at Thoresby's behest. In 1370, not long before the Archbishop's death, he acquired the Minster prebendary of Fenton. His diplomatic duties on the Archbishop's behalf undoubtedly assisted him in his subsequent career in the royal service and in 1386 he was made keeper of the

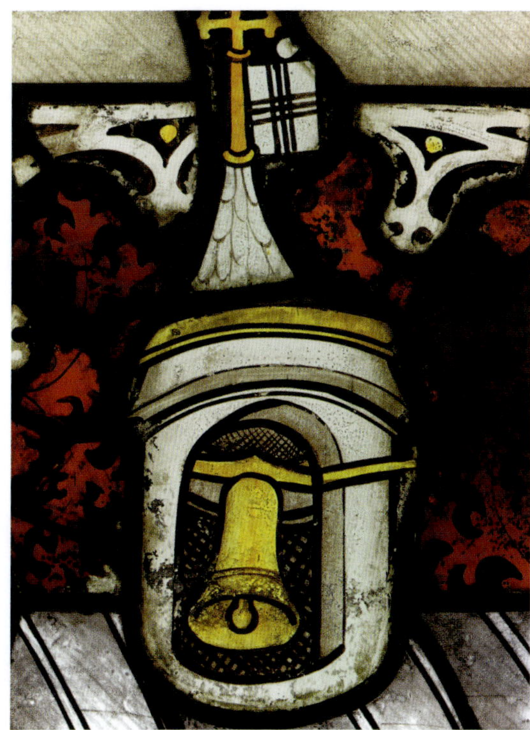

privy seal. The first of his episcopal appointments followed shortly afterwards. His distinctive coat of arms was once painted alongside those of St William of York, St Edward the Confessor and the arms of the three Magi on the blank tracery above the door from the chapter house vestibule into the north transept. The dating of this now-lost scheme is not without its problems, but it has been suggested that it was painted in association with one of King Richard II's visits to York Minster, the last of which took place at Easter 1396. Nor was the Great East Window Skirlaw's only act of generosity to the Minster. His late medieval biographer recorded his patronage of the central tower, where his coat of arms is prominently displayed on the south wall, a position that echoes the crowning location of the pennant in panel 7e (Fig. 2.4). The redating of the fall of the central tower to 1405 rather than 1407 means that this was probably another major gift made during his lifetime and donated in response to an architectural emergency. In fact, Skirlaw's generosity to York Minster was to continue after death. In his will he bequeathed 100 marks to the fabric and a whole set of vestments embroidered in gold with crowns and stars, valued at 120 marks (a set which included five copes with embroidered golden orphreys), at the top of the list in the post-mortem inventory of his vestments. In 1416 his executors released a further donation of £52 to the Minster fabric fund, and his soul was remembered at a chantry attached to the altar of St Cuthbert, which was probably located on the south-east side of the south-west crossing tower, close to the image of his arms in the tower above.

Skirlaw's motives in giving the Great East Window have sometimes been called into question. In 1398 the canons of York had elected him archbishop, but they were overruled by the Pope, and Richard Scrope, the candidate favoured by King Richard II, who had been active in the king's campaign to secure the canonisation of Edward II, was appointed instead. It has been suggested that Skirlaw offered the

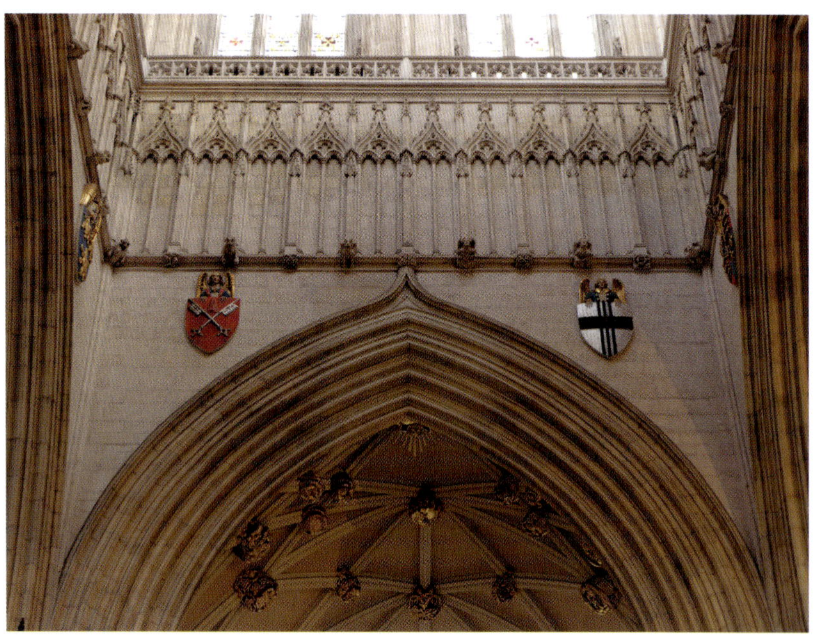

Fig. 2.4
The south face of the central tower (rebuilt after a partial collapse in 1405), with the arms of St Peter, the saint to whom the Minster is dedicated, alongside those of Bishop Skirlaw.

money for the window either *c.*1398 as leverage to secure his election, or perhaps even in the summer of 1405 when the see was once again vacant following Scrope's death. While this cannot be discounted, his donation of the Great East Window must be seen in the wider context of his interest in buildings and stained glass, for he was also associated with glazing projects at Durham, in the chapel of the Nine Altars, glass which no longer survives. The evidence is rather that Skirlaw and Scrope worked collaboratively to bring about the completion of Thoresby's vision of the Minster. As we have seen, Skirlaw's early career and advancement owed a great deal to Thoresby's patronage and, as his secretary and chaplain in the years when the Lady Chapel project came to fruition, Skirlaw would have been privy to the Archbishop's plans for the mother church of the northern province. By 1401 Bishop Skirlaw, prince-bishop of Durham and esteemed royal diplomat, had retired from public life on the grounds of ill health. He remained close to home for the rest of his life. His will and its inventory reveal his quite extraordinary wealth, and his gift of the Great East Window

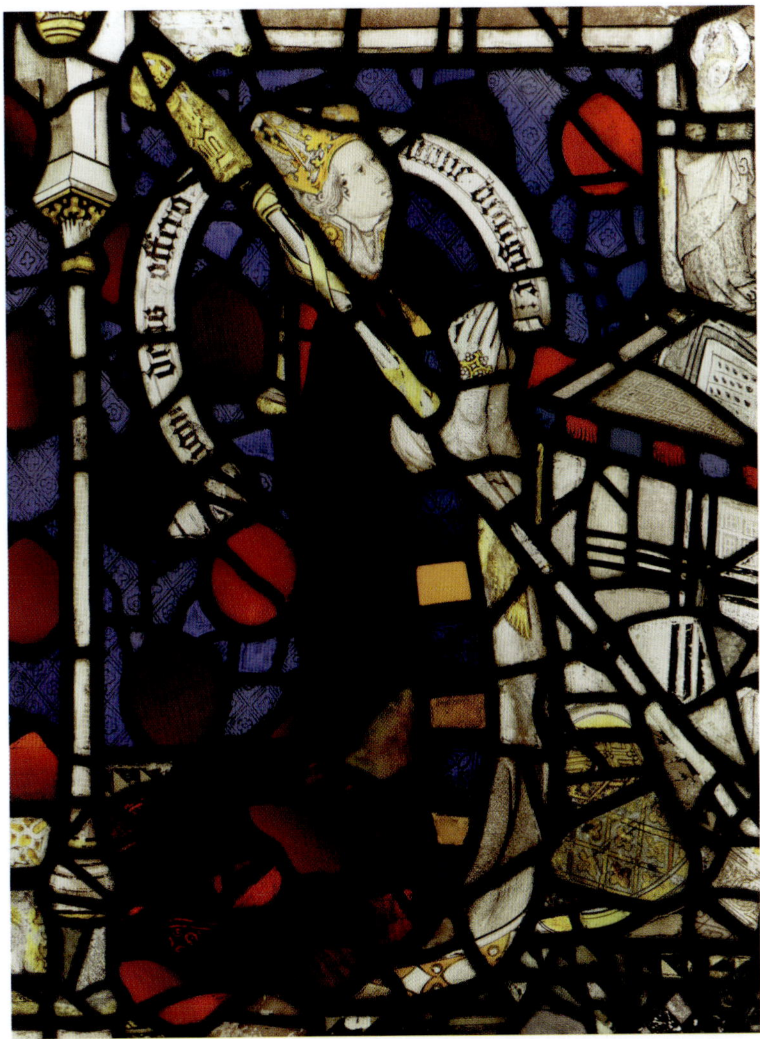

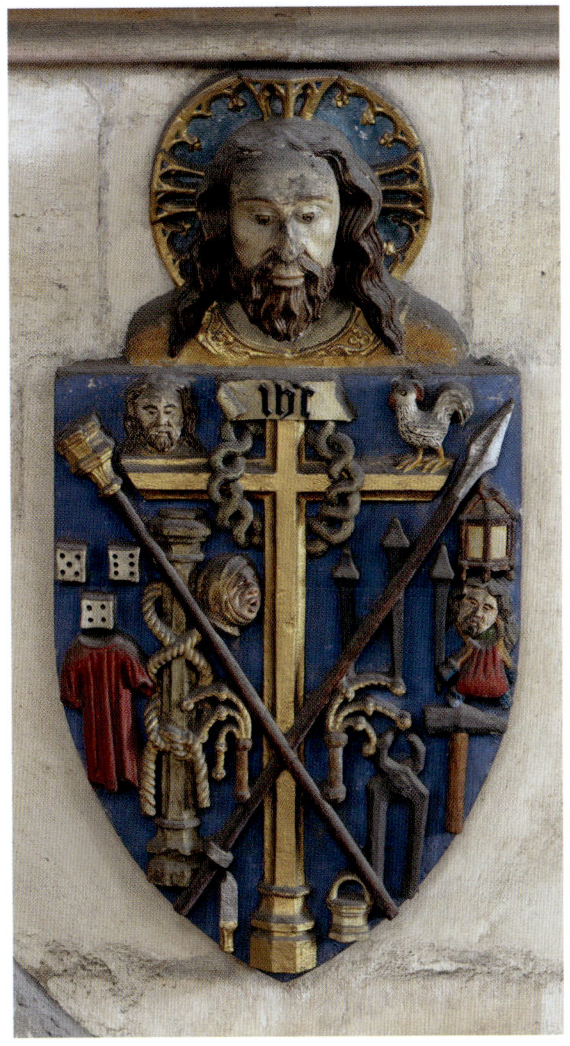

Fig. 2.5
The donor image of Bishop Skirlaw before recent conservation. The original head of the Bishop had been lost by the 1820s and was replaced with a medieval insertion too small in scale.

Fig. 2.6
The Arma Christi shield carved into the north choir arcade, directly opposite the shield of Archbishop Richard Scrope.

makes a great deal of sense in the context of ailing health, great wealth and a long-standing interest in building and glazing, as a generous gift to the mother church of York, fulfilling the vision of a fondly remembered patron. The window also provided a prominent donor image close to the final resting place of Archbishop Thoresby that would elicit the grateful prayers of the canons of York, offering a compelling mixture of the 'provident stewardship' of his earthly goods to which reference is made in the opening paragraph of his will, and the spiritual benefit sought by all those close to death.

In *c.*1670 the antiquary Henry Johnston drew Skirlaw's figure with his original head intact, wearing a mitre with two crosses on its gabled peaks. Sadly, this head had been lost by the 1820s, when a too-small medieval head of a bishop, inserted inside out, was supplied from elsewhere to patch the figure (Fig. 2.5). During recent conservation one of the crosses that adorned the mitre was located in the surviving glass, helping to establish the location, size and aspect of the missing head of Walter Skirlaw. It was clear that the head of the donor had been drawn from the same cartoon as a number of other heads of episcopal figures in the bottom row of the window. After considerable discussion and reflection (a process discussed in Chapter Three), a new head of the right scale was created, based on one of these original heads, restoring to Skirlaw's figure a degree of gravitas and presence. We must conclude, however, that Skirlaw was identified by his dress and his coat of arms rather than by any attempt at a living likeness of the bishop. That we honour Skirlaw's memory as a great builder and benefactor at both York and Durham shows his gifts to have been a sound investment.

Archbishop Richard Scrope

It has been suggested that Skirlaw may have been instrumental in introducing John Thornton to the Chapter of York, for not only was he patron of the project, but he had served as bishop of Coventry and Lichfield for a year in 1386, nearly 20 years before the commissioning of the Great East Window. Perhaps a stronger contender for this role is Archbishop Richard Scrope, who served as bishop of the Coventry and Lichfield diocese from 1386 until he came to York in 1398, just as work on the choir got under way again. As mentioned in Chapter One, Archbishop Richard personally promoted the newly resumed building work, in 1405 providing the annual wages for an additional mason, and his arms are paired with those of Bishop Skirlaw in the spandrel of the south choir arcade, in the first bay of the new work. The Archbishop's sudden and unexpected death (some would say murder), executed for rebellion on 8 June 1405 on the order of King Henry IV, cut short whatever personal plans Scrope may have had for the Minster. That his body could be buried immediately in a grave so prominently located on the boundary between the Lady Chapel and St Stephen's Chapel, close to the line of archiepiscopal burials established by Archbishop Thoresby, suggests that he had already initiated his own plans for the area illuminated by the Great East Window. At least

eight members of the Archbishop's family, the Scropes of Masham, were buried in St Stephen's Chapel, so that by the middle of the 15th century it was known as 'Scrop Chapell', an unprecedented and never-again matched appropriation of a Minster chapel as a family mausoleum. By 1500, if not before, the hangings for the choir included 12 pieces of red tapestry woven with the arms of the Scropes of Masham, of which a few fragments survive to this day. It must be assumed that had he lived, the Archbishop would have been commemorated with an appropriately splendid tomb, such as Archbishop Bowet commissioned in the equivalent position on the south side of the Lady Chapel.

But did Scrope also have plans for the stained glass of the choir? There is certainly circumstantial evidence to suggest that he did. He was probably the donor of a sophisticated typological window in the north choir aisle (window n4) close to St Stephen's Chapel (since lost). He came from a family who owned many books, including an illuminated Apocalypse (although probably not one of those that informed the imagery of the Great East Window). He had borrowed from Durham the illuminated life of St Cuthbert which certainly provided one of the source books for the St Cuthbert window. Professor Norton has suggested that the two episcopal colleagues collaborated closely in the provision of glass for the great windows of the east end, with Skirlaw offering the Great East Window and Scrope intending to offer the St Cuthbert window, a plan confounded by his untimely death. Is it even conceivable that Archbishop Richard Scrope, perhaps with the assistance of his own family, intended to provide *both* of the great windows that shine the light of the saints of the north on the high altar? To the south of the high altar Archbishop Scrope's personal arms are displayed (with those of Bishop Skirlaw). On the north are the instruments of Christ's Passion, arranged on a shield of arms, known as the Arma Christi, the 'heraldry' attributed to Christ himself since the late 13th century (Fig.

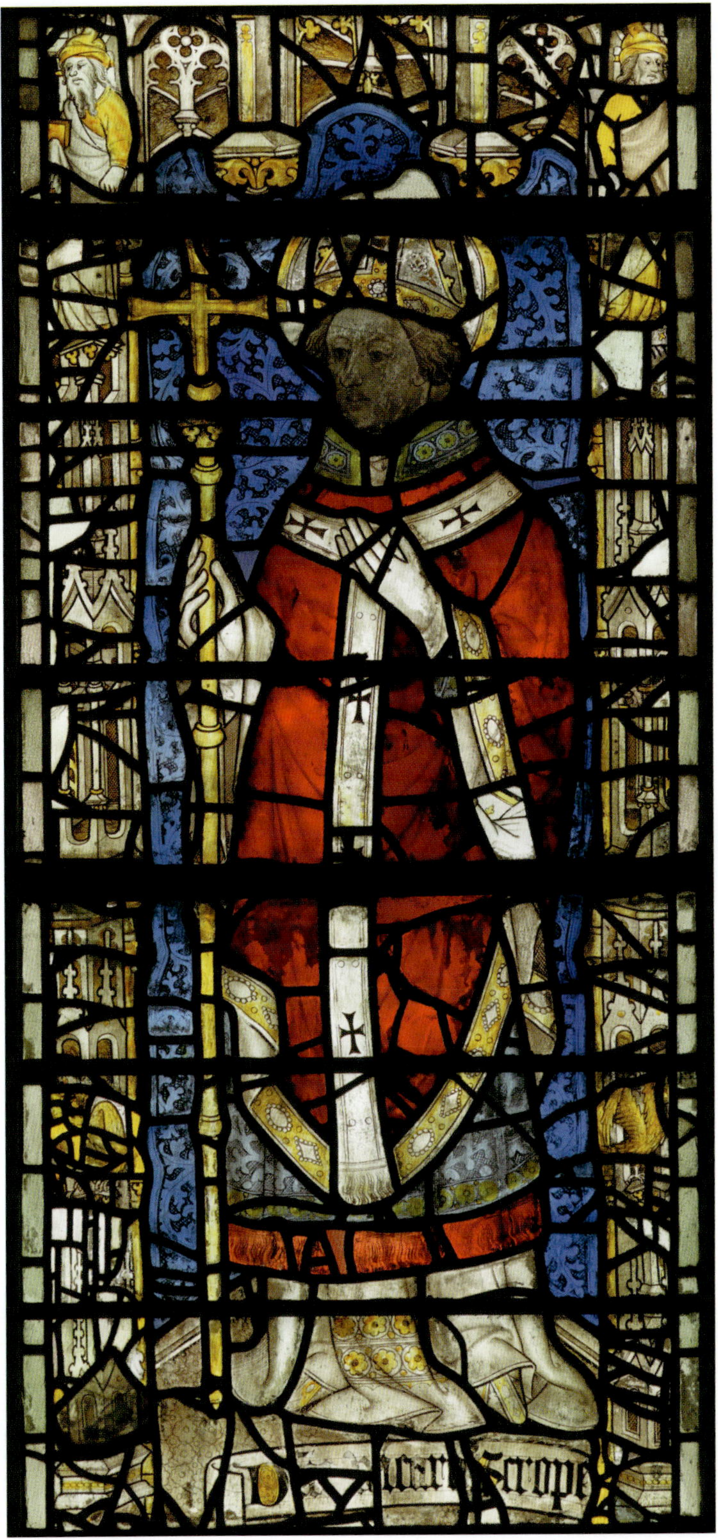

2.6). The popularity of the Arma Christi reflects the importance of late medieval devotion to the suffering of Christ, and especially to the wounds inflicted during his Passion and Crucifixion. Archbishop Scrope is known to have had a personal devotion to the wounds of Christ. He is said to have used them to adorn the banner that he took onto the field of battle in 1405, and invited his executioner to cut off his head with five blows in memory of Christ's five wounds. It has been suggested that the stone shield, albeit probably installed only after Richard Scrope's death, reflects his devotion to Christ's wounds, as it is 'viewed' by the Archbishop's proxy, his own heraldry, on the opposite side of the choir. Gazing on the Arma Christi afforded the viewer an indulgence – release from time in purgatory – so this placement is likely to have been deliberate. But could it also imply a closer connection between Scrope and this particular bay of the choir? The great window in the north-east transept, devoted to the life and miracles of St William, Archbishop of York (d.1154), was actually given after 1414 by Beatrice, dowager countess of Ros (d.1415), and she and her family appear at the base of the window. But was this always the intention, or did Beatrice step in to fill a patronage gap left by Scrope's death? This remains a speculation, but the devotion of one archbishop for his saintly predecessor would not be remarkable and while still bishop of Coventry and Lichfield, Richard Scrope had founded a chantry at Worfield in Shropshire dedicated to Christ, St Chad of Lichfield and St William of York. That members of the Scrope family may have shared a devotion to St William might be suggested by the fact that the arms of Henry, Lord Scrope, the Archbishop's nephew (d.1415), accompany the arms of St William in the seventh bay of the north choir arcade. Henry was executed for treason in 1415, extinguishing any lingering chance of Scrope patronage of a major Minster window. However, after declaring his devotion to the Virgin Mary, St John the Baptist, St Katharine and all the saints, his will requested a preference for burial in York Minster, not in the 'Scrop Chapell'

but between two columns on the north side behind the high altar, which would have placed him close to the place where the head shrine of St William was kept, and the place where the shrine of 1472 would eventually stand. The authorship of the St William Window is undocumented, but the development of such a huge image cycle out of a number of different sources required considerable ingenuity. On the grounds of style and quality the window has traditionally been attributed to John Thornton, long ago suggested by J. A. Knowles and an association that closer scrutiny of the Great East Window has tended to confirm. But even if the Ros family had already been secured as donors of the St William Window, it is not difficult to imagine Richard Scrope inviting John Thornton to York to take charge of the creation of three of the largest and most ambitious stained-glass narratives ever created. One final piece of evidence serves to link Thornton to the wider Scrope family circle. In 1406 the Archbishop's brother, Stephen, second Lord Scrope of Masham, bequeathed to him 6*s*. 8*d*. in his will.

Archbishop Scrope was eventually to be associated with a St William Window, although probably not in a way he had ever imagined. In the clerestory windows of the south-east transept, flanking the St Cuthbert window (s7), are images of Richard Scrope (S6), given by his nephew Stephen Scrope, archdeacon of Richmond (d.1418), facing an image of St William (S7), the gift of Robert Wolveden, treasurer of York (1426–32) and a former close associate of Archbishop Scrope. Archdeacon Stephen Scrope was buried next to his uncle in St Stephen's Chapel, and his windows contains the only image in the Minster to call Richard Scrope 'Sanctus Ricarde' (Fig. 2.7).

According to the Best of His Skill and Cunning

Whether it was an increasingly infirm Bishop Skirlaw or the ill-fated Archbishop Scrope who had invited John Thornton to come to York, in the winter of 1405, as the contract was signed, the project must have seemed an extremely daunting one. The city was still in uproar after the rebellion and death on 8 June of Archbishop Scrope. A number of the Archbishop's close circle, including the future Minster treasurer Canon Robert Wolveden, had to seek a royal pardon. The choice of Scrope's successor was not quickly resolved, and the new archbishop, Henry Bowet, a loyal supporter of Henry IV, was only enthroned in November 1407, by which time work must have been well under way. Nor was the Dean available to drive the project. Thomas Langley, another Lancastrian royal servant appointed dean in 1401, was frequently away on diplomatic business. In March 1405 he was made chancellor of England and in 1406 was promoted to episcopal status at Durham. His successor, John Prophete (1406–16), was another administrator and pluralist, with a licence to be absent from this cathedral for much of his tenure. In this administrative power vacuum the question arises as to who was able to maintain the momentum of the building and glazing projects, a situation made all the more acute by the fall of part of the central tower in the winter of 1405. Four of the residentiary canons, John Neuton (who had been treasurer since 1393), Thomas Haxey (who became treasurer in 1418), and canons Thomas Walleworth and William Waltham were all active in managing the Minster's affairs in these difficult years. These are the men most likely to have been on hand to offer advice, direction and even encouragement, providing the link between Thornton and his client, the Chapter of York. At least until his death in 1406 there may also have been a requirement to report progress to the donor, Bishop Skirlaw, and it is perhaps important to note that both John Neuton and William Waltham were beneficiaries of Bishop Skirlaw's will. When Neuton died in 1414 he bequeathed his very considerable library to the Minster, an act of generosity that resulted in the building of the Minster's free-standing library, its well-equipped reading room glazed with the shields of Minster benefactors, including those of Bishop Walter Skirlaw. Neuton's colleague and successor in the treasurership,

Thomas Haxey, who had supervised the repair of the fourth pier of the central tower, paid for the lead for the library roof. Neuton's literary and theological interests would have fitted him well for the role of intermediary between the stained-glass workshop and those who devised the glazing scheme. However, the contract makes it clear that a great deal of entrepreneurial and managerial responsibility was expected of John Thornton. He was required to recruit a team of craftsmen and glass painters to assist him. He was also to source and acquire the glass and other materials, which would have included glass paint, silver filings for the silver stain, lead for the casting of the calmes, solder and tallow, in addition to the tools and equipment needed in the workshop. He would also be required to liaise with the masons concerning the templates of the stone and the cutting of the glazing grooves to receive the stained glass, and with the blacksmith concerning the making of the window bars and the provision of tools for the glaziers, including dividing irons and grozing irons. Matthew Hutton records that Thornton was to manage these affairs on the Dean and Chapter's behalf 'in the same manner as he would have done if the like had to be done at his own costs and charges', a bid for good value for money, but also underlining the considerable trust that they reposed in him.

He Shall Portray the Said Window with His Own Hand: The Cartoons

It is probably those terms of the contract that relate to Thornton's work as an artist that have excited the greatest interest (see pp. 48–9). It is also the part of the document that can be most easily misunderstood when viewed from a modern perspective. After specifying the three-year duration of the project, the contract specifies that Thornton must portray 'with his own hand' (*manu sua propria portroiabit dictam fenestram*), all the specified historical images and painted work. Of the glass painting, also within his remit, he needed only to 'paynt the same as necessary

according to the Ordination of the Dean & Chapter'. In other words, the first operation could *only* be undertaken by Thornton himself, while he was expected to undertake only *some* of the glass painting, presumably delegating those things not ordained by the Dean and Chapter to other team members. What exactly does 'portraying' mean in this context? In the medieval stained-glass workshop, the task of 'portraying' a subject meant the act of translating a small-scale design (sometimes called a vidimus) into the full-scale 1:1 working drawing or cartoon from which the stained glass was made. As the 12th-century writer Theophilus explained, a stained-glass cartoon was usually drawn out at full scale on a whitened wooden table top, which combined the functions of cartoon, cut-line drawing and workbench for the reassembly and leading-up of the final panel. An inventory of stores for Westminster and Sheen palaces made in 1443 describes wooden 'portraying tables' of wainscot (oak) and poplar for the use of the glaziers and the trestles on which to support them.

That the task of 'portraying' was the skill most highly prized by Thornton's clients is implicit in the stipulations of his contract, but the status of this process is confirmed in the extremely detailed mid-14th-century accounts for the prestigious and costly royal glazing of St Stephen's Chapel, Westminster. Master John de Chestre, the man in overall charge, consistently received the highest wages of all the glaziers (7*s.* per week, irrespective of the number of working days in a week). He worked with five others, also termed master, all of them defined by their responsibilities for 'designing and painting on white tables', which were washed with ale at regular intervals throughout the project, allowing new designs to be drawn up on their whitened surfaces. In the hierarchy of payments made to the glazing team employed at Westminster, only those described as 'master' were entrusted with the designing on the white tables and they were most generously rewarded, at 12*d.* per day worked. Glass painters, by comparison, were

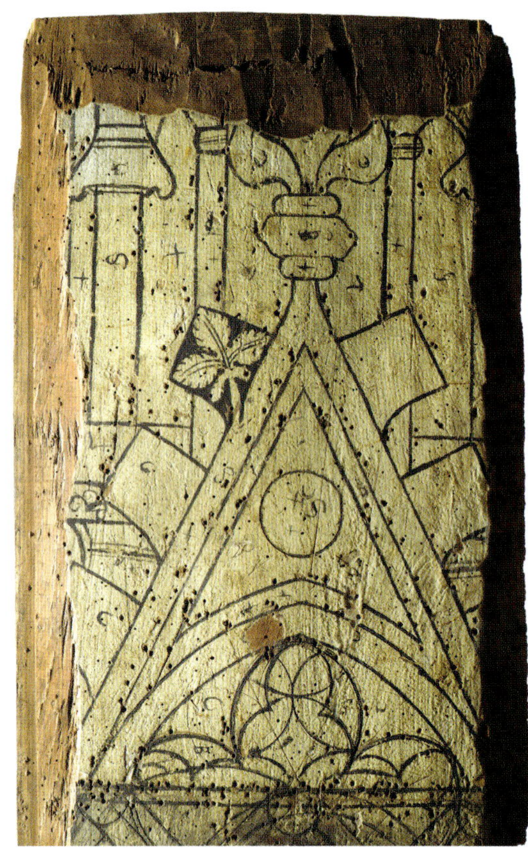

he claimed his well-earned bonus in 1408.

It is not hard to see why this process was so important. First of all, it is the cartoon that ensures that the small-scale preparatory drawings that have been approved by the client are accurately translated into a full-scale version in glass and lead. No preparatory drawings (vidimuses) for the Great East Window have survived, but given the complexity and sophistication of the subject matter, we can be sure that they must have existed in some form and they may even have formed an adjunct to the formal contract, as can be documented at the Beauchamp Chapel, Warwick (1447), the Lady Chapel of Westminster Abbey (1509) and King's College, Cambridge (1527), where patterns on paper were supplied by the client. The cartoon was also a highly technical 'document' crucial to the smooth operation of the glazing workshop. Every stained-glass panel must be made to the exact dimensions of the masonry opening prepared for it. Too large and it will not fit the tracery. Too small and it will fall out! The craftsmen who cut the glass, the painters who decorate it and the glaziers who reassemble it after firing in the kiln, all require the cartoon to guide them. While John Thornton may well have delegated a great deal to a skilled team of collaborators, in a very real sense he was the author of every single panel in the window.

Only two medieval glaziers' tables have survived. One, cut into two pieces, is all the more remarkable because stained-glass panels made on it have also been preserved, in the choir clerestory of Girona Cathedral (in Catalonia). The Girona table (Fig. 2.8), whitened with a gesso-like coating, bears the outline of a number of designs easily identified in the cathedral's stained glass, and the pattern of nail holes shows that the table was used from the first setting-out of the design through to the leading-up of the panels, as described by Theophilus. Ultraviolet examination of the table's surface has also revealed that more than one design was manufactured on the table, with the first design being washed off to allow another to be set out, although whether ale was

paid only 7*d*. per day, while those engaged in 'breaking and fitting glass' were paid 6*d*. and glaziers' mates received only 4½*d*. per day. While the wage rates at Westminster were apparently higher than those enjoyed by Thornton nearly 50 years later, this is probably explained by post-Black Death wage inflation and the prestige of a royal project. While the sums of money involved at York were different, the Westminster accounts are nonetheless invaluable in helping us to understand the hierarchy of status within a medieval glazing workshop, and to appreciate that it was the cartooning process that was most highly prized, and earned the recognition of mastery. Unlike John de Chestre, John Thornton had no assistance in this onerous task and so personally had cartooned well over 300 individual panels of stained glass by the time

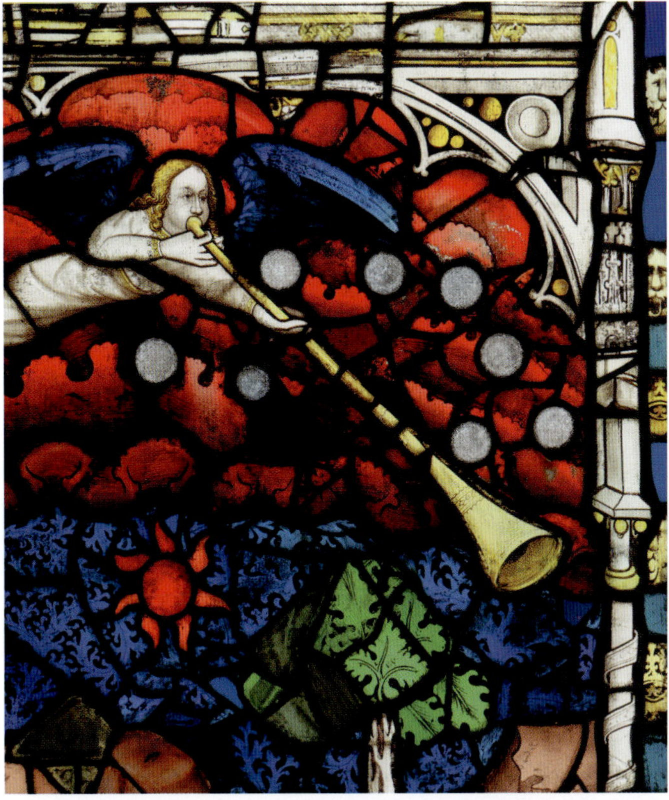

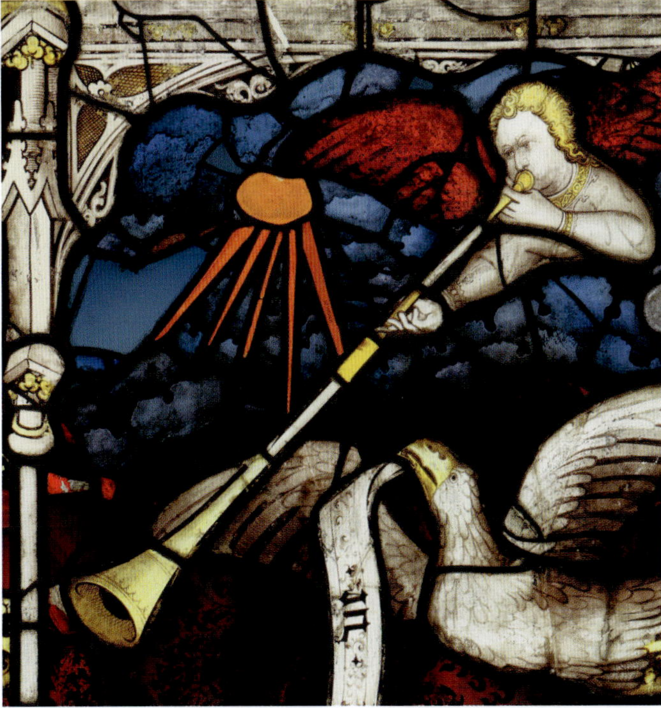

used, as at Westminster, cannot be determined! The most noticeable 'washed' area, in which the shadow of an earlier design of a standing figure of the Virgin Annunciate is discernible with the benefit of UV light, is immediately below the very well-preserved drawing of a canopy head. This shows that the cartoon of the canopy head, used to frame several of the standing figures in the choir clerestory glazing, was carefully retained, while the area immediately below was washed to receive new figures as the project progressed, minimising the amount of new work required of the workshop master. This observation of the Girona table has helped to shed light on a long-standing puzzle in the Great East Window.

Writing in the 1690s, antiquary James Torre had noted that four panels, at the end of row 9 and beginning of row 8, depicting the angels blowing four of the seven trumpets described in Revelation 8:7–13, were in the wrong biblical order. Torre had recorded them in the order Second Trumpet (in 9j), Third Trumpet (in 8a), Fourth Trumpet (in 8b), First Trumpet (in 8c). This was long assumed to represent some undocumented intervention in the window's past in which the panels had all been removed at the same time, only to be returned in the wrong order. Accordingly, after the Second World War, Dean Milner-White returned the panels to what is undoubtedly their correct biblical order. During the recent conservation of the window, it was realised that this could not be the correct explanation of the apparent error. Each of the top six rows of the Apocalypse section of this nine-light window was designed to have its own distinctive canopy design. It was observed, however, there are actually ten panels framed in a 'row 9' canopy design and only eight panels framed in a 'row 8' canopy (Figs. 2.9 and 2.10). The second and fourth angels in the biblical sequence have both been framed in row 9 canopies whereas they should both be framed ready to go into row 8. The first angel, which should be framed for row 9, is framed for row 8. Only the third angel is correctly framed for its location in row 8. The problem was probably compounded by the location of the sequence in the overall narrative, which required the first four angels to be split between two rows, while at least two of the panels are also compositionally similar. Nor was this an isolated example of a 'production error'. From row 5 downwards, canopy arrangements become more complicated, with alternating designs used across the row. This is maintained without a problem until row 2. In this row panel 2c is not framed for its row 2 location, but in the same frame as panels 3b, 3d, 3f and 3h in the row above.

The most likely explanation of this error is that in preparation for the creation of a new design it was the glaziers' normal practice to wash the table area *inside* the framing canopy, as appears to have been the case at Girona, thereby minimising the amount of work that the master had to set out anew. In these few instances, it looks as if Master John Thornton drew out the narratives inside the wrong architectural frame. This explanation also implies that the workshop had more than one row in production at the same time, or at very least that the execution of one row overlapped with the execution of its successor, and that, as we might have expected, the rows were worked on in numerical order. In rows 8 and 9 these problems cannot have gone unnoticed, as the order of the biblical narrative and the correct ordering of the canopy design can never be reconciled. How Thornton resolved the problem with his clients we cannot know and it has taken over 600 years for it to be noticed again!

The recent re-examination of the Girona table has also challenged earlier assumptions derived from Theophilus's 12th-century description of medieval glazing practice, which implies that *all* details required to make the stained-glass panel were supplied on the table. The Girona table shows rather that the master in overall charge of this project afforded a significant degree of autonomy to the individual team members, even after the full-size 'skeleton' of the window design has been determined.

The designs on the Girona table do not actually indicate all the necessary glass cut-lines (and thus the lead lines) and, indeed, leave out altogether some lines that would be critical to the cutting and leading of glass for a viable stained-glass panel. The superimposition of the cut-line of several of the Girona Cathedral canopies as they were actually made, onto the lead lines indicated on the table, shows that glass was cut and leaded in a variety of different combinations. The master therefore allowed the individual craftsman to judge where best to place subsidiary lead lines and thus how best to cut a piece of glass, ensuring that sheets could be cut economically and without waste. This realisation has important implications for our understanding of working relationships within a tight-knit team, and also for the status of individual components within the whole. While based on a single design 'template', the Girona table reminds us that stained-glass panels, even when made to a repeated cartoon, were anything but a mass-produced product. Each one is, in effect, unique, a version of the master's cartoon rather than a replica of it. How much more is this true of John Thornton's designs for the Great East Window, each panel a complex narrative with only limited areas of repetitive design, predominantly in the architectural frames.

Paint the Same as Necessary

That the Dean and Chapter required Thornton to paint at least some of the window himself shows that his skills in this regard were prized. On the other hand, it also means that some of the work could be delegated to his hand-picked collaborators, and as we can see from the Westminster accounts, painters were paid significantly less than the masters who cartooned the designs. A question that continues to intrigue us is the meaning of the words 'paint the same where need required according to the Ordination of the Dean & Chapter'. In other words, can we identify the hand of John Thornton himself in the painting of the Great East Window? Sadly

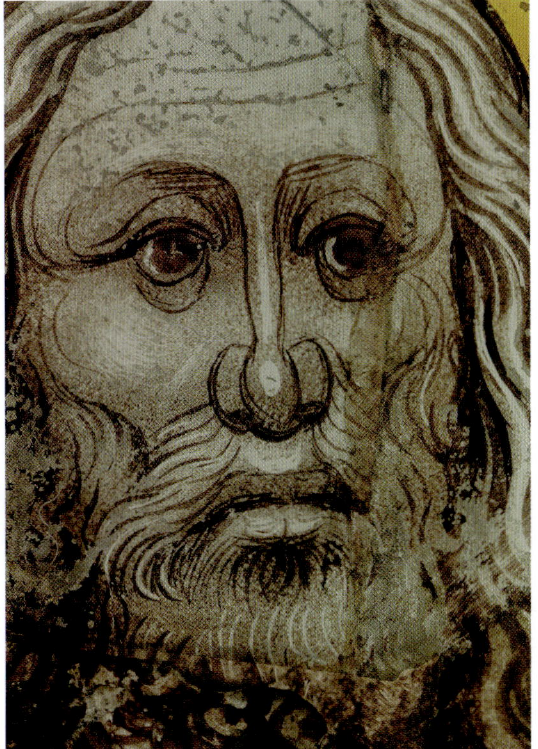

Fig. 2.11
The head of Christ in panel 2h.

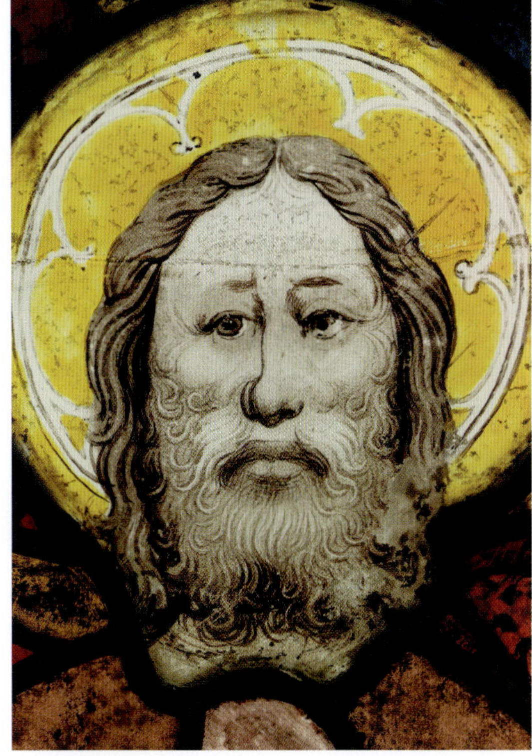

Fig. 2.12
The head of Christ in panel 2j (the adjoining panel).

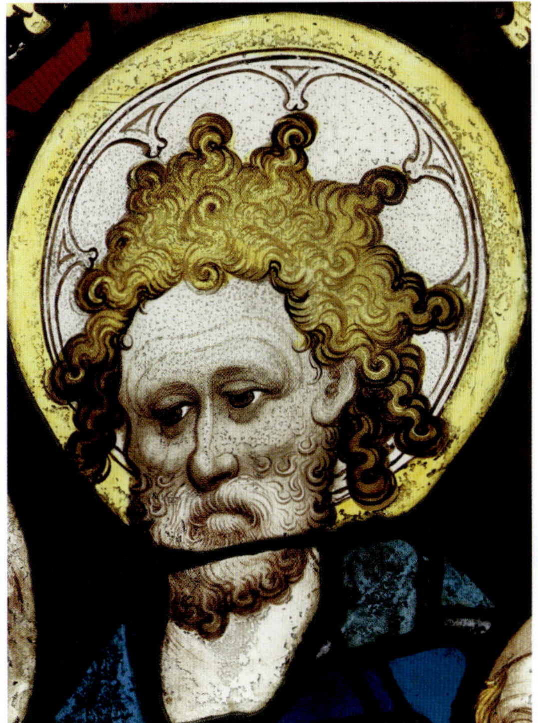

Fig. 2.13
The head of St John in panel 11c.

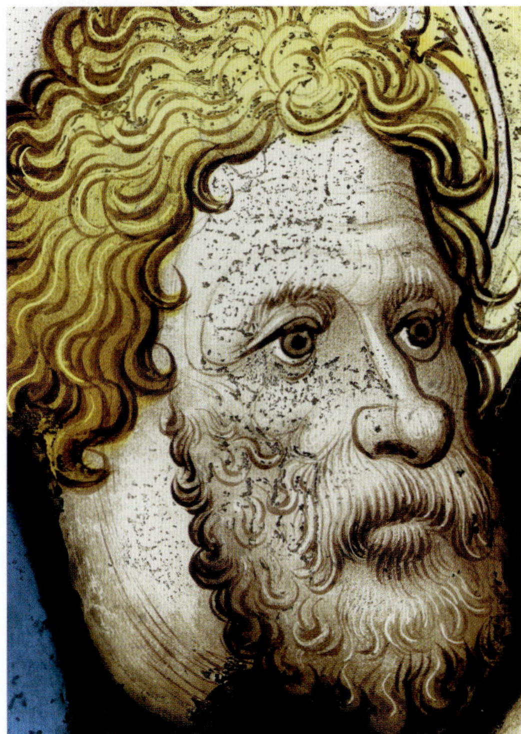

Fig. 2.14
The head of St John in panel 10f.

the answer is no! Even a superficial study of the painting styles shows that there are several hands at work. The conservators of the York Glaziers Trust (YGT) have identified at least three painters, if not four, working on the heads of figures, traditionally that part of any painting carrying the greatest emotional and symbolic significance and thereby calling upon the greatest artistic skill. Another painter probably worked on the architectural structures in the window, and there are at least two variations in the painting of the background 'seaweed' foliage. Another potentially specialist role may have been assigned to whoever painted the scrolls and inscriptions in the window. While some painted 'words' are merely lines designed to look like writing when seen from a distance (the open books in panels 10c and 8g, for example), the many lettered scrolls of Latin text are executed expertly, with a high degree of textual accuracy, set out between fine guidelines such as scribes would have prepared in the copying of a manuscript, while the Latin is punctuated with appropriate abbreviation marks and word spacers. The enrichment of capital letters and the pen flourishing embellishments are also comparable to the work of a professional scribe. In panel 1b on the fur collar of the central king, the name 'Lucius' has been painted on top of the ermine tails, supporting the suggestion that the lettering was a specialist task assigned to a particular painter. An *extremely* fine brush must have been used to achieve these inscriptions, and in only one instance has a smudge been allowed to remain!

No attempt at a detailed analysis of artistic or stylistic hierarchy within the Great East Window has yet been attempted and the problem is compounded by the fact that all of the work is characterised by the consistently high standard of painting, so that no distinctions can easily be made in purely qualitative terms. Thornton clearly picked his collaborators with great discernment, and applied strict quality control over the whole work, as his contract required. It is also clear, however, that the Dean and Chapter

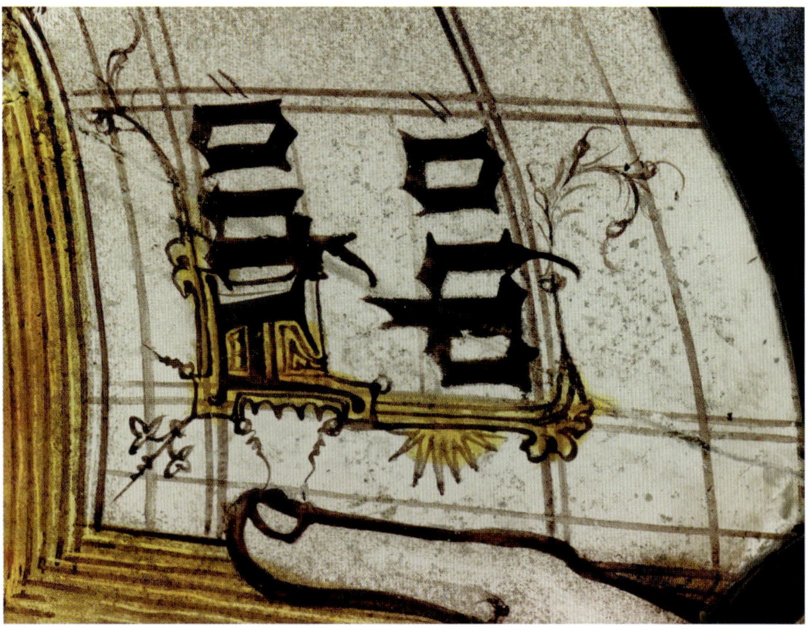

expected Thornton himself to paint some glass 'as necessary' and that this contribution was somehow to be defined by the client ('according to the Ordination of the Dean & Chapter'). Can we interpret what might have been ordained by the Dean and Chapter? Could the status of the figure depicted be a guide? By this reckoning all of the figures (and especially the heads) of God himself, and by extension those of Christ, might fall into this category. However, more than one hand can be detected in the work, even when the figures in question are in adjoining panels, and they cannot all be the work of Thornton (Figs. 2.11 and 2.12). Nor are the figures of St John, the narrator of the Apocalypse narrative, all by the same painter (Figs. 2.13 and 2.14). The proximity of the figure to the viewer might be another criterion of interest to the client. Unfortunately, one panel that combines proximity to the viewer and a figure of Christ in Judgement, a panel occupying the axial location in the window (2e), directly beneath the figure of God as the Alpha and the Omega at the very apex of the window (DD1) and thus a prime candidate to have been the work of Thornton, has suffered catastrophic damage and the original head and much of the figure of the enthroned Judge have been lost. The client might also have requested that Thornton paint the head of the donor, Walter Skirlaw, in 1e. Sadly, this panel has also been badly damaged and the original head had been lost by the early 19th century. The image of St Edward the Confessor in panel 1d is undoubtedly one of the most accessible and also one of the most admired 'portraits' in the whole window and remains a strong candidate to have been by the master. On the other hand many of the figures in the highest reaches of the tracery are also exceptionally fine. The lettered Latin scrolls are also consistently painted to a very high standard (Fig. 2.15) and the Word of God would surely have been considered of the utmost importance to the Dean and Chapter, so they must be included among the list of candidates. We are forced to conclude, therefore, that we can only guess as to which pieces of glass were painted by Thornton himself. On the other hand, the outstanding quality of all of the glass painting, whether by Thornton or others, can be attributed to him, as he was charged with the recruitment and oversight of this exceptional team of glass painters, and had established a very high benchmark of quality.

Despite the anonymity of Thornton's collaborators and our ignorance as to their number and their origins, the Great East Window still has a great deal to tell us about medieval stained-glass workshop practice. In a modern workshop it is common for all the glass pieces to be stuck to a plate glass easel, an invention of the 19th century, or laid out on an illuminated table, so that the glass painter can work against the light on large sections of the window at once and at times when natural light is in short supply. This was impossible in a medieval workshop because of the limited size of glass sheets and the lack of suitable artificial illumination. In the 12th century Theophilus implies that *all* details to be painted were first marked out on the glaziers' table, something which is actually contradicted by the evidence of the Girona table, on which only one vine-leaf crocket is filled in. While Theophilus

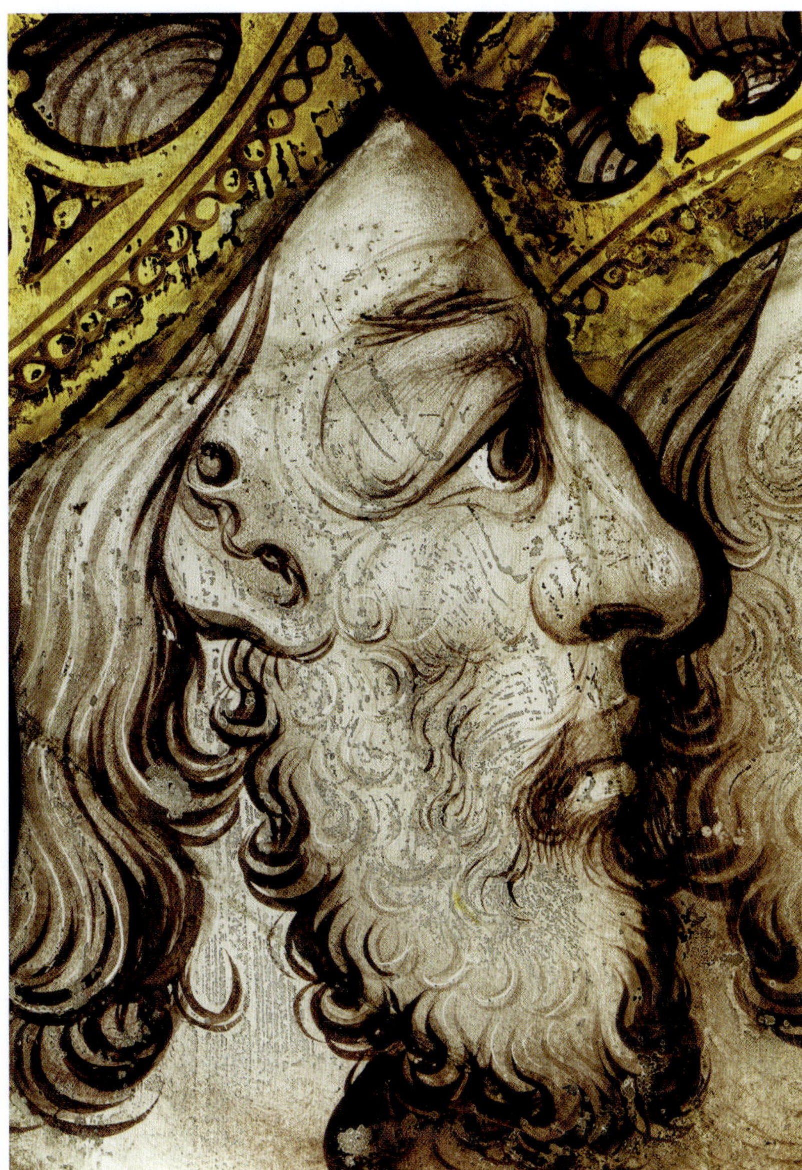

Fig. 2.16
Darker trace lines applied over the softer modelling washes: Detail of heads of kings in panel 11g.

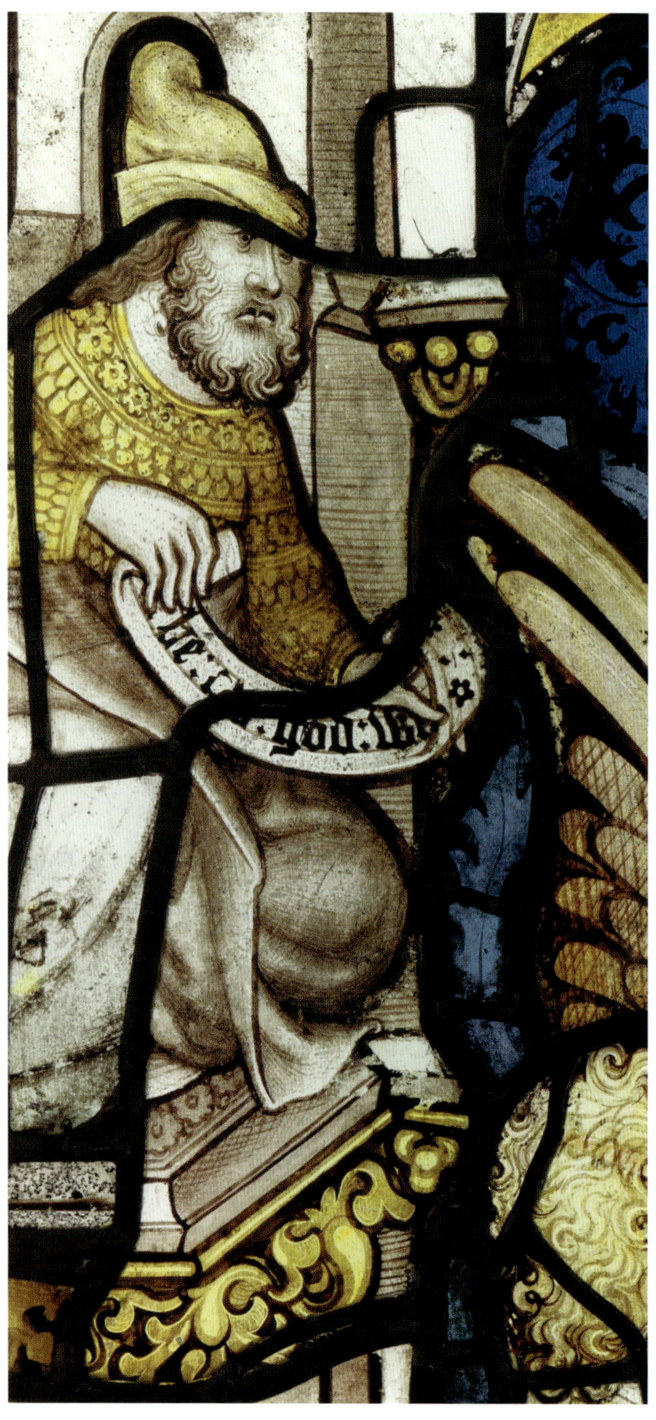
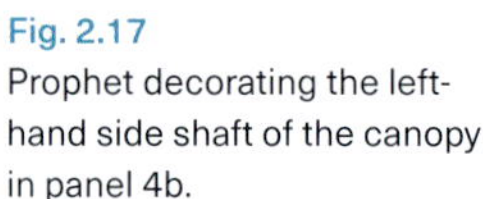

Fig. 2.17
Prophet decorating the left-
hand side shaft of the canopy
in panel 4b.

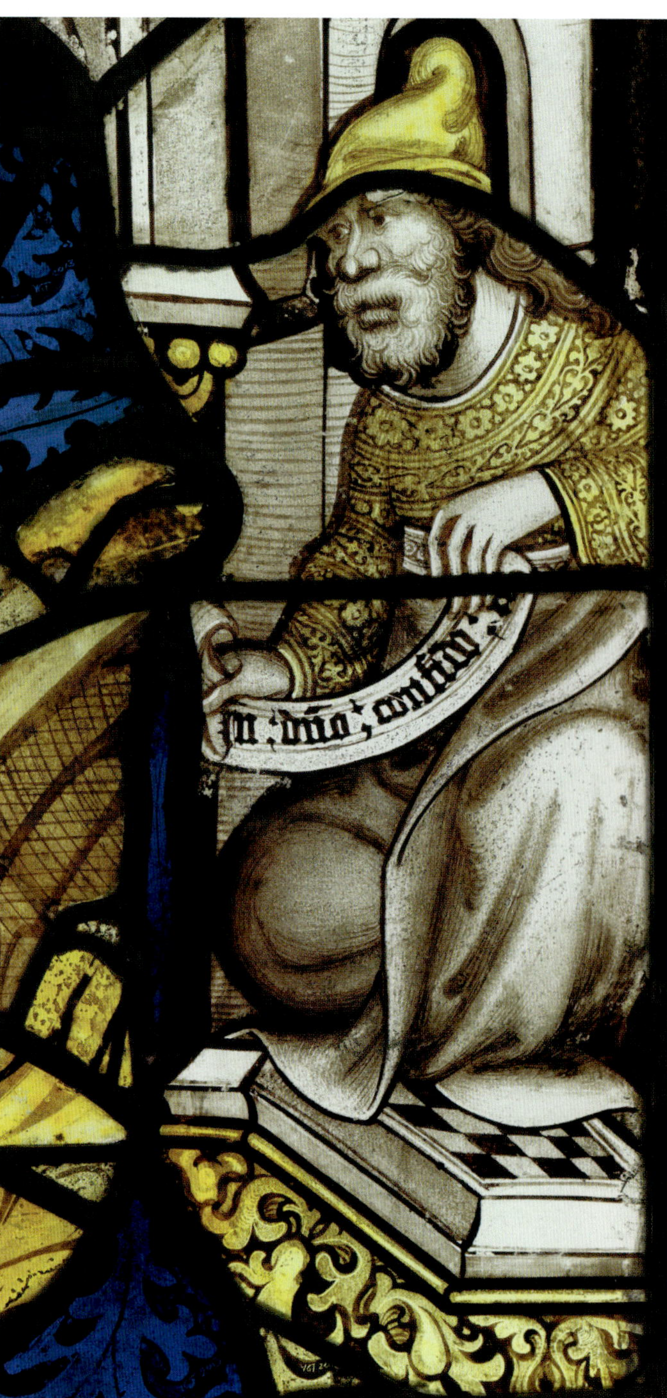

Fig. 2.18
Prophet decorating the right-
hand side shaft of the canopy
in panel 4b.

also provides rather elaborate instructions as to how to transfer information from the glaziers' table to the glass, the way glass is painted makes it rather unlikely that all glass-painting detail was created directly on top of the table, with the glass laid over the cartoon, something which anyway does not work well with darker-coloured pieces.

Stained glass works by allowing light to be coloured and modified by the application of differing amounts of glass paint. The delicate layering of paint typical of Thornton's workshop makes it all the more unlikely that the painters worked on top of the tables. It can also be observed that their painting is actually applied 'in reverse', with modelling washes applied before solid trace lines, which are applied last, on top of the modelling (Fig. 2.16). Without the benefit of underlit light tables or large-scale plate glass easels, complex, multilayered glass painting could only be done on the *front* of the piece of glass by following a framework of visible guidelines applied to the *back* of it. This would allow the glass painter to work away from the opaque cartoon and against the light at a window. Once the painting was complete, the temporary guidelines could be wiped off prior to the application of any modifying back-painting and the application of any silver stain, which is almost always applied to the exterior surface. On some pieces from the Great East Window (and in other Minster windows), these temporary guidelines have been overlooked or only partially wiped away, and because they too had been applied using fusible glass paint, they have also been fired and made permanent, inadvertently providing clues as to how designs were translated from cartoon to glass and how the glass painters achieved such astonishingly sophisticated layered effects.

In the painting of the architectural canopies there are numerous instances where the left- and right-hand side of a panel are mirror images of one another, with a degree of precision that free-hand copying could not achieve. This precision is best explained through the transfer of a 'master

detail' from the table in the form of guidelines on the back of the glass as just described, but might also suggest that this level of detail was supplied only once on the cartoon and was then reversed, something seen in a small number of surviving late medieval paper cartoons, in which the master has only worked up one side of the drawing. In those architectural designs with figures standing in niches, the exact replication of detail even extends to the main lines of drapery folds. Within these identical guidelines, however, there is a considerable amount of variation in the execution of shading, details of decoration and the application of silver stain, indicating the degree of licence afforded to individual painters (Figs. 2.17 and 2.18). Occasionally mistakes were made, as when the shadowing of an architectural feature is applied to the wrong side. In some cases it is also possible that different painters have worked on opposite sides of the panel.

It is perhaps not surprising that the evidence of close copying is found most

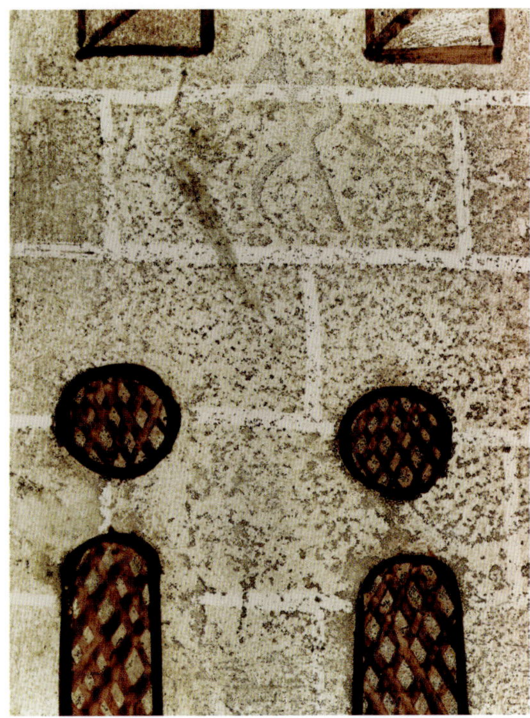

An early 16th-century 'vidimus' (approved sketch design) for a 13-light window. Probably made for an unrealised glazing project for Cardinal Thomas Wolsey.

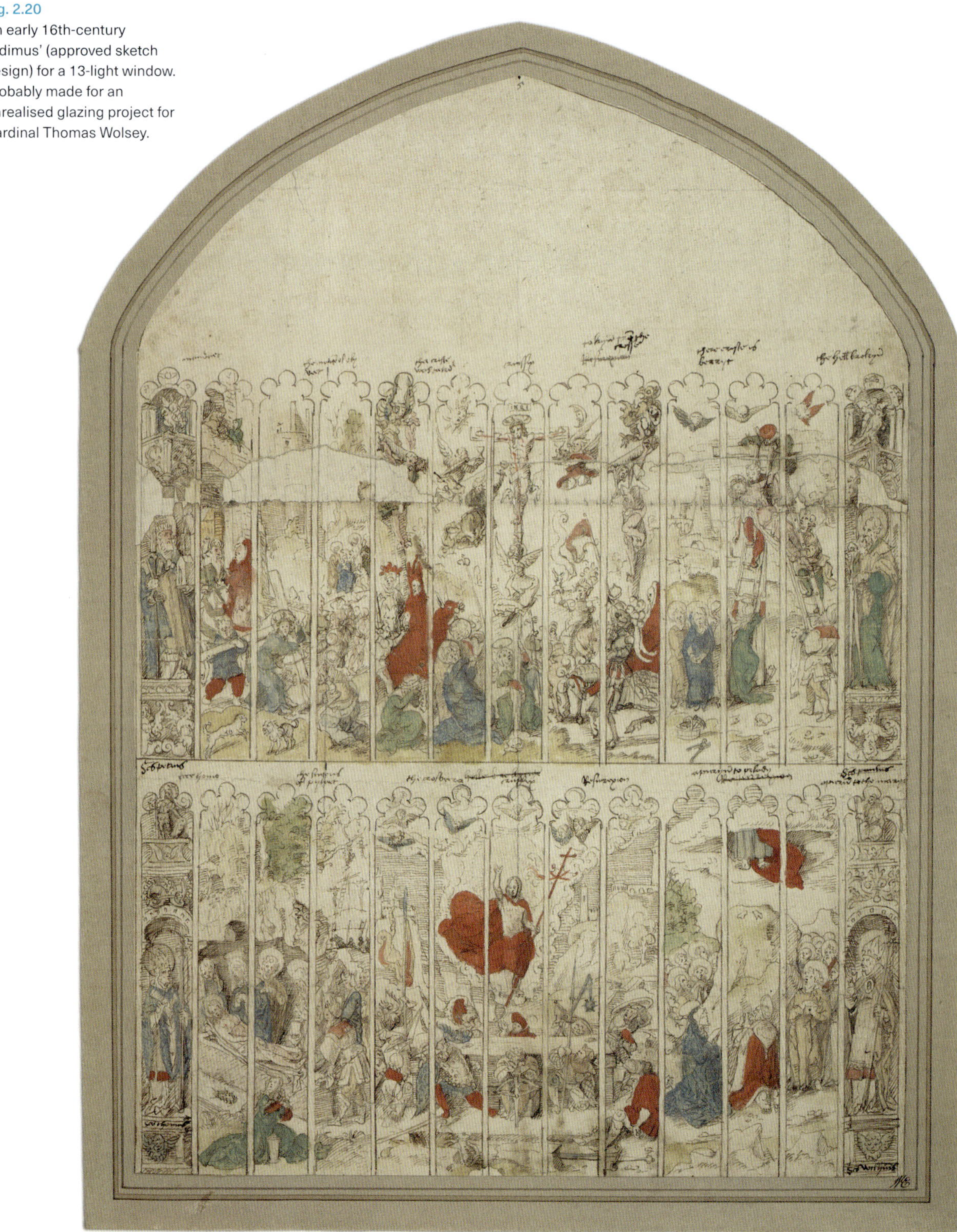

frequently in connection with the more 'mechanistic' aspects of the design, as these are the parts of the project that would have been assigned to the less expert or experienced members of the glazing team. The canopies are also, of course, one of the few parts of the window that are made up of repeated elements and allow, therefore, for a streamlining of production methods. We can imagine that Thornton would entrust the execution of the more challenging and individualistic aspects of the cartoon, and especially the figurative narratives, to his most expert and trusted collaborators who probably had access to the vidimuses on which the master had worked in collaboration with the client at the earliest stage of the design process. Paper patterns for the use of glaziers can be documented in England from the 1440s onwards and probably existed at a much earlier date. However, examination of a vidimus reveals the huge gap between the sketch design and the window design as executed (Fig. 2.20). With the major outlines of the designs marked out at full scale on the glaziers' tables, with an indication of critical colour choices and the correct text selections, it would be an easy matter for a team of highly expert and close-knit colleagues to retrieve finer details from a set of reference drawings, with a degree of artistic licence allowed in matters such as the choice of decorative motif for drapery and the choice of vegetation for landscape details.

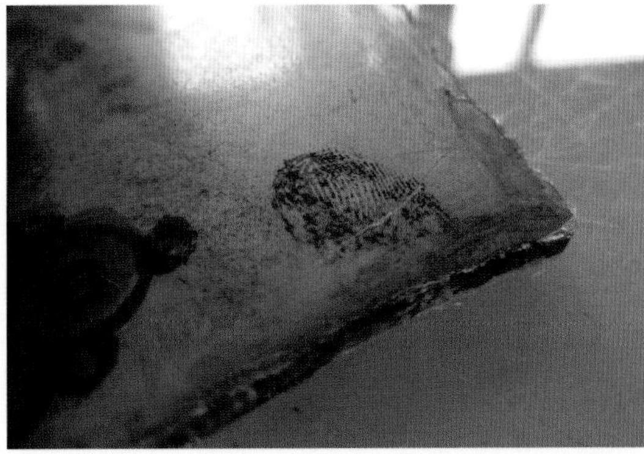

Fig. 2.21
A glazier's fingerprint accidentally preserved in a smear of glass paint on the edge of a fragment in panel 11g.

This adaptive and fluid approach to manufacture goes a long way to explain the ambiguous 'glaziers' marks', discreet and barely visible marks which in the Great East Window are wiped out of a fired paint layer, and predominantly found in the more 'anonymous' areas of a panel, including architectural frames and backgrounds (Fig. 2.19). Comparisons have been made with masons' marks (which informed the payment of the masons) and carpenters' assembly marks. While some glaziers' marks may have indicated the order of assembly, for architectural elements, for example, this cannot explain the large numbers of the same mark scattered widely across a single panel, and all orientated in the same direction. However, once the 'bespoke' nature of the cutting of the glass for each panel is appreciated, it can be seen that, after firing, the glaziers needed to reassemble the pieces belonging to each specific 'jigsaw puzzle' of painted and fired glass with speed and precision. While large, distinctive pieces belonging to unique figures or narrative compositions could be recognised with relative ease, repeated elements within a scheme could be less easily distinguished from one another, and although there were superficial similarities, glass pieces were not readily interchangeable from one panel to another, even if prepared on the same glaziers' table.

The final stage in the process of manufacture involved the reassembly of the fired pieces and their glazing up, using strong and malleable lead calmes. This process was carried out on top of the cartoon marked out on the glaziers' table, and the Girona table is covered in the holes (some with the tips of the nails still in them) made by the 'closing nails' that held the glass pieces in place until they could be soldered to make a strong, unbreakable matrix. Medieval window leads were cast rather than milled, which gave them great strength; window leads made in the second quarter of the 14th century are still fulfilling their function in the windows of the choir clerestory of Cologne

Cathedral. Unfortunately, very little medieval lead has survived in the Minster's windows. Only a small section of the shield of St William in panel 1j retains its delicate medieval leads (see Fig. 4.19). Even in this functional process we can discern the evidence of the designer's skill, for example, in the introduction of some subtle deviation from the strictly vertical in order to avoid the creation of weak 'hinge points' in the leading patterns, in the creation of intersections in the leading to allow for the fixing of the ties that enable the panels to be connected to the support bars, and in locating the support bars so that they perform their structural function and yet avoid cutting across faces or key iconographic features. The final quality control and checking to ensure that every panel in the window was of the highest technical quality and correct in all its iconographic and textual detail must have been one of Thornton's most onerous responsibilities. There are very few signs of careless execution in the window – the occasional fingerprint and the marks left by filaments of cloth from a glazier's clothing trapped in the unfixed paint are rare but precious links to a team of exceptional artists and craftsmen (Fig. 2.21).

We are forced to conclude that we will probably never know which parts of the Great East Window were actually painted by John Thornton's own hand. The status of the figure and the scene to be represented, its iconographic or technical challenges, and its proximity to the viewer may all have played a part in determining his contribution to the painting of the glass 'according to the ordination of the Dean and Chapter'. But through the agency of the cartoon and in his role as designer, mentor, manager and leader, John Thornton's influence must have pervaded the spirit of every panel and influenced every stage in the conduct of the work.

Thornton as Designer

The parallels between the stained glass of the Great East Window and that of a number of illuminated manuscripts, explored more fully in in Chapter 5, do not mean that Thornton merely slavishly copied from the sources to which he was introduced by someone well versed in theology and conversant with a number of illuminated manuscripts. The extraordinary power of the biblical narrative in the Great East Window can undoubtedly be attributed to the genius of John Thornton, and for his skill in envisioning and reinvigorating well-established pictorial models, we can call him the author of this medieval masterpiece. With a limit placed upon the number of scenes that could be accommodated in the window – 81 assigned to the Apocalypse – a process of selection and editing was called for and it is likely that it was in this process that Thornton the designer exercised his particular skills. The manuscript apocalypses could vary widely in the number of their illustrations and both of the manuscript models identified by Professor Nigel Morgan had more scenes than Thornton could accommodate in the window. The Douce MS, for example, has 97 surviving pictures (with three leaves lost). Some of Thornton's compositional decisions were designed to shape the narrative to suit its architectural context (Fig. 2.22). A book can present its illustrations across no more than two open pages at a time, meaning that the reader must turn a page to advance the narrative. The 'reader' of the Great East Window, on the other hand, has the total narrative laid out in rows across the window's nine lights. The division of the window into rows of nine scenes meant that the standard iconography of the ages of the world was subtly adjusted so that each age could be represented by a distinct row in the window. The stained-glass narrative follows the order of the biblical text, reading from left to right, starting at the top left-hand corner and working down, while the window offers a completely different reading mode, allowing a 'sampling' of the entire narrative. It allows the

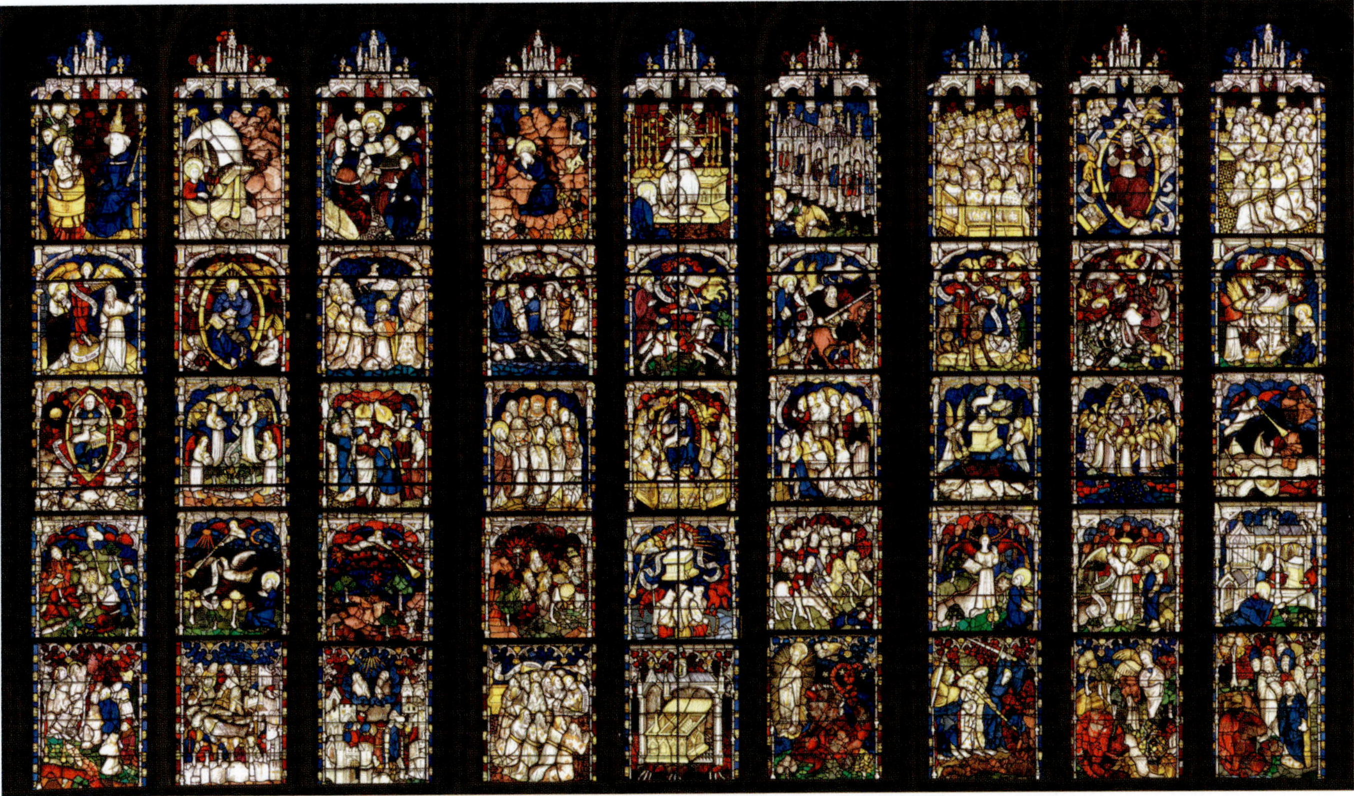

Fig. 2.22
Rows 7 to 12 of the Great East Window following the 2011–17 conservation.

'reader' to construct the typological relationships between scenes in the Old Testaments section of the window and the tracery above, and lends itself especially well to the non-linear and visionary nature of the Apocalypse text.

Where episodes are spread over more than one scene – God enthroned in the midst of the elders (Revelation 4:4–11 in 11g, 11h and 11j), or the story of the two witnesses (Revelation 11:3–13 in 7a, 7b, 7c), for example – Thornton favoured triplets of panels and ensured that they were always confined within one of the main three-light window subdivisions. This means that the thicker mullions act as a kind of stone 'bookmark' helping the viewer to group the scenes that are to be read together. In each one of three main blocks of the window, particular use is made of the central light for emphasis, especially for images of God. This preference is especially apparent in the Apocalypse section and has been even

more strongly underlined by the repositioning of panels into their correct location as a result of the recent conservation. The panel depicting God, the Lamb and the Book (Revelation 5:6–7), for example, wrongly placed in panel 10c by Dean Milner-White, has returned to its central location (10b) in the left-hand block of the window. The axial light (light e), in particular, contains the largest number of enthroned and raised-up images of the Godhead and this axial line also connects God the Father at the window's head (DD1) with Christ as the Judge at its base (2e). It is no accident that the window's donor, Walter Skirlaw, is also in this light (1e), at the feet of the Judge, in a line that unites heaven and earth.

Other episodes are compressed into single scenes. In the opening sequence, for example, Thornton combines into a single scene John's vision of the seven churches of Asia (Revelation 2:1–2) and subsequent verses in which John is instructed to write to each one of them (eight separate images in the Douce Apocalypse). Thornton devised a unique composition (panel 11f) in which he took the tabernacle structure of the vision employed in several of the manuscript versions, but instead of filling it with the angels of the biblical text, as the illuminators always do, he populated the structure with figures of bishops, representative of ecclesiastical authority, an adjustment rather appropriate for the east window of a metropolitan cathedral. Another compressed design illustrates Revelation 8:8–10, where John is told first to take the book from the Mighty Angel and then is instructed to eat it. In panel 8h Thornton shows the angel thrusting the book directly into John's mouth, and the accompanying scroll combines the words of the Mighty Angel's two separate instructions to John into a single command: 'Take the book and prophesy.'

The Great East Window, unlike an illuminated manuscript, must work as image without text. Even the Westminster chapter-house paintings, which unlike the window could be viewed at almost eye level, closely replicate the page layout of their manuscript model, with extracts of the text written on vellum actually pasted onto the wall beneath the relevant illustration so that they have the appearance of oversized pages in a picture book. Thornton could accommodate neither the extensive extracts from the biblical text nor the commentary that is a hallmark of every illuminated-manuscript Apocalypse. That is not to say that the window is devoid of text, however. Many of the figures in the tracery have labels that identify the figures. In the main lights 28 scenes have elaborate scrolls lettered with carefully penned and accurate Latin texts, 26 of them relating to the Apocalypse narrative. Some Apocalypse panels have more than one elegantly curling scroll, which adds to the decorative quality of the design. They are in the regular 'black-letter' script of the 15th century and are written as a professional scribe would write, with evenly spaced letters balanced between delicately painted guidelines, with

appropriate Latin abbreviation marks and word spacers. In places there are even pen flourishes and decoration added to initial letters. There are also five open books inscribed with legible text (panels 5f, 2d, 2h, 2j), while Moses' tablets are inscribed with words for the Gospel of St Luke (Q2), and the robe of the leading rider in 3e and 3g is decorated with the Latin words 'King of Kings and Lord of Lords', required by the biblical text. The scrolls in the narrative panels bear the specific words of reported speech. Only two of the Old Testament scenes use this device (14j and 13b), but they are used extensively in the Apocalypse scenes, bearing the words heard and recorded by John. A significant number of the words, such as the instruction 'Come and See' in panels 11h, 10e, 10f, 10g and 10h, are specifically addressed to him. The majority of scrolls record the words emanating from a single speaker, comparable to a speech bubble in a cartoon, suggesting that the window is conceived as a giant drama with speaking parts. In some of the scenes the artist includes scrolls that record the words spoken by more than one person, as in 11h where the words 'Holy, Holy, Holy' (*Sanctus, Sanctus, Sanctus*) spoken continuously by the four living creatures, flutter through the background. In 10d, a panel much damaged, the single word 'Amen' is spoken by every creature in heaven. There are some scenes in which the Apocalypse text records the spoken word but there are no scrolls, which initially seems a strange omission. However, these omissions all seem to occur where a large group join in singing or proclaiming in unison, and perhaps as a designer sensitive to the legibility of his monumental Apocalypse, Thornton could find no easy solution to the challenge of attributing speech to a large group of characters without making a scene confused and illegible.

The indebtedness of the Great East Window to older, well-established iconographic formulae cannot detract from its creative responsiveness to the demands of its subject matter. Some of the adaptations reflect the cleverness of a designer steeped in experience of this challenging medium.

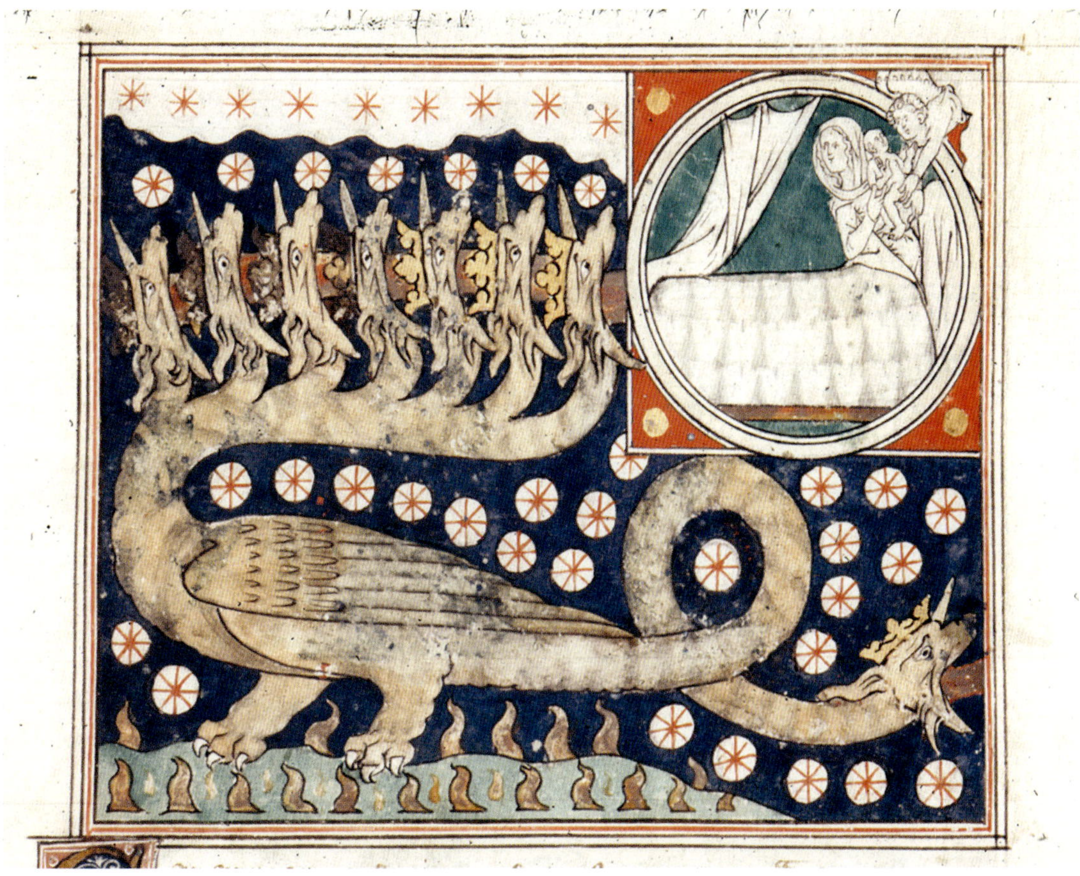

Fig 2.23
The dragon pulls down one third of the stars (Revelation 21:1–5), as depicted in the 14th-century Queen Mary Psalter (London, British Library, Royal B XV, fol. 21r).

In panel 11e, for example, Thornton skilfully manages to juggle most of the key elements required of the image of the vision of the Son of Man seated in the midst of the seven candlesticks, a feat that few illuminators achieved. The mouth of the Son of Man is pierced by the sharp two-edged sword in accordance with the text. The skilful application of silver stain has ensured that his face shines like the sun while his hair remains white 'as white wool, and as snow' (Revelation 1:14). Realising too, that the seven stars would be well-nigh invisible if held in His right hand, Thornton has scattered them amongst the right-hand candlesticks, where they are silhouetted against the ruby background, making them legible from a distance. Other devices suggest a thoughtful response to the demands of the text. In panel 7f, for example, Thornton has combined an episode illustrated in two scenes in his manuscript models. The woman clothed in the sun (Revelation 12:1–5) stands on the moon, her head wreathed in a crown of stars. She is menaced by a seven-headed ruby dragon, and her pregnant state is indicated by her gesture and her loosely laced dress, although her son is safely raised to heaven by an angel. The stained-glass scene shares with the manuscripts the depiction of a dragon with an elaborately curling tail. Prior to restoration the stars in the heaven mentioned in the text, and numerous in the manuscript images (Fig. 2.23), were nowhere to be seen. Careful examination of the grozed edges of the original glass revealed that Thornton's heaven once contained only three stars, one of which was caught in the coils of the dragon's tail, allowing a very literal visualisation of the text: 'And his tail drew the third part of the stars of heaven, and cast them to the earth.' The careful placing of text scrolls is also suggestive of a direct response to the text: in panel 10g depicting the rider on the black horse (Revelation 6:5–6), John 'heard as it were a voice in the midst of the four living creatures, saying: Two pounds of wheat for a penny, and thrice two pounds of barley for a penny, and see though hurt not the wine and the oil.' In Thornton's depiction the elegantly unfurling text scroll emanates from the midst of the cloud in which the four creatures are clustered. In panel 9a, Thornton depicts Revelation 6:12–17, the opening of the sixth seal, in which the kings, princes, tribunes, the rich and the strong, the bondman and the free, hide themselves from the Day of Wrath in holes in the ground, and address the rocks with words that Thornton shows emanating from symmetrically placed scrolls, lettered 'Who shall stand?' (*Quis poterit stare?*). Through the orientation of the letters, ascending on the left and descending on the right, the words seem to rise out of the rocks on one side and descend into the rocks on the other.

While some of these details may reflect the input of Thornton's theological adviser, some must surely be attributable to Thornton himself, and this raises the question of the degree to which he was able to access the biblical text directly. The level of Latin literacy among craftsmen is a subject that has received little scholarly attention, and the precision of the Latin scrolls suggests that at least one person working on the window was proficient in the language. By the time the window was being designed, an English translation of the Bible was available, the Wycliffe Bible of 1388. It had been outlawed by 1401, but it is conceivable that Thornton was familiar with the Apocalypse text in his own language.

Thornton after the Great East Window

In 1956 Coventry historian Joan Lancaster published documentary evidence that demonstrated that John Thornton maintained a residence, if not a workshop, in his native city, in 1413 taking out a lease on a house on St John's Bridges for 60 years, a house in which he is said to have been living in 1411. The large amount of glass in what has been loosely termed a 'Thornton style' surviving in the Midlands counties persuaded Lancaster that Thornton did not settle permanently in York. Similarities between the Minster's St William Window and the east window of Great Malvern Priory, for example, had been noted in the 1930s. It is certainly true that the only documented work by Thornton in York, indeed anywhere at all, is the Great East Window of 1405–8. On the other hand, in 1410, not long after the window was finished, 'Johannes Thornton glasyer' became a freeman of the city of York, allowing him to work throughout the city and not just within the jurisdiction of the Dean and Chapter. It is clear that he maintained a residence in York, for in 1433, the last documented reference to him in either city, he was repairing a house in Stonegate that belonged to the Dean and Chapter. Stonegate was a street in which many glaziers and craftsmen resided, and a number of them (although not, apparently, John Thornton) were buried in St Helen's church at the south end of the street.

However, already in the 1920s J. A. Knowles had observed some close design similarities between the Great East Window and the St William Window of *c.*1414, arguing that this window was also entrusted to John Thornton (see Fig. 3.11). This is a very credible hypothesis, for like the Great East Window, the St William Window required considerable design ingenuity. While the Minster had two earlier St William narratives, in the chapter house (CHn3, *c.*1290) and in the north nave aisle (n24, *c.*1320–30), these were sequences of 20 scenes and three scenes respectively, and the window in the north-east transept requires 95 narrative panels, with accompanying saints in the tracery. The window's designer therefore needed to be able to expand the existing visual material very considerably, and as Professor Norton has shown, two separate sources were collated in order to create an expanded and coherent narrative, affording a talented designer an even greater challenge than that of adapting existing well-established visual models. Even so, in common with the Great East Window, the St William Window expands and contracts the source material to place particular emphasis on specific episodes. The story of Ralph and Besing, for example, afforded two or possibly three scenes in the chapter house window, is the subject of an entire row of five scenes (row 12). Perhaps even more comparable to the design skills displayed in the Great East Window by Thornton is the ingenious way in which the St William Window designer compresses three episodes, the death in the same year (1153) of William's opponents Archbishop Murdac, Abbot Bernard and Pope Eugenius III, into a single panel (panel 5c), while the woman poisoned by eating a frog (panel 17a), is shown first eating the frog and then suffering the consequences in a single scene (see Fig. 3.13). It is also clear that some of those who painted the Great East Window also painted the St William Window, as well as some of the glass in the choir aisle windows. However, as we cannot identify Thornton's hand in the Great East Window, on the basis of painting styles, we cannot attribute definitively later Minster windows (or windows elsewhere, for that matter) to Thornton himself. During the recent conservation of the Great East Window even more cartooning parallels with the later St William Window have been noted. Given the relatively unwieldy nature of a glaziers' table and the very specific iconography of the window, it is unlikely that East Window cartoons were directly copied for the St William Window. It is however, very likely that pattern books produced under Thornton's supervision and familiar to the glaziers and glass painters who worked closely with him on the Great East Window continued to be used over long periods of time. Knowles has shown how popular cartoons were used and reused in the city over long periods and were even bequeathed to the younger generation. In 1503, for example, Robert Preston left 'all my scrowles' to fellow glazier Thomas English. Through his leadership, standards of craftsmanship and skill in narrative design, expressed in his greatest masterpiece, the Great East Window, Thornton can be said to have left his mark on the later glazing of York Minster in ways that transcend unanswerable questions of specific attribution.

The actual contract for the making of the window has not survived. In the late 17th century antiquaries James Torre and Matthew Hutton both made Latin précis of the record of it enrolled in a book of Chapter Acts of 1390–1410, since lost. Slight discrepancies in the two Latin texts suggest that Torre and Hutton were summarising rather than transcribing the text verbatim, but the texts agree in their most important details.

Oct 1405

Indentura facta inter decanum et Capitulum Ebor ex parte una et Johannem Thornton de Coventre glasier ex parte altera testatur &c quod Johannes bene & fideliter as sufficienter servi posse & scienta sua magnam fenestram in gaviolo Chori Eccleie Cathedralis Ebor faciet & vitreabit de vitro plumbo, stagno & omni alia material requisite simul cum operariis sufficientibus expensis dictorum Decani & capituli disponendum & ordinandum infra triennium ab incoatione hujus modi operis sui quantum ad ipsum attinet in arte sua finaliter perimplendum.

Et Prefatus Johannes portreiabit manu sua propria melioribus modo & forma quibus servierit & poterit dictam fenestram & historias ymagines & alia quaecumque pingenda in eisdem.

Et etiam depinget quatenus opus fuerit secundum ordinationem Decani & Capituli &c.

ad quod idem Johnannes prestiterit Juramentum et idem percipient de Decano & Capitulo singulis septimanis quibus laborabit in arte sua durante dicto temino 4s sterlingorum & quilibet anno ejusdem triennij 100m solidos sterlingorum.

Et si idem Johannes opus hujus modi bene & fideliter & subtiliter &c & secundum conventiones premissas adimplevereit &c Decanus & Capitulum solvent prefato Johanni pro regardo suo 10ll argenti.

York Minster Library and Archive MS LI/2, part II, 34

On 10 Aug[u]st Ad 1405 6H4

An indenture was made between the Dean & Chapter on the one p[ar]t And John Thornton of Covintry glazier on the other Whereby The s[ai]d John covenanted to make a Great Window at the E: end of the Quire, according to the best of his skill & Cunning And undertook to glaze the same w[i]th Glass, Lead, Sodder & other necessaries requisite, & to find all sufficient workmen to be disposed at the Costs of the s[ai]d Dean & Chapter. And to finish the same w[i]thin 3 years from the date hereof And obliging himself w[i]th his own hands to portrature the s[ai]d window w[i]th Historicall Images & other painted work, in the best Mannor & form that he possibly could And likewise paynt the same where need required according to the Ordination of the Dean & Chapter. For all w[hi]ch the Dean and Chapter should pay him 4s Sterling a week during the term afores[ai]d that he wrought in his Art. And besides that 100s sterling every one of those 3 years. And if he performed his work well & truly, & perfect it according to the tenor of these Covenants, then he should receive more of the Dean & Chapter for his care therein, the sum of 10ll in silver

York Minster Library and Archive, MS LI/7, 7

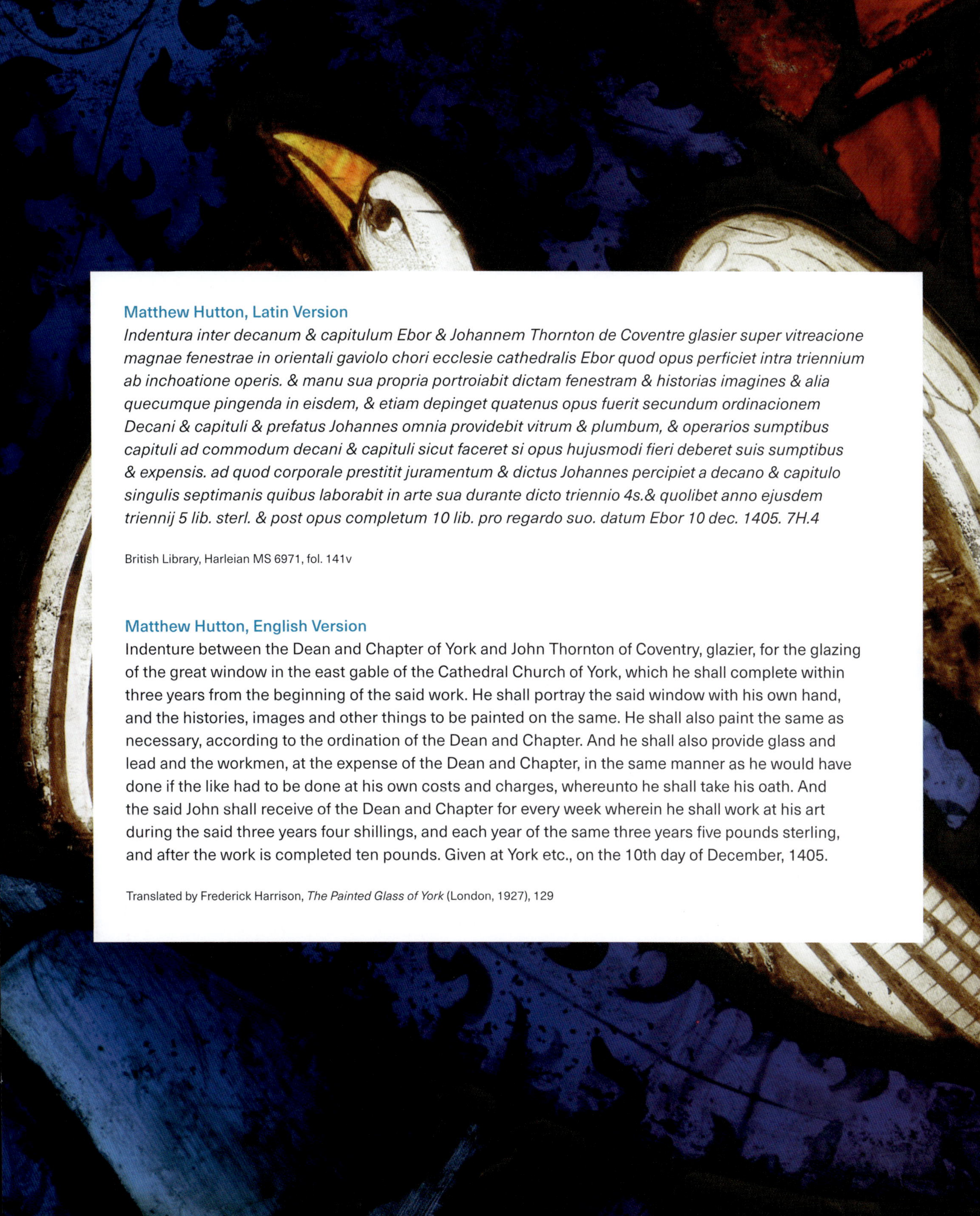

Matthew Hutton, Latin Version

Indentura inter decanum & capitulum Ebor & Johannem Thornton de Coventre glasier super vitreacione magnae fenestrae in orientali gaviolo chori ecclesie cathedralis Ebor quod opus perficiet intra triennium ab inchoatione operis. & manu sua propria portroiabit dictam fenestram & historias imagines & alia quecumque pingenda in eisdem, & etiam depinget quatenus opus fuerit secundum ordinacionem Decani & capituli & prefatus Johannes omnia providebit vitrum & plumbum, & operarios sumptibus capituli ad commodum decani & capituli sicut faceret si opus hujusmodi fieri deberet suis sumptibus & expensis. ad quod corporale prestitit juramentum & dictus Johannes percipiet a decano & capitulo singulis septimanis quibus laborabit in arte sua durante dicto triennio 4s.& quolibet anno ejusdem triennij 5 lib. sterl. & post opus completum 10 lib. pro regardo suo. datum Ebor 10 dec. 1405. 7H.4

British Library, Harleian MS 6971, fol. 141v

Matthew Hutton, English Version

Indenture between the Dean and Chapter of York and John Thornton of Coventry, glazier, for the glazing of the great window in the east gable of the Cathedral Church of York, which he shall complete within three years from the beginning of the said work. He shall portray the said window with his own hand, and the histories, images and other things to be painted on the same. He shall also paint the same as necessary, according to the ordination of the Dean and Chapter. And he shall also provide glass and lead and the workmen, at the expense of the Dean and Chapter, in the same manner as he would have done if the like had to be done at his own costs and charges, whereunto he shall take his oath. And the said John shall receive of the Dean and Chapter for every week wherein he shall work at his art during the said three years four shillings, and each year of the same three years five pounds sterling, and after the work is completed ten pounds. Given at York etc., on the 10th day of December, 1405.

Translated by Frederick Harrison, *The Painted Glass of York* (London, 1927), 129

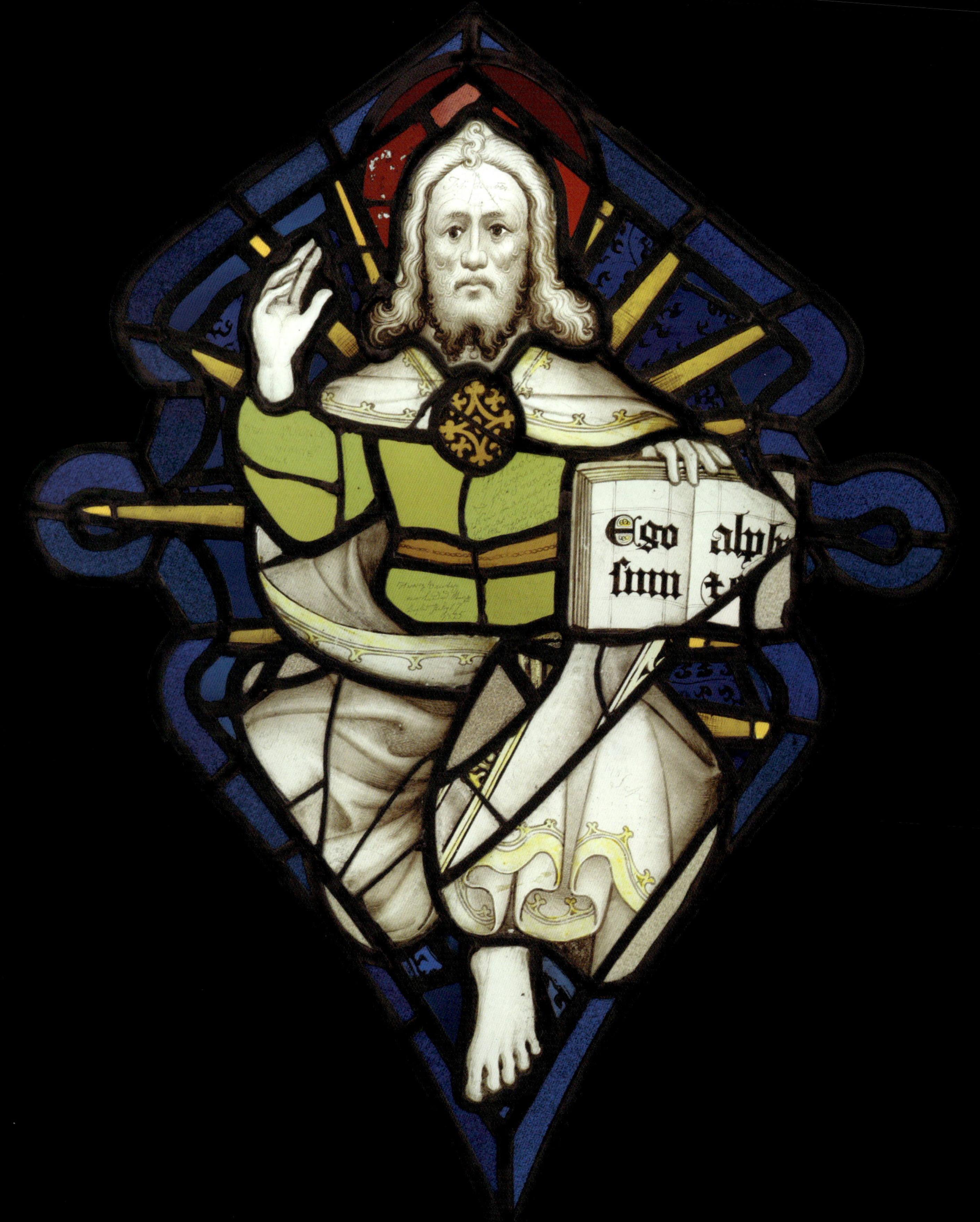
Ego alph
sum

Chapter 3

Sacred Time and a Holy Place

The Meaning of the Great East Window

The evidence of later structural changes discernible in the stone framework that holds the Great East Window, discussed in Chapter One, makes it unlikely that the stained-glass content of the window, if planned at all, had been designed in any detail as part of Archbishop Thoresby's original plan for the eastern arm of the cathedral. But the sheer scale of the window opening and its close iconographic relationship to the rest of the new glazing of the eastern arm suggest that at a relatively early date some thought had been given to the glazing of the new building. We can be reasonably confident that by 1399, a year immediately after Richard Scrope's arrival, the scheme was in the active planning stage. However, if we have some slight evidence of the research that went into the St Cuthbert window, in the form of a borrowed illuminated life of the saint, we have no indication of how or by whom the Great East Window was planned. Nor can it have been conceived in isolation, for as we shall see, its content relates closely to the wider scheme of choir glazing for which it provides a key. While we might safely assume that the donor, Bishop Skirlaw, approved the subject matter of the window he was gifting, we must also assume that the subject of the window that illuminated the liturgical heart of the mother church of the northern province had the support and engagement of the Archbishop and members of the Chapter of York, and it was with the Dean and Chapter rather than the donor that John Thornton entered into his contract.

The window offers a complex and multilayered iconography, and it can be shown that, contrary to earlier commentaries, it is far from arbitrary in its choice of subject matter. While the window is undoubtedly about the Bible, deriving its main-light subject matter directly from biblical texts, it is also about time, and the movement from an earthly temporality into eternity, a transition made possible by the Last Judgement and the Second Coming of Christ, events depicted in panels 2e to 2j. It is also a story in which the cathedral of York and the kings, popes and prelates associated with the evangelisation of the northern province have their place.

Fig. 3.1
'I am Alpha and Omega, the beginning and the end, saith the Lord God, who is, and who was, and who is to come, the Almighty' (Revelation 1:8). God the Father at the apex of the Great East Window (DD1).

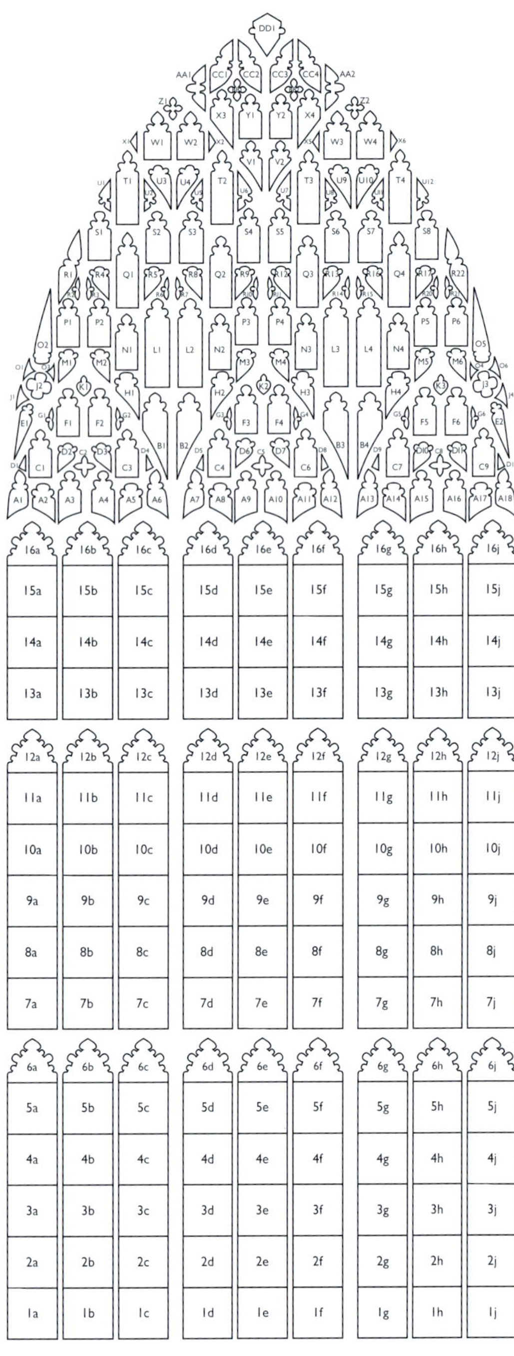

Fig. 3.2

The tracery of the Great East Window articulates the divisions in the narrative. The super-mullions subdivide the overall window opening into three windows within one, establishing the importance of the number 3 in the window's underlying numerology.

The window is divided up into clearly defined sections (Fig 3.2), articulated by the architectural framework of the tracery, and the size and number of panels assigned to each one is of considerable significance in understanding its overall meaning, a matter to which we will return later. Unlike most of the Minster's windows, it was designed to be read from the top down, with the company of heaven arranged at God's feet at the apex of the window. Immediately below the tracery, in the first three rows of the window's main lights (rows 15, 14 and 13), are 27 scenes of Old Testament history, from Creation to the time of King David. Row 15 depicts the seven days of Creation, the temptation and fall, and the expulsion of Adam and Eve from paradise. Row 14 begins with Cain's murder of Abel and concludes with Jacob blessing his sons. Row 13 opens with the infant Moses found by Pharaoh's daughter, followed by five more Moses scenes, Samson in the house at Gaza, concluding with two scenes from the time of King David. Below the transom, and occupying the largest part of the window (rows 12 to 2), is the famous Apocalypse cycle for which the window is perhaps best known. Eighty-one scenes are devoted to this subject, although the first three concern the life, torture and banishment of St John the Divine to the island of Patmos. In the fourth scene John sleeps and is visited by the angel who conducts him through a series of dreamlike encounters, the narrative of the Apocalypse or book of Revelation. While this Apocalypse cycle is by no means the most extensive in English art, in terms of scale it is surely the largest and most ambitious. At the window's base is a gallery of historical figures, including the image of the donor, William Skirlaw. The correct reordering of these important panels as a result of recent research and conservation enables the significance of this row to emerge once again. On the left-hand side of Bishop Skirlaw are ten royal figures, from the legendary King Ebrauk (1a) to the historical figure of King Edward

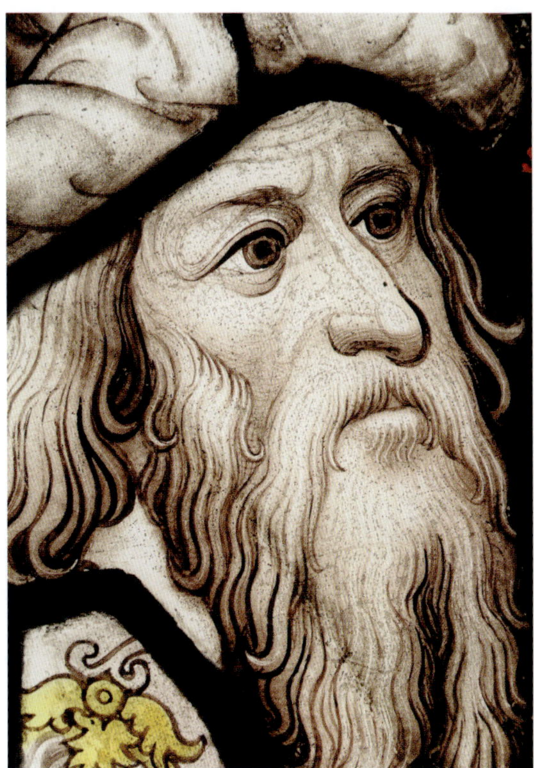

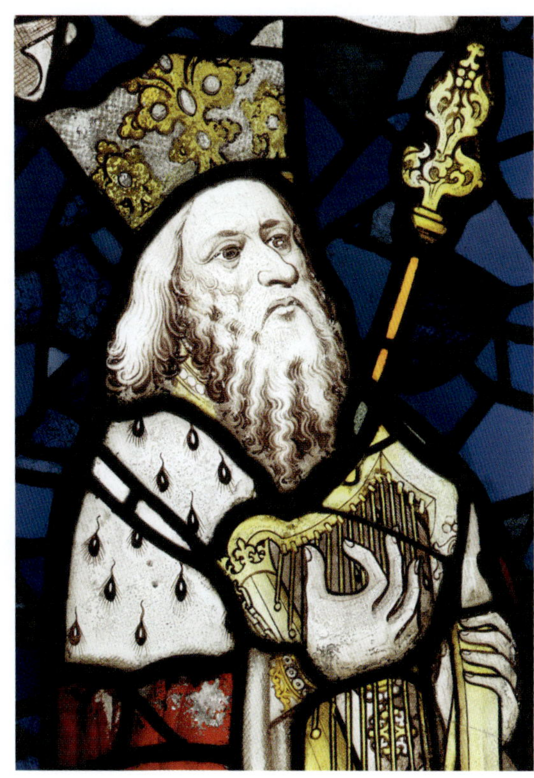

III (1312–77, 1d) in whose reign Archbishop Thoresby's great project began. To the right of Bishop Skirlaw are 12 enthroned ecclesiastics, in each panel a pope flanked by two archbishops, culminating with the figure of St William of York (d.1154, 1j). The figures are all accompanied by coats of arms that help to identify them, although the glaziers were unable to attribute shields to many of the centuries-dead popes, who were therefore assigned shields bearing Bishop Skirlaw's arms, another mark of distinction accorded to the generous donor. The choice of these 'historical' figures can now also be shown to be part of the carefully considered scheme.

The key to the window's overall meaning is actually found at its very apex, barely visible from the ground. Here, God is seated amidst the company of heaven (panel DD1, Fig. 3.1), an open book upon his knee inscribed with the words *Ego sum α[lpha] et Ω[mega]'* . This is abbreviated from chapter 1, verse 8 of the

book of Revelation (always called Apocalypse in the Middle Ages): 'I am Alpha and Omega, the beginning and the end, saith the Lord God, who is, and who was, and who is to come, the Almighty.' This signals the theme of the whole window, which depicts the beginning (Creation, described in Genesis, the first book of the Old Testament, in row 15) and the end of earthly time (Apocalypse and the Second Coming of Christ, from the book of Revelation, the last canonical book of the New Testament, depicted in rows 2–11). The very same words are inscribed on the open book in the window's final Apocalypse scenes (panels 2h and 2j), in which the heavenly Jerusalem has descended to earth, presaging the entry into eternity. These sentences underline another important characteristic of the Apocalypse, which is that it is simultaneously about the past, the present and the future. It was for this reason that the book of Revelation was (and is) the subject of constant reinterpretation

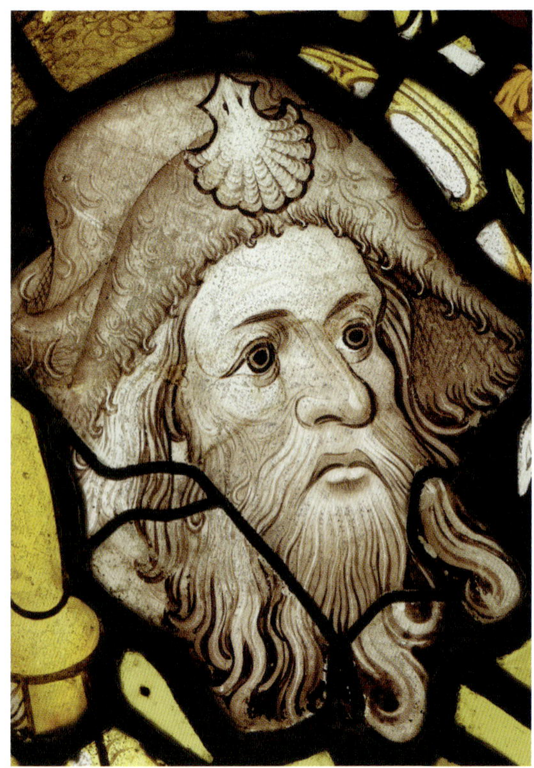

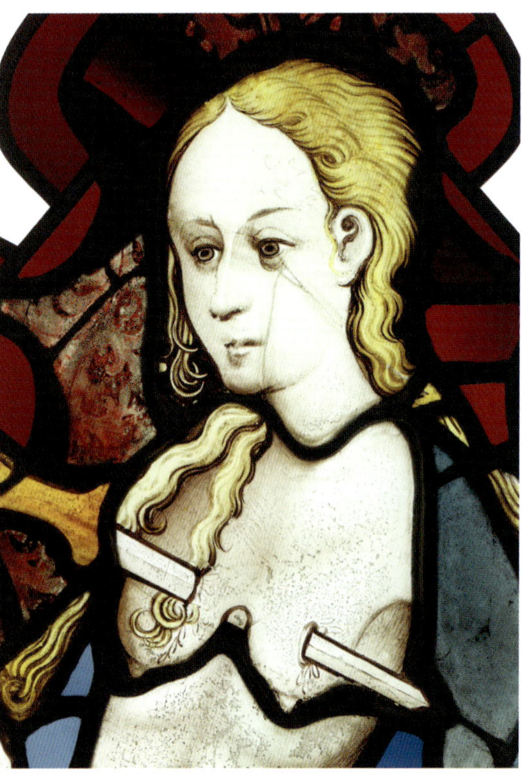

and commentary, for unlike the rest of the New Testament it is not a linear narrative, but a visionary book of prophecy, believed by its medieval commentators to far exceed the prophetic qualities of the Old Testament, which is probably one of the reasons why the Apocalypse section of the window considerably exceeds that of the Old Testament in terms of its size.

The Company of Heaven

In 1927 Canon Chancellor Frederick Harrison declared that the single figures of the tracery 'are not important in the scheme of the window'. In fact, the tracery not only heralds the window's overall meaning, but also plays a key role in articulating its typological significances. The heavenly host is arranged at the feet of God the Father. He is most closely surrounded by the angelic orders, underlining their physical proximity to the heavenly throne of God, but also

a reminder that they existed before the creation of the world. Indeed, figures throughout the tracery are arranged not in a hierarchy of status, with the Apostles and Evangelists closest to God and lesser prophets and saints further away, but in chronological order across time and down through the layers of the tracery. Consequently, the Old Testament patriarchs Adam, Noah, Abraham and Jacob (T1–4) all appear in the top row immediately below the angels. In the next row down are the sons of Jacob, representing the 12 tribes of Israel (S1 (Fig. 3.3)–S8, Q1 and Q4), including Judah (Q1), who is named and accompanied by a lion, and Joseph (Q4) who is regally dressed as the Pharaoh's viceroy. Through Joseph the Israelites entered the kingdom of Egypt and were eventually enslaved. Through Moses and Aaron, who also appear centrally in the same row as full-length standing figures (Q2 and Q3), they were led to freedom. Moses (Q2), is immediately recognisable thanks to the

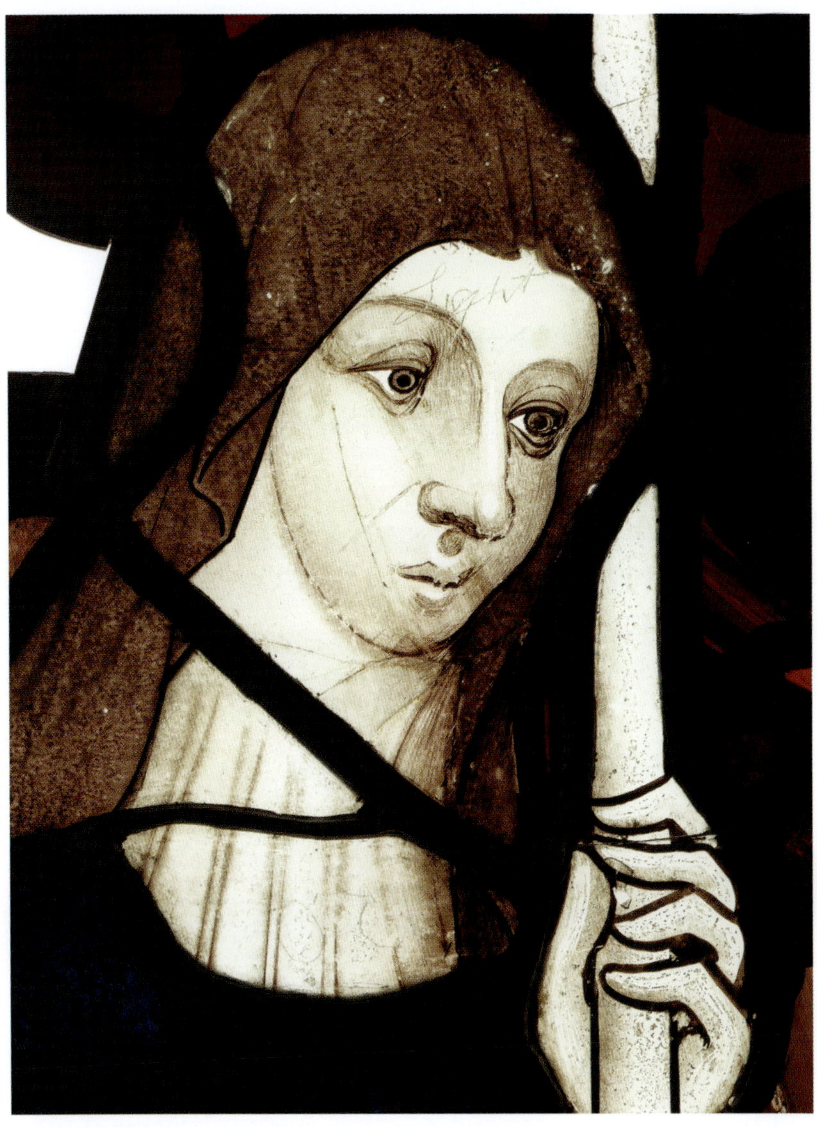

Fig. 3.7
An unidentified saintly abbess (A13).

tablets of the law that he holds in his left hand, their stone surfaces legibly inscribed with the words (in Latin) 'Thou shalt love the Lord thy God with thy whole heart, and with thy whole soul, and with all thy strength, and with all thy mind; and thy neighbour as thyself' (Luke 10:27). In the next level are the 12 major prophets, most of them named in scrolls (P1–N4), together with the four righteous kings – David (Fig. 3.4), Solomon, Hezekiah and Josiah (L1–4). In the next layer are the Apostles and Evangelists who bore witness to Christ as Messiah and Saviour. The four Evangelists are represented by their well-known symbols (J2–3 and E1–2). Most of the Apostles (H1–4 and B1–4), including St Peter (B1), St James the Great (B3, Fig. 3.5) and St Thomas (B4), can be identified from their standard attributes. In the lowest zones, below the heads of the three subsidiary traceries that divide the window into three windows in one, are those saints who bear witness to Christ. On the left are male saints. In the middle are the sainted prelates and ecclesiastics and on the right, the female saints. While some are easily identifiable from their attributes (St Stephen, F1 (Fig 3.8); St Clement, C1; St Katharine, A16; St Agatha, F6, Fig. 3.6), others are only identifiable in very general terms as popes, archbishops or saintly abbesses (Fig 3.7), although we may speculate as to their identities. It is surely no coincidence that figures given full-length prominence in the tracery panels – notably Adam, Noah, Abraham, Isaac, Jacob, Moses and David – are the subject of significant narrative sequences in the main-light panels below.

The Old Testament Narrative

While most early students of the Great East Window could identify the Old Testament stories depicted in this part of the window, until recently this has been the least studied and least understood section of the window. This may be because it has been overshadowed by the size and spectacle of the Apocalypse cycle

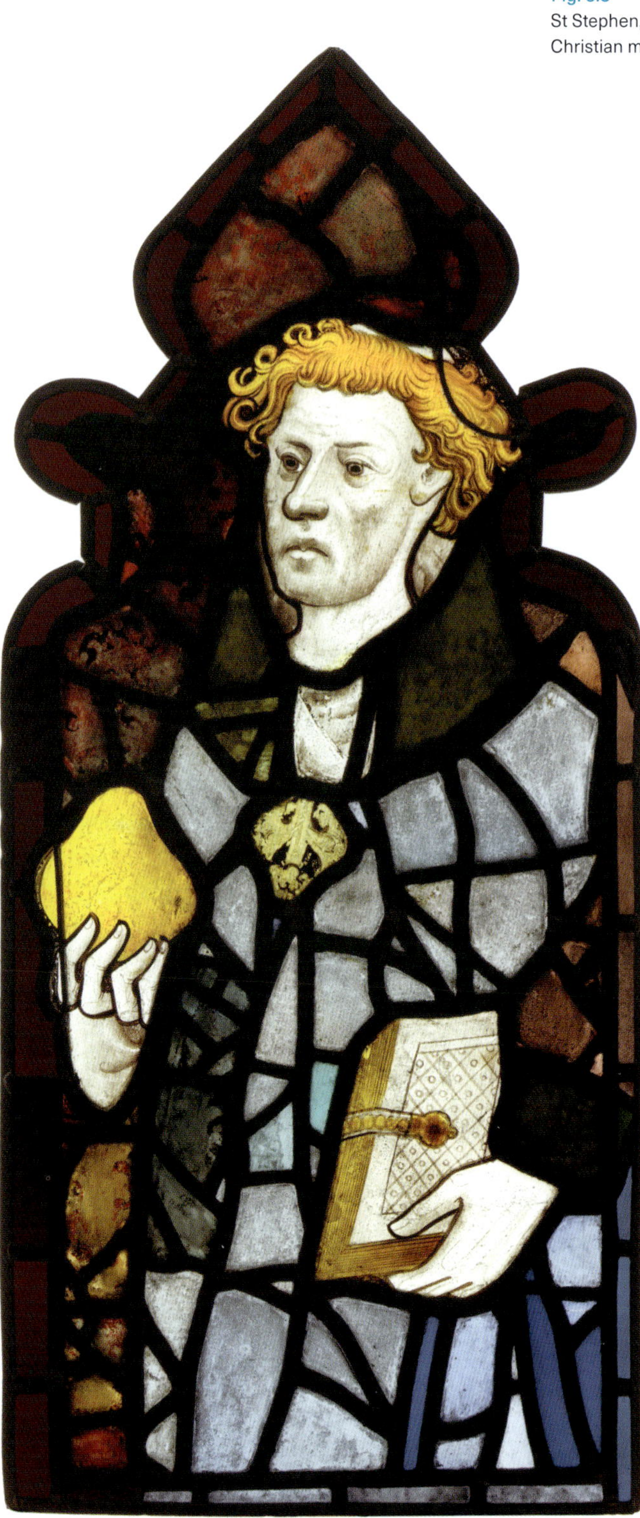

Fig. 3.8
St Stephen, the first
Christian martyr (F1).

below, but also because some of it has been badly damaged and much of it is hard to see from the ground. Benson and Harrison (in accounts published in 1914 and 1927 respectively) offered only a listing of the subjects, although Harrison commented on the fact that the drunkenness of Noah was in the wrong position. J. A. Knowles went so far as to suggest that there was no intent at all behind the selection of biblical subjects in the window as a whole: 'one hundred and eight scenes from the Bible, which were probably used only because of the difficulty of finding from any source a series of subjects sufficiently extended to fill so large a window'! As we have seen, the adjustment of the position of the transom walkway to create a division at this point between the two main narrative sections of the window, and the insistence on glazing row 13, which is almost obscured by it, suggests that this was a deliberate and carefully considered decision in which the choice and number of scenes was very important. It is clear that this was a planned scheme, even if its meaning has eluded modern onlookers until very recently.

The renewed study of the window in preparation of the Corpus Vitrearum volume published in 1995 brought this subject into sharper focus. David O'Connor challenged the idea that the Old Testament scenes were an arbitrary selection. He pointed out the obvious typological significance of many of the scenes, especially when related to the Apocalypse to which they serve as a preface. Many would have been extremely familiar from the wealth of English typological texts such as the *Biblia Pauperum*, *Speculum Humanae Salvationis* and the *Pictor in Carmine*, which from the 12th century onwards matched Old Testament history with New Testament events. This is a dramatic device used in the York mystery plays, for example. Moses and the burning bush (13b) was explained as foreshadowing the Nativity, while Melchisedech offering bread and wine to Abraham (14e) was compared to the Last Supper. The mocking of Noah's nakedness (14c) was paired with the mocking of Christ, while the raising of the serpent of brass (13f) was a common type of the Crucifixion. St Augustine had compared Noah's ark (14b) to the city of God. In panel 14j Jacob blesses his 12 sons, who prefigure the 12 Apostles, summoning them to his bedside with the words 'Gather yourselves together that I may tell you the things that shall befall you in the last days', a summons that could easily be a call to those who look upon the depiction of the Apocalypse in the panels below. Samson's destruction of the Philistines (13g) and David's triumph over Goliath (13h) both symbolise God's victory over evil that presages the Second Coming and the establishment of the New Jerusalem, the triumphant conclusion of the Apocalypse sequence that occupies the main narrative of the Great East Window. However, it is also the case that some of the most familiar Old Testament types – the Sacrifice of Isaac, for example – are absent from this part of the window, although it appears in the tracery (T3). The death of Absalom, like the raising of the serpent of brass, was a type of the Crucifixion of Christ.

O'Connor also noted the importance of the writings of the Venerable Bede (623–735) in the medieval interpretation of the Apocalypse. Together with St Augustine's *City of God*, his *Explanatio Apocalypsis* is likely to have been very familiar to the members of the Minster clergy who daily viewed the Great East Window. Bede's writings were undoubtedly an important source for much of the biblical and historical imagery in the glazing of the choir of York Minster. He lived and worked all his life at the monastery of Jarrow in the Anglo-Saxon kingdom of Deira, of which York was the capital. His famous *Ecclesiastical History of the English People* was unsurprisingly a source for the depictions of both historical figures at the base of the Great East Window and the windows in the western choir clerestory (N8–11 and S8–11). He was also, of course, the author of *De Temporum Ratione*, the seminal text on the computation of time and the calculation of Easter, central to the Christian year. Bede's work concluded with a reflection on the Six Ages of the World (also derived from St Augustine) and a chronicle from Creation to his own time, with speculations on the current age, the end of the world and the seventh age to come. These are ideas embedded in the underlying architectural and numerological symbolism of the Great East Window.

In important and as yet unpublished research undertaken alongside the conservation of the Great East Window, Professor Nigel Morgan has revisited the question of the significance of the Old Testament scenes in terms of medieval concepts of time. He has argued that the three rows of Old Testament scenes would have been read on one level as a linear history of the first three ages of the world, from Creation to the time of King David, although the division of the ages is most closely aligned to the chronology proposed by Berengaudus, author of the most widely read commentary on the Apocalypse. For Berengaudus the first age began with Creation and ended with the Flood, the second ran from Noah to the birth of Moses (*ante legem* – the age before God gave Moses the Law) and the third ran from Moses to the time of King David (*sub legem* – the time in which the kingdom of Israel operated under God's Law). However, the window does not follow this order without question, but edits the story for dramatic effect and to take advantage of the architectural framework in which the narrative unfolds. For example, the first row (or age) does not conclude with Noah and the Flood, but more dramatically with the expulsion from paradise, in which the woeful Adam and Eve are driven literally out of the window frame. The second age fills most of row 2, opening with the murderous consequences of mankind's sin, the slaying of Abel by his brother Cain, and then proceeds from Noah to the time immediately before the birth of Moses. The third age, from Moses to David, fills the third row. The fourth age, that of prophecy, is most dramatically represented by the Apocalypse, considered by

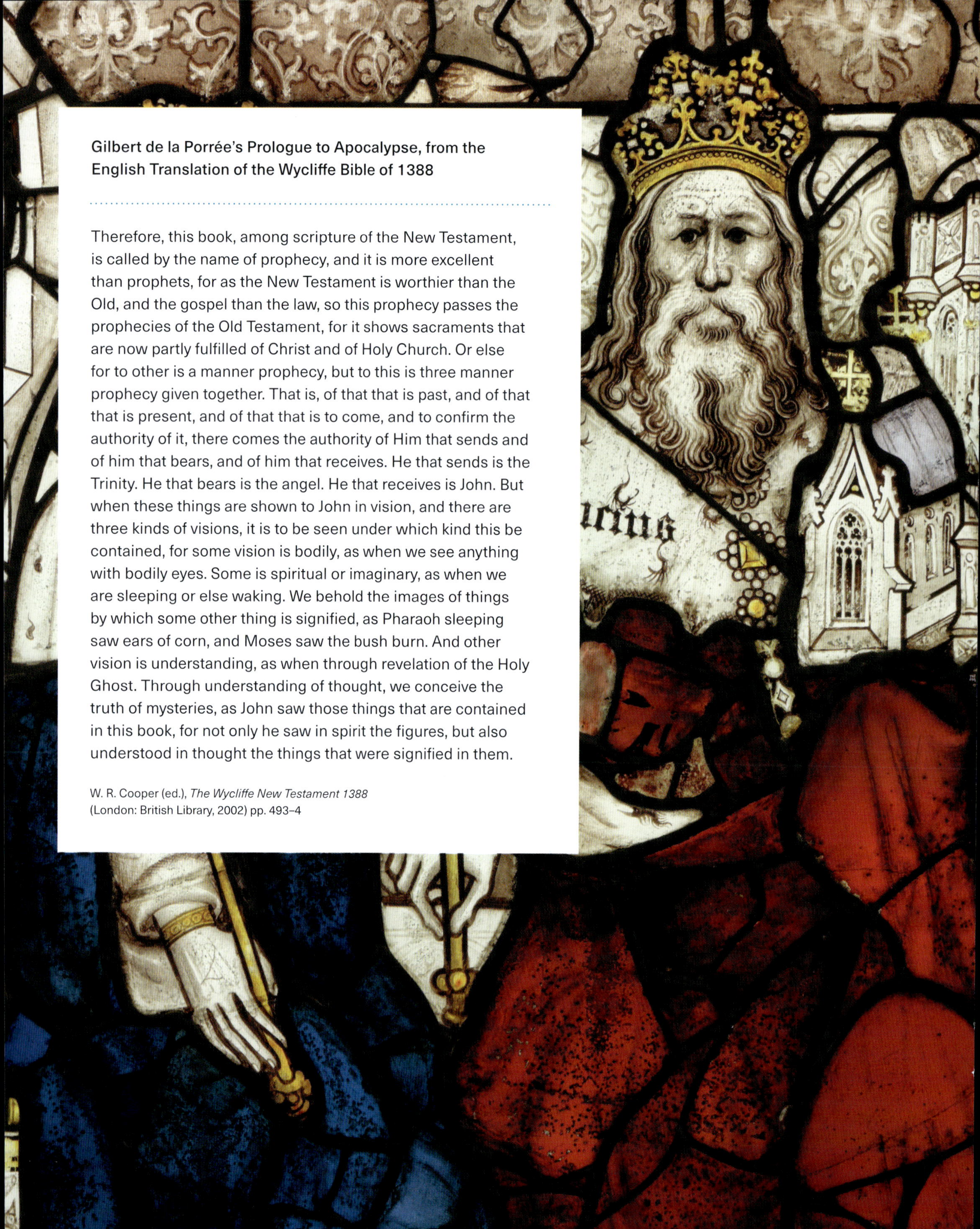

Gilbert de la Porrée's Prologue to Apocalypse, from the English Translation of the Wycliffe Bible of 1388

Therefore, this book, among scripture of the New Testament, is called by the name of prophecy, and it is more excellent than prophets, for as the New Testament is worthier than the Old, and the gospel than the law, so this prophecy passes the prophecies of the Old Testament, for it shows sacraments that are now partly fulfilled of Christ and of Holy Church. Or else for to other is a manner prophecy, but to this is three manner prophecy given together. That is, of that that is past, and of that that is present, and of that that is to come, and to confirm the authority of it, there comes the authority of Him that sends and of him that bears, and of him that receives. He that sends is the Trinity. He that bears is the angel. He that receives is John. But when these things are shown to John in vision, and there are three kinds of visions, it is to be seen under which kind this be contained, for some vision is bodily, as when we see anything with bodily eyes. Some is spiritual or imaginary, as when we are sleeping or else waking. We behold the images of things by which some other thing is signified, as Pharaoh sleeping saw ears of corn, and Moses saw the bush burn. And other vision is understanding, as when through revelation of the Holy Ghost. Through understanding of thought, we conceive the truth of mysteries, as John saw those things that are contained in this book, for not only he saw in spirit the figures, but also understood in thought the things that were signified in them.

W. R. Cooper (ed.), *The Wycliffe New Testament 1388*
(London: British Library, 2002) pp. 493–4

the medieval commentators to outshine the Old Testament in its prophetic qualities, but it is also expressed through the prophets in the tracery.

Morgan has demonstrated that the fifth age, that of Christ and those who bore witness to him (the Apostles, Evangelists, Saints and Martyrs), is also present, but typologically rather than literally. While the cloud of witnesses was very much in evidence in the tracery, the Old Testament panels and the tracery figures when taken together could easily be read typologically by the educated medieval theologian as representing the early life, Passion, Resurrection and Ascension of Christ, the fifth age. We know that these ideas preoccupied the late medieval Minster community, because a version of the chronology of the Seven Ages was one of the subjects once displayed in the Minster on the so-called tables of the Vicars Choral, a compendium of all sorts of historical information about the cathedral and the see, including extracts from charters and excerpts from chronicles.

The recent re-examination of this section of the window has raised the intriguing possibility of another source to which the window's narrative may have been indebted – that of medieval drama. In panel 13c it is Moses rather than Aaron who takes the lead in confronting Pharaoh. This scene has traditionally been identified as depicting events described in Exodus 7, in which Aaron turns his staff into a serpent as a sign of the power invested in him by God, although in this panel it is Moses rather than Aaron who holds the staff. The serpent-shaped end of the staff was recorded by the 18th-century antiquarian draughtsmen who drew the window, although this glass is now entirely a recreation by Dean Milner-White. If the serpent-ended staff cannot be substantiated, this might point to an alternative attribution of the scene, to events in Exodus 12, when permission is finally granted to Moses to lead the children of Israel out of Egypt. However, as Professor Richard Beadle has shown, in the Hosiers' Corpus Christi pageant (first mentioned in 1403), it is Moses who carries the serpent staff as in panel 13c, and this dramatic motif was derived from an even older 14th-century Middle English metrical paraphrase of the Old Testament which was used as a source for several of the York Old Testament pageants performed in the city's streets at the feast of Corpus Christi.

The Apocalypse

The book of Revelation, or the Apocalypse as it was known to the medieval reader, is not only the last canonical book of the Bible, but also the last to be accepted into the canon. Notwithstanding, in the Middle Ages it was a book that attracted an enormous amount of theological interest precisely because its meaning defied easy interpretation. Its prophetic qualities and its capacity to encompass past, present and future time made it a fruitful focus for theological debate and for artistic interpretation. While the identity of John, the narrator, witness and author of the book, remains a matter of scholarly debate, in the Middle Ages he was identified as John the son of Zebedee and the beloved disciple of John's Gospel. Despite their stylistic differences, in the Middle Ages the Gospel of St John, the three Johannine epistles and the book of Revelation were all attributed to John the Evangelist and Apostle.

It is estimated that by 1400, there were at least 500 illuminated manuscripts in England devoted to the Apocalypse, of which 47 survive. None of the surviving copies is identical, although scholars have been able to suggest 'family' relationships between some of them. Some are in Latin, some are in Anglo-Norman French, and so far only the 13th-century manuscripts have been the subject of sustained and detailed research. For a brief time at the end of the 14th century the text could also be read in English, in the translation of 1388 associated with the followers of John Wycliffe (d.1384). It is in this section of the window that the age of prophecy is made manifest, a cycle culminating in the scenes that point the way to the seventh age of the world

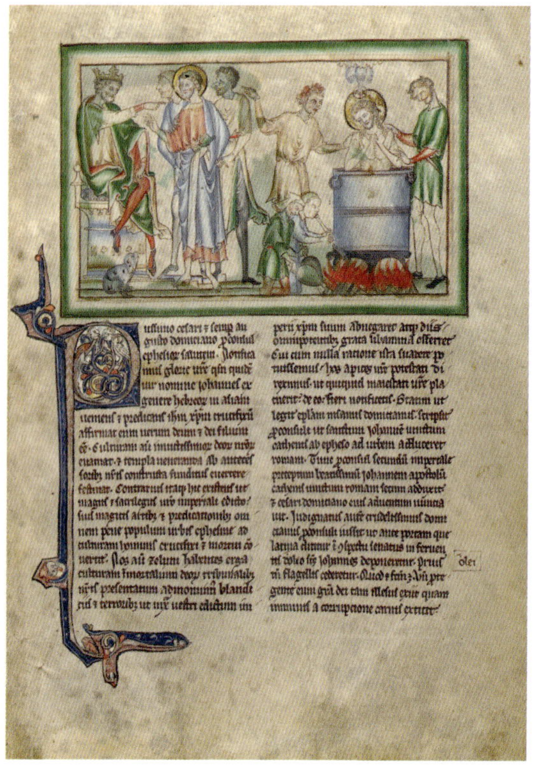

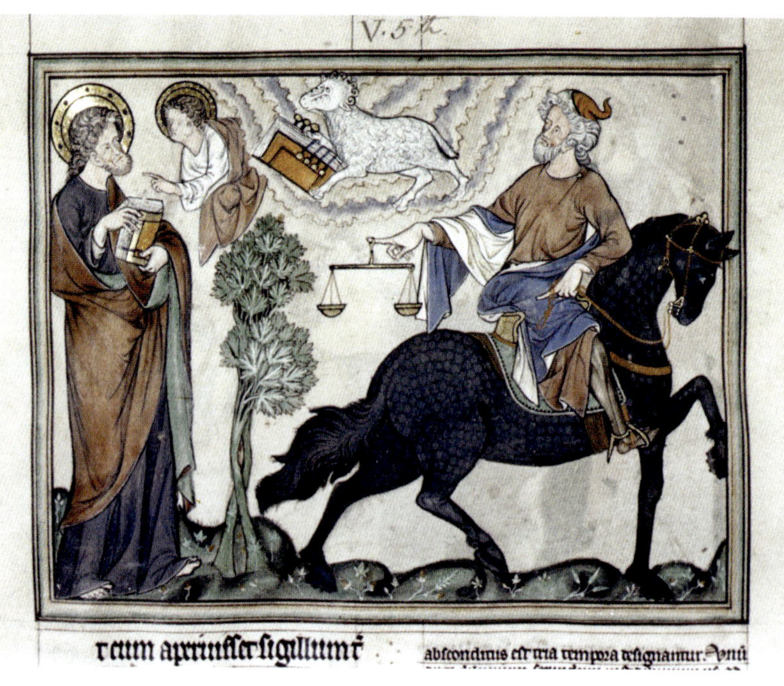

in which there will be Judgement and all will be made new in the New Heaven and the New Earth.

The manuscripts, unlike the window, were usually accompanied by commentaries that offered the reader a means of understanding the biblical text. The manuscript versions of the Apocalypse vary considerably in the number of scenes that they illustrate, but of course, in every case an image related directly to a specific text and the two could be read together, although only across two open pages at a time. The Great East Window has its own 'reading structure'. Like a book, it is read from left to right, and from top to bottom, but the 'reader' can sample the narrative in different ways, across rows and even across whole sections of the window in a non-linear way that suits the visionary nature of the Apocalypse text. In fact, the ability to read across the entire narrative of the window in a non-linear as well as a linear manner is essential for anyone wanting to digest the overall meaning of the window as a whole.

It has long been realised that the Great East Window was indebted in some way to the Apocalypse imagery found in medieval manuscripts and reference to a very limited number of published manuscripts available in the 1940s and 1950s influenced Dean Milner-White's restoration. Research by the late Jill Rickers examined the wider art-historical context in which the window was made and concluded that no single text could be identified as the source from which the window was derived. This is in contrast, for example, to the wall-paintings cycle in the chapter house of Westminster Abbey, completed before 1404. Comprising 96 scenes, this huge cycle was derived from one particular manuscript (Cambridge, Trinity College, MS B.10.2 of c.1380–90), and works almost like a supersize picture book, as the blocks of images resemble the opened pages of a book, and deep strips of the biblical text, painted onto parchment, are pasted onto the wall immediately underneath the relevant images.

Through meticulous scrutiny of the iconographic idiosyncrasies of the window, Professor Morgan has demonstrated that John Thornton was familiar with imagery found in two groups of illuminated Apocalypse manuscripts. One source must have been associated with the 'Westminster group' of Apocalypses dating from the 1260s–70s. These are in Latin and include the famous Douce Apocalypse (Oxford, Bodleian Library, Douce MS 180) and the Getty Apocalypse (Los Angeles, J. Paul Getty Museum, MS Ludwig III, 1). The second group that shares features with the York window is in Anglo-Norman French, comprising manuscripts produced probably in the 1330s. The so-called Queen Mary Apocalypse (London, British Library, Royal MS 19 BXV) is perhaps the best-known member of the group. The books were all luxury items produced for elite patrons: the Douce Apocalypse was made for Prince Edward (later Edward I), and the Queen Mary Apocalypse can be shown to have been in the royal collection by the first half of the 16th century. It is unlikely, therefore, that it was these books to which Thornton had access. We shall probably never know how Thornton was introduced to these visual models. Perhaps Scrope, Skirlaw or even Minster treasurer and bibliophile John Neuton may have borrowed manuscripts to assist in the designing. Given the costs involved in making a window of this size it is likely that someone was given the task of making preparatory drawings from manuscript sources from which the cartoons could be drawn up, and we know that it was common practice for glaziers to be provided with small-scale drawings, sometime called vidimuses, from which their cartoons could be prepared. These were probably appended to the original contract, which makes no mention of the specific subject matter of the window, and concerns itself with financial and logistical matters. At what stage the stylistic differences inherent in sources of such different dates were harmonised we cannot know, and even if we compare the same scenes in window and relevant manuscript 'family' it is clear that the sources underwent considerable transformation in the hands of John Thornton (the subject of Chapter Two).

A small number of distinctive iconographic details from among those identified by Professor Morgan serve to underline the points of contact between the window and the two relevant manuscript groups. The Great East Window, in common with some Apocalypse manuscripts, prefaces the scenes of the Apocalypse with episodes from the life of St John, who is the witness and narrator of the book. Both the Westminster and Anglo-French prose groups contain these prefatory scenes, which include John's persecution at the hands of the Emperor Domitian (panel 11a) and his exile on Patmos (Revelation 1:9, panels 11b and 11d) although only the latter includes the scene in which John preaches (panel 11c), derived not from the Apocalypse itself, but probably from the *Golden Legend* and perhaps the letter, purporting to be from the proconsul of Ephesus to the Emperor Domitian, used as the prologue in some Latin Apocalypses (including Getty from the Westminster group) (Fig. 3.9). In the scenes of the four horsemen (Revelation 6) depicted in panels 10e–h, Thornton has included the Lamb opening the seals (found in some members of both the Westminster and the Anglo-Norman French prose Apocalypses) (Fig. 3.10), but in 10e and 10g he also incorporates all four of the 'living creatures', a detail found in some of the Anglo-Norman prose manuscripts, but not in the Westminster ones. At the fall of the wicked city of Babylon (Revelation 18:9–19), the merchants stood afar to lament the loss of their riches. As Professor Morgan has pointed out, this scene is only rarely depicted in English Apocalypse manuscripts, but tellingly is found in both groups to which we believe Thornton had access and is depicted in panel 3b of the Great East Window. Indeed, it is easy to see how such an admonitory scene might have had special resonance in a bustling urban, mercantile centre like late medieval York.

Kings, Popes, Prelates: The Bottom Row

Row 1, at the base of the window, attracted the attention of post-medieval antiquaries (notably Torr and Henry Johnston), who were drawn to its gallery of 22 shields of arms, but had less interest in the identity of the enthroned figures above. Apart from the central kneeling figure of Bishop Walter Skirlaw, each of the eight panels depicts three enthroned male figures, the majority identified by his heraldry. Recent research undertaken alongside the conservation of the window has allowed us to reorder these historical figures correctly and to reposition or restore them. It is now clear that to the left of Bishop Skirlaw are images of kings significant to the history of the cathedral and the see of York, running from the mythical King Ebrauk to King Edward III (1312–77) in whose service Archbishop Thoresby, Bishop Skirlaw and the Scrope family had prospered. His arms appear in the first southern bay of the Lady Chapel arcade, accompanied by those of his son, Edward, the Black Prince (1330–76). To the left are popes and prelates of roughly corresponding periods, probably running from St Sampson to St William (d.1154). Many of the figures were originally labelled. Some of the panels have been heavily disturbed and retain only a small proportion of their original glass (notably 1g). Originally running along the base of each panel was a metrical Latin text, which can now be identified as an adapted version of a late 14th-century metrical chronicle composed in York and usually attributed to John of Allhallowgate, a priest at Ripon. This chronicle was, of course, indebted to earlier sources, including Bede and Geoffrey of Monmouth, and was also displayed in the Minster on the tables of the Vicars Choral.

The chronicle is conceived in a structure that emulates the ideas already discussed, presenting history in a series of distinct ages, in this case pre-Christian, British, Anglo-Saxon and medieval (from the 11th to the 14th century). The kings fit the metrical chronicle's chronology very closely: in the time of King David, King Ebrauk (1a) founded the city of York, built its

walls and founded the first temple manned by the *archeflamen* and *protoflamen* (priests). King Lucius (1b) turned the temple into a Christian church and sent to Rome for pastoral support. King Edwin (1c) was the first king of the Anglo-Saxon kingdom of Northumbria to be converted to Christianity and refounded the church of York. In the reign of William I (1d) the Minster was rebuilt in stone and during that of Edward III (in the same panel) the reconstruction of the choir was begun. The choice of ecclesiastical figures mirrors the content of the chronicle less closely, but presents a parallel narrative in which the confirmation of York's privileges and status is the key. Pope Eleutherius is flanked by the metropolitans he sent to the aid of King Lucius (1f); Pope Gregory the Great (d.604, 1g) is flanked by St Paulinus (d.644) and St Wilfrid (634–710), who re-established York as the principal see of Northumbria, and whose stories were made famous in Bede's *Ecclesiastical History.* Panel 1h depicts two of 8th-century York's illustrious sainted (arch)bishops, John of Beverley (d.721) and Egbert (d.766), accompanied by Pope Calixtus (1119–24). This initially surprising inclusion illustrates how the choice of figures was edited to convey particular messages about the status of the see of York that would have resonated with the window's principal audience, the canons of the Minster. As Professor Norton has observed, Calixtus was the pope who consecrated Archbishop Thurstan (1070–1140) after he had refused to swear allegiance to Canterbury, thereby effectively ending the dispute for overall primacy in England. It is possible that saintly Thurstan is the unidentified figure in 1j, accompanying Pope Celestine III (1106–98), who confirmed Durham's subservience to York. William of York (d.1154), canonised in 1224 and enshrined in the Minster, was an obvious choice (Fig. 3.11) and it is likely that as Thornton began work on the Great East Window, the decision to devote one of the 'great windows of the choir' to his life and miracles had already been made.

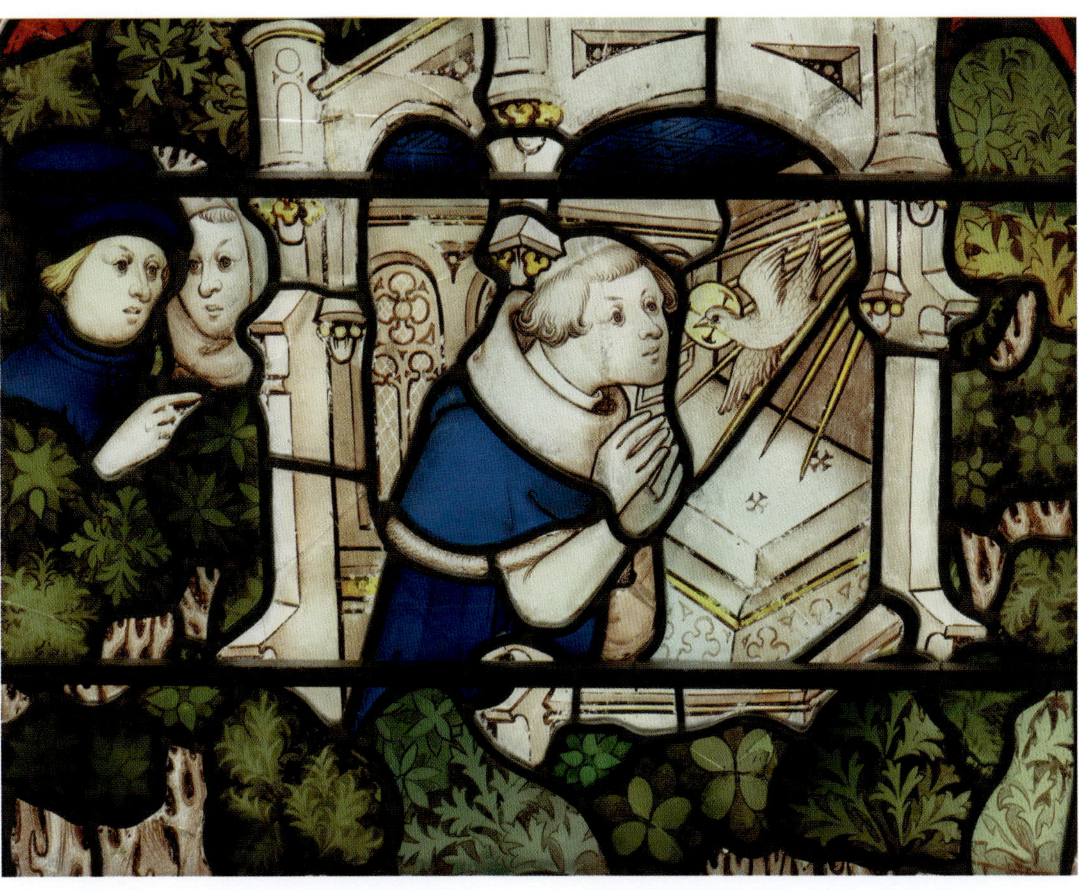

Foreshadowing the Heavenly Jerusalem: Architectural and Numerological Symbolism

As has been mentioned above, the adaptation of the internal tracery skin of the window was to have significant implications, for the subdivision of the subject matter creates an additional layer of numerological significance within the window. The subdivision of the tracery into three main sections, vertically by the insertion of heavier super-mullions, and horizontally by the inclusion of transoms, has long been observed, and the idea of 'three in one' has obvious Trinitarian significance.

The number 3 also unlocks a far more sophisticated message: 3x3 accounts for the nine panels of historical figures at the window's base; 9x3 is 27, the number of Old Testament scenes, which we can now see was made possible by a very deliberate alteration to the architectural framework; 3x27 is 81, the number of panels in the Apocalypse cycle, which as has been discussed above, was edited to fit the specific space allocated to it. In other words, each section of the narrative cycle is three times larger than the one before. The number 3, representing the Holy Trinity, can therefore be seen to be the fount of Creation and of all of human history. Professor Norton has also pointed out that the multiplication of all of these numbers (9 x 27 x 81) results in the figure 19,683 which according to some medieval calculations was the number of years between Creation and the end of the world, promised in the book of Revelation as a precursor to the creation of a new heaven and a new earth, the subject with which the window's narrative concludes.

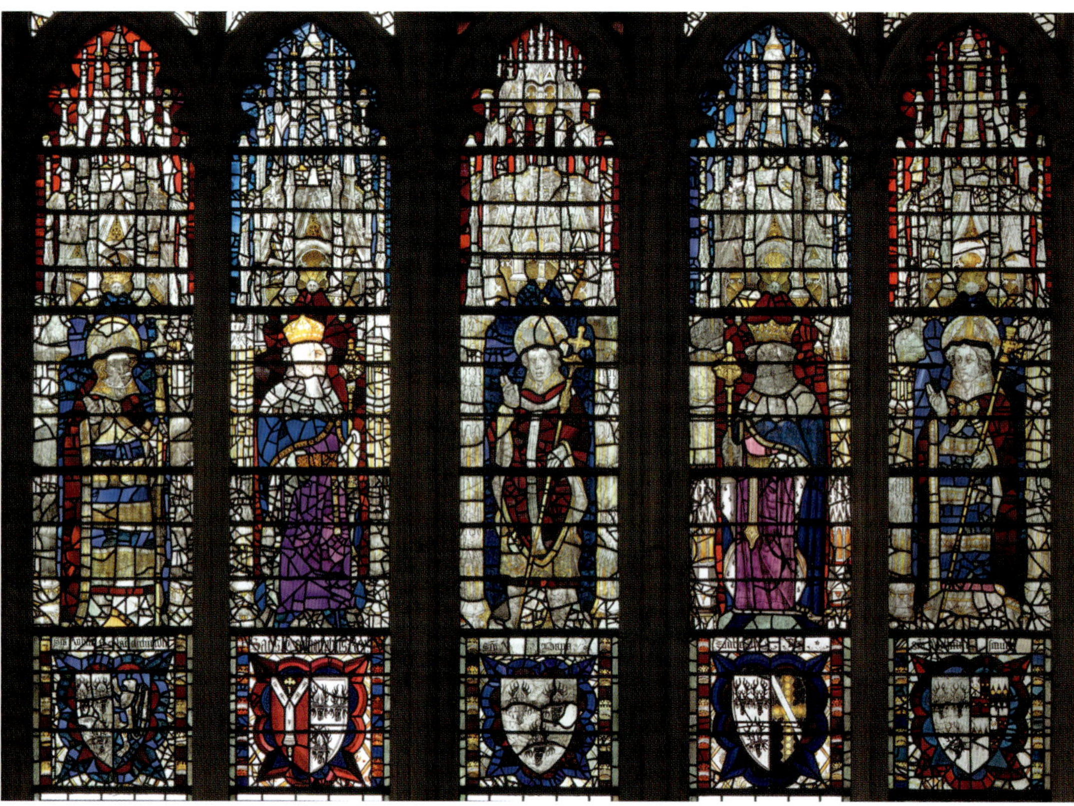

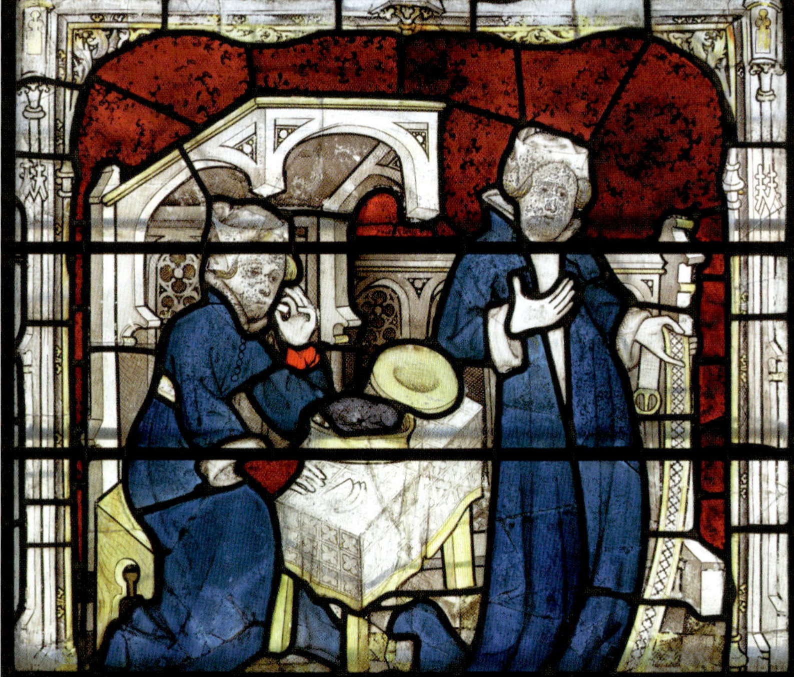

Fig. 3.12
Choir clerestory window N8, the gift of Archbishop Henry Bowet (1407–23).

Fig. 3.13
A woman is poisoned by accidentally eating a frog concealed in a loaf. The narrative unfolds in two parallel scenes, as she ingests the frog and then suffers the consequences and is forced to undo her belted robe. Panel 17a of the St William Window.

Reading the Choir

The creation of the Great East Window was just the start of an enormous programme of glazing that between *c*.1408 and *c*.1420 filled the western choir aisles and clerestory with what is clearly a coherent and planned scheme, although funded by a wider range of individual patrons and donors, some of them laypeople and some ecclesiastics. If the Great East Window is the story of universal human history and salvation, the rest of the choir glazing adds a layer of localised historical texture and detail. The eight windows of the western choir clerestory (N8–11 and S8–11) explore the history of the evangelisation of the kingdom of Northumbria and the relationship of the Church in the northern province to the Universal Church in general and to Rome, the see of St Peter, to whom the Minster itself is dedicated, in particular. We have seen how the base of the Great East Window presents key figures in the history of York's past. This theme is developed in far greater depth in the choir clerestory windows, with an emphasis on the historical strand that receives least attention in the east window, namely the story of the Anglo-Saxon conversion of the seventh and eighth centuries. This is the story so vividly told in Bede's *Ecclesiastical History of the English People* (completed in 731), a principal source for this cycle, and one which was written with a strong northern emphasis. Each window contains standing figures under canopies, arranged above shields of arms that suggest the identity of the patrons who helped to pay for the scheme. In the five-light windows the order is archbishop, king, pope, king, archbishop, and originally every figure was identified by a label. The heraldry suggests that they were made between *c*.1408 and 1415, in a sequence book-ended by the Great East Window and the St William Window. Window N8 (Fig. 3.12), for example, was the gift of Archbishop Henry Bowet (1407–23), whose personal arms and those of his family, are located below figures of St John of Beverley (705–17), King Ceolwulf (729–37), Pope Gregory II (715–31), St Wilfrid II (717–44) and

King Eadberht (737–48). The damage caused by the fire of 1829 makes it difficult now to identify all the figures, and after the Second World War Dean Milner-White moved some of the panels. However, in the better preserved windows on the north side, the care taken to develop the narrative can be seen in the careful arrangement of the figures. In window N9, for example, the two archbishops are St Wilfrid, Bishop of York in 669 (d.709) and his successor St Bosa (d.705). In the centre light is Pope Agatho (678–81), to whom Wilfred appealed his deposition in 679, who found in his favour. The kings are Oswiu (655–70), who presided over the critical synod of Whitby of 664, which found in favour of the Roman over the Celtic tradition for the celebration of Easter, an event in which Wilfrid played a decisive part, and his son King Aldfrith (685–705). While this is a period in which the bishops and archbishops of York are remembered for their sanctity, historical circumstances mean that very few had actually died in York or had been buried there. This scheme ensured, therefore, that this most illustrious chapter in York's history is celebrated in the liturgical heart of the church, complementing the later medieval archbishops, including St William of York, who were entombed in the Minster in person. Archbishop Thoresby had enhanced the choir as a place of episcopal burial by arranging to be buried before the Lady Chapel altar with six of his most illustrious immediate predecessors. At this time the main focus of the cult of St William was at the east end of the nave, although the head shrine of the saint was kept close to the high altar and the north-east transept window was filled with a large narrative cycle dedicated to the life and miracles of St William, with a strong emphasis on the efficacy of pilgrimage to the Minster shrines (Fig. 3.13). He was accompanied next to the high altar with a window dedicated to the life of St Cuthbert, although this window (s7, Fig. 3.15) was only filled with glass a generation later, probably in the 1440s. These two great windows can only be seen properly when standing in the bay occupied

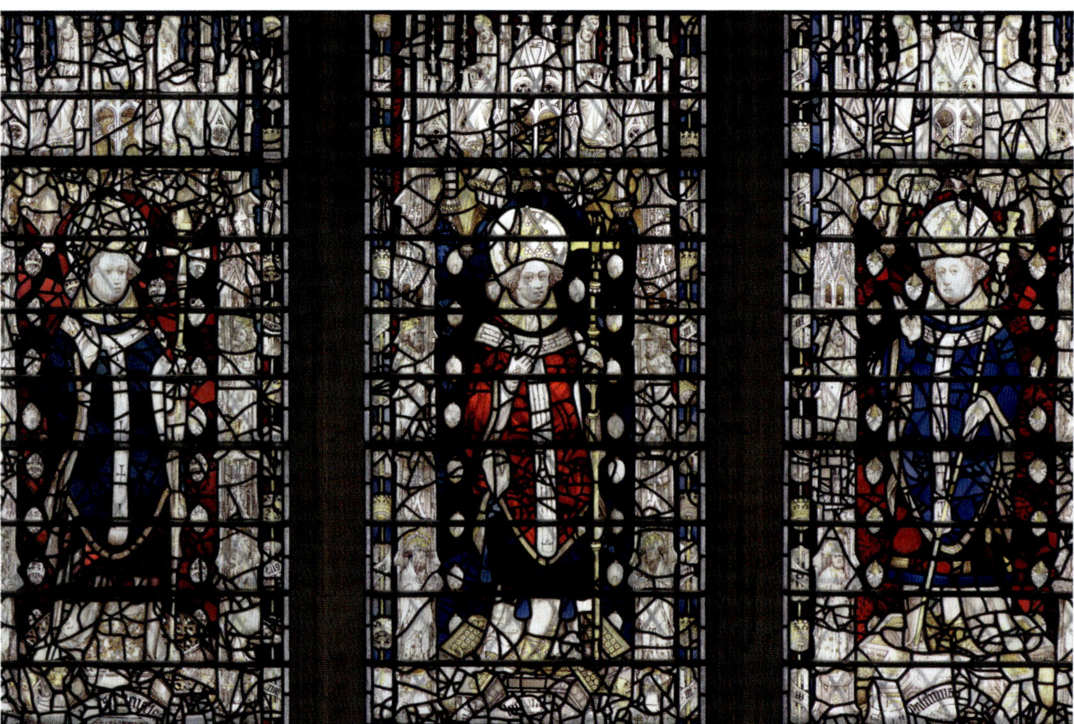

by the high altar, meaning they were designed to be viewed primarily by the Minster clergy rather than by visiting pilgrims. This community of northern saints was augmented by windows in the adjoining choir aisles, in which the personal devotional preferences of the individual donors can more easily be discerned and once again it is on the better-preserved north side that the coherence of the scheme can best be seen. Archbishop Henry Bowet, who as we have seen, donated a choir clerestory window, also gave aisle window n10, celebrating the Virgin Mary, St Peter and St Paul, the two saints most commonly represented on the seals of York Minster. Canon Thomas Parker (n9, Fig. 3.14) chose St John of Beverley (Archbishop of York, 705–21), St William of York (d.1154) and St Thomas of Canterbury (d.1170), his own name saint. Canon Treasurer Robert Wolveden (n8) chose St Paulinus, the first bishop of York (d.644), St Chad (d.672), briefly bishop of York and then first bishop of Lichfield where Wolveden had served as precentor, and St Nicholas of Myra.

The glazing of the western choir is of variable quality and is not all as outstanding as that seen in the Great East Window. However, the stylistic imprint of the workshop assembled by Thornton can clearly be seen throughout the choir glazing and it seems likely that in liaison with the Dean and Chapter he was involved in the overall planning. It is clear that in the ingenuity of design and the quality of the glass painting, the St William Window (n7) is his work. The need to plan and implement this second great narrative must have absorbed much of his time after the completion of the Great East Window. For the slightly later St Cuthbert window (s7), there were comparatively rich visual sources to be drawn upon , although they too required careful editing, and if Thornton was not to live to see this window made, his example as a master storyteller would not have been wasted on those glaziers entrusted with the final great work to be commissioned for the choir.

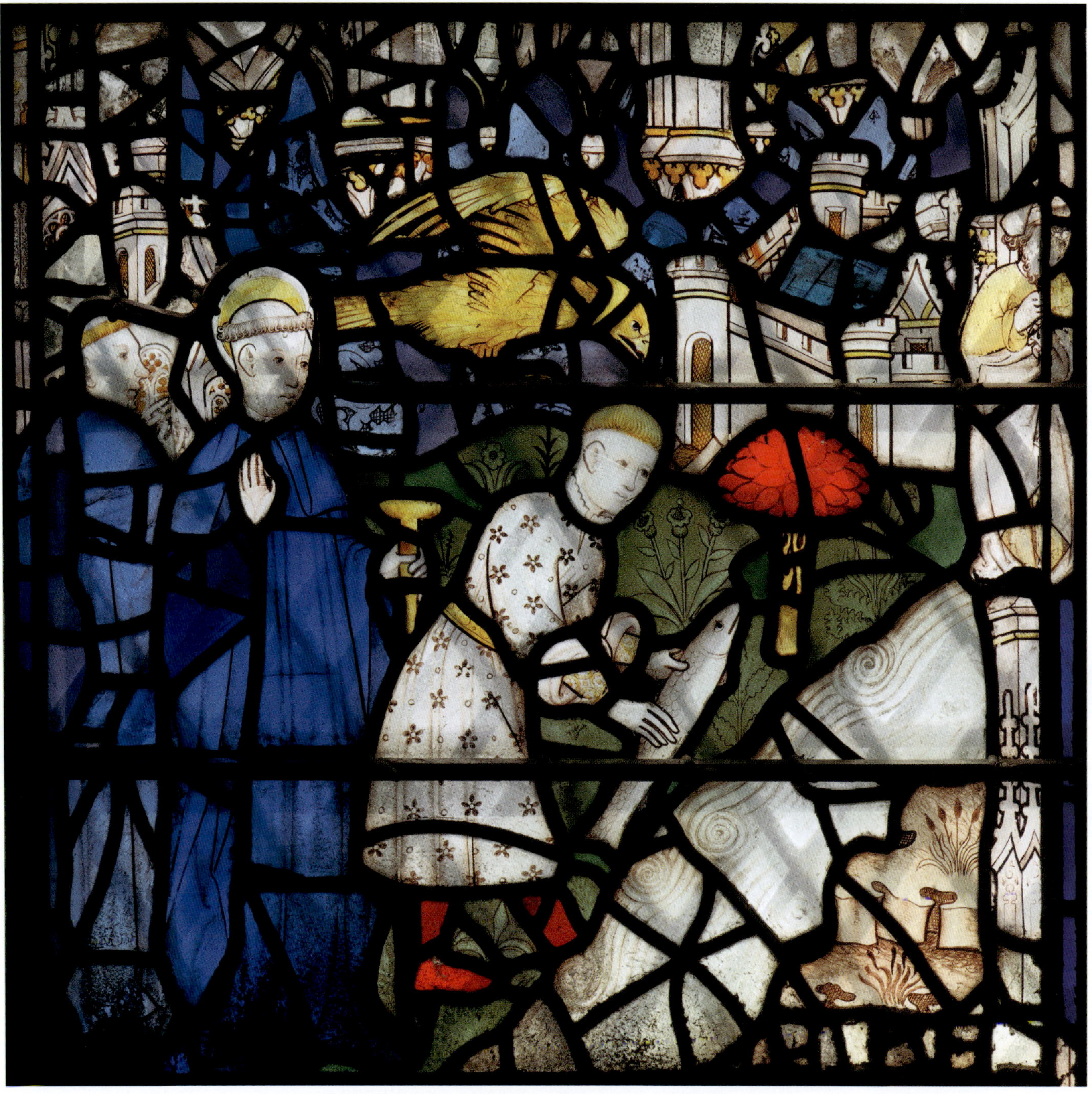

Fig. 3.15
St Cuthbert receives a
fish from an eagle, in
the St Cuthbert window
(s7, panel 13b).

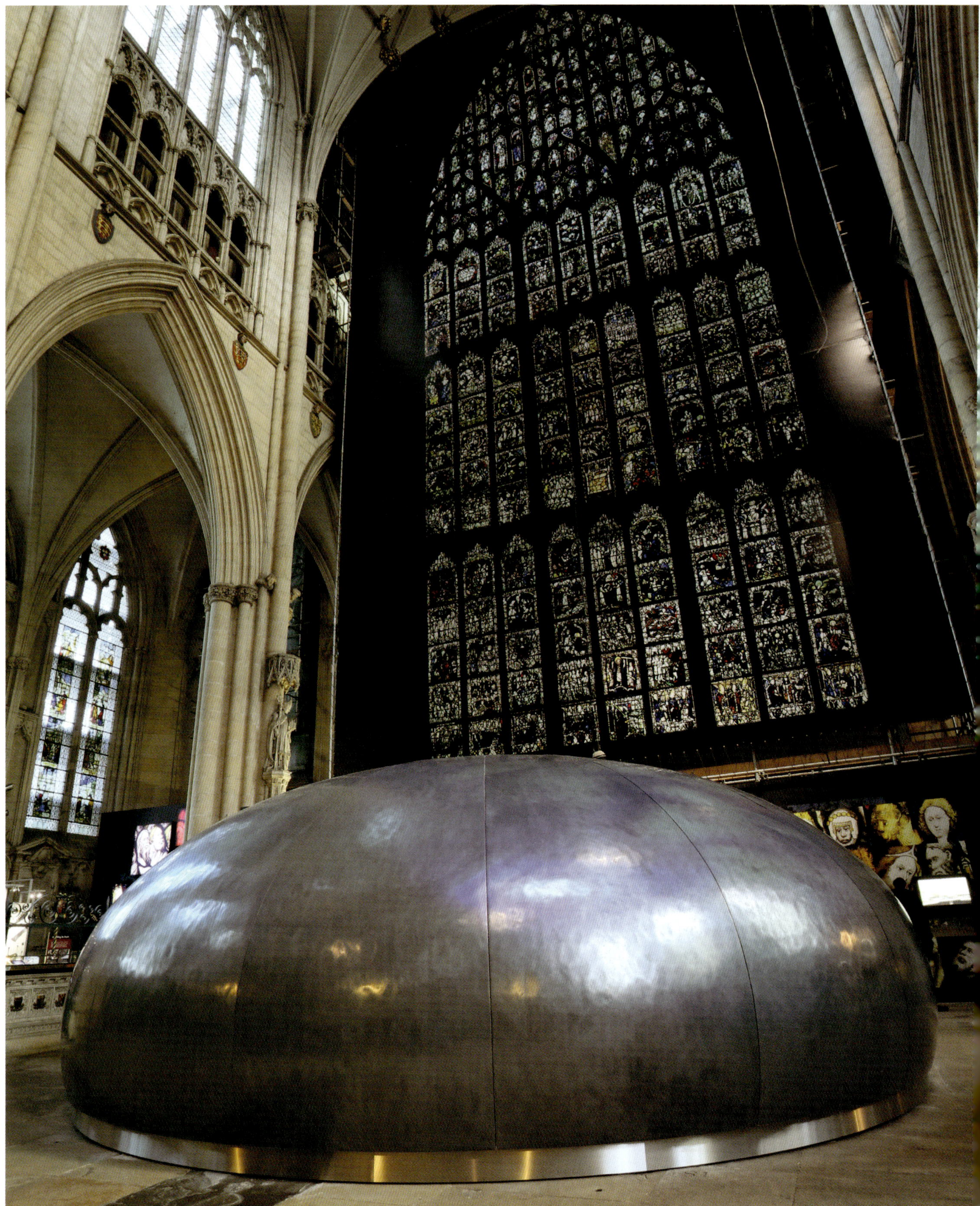

Chapter 4

Preserving a Medieval Masterpiece
The Conservation Programme of 2011–2017

In 2005, as work on the conservation of the St William Window was drawing to a close, the urgent need to conserve the masonry of the east façade of the cathedral first became apparent and the removal of the stained glass of the Great East Window to a place of safety for the duration of the work was an obvious requirement. Every five years the condition of the Minster's windows is assessed as part of the quinquennial inspection of the building. Having been restored and provided with external glazing relatively recently, the Great East Window had not been identified as one of the highest priorities. The high-level windows of the building represent the greatest conservation challenge, as access to them for maintenance and repair can only be safely achieved from scaffolding on *both* sides of the window, something that happens infrequently and at very great cost. The need for urgent masonry repair put the conservation of the stained glass back on the agenda for the first time since 1953. The prospect of being able to examine and study at close quarters and in its entirety the Great East Window, the jewel in the Minster's crown, at a time when conservation expertise and art-historical scholarship in York is at its height, was recognised as an opportunity not to be missed (Fig. 4.1). Would any conservation work other than a gentle clean and the renewal and improvement of its external protective glazing be necessary or justifiable? In 2005 this was the first issue to be addressed by a newly appointed advisory group made up of conservators, art historians and representatives of the Chapter.

Fig. 4.1
The Orb, introduced into the Lady Chapel in October 2012, an exciting modern structure in which conserved panels from the Great East Window could be viewed at close quarters, against the backdrop of an enormous digital photograph of the absent window.

The East Window Advisory Group
The conservation of the St William Window in the north-east transept (window n7), undertaken between 1998 and 2007, was the biggest single stained-glass conservation project undertaken since the post-war campaigns overseen by Dean Eric Milner-White. The conservators of the York Glaziers Trust (YGT) had benefited enormously from the support of an informal advisory committee, the St William Window Advisory Group

(SWWAG). The group had met at regular intervals throughout the conduct of the project and a careful record of the decision-making processes was maintained alongside the conservation documentation. In 2005 the advisory group model was revived by the Dean, the Very Revd Keith Jones, and rechristened the East Window Advisory Group (EWAG). The group's remit was to work with the conservators of YGT to develop a robust conservation methodology for the window, to provide independent advice to the Chapter and to assist it in conducting the national consultation processes that would underpin applications to the national regulatory body (the Cathedrals Fabric Commission for England) and to external funders. Between 2005 and 2010 EWAG produced four reports on the developing methodology and has met over 90 times since 2011 when the project began in earnest.

The Condition of the Window

The removal of a small number of panels from the Minster in 2005 meant that the condition of the window could be evaluated in greater detail and most importantly, the exterior surfaces, hidden behind the external quarry glazing, could be accessed for the first time since 1953. Needless to say, the window was very dirty, its surfaces covered in a mixture of dust, cobweb and the greasy soot that accumulates in a heated building visited by hundreds of thousands of people every year. The most striking thing was the excellent state of preservation of all the uncoloured ('white') glasses, which displayed only light pitting (Fig. 4.2). Elsewhere, the problems associated with 600 years of exposure to the environment were immediately apparent. Some coloured glasses were heavily corroded, notably those in the purple-red and pale-green colour range, and where the original glass survived, it was often only with significant paint loss (Fig. 4.3). There was almost no original pot-metal yellow glass remaining in the window and the pale greyish blue favoured for the depiction of lead roofs

displayed internal micro-cracks (e.g. in panel 8j) and in places had disappeared altogether (e.g. panel 7e). The flashed ruby glass displayed widely varying patterns of corrosion. By the 15th century a 'flashed' ruby glass was usually made by blowing a small gather of pure red glass with a gather of white glass, so that a thin layer of ruby formed over the white base. It is therefore very susceptible to surface corrosion, which can render it pale or even colourless, depending on the degree of corrosion of its ruby layer (Fig. 4.4). A great deal of it was extremely well preserved, while elsewhere adjoining pieces of ruby glass in the same figure displayed widely differing rates of decomposition. In contrast, the darker blues used for the seaweed backgrounds were generally well preserved. Paint loss had occurred across the window, in places as a result of the corrosion of the surfaces of less durable coloured glasses, but elsewhere as a result of the overzealous cleaning in the past, when abrasive brushes were used, as evidenced by scratch marks in closely set parallel lines. Silver stain (always applied on the exterior) was generally well preserved.

The results of the post-war restoration were also very apparent. The thick leading favoured by the 20th-century Minster glaziers meant that apart from a small number of panels in row 13, which exhibited buckling along their lower edges, panels were generally in a very stable state. However, uniformly thick leads had been used indiscriminately throughout the panels, so that principal outlines and mended breaks had been treated in the same way, often with disastrous visual results (Figs. 4.5 and 4.6). Attempts had been made to avoid the most invasive and disfiguring of mending leads across key features (especially heads), and a common 20th-century approach was to create a plated 'sandwich' of modern plain glass encapsulating the broken medieval pieces. Animal glue was used to hold the broken medieval pieces in place, but in numerous places these thick 'packages' of glass (which also needed deep-hearted leads to hold them together) had admitted dirt and

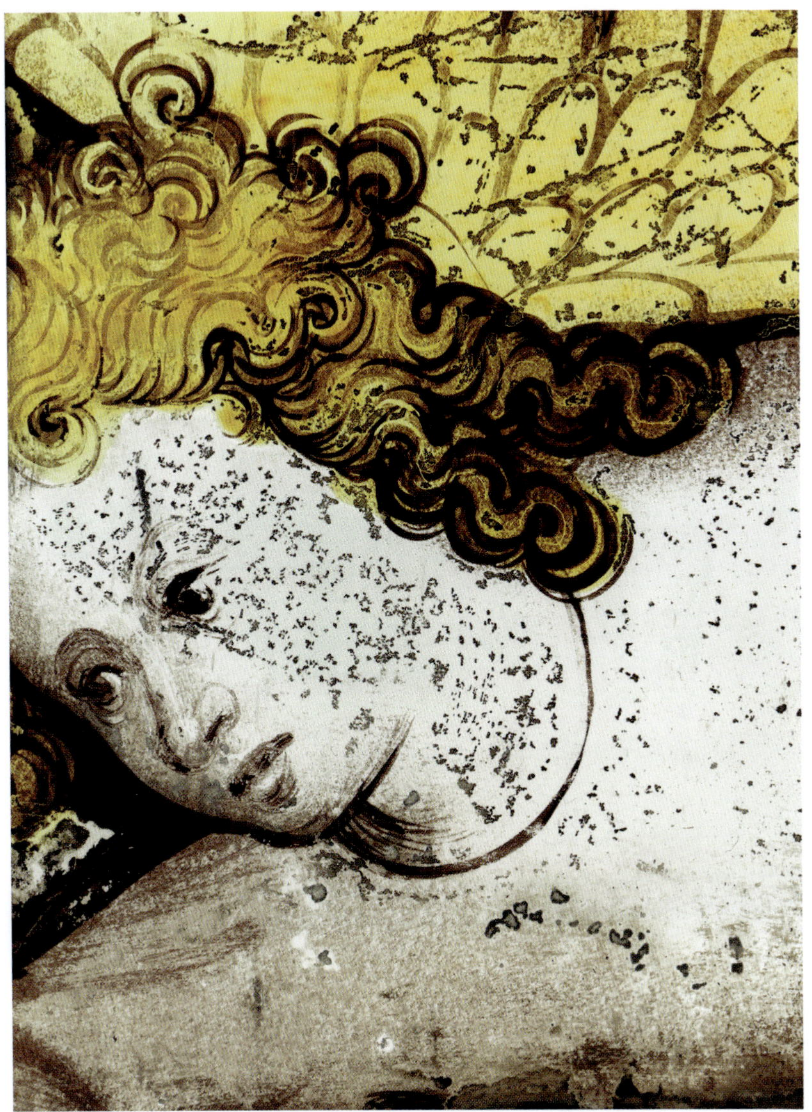

Fig. 4.2
Light pitting affecting the otherwise excellently preserved 'white' glass of the Great East Window (detail of panel 9b). By 1399 large quantities of white glass had been stockpiled for the making of the great windows of the choir.

moisture, creating a moist microclimate which dissolved the glue and allowed unsecured medieval pieces to move about inside the plates, with a considerable risk of damage and moisture-induced corrosion. It had long been common practice at York Minster to use pieces of medieval glass from other windows to patch damaged windows or to replace individual glass pieces considered too corroded or opaque to be retained (these are known as 'stopgaps'). These had often been very skilfully chosen and were in harmony with the surrounding original glass, matching it well in terms of tone and character. Under Dean Milner-White, this practice had continued, although if no suitable pieces could be found, unpainted modern glass was used instead. These insertions were very thick compared to the medieval material, requiring thick leads to hold them, and the absence of any surface paint meant that the pieces were often visually very obtrusive, especially when viewed from a distance (Fig. 4.7). The conservation trials also found them to have been very imprecisely cut, so that very wide leads were needed to make them fit into the medieval panels.

Compared to the St William Window, last restored in 1895, the Great East Window presented a far more complex mix of original and intruded glass. During the restoration of the St William Window, almost all glass judged to be alien to the window was removed by the restorer J. W. Knowles (1838–1931), who supplied a number of very-well-painted new pieces. The original configuration of medieval glass (the 'cut-line') was, however, relatively well preserved. The window was consequently essentially of two dates: c.1414 and 1895. While Milner-White's unpainted glass inserts in the Great East Window were easily identified, other insertions of medieval, 18th-century and early 19th-century glass represented a far more complex picture. The situation was further exacerbated by Dean Milner-White's readiness to substitute one collection of stopgaps with another, to rearrange original glass, in many instances moving it from

Fig. 4.3
Heavy internal corrosion and associated loss of painted detail affects the small amount of surviving green glass in the window (detail of panel 4e). Much of the original green has been lost altogether.

Fig. 4.4
Corrosion of the internal glass surface has removed the thin layer of ruby 'flash' on this red sleeve, revealing the white base glass beneath (detail of panel 4c).

Fig. 4.5
The head of St John (panel 10e), broken and with pieces missing, repaired with heavy mending leads which disfigure and distort the original design.

Fig. 4.6
The same piece following conservation. A new painted insertion has restored the original shape and proportion of the head.

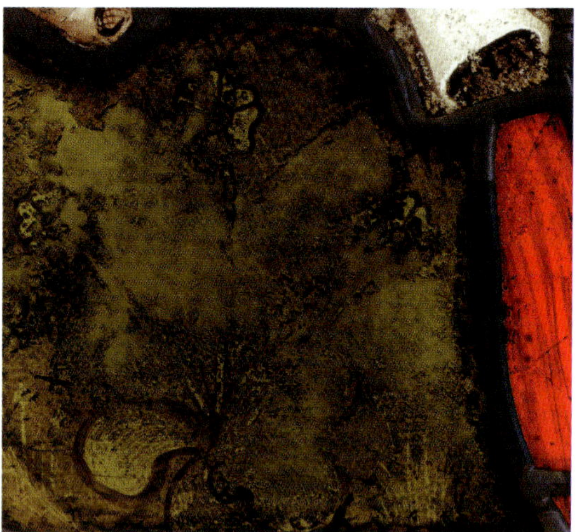

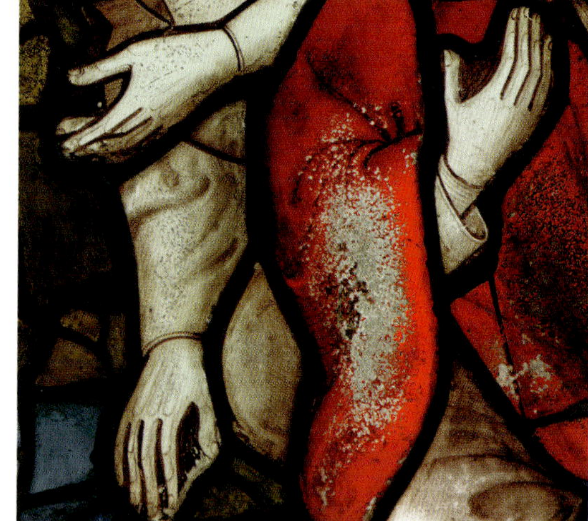

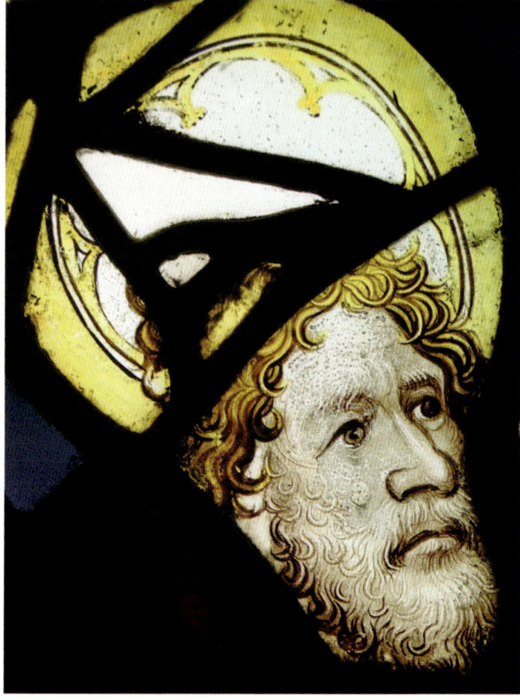

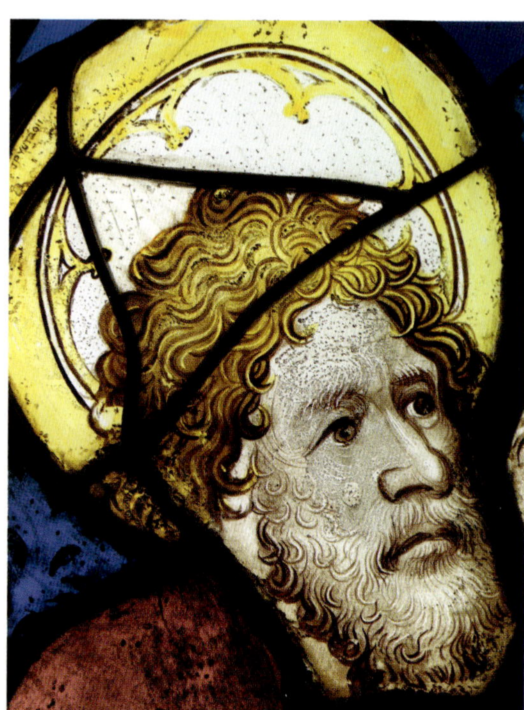

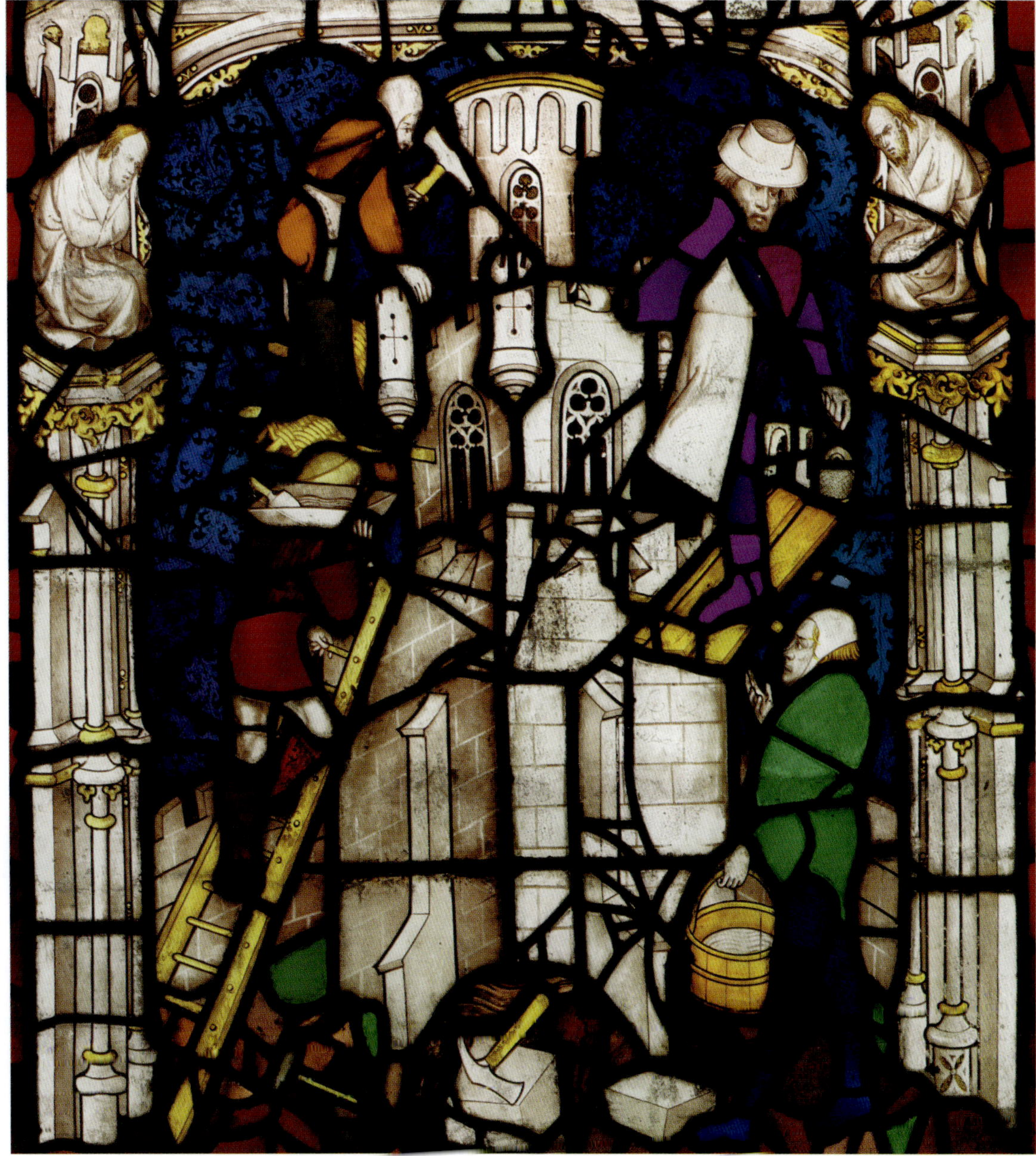

Fig. 4.7
The Tower of Babel (panel 14d), before conservation. Heavy mending leads and very bright, unpainted green and purple modern glass disrupt the legibility of the original design.

its correct original location, in order to fill a gap created by the removal of a discarded earlier repair, and in some instances allowing original pieces to be cut to make them fit into a new 'cut-line'. There was scant respect for the work of the early 19th-century restorers, who had tended to preserve the original medieval leadlines, even if they introduced stopgaps to make good any holes in the window. Very little research was done before the glazing team led by the Dean embarked upon quite significant interventions in the complex panels. As a theologian the Dean was undoubtedly familiar with the biblical texts on which the window is based. He also had access to at least one of the facsimile editions of English medieval Apocalypse manuscripts, a subject on which his Cambridge mentor M. R. James (1862–1936) was an acknowledged expert. Nonetheless, the understanding of the relationships between 'families' of Apocalypse manuscripts and their relationship to John Thornton's window was poorly understood and the Dean seems to have relied on his own judgement in all things. The late 17th-century description of the window by antiquary James Torre (1649–99), a seminal source for the recent conservation project, was dismissed out of hand: 'Alas that he did not better understand what he was describing.' He reported on the progress of the work in the pages of the Friends of York Minster annual reports, but these lively and exciting descriptions of triumph and discovery are no substitute for the almost complete lack of any documentation of what was done in the years 1941–53.

'In the Beginning':
Or What to Do and How to Do It

The conservation of the Great East Window in the 21st century would be the biggest project ever undertaken by the YGT and the risks, the challenges and the costs were likely to be greater than anything experienced before. A series of conservation trials were identified as the best means of arriving at a well-informed conservation methodology that would stand up to the scrutiny of both the national regulatory bodies and the international conservation community. The method statement would need to address both technical issues (structure of the panels, likely remaining lifespan of the inherited lead nets, cleaning methods, edge-bonding materials and techniques, design of environmental protective glazing, standards of documentation, the role of digital media) and ethical concerns (the nature and extent of historical evidence, criteria for retention or replacement of later additions, the balance of conservation and restoration). The project would need to take account of the latest technical developments in stained-glass conservation, which offered a number of techniques unavailable to our predecessors, but also required that the conservation be conducted in line with the highest ethical standards, as defined in international guidelines such as the International Council on Monuments and Sites' (ICOMOS) *Venice Charter* of 1964 and its successors and, more specifically, the *Guidelines for the Conservation and Restoration of Stained Glass* published by the international Corpus Vitrearum in 2004.

Two guiding principles underpin the Corpus Vitrearum *Guidelines*: the paramount importance of research in the conduct of conservation and the role of environmental protection as an integral part of any stained-glass conservation strategy. With Heritage Lottery Fund (HLF) support for a project entitled 'In the Beginning', the YGT commissioned new background research into the restoration history of the window (undertaken by Dr Joseph Spooner) and benefited from new research into the iconographic sources of the window (undertaken by Professors Nigel Morgan and Christopher Norton). The benefits of external protection, first installed in 1861, was already acknowledged and EWAG defined ventilated external protective glazing (sometimes called isothermal glazing) as an essential component of any future conservation project. The HLF grant allowed a new internally

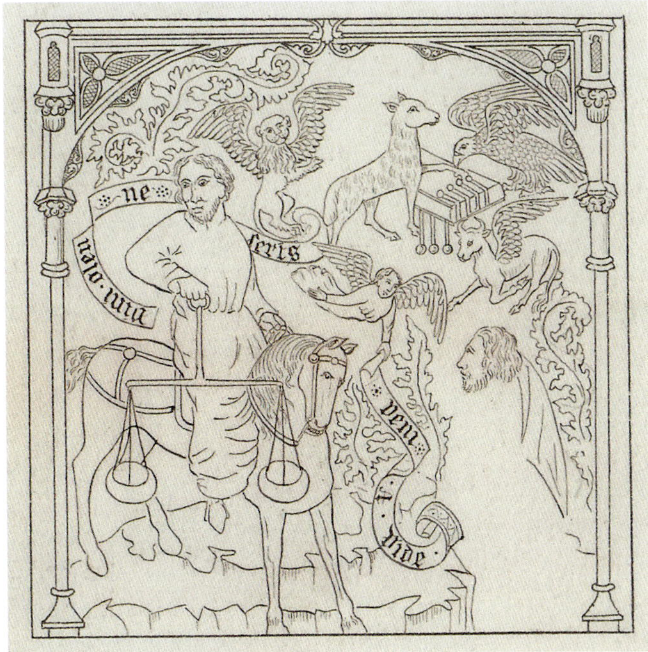

Fig. 4.8
One of Henry Crump
Camidge's 1884 drawings
(of panel 10g).

ventilated environmental protective glazing system to be designed and a test installation at the east end of the building to be trialled, using the glass sensors of the Fraunhofer Institut für Silikatforchung in Germany, and temperature and humidity data loggers. The results were analysed by Dr Ivo Rauch and Dr Erhard Jaegers.

The historical and antiquarian research ensured that the history of the Great East Window in the years after its creation and installation was more fully understood and the significance of the surviving traces of successive interventions (outlined in Chapter One) could be properly evaluated. The research also identified the main descriptions and images of the window over time, providing a series of informative 'snapshots' of its state at key points in its history, the most important sources being those of James Torre (a detailed and objective unpublished description of *c*.1690), Thomas Gent (descriptions published in 1730 and 1762), the Hayes/Toms large-scale engraving of *c*.1736, the H. C. Camidge drawings (*c*.1884, Fig. 4.8) and the photographs of 1939–40. As no work was

done on the window between the 1820s and the 1940s, these photographs, taken on large-format glass negatives as the panels were removed to safety at the outbreak of the Second World War, provide an exceptionally clear record of the state of the panels following the restoration of the 1820s. During the recent conservation programme, we have printed them at the same scale as the actual stained-glass panels, allowing individual pieces of glass to be tracked over time.

The trial allowed three conservation approaches to be put to the test. The members of EWAG collaborated with the conservators on their implementation and assessment, and then reported to the Chapter on their relative merits. In the first trial, representing minimal intervention, glass was cleaned in the leads, cracks were stabilised and any broken solder joints were mended. The condition of the trial panel was mapped fully and it was photographed with high-resolution digital photography. This was, of course, the least expensive approach, and would have seen the window returned to the Minster, fully protected, but with no improvement in terms of levels of iconographic integrity and legibility. In the second trial, a panel was carefully dismantled from its leading. The individual glass pieces were cleaned and wherever possible mending leads were removed and clean breaks were edge-bonded. The panel was then releaded using a lighter gauge of lead throughout. This approach was close to the 'relead as found' approach pursued by Minster glaziers throughout the late 19th and early 20th centuries, and only abandoned under Dean Milner-White's restorations. The dismantling process revealed the poor fit of many of the pieces of glass introduced into the panel by the Milner-White campaign and meant that this approach was far less straightforward than anticipated. Notwithstanding the difficulties, the approach meant that after conservation the trial panels were visually lighter and weighed less (by 4–5 kg) than in their pre-conservation state. In the third trial, by far the most interventive and potentially the most controversial, the panel was also dismantled from its thick leads. Glass was cleaned, mending leads removed where possible, and glass edge-bonded as appropriate. In addition, it was agreed that through the combination of art-historical research and the forensic examination of the glass itself, an attempt should be made to recover the original cut-line of the panel, in other words the original configuration of glass within Thornton's cartoon.

This meant that a clear and robust set of principles for the handling of two main issues was required. First of all, the treatment of stopgaps, those pieces of glass of all dates and types, introduced as repairs and replacements by previous restorers. The recovery of Thornton's original design often displaced some of the stopgaps, especially those introduced by Milner-White. A note of caution was sounded by Cesare Brandi (1906–88), writing in 1963 in the context of wall- and panel-painting conservation: 'From the historical point of view, only the conservation of an addition is unconditionally legitimate, while removal always requires justification.' The ICOMOS *Venice Charter* of 1964 stressed that 'the valid contributions of all periods to the building of a monument must be respected, since unity of style is not the aim of a restoration' (article 11), to which the Corpus Vitrearum *Guidelines* of 2004 added the observation that 'Losses, stopgaps, rearrangements and later additions provide evidence of the history of a stained-glass panel and must be fully studied and documented' (article 4.4.1). The third option also raised the question of the appropriate balance to be struck between conservation and restoration. The objective of restoration was defined thus by ICOMOS in 1964: 'to preserve and reveal the aesthetic and historic value of the monument and is based on respect for original material and authentic documents. It must stop where conjecture begins' (*Venice Charter*, article 9). Cesare Brandi warns us that 'Contrary to general belief, the most serious aspect in regard to a work of art is not what is

missing but what is inserted inappropriately', a description that certainly fitted some of the most aesthetically obtrusive of stopgaps, but also set the bar very high in the consideration of the treatment restoration infills. The Corpus Vitrearum *Guidelines* require that 'The insertions of infills, inpainting and restoration of missing paint, rearrangements of replacement of later additions should only be undertaken when fully justifiable based on thorough art-historical and technical research' (article 4.4.1). Working with these underlying principles, it was clear that the third option could only be adopted if supported by thorough and continuing research throughout the project and that a set of strong criteria to govern the retention or removal of stopgaps, and a fully justified rationale for this replacement, would be required. These were developed, based on fit, colour and tone. The impact of a stopgap on the iconographic meaning of a panel was also recognised to be a factor in some instances. Any proposed alteration to the arrangement inherited from Milner-White required careful consideration and justification to members of EWAG and any restoration of lost details required the support of art-historical and/or technical evidence.

Mindful of Brandi's definition of 'appropriateness', the style of restoration painting to be employed was also given careful consideration. Stained glass as a medium works through the manipulation of the passage of light through colour by means of the addition of glass paint. Indeed, it is actually both an additive and reductive process, as glass painters also reveal contrasting highlights through the careful removal of areas of paint to reveal raw glass beneath. Unpainted pieces, such as many of the Milner-White insertions, are visually obtrusive because they are usually far brighter than the surrounding glass, and interrupt the passage of the eye across the composition as a whole. The application of some modifying paint was therefore agreed to be necessary. What form it should take was another matter. International conservation guidelines are all in agreement that new additions must be both

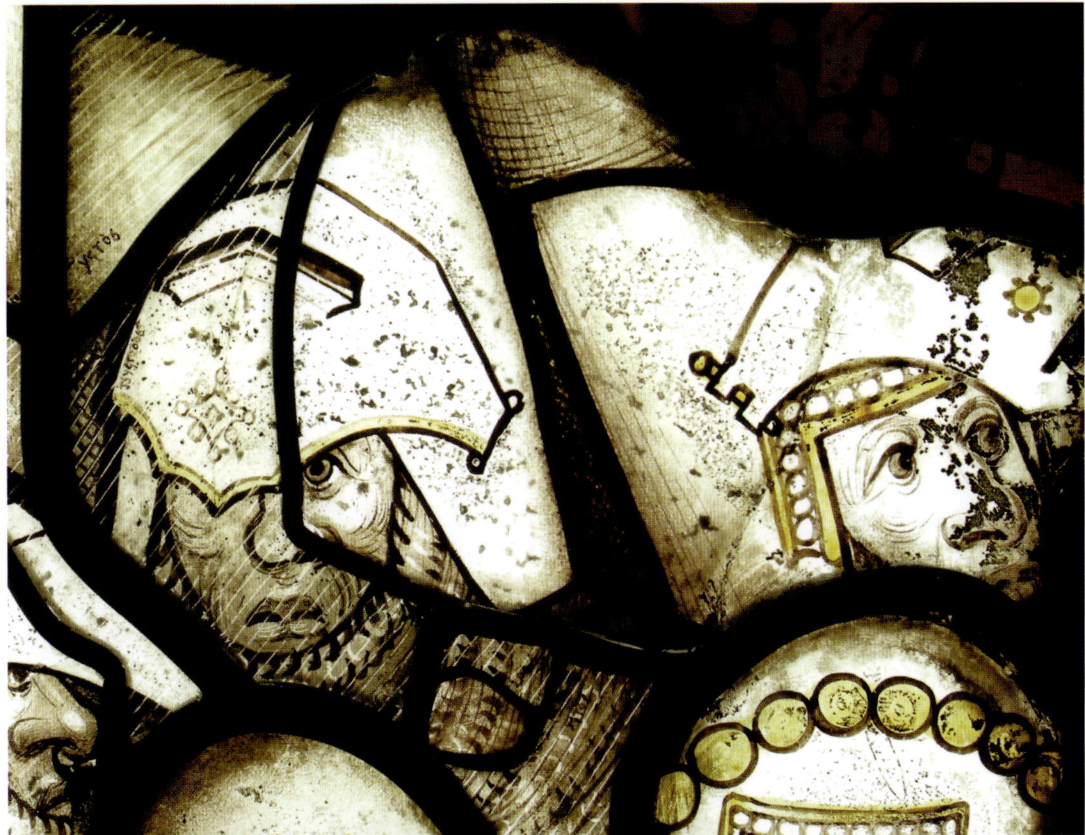

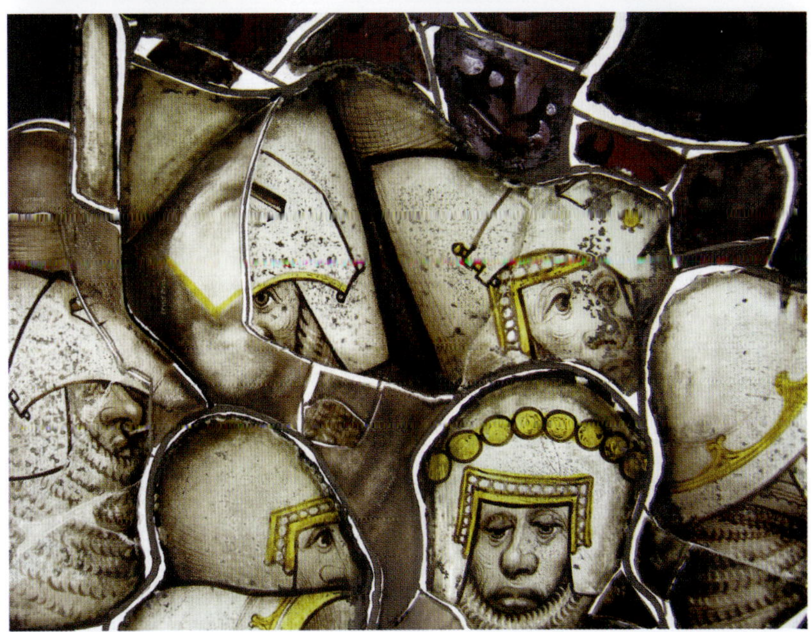

Fig. 4.9 and Fig. 4.10
Conservation painting trials. During the development of the conservation methodology, the YGT explored different approaches to the creation of restoration infills, testing the impact of scribed (top) and toned (bottom) painting techniques as a means of distinguishing new glass from old (trials of panels 8f).

unobtrusive and readily identifiable. The *Venice Charter* requires that 'replacements of missing parts must integrate harmoniously with the whole, but at the same time must be distinguishable from the original' (article 12). Brandi offers a more nuanced interpretation of what this means in practice: 'Any integration must always be easily recognisable, but without interfering with the unity that one is trying to reestablish. Thus at the distance from which the work of art will be viewed, the integration should be invisible. From a closer view point it should be immediately recognisable, without the aid of special equipment.' The Corpus Vitrearum *Guidelines* require that any addition must 'be identified in a permanent manner with a date and signature or other identifying symbols' (article 4.4.1).

A wide variety of treatments of restoration insertions are possible, including stippled shading, microdots and cross-hatchings (the last two commonly used in wall-painting restoration). Initially, the YGT team and EWAG favoured a stippled shading for the restoration infills. This approach was applied to panel 8f, in areas of both light and dark glass. As anticipated, in areas of darker colour, the exact character of the paint application was not too critical visually. In the light areas, on the other hand, the misty, indistinct nature of the end result was found to be visually disturbing and detracted from the reading of the original composition (Fig. 4.10). A return to the more traditional 'facsimile painting' favoured in the 19th century, and used to good effect in the conservation of the St William Window, was therefore also trialled. In every instance a new infill required rigorous evidence, together with a thorough understanding of the painting techniques of the medieval painters, in order to ensure that the new pieces achieved the visual harmony advocated by Cesare Brandi and the *Venice Charter*.

For many years it has been normal practice for stained-glass conservators to sign and date any new pieces in a discreet location which is visible to close scrutiny and photography. The

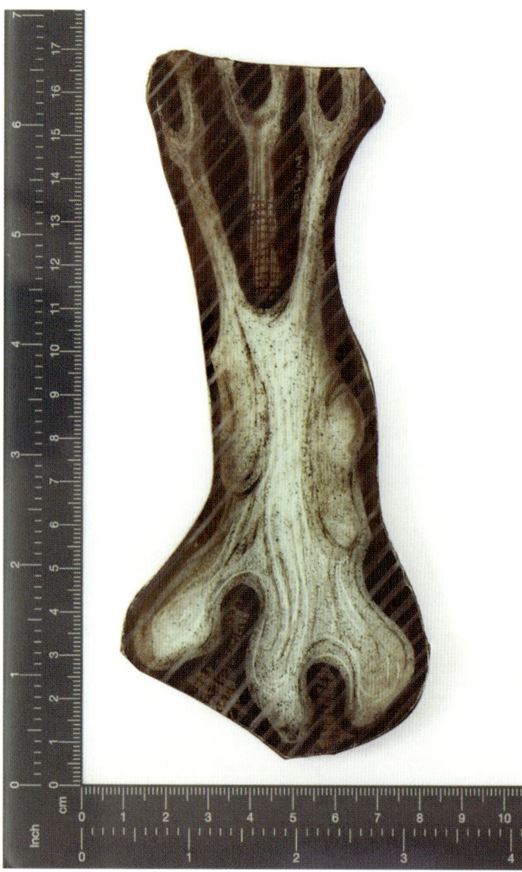

Fig. 4.11
The preferred option for restoration painting – a close facsimile of the medieval painting style, signed and dated, and with a distinguishing 'water-mark' of fired white lines on the exterior surface (sample piece).

YGT has traditionally used the initials of the individual painter together with 'YGT' and the year. Given the decision to paint in a 'facsimile' manner, it was also agreed that all new pieces should be marked with an overall signifier that would distinguish them immediately from both original pieces and from stopgaps of all previous interventions. Initially this was achieved by scoring diagonal lines through the paint of any new piece immediately prior to firing (Fig. 4.9), but as the sophistication of the painting techniques in the team developed, it became more and more difficult to score through the sophisticated layers of unfired paint without damaging the piece. The scoring also generated glass-paint dust, which can be hazardous to health. In places, the scored lines were also found to be difficult to distinguish from the cross-hatched modelling techniques used by the medieval glass painters. The team experimented with a variety of marking techniques based on the concept of the watermark found in hand-made paper. The eventual solution was the painting of fine diagonal lines across the entire exterior surface of each new piece, using a white glass-paint (Fig. 4.11). These are clearly legible from the back of the panel and can easily be seen in exterior photographs. From the interior they can be clearly seen when the panel is viewed at close quarters, although more so in light areas than in dark ones. As a result, all new glass from the current project will be easily distinguishable visually, as well as through the thorough documentation of each panel.

Unsurprisingly, this third conservation approach was also shown to be the most costly, requiring the greatest input of conservation expertise and art-historical research, and extensive deliberation between the conservators and the advisory group, not to mention the meticulous mapping of condition, conservation treatment and end result. Nonetheless, it was the third approach that was adopted by the Chapter of York, on the grounds that, while it was undoubtedly the most costly option, it also yielded the greatest benefits. The conservation approach ensures that while the work is not entirely reversible (only a sample of the 1950s lead was retained, for example), the window is re-treatable. In contrast to earlier restoration campaigns in York Minster, no stopgaps removed from a panel have been 'recycled'. They have been recorded, their former location noted, and have been retained in the Minster glass archive. While most are of unpainted glass of *c*.1950, a smaller number are medieval in origin and in some cases it is even possible that eventually their original location in another Minster window will be identified.

The Conservation Objectives

1. To conserve the medieval glass and to prevent further deterioration through the installation of an appropriate system of ventilated external protective glazing.

2. To identify and retain all original glass.

3. To restore the original cut-line, where there are sufficient grounds to do so.

4. To respect and preserve, as far as is reconcilable with objectives 3 and 5, the physical evidence of past restorations of the window.

5. To respect the medieval palette of colour (and range of tones within that palette), sympathetic to the John Thornton scheme.

6. To maintain consistency of approach through the lifespan of the project.

East Window Advisory Group, Final Report to the Chapter of York

From Beginning To End:
Conservation 2011–2017

Formal approval for the conservation of the window according to this methodology was secured from the Cathedrals Fabric Commission for England in the autumn of 2008. In 2011 an application by the Chapter of York and the York Minster Fund to the HLF for support for a wide-ranging package of work under the title 'York Minster Revealed' (including conservation of the east façade and Great East Window, redisplay of the undercroft collections, interpretation and outreach, creation of a new public space on the south side of the cathedral, and provision of new toilets for visitors) was successful. The glass and stone conservation informed exciting new interactive interpretation schemes at the east end of the Minster, including 'The Orb', which allowed visitors to see conserved panels at close quarters (see Fig. 4.1). In the converted Bedern Chapel, visitors were able to see the YGT conservators at work, while in a specially constructed masons' lodge, the masons could be seen at work in all weathers. At both the YGT and in the Minster stone yard, the project created new training opportunities for the next generation of conservators and craftsmen, young people who will continue to care for the building well into the future, handing on traditional and now increasingly rare heritage skills (Fig. 4.12).

By March 2016 the Apocalypse cycle, the historical figures in row 1 and the uppermost section of the tracery lights had been conserved and returned resplendent to the window, protected from the negative impact of the environment with state-of-the-art protective glazing. Work on the second phase of the project, supported by the York Minster Fund, began immediately, conserving the remaining tracery panels and the 27 Old Testament scenes. These panels were all returned to the window by the end of 2017, allowing the final removal of scaffolding and the revelation of the fully conserved window, its panels restored to the order in which they were installed by 1408. The antiquarian, art historical and iconographical research that has underpinned the conservation work has provided the foundation of a new understanding of John Thornton's medieval masterpiece.

In both phases of the project it was decided that conservation work should proceed in the same order as the biblical narrative (i.e. working from top to bottom and left to right). While Milner-White had corrected some mistakes in the order of the Old Testament and Apocalypse panels, he had introduced other errors as a consequence of mistaking some of the subjects depicted. He had been convinced that at least 30 panels in the window, including 24 in the Apocalypse sequence, were in the wrong order. The 1820s restorers had carefully returned every panel to the location in which they had found them, a sequence ignored in the 1940s, leading to the relocation and consequent resizing of a large number of panels, especially in the first three rows of the Apocalypse. We now know that only four Apocalypse panels were out of sequence when James Torre recorded the window *c.*1690, and that these four panels had probably always been in the wrong order as a consequence of a medieval production error. The Dean's interpretation of the Apocalypse was based predominantly on his own reading of the biblical text, perhaps augmented by reference to the facsimile editions of the Douce and Dyson Perrins (now Getty) Apocalypses, published by the Dean's former mentor M. R. James (in 1922 and 1927 respectively). Recent iconographic research has reassessed the subject matter of the Apocalypse panels in question and it was realised that apart from four panels in rows 8 and 9 (9j, 8a, 8b and 8c), the Apocalypse panel order recorded by James Torre *c.*1690 was not only the earliest description of this part of the window, but was also likely to be the original order in which Thornton installed the glass. The confusion in rows 8 and 9 had probably arisen, as discussed above, out of a medieval production error. The Chapter has decided to preserve this in the interest of the historical integrity of the window

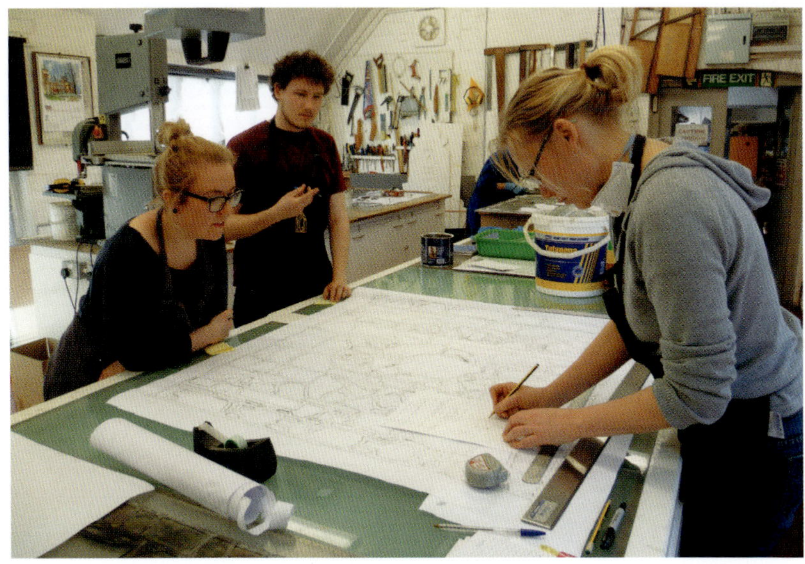

Fig. 4.12
A senior YGT conservator instructs Heritage Lottery Fund trainees in the preparation of documentation.

Fig. 4.13
The original grozed edge of a medieval fragment (from the canopy side-shaft of panel 5b).

and all the panels have been returned to the order in which they were installed in 1405. In the bottom row, so vulnerable to damage, in which legendary and historical figures accompanying the donor, Walter Skirlaw, are depicted, there had been some disruption of the panels by the time Torre recorded them. However, taken together, the evidence of Torre and his fellow antiquary Henry Johnstone (d.1723) who recorded the Minster in 1670, has enabled us to reconstruct the order of the panels, their heraldry and thus the identity of 21 out of the 24 figures represented with a degree of certainty.

Before conservation began, every panel was photographed (interior surface, exterior surface, with transmitted and reflected light) and its condition was mapped carefully. A rubbing was made to record the inherited lead net and the position of glass within it before the panel was dismantled and each piece of glass was placed back on the rubbing. Initial cleaning trials had demonstrated that surviving glass paint and silver stain were generally well adhered throughout the window. Sadly, however, overzealous cleaning in the past has removed any fragile or lifting paint. Nonetheless, all glass cleaning was conducted under binocular microscopes, ensuring complete control of the process. Dry cleaning with soft brushes was followed by gentle swabbing with a 50:50 mix of deionised water and ethanol. Particular care was taken on any heavily corroded pieces, which thankfully were in the minority.

Once all glass pieces within a panel had been cleaned, a forensic examination of their character could be undertaken. Thornton pieces were initially separated from all other glass, allowing the extent of survival to be judged. The identification of all original 'grozed' edges, cut with extraordinary precision using the distinctive grozing iron (Fig. 4.13), enabled the process of recognising the original cut-lines of the cartoon to begin. Whenever possible, the identification of a complete sequence of medieval glass from the top to the bottom and from one side of a panel to the other is especially helpful. A modern cartoon of the architectural canopy design appropriate to the row was drawn up from the accumulated evidence from all relevant panels, as experience has shown that there is a high level of replication in the architectural framing, which provides

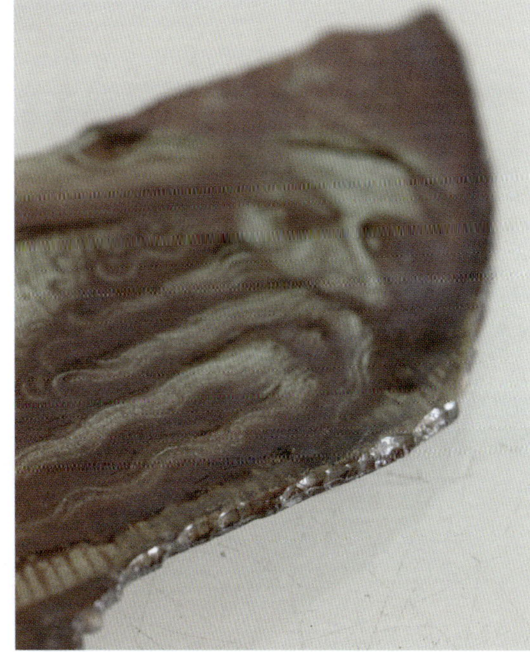

visual coherence across the entire row of related narrative scenes. This cartoon also assisted in the recognition of fragmented architectural pieces. Once the original cut-line had been recovered as much as possible, a consideration of the stopgaps could begin. Medieval pieces that fitted within the Thornton design were retained with very few exceptions, although in some instances the correct repositioning of original pieces of glass displaced an inserted stopgap. EWAG met in the YGT workshops every six to eight weeks throughout the conduct of the project (Fig. 4.14), to discuss proposals for each panel in turn, based on a dossier of historical and antiquarian evidence and one that summarised the physical evidence from each panel. Only if the evidence for lost original glass was extremely strong, and justified to EWAG's satisfaction, were stopgaps replaced with newly painted pieces. A description of the treatment of a selection of panels will be used to exemplify this process.

In the post-war restoration of panel 11h Milner-White had recovered from the very jumbled panel the pieces that made up the head of St John looking through a trapdoor into heaven, fulfilling the words 'I looked, and behold a door was opened in heaven' (Revelation 4:1). He had also, however, removed stopgaps inserted in the 1820s from the figure of God enthroned in majesty and substituted different stopgap pieces, particularly in the robes of God. Writing *c*.1690, Torre had recorded these as being purple, a colour with imperial symbolism. The 1820s restorers had maintained the colour of the robes, although they had replaced the 15th-century glass, perhaps because it was heavily corroded and no longer transparent (as recorded by J. W. Knowles *c*.1890–1920), but the robe was rendered ruby by Milner-White (Figs. 4.15 and 4.16). In 2010 when all the Thornton glass was laid out in its correct position within the correctly realigned pieces of the mandorla, the shape, proportion and size of the missing outer garment of God was revealed quite clearly. The grozed edges of the white garments at neck,

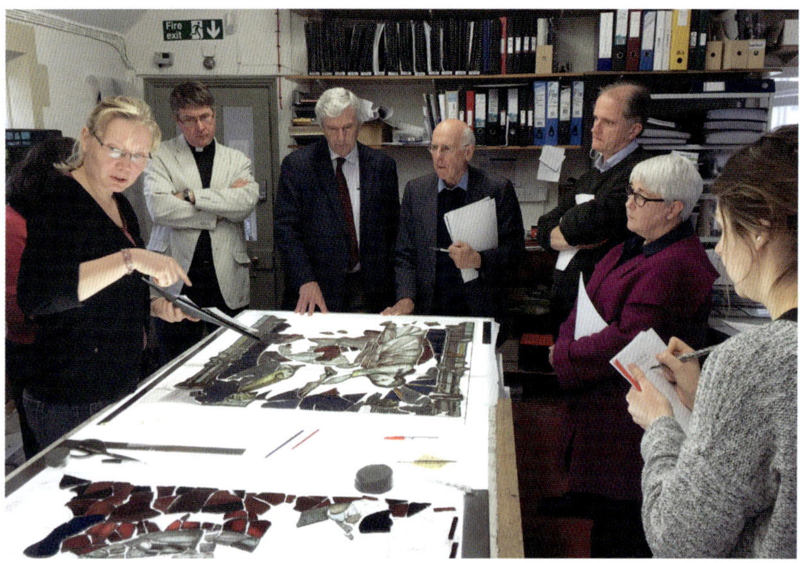

Fig. 4.14
A meeting of the East Window Advisory Group (EWAG) discusses panel 15a.

sleeve, waist and ankles, taken with the evidence of Torre and Knowles, made it clear that God had been clothed in a white vestment worn under a purple robe, which was draped across the knees and fell to the ankles, with white drapery visible at the hem. After discussion and preparation of a cartoon, it was agreed that the purple drapery of God should be restored, based on the treatment of the drapery of a complete enthroned figure elsewhere in the window (e.g. 11e). The importance of the enthroned figure of God in majesty, the centrepiece of a triplet of panels (11g, 11h and 11j) occupying the right-hand block of the row, was felt to justify this restoration.

The conservation and restoration of panel 10g dealt with evidence of rather a different nature. In both the 1884 Camidge drawing and in the black-and-white photograph taken *c*.1939–40, all four of the 'living creatures' can be seen hovering in a cloud around the Lamb, who opens the fourth seal (Revelation 6:5–6). And yet by 1953 the winged ox of St Luke had been lost. Only its outstretched foreleg survived, albeit relocated by Milner-White. The quality of the pre-restoration photograph (Fig. 4.17) enabled a photographic cartoon of the lost ox to be created with confidence and EWAG approved its re-creation for reasons of both iconographic significance and aesthetic impact.

More extensive interventions were approved in the case of panel 5b. Dean Milner-White was convinced that the scene represented Revelation 13:11–13: 'And I saw another beast coming up out of the earth, and he had two horns like a lamb and he spoke as a dragon', etc. In his own words:

> *Comparison with the medieval illustrated apocalypses recorded that the False Prophet or Second beast should have been there [by which he meant in the patched centre of the panel]. We had to reconstruct him, guided by somewhat varied versions of him given in the MSS. ... The traditional lion head came from a patch in the Chapter House windows, his original teeth we found and replaced; the red brown body was built out of Peckitt patches removed from the foreground of the next but one panel. For the remainder – the grey blue sword, tail and wings – we went to the 1862 Clayton & Bell medallions removed from the North Transept.* [Fig. 4.18]

It is the inclusion of the label *Quis similis besti(ae)* ('Who is like the beast') that makes this iconographic error all the more surprising, as it establishes unequivocally that it is actually verse 4 that is illustrated. Indeed, the juxtaposition of panels 5a and 5b together illustrate Revelation 13:1–4:

> *And I saw a beast coming up out of the sea, having seven heads and ten horns, and upon his horns ten diadems, and upon his heads names of blasphemy. And the beast which I saw, was like to a leopard, and his feet were as the feet of a bear, and his mouth as the mouth of a lion. And the dragon gave him his own strength, and great power ... And they adored the dragon which gave power to the beast [the subject*

> *of panel 5s]: and they adored the beast, saying: Who is like to the beast? And who shall be able to fight with him? [panel 5b]*

This reconstruction was recently judged by EWAG to be both iconographically and aesthetically intrusive into Thornton's medieval narrative. Milner-White's inserted beast was removed and the gap left in the centre of the panel was closed up by the correct realignment of the beast's upraised foreleg and with a modern replacement of the corroded flashed-ruby background diaper, which was surely what the 'blank mass of 19c. magenta sheet glass' removed by the Dean had been intended to replicate.

Compared to the Apocalypse panels, some of the Old Testament panels (conserved in the second phase of work, 2016–17) have suffered significant loss and disturbance, although whether this can be attributed to the fire of 1829 is by no means certain. In panel 15j (the expulsion from paradise), for example, the figures of the Angel, Adam and Eve had all suffered damage. The crown of Adam's head and his forehead survived, but not his face, and the long hair on his surviving left shoulder did not match the short hair of the inserted head provided for him in the 1820s. In this instance EWAG approved the re-creation of the lower half of the head, based on the other images of Adam in the window. Once dismantled, the outline of the lost fig leaf with which he covered his genitals, as described in the Bible, was clearly discernible in the grozed edges of the glass, and this too was re-created.

The identity of the subject of at least one, and possibly two, of the Old Testament panels have been reconsidered as a result of the careful scrutiny of the glass and its previous states. Panel 14h, for example, had formerly been identified as the scene in which Joseph and his brothers, including Benjamin, are joyfully reunited (Genesis 45). The leadline of the missing head of the brother leading the group, a shape

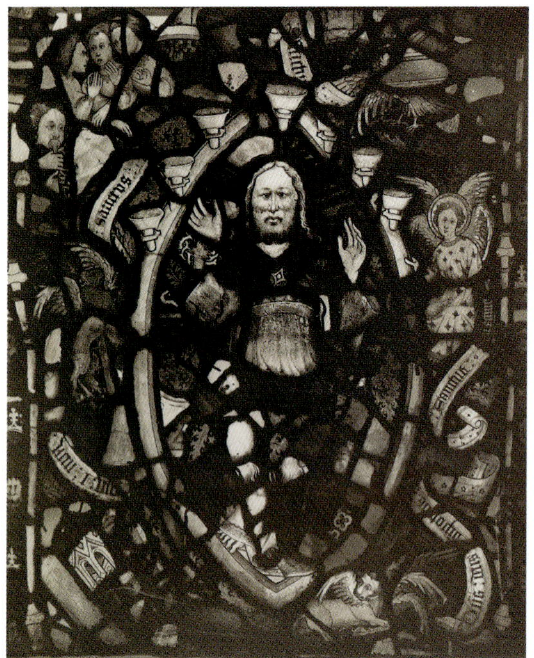

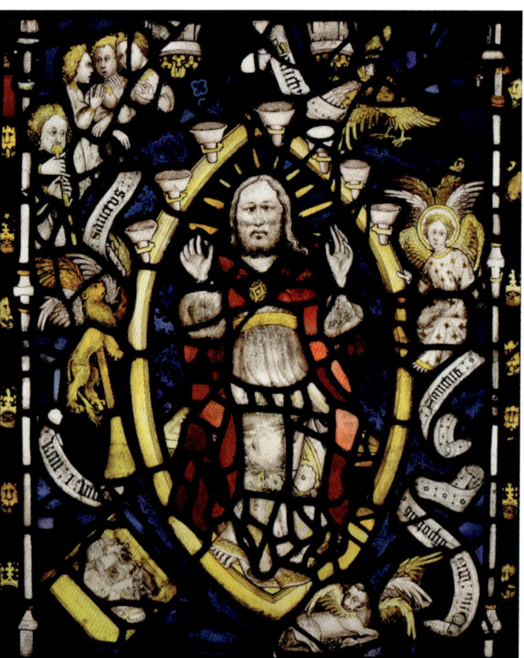

Fig. 4.15
Panel 11h photographed *c*.1939, showing the state of the panel following restoration in the 1820s but prior to the post-war restoration directed by Dean Eric Milner-White.

Fig. 4.16
Panel 11h as configured by the restoration team led by Dean Milner-White.

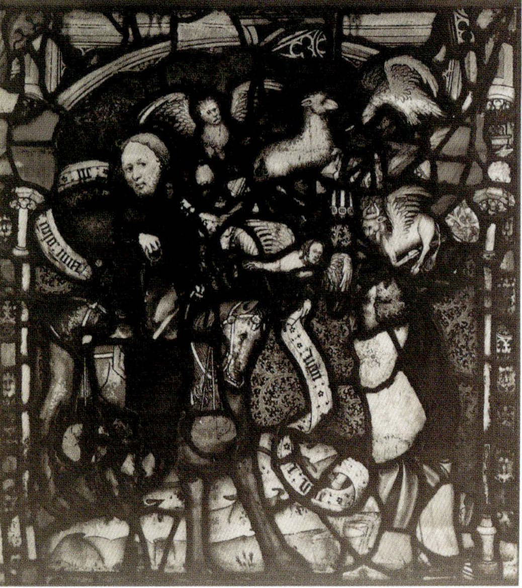

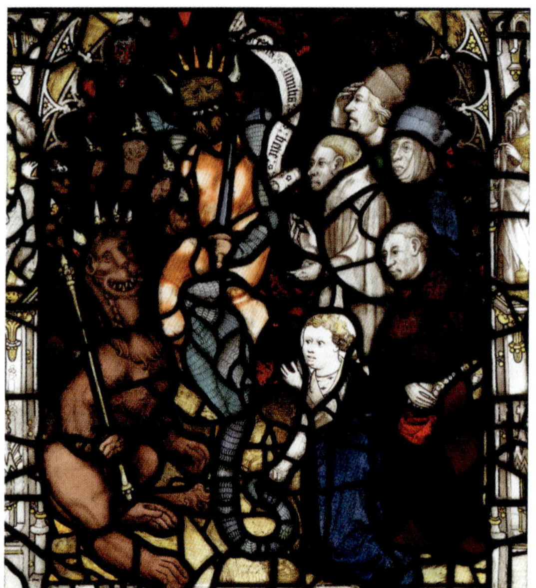

Fig. 4.17
Panel 10g photographed *c*.1939. The winged ox symbol of St Luke remains intact, a photographic detail used to restore the lost detail during the conservation programme of 2011–17.

Fig. 4.18
Panel 5b as incorrectly restored by Dean Milner-White. The central serpentine beast was created out of miscellaneous fragments from the 'glass-bank'.

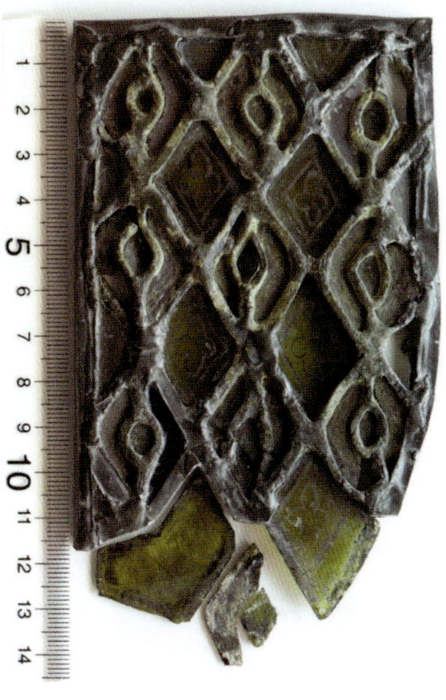

Fig. 4.19
The only surviving medieval lead in the Great East Window – the extraordinarily delicate leading of the shield of St William of York (panel 1j).

suggesting a bearded older head in profile, together with the stern demeanour of Joseph, who still wields his staff of office, suggested an alternative attribution, an earlier point in the narrative (Genesis 42:6–8), when his brothers first meet Joseph and do not know him. This would have a typological significance in the Great East Window, with Joseph understood to represent Christ, unrecognised by the tribes of Israel.

In many respects, it is the reglazing that results in the most noticeable difference in the final appearance of the conserved panels. Wholesale replacement of lead during successive campaigns of past restoration means that there is now very little medieval lead remaining in any Minster windows. Europe-wide research into the manufacture and character of medieval window lead confirms that they were cast in moulds rather than milled, and suggest that they were remarkably narrow, generally between 4mm and 6mm across the leaf. This is borne out by examples of 'painted' lead lines in the Great East Window, where the glass painter has created a fictive lead line that emulates the real thing, thereby confirming the size of the now-lost originals. Finally, the character of the

original leading can now be confirmed by the discovery of a small area of original lead, in panel 1j (Fig. 4.19). The leads that hold in place the tiny glass pieces that make up St William's shield are between only 2mm and 3mm in breadth. After reglazing and soldering on both sides, panels are then waterproofed by hand using a traditional linseed putty pushed up under the leaf of the lead. This gives the panels additional strength, but was probably not a process observed by the medieval glaziers. Finally, any resin bonds and resin infills are touched in with cold paint to ensure that they do not glitter or 'read' as holes once the panel is reinstalled in the window.

For the Record

One of the greatest problems faced in unravelling the story of the window's past has been the lack of any comprehensive record of past restorations. Modern conservation practice places considerable store by the compilation of detailed records of the condition of the object undergoing treatment before, during and after conservation. High-resolution, medium-format digital photography has been used throughout the project to ensure that even the smallest detail can be studied long after the panels have returned to their elevated locations in the Minster. All alterations, adjustments, additions and treatments have been meticulously recorded, initially on annotated rubbings but subsequently in a digital documentation system tailor-made for the Great East Window project. The system was designed in-house, but refined with input from colleagues at Lincoln and Cologne Cathedrals and commercial studios in Germany and Belgium. This allows layers of information to be built up to create an in-depth record of the 2011–17 conservation programme and will ensure that future students and conservators of the window will be able to unravel the nature of the recent treatment of every panel. The photographs will also enable future researchers to have full access to the window without recourse to scaffolding.

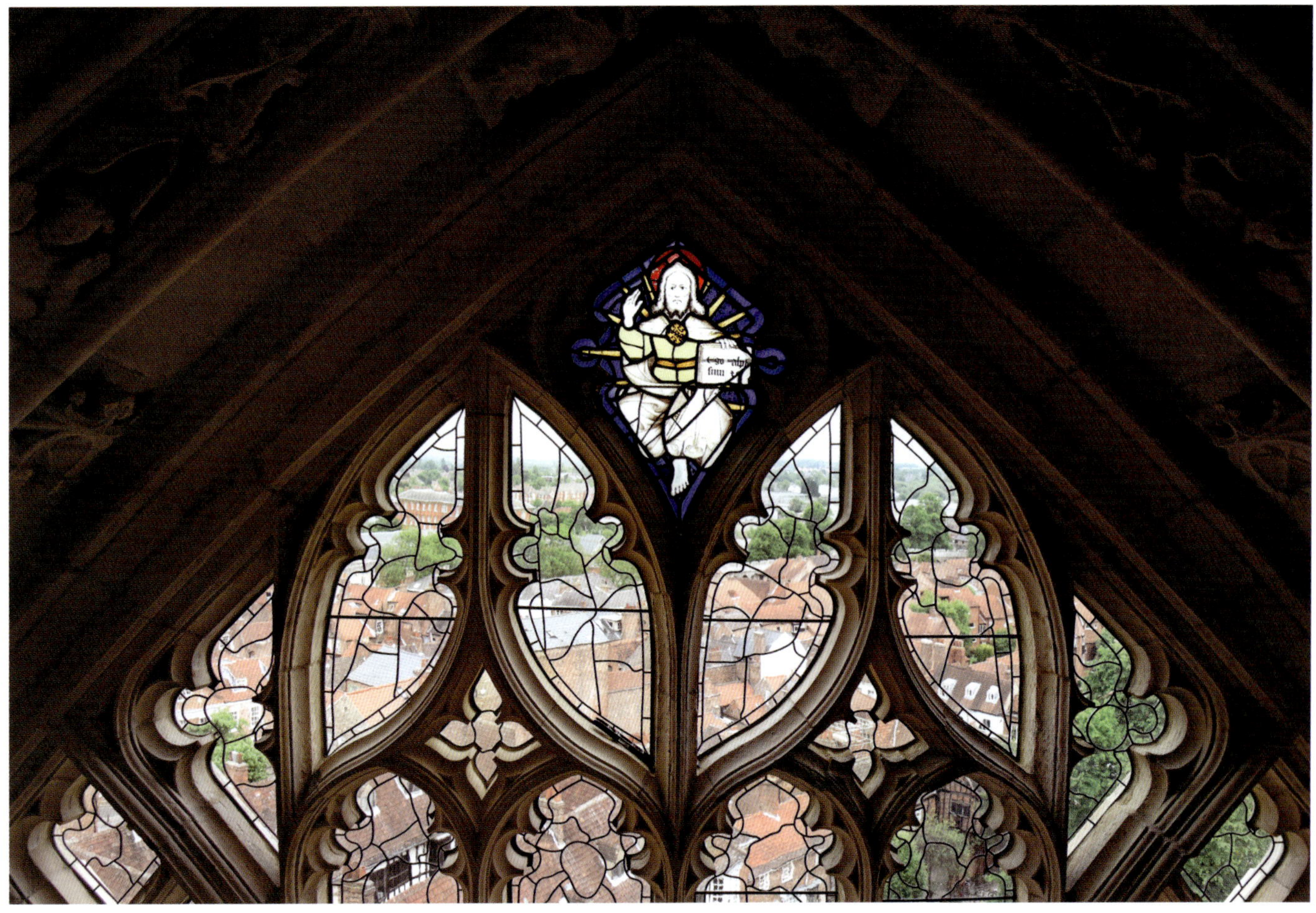

Future-Proofing the Great West Window

Ventilated environmental protective glazing as a means of halting glass deterioration now has a proven track record of over 75 years. The principle is simple, although every project requires a custom-designed solution. New panels of unpainted modern glass, in this case in a leading pattern based on a simplified version of the historic lead net, are set on t-bars in the window opening and are mortared into the outer glazing groove, taking the place of the historic glass as the weather shield to the outside of the building. This immediately removes the medieval glass from contact with external moisture and the potentially damaging effects of wind pressure on corroded glass. The historic glass is placed inside a custom-made bronze frame with integral saddle-bars, and is brought inside the window opening, also supported on a t-bar set into the stonework. Pins are inserted into holes drilled at intervals into the t-bar, ensuring that the framed panels sit securely. Lead strips soldered on the sides of the frames can be tamped against the stone at the panel edges to ensure that there is no glimmer of light at the sides. Gaps at the top and bottom of each light allow air from inside the building to be drawn into the interspace between historic glass and outer glazing, which in the Great East Window is a depth of approximately 40mm. Warm air rises, to be replaced by cooler air, keeping the air moving in and out of the interspace. This ventilated double-glazing

Fig. 4.20
June 2015: The window opening filled with new outer glazing and with God the Father (DD1) reinstalled at the apex of the window. This state-of-the-art ventilated environmental protective glazing was the first in the UK to use this kind of UV-resistant glass.

protects the historic glass from its greatest environmental enemy, surface moisture in the form of condensation. If the interior building temperature drops to below dew point (when moisture-laden air cools to the point at which it can no longer carry water) condensation will form, no longer on the medieval glass but on the outer protective glazing. Condensation trays at the sill allow moisture to be conducted out of the building, thereby also protecting the stonework. Environmental monitoring of the protected Great East Window undertaken in 2016–17 has shown that this system is working very well and that on the few days when the internal air has reached dew point, condensation has always formed on the protective outer glazing and never on the historic stained glass.

Until very recently the only aspect of the conservation treatment against which this form of environmental glazing has afforded no protection has been the effects of ultraviolet radiation on light-sensitive materials, and in particular on epoxy resins, which can discolour and embrittle after long periods of exposure. There have been a number of approaches to the reduction of UV exposure. In many museums with mixed media displays, for example, UV-resistant films are applied to the window glass. This is not an option suitable for in situ stained-glass conservation, as the films require regular replacement. An alternative has been the use of UV-protective glasses, traditionally a lamination of two sheets of glass with a UV-resistant film sandwiched inside. These glasses are consequently thick (and relatively heavy), difficult to cut (as both glass layers and the interior film require cutting separately) and the inner film is susceptible to the ingress of moisture or oil from glazing cement. They are not suitable, therefore, for incorporation in the style of protective glazing favoured at York Minster, in which the lead lines of the historic glass are followed in a simplified form.

In 2013 the world-famous Lamberts glasshouse in Waldsassen in Germany, manufacturers of most of the mouth-blown pot-metal glasses being used for the restoration of the Great East Window, successfully launched a new kind of glass. The UV resistance is blown as a thin 'flash' onto the mouth-blown cylinder and its therefore integral to the body of the glass. It is able to eliminate the invisible but damaging UV spectrum. Like the other cylinder glasses made at Lamberts, the glass has all the movement and character of a mouth-blown material and can be cut and leaded in the same way. In common with other mouth-blown traditional glasses, it is not indestructible, but it will perform like any other glass in a protective glazing system, keeping the medieval glass dry and protected from wind pressure, while providing additional long-term protection from UV radiation for light-sensitive conservation materials (Fig. 4.20). A window that set new standards of artistic quality and iconographic ambition is now protected by one of the world's most sophisticated stained-glass protection systems.

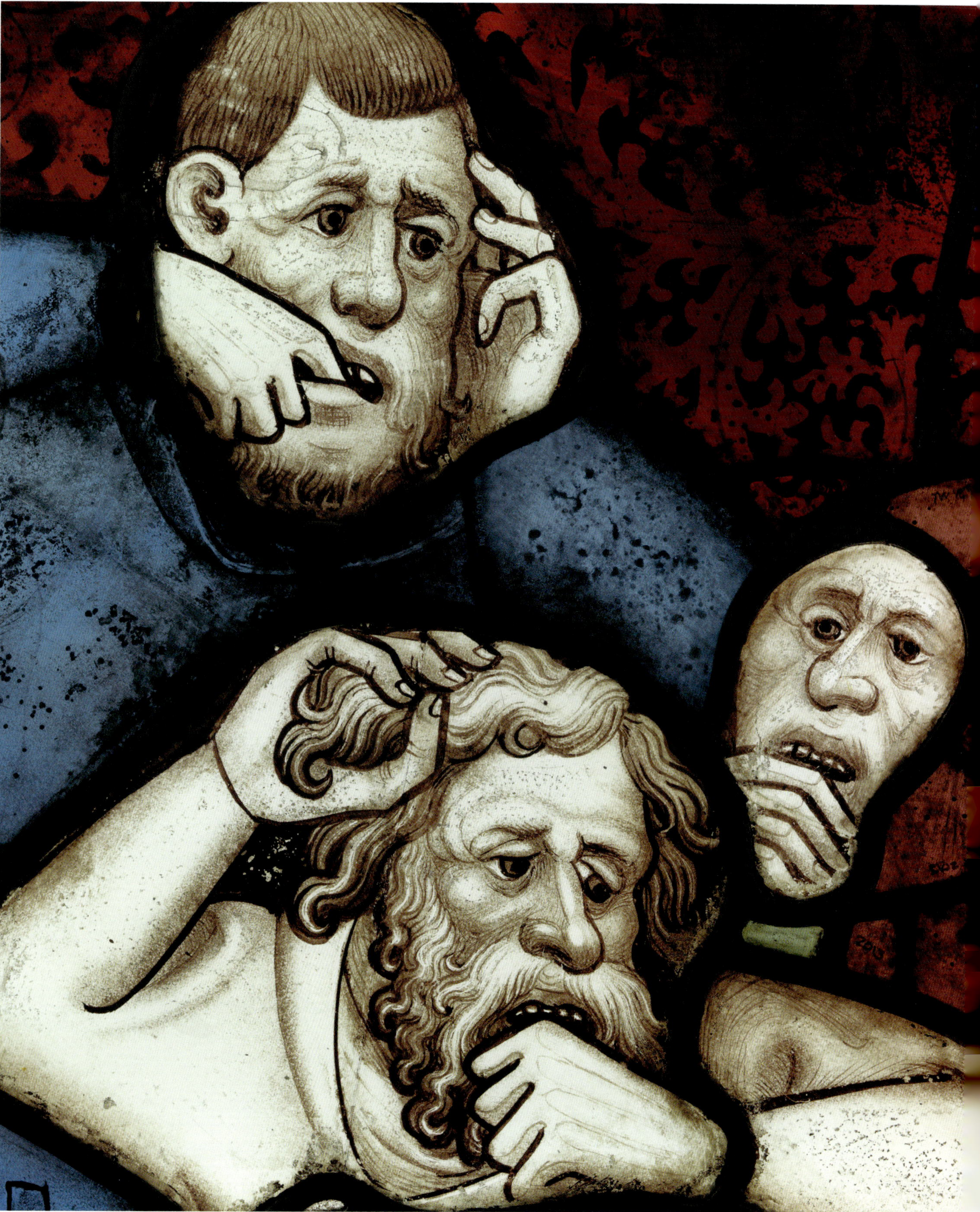

Chapter 5

A Medieval Masterpiece?
The Great East Window in Context

What may justly be called the wonder of the World
Francis Drake, 1736

It is solemn, monumental and majestic
Jill Rickers, 1996

The 'Sistine Chapel of Stained Glass'?

When the structural emergency at the east end of York Minster first became apparent in 2005, the conservation of the Great East Window was not the first priority. However, the removal of a small number of panels for closer examination and evaluation quickly excited everyone involved in the project, not simply because of the sheer artistry of the work, but also because of the potential to rediscover and reinterpret this long-overlooked medieval masterpiece. The chance to put John Thornton, whose name was barely known outside York, 'on the map' became one of the explicit objectives of the York Minster Revealed project, for which Heritage Lottery Fund (HLF) support was secured in 2011. In seeking to engage public interest, and convey a sense of the scale and importance of the window, Dean Keith Jones compared it to the Sistine Chapel, famous for Michelangelo's majestic painted ceiling of 1508–12, a world-famous artwork that is now imperilled by the impact on its environment of its huge international audience. Throughout the project the Great East Window was often referred to as York's 'Sistine Chapel of Stained Glass'. While this began as a handy tool for promoting public interest in a project of unprecedented scale, we can now reconsider the validity of Thornton's claim to authorship of a masterpiece in the light of the window's rediscovery through conservation and research. As panels re-emerged lighter, brighter and less heavily leaded, Thornton's true genius as designer, storyteller and leader of a workshop of astonishing artistic talent, was confirmed afresh.

Fig. 5.1
'And they gnawed their tongues for pain' (Revelation 16:10). A group of expressive, grimacing heads from the scene of the pouring of the fifth vial (panel 4g).

An Invisible Masterpiece: The Great East Window in Print

While Thornton's genius was acknowledged in York from the late 18th century onwards, he has been less well served in the literature about English medieval art more generally, and it is hard to escape the conclusion that the relative inaccessibility of his great work is part of the explanation. In common with most English stained glass, York Minster's Great East Window has been something of a well-kept secret, known and appreciated by only a relatively small circle of specialists in the medium. York Minster's windows were listed in locally authored guides to the city's glass but, with the exception of Gent's eccentric 1762 guide (see Fig. 1.8), only sparsely illustrated, and the great height of the Great East Window, darkened by the exterior quarry glazing on which Hugh Arnold commented in 1913, was a significant barrier to visual access and scholarly interest. Arts and Crafts designer and writer Lewis Foreman Day (1845–1910), in a sweeping survey volume of 1897, illustrated with his own evocative and accurate sketches that took his readers all over Europe in search of stained-glass masterpieces, devoted a whole chapter to 'story windows' but made no mention of the Great East Window. In his book of English stained-glass tours first published in 1909, retired American diplomat Charles Hitchcock-Sherill (1867–1936) urged his readers to visit the Minster, 'one of the most notable points of interest in the world for the lover of stained glass' in which the Great East Window was 'the crowning glory'. A black-and-white plate of the choir looking towards the window gave a sense of the scale of the window but no impression of its artistry. Philip Nelson's 1913 *Ancient Stained and Painted Glass* was similarly enthusiastic, but illustrated the window only with a monochrome version of Francis Bedford's highly fanciful lithograph of 1850. A far more measured and scholarly approach to the discussion of stained glass as an artistic medium was adopted by the art historian and critic Sir Herbert Read (1893–1968). His 1926 monograph

English Stained Glass also generally made better use of detailed photography, but in his discussion of York Minster he was reliant on images made available to him by J. A. Knowles, and singled out the St William Window at the expense of the Great East Window. This was in significant contrast to the treatment of the stained glass of Great Malvern Priory and Canterbury Cathedral, which were the subjects of well-researched and generously illustrated monographs by Gordon Rushforth (1936) and Bernard Rackham (1949) respectively. It is hard to escape the conclusion that the absence of good photography was responsible for consigning Thornton's masterpiece to relative obscurity. Rushforth was very well served by Gloucester-based professional photographer Sydney Pitcher (1884–1950), himself a stained-glass enthusiast and author, while Rackham took advantage of wartime storage of the Canterbury glass to commission new photographs from the Victoria and Albert Museum, where he was curator of ceramics and glass. Despite the post-war conservation of the Great East Window under Dean Milner-White, surprisingly few photographs of the window made their way into print, and the Dean included only a small number in his own *Antiquaries Journal* article of 1950. In her survey of English medieval painting, first published in 1954 as part of the landmark Pelican History of Art series, Margaret Rickerts illustrated a single detail from the largest medieval window in England, of the upper half of King David (L1) from the tracery, together with one panel from the St William Window, in her discussion of the international style. Thanks to Sydney Pitcher, whose collections had been acquired by the National Monuments Record, Great Malvern, the Beauchamp Chapel in Warwick and All Souls College in Oxford were all rather better represented in her second edition (1965). In the same period the very first doctoral thesis devoted to stained glass, Peter Newton's 1961 Courtauld Institute study, 'Schools of Glass Painting in the Midlands 1275–1430', was undertaken, a work that continues to be cited but was never published and has only recently become available as an online resource. Newton placed Thornton in a wider English and Midlands context, a much-needed counterbalance to J. A. Knowles's arguments for an unbelievably prolific 15th-century 'York School' of glass painting.

The huge programme of engineering to underpin the Minster that took place between 1966 and 1973 meant that much of the interior was scaffolded, and the Royal Commission on Historical Monuments seized the opportunity to conduct a new programme of investigation and photography. The new photographs, lodged in a publicly accessible national archive, the National Monuments Record, were a revelation, although very few had been taken in colour. In 1977, in a groundbreaking essay by David O'Connor and Jeremy Haselock, the stained glass of York Minster was discussed in a national and international art-historical context for the first time, and Thornton's Great East Window was fully acknowledged as a masterpiece of medieval design, with appropriate illustrations. In 1995 the Corpus Vitrearum catalogue by Tom French with a contribution on iconography by David O'Connor presented images of almost all of the panels for the first time, although the record was predominantly still in black and white. Within the constraints of a scholarly series with a very small print run and a high price, only 18 full panels and 12 details were reproduced in colour. Thornton's reputation was growing, however, and the book has the distinction of being the only British Corpus Vitrearum volume to warrant a second edition, in a more affordable paperback format!

The Thornton Apocalypse in Context

It has always been Thornton's treatment of the Apocalypse that has attracted the greatest attention, from visitors and scholars alike. He was certainly not alone in working on a monumental scale and the window has been referenced in the wider art-historical literature most commonly in the context of the discussion of late medieval monumental Apocalypses. The Great East Window is one of four late medieval English works of art to explore the book of Revelation on a monumental scale, a number increased only recently by the discovery in 2000 of fragments of a lost scheme at the demolished cathedral priory of St Mary at Coventry. This means that almost half of the known surviving monumental examples originated in England, and to date the Great East Window is the only surviving example in stained glass.

Three of the four schemes – at Norwich Cathedral priory, at Westminster Abbey and at Coventry – were made for Benedictine monastic communities and were displayed in places accessible predominantly, if not exclusively, to the monks (in the cloister at Norwich, and in the chapter houses at Westminster and Coventry). Indeed, in the case of Westminster, it has been suggested that the decoration of the walls at the behest of John of Northampton (a monk at Westminster between 1372 and 1404), was undertaken to mark the reclamation of the chapter house by the monastic community after its use by Parliament. Its great size and prominent location meant that by comparison the Great East Window was always more accessible, both visually and intellectually, although its principal medieval audience would always have been an educated clerical elite worshipping in the Minster's choir.

Compared to these other English examples, the Great East Window is certainly not the largest Apocalypse cycle, precisely because, as we have seen, the Apocalypse is but one component in a more ambitious story. The Norwich scheme covers 100 bosses in the south and west cloister walks. The cloister was reconstructed over a long period between 1297 and the 1440s. In 1346 the masons asked the priory to buy for them 'A History of the Apocalypse', revealing that the scheme was conceived some time before the no-doubt apocalyptic experiences wrought by the arrival of the plague known as the Black Death, and was completed only some years after its passing into memory. The Norwich bosses are one of the largest and most ambitious monumental explorations of the Apocalypse in European art, although this has perhaps been overlooked because they can be difficult to read; the designs give the impression of having been flattened from their two-dimensional models and wrapped around the broadly domed format of the boss. In this regard, they lack the ingenuity of the roughly contemporary bosses running down the central rib of York Minster's nave vault, which share with Thornton's later stained-glass window a skilfulness in designing for a specific medium and a specific context.

The Westminster Abbey chapter house scheme (Fig. 5.2) was also larger than the York cycle, probably originally comprising 96 scenes. They are close in date and content to a late 14th-century Apocalypse manuscript now in Cambridge (Trinity College MS B.10.2; Fig. 5.3). This book was probably made at and for Westminster Abbey, as it also contains scenes from the life of St Edward the Confessor and is linked by its style to another book made for the abbey, the famous Litlyngton Missal, made for Abbot Nicholas Litlyngton (1362–86; Westminster Abbey MS 37). The painters responsible for the mural scheme were probably German or Flemish, although Paul Binski has accused the scheme of being 'qualitatively routine'. Comparison of the wall paintings with the manuscript shows that the painters certainly did not stray very far from their model.

The size of the Coventry cycle cannot be known. However, reconstructions of the building (which resembled the near-contemporary Lady Chapel at Lichfield Cathedral) from the remaining archaeological evidence suggests that there could have been as many as 104 painted scenes, although the Apocalypse might have been accompanied, as at Westminster, by a depiction of the Last Judgement. The Coventry fragment has also been compared to the St Stephen's Chapel paintings at Westminster.

What all the schemes, including Thornton's, have in common, is their interaction with an earlier English Apocalypse tradition dating back to the mid-13th century, when English artists created large numbers of illuminated Apocalypses for elite patrons. The large number of mid-13th-century examples may well be accounted for by the currency of the writings of theologian Joachim of Fiore (d.1201), who foretold the end of the world in 1260, but illuminated Apocalypses continued to appeal to readers through the vitality of their storytelling. They did not require apocalyptic times to be a subject of interest, and in the case of the Westminster paintings, it has been suggested that it was the prominence of the role played by his name saint, St John, that appealed to the donor, John of Northampton, who also gave images of St John the Baptist. In the layout, with two rows of narrative, one above the another, with strips of explanatory text beneath, the Westminster painters were creating a supersized picture book, presented conveniently at eye level in a building frequented daily. It was also a layout employed at Westminster on the walls of the so-called painted chamber in the nearby royal palace, first decorated by Henry III in the 1260s and 1270s and repaired or completed by Edward I in 1307–8, and also in St Stephen's Chapel, a scheme completed by 1363. The Old Testament narratives in the painted chamber were accompanied by explanatory inscriptions. In the sumptuously decorated St Stephen's Chapel, designed to rival in splendour the Sainte-Chapelle in Paris, the walls below the side windows were painted with two tiers of narrative, with Latin texts beneath each scene. The decoration of the painted chamber is known only from the antiquarian record, but fragments of the lives of Job and Tobit are preserved in the British Museum. It is unlikely that John of Northampton and the monks of Westminster Abbey had access to elite royal space, but we can see that this style of narrative presentation was current among wall painters.

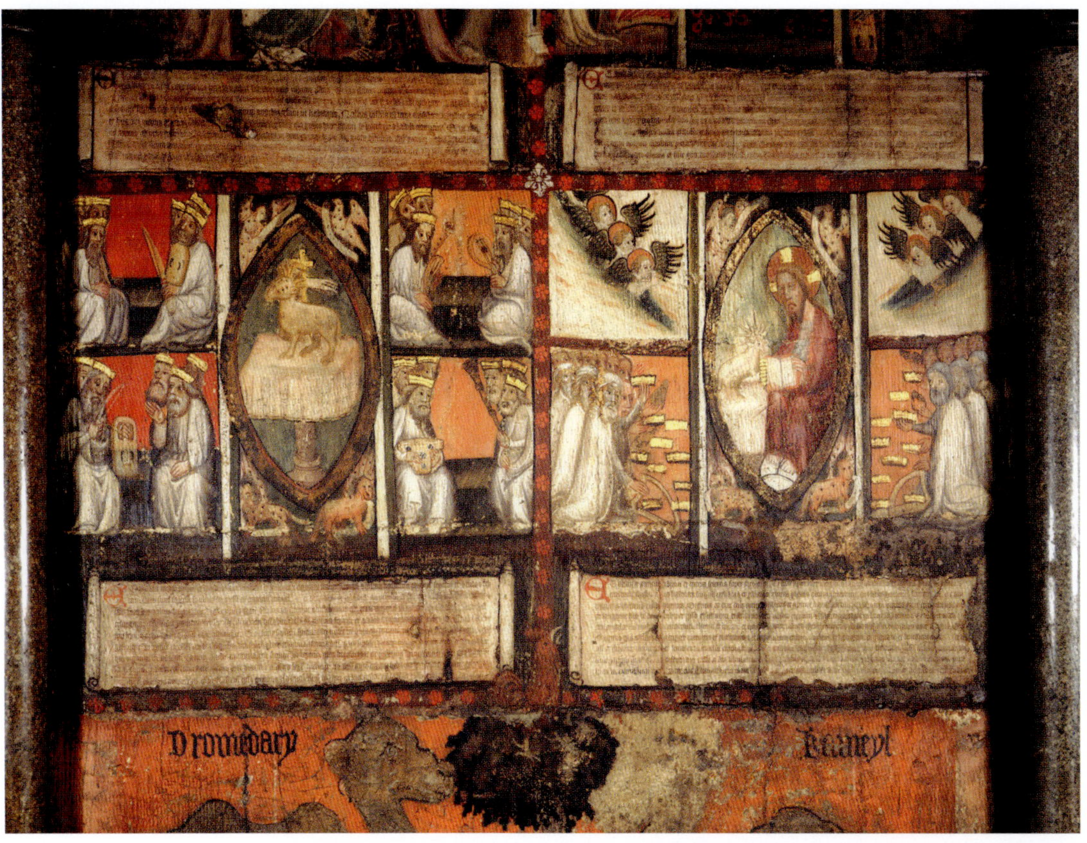

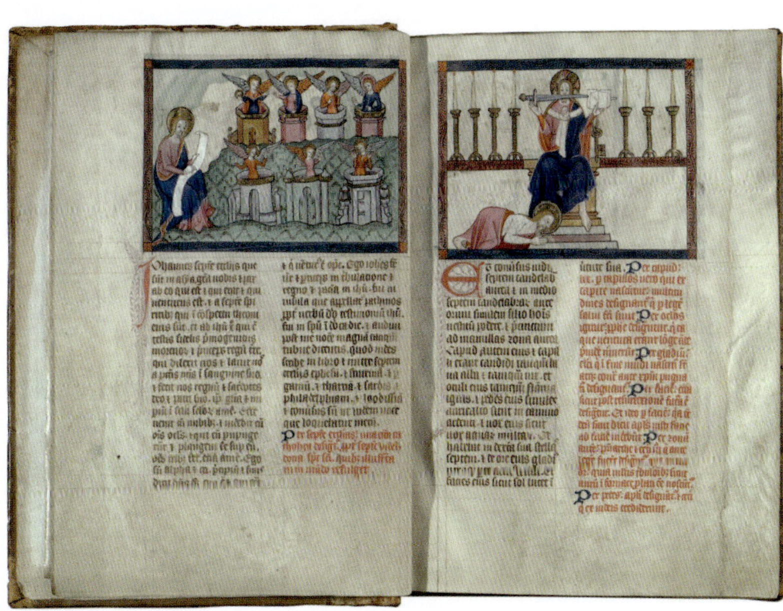

Fig. 5.2
The Westminster Abbey chapter house wall paintings, made at the behest of John of Northampton (monk at the abbey 1372–1404), originally comprising 96 Apocalypse scenes (the animals were added later).

Fig. 5.3
The probable source for the Westminster wall paintings, an illuminated Apocalypse manuscript made at Westminster Abbey and associated with illuminations of the life of St Edward the Confessor (Cambridge, Trinity MS B.10.2, f. 3v).

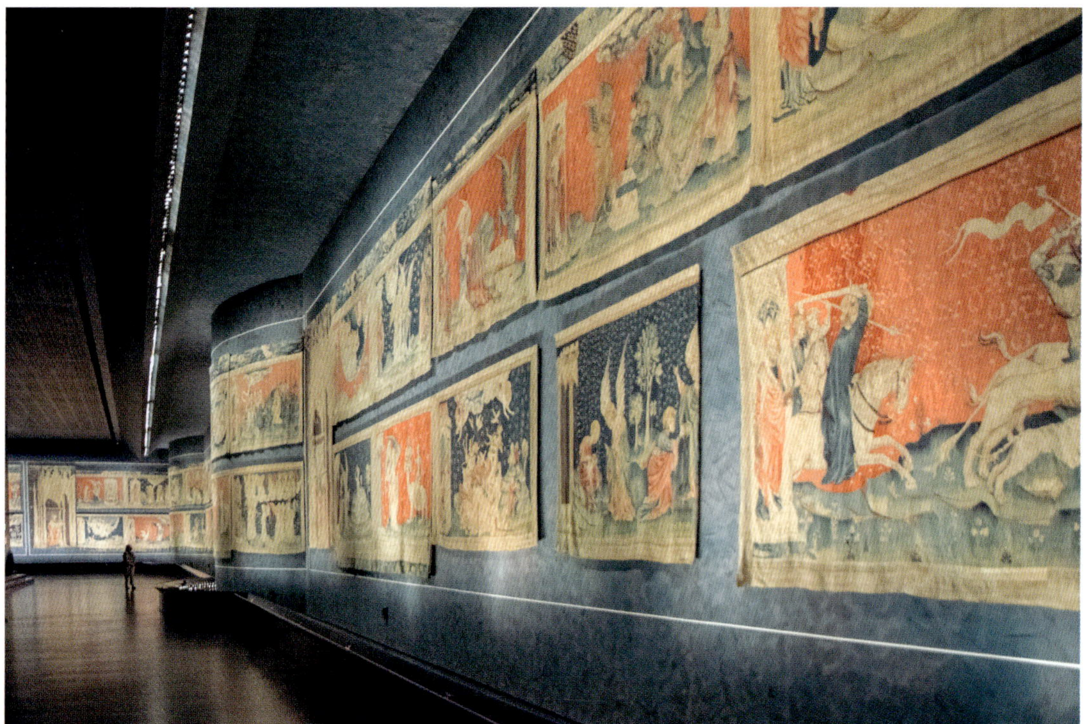

Fig. 5.4
The Angers Apocalypse tapestry, originally 104m long and 4.5m high and covering 850m^2. The restored tapestry can now be viewed in an environmentally controlled gallery in the castle of Angers.

The Angers Apocalypse (Fig. 5.4)

The influence of the English 13th-century Apocalypse tradition was not confined to English art, however. The famous Angers Apocalypse tapestries, made *c*.1373–80 for the palace chapel in Angers of Louis I, duke of Anjou (d.1384), brother of King Charles V of France, have been compared to the scenes in a mid-13th-century English manuscript (the Burckhardt-Wildt Apocalypse), although the king had also lent his brother a French manuscript of the same subject. The Angers Apocalypse, made by the royal tapestry workshop of Nicolas Bataille (d.1405), to cartoons by Charles V's painter Jean Bondol (d.1381), was close in size to the York Minster Apocalypse, comprising 84 scenes. Like John Thornton, in designing the Angers tapestries Jean Bondol freed himself from the text-reliant layout found in the manuscripts and in the wall paintings, depicting the visionary narrative in a vigorous and naturalistic manner typical of what has come to be known as 'International Gothic' style. Like Thornton's Great East Window, the tapestry does not attempt to 'caption' scenes with blocks of text but drives the narrative by movement, gesture and expression, and by the sheer force of its scale – originally 140m long, and 4.5m high.

The public profile of the Angers tapestries makes for an interesting comparison with the Minster's east window. Louis's successors gave them to Angers Cathedral and they continued to be displayed there until the 18th century. Thereafter, they disappeared from public view. They were cut up during the French Revolution and used for a variety of ignominious purposes, including at one time being used to protect orange trees from frost! Their reputation (and their physical fabric) was rehabilitated from the middle of the 19th century onwards, and since the 1950s they have been displayed in a special gallery in the castle of Angers, where they may now be viewed in a fully conserved state in a state-of-the-art environment, celebrated

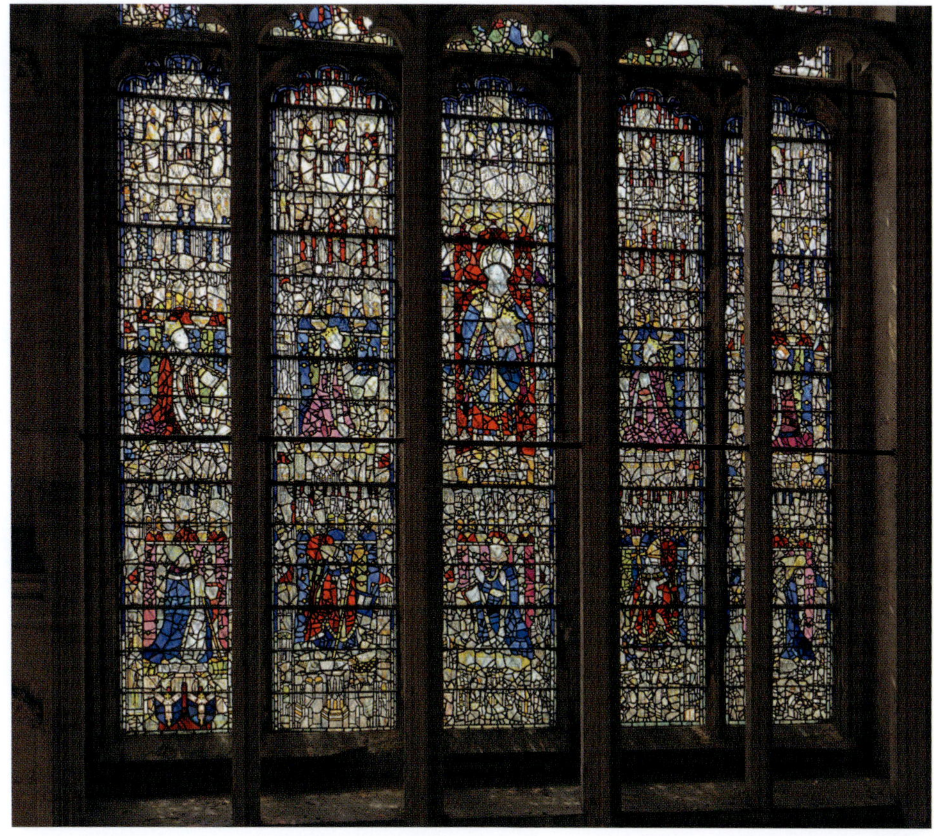

as a unique medieval treasure (Fig. 5.4). While the tapestries have been removed from the cultural and architectural context for which they were conceived and made, they have been elevated from decorative art to fine art by their presentation on the walls of a gallery space, making few physical demands on the viewer.

A Bigger Picture

Until recently, the focus on the Great East Window as part of a family of medieval Apocalypses has perhaps detracted from an appreciation of the window as far more than a version of a manuscript in glass. The work of O'Connor, Morgan and especially Norton has revealed the true scale of the window's ambition, as a key to unlocking one of Europe's largest and most carefully planned late medieval glazing schemes, filling over 20 windows, three of them (the Great East Window, the St William Window and the St Cuthbert window) of exceptional size (Fig. 5.5). It has also meant that the significance of the window as harbinger of a revival in the medium of stained glass as a vehicle for narrative unprecedented since the 13th century has been overlooked. Not since the glazing of the Trinity Chapel of Canterbury Cathedral in the first quarter of the 13th century and the glazing of York's chapter house in the years around 1285 had anything like 'the great windows of the choir' been attempted in England.

The development of the Gothic window with subdivided bar tracery had posed new challenges in stained-glass design. The 'band window' format that emerged in France in the years around 1260 and reached England in the last quarter of the 13th century offered a formula that balanced the need for light with the opportunity to use stained glass as a storytelling medium. It was employed very successfully in the chapter house of the Minster and is the format that dominates the nave aisle glazing. Gradually, however, the single figure under a canopy came to dominate at the expense of narrative – majestically exemplified by the West Window of the Minster itself, commissioned in 1339, and exploited to the full with an ethereal silvery aesthetic in the east window of Gloucester Cathedral, glazed *c*.1350. It was probably this kind of glazing that filled the windows of St Stephen's Chapel in Westminster, so that 'the community of saints' occupied the windows, while the biblical narrative covered the painted walls below. Indeed, the lower parts of the windows were filled in in order to create more space for the wall paintings.

In the choir of York Minster, and in the hands of John Thornton, we see stained glass seize the narrative initiative once more, first with the Great East Window, and then with the St William Window. The figure and canopy format is, of course, maintained in the choir clerestory and in the aisle windows, although here too, small-scale narratives fill 'predella' panels under the standing figures. Thornton's windows must surely have been 'must see' works of art for patrons and artists alike, showing what stained glass was capable of, and setting new standards in stained-glass design in York and much further afield. In the city churches, narrative windows were commissioned at All Saints, North Street ('The Pricke of Conscience', the Corporal Works of Mercy (Fig. 5.6), the Nine Orders of Angels) and St Martin le Grand (the life of St Martin of Tours). At Great Malvern Priory in Worcestershire, a new east window devoted to the Passion of Christ bears remarkable similarities to the St William Window of York Minster and may have been painted by some of the same glass painters (Fig. 5.7). Whether we can go as far as to say that either window is actually by the hand of John Thornton himself is debatable, but without the example set by Thornton and his workshop, the

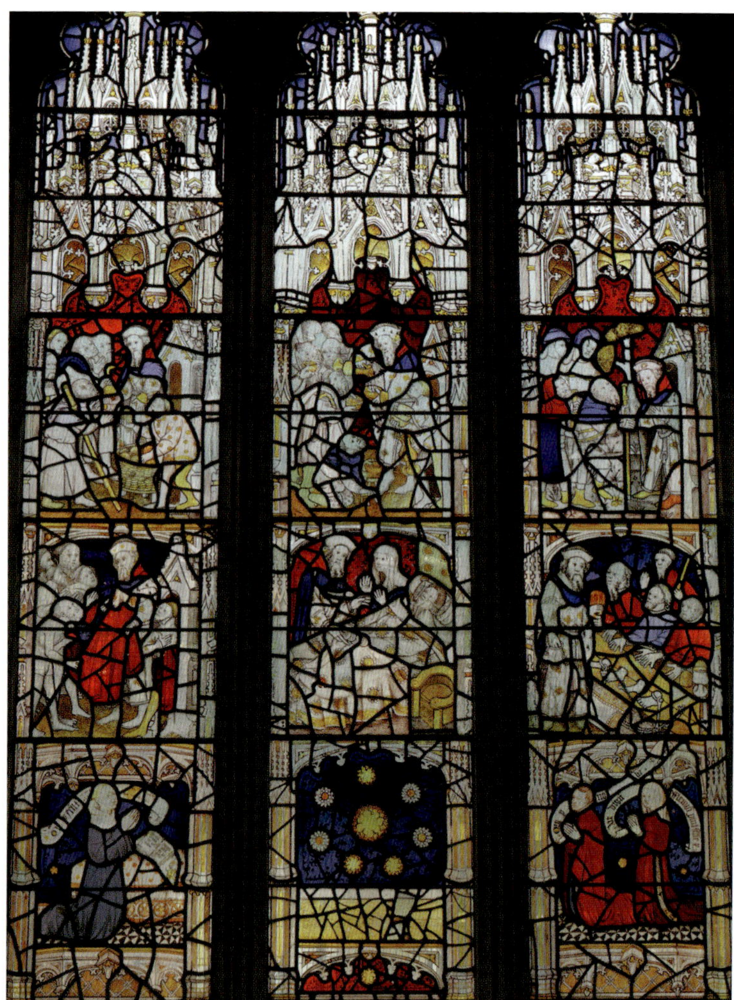

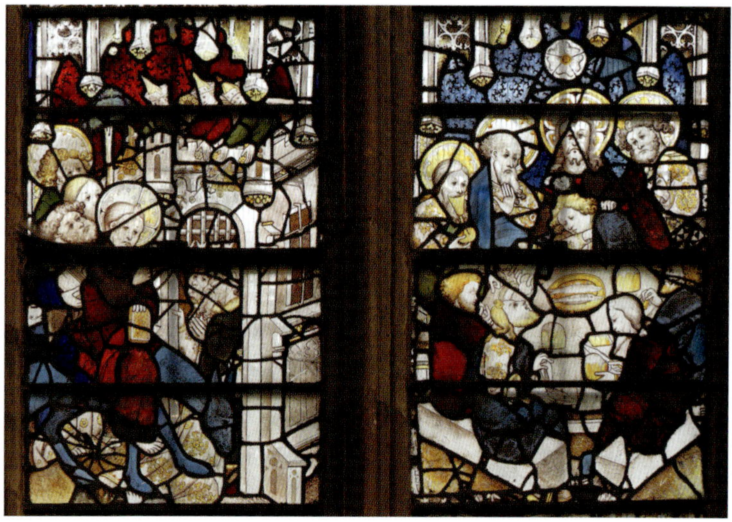

east window of Great Malvern is inconceivable. In the second half of the 15th century, the narrative in stained glass was resurgent. Some of these schemes were made for the chantry foundations of great lords, like the collegiate church of Holy Trinity Tatteshall, glazed with the legend of the Holy Cross, St James, the Creed, the Magnificat and the Seven Sacraments in memory of Ralph, Lord Cromwell (d.1456). In cities like Norwich, the mercantile urban elites were the patrons, exemplified by the huge parish church of St Peter, Mancroft, with glass narratives of St Peter, the Virgin Mary, the Passion, St John the Evangelist and St Margaret. In rural Shropshire, the church of St Laurence at Ludlow was provided with an east window of cathedral-like proportions (Fig. 5.8) celebrating the life of its patron saint. In more humble parish settings, at Morley in Derbyshire and at Greystoke in Cumbria, for example, the lives of St Robert of Knaresborough and St Andrew were narrated in glass.

'A Work of Outstanding Artistry or Skill'

This is how the *Oxford English Dictionary* defines a 'masterpiece', and by this definition, the Great East Window of York Minster surely makes the grade. However, it is its power to engage and delight which gives it its abiding appeal to audiences over 600 years after it was first installed. The feeling that in the faces of John Thornton's characters we are glimpsing the faces of his family, his friends, his neighbours and even his patrons in the medieval city is inescapable. The late medieval walled city is almost a character in itself; it is probably no accident that the apocalyptic collapse of urban structures described in the book of Revelation is restrained and circumspect in Thornton's window (7b, 7c, 5g, 4j, 3b), with a few tumbled stones. The natural world is also wonderfully conveyed: the dogs that accompany Noah (T2 and 14b), the animals, birds and fish that worship God (15e, 15g, 10d), the lamb who opens the seals (10c, 10e, 10f, 10g, 10h, 10j, 9a), and above all the

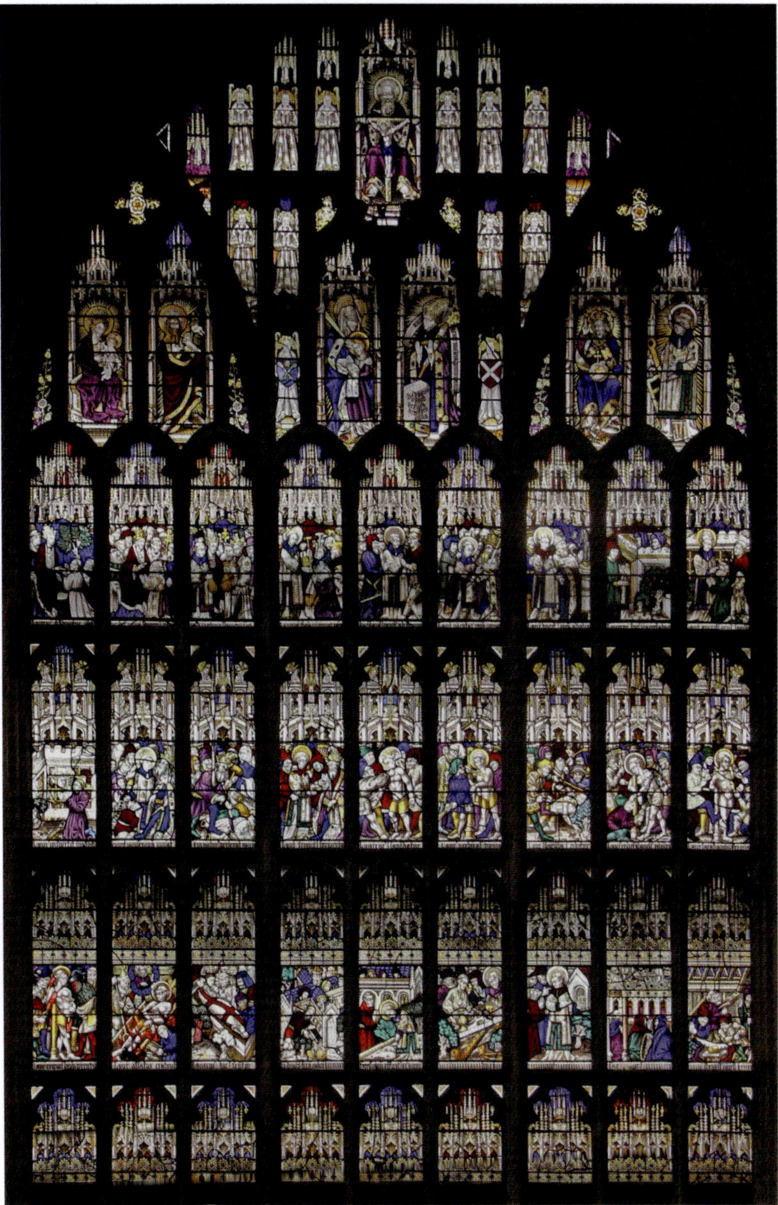

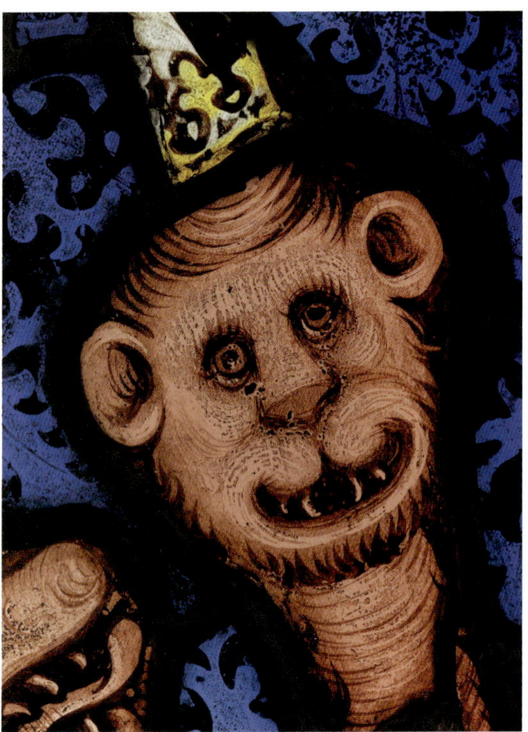

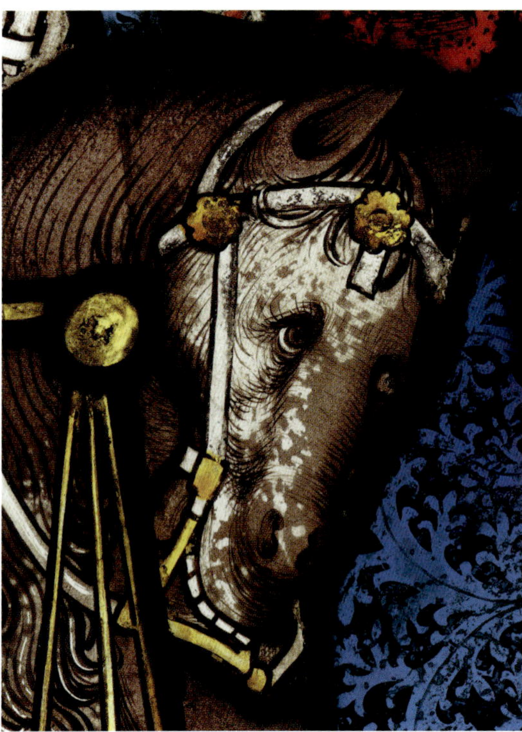

Fig. 5.9
One of the seven heads of the Beast who makes war with the saints in Revelation 13:7 (detail of panel 5c). Far from being a terrifying creature!

Fig. 5.10
One of many characterful horses found in the Great East Window – this dark one is ridden by the third of the Apocalyptic horsemen (panel 10g).

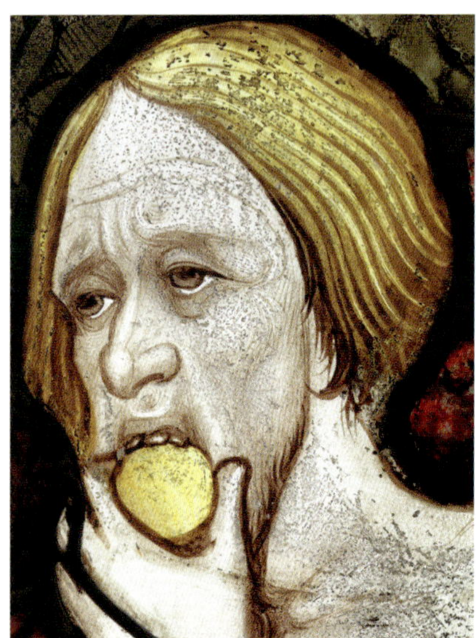

Fig. 5.11
The doleful face of Adam as he succumbs to sin and bites the fruit from the Tree of Knowledge (panel 15h).

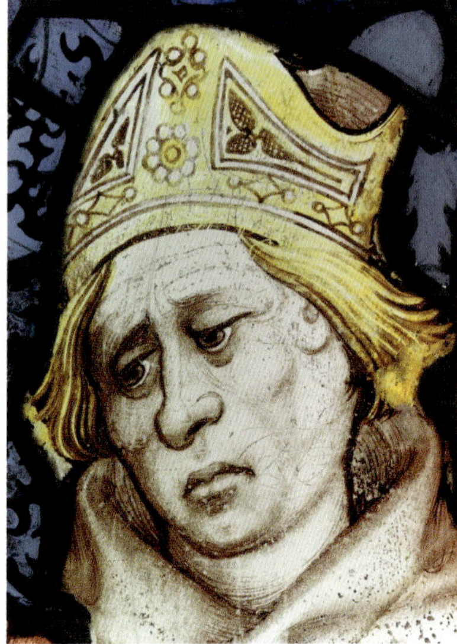

Fig. 5.12
Dignified in the face of danger – one of the saints menaced by the powerful Beast in Revelation 13:7 (panel 5c).

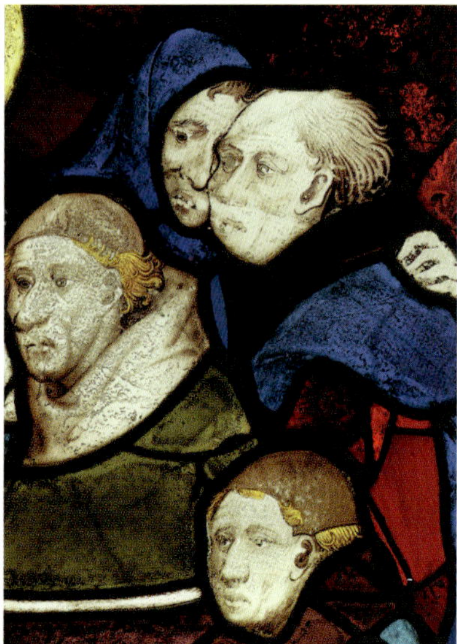

Fig. 5.13
Whispering in the background – a detail of the audience to St John's preaching in panel 11c.

horses in which the artists took such delight (15f, 13j, 10e, 10f, 10g (Fig. 5.10), 5j, 4h, 3e, 3g), are all rendered with an affectionate attention to detail that makes them memorable and believable. Even the beasts and dragons – creatures that in the hands of others are imbued with a terrifying, nightmarish quality – are, in Thornton's hands (8f, 7f, 7g, 7h, 7j, 5a–5d; 4c, 4h (Fig. 5.9)) treated with empathy and even a touch of humour.

But above all it is in the treatment of the human condition that the window excels. Descriptions of the characteristics of Thornton's 'style' almost always refer to bulbous noses, and this is certainly a conspicuous feature of many of his figures. There is so much more, however, for in many of the window's faces we glimpse emotion and internal turmoil. Adam's doubt as he bites the apple (15h, Fig. 5.11), the sorrow and bewilderment of Jacob's sons as he blesses them from his deathbed (14j), Absalom's sorrow as he is suspended from the tree, the calm resignation of the saints as they face the Beast (5c, Fig. 5.12), the despair of those who are afflicted by the fourth and fifth vials (4f and 4g, Fig. 5.1), the dismay of the kings of the earth who witness the fall of Babylon. The window has very few female figures, but the calm loveliness of the female figures in the tracery (F5, F6, C9, C7 C9, A13, A14, A15, A16, A17, A18) effortlessly conveys their saintly nature. The interaction between individuals – whispering (Fig. 5.13), plotting, sharing secrets, sharing anxieties – is another hallmark of the window's design. Thornton's ability to convey these emotions may seem commonplace from a modern perspective, but it is remarkable in a work of this date and presages the characteristics associated with the work of the famed panel painters of the northern Renaissance – Van Eyck (d.1441), Van der Weyden (d.1464), Van der Goes (d.1482) and Memling (d.1494) – with whom Thornton deserves to be compared.

Thanks to conservation and modern photography, John Thornton and his unnamed collaborators are only now receiving the international acknowledgement that they deserve. Ironically, had they painted walls or panels rather than glass, their work might not have survived at all, and could well have been lost to the iconoclasts of the Reformation or Civil War and Commonwealth. The very inaccessibility of their work and the essential function they play as part of the weatherproof envelope of the cathedral church have ensured their survival, if also disguising their splendour. At long last we can enjoy their achievements again, safeguarding them from the risks posed by their environment and the impact of the many more visitors who now wish to see this medieval masterpiece for themselves. In this regard at least, Thornton's great achievement is safer than Michelangelo's Sistine Chapel ceiling to which it was once, half in jest, compared.

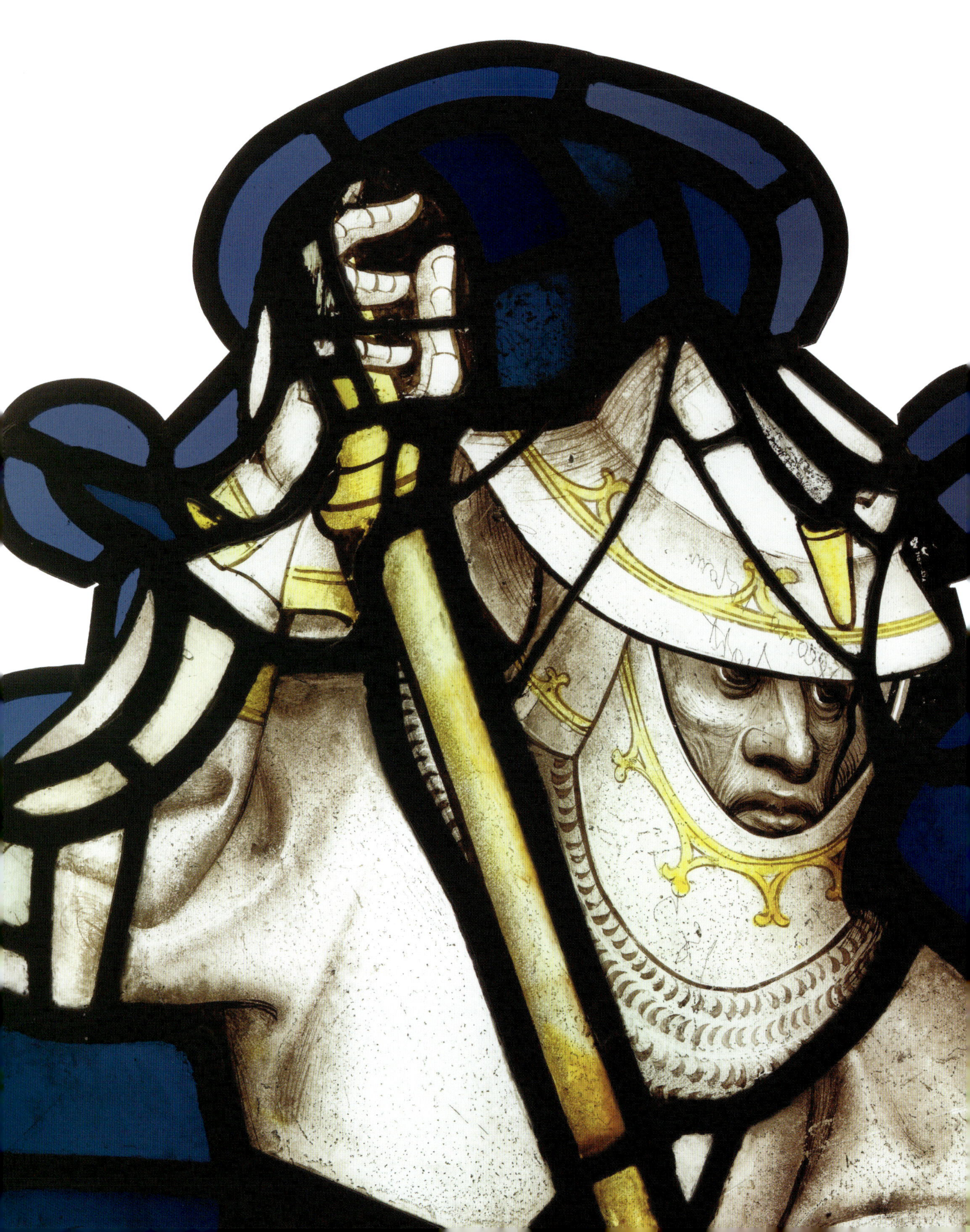

Catalogue

Catalogue
The Tracery

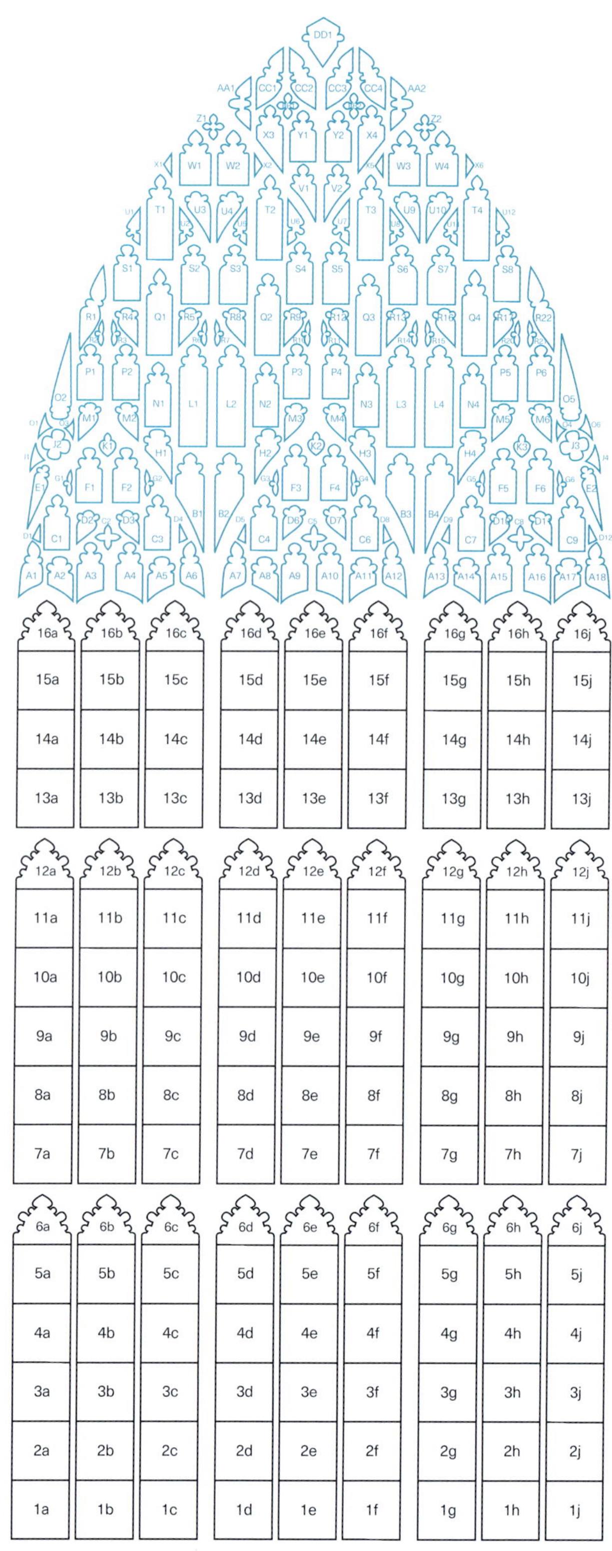

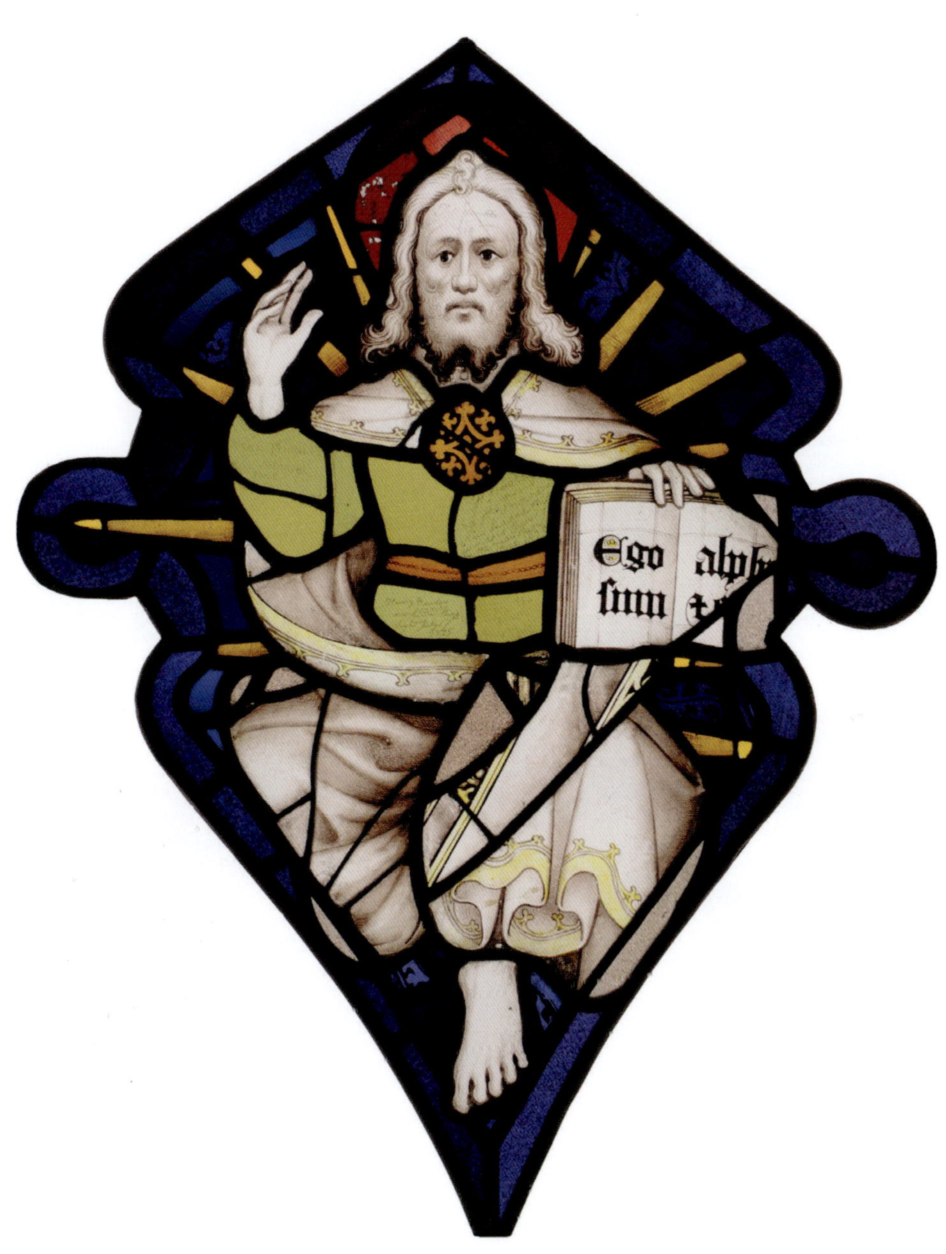

DD1
God as Alpha and Omega

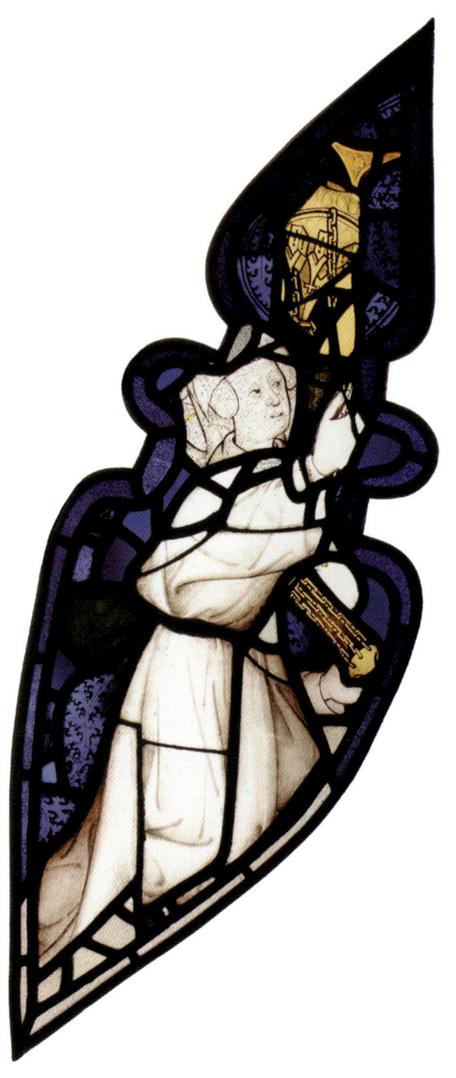 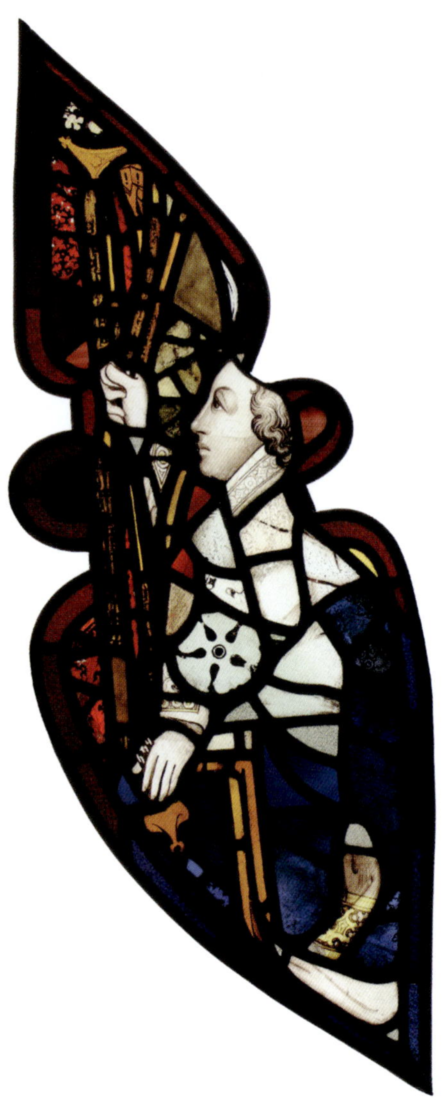

CC1 and CC2
Censing Angels

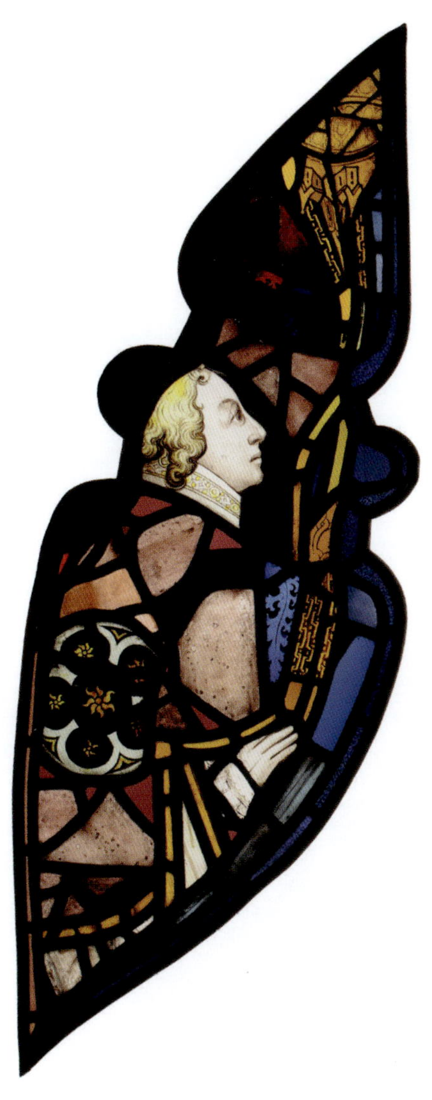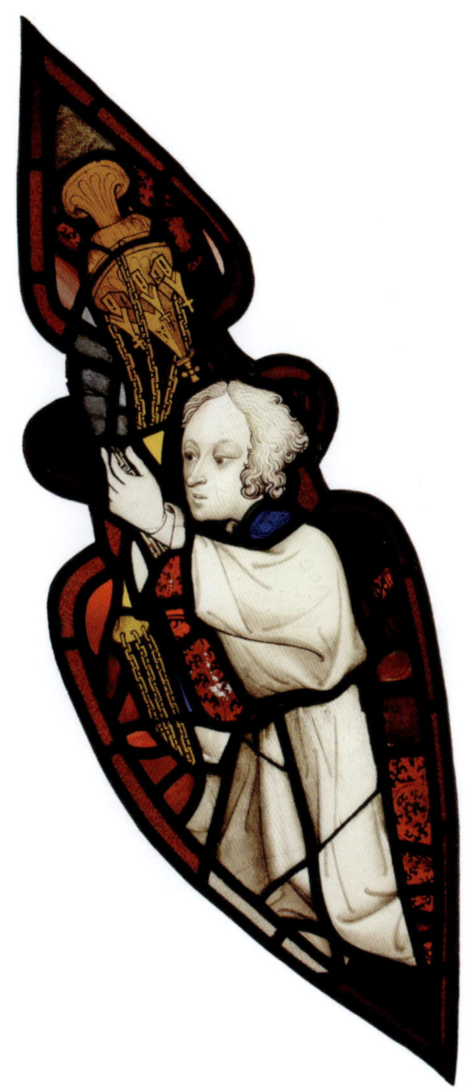

CC3 and CC3
Censing Angels

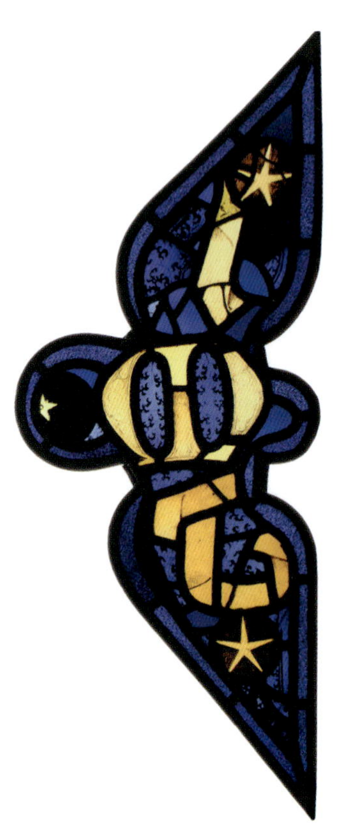

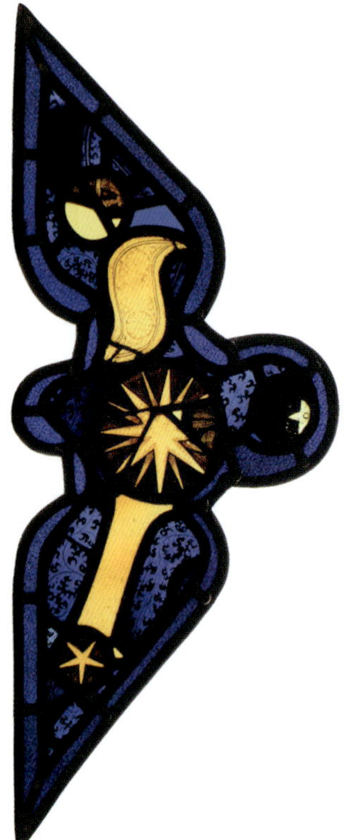

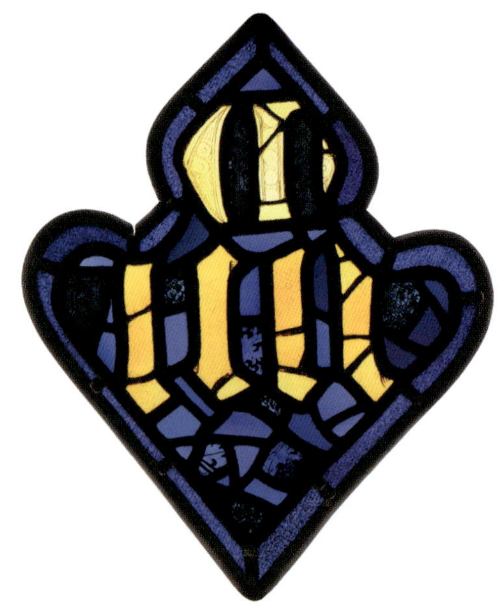

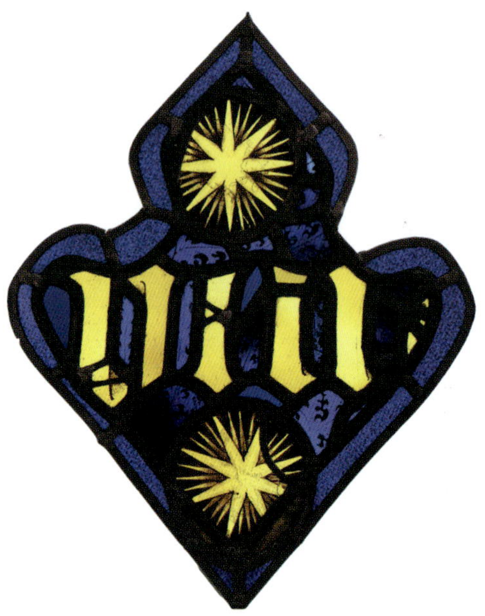

AA1
Lettering

AA2
Sunburst

Z1 and Z2
First and second half of date 1408

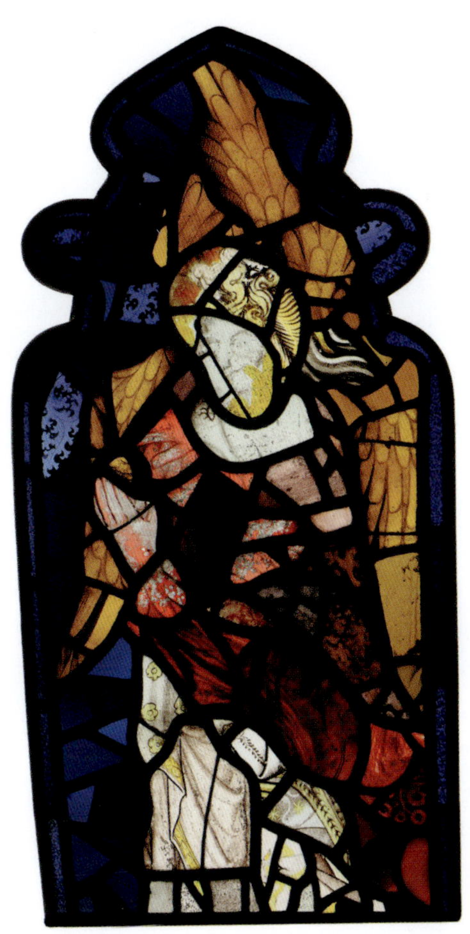 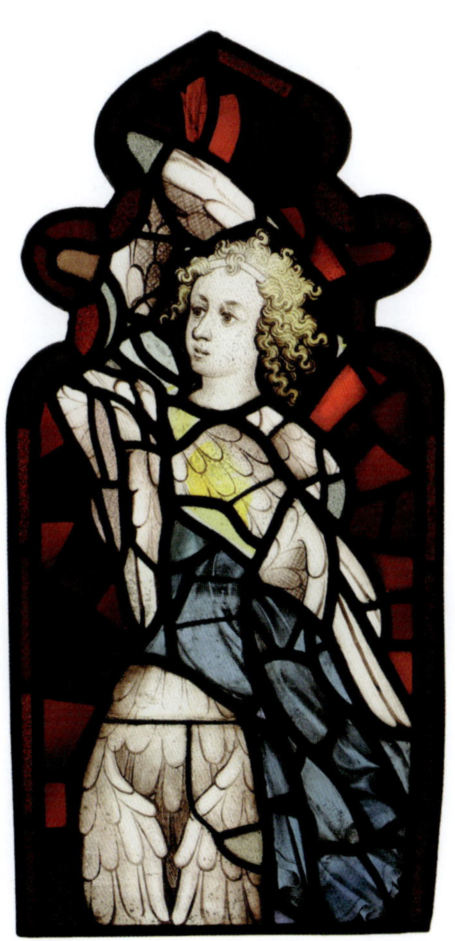

Y1 and Y2
Angels

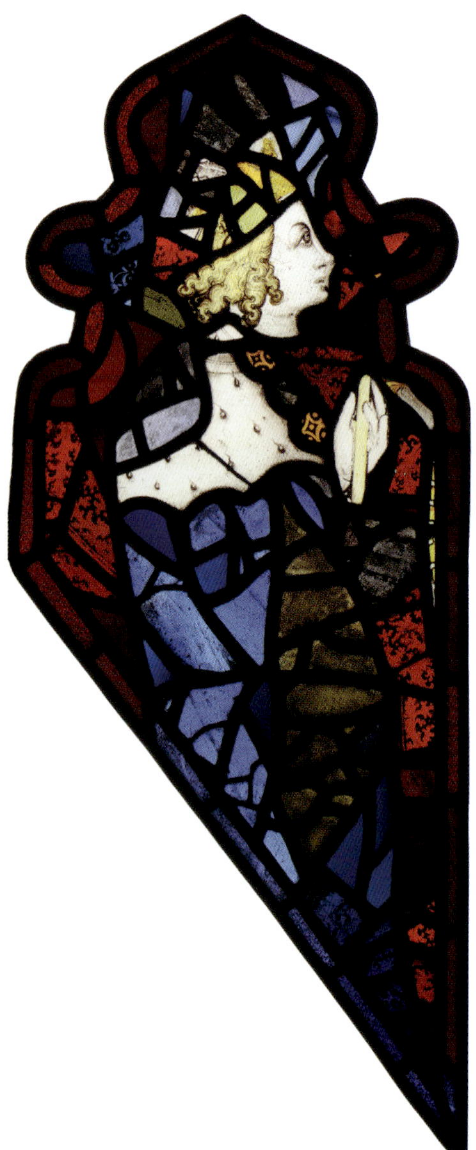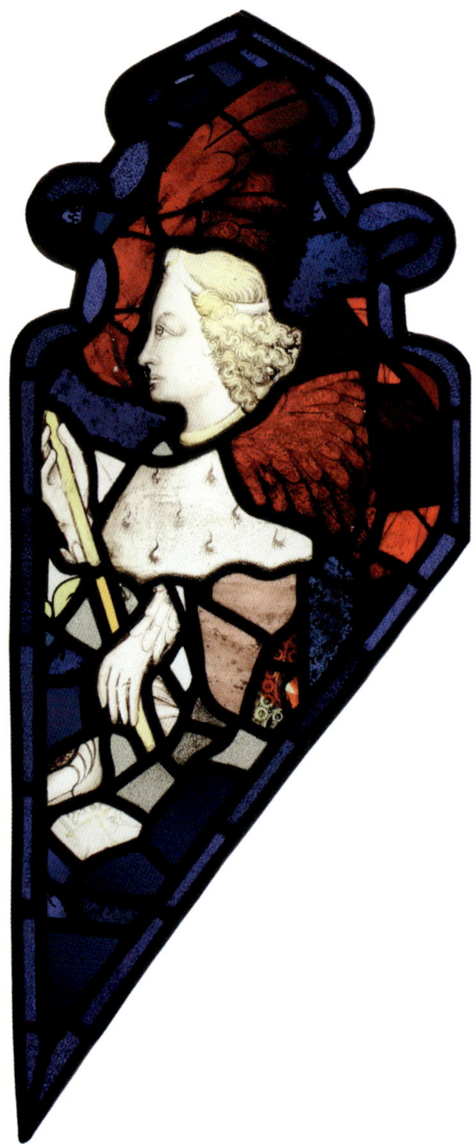

X3 and X4
Angels

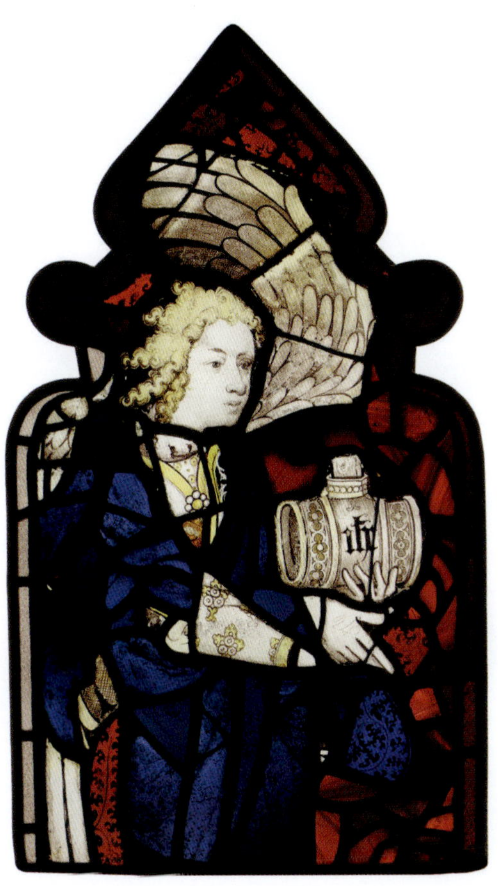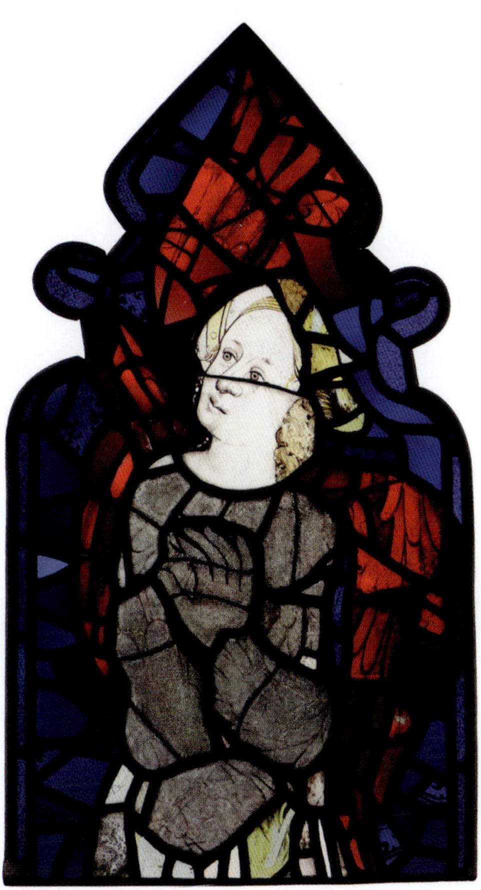

W1 and W2
Angels

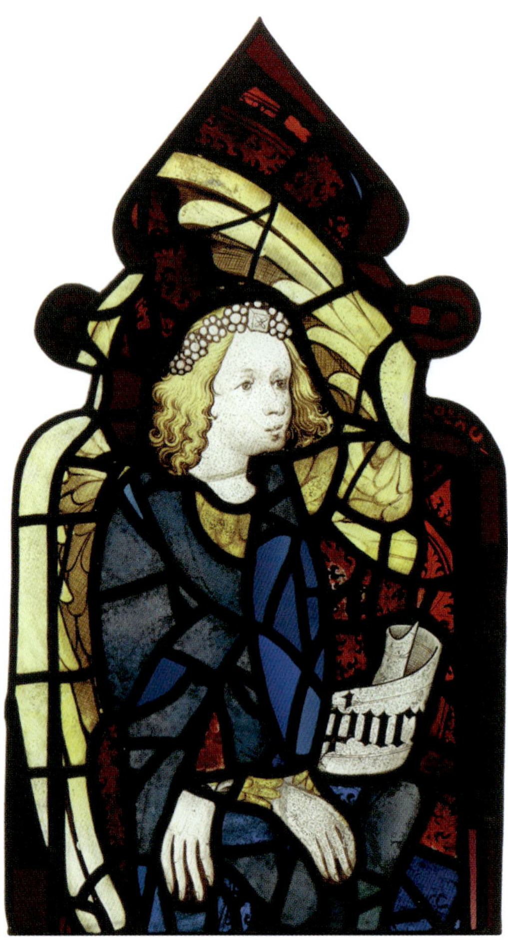 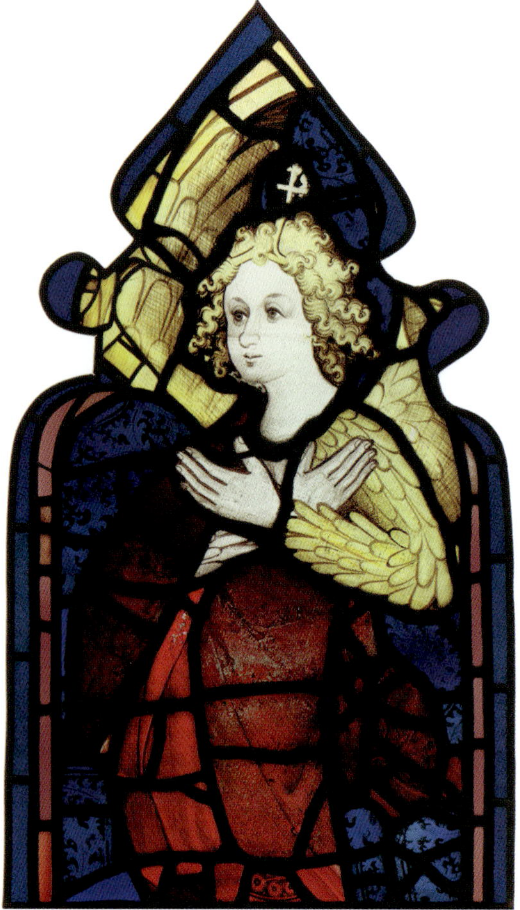

W3 and W4

Angels

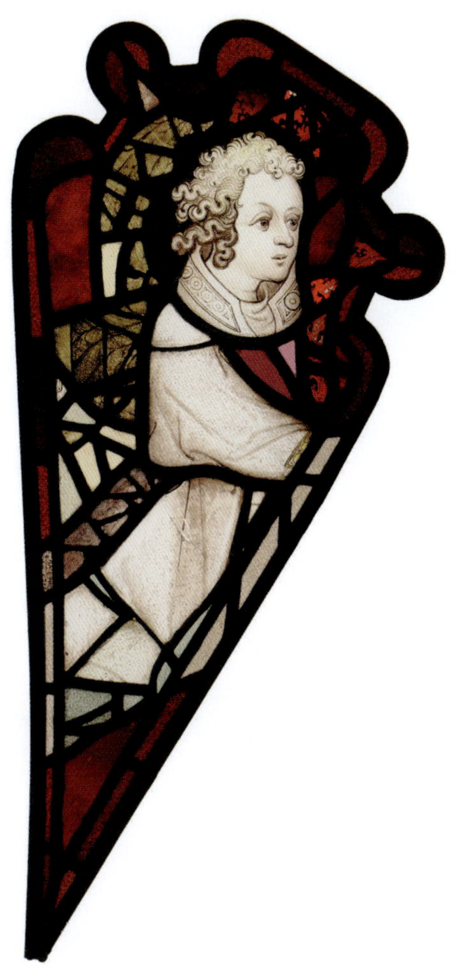 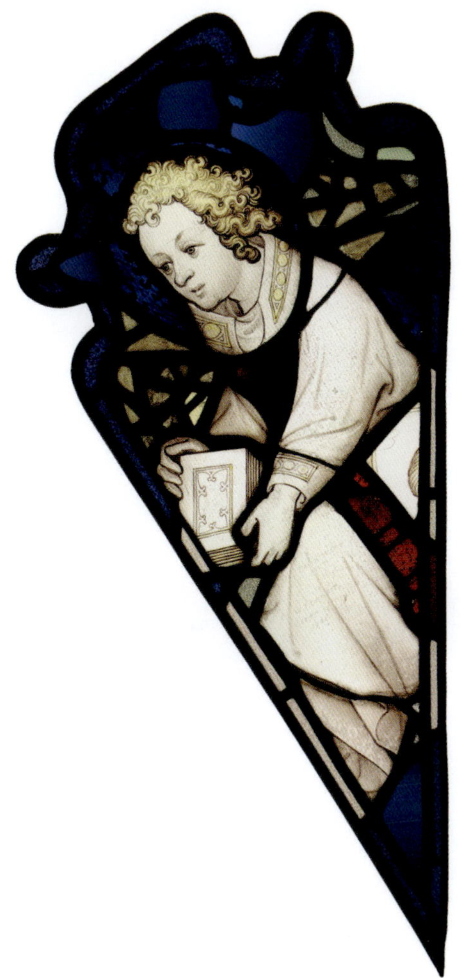

V1 and V2
Angels

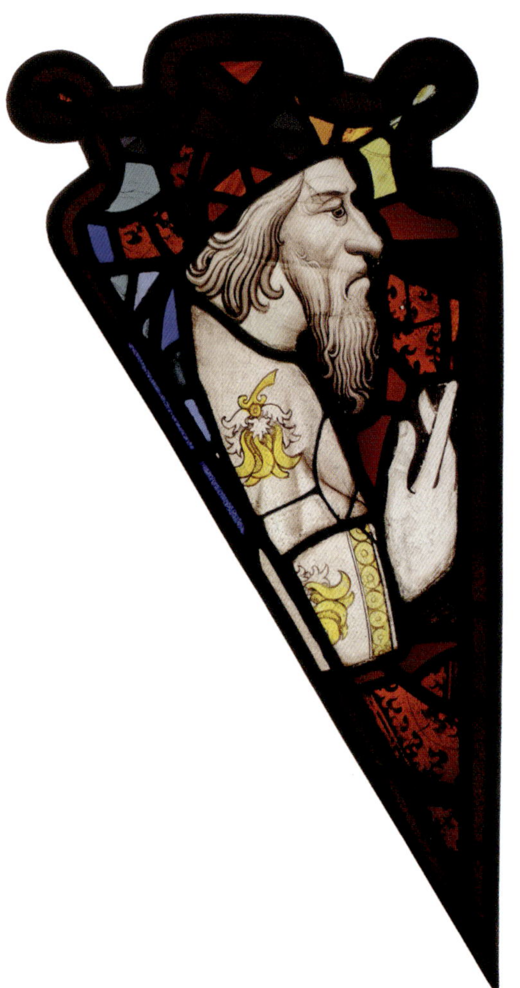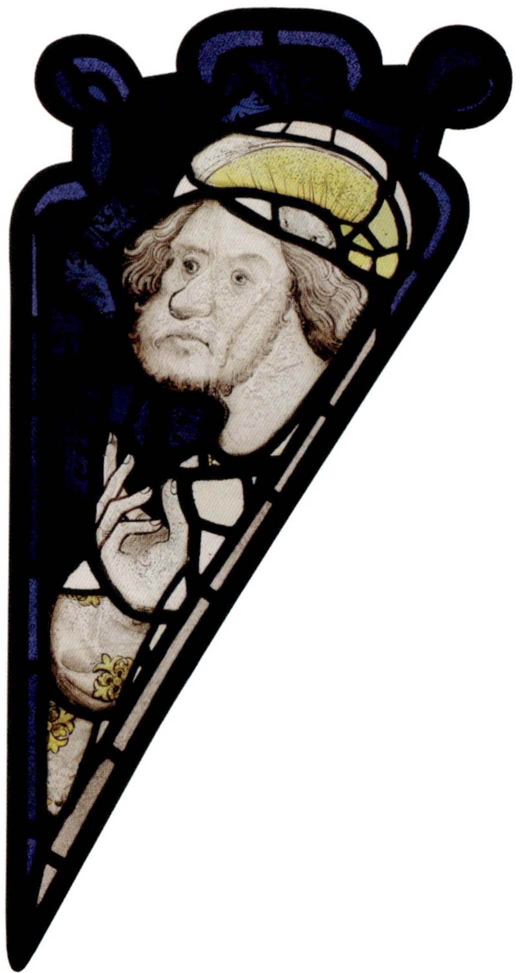

U3 and U4
Male figures

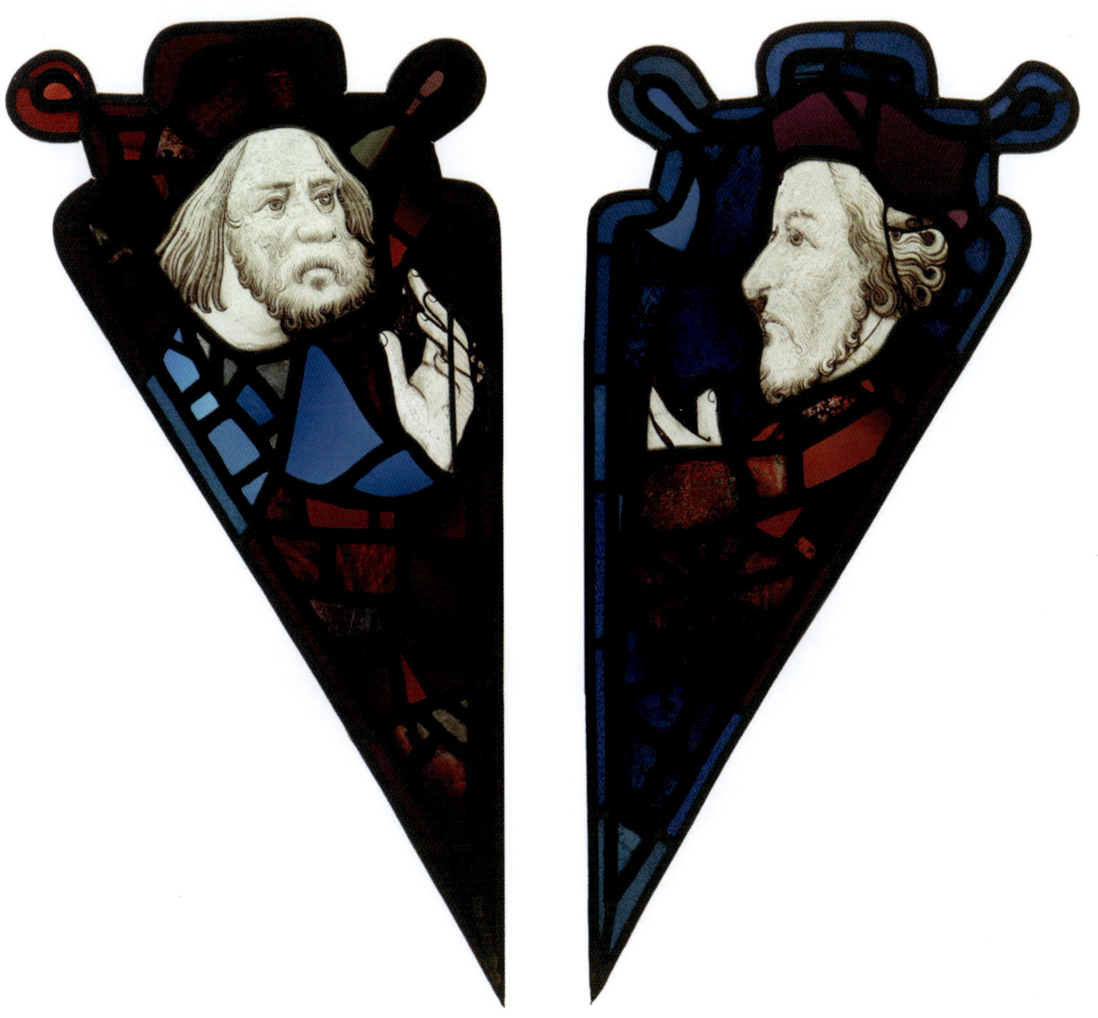

U9 and U10
Male figures

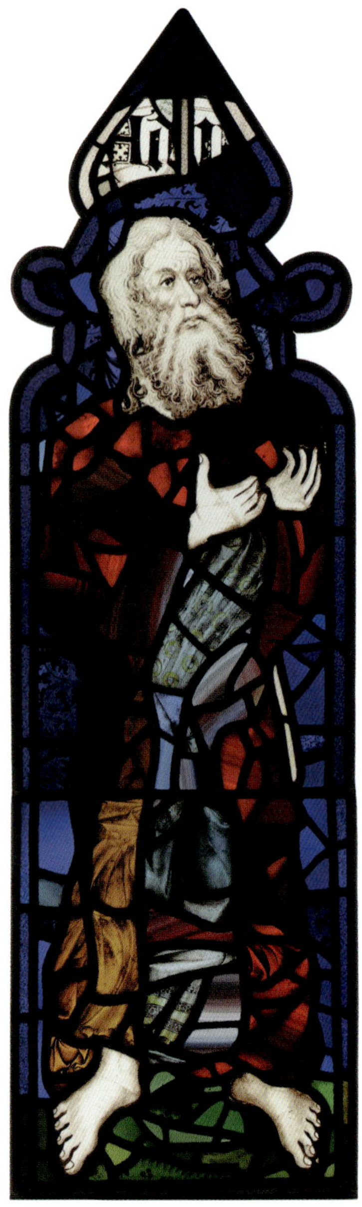

T1
Adam: **Ad[a]m**

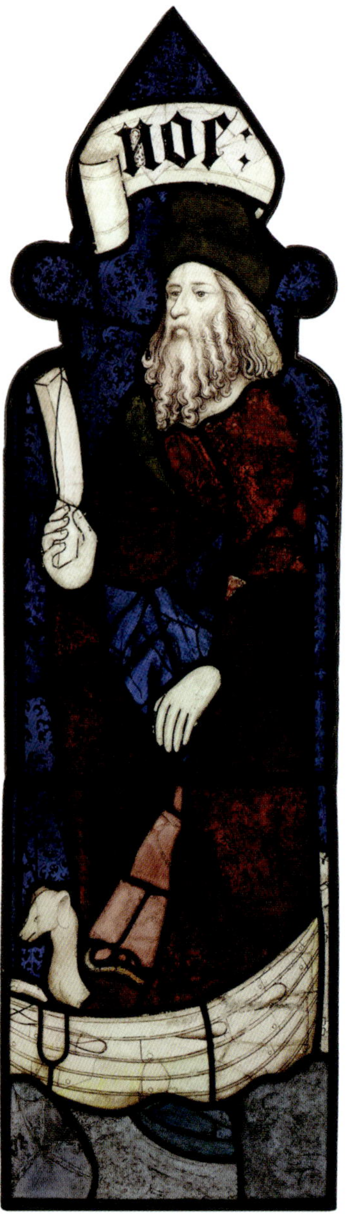

T2
Noah and the Ark: **noe**

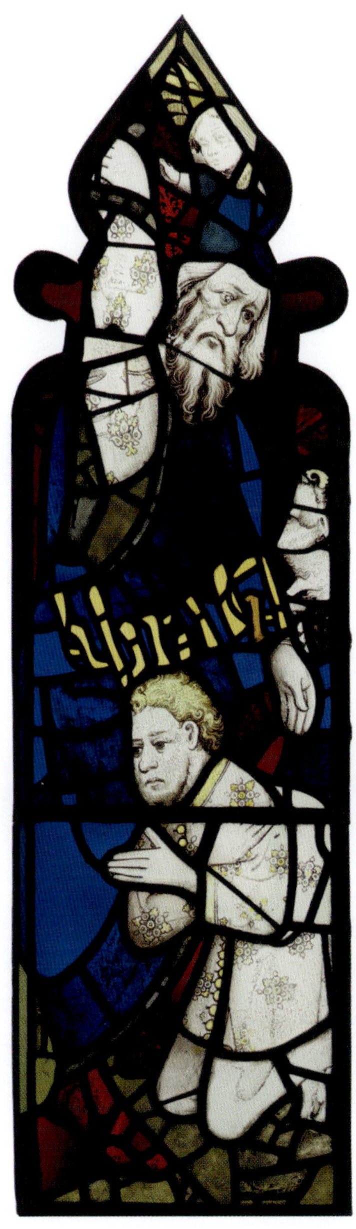

T3
Abraham about to sacrifice
Isaac (**Abrah** created in 1953)

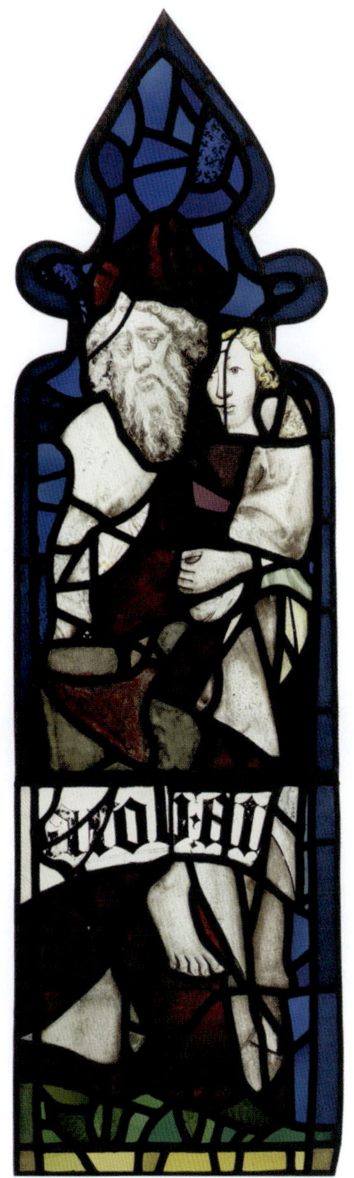

T4
Jacob wrestling with the angel,
[I]acob: an

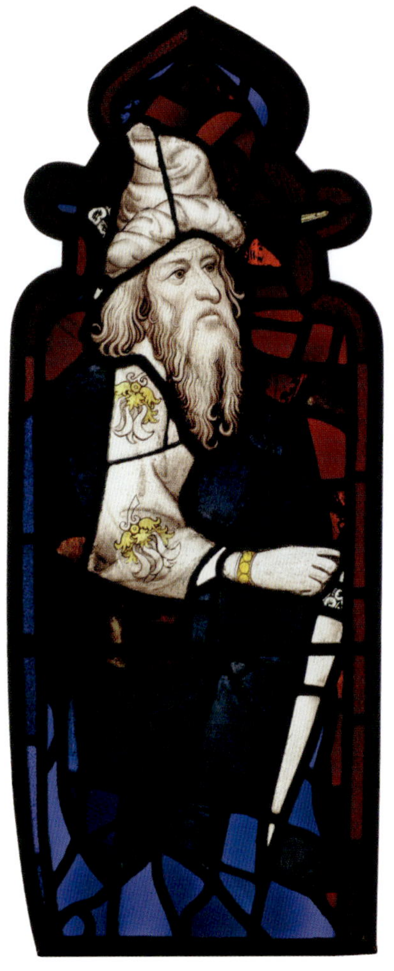

S1
Male Figure

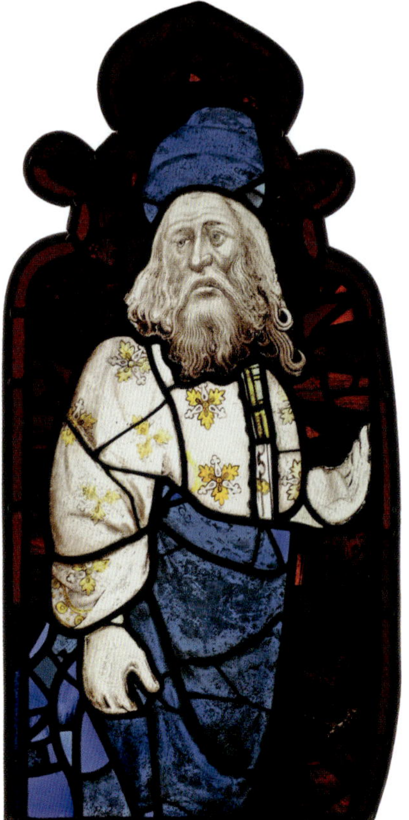

S2
Male Figure

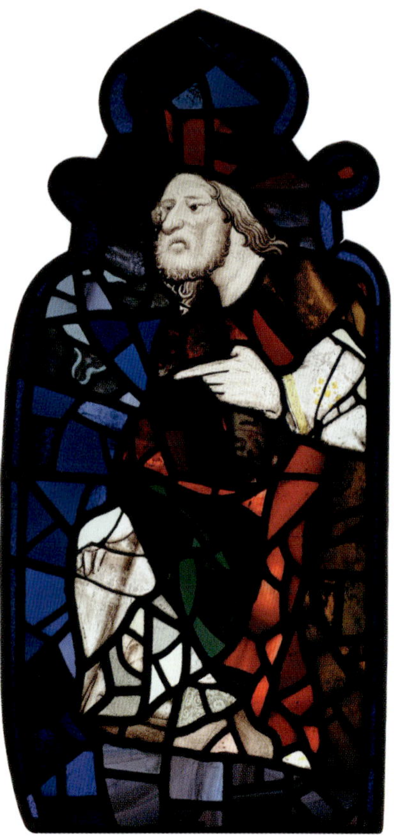

S3
Male Figure

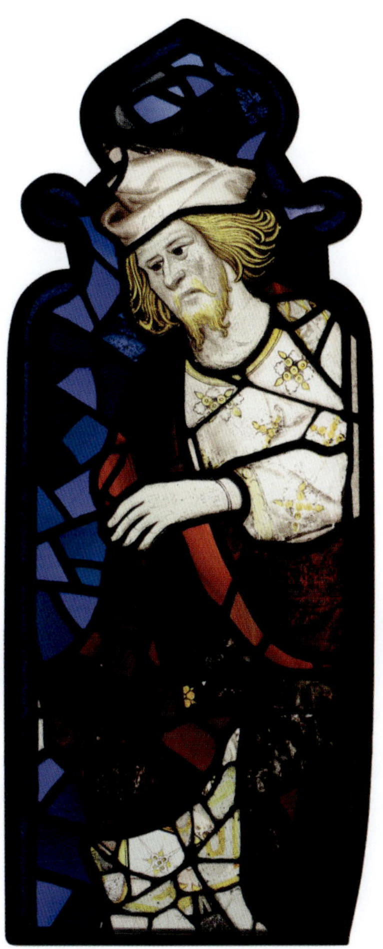

S4
Male Figure

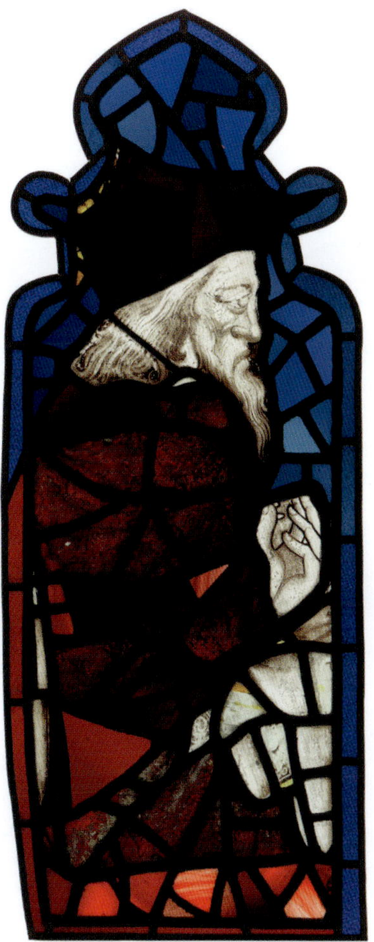

S5
Male Figure

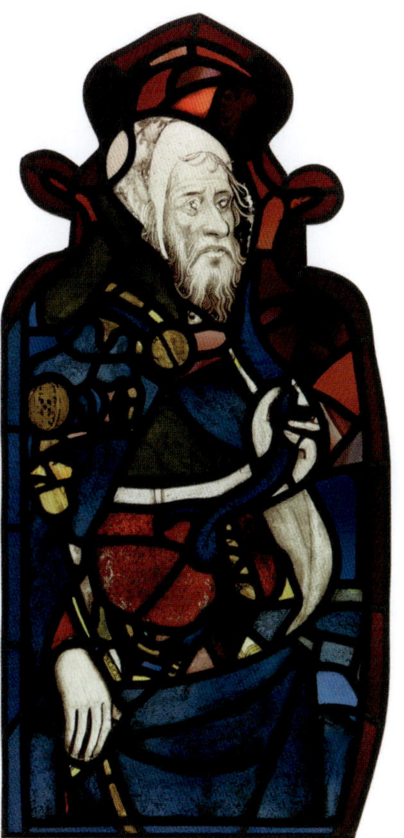

S6
?Dan

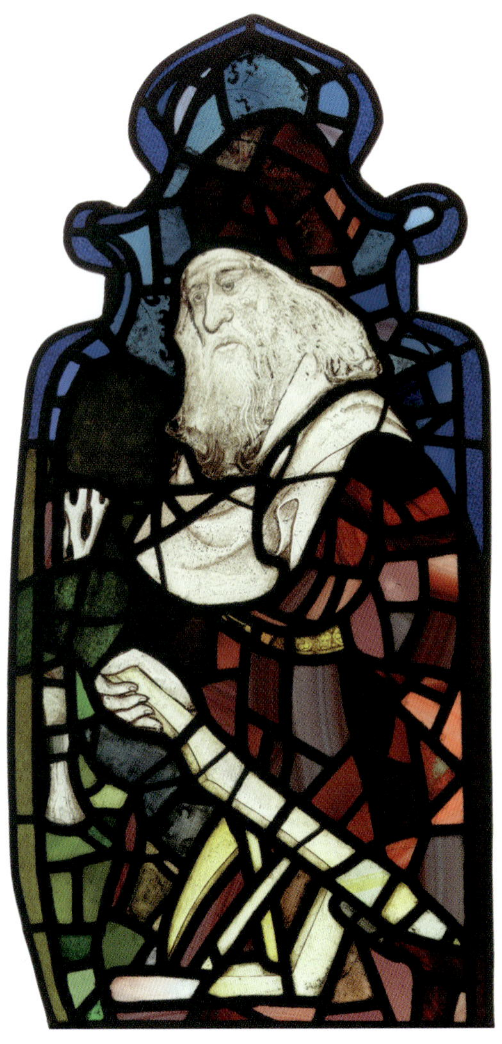

S7
Male Figure

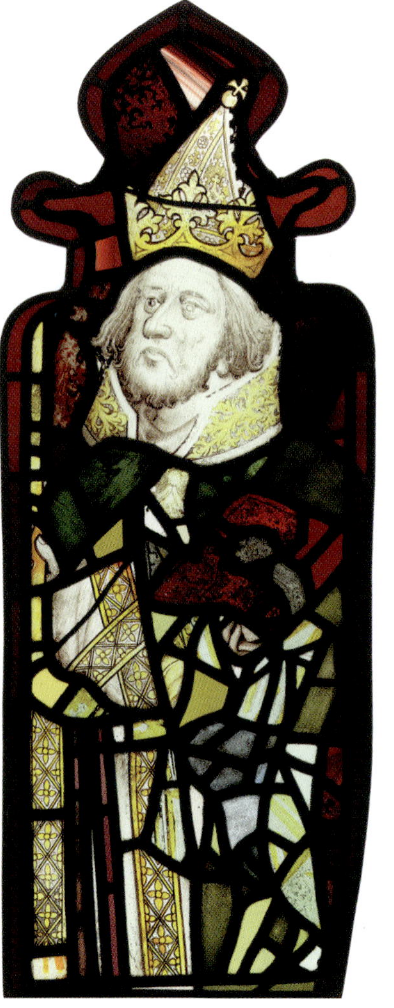

S8
Pope

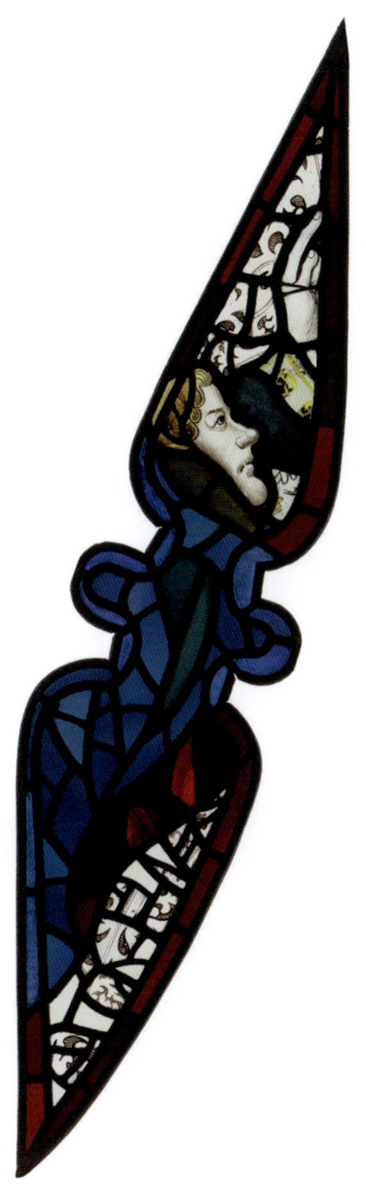

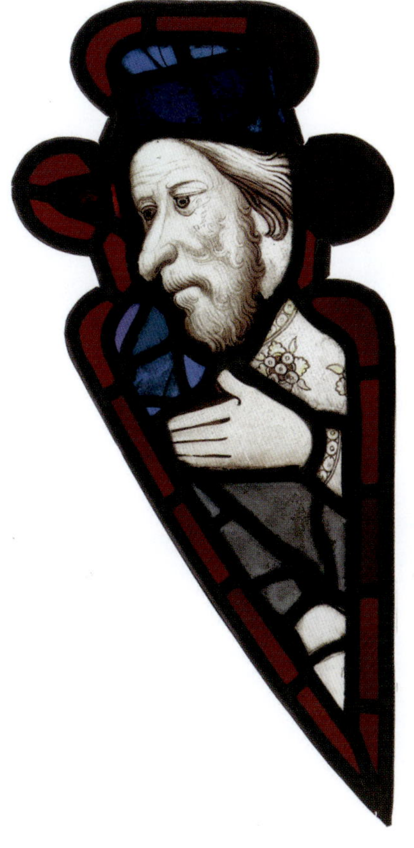

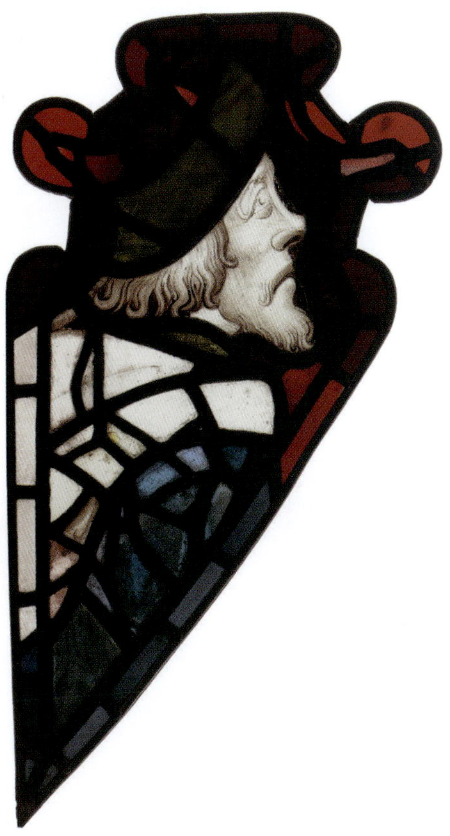

R1
Male Head

R4
Male Figure

R5
Male Figure

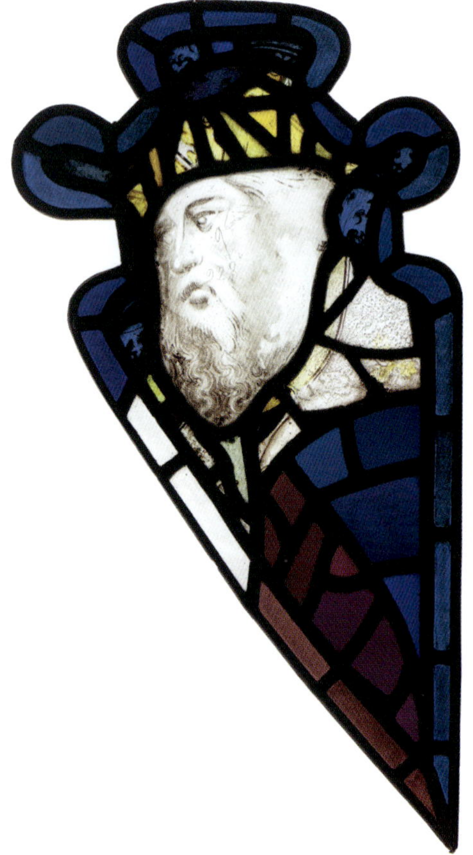

R8
Male Figure

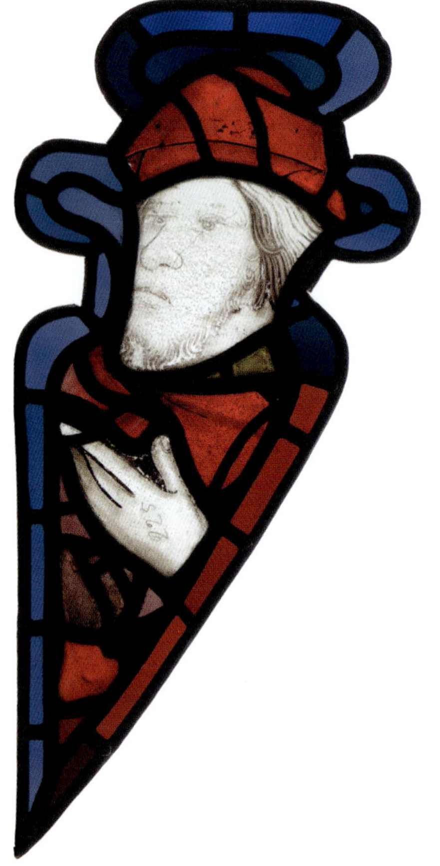

R9
Male Figure

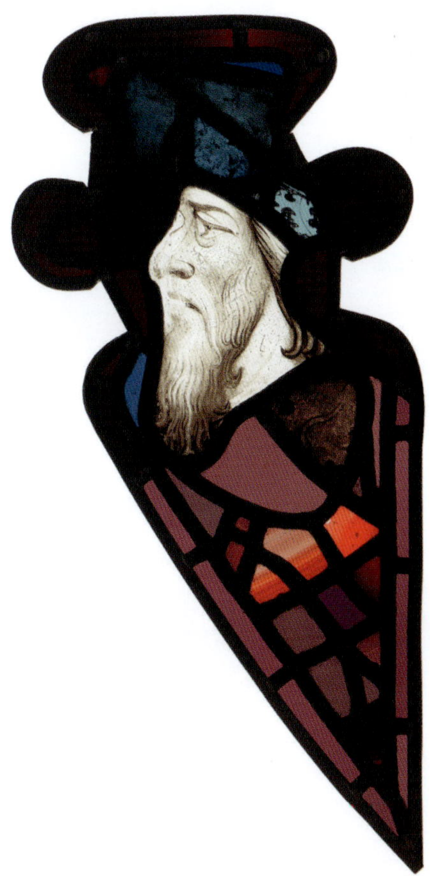

R12
Male Figure

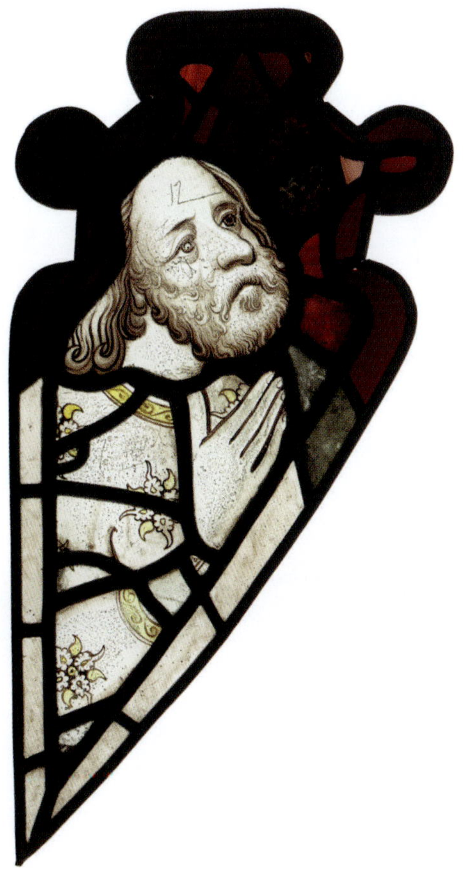

R13
Male Figure

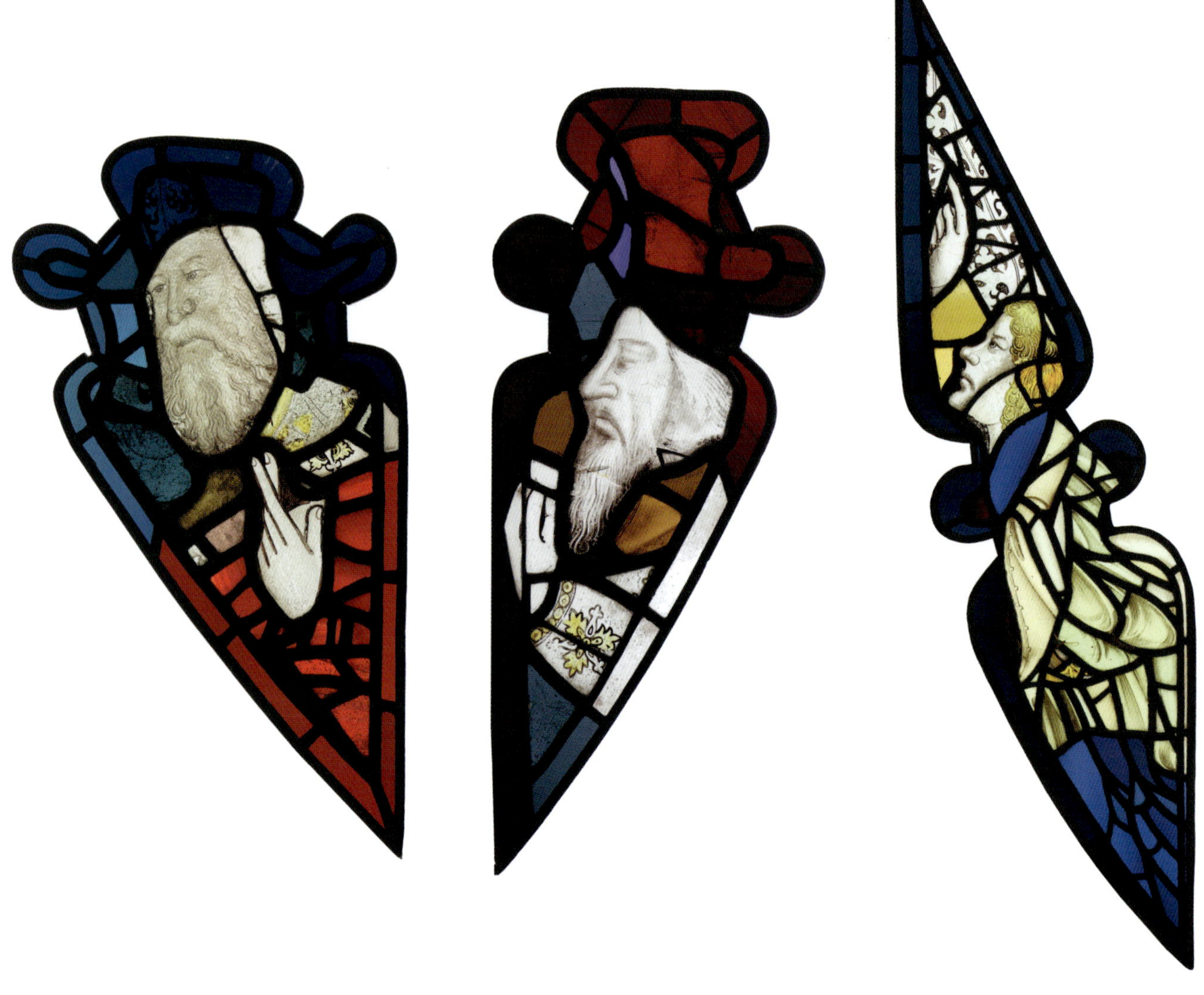

R16
Male Figure

R17
Male Figure

R20
Male Figure

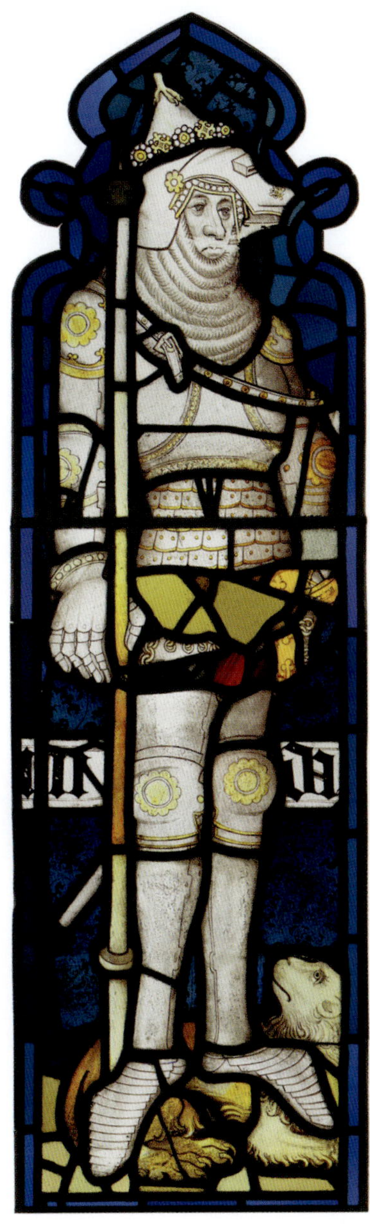

Q1
Judah: [I]uda

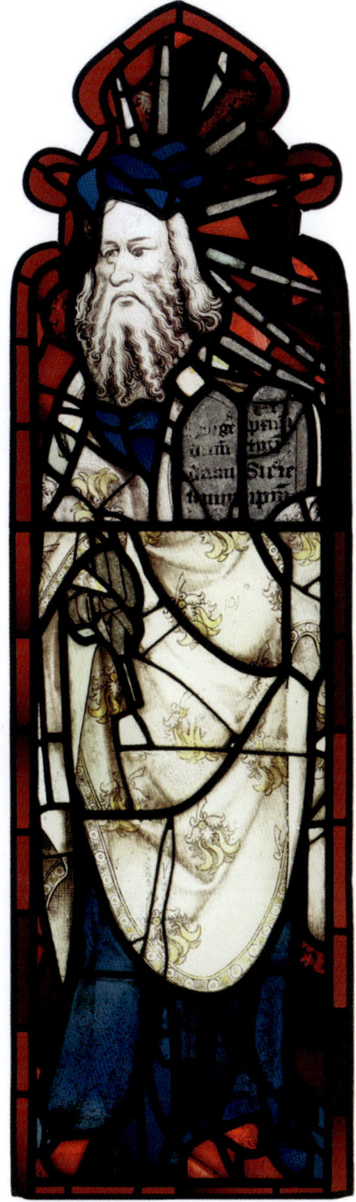

Q2
Moses, tablet inscribed **Diliges/ d(omi)n(u)m/ deum/ tumum** and **Et/ p(ro)x(imum)/ tuu(m)/ Sic(ut) te/ ip(su)m** (Luke 10:27)

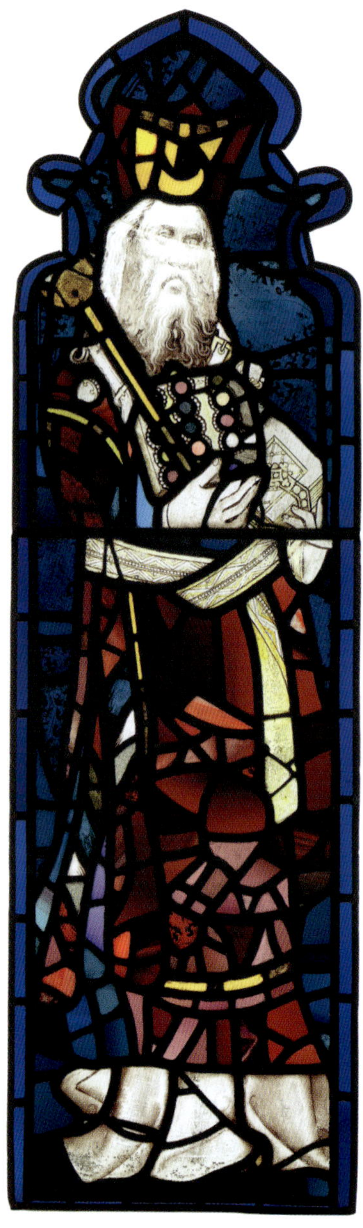

Q3
Aaron

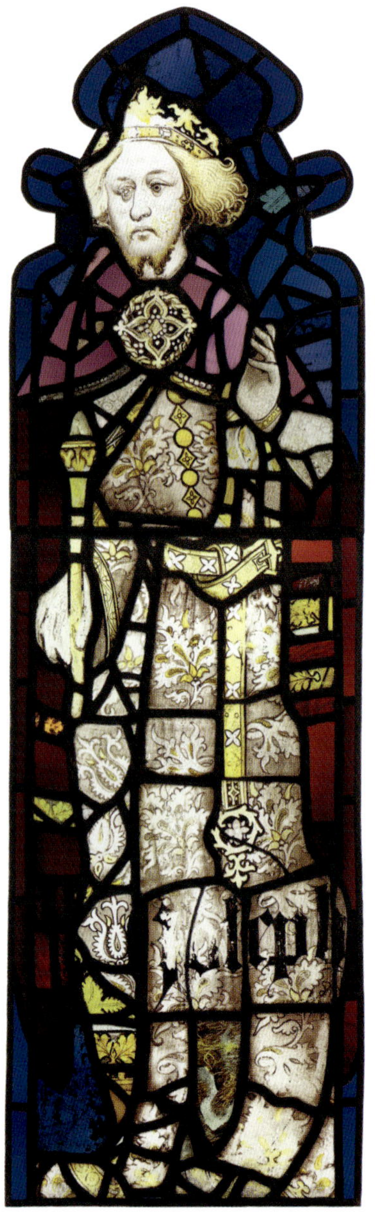

Q4
Joseph: **Ioseph**

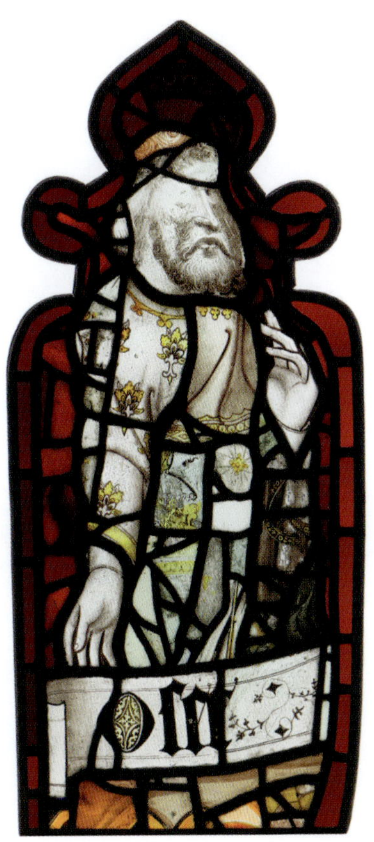

P1
Hosea: Osee

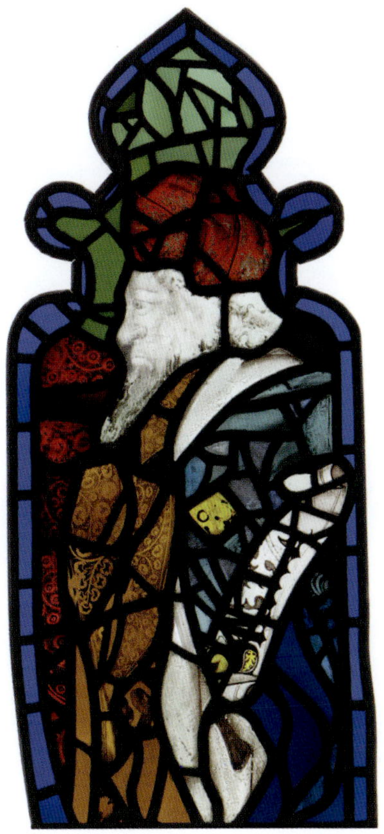

P2
Prophet (?Samuel): S…

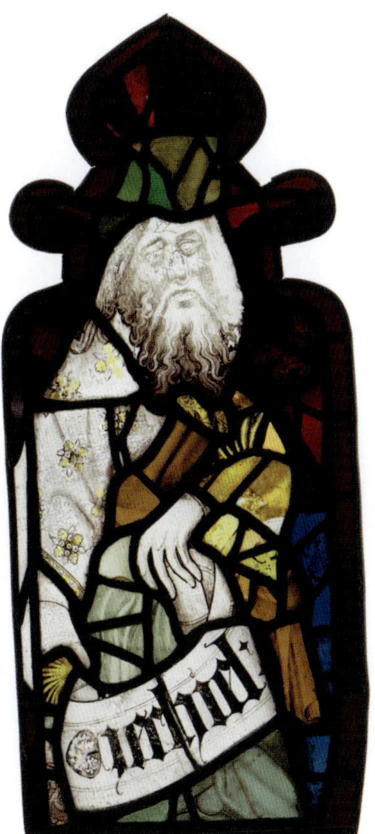

P3
Ezekiel: Ezechiel

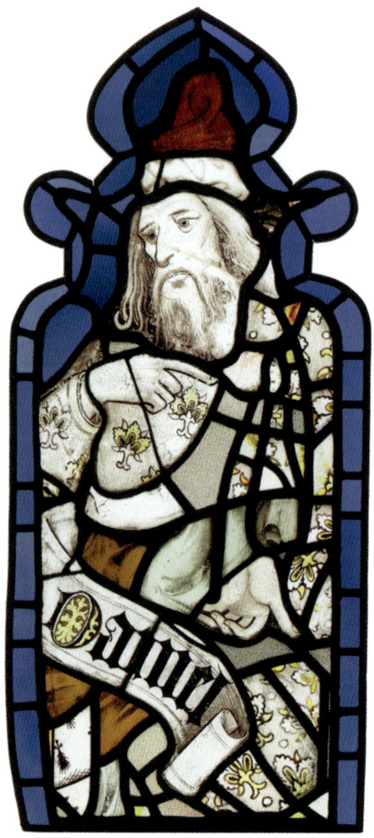

P4
Daniel: **Daniel**

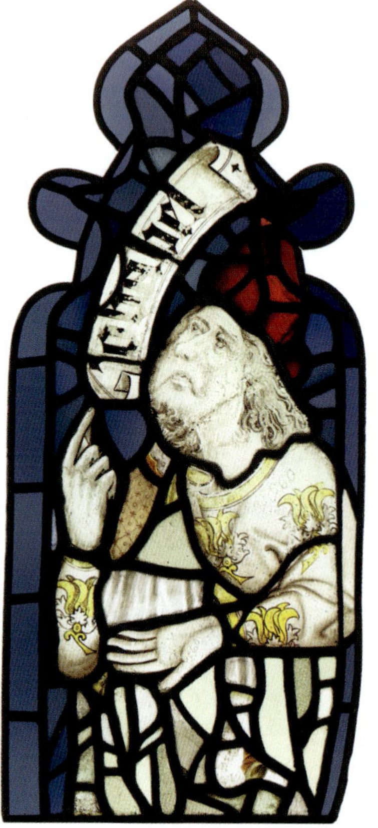

P5
Zerubbabel: **Z[er]obabel**

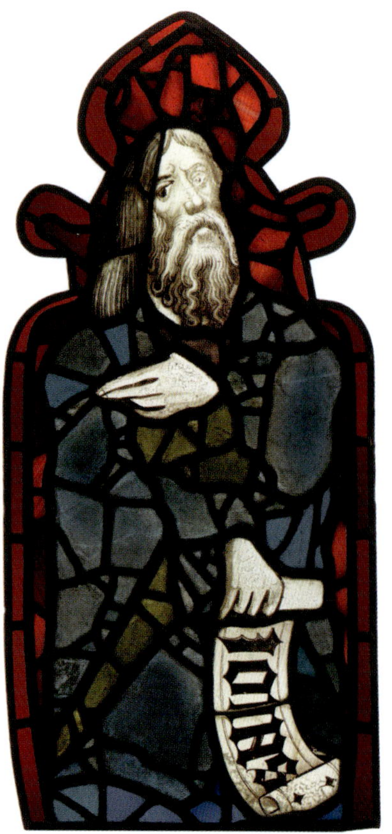

P6
Jonah: **Ionas**

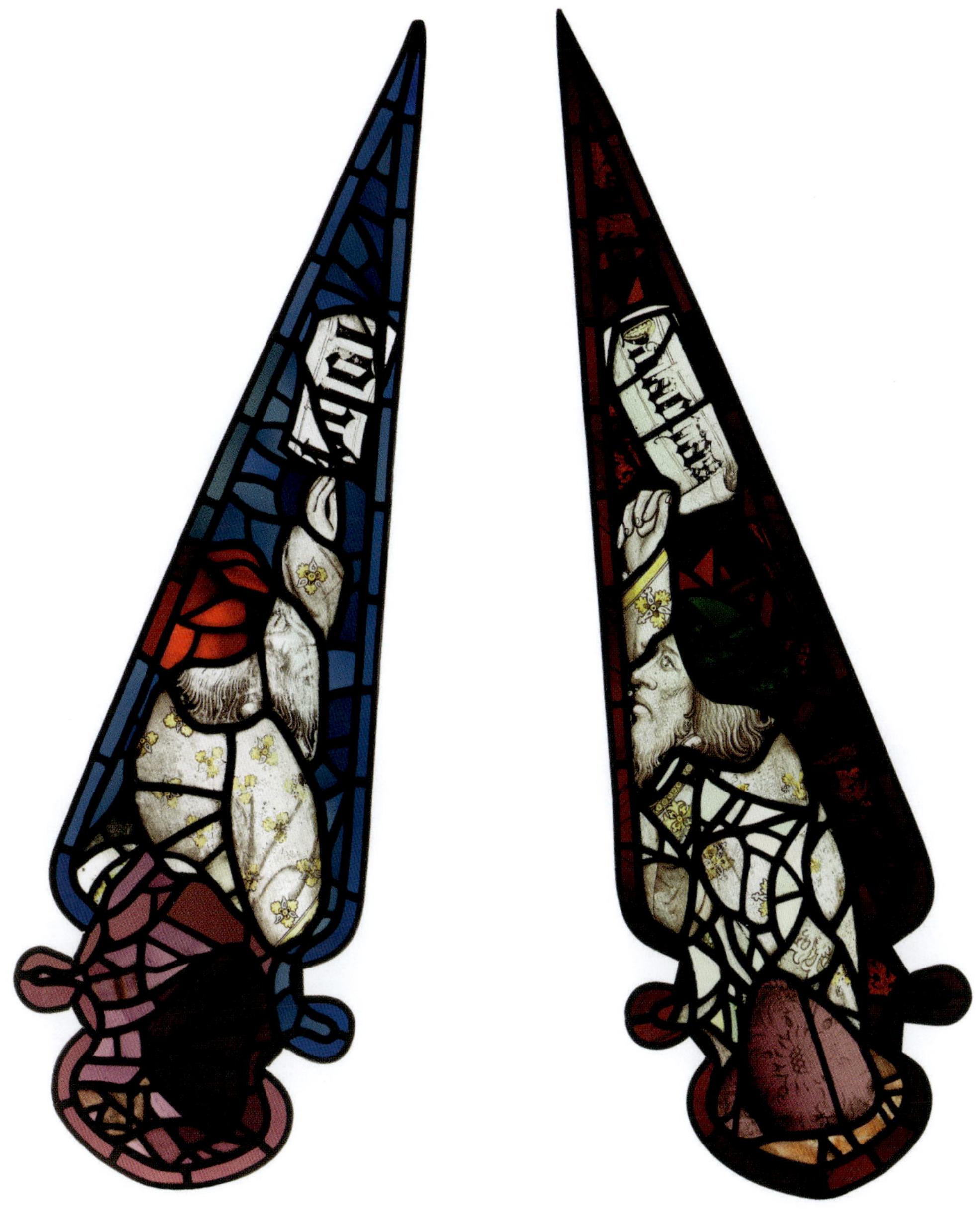

O2
Joel: **Iohel**

O5
Malachi: **Malachas**

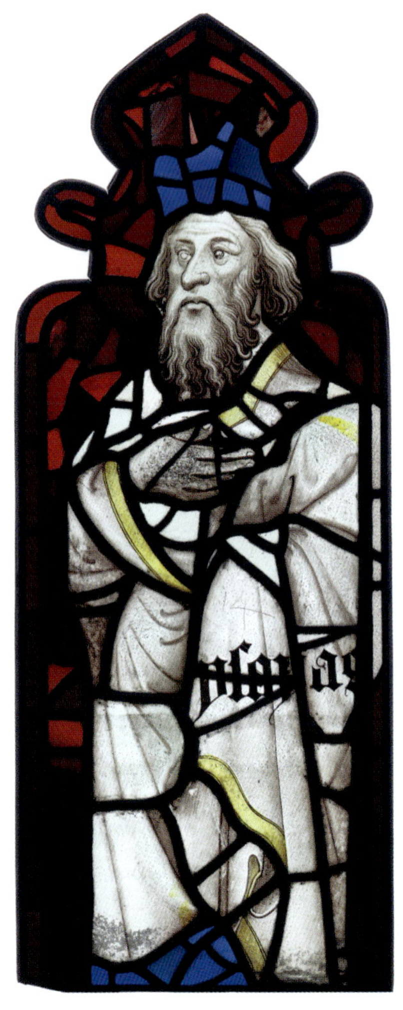

N1
Isaiah: **ysaas**

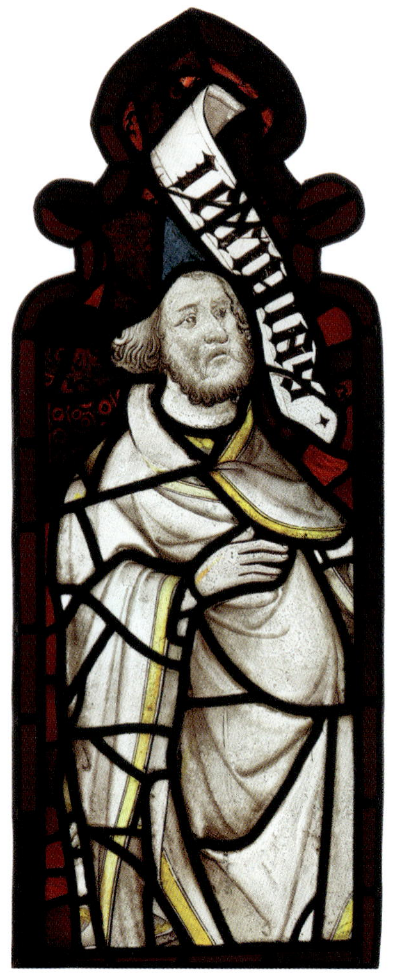

N2
Jeremiah: **Ieremias**

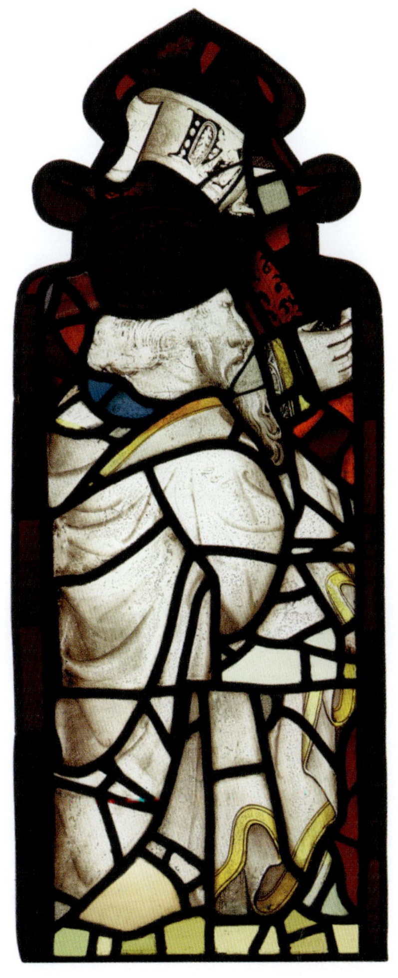

N3
Prophet, probably Nahum: **Na ...**

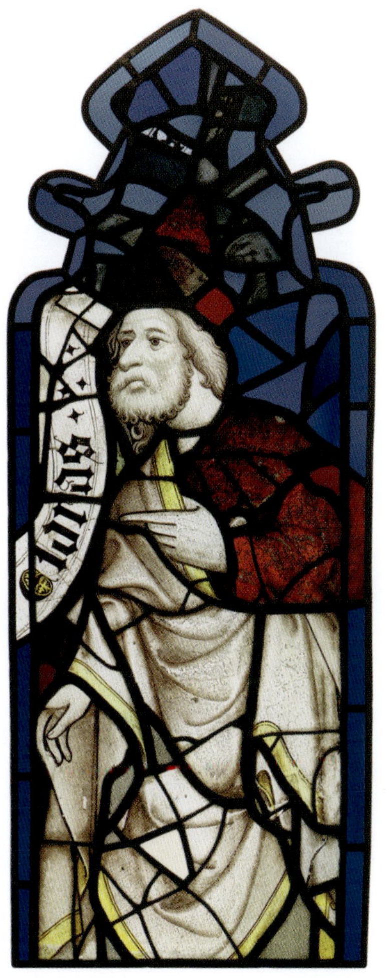

N4
Esdras: **E[s]dras**

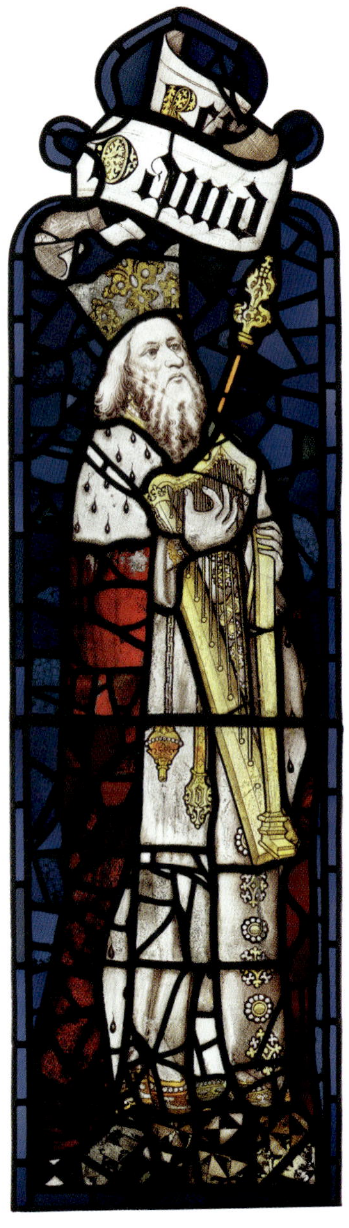

L1
King David: **Rex David**

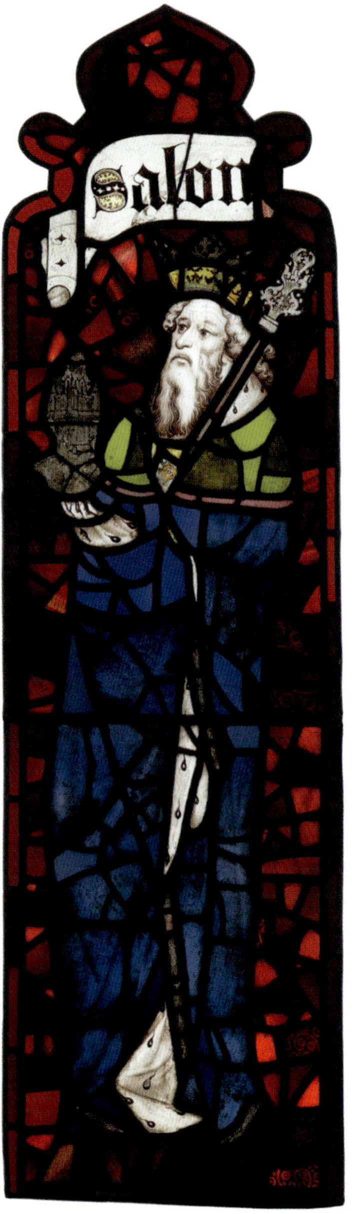

L2
Solomon: **Salom[on]**

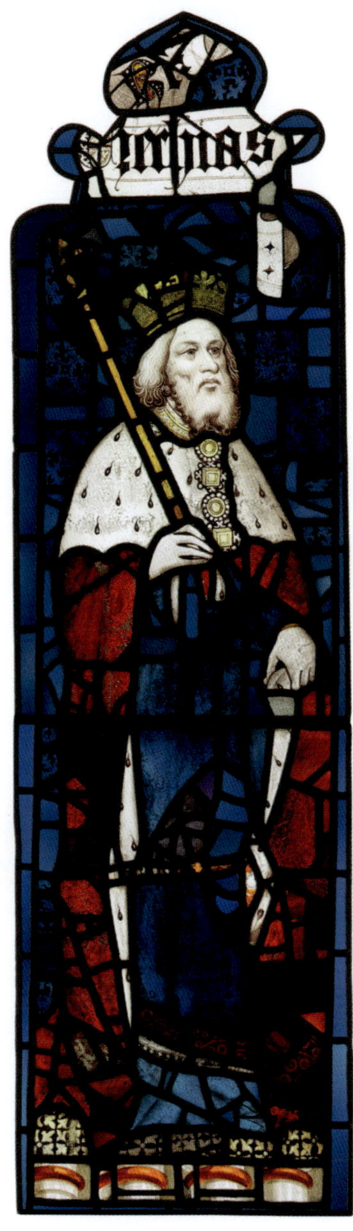

L3
King Hezekiah: **Re[x] Ezechias**

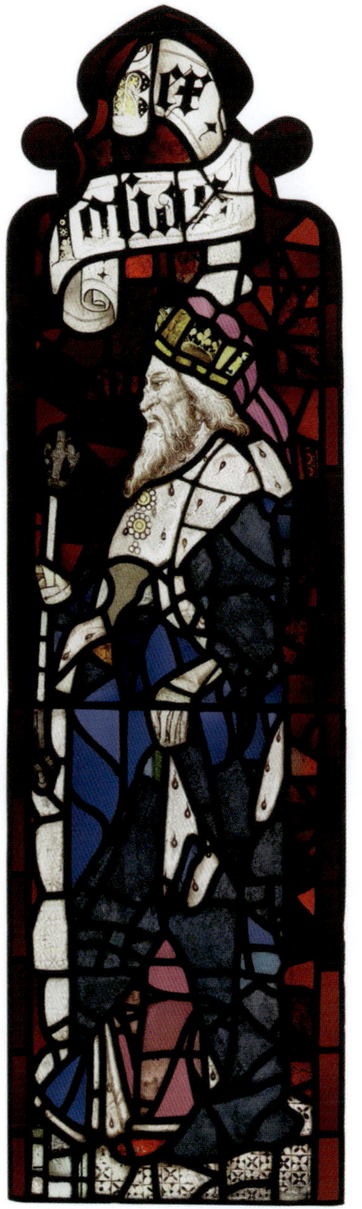

L4
King Josiah: **Rex**

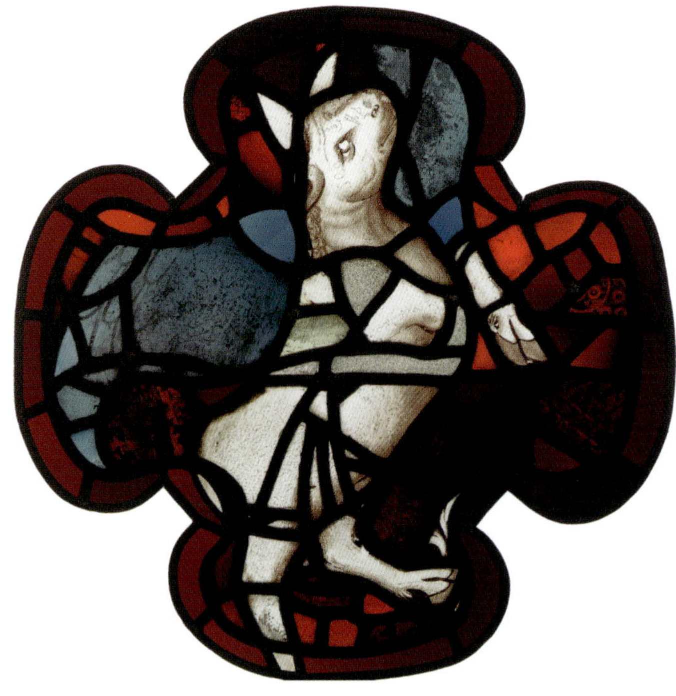

J2
Bull of St Luke

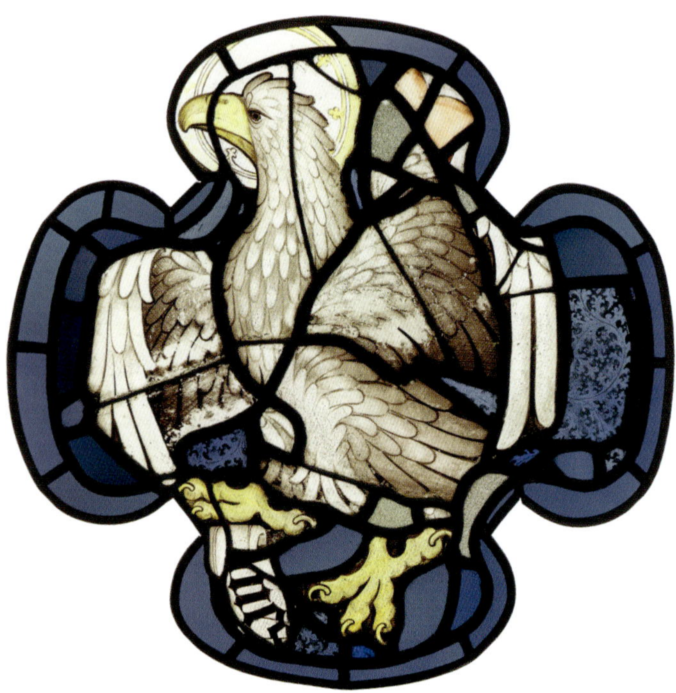

J3
Eagle of St John: [Iohan]nes

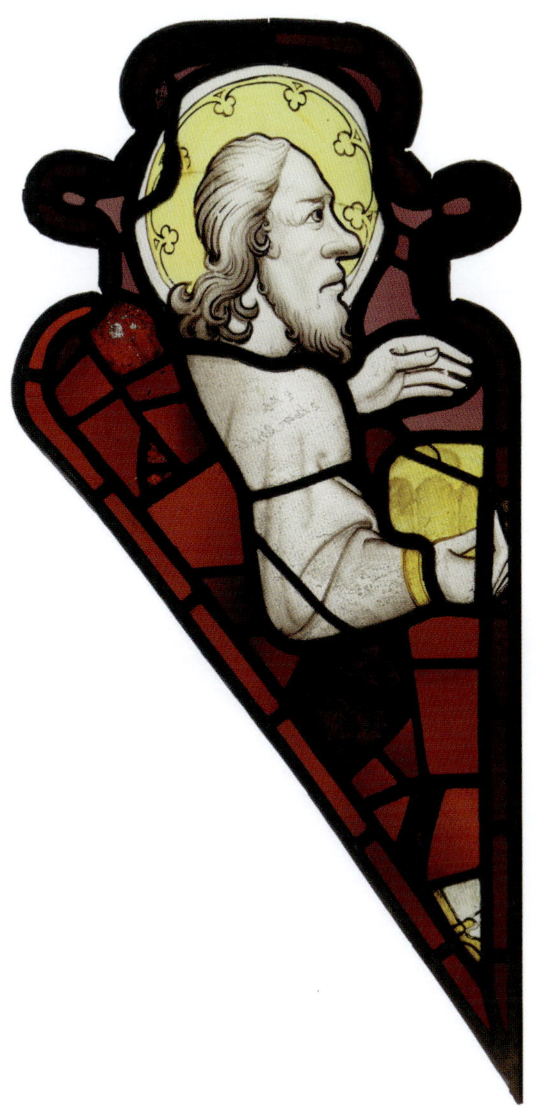

H1
St Philip

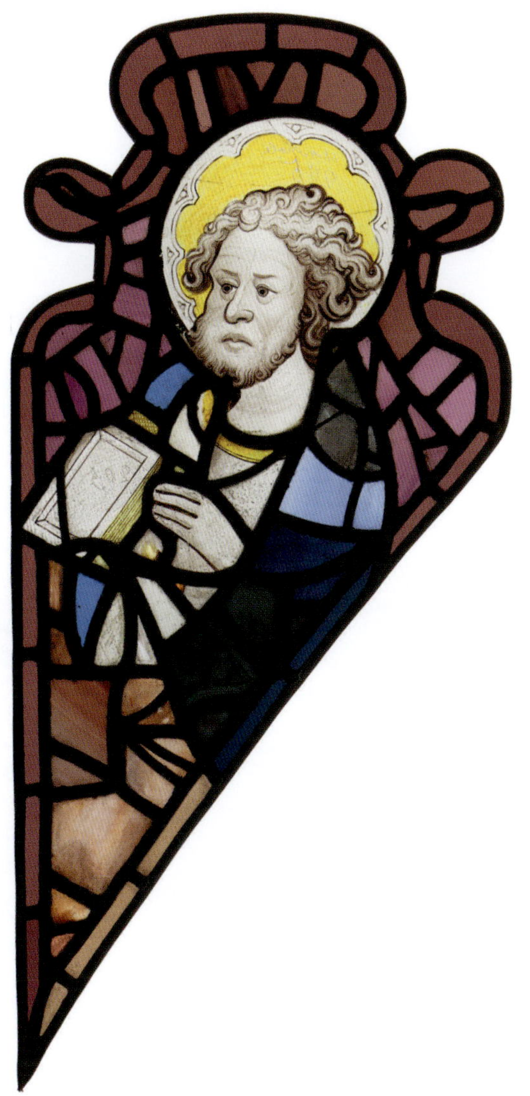

H2
Apostle

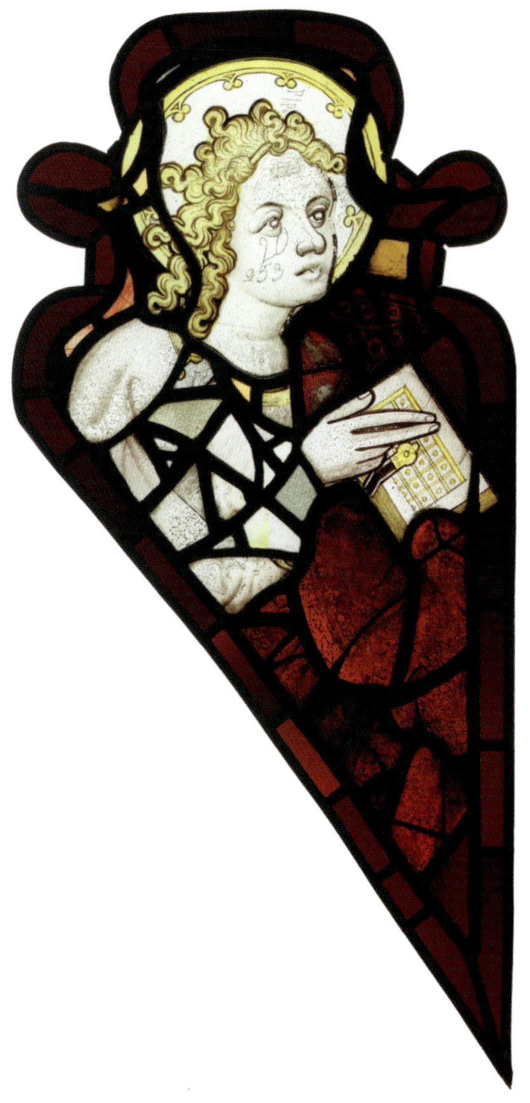

H3
Apostle

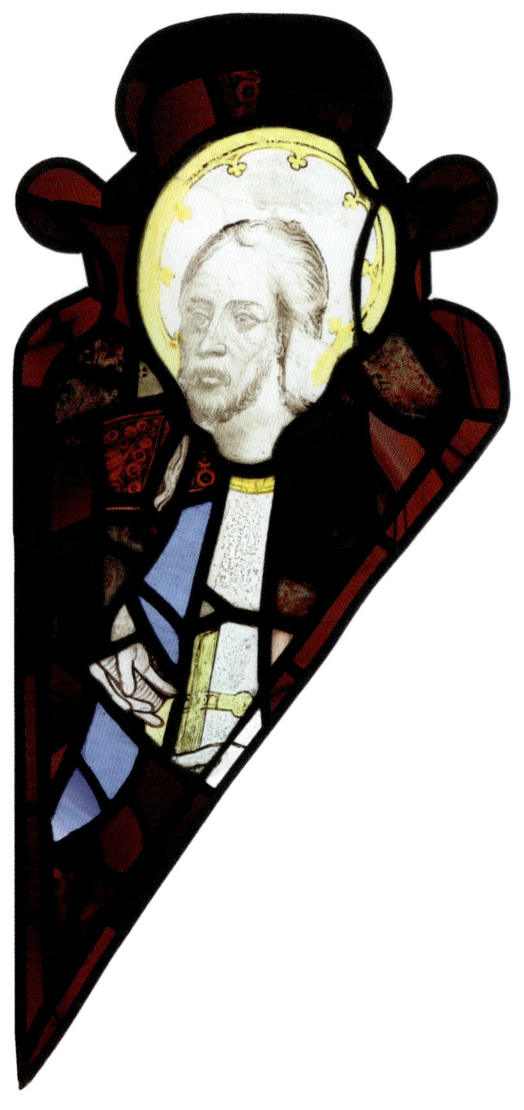

H4
St Bartholomew

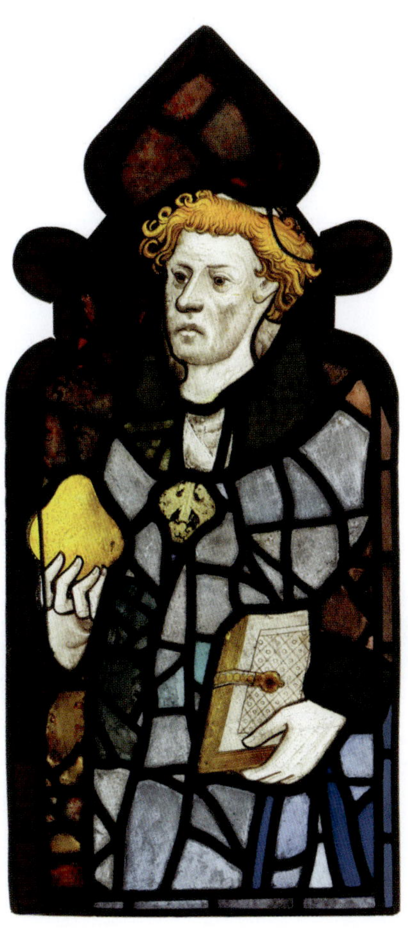

F1
St Stephen

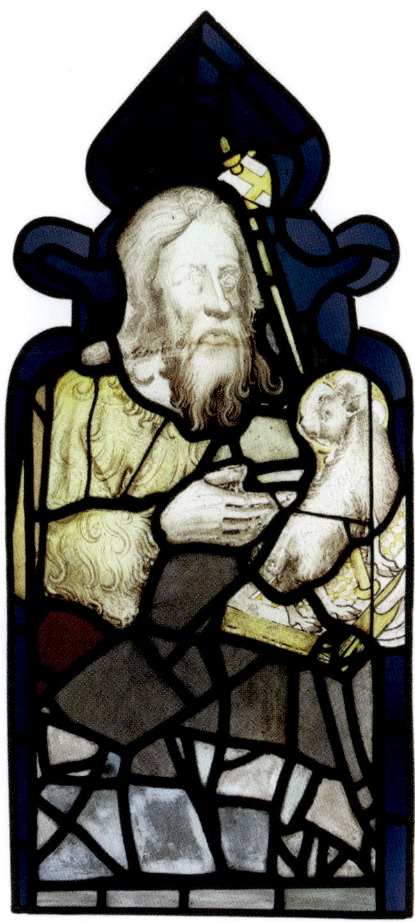

F2
St John the Baptist

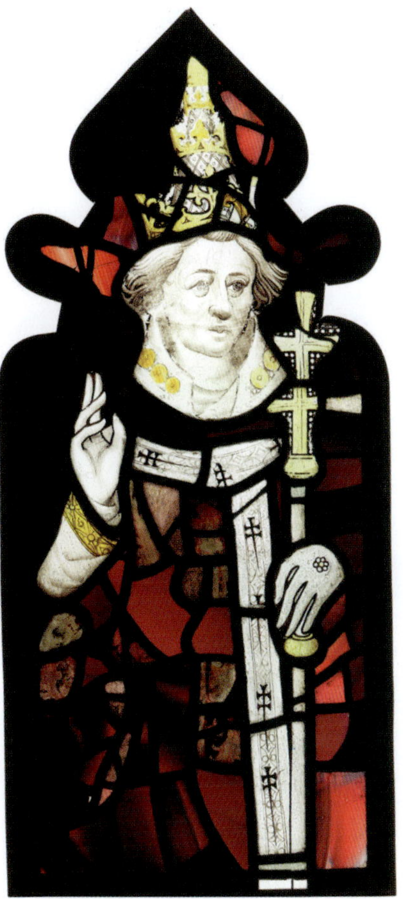

F3
Pope

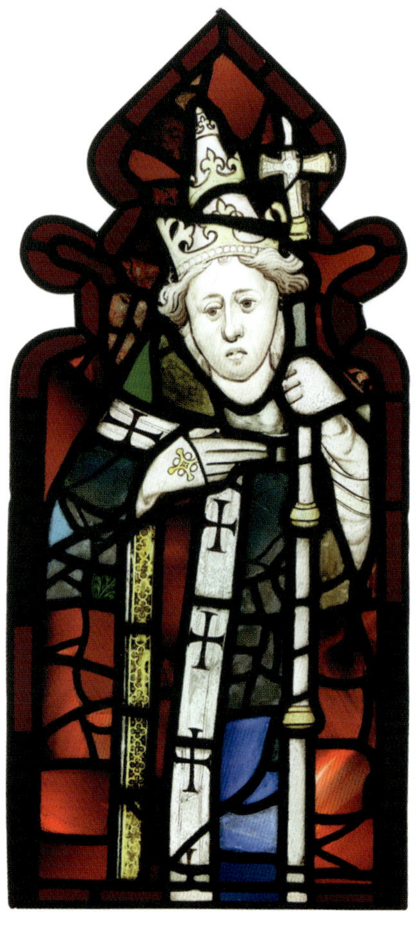

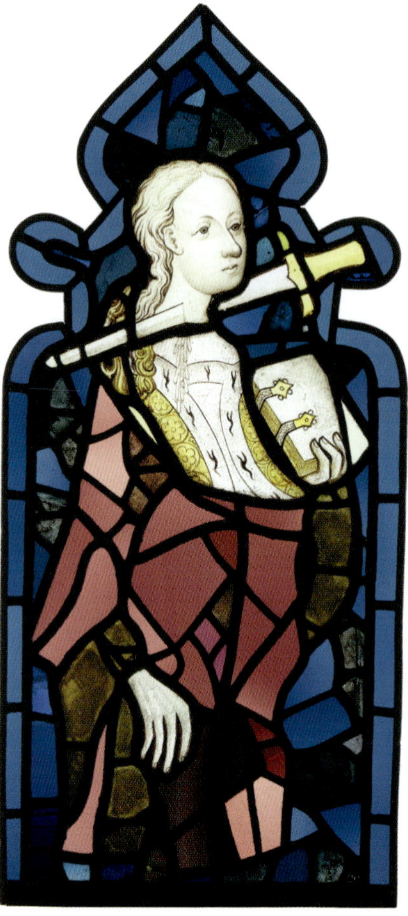

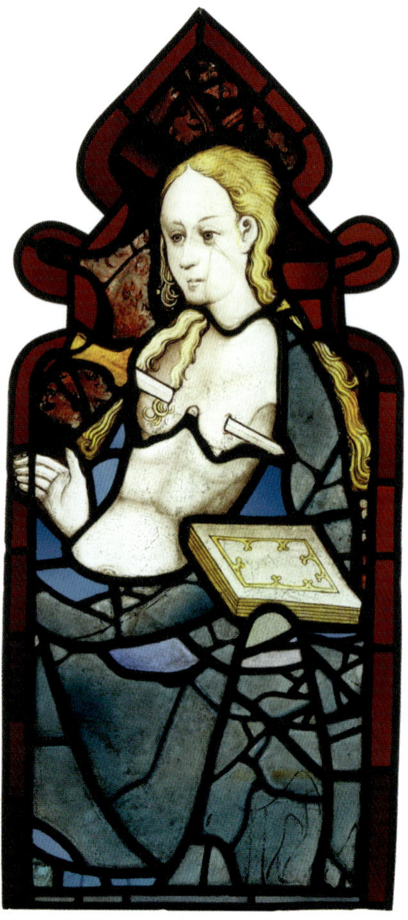

F4
Pope

F5
St Agnes or St Lucy

F6
St Agatha

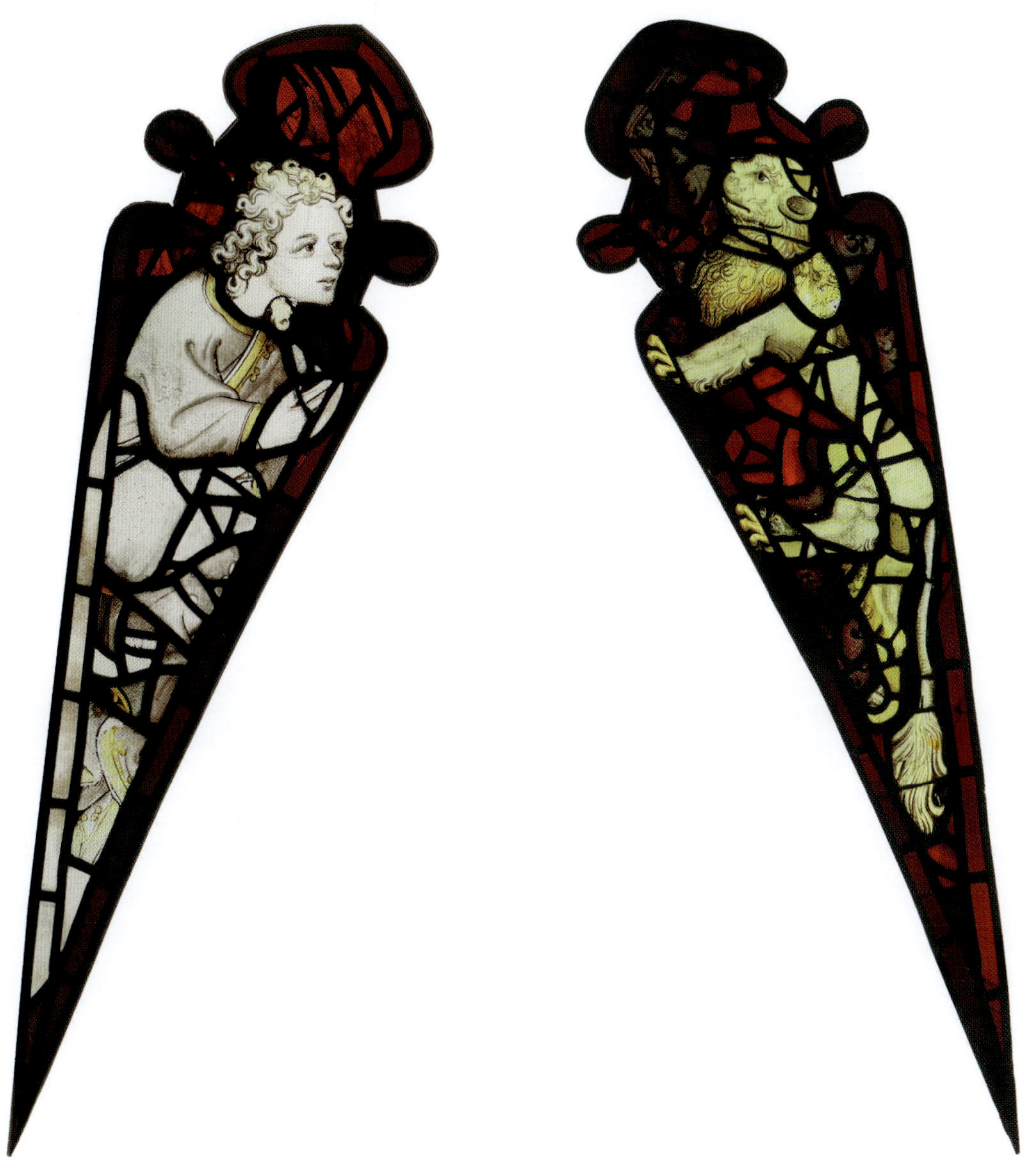

E1
Angel of St Matthew

E2
Lion of St Mark

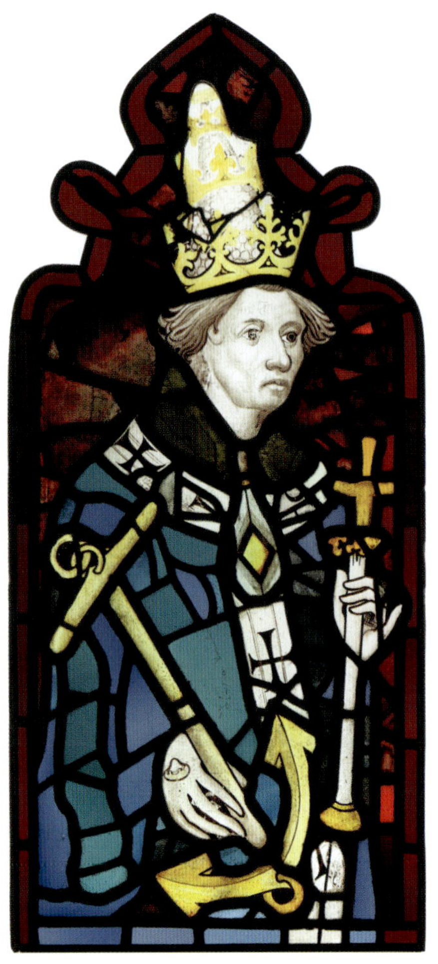

C1
St Clement

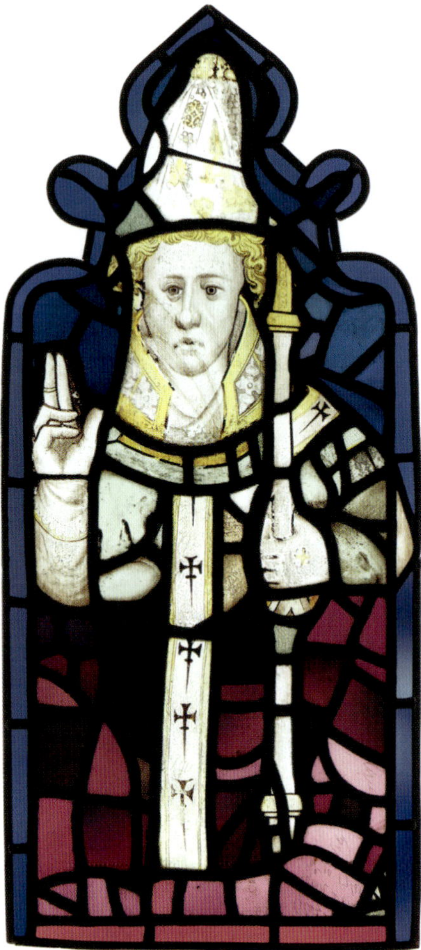

C3
Archbishop

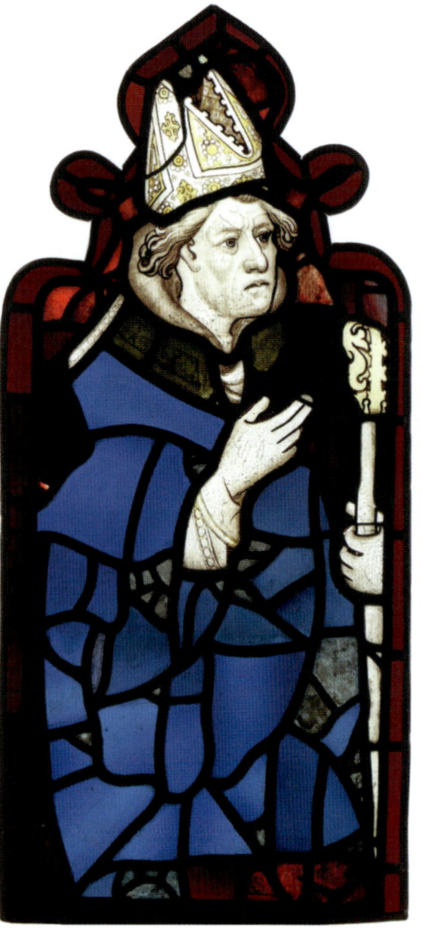

C4
Bishop

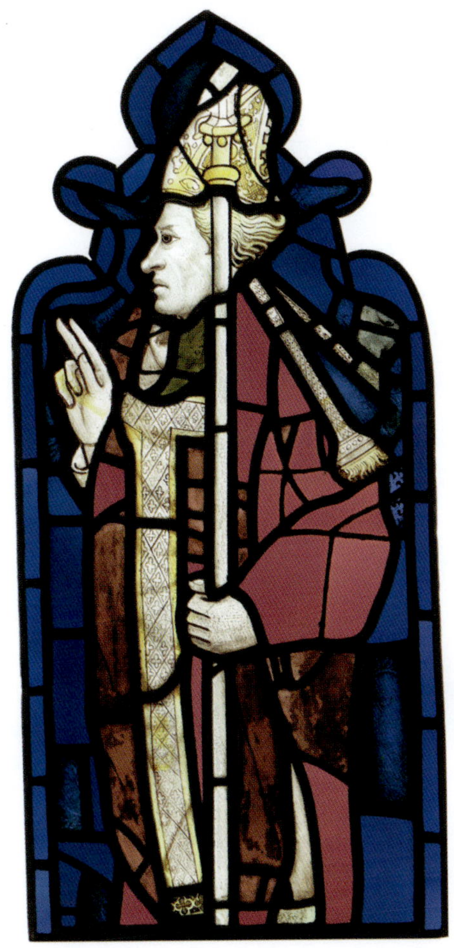

C6
Archbishop

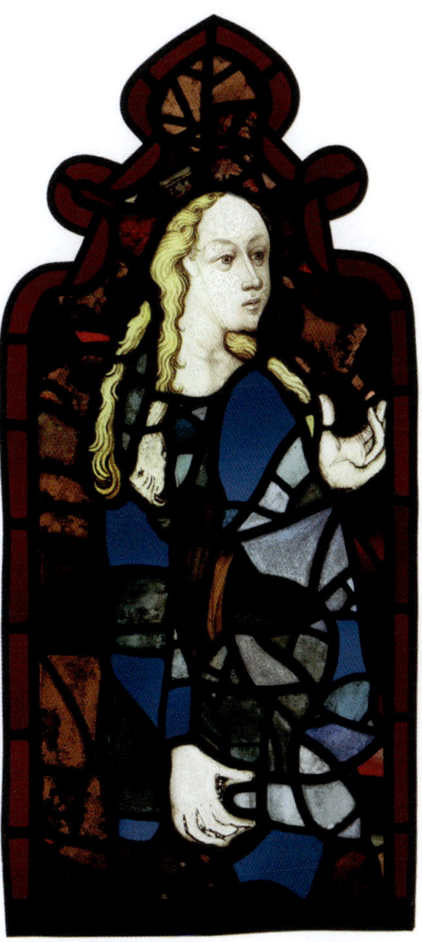

C7
Female Saint

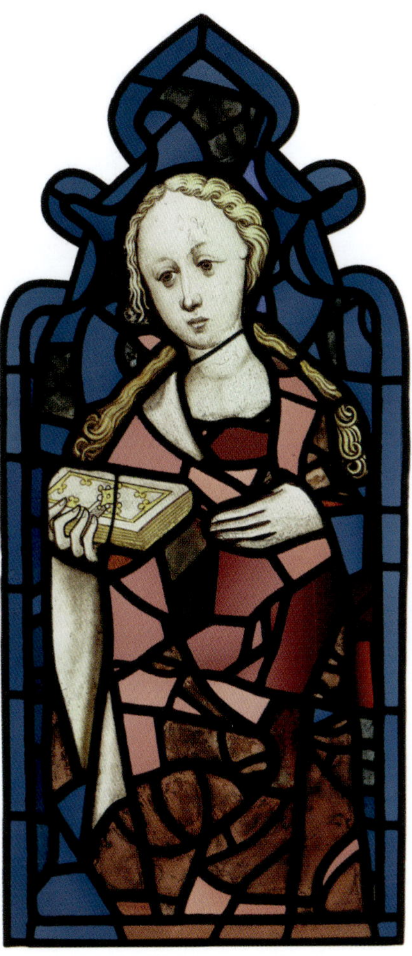

C9
Female Saint

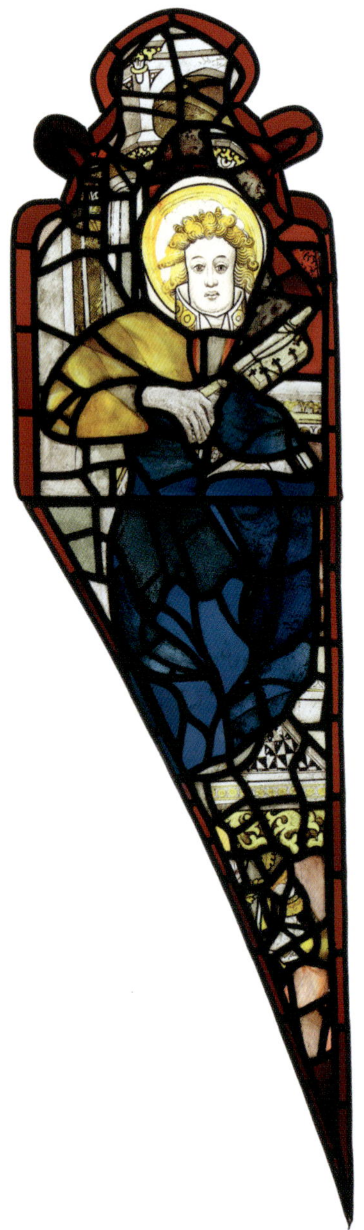

B1
St Peter

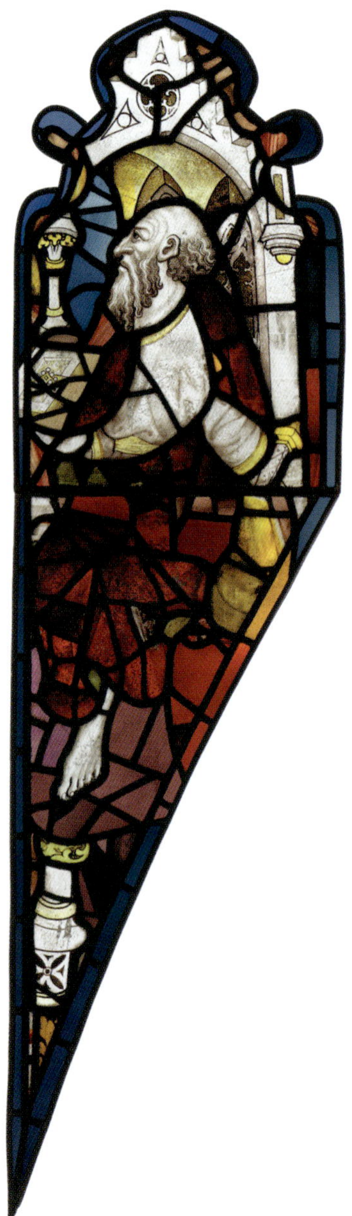

B2
St Paul

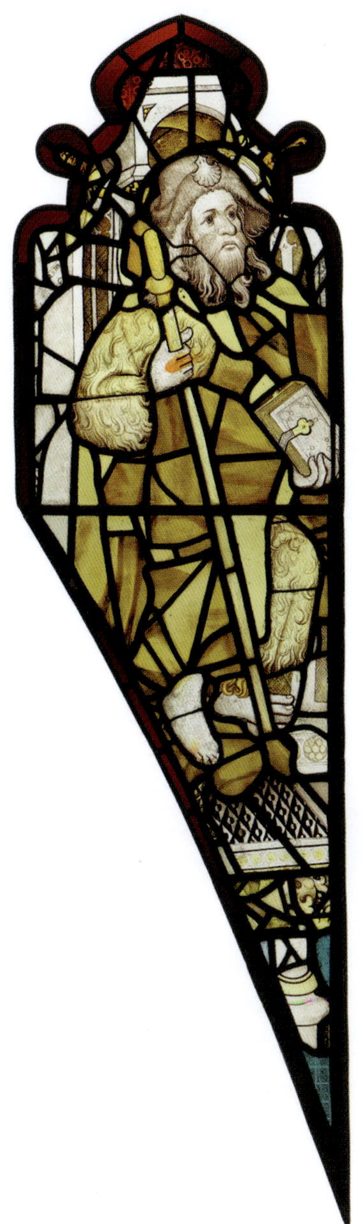

B3
St James the Greater

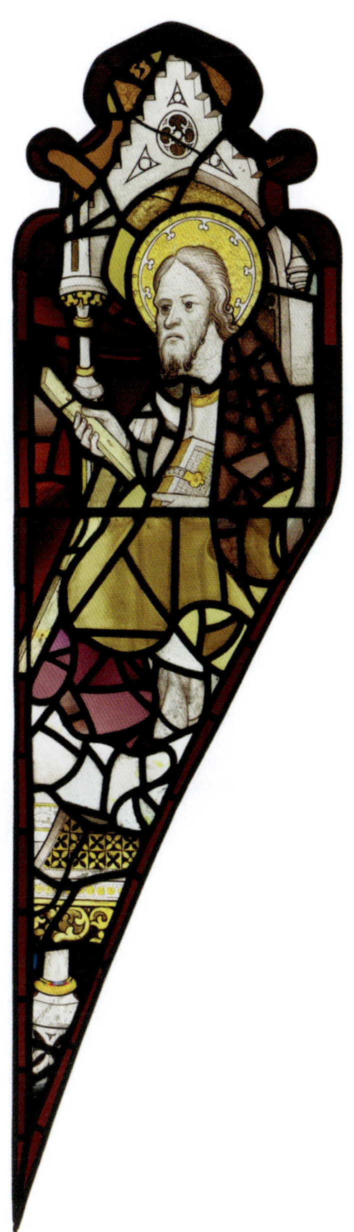

B4
St Thomas

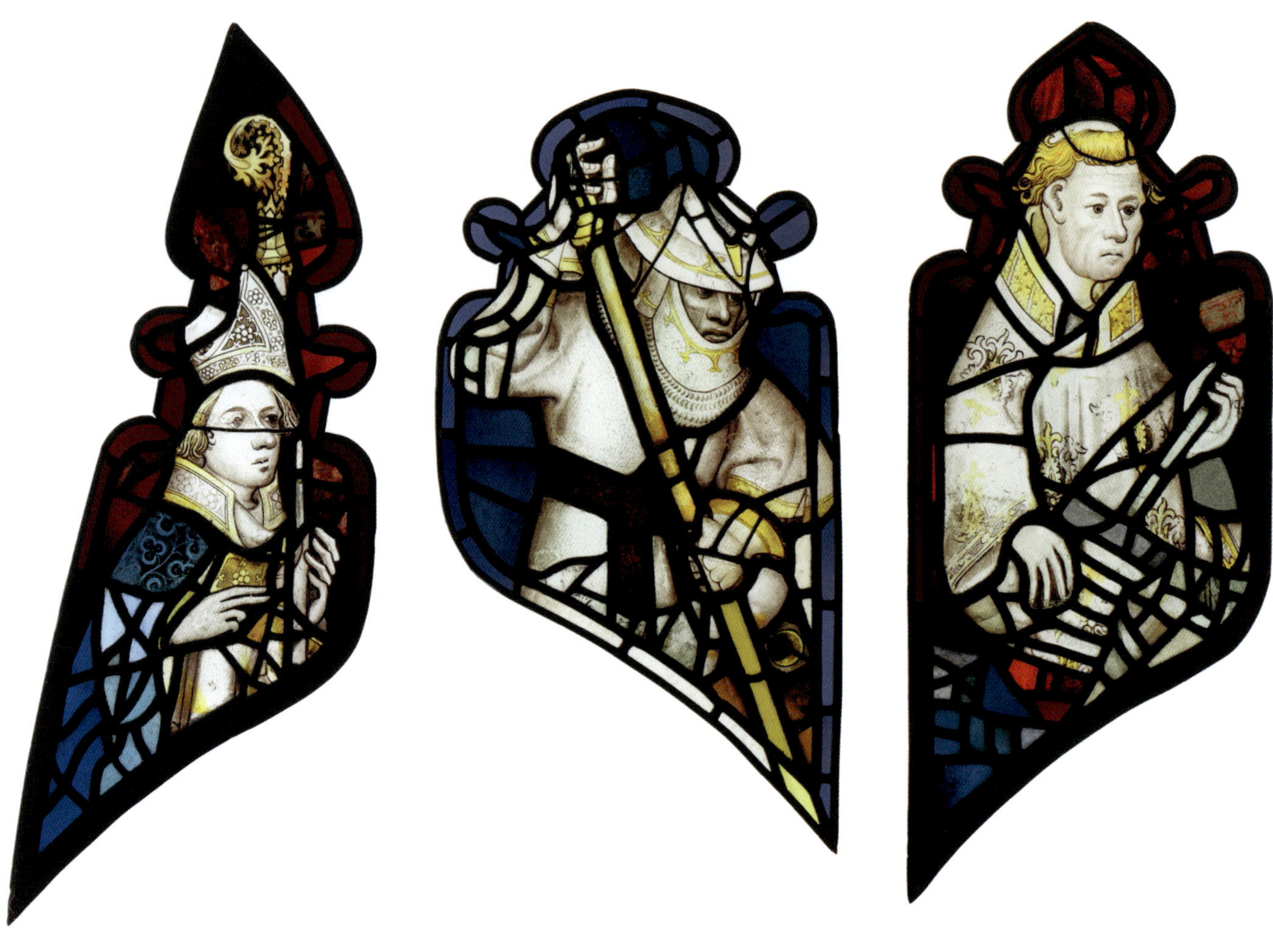

A1
Bishop

A2
St George

A3
St Lawrence

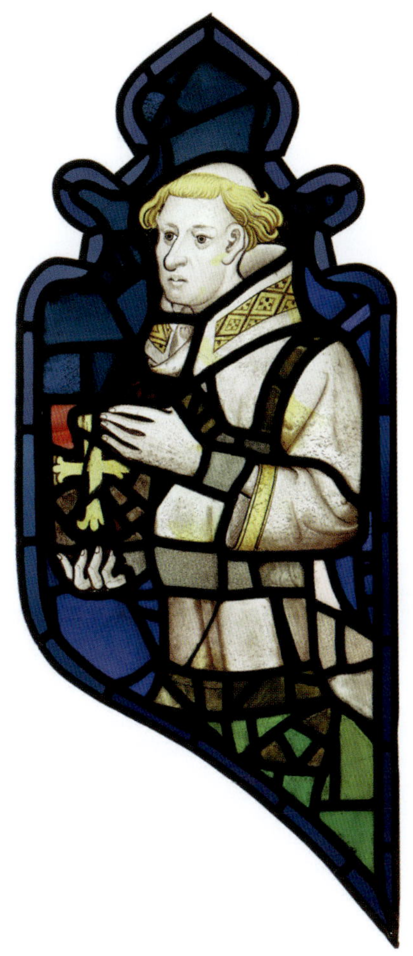

A4
Priest

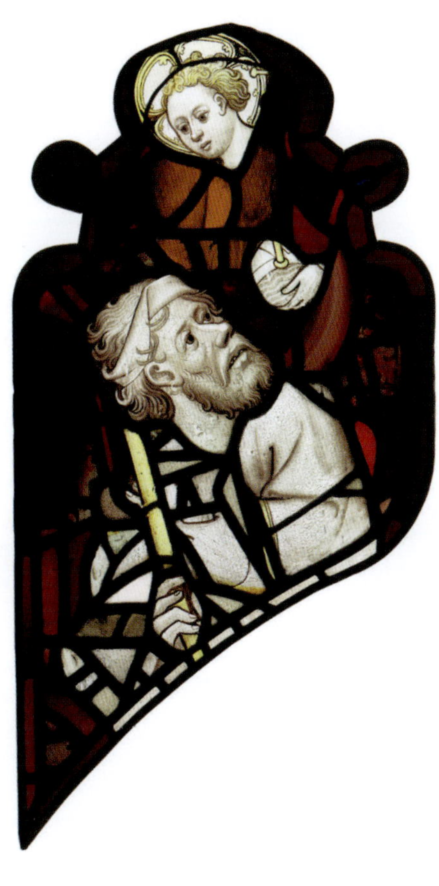

A5
St Christopher

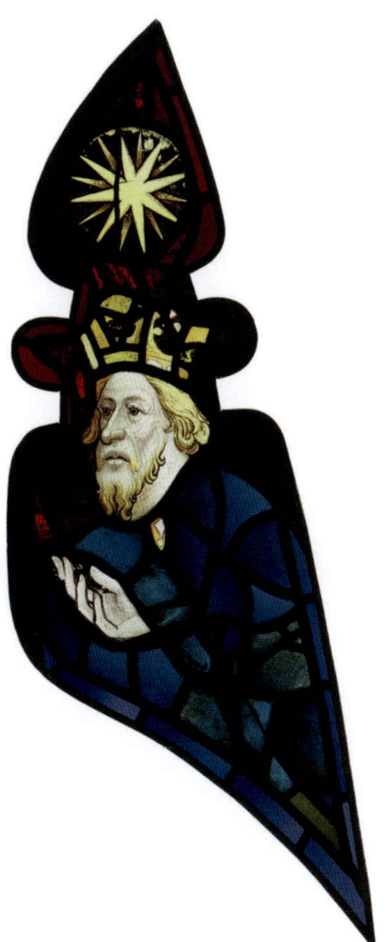

A6
King

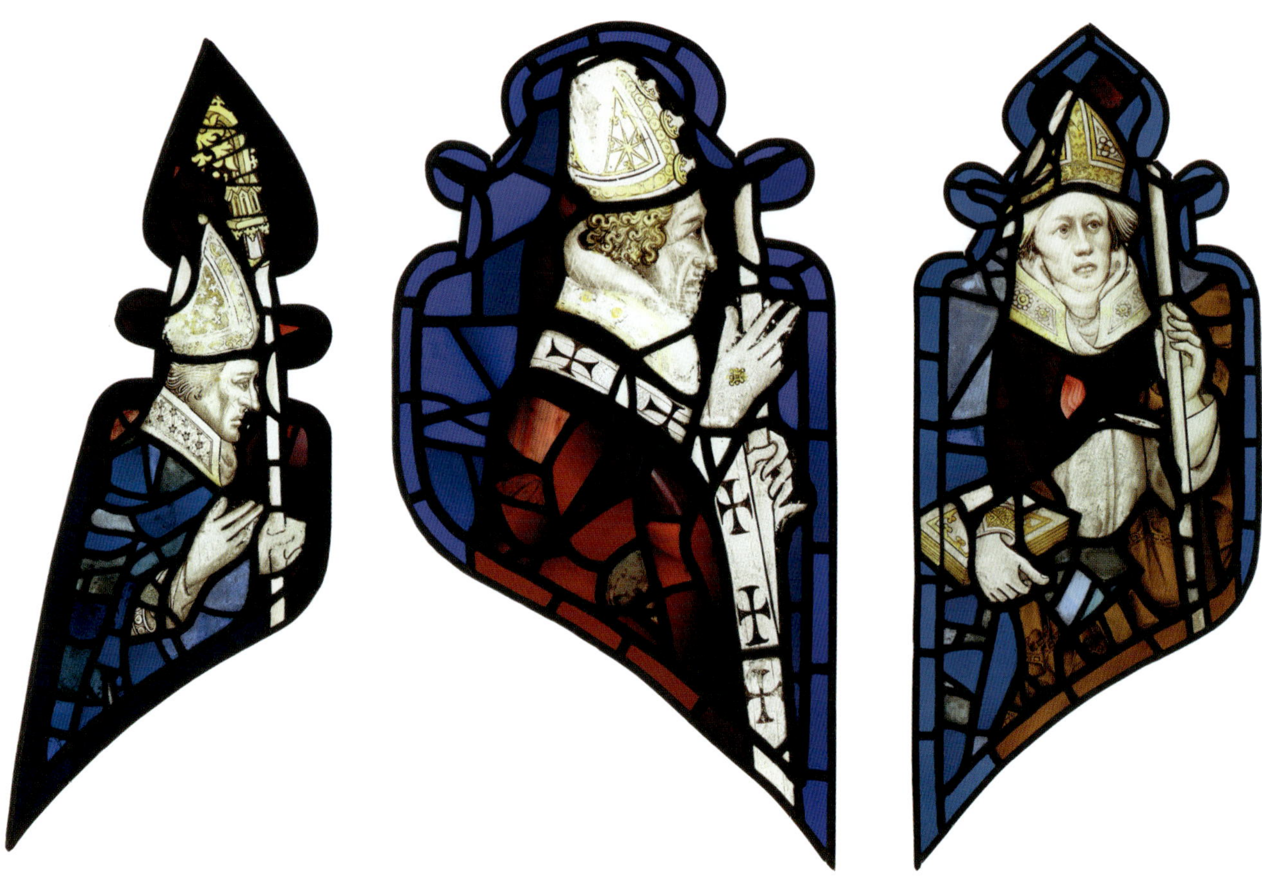

A7
Bishop

A8
Archbishop

A9
Bishop

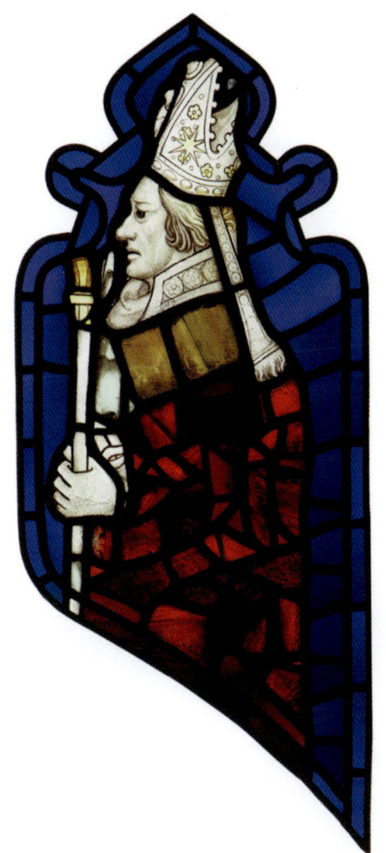

A10
Bishop

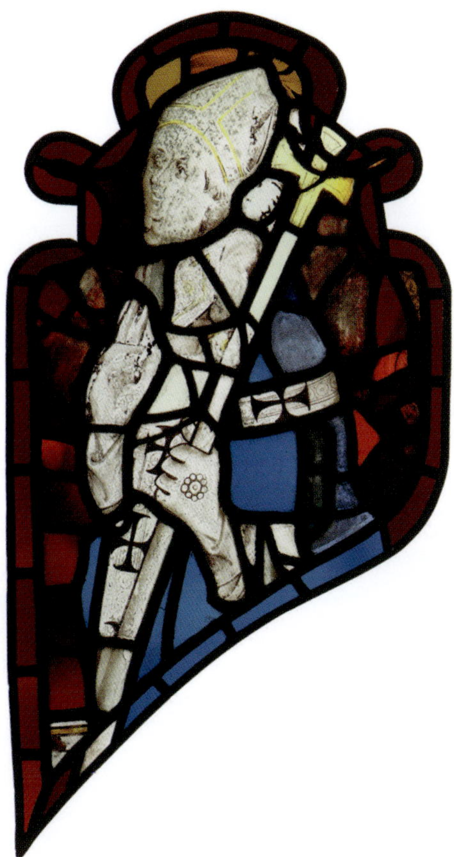

A11
Archbishop

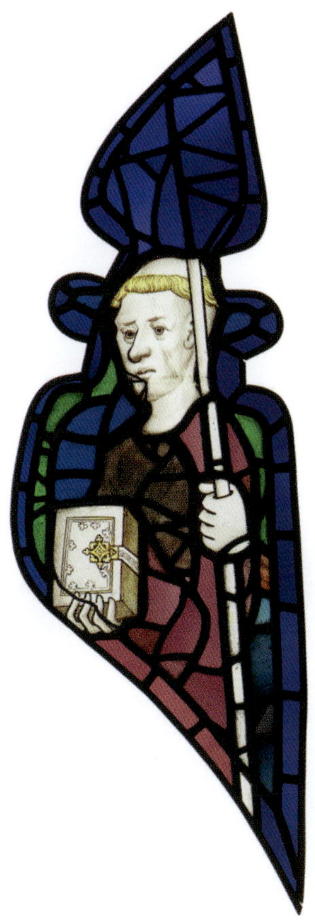

A12
Abbot

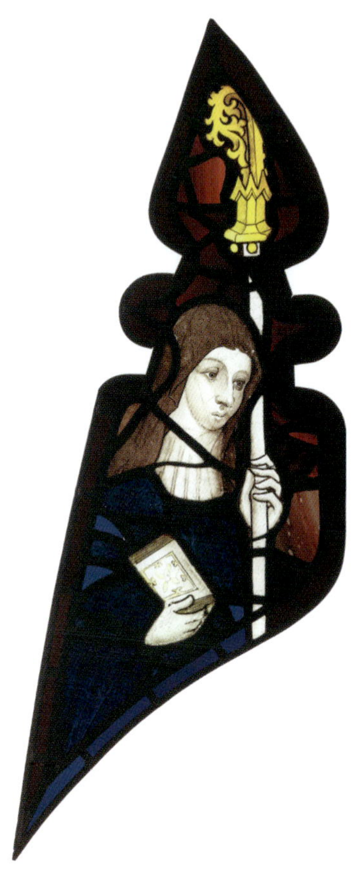

A13
Abbess

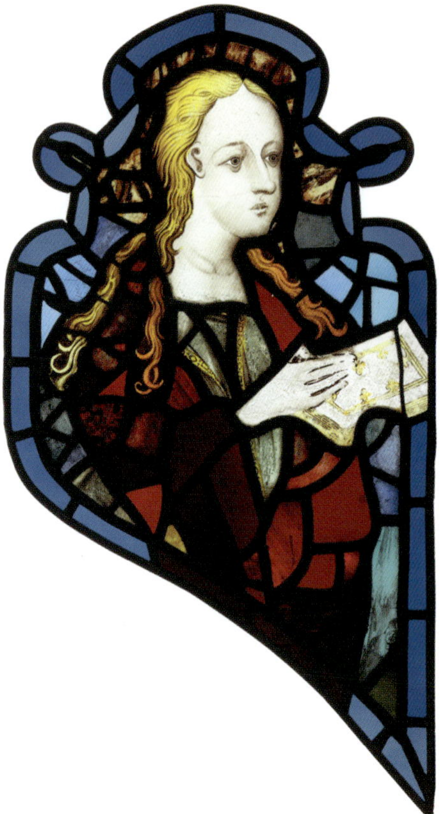

A14
Female Saint

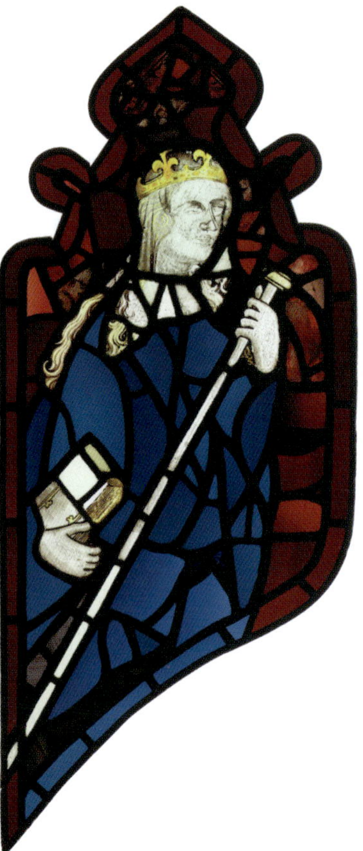

A15
St Margaret

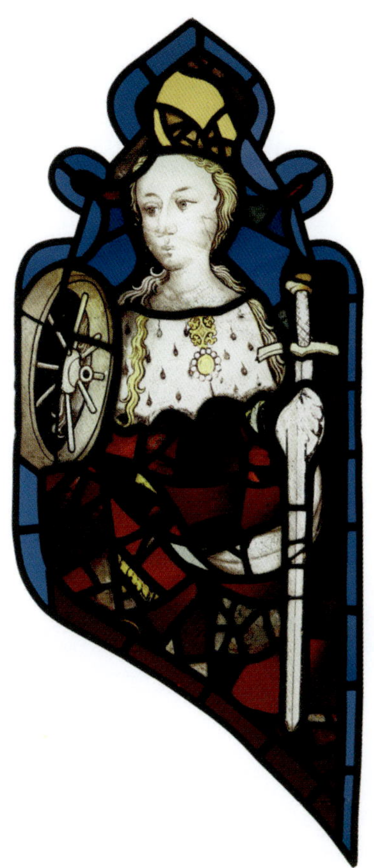

A16
St Katharine

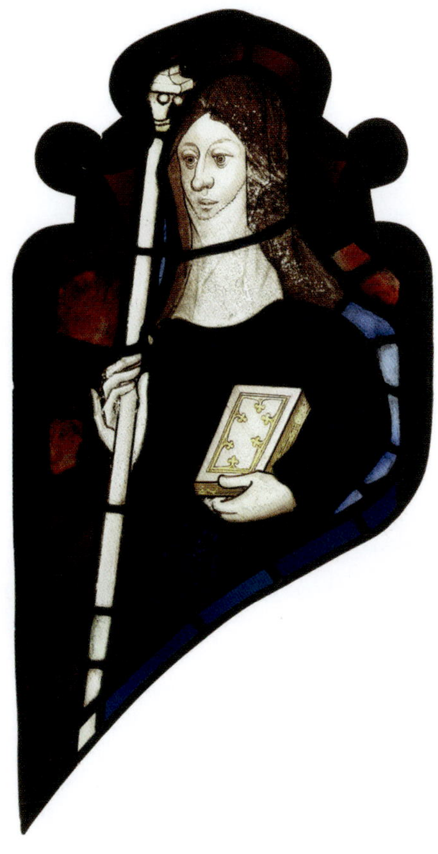

A17
Abbess

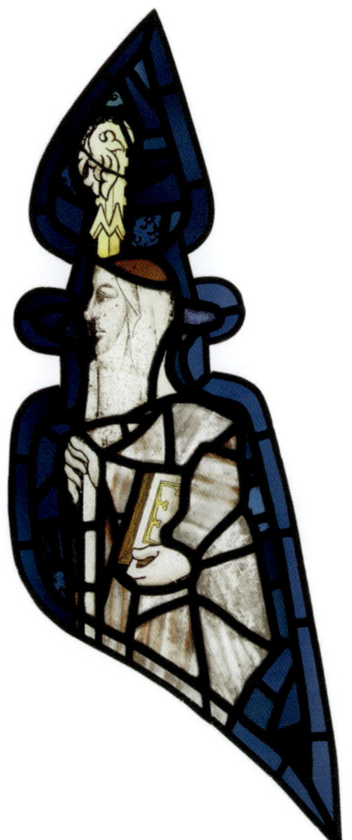

A18
Abbess

Catalogue

The Old Testament

The text used is that of the Douay-Rheims Bible, as this English translation is closest to the Latin Vulgate with which Thornton and his clients and collaborators would have been familiar.

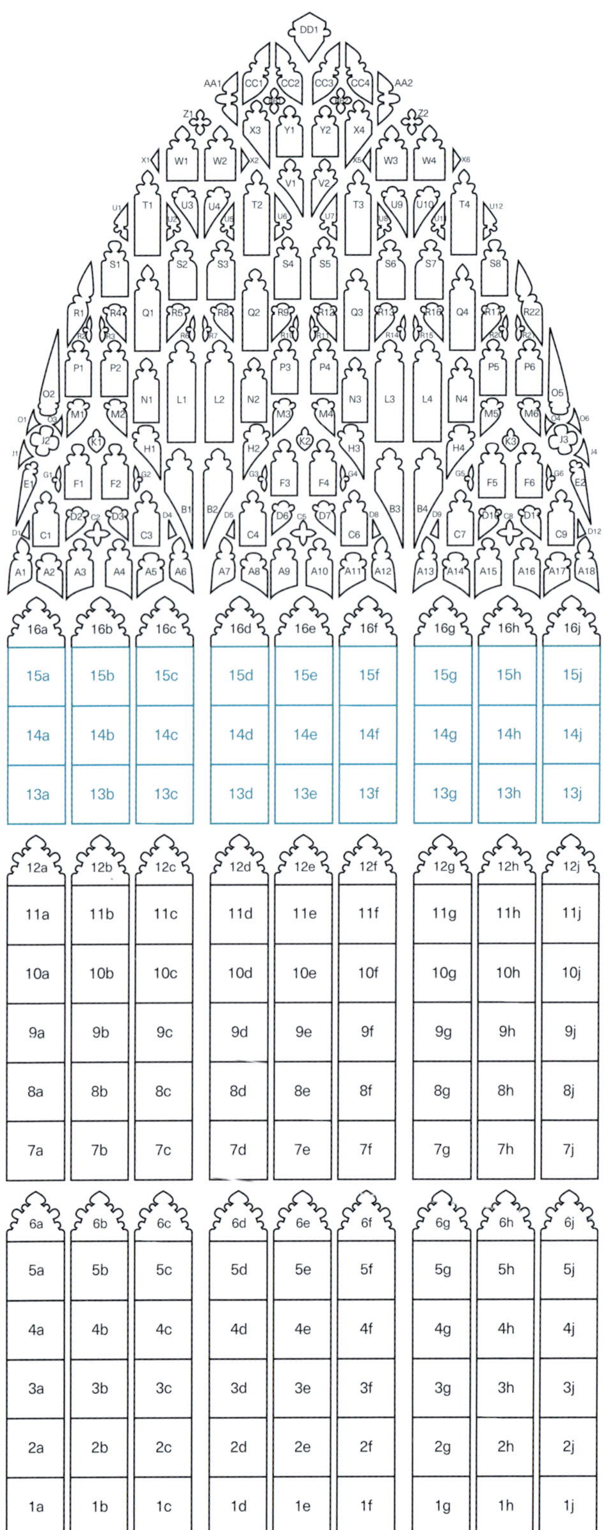

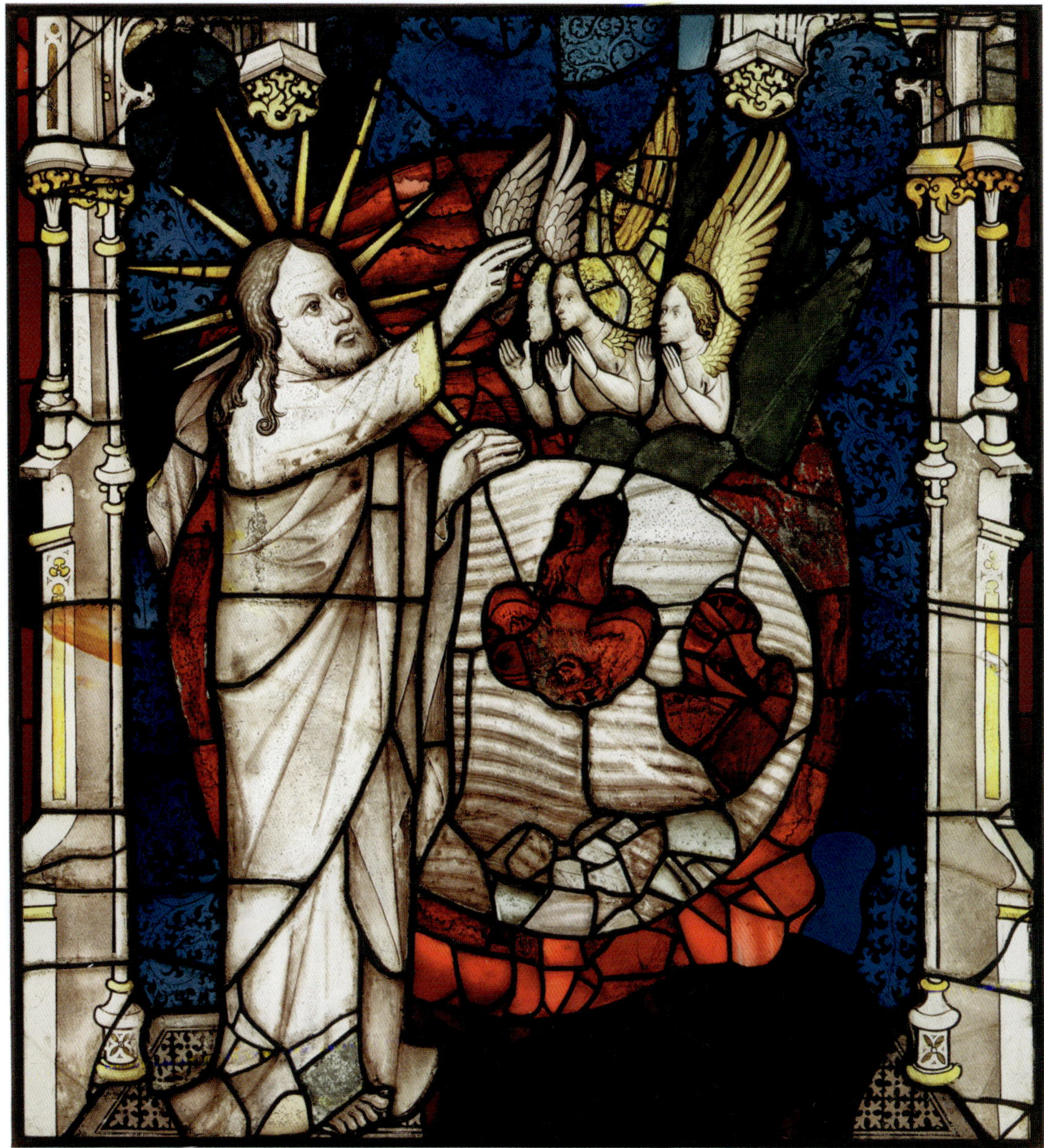

15a The First Day of Creation

In the beginning God created heaven, and earth. And the earth was void and empty, and darkness was upon the face of the deep; and the spirit of God moved over the waters. And God said: Be light made. And light was made. And God saw the light that it was good; and he divided the light from the darkness. And he called the light Day, and the darkness Night; and there was evening and morning one day.

Genesis 1:1–5

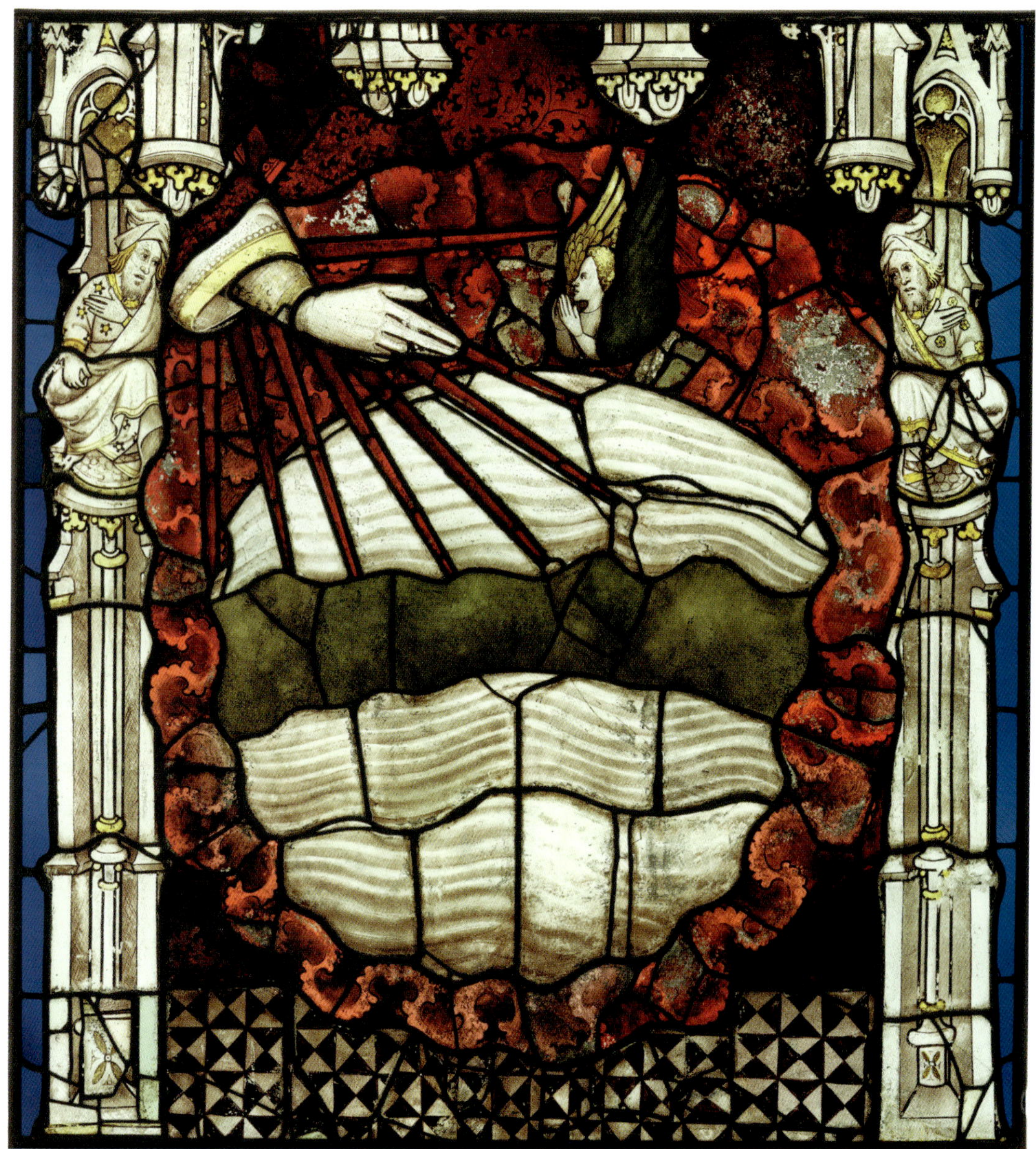

And God said, Let there be a firmament made amidst the waters, and let it divide the waters from the waters. And God made a firmament, and divided the waters that were under the firmament, from the waters that were above the firmament: and it was so. And God called the firmament, Heaven. And the evening and the morning were the second day.
Genesis 1:6–8

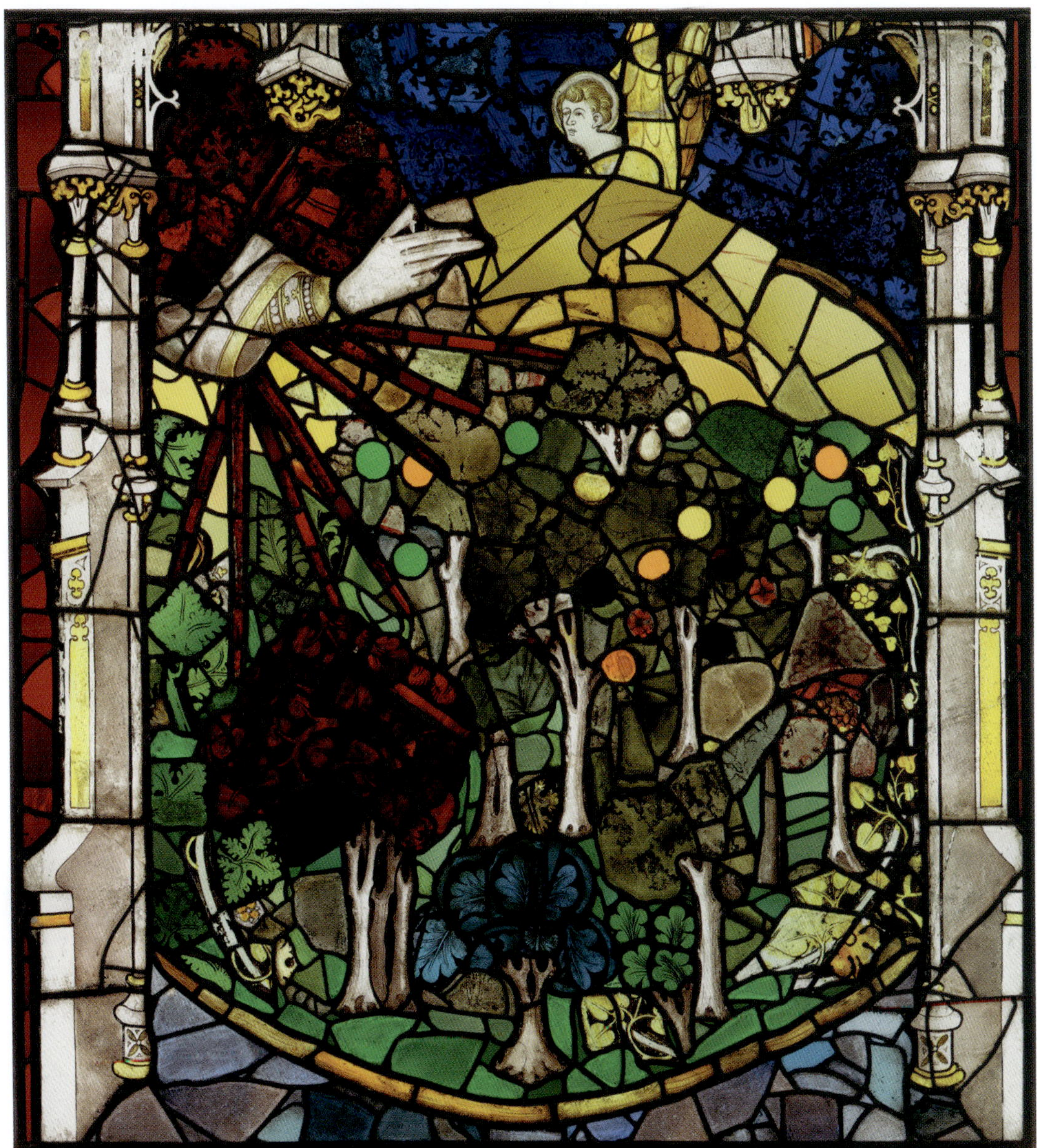

15c The Third Day of Creation

God also said: Let the waters that are under the heaven, be gathered together into one place, and let the dry land appear. And it was so done. And God called the dry land, Earth; and the gathering together of the waters, he called Seas. And God saw that it was good. And he said, Let the earth bring forth the green herb, and such as may seed, and the fruit tree yielding fruit after its kind, which may have seed in itself upon the earth. And it was so done. And the earth brought forth the green herb, and such as yieldeth seed according to its kind, and the tree that beareth fruit, having seed each one according to its kind. And God saw that it was good. And the evening and the morning were the third day.

Genesis 1:9–13

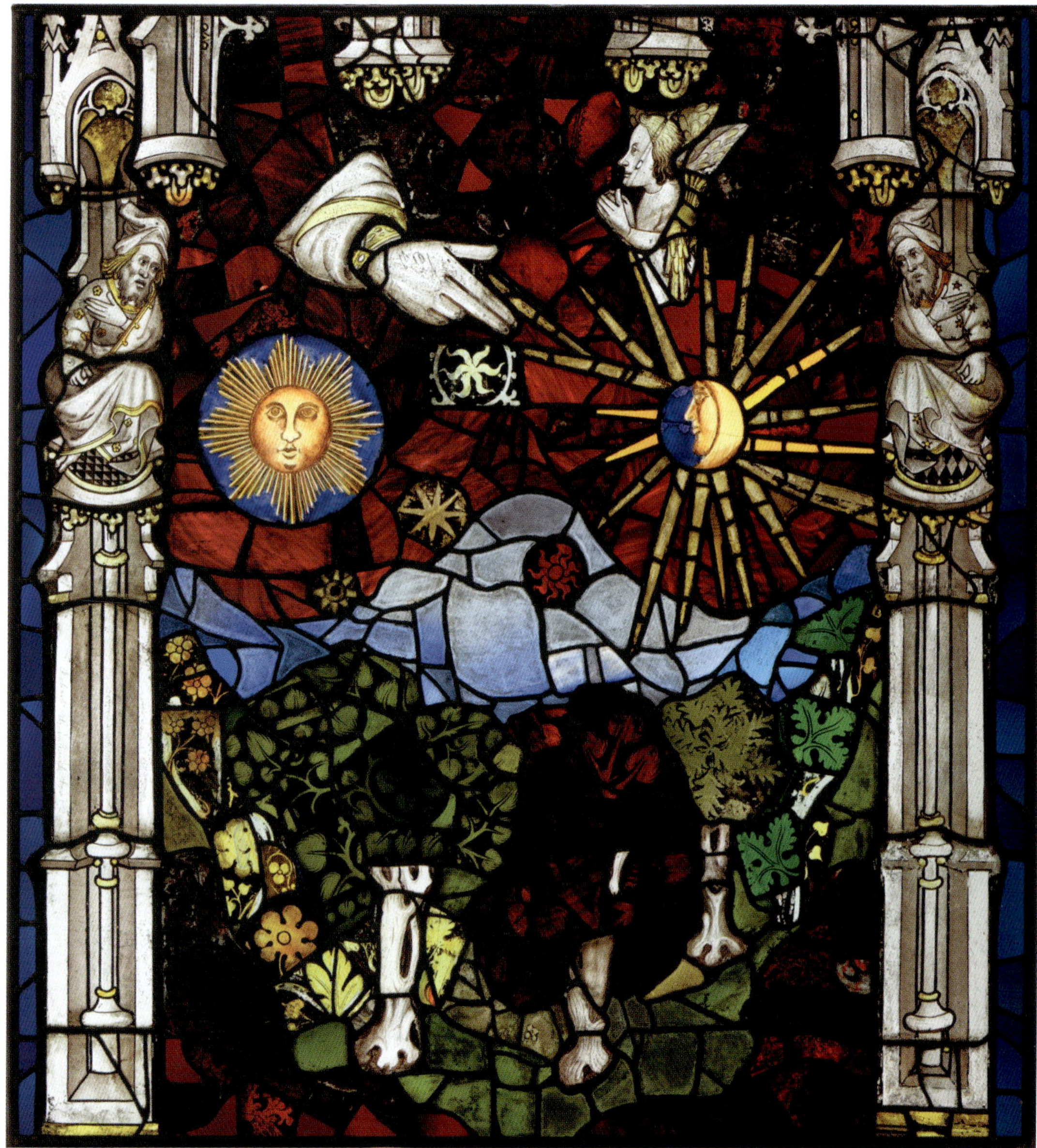

15d The Fourth Day of Creation

And God said, Let there be lights made in the firmament of the heaven, to divide the day and the night, and let them be for signs, and for seasons, and for days and years: To shine in the firmament of heaven, and to give light upon the earth. And it was so done. And God made two great lights: a greater light to rule the day, and a lesser light to rule the night: and the stars. And he set them in the firmament of heaven to shine upon the earth. And to rule the day and the night, and to divide the light and the darkness. And God saw that it was good. And the evening and morning were the fourth day.

Genesis 1:14–19

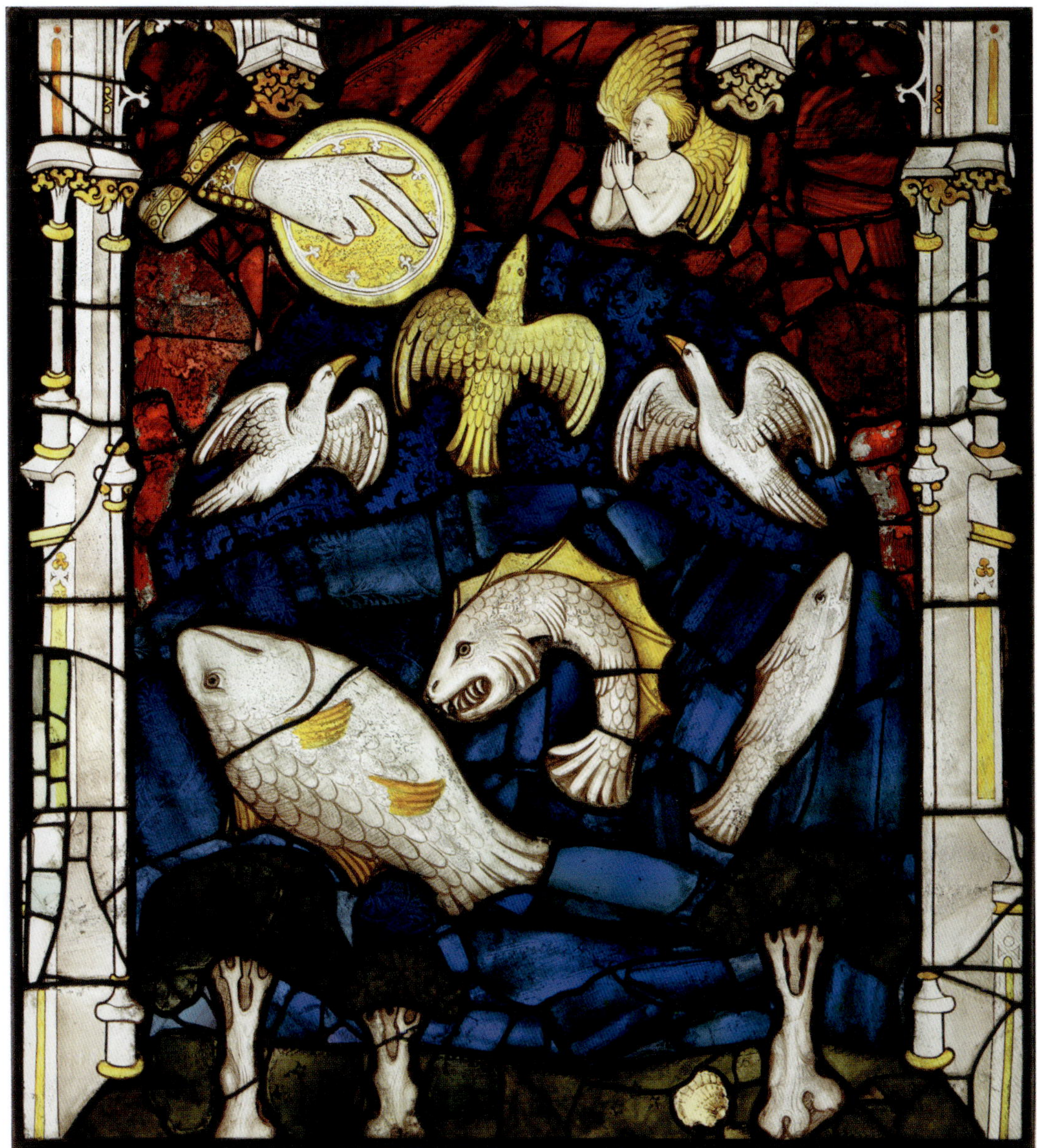

15e The Fifth Day of Creation

God also said, Let the waters bring forth the creeping creature having life, and the fowl that may fly above the earth under the firmament of heaven. And God created the great whales, and every living and moving creature, which the waters brought forth according to their kinds, and every winged fowl according to its kind. And God saw that it was good. And he blessed them, saying: increase and multiply, and fill the waters of the seas: and let the birds be multiplied upon the earth. And the evening and the morning were the fifth day.

Genesis 1:20–3

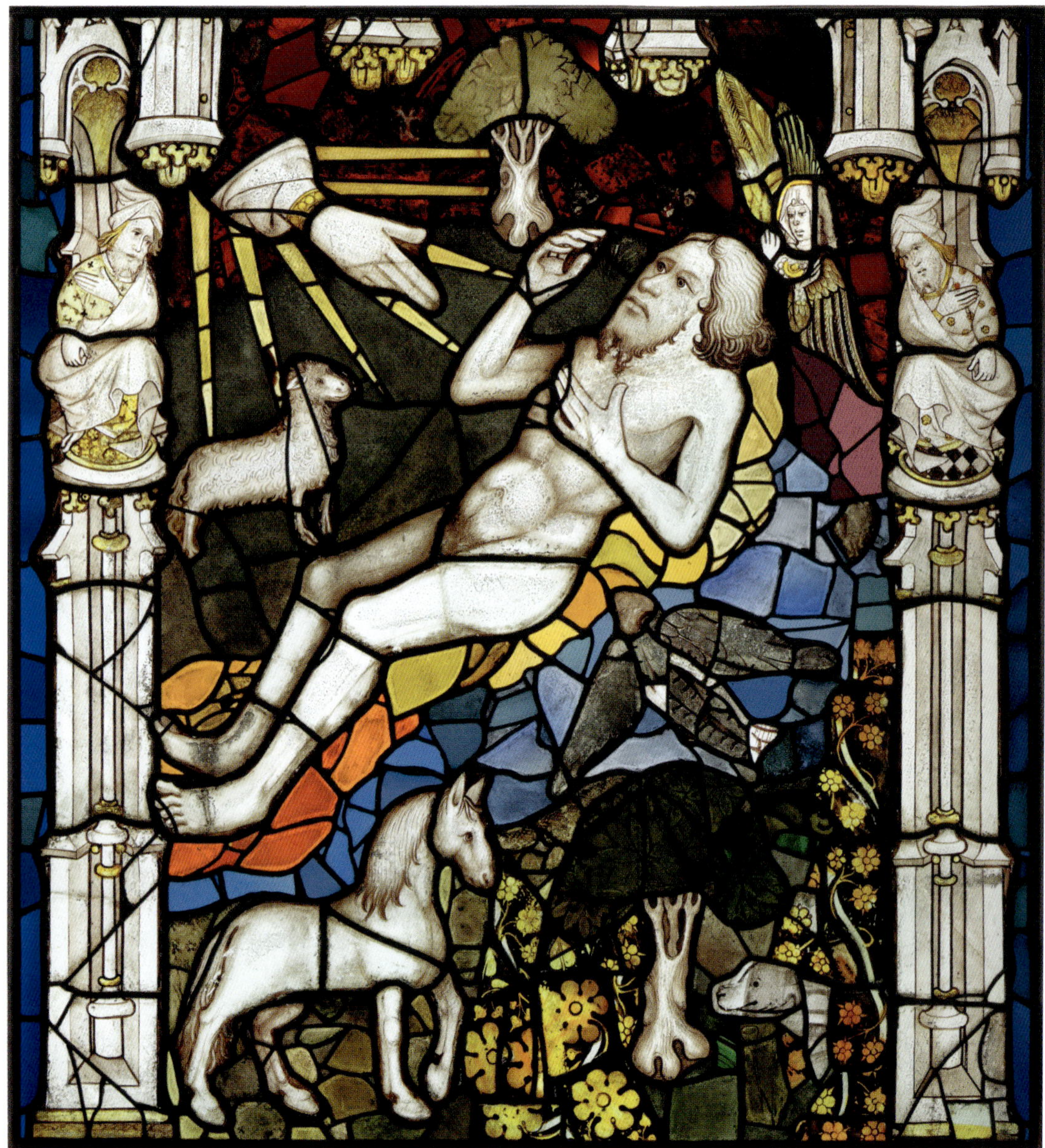

15f The Sixth Day of Creation

And God said: Let the earth bring forth the living creature in its kind, cattle and creeping things, and beasts of the earth according to their kinds. And it was so done. And God made the beasts of the earth according to their kinds, and cattle, and every thing that creepeth on the earth after its kind. And God saw that it was good. And he said, Let us make man to our image and likeness: and let him have dominion over the fishes of the sea, and the fowls of the air, and the beasts, and the whole earth, and over every creeping creature that moveth upon the earth. And God created man to his own image: to the image of God he created him: male and female he created them. And God blessed them, saying: Increase and multiply, and fill the earth, and subdue it: and rule over the fishes of the sea, and the fowls of the air, and all living creatures that move upon the earth. And God said: Behold I have given you every herb bearing seed upon the earth, and all trees that have in themselves seed of their own kind, to be your meat: And to all beasts of the earth, and to every fowl of the air, and to all that move upon the earth, and wherein there is life, that they may have to feed upon. And it was so done. And God saw all the things that he had made, and they were very good. And the evening and the morning were the sixth day.

Genesis 1:24–31

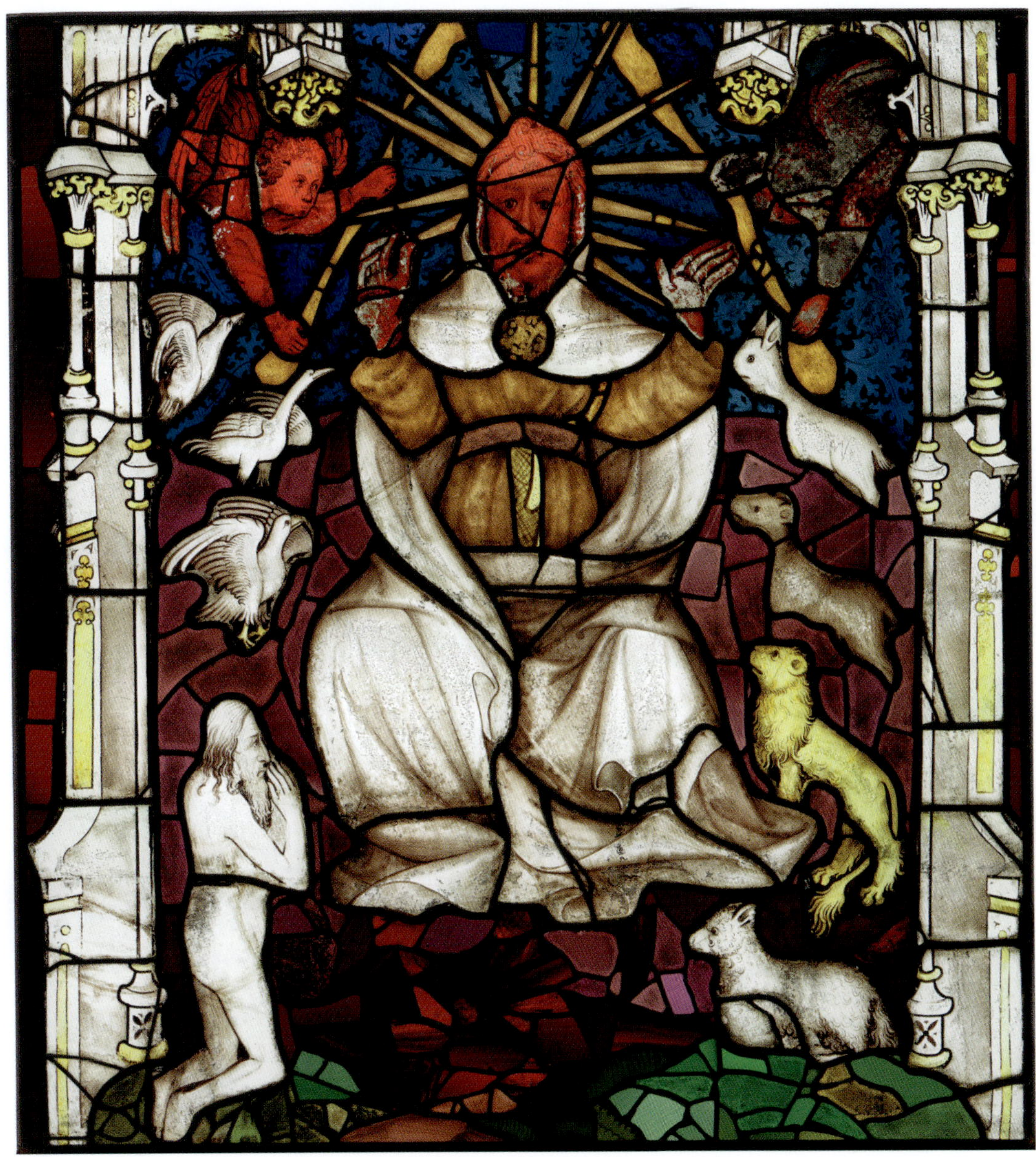

15g The Seventh Day

So the heavens and the earth were finished, and all the furniture of them. And on the seventh day God ended his work which he had made: and he rested on the seventh day from all his work which he had done. And he blessed the seventh day, and sanctified it: because in it he had rested from all his work which God created and made.

Genesis 2:1–3

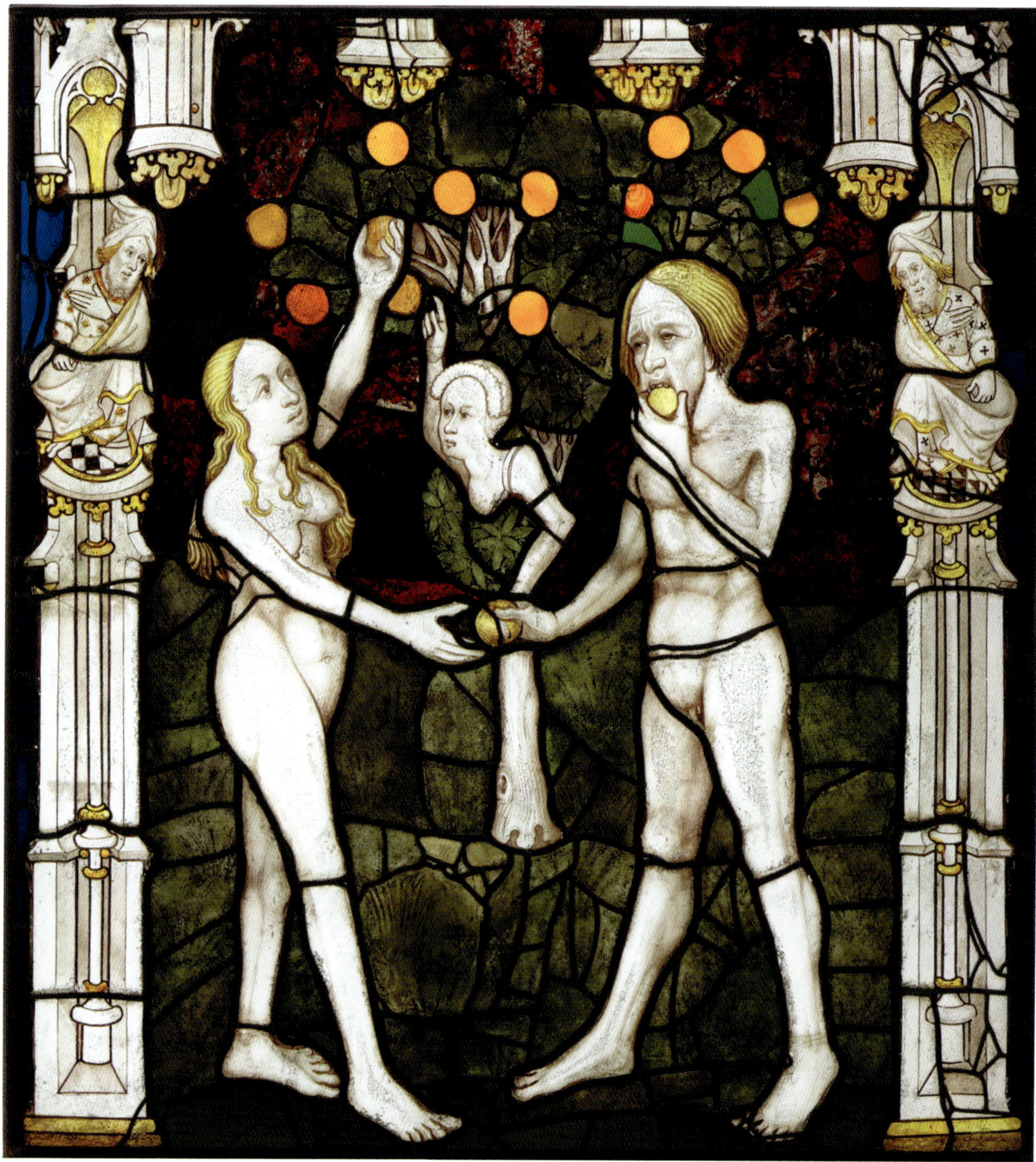

15h The Temptation and Fall

Now the serpent was more subtle than any of the beasts of the earth which the Lord God had made. And he said unto the woman, Why hath God commanded you, that you should not eat of every tree of paradise? And the woman answered him, saying, Of the fruit of the trees that are in paradise we do eat: But of the fruit of the tree which is in the midst of paradise, God hath commanded us that we should not eat; and that we should not touch it, lest perhaps we die. And the serpent said to the woman: No you shall not die the death. For God doth know that in what day soever you shall eat thereof, your eyes shall be opened: and you shall be as Gods, knowing good and evil. And the woman saw that the tree was good to eat, and fair to the eyes, and delightful to behold: and she took of the fruit thereof, and did eat, and gave to her husband who did eat.

Genesis 3:1–6

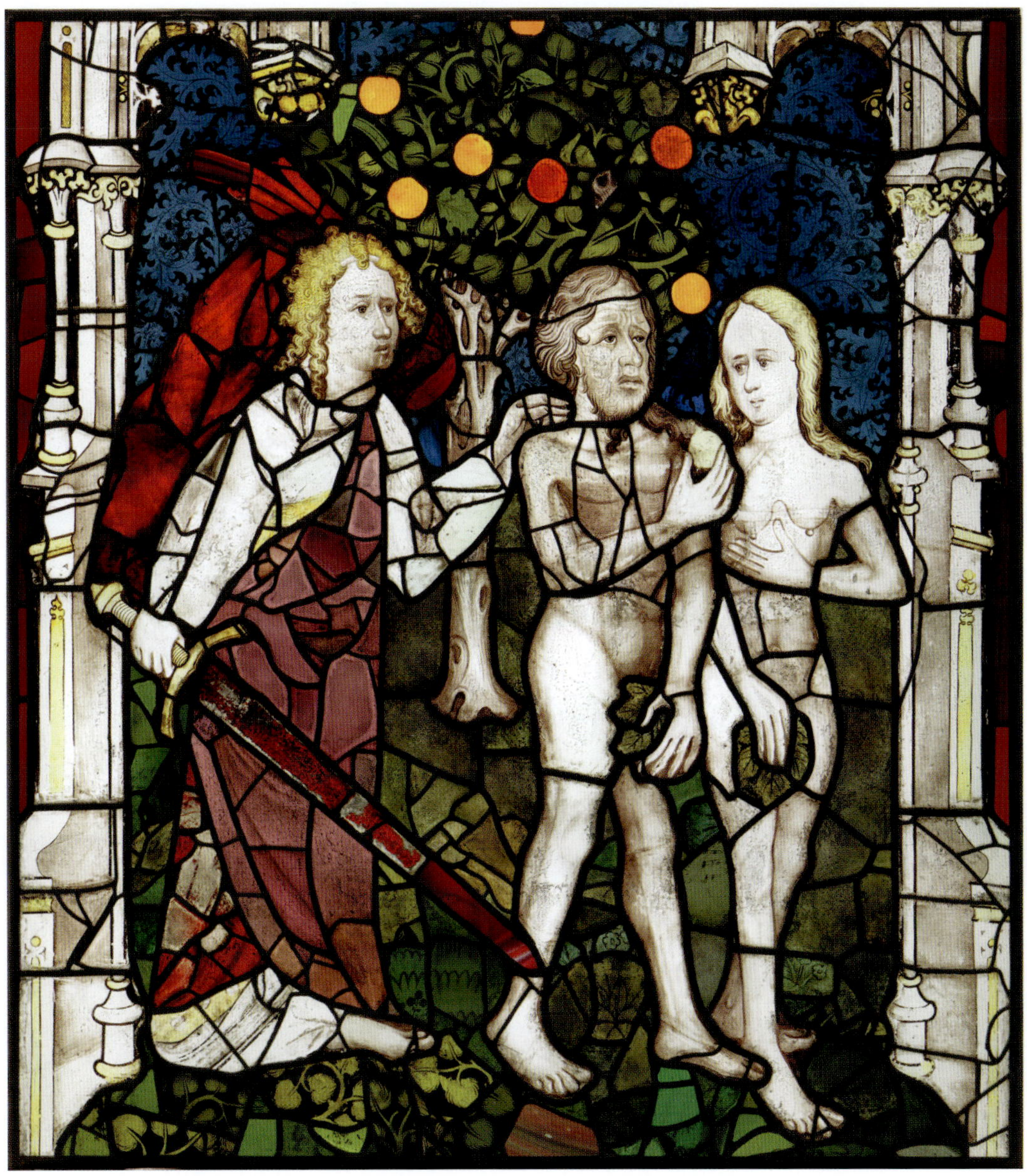

15j The Expulsion of Adam and Eve from Paradise
And the Lord God sent him out of the paradise of pleasure, to till the earth from which he was taken. And he cast out Adam; and he placed before the paradise of pleasure Cherubims, and a flaming sword, turning every way, to keep the way of the tree of life.
Genesis 3:23–4

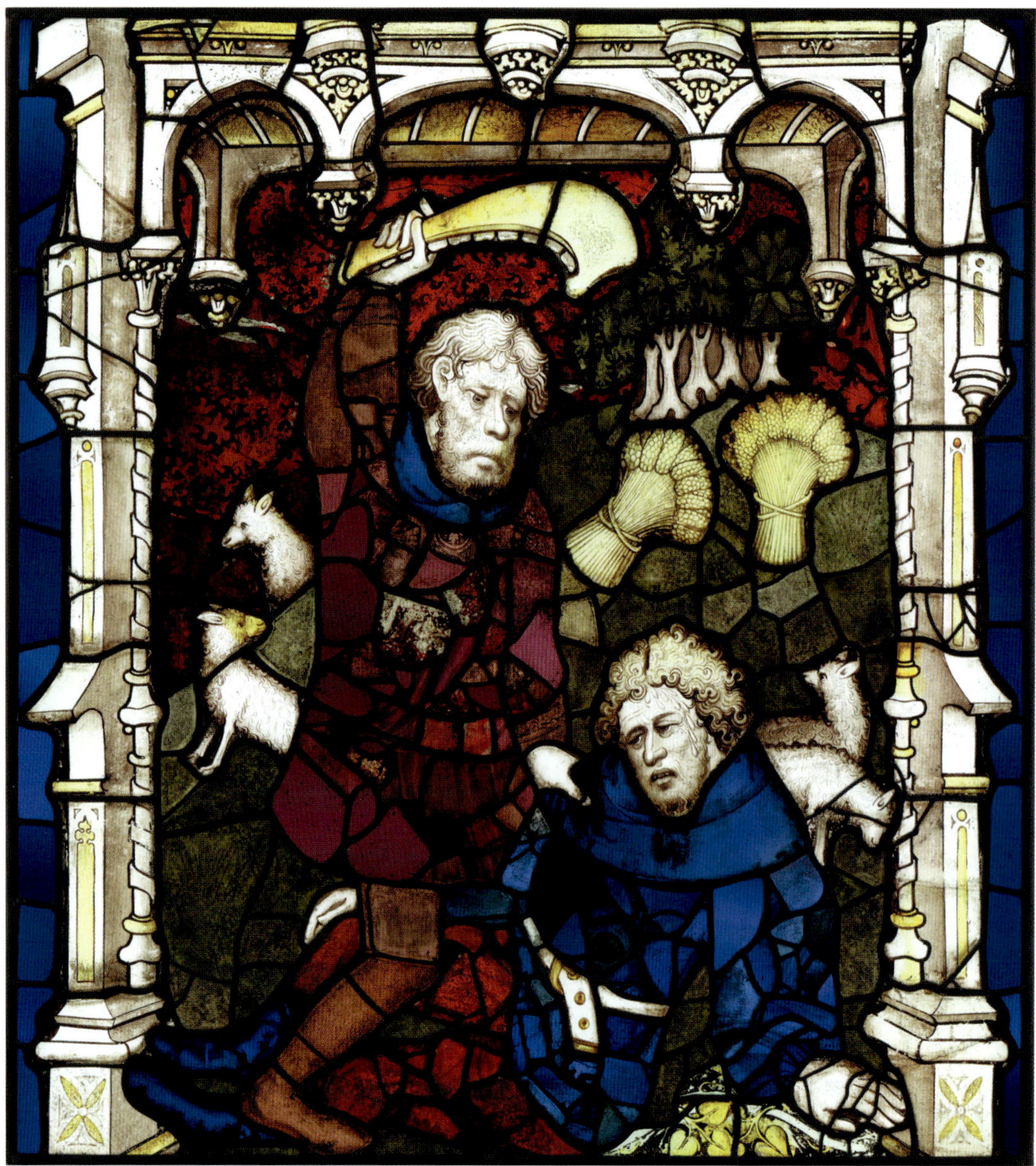

14a Cain Murders Abel

And Adam knew Eve his wife: who conceived and brought forth Cain, saying: I have gotten a man through God. And again she brought forth his brother Abel. And Abel was a shepherd, and Cain a husbandman. And it came to pass after many days, that Cain offered, of the fruits of the earth, gifts to the Lord. Abel also offered of the firstlings of his flock, and of their fat: and the Lord had respect to Abel, and to his offerings. But to Cain and his offerings he had no respect: and Cain was exceedingly angry, and his countenance fell. And the Lord said to him: Why art thou angry? and why is thy countenance fallen? If thou do well, shalt thou not receive? but if ill, shall not sin forthwith be present at the door? but the lust thereof shall be under thee, and thou shalt have dominion over it. And Cain said to Abel his brother: Let us go forth abroad. And when they were in the field, Cain rose up against his brother Abel, and slew him.
Genesis 4:1–8

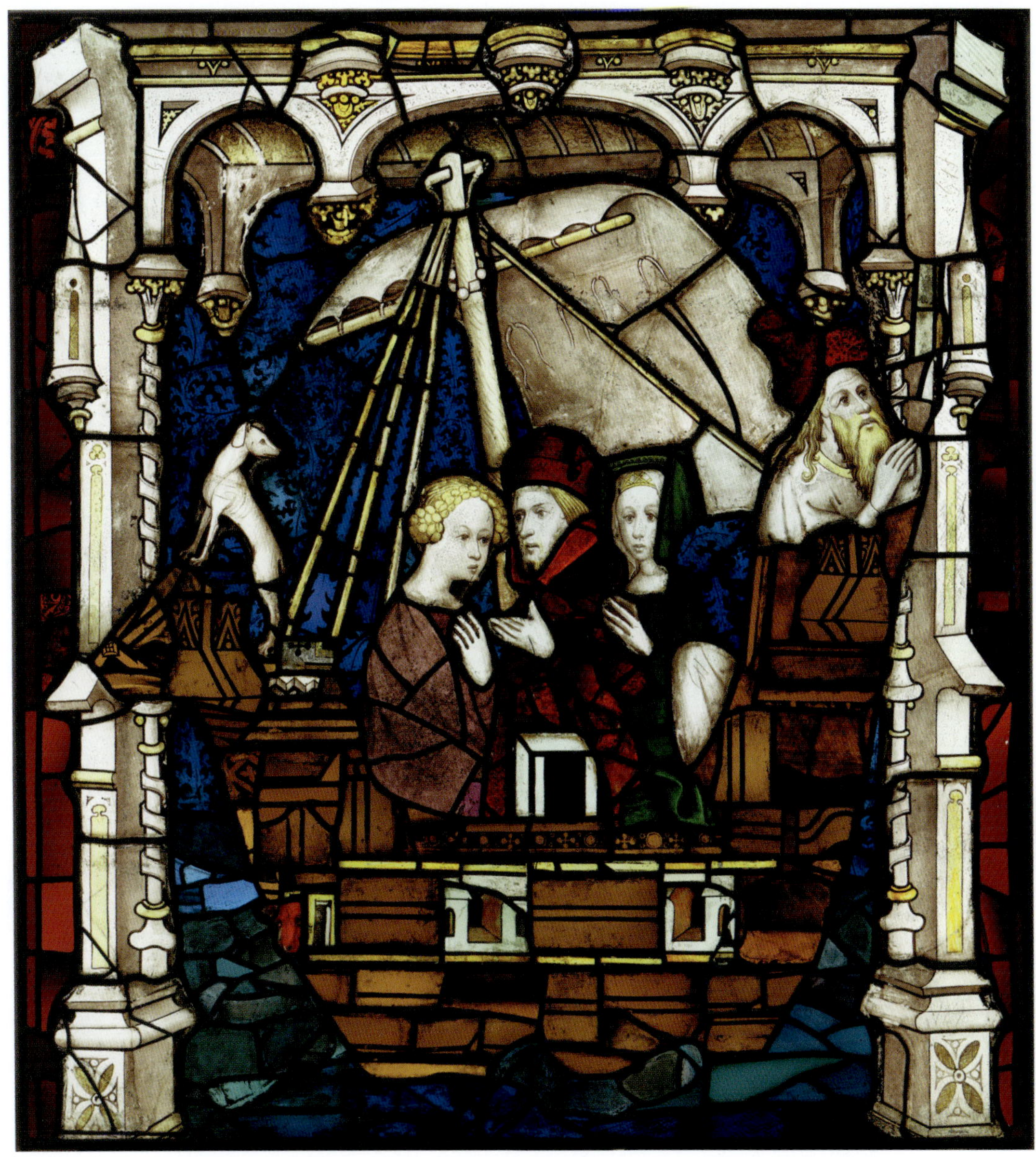

14b Noah in the Ark

And God remembered Noe, and all the living creatures, and all the cattle which were with him in the ark, and brought a wind upon the earth, and the waters were abated. The fountains also of the deep, and the flood gates of heaven were shut up, and the rain from heaven was restrained.

Genesis 8:1–2

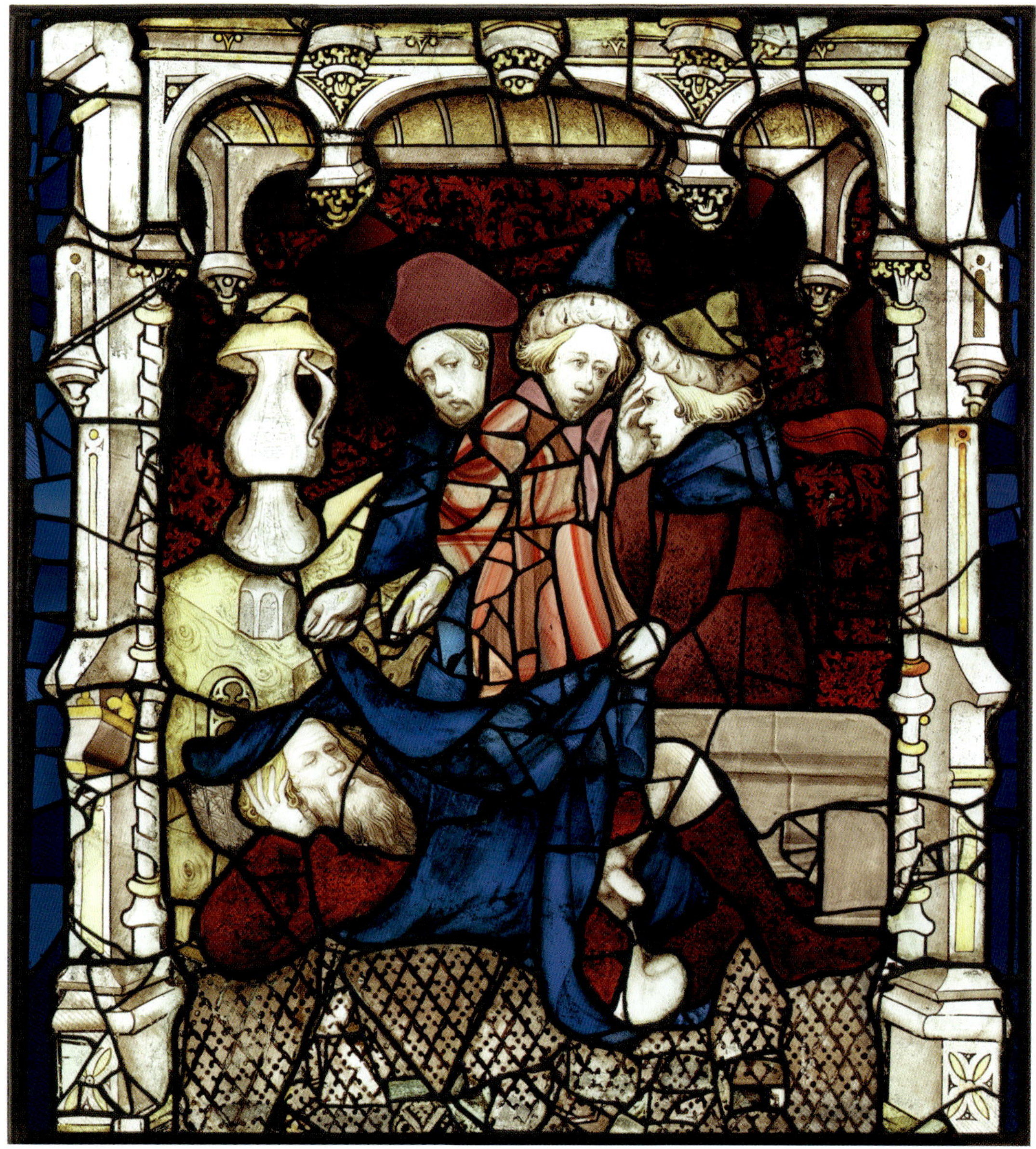

14c The Drunkenness of Noah

And drinking of the wine was made drunk, and was uncovered in his tent. Which when Cham the father of Chanaan had seen, to wit, that his father's nakedness was uncovered, he told it to his two brethren without. But Sem and Japheth put a cloak upon their shoulders, and going backward, covered the nakedness of their father: and their faces were turned away, and they saw not their father's nakedness.

Genesis 9:21–3

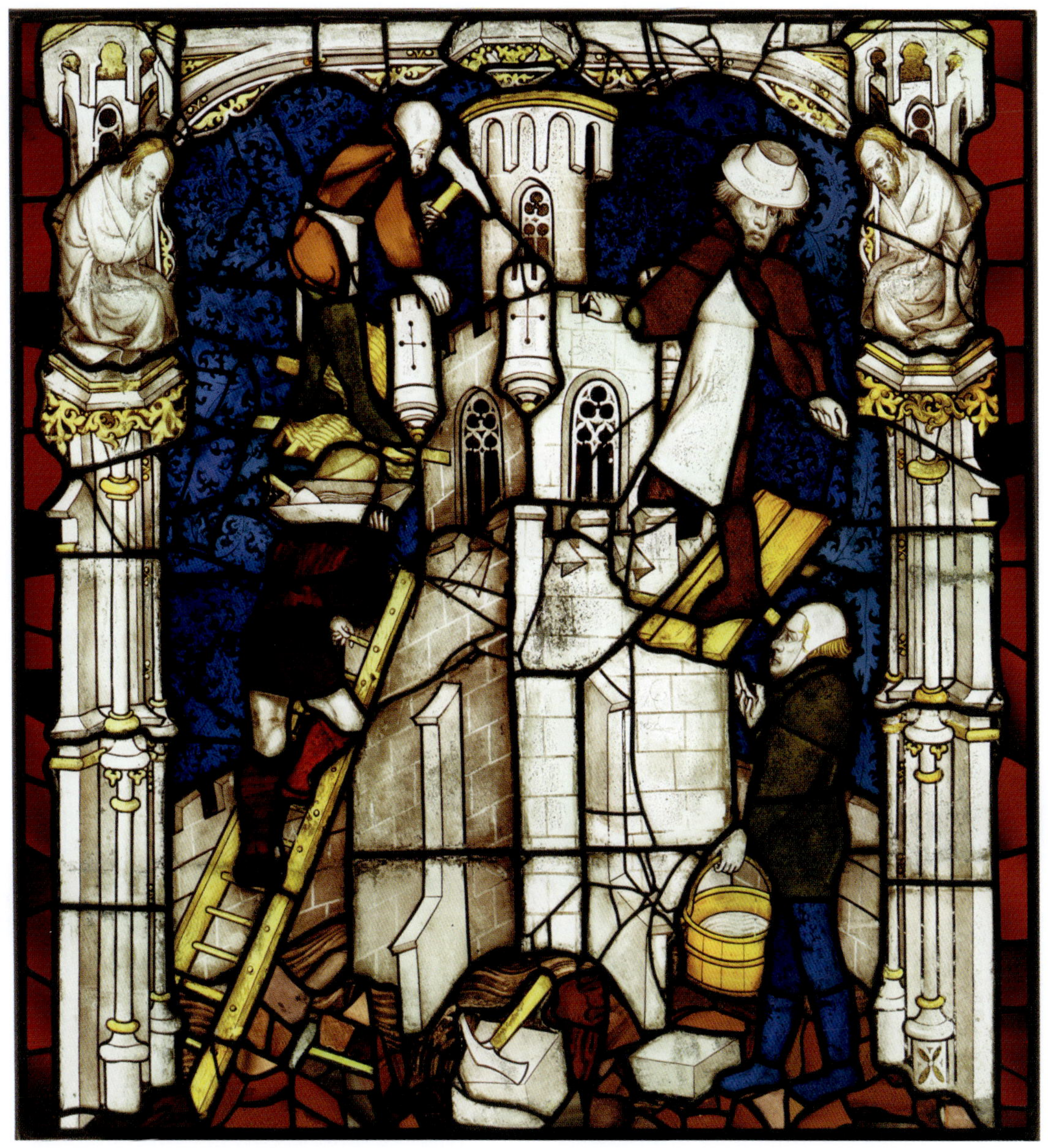

14d The Tower of Babel

And they said: Come, let us make a city and a tower, the top whereof may reach to heaven: and let us make our name famous before we be scattered abroad into all lands.

Genesis 11:4

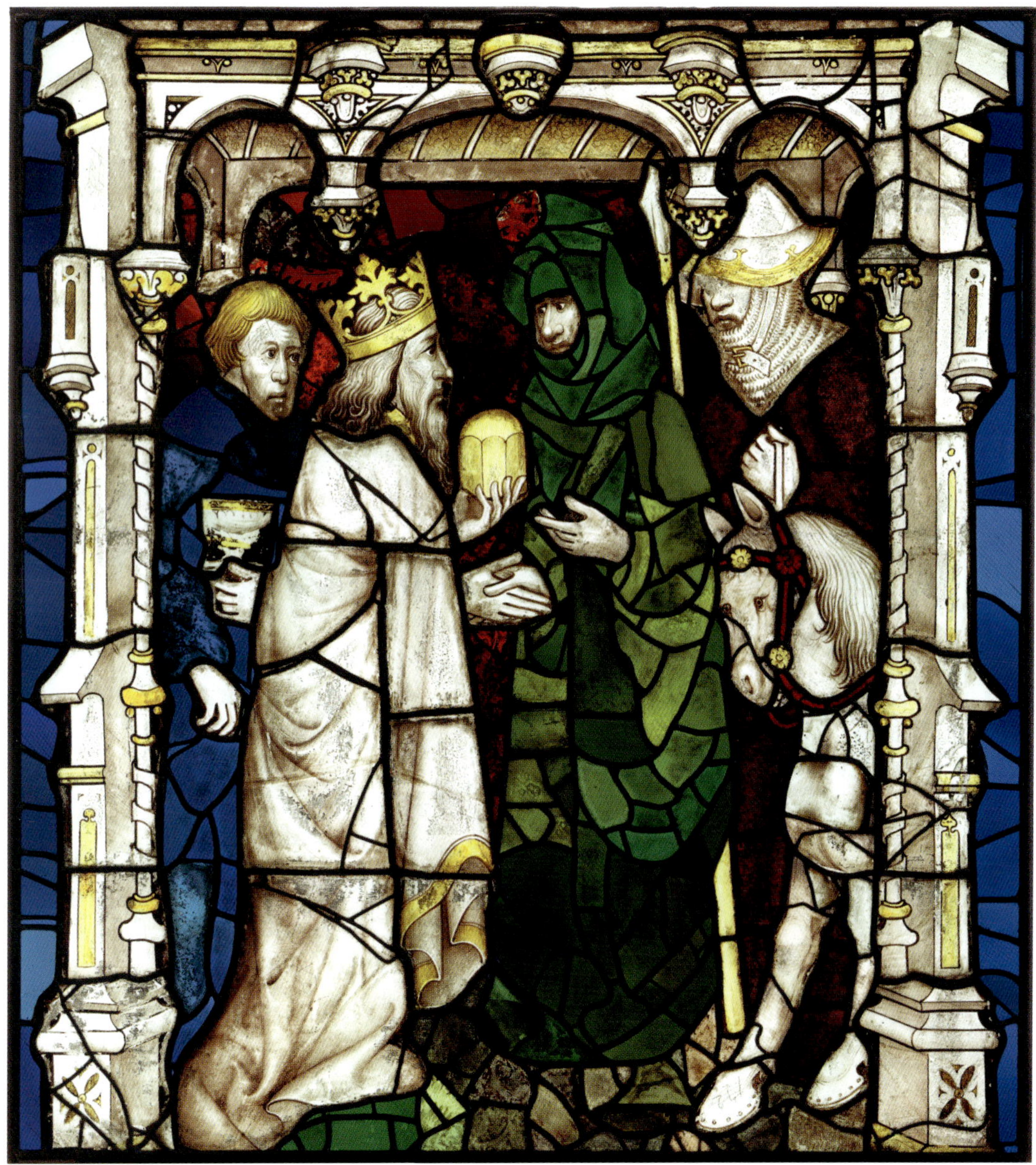

14e Abraham Greeted by Melchisedech

But Melchisedech the king of Salem, bringing forth bread and wine, for he was the priest of the most high God, Blessed him, and said: Blessed be Abram by the most high God, who created heaven and earth. And blessed be the most high God, by whose protection the enemies are in thy hands. And he gave him the tithes of all.
Genesis 14:18–20

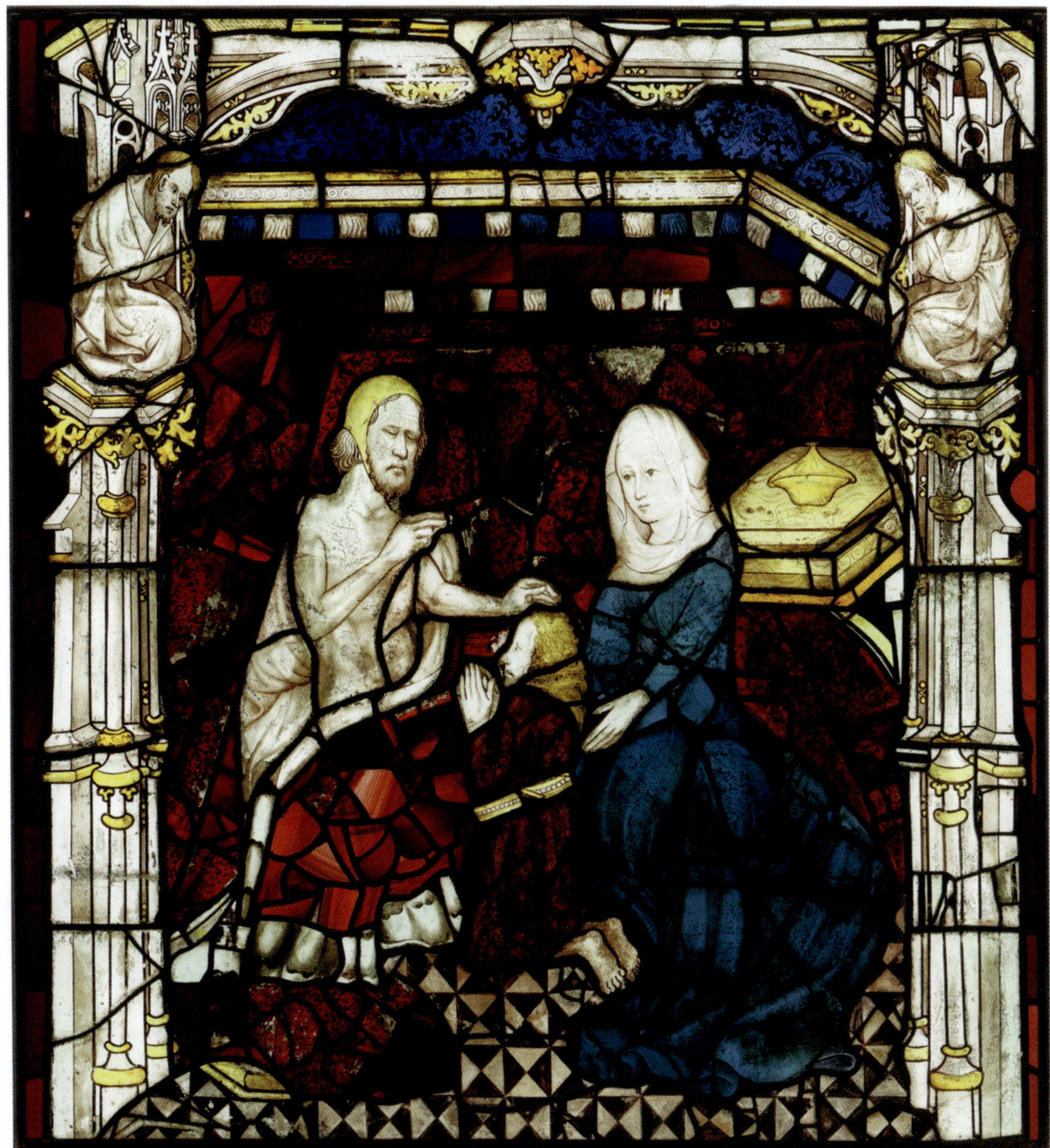

14f Isaac Blesses Jacob

He came near to his father, and when he had felt him, Isaac said: The voice indeed is the voice of Jacob; but the hands are the hands of Esau. And he knew him not, because his hairy hands made him like to the elder. Then blessing him, He said: Art thou my son Esau? He answered: I am. Then he said: Bring me the meats of thy hunting, my son, that my soul may bless thee. And when they were brought, and he had eaten, he offered him wine also, which after he had drunk, He said to him: Come near me, and give me a kiss, my son. He came near, and kissed him. And immediately as he smelled the fragrant smell of his garments, blessing him, he said: Behold the smell of my son is as the smell of a plentiful field, which the Lord hath blessed.

Genesis 27:22–7

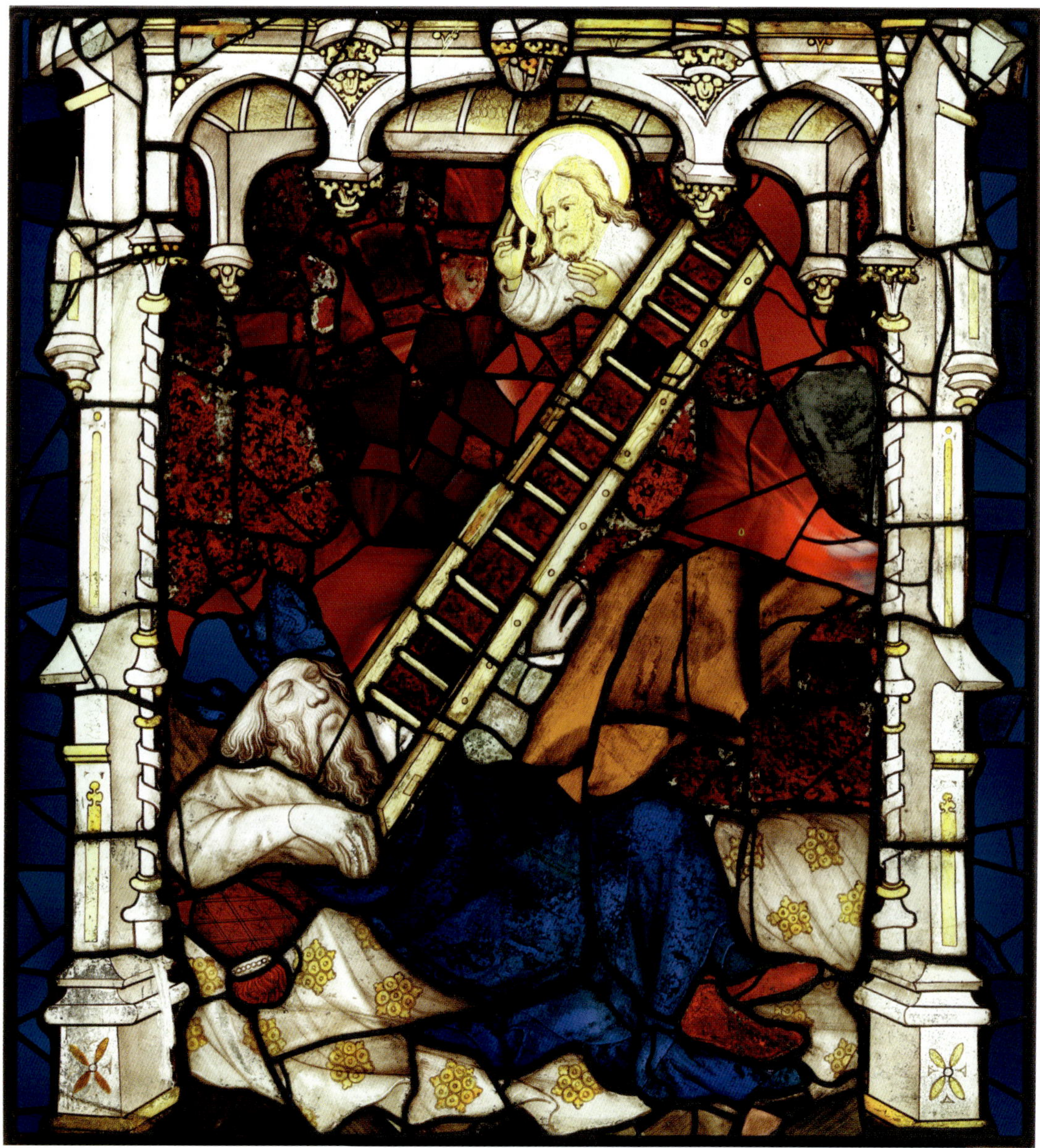

14g Jacob's Dream

And he saw in his sleep a ladder standing upon the earth, and the top thereof touching heaven: the angels also of God ascending and descending by it; And the Lord leaning upon the ladder, saying to him: I am the Lord God of Abraham thy father, and the God of Isaac; the land, wherein thou sleepest, I will give to thee and to thy seed. And thy seed shall be as the dust of the earth: thou shalt spread abroad to the west, and to the east, and to the north, and to the south: and IN THEE and thy seed all the tribes of the earth SHALL BE BLESSED. And I will be thy keeper whithersoever thou goest, and will bring thee back into this land: neither will I leave thee, till I shall have accomplished all that I have said.
Genesis 28:12–15

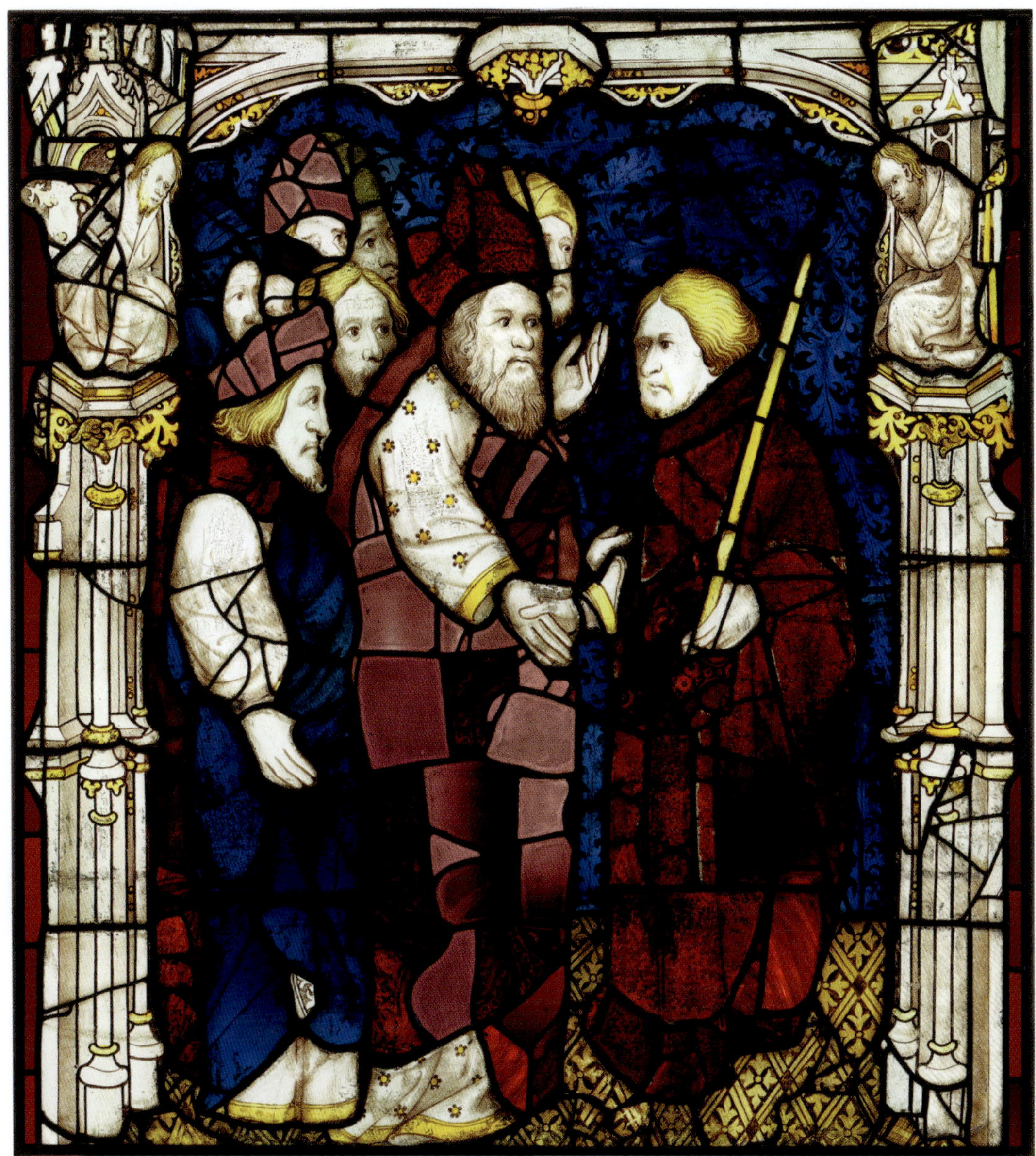

14h Joseph and His Brethren

And Joseph was governor in the land of Egypt, and corn was sold by his direction to the people. And when his brethren had bowed down to him, And he knew them, he spoke as it were to strangers somewhat roughly, asking them: Whence came you? They answered: From the land of Chanaan, to buy necessaries of life. And though he knew his brethren, he was not known by them.
Genesis 42·6–8

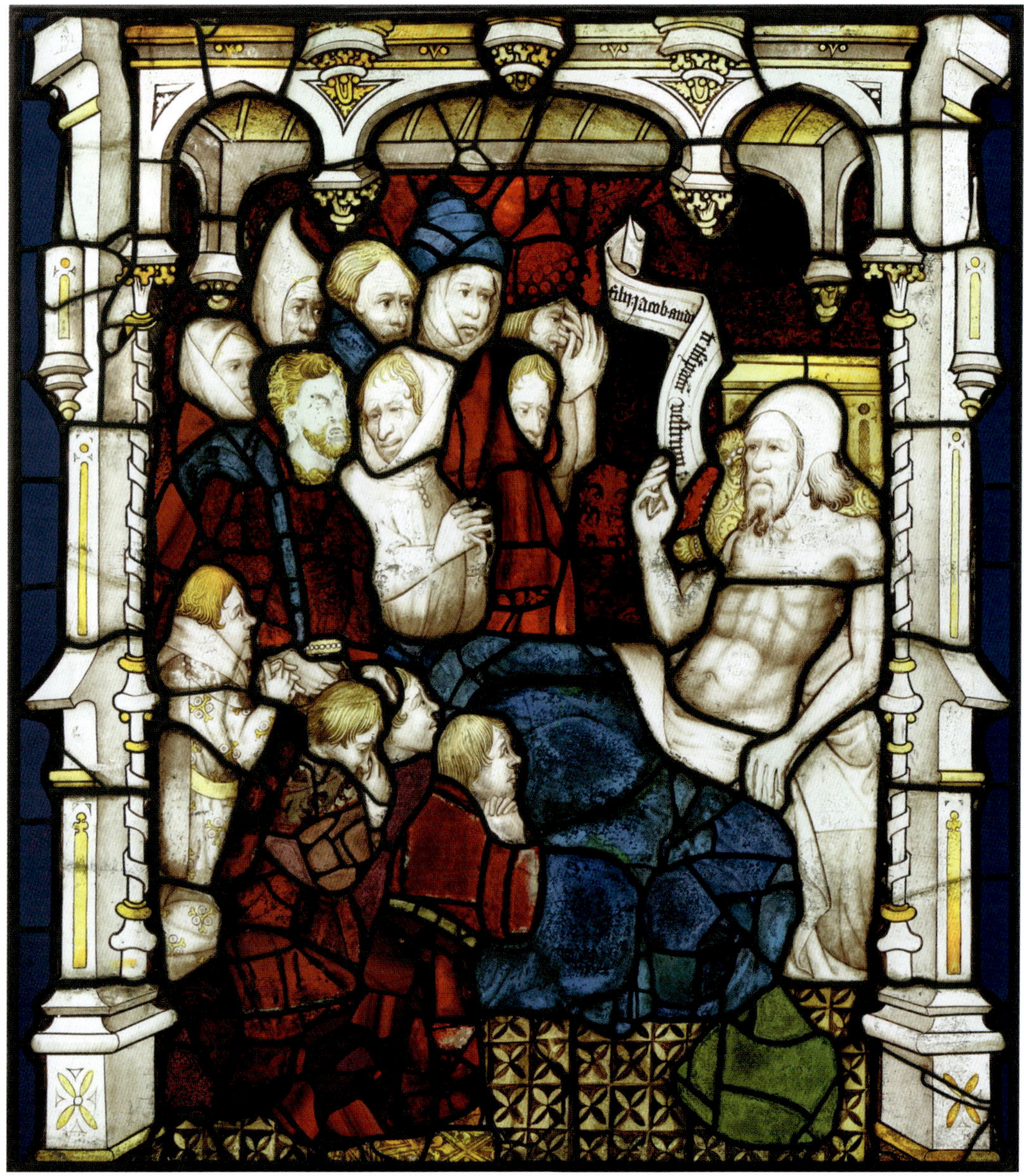

14j Jacob Blesses His Sons

And Jacob called his sons, and said to them: Gather yourselves together that I may tell you the things that shall befall you in the last days. Gather yourselves together, and hear, **O ye sons of Jacob, hearken to Israel your father.**
Genesis 49:1–2

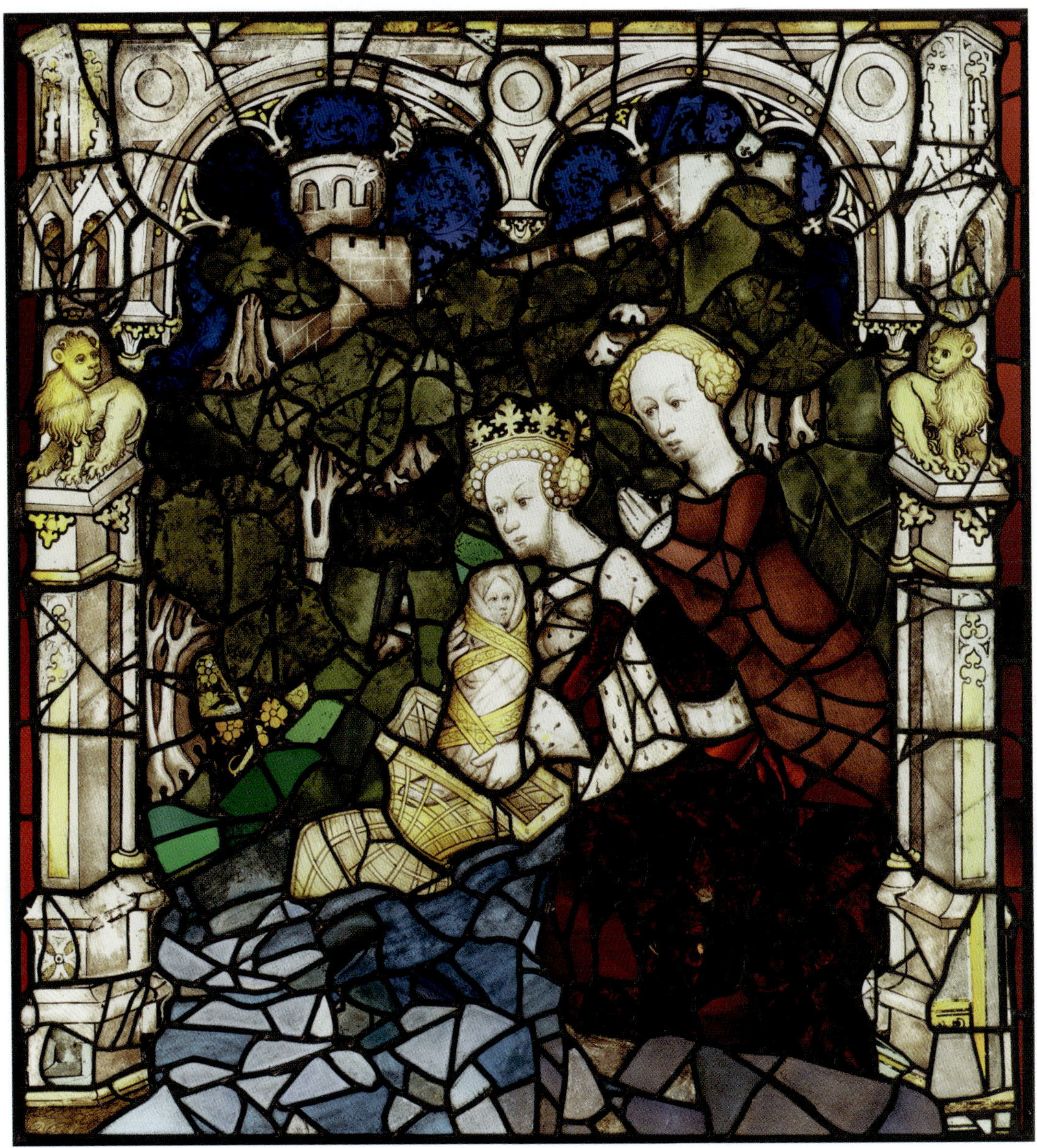

13a Moses Discovered by Pharaoh's Daughter

After this there went a man of the house of Levi; and took a wife of his own kindred. And she conceived, and bore a son; and seeing him a goodly child hid him three months. And when she could hide him no longer, she took a basket made of bulrushes, and daubed it with slime and pitch: and put the little babe therein, and laid him in the sedges by the river's brink, His sister standing afar off, and taking notice what would be done. And behold the daughter of Pharao came down to wash herself in the river: and her maids walked by the river's brink. And when she saw the basket in the sedges, she sent one of her maids for it: and when it was brought, She opened it and seeing within it an infant crying, having compassion on it she said: This is one of the babes of the Hebrews.

Exodus 2:1–6

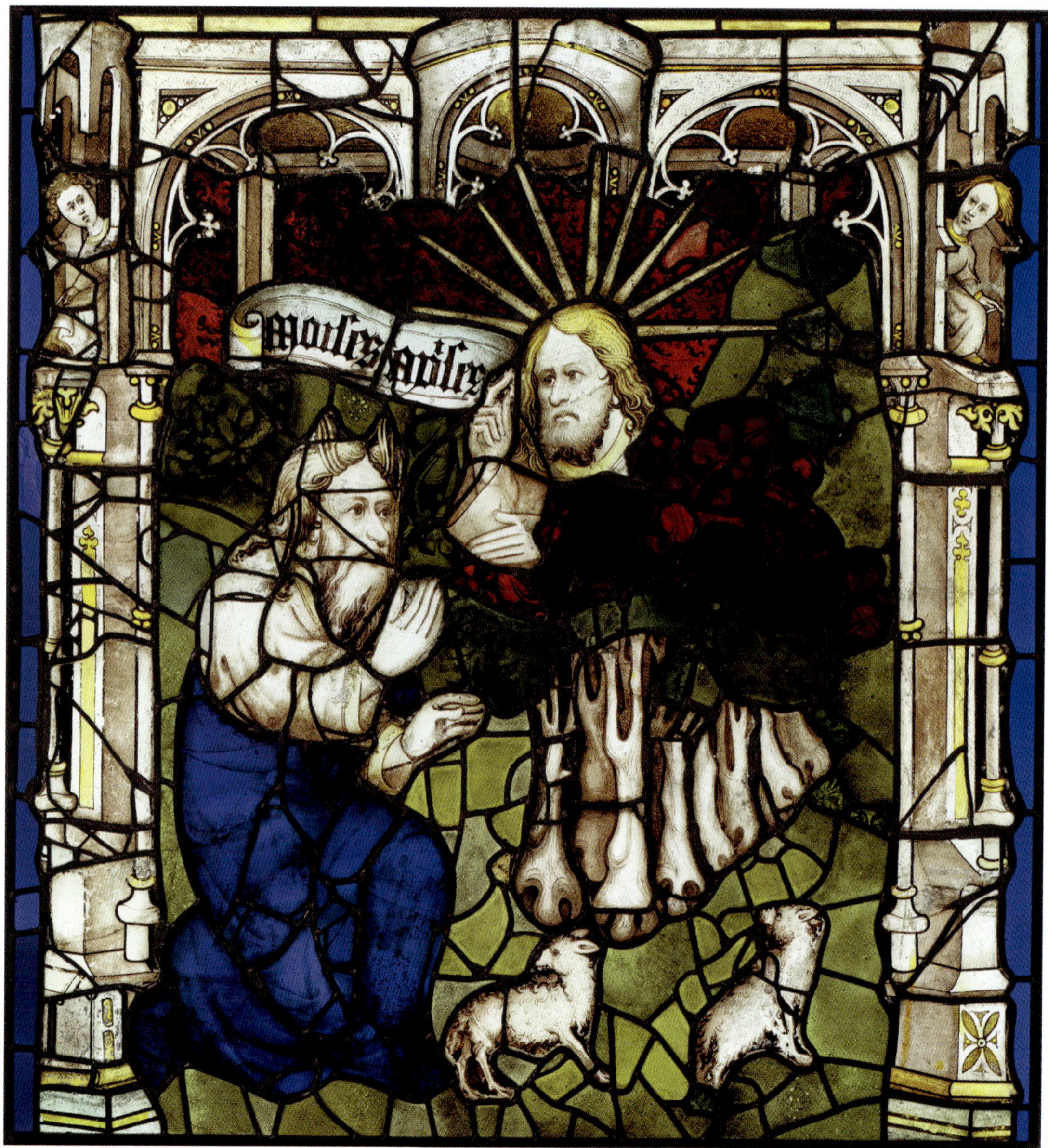

13b Moses and the Burning Bush

Now Moses fed the sheep of Jethro his father in law, the priest of Madian: and he drove the flock to the inner parts of the desert, and came to the mountain of God, Horeb. And the Lord appeared to him in a flame of fire out of the midst of a bush: and he saw that the bush was on fire and was not burnt. And Moses said: I will go and see this great sight, why the bush is not burnt. And when the Lord saw that he went forward to see, he called to him out of the midst of the bush, and said: Moses, Moses. And he answered: Here I am. And he said: Come not nigh hither, put off the shoes from thy feet: for the place whereon thou standest is holy ground. And he said: I am the God of thy father, the God of Abraham, the God of Isaac, and the God of Jacob. Moses hid his face: for he durst not look at God.
Exodus 3:1–6

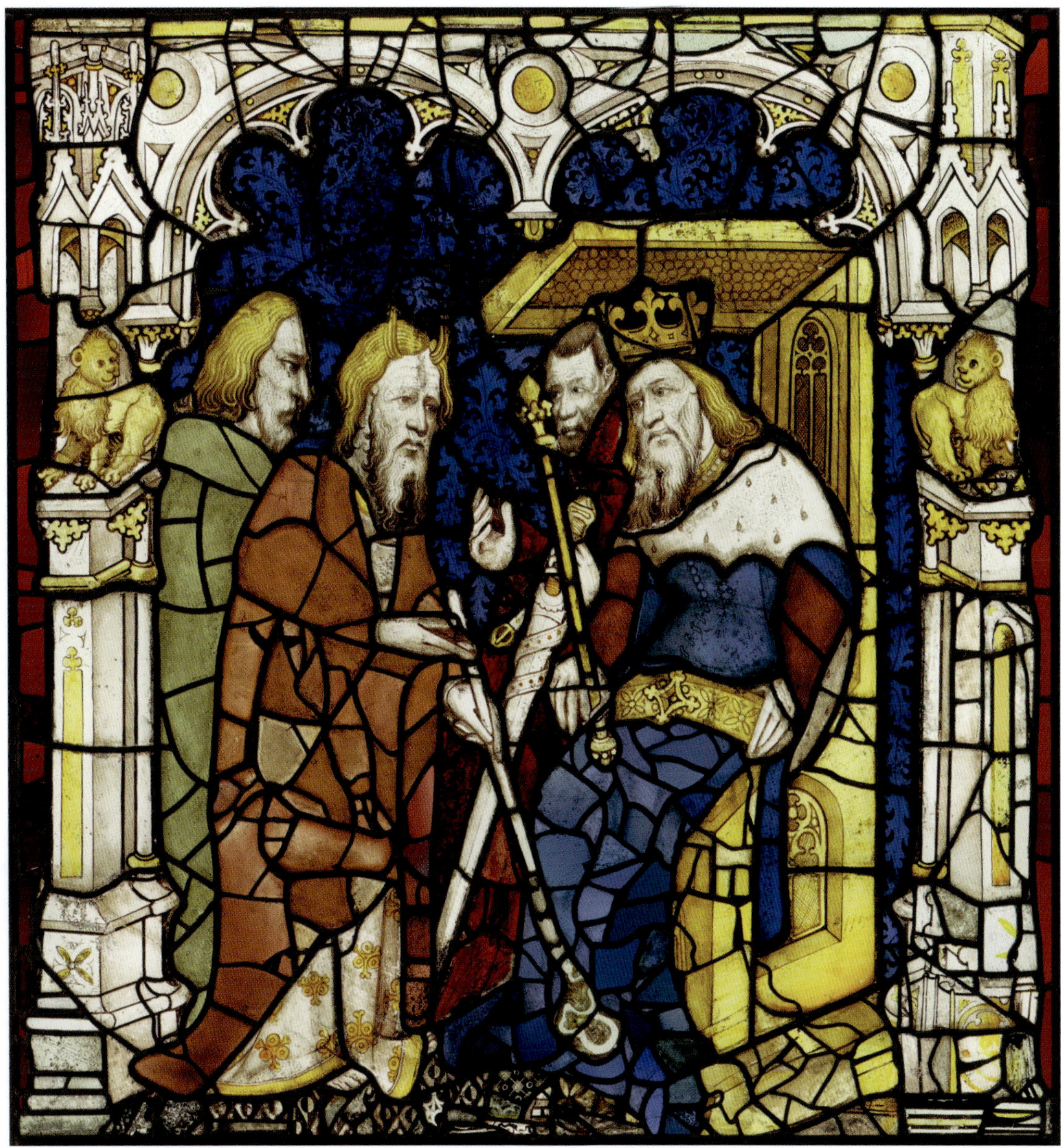

13c Moses and Aaron before Pharaoh

So Moses and Aaron went in unto Pharao, and did as the Lord had commanded. And Aaron took the rod before Pharao, and his servants, and it was turned into a serpent.

Exodus 7:10

or

And Pharao calling Moses and Aaron, in the night, said: Arise and go forth from among my people, you and the children of Israel: go, sacrifice to the Lord as you say.

Exodus 12:31

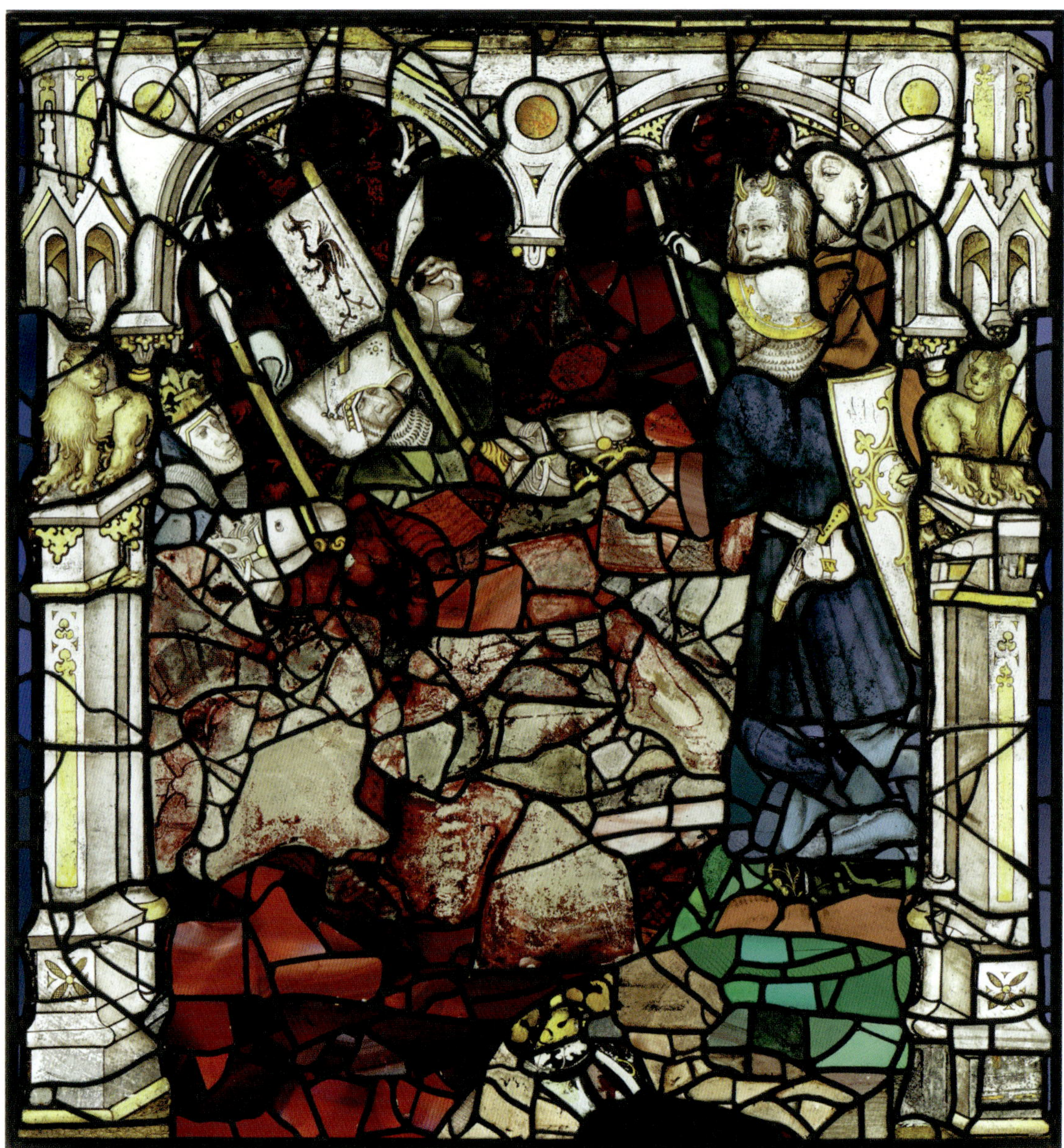

13d The Egyptians are Drowned in the Red Sea

And the Lord said to Moses: Stretch forth thy hand over the sea, that the waters may come again upon the Egyptians, upon their chariots and horsemen. And when Moses had stretched forth his hand towards the sea, it returned at the first break of day to the former place: and as the Egyptians were fleeing away, the waters came upon them, and the Lord shut them up in the middle of the waves. And the waters returned, and covered the chariots and the horsemen of all the army of Pharao, who had come into the sea after them, neither did there so much as one of them remain.

Exodus 14:26–8

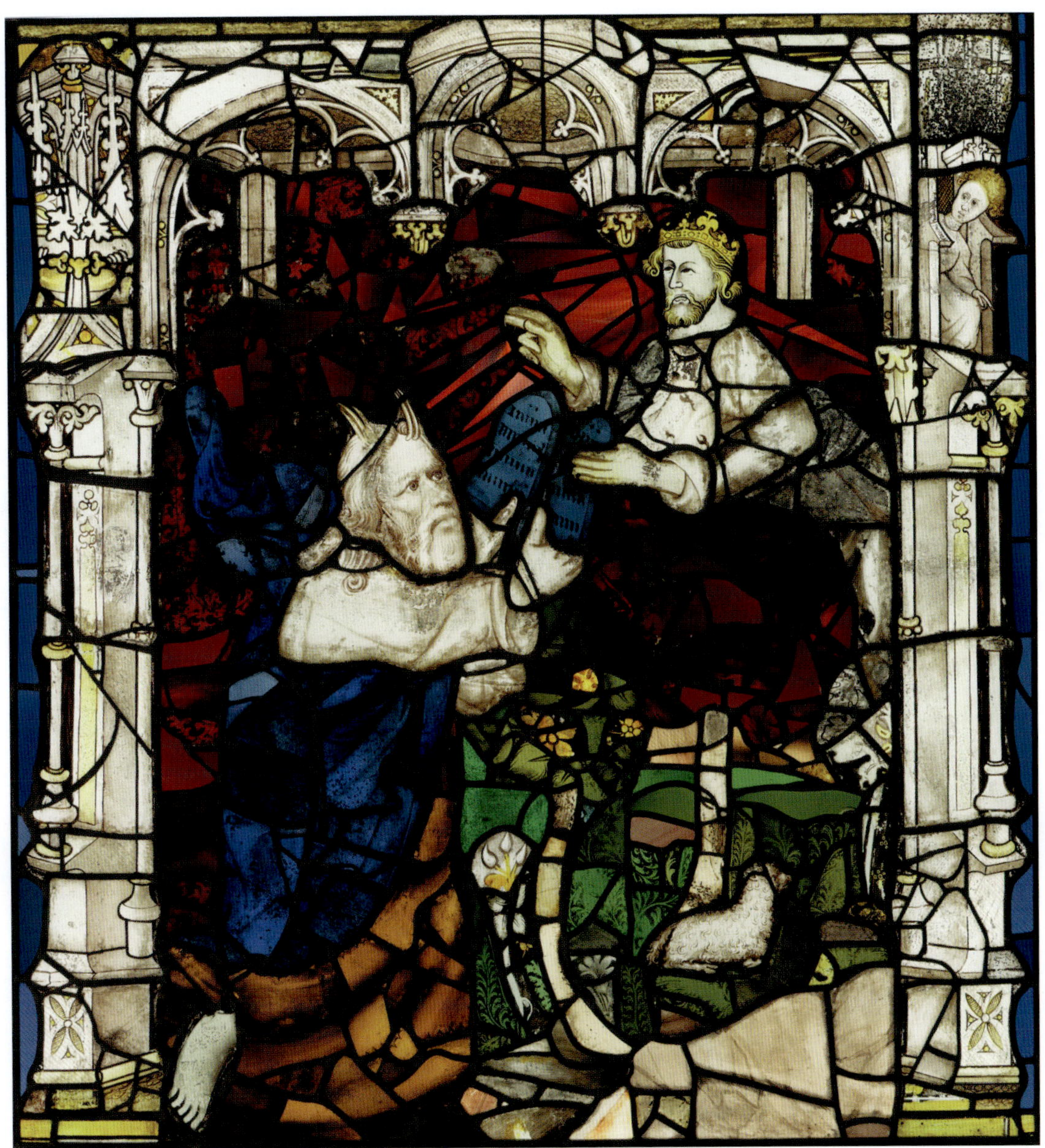

13e Moses Receives the Tablets of the Law
And the Lord, when he had ended these words in mount Sinai, gave to Moses two stone tables of testimony, written with the finger of God.
Exodus 31:18

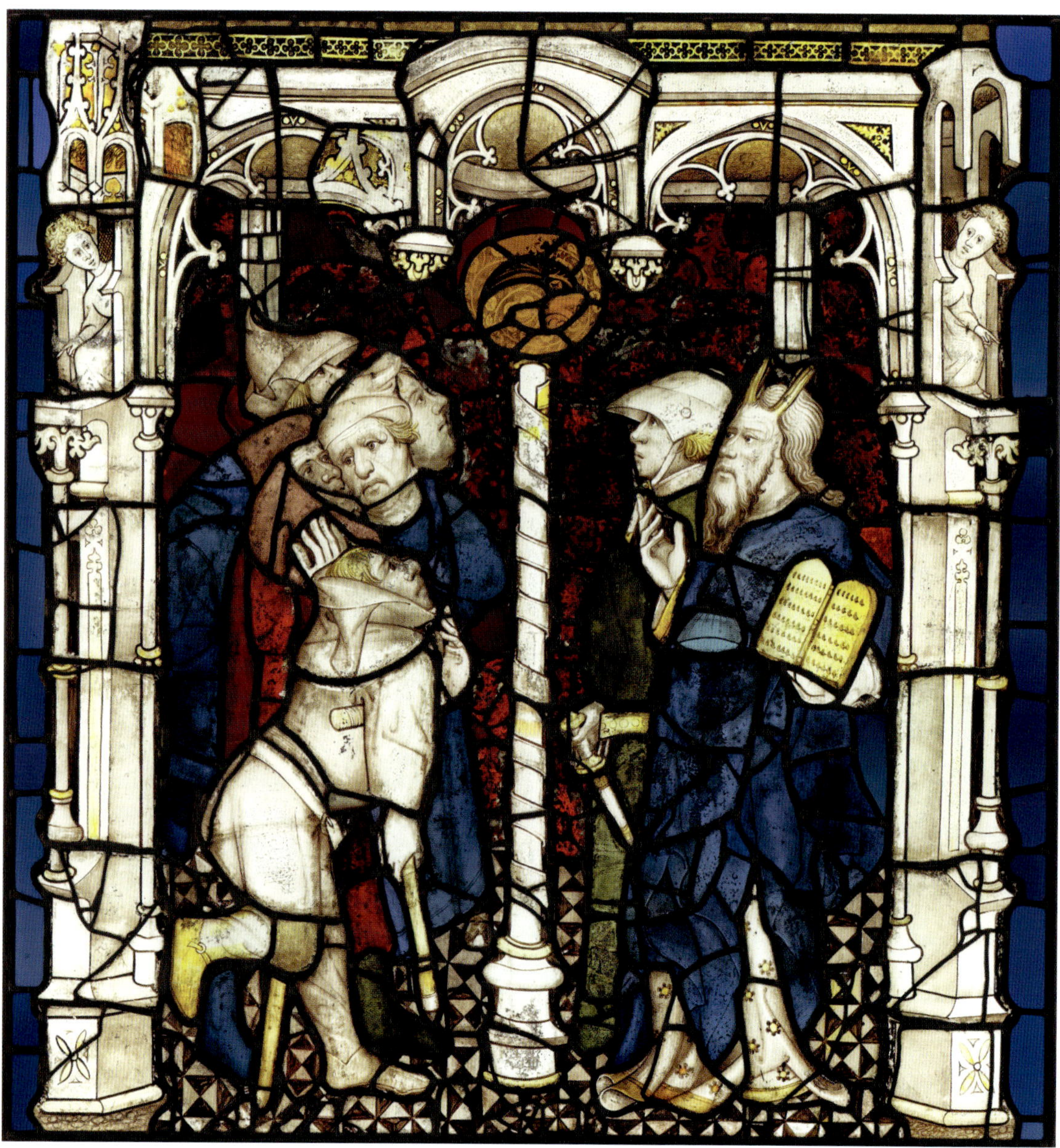

13f Moses and the Serpent of Brass

And the Lord said to him: Make a brazen serpent, and set it up for a sign: whosoever being struck shall look on it, shall live. Moses therefore made a brazen serpent, and set it up for a sign: which when they that were bitten looked upon, they were healed.
Numbers 21:8–9

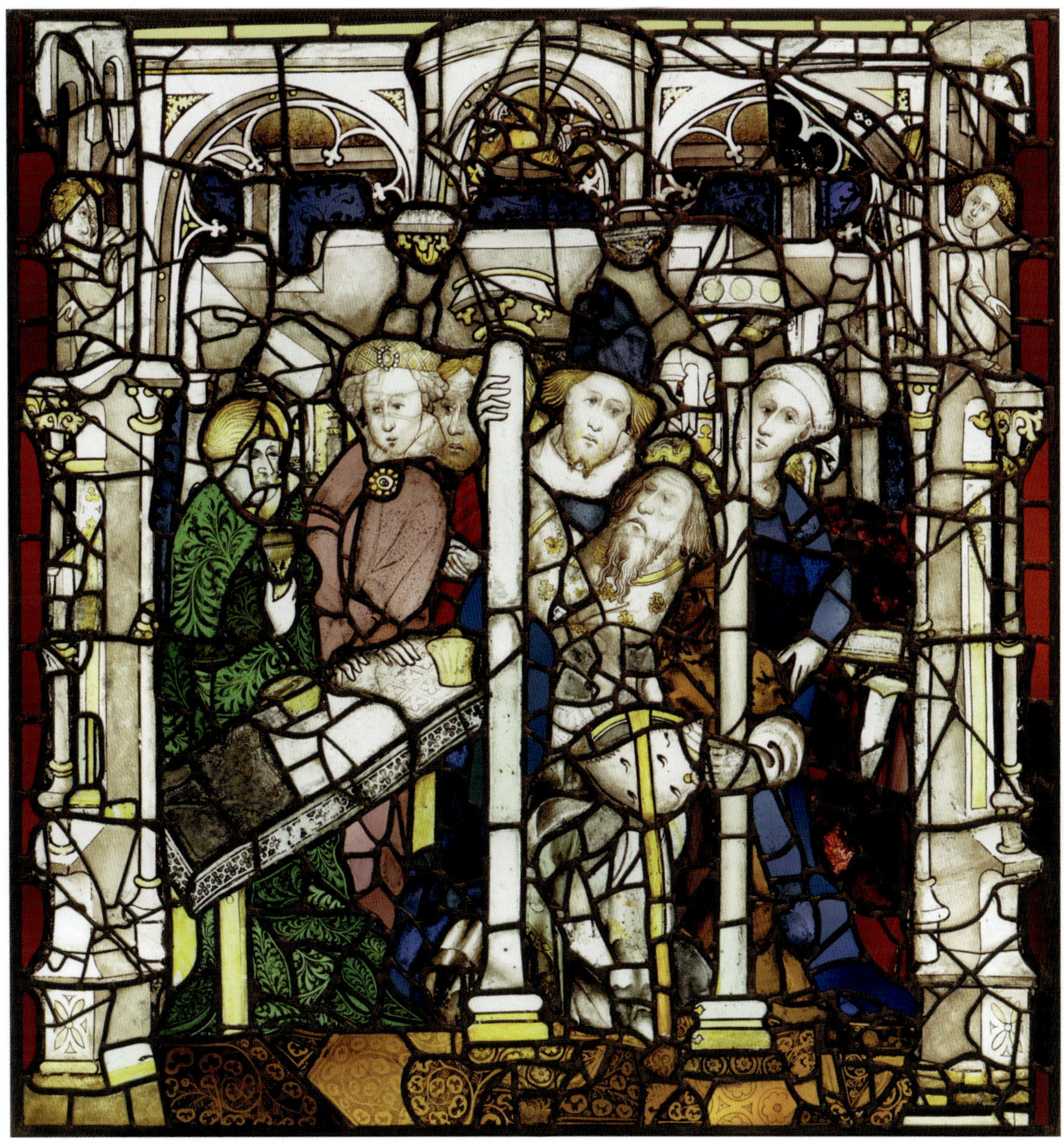

And rejoicing in their feasts, when they had now taken their good cheer, they commanded that Samson should be called, and should play before them. And being brought out of prison he played before them, and they made him stand between two pillars. And he said to the lad that guided his steps: Suffer me to touch the pillars which support tho whole house, and let me lean upon them, and rest a little.
Judges 16:25–6

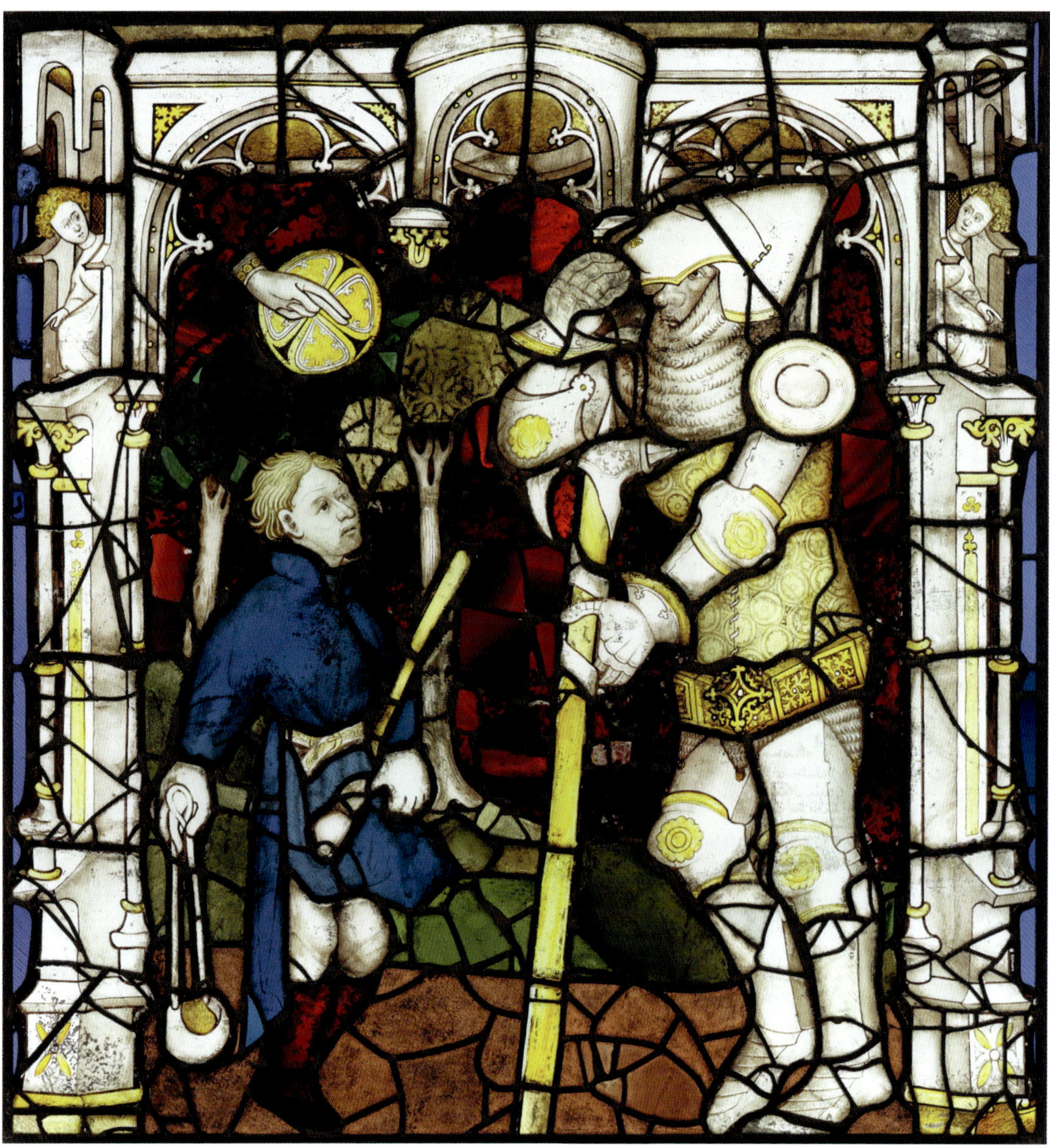

13h David and Goliath

And he put his hand into his scrip, and took a stone, and cast it with the sling, and fetching it about struck the Philistine in the forehead: and the stone was fixed in his forehead, and he fell on his face upon the earth. And David prevailed over the Philistine, with a sling and a stone, and he struck, and slew the Philistine.
1 Samuel 17:49–50

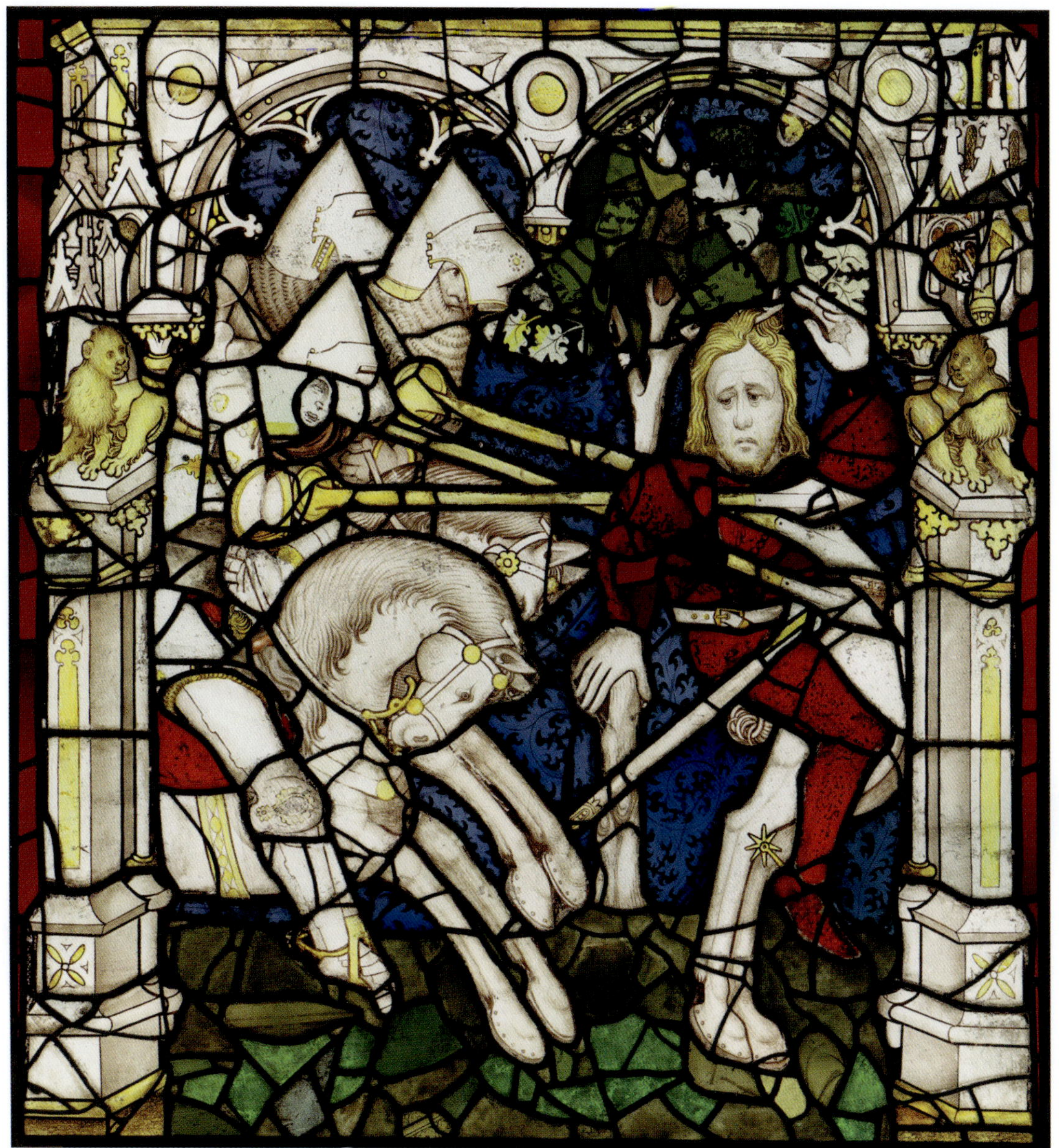

13j The Death of Absalom

And it happened that Absalom met the servants of David, riding on a mule: and as the mule went under a thick and large oak, his head stuck in the oak: and while he hung between the heaven and the earth, the mule on which he rode passed on. And one saw this and told Joab, saying: I saw Absalom hanging upon an oak. And Joab said to the man that told him: If thou sawest him, why didst thou not stab him to the ground, and I would have given thee ten sicles of silver, and belt? And he said to Joab: If thou wouldst have paid down in my hands a thousand pieces of silver, I would not lay my hands upon the king's son: for in our hearing [t]he king charged thee, and Abisai, and Ethai, saying: Save me the boy Absalom. Yea and if I should have acted boldly against my own life, this could not have been hid from the king, and wouldst thou have stood by me? And Joab said: Not as thou wilt, but will set upon him in thy sight. So he took three lances in his hand, and thrust them into the heart of Absalom: and whilst he yet panted for life, sticking on the oak.

2 Samuel 18:9–14

The Apocalypse

The texts highlighted in bold are the English translations of the Latin words represented on scrolls in the panels.

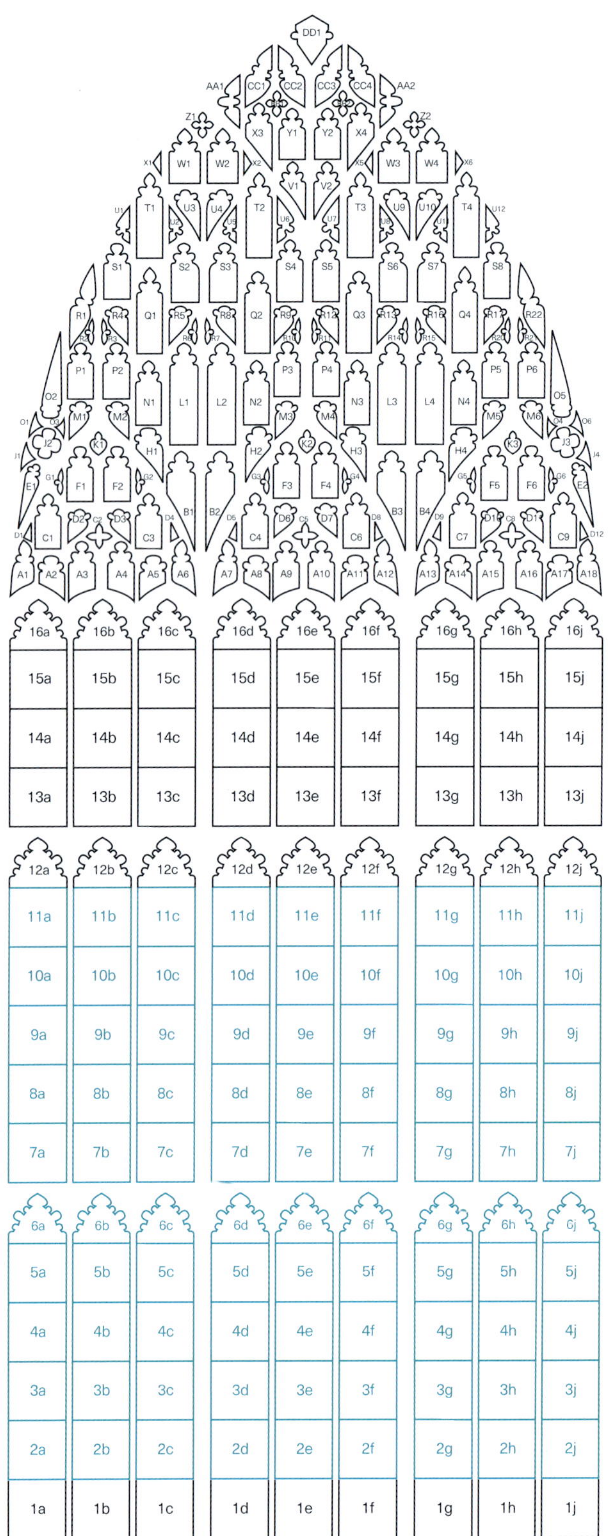

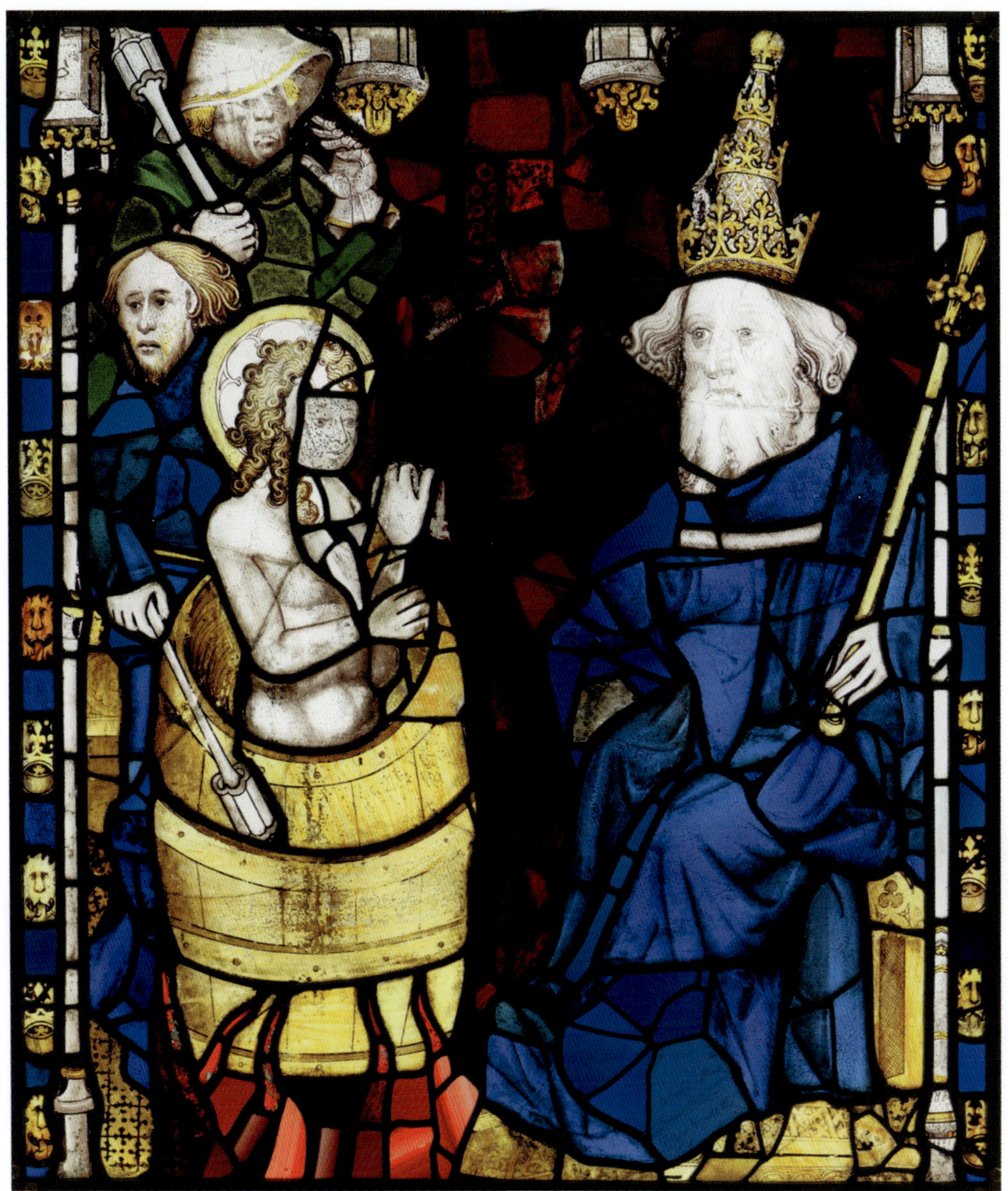

11a St John tortured before Domitian
The emperor Domitian, hearing of his fame, summoned him to Rome and had him plunged into a caldron of boiling oil ... but the blessed John came out untouched, just as he had avoided corruption of the flesh.
The Golden Legend

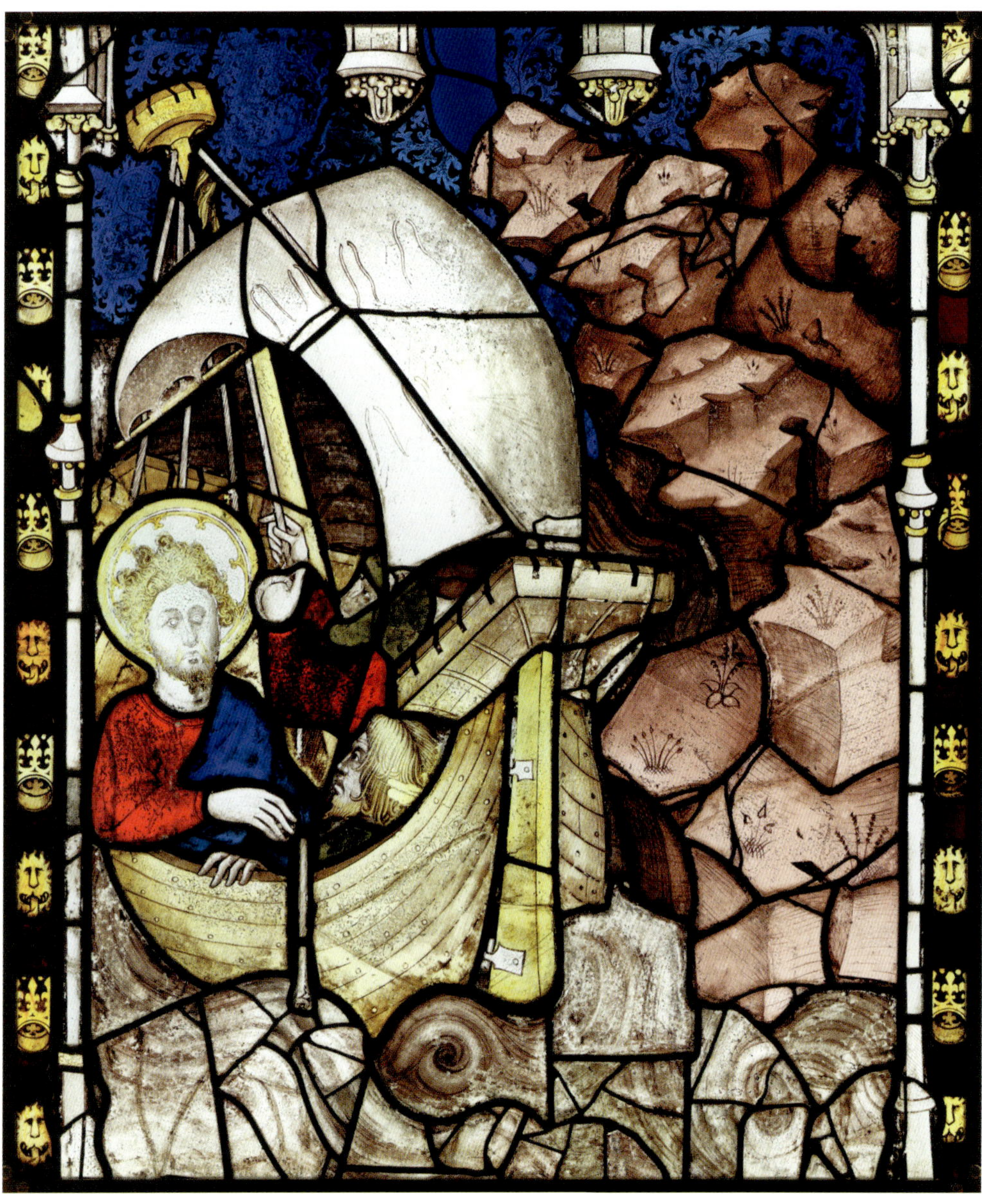

11b St John sails to the island of Patmos
Seeing that this treatment had not deterred him from preaching, the emperor exiled him to the island of Patmos.
The Golden Legend

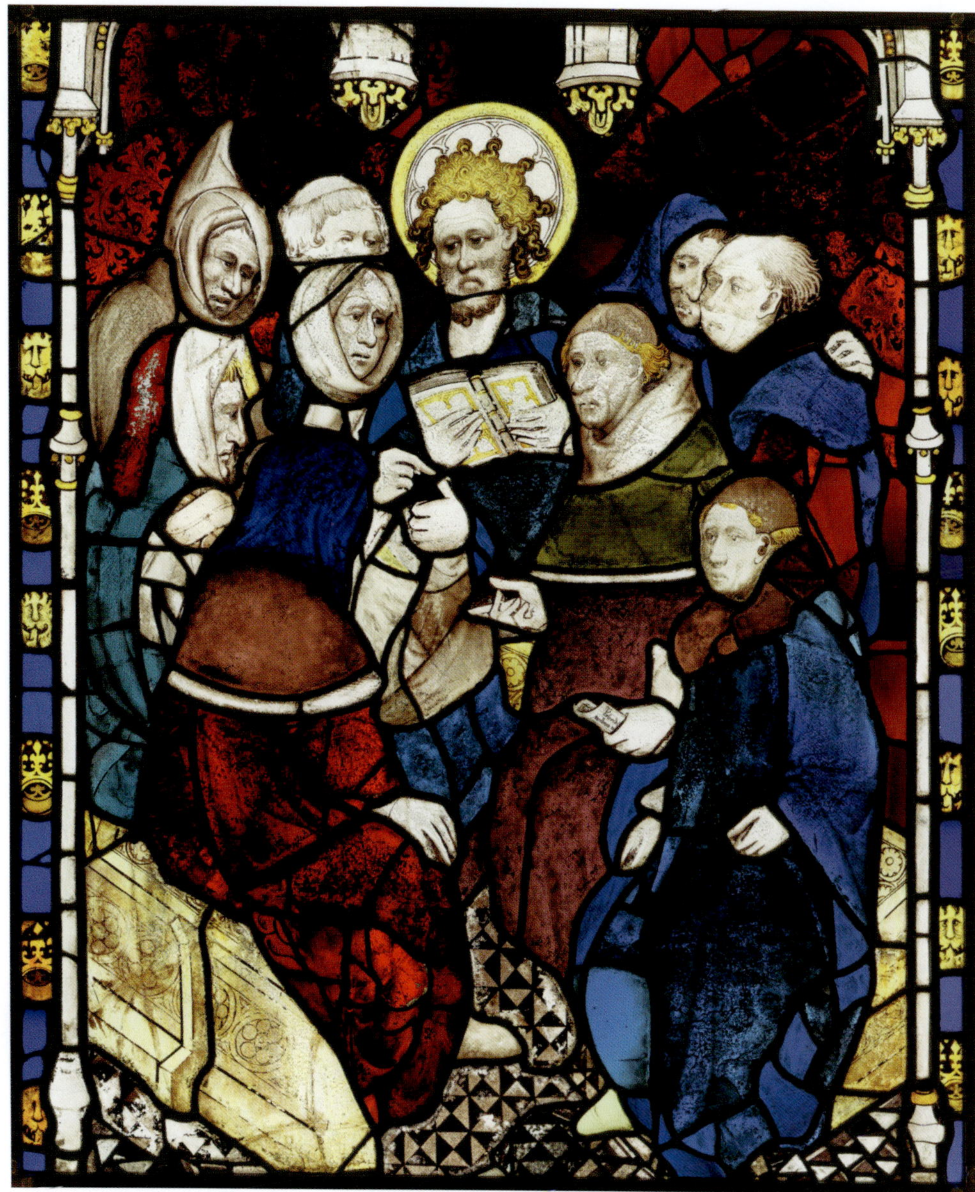

11c St John teaching

There is no specific textual source for this scene, which appears to depict St John preaching from a book. Its location in the narrative sequence has also been questioned, but earliest records of the window record it in this position, so its location has remained unchanged during the recent conservation project.

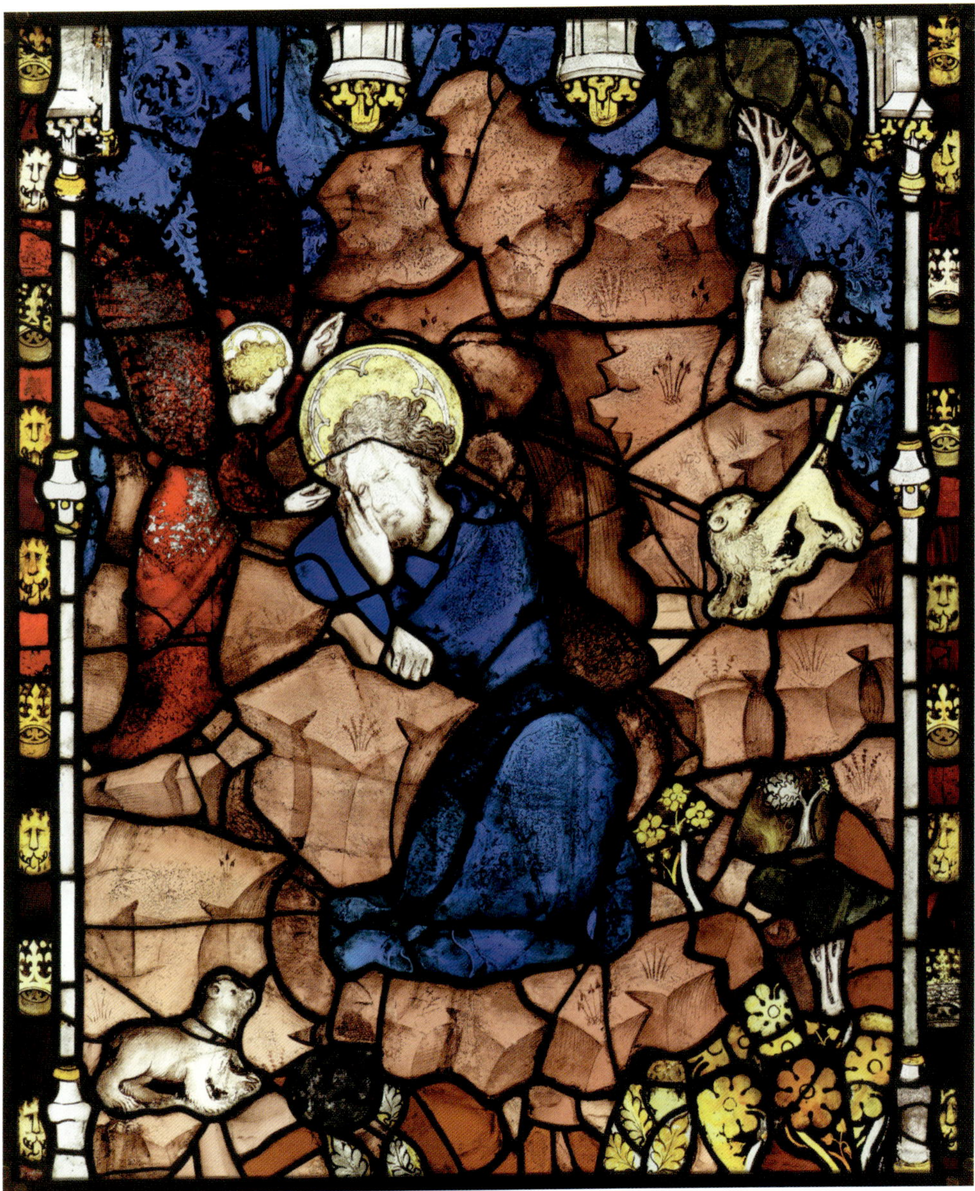

11d St John and the Angel
The Revelation of Jesus Christ, which God gave unto him, to make known to his servants the things which must shortly come to pass: and signified, sending by his angel to his servant John, Who hath given testimony to the word of God, and the testimony of Jesus Christ, what things soever he hath seen.
Revelation 1:1–2

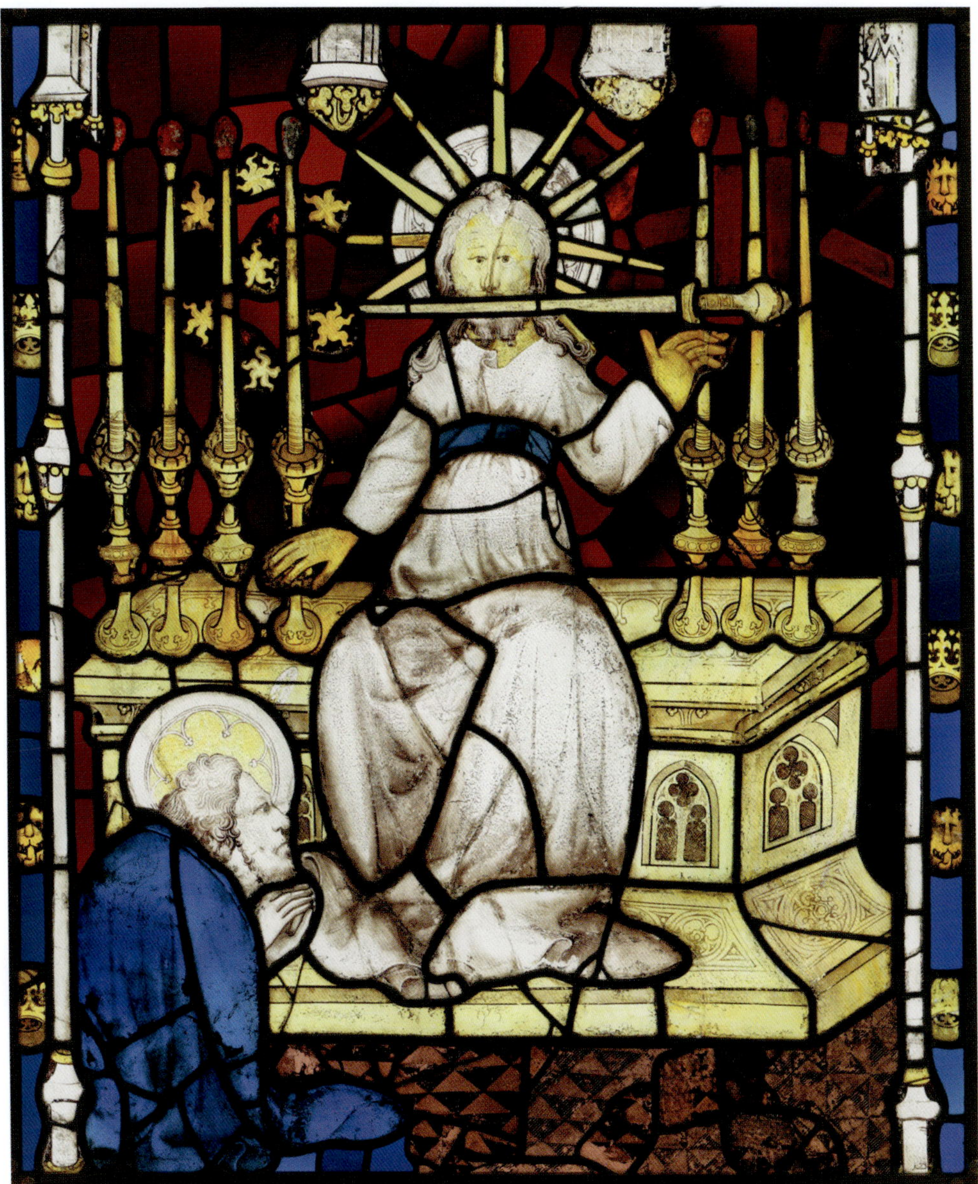

11e The Vision of the Candlesticks

And I turned to see the voice that spoke with me. And being turned, I saw seven golden candlesticks: And in the midst of the seven golden candlesticks, one like to the Son of man, clothed with a garment down to the feet, and girt about the paps with a golden girdle. And his head and his hairs were white, as white wool, and as snow, and his eyes were as a flame of fire, And his feet like unto fine brass, as in a burning furnace. And his voice as the sound of many waters. And he had in his right hand seven stars. And from his mouth came out a sharp two edged sword: and his face was as the sun shineth in his power. And when I had seen him, I fell at his feet as dead.

Revelation 1:12–17

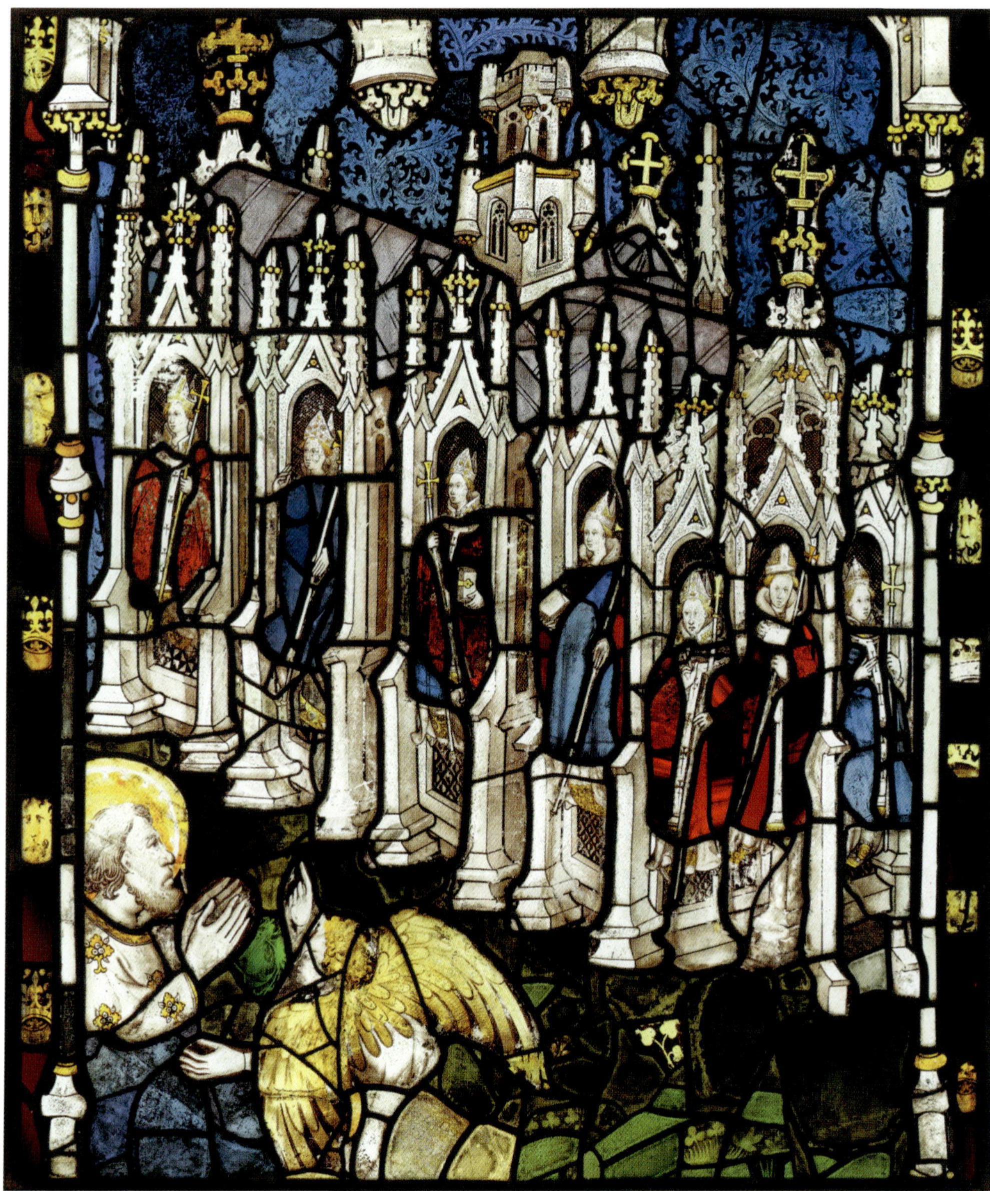

11f The Seven Churches

What thou seest, write in a book, and send to the seven churches which are in Asia, to Ephesus, and to Smyrna, and to Pergamus, and to Thyatira, and to Sardis, and to Philadelphia, and to Laodicea ... The seven stars are the angels of the seven churches. And the seven candlesticks are the seven churches.

Revelation 1:11 and 20

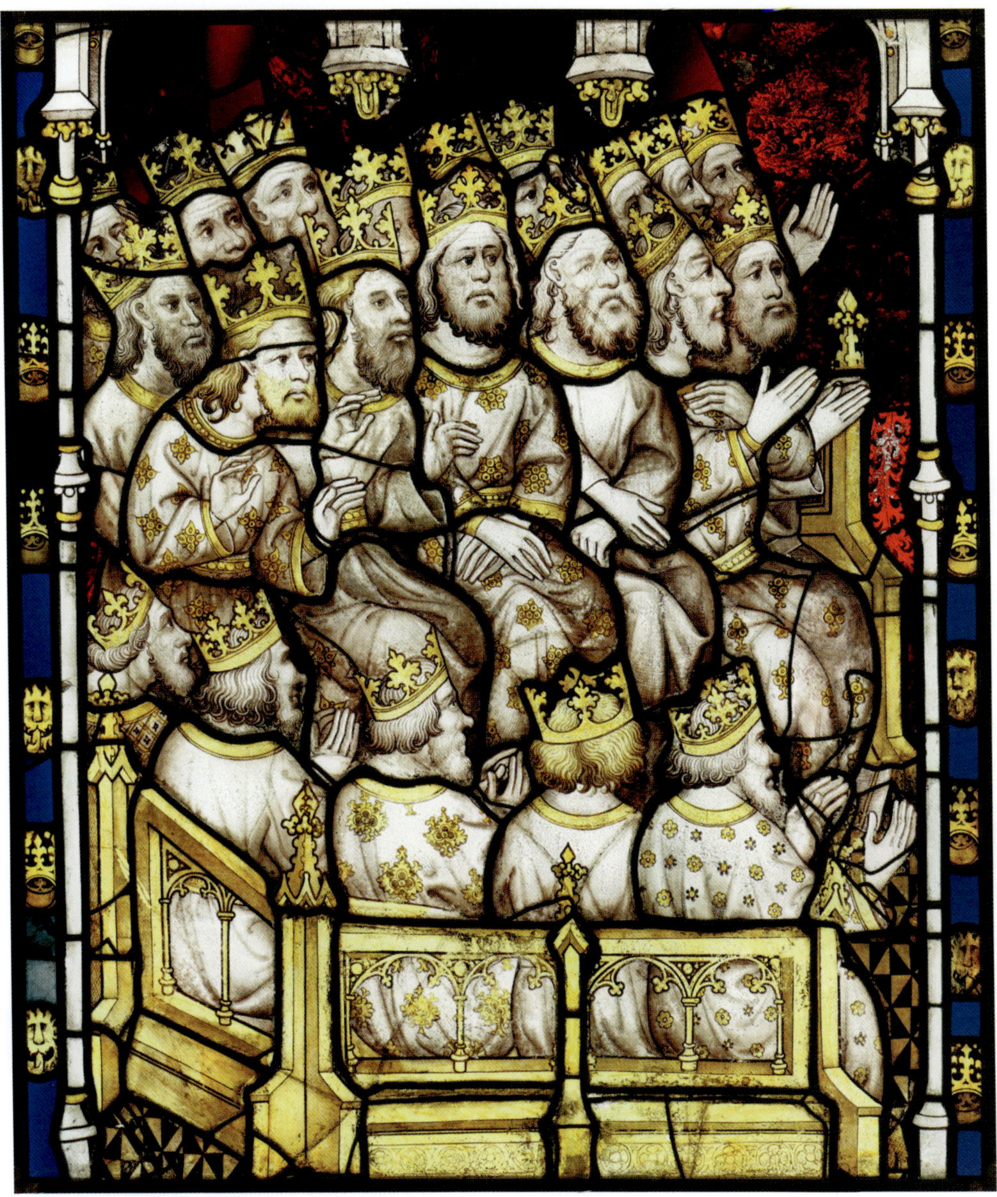

11g The Elders worship God
And round about the throne were four and twenty seats; and upon the seats, four and twenty ancients sitting, clothed in white garments, and on their heads were crowns of gold.
Revelation 4:4

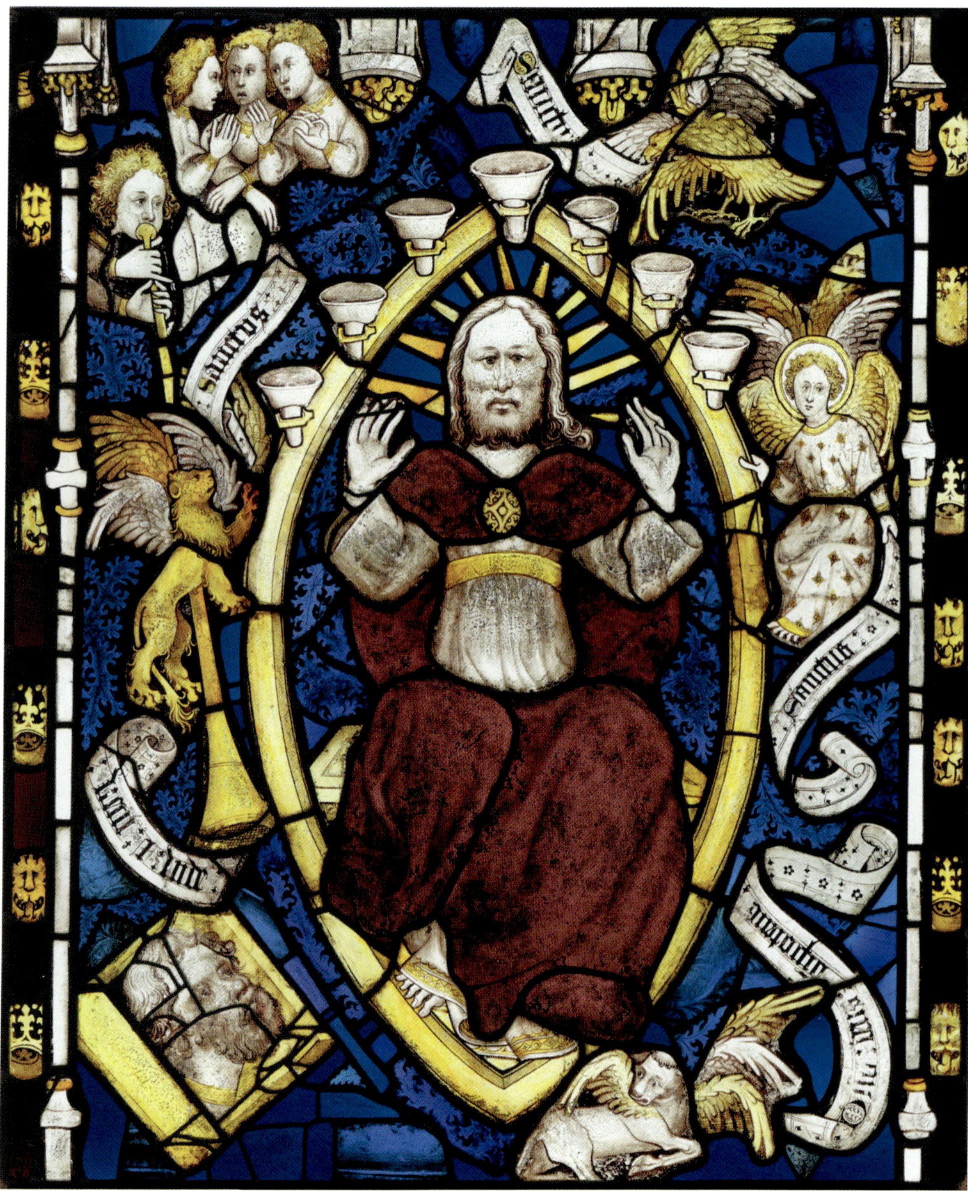

11h God in Majesty

After these things I looked, and behold a door was opened in heaven, and the first voice which I heard, as it were, of a trumpet speaking with me, said: Come up hither, and I will shew thee the things which must be done hereafter. And immediately I was in the spirit: and behold there was a throne set in heaven, and upon the throne one sitting. And he that sat, was to the sight like the jasper and the sardine stone; and there was a rainbow round about the throne, in sight like unto an emerald ... there were seven lamps burning before the throne, which are the seven spirits of God. And in the sight of the throne was, as it were, a sea of glass like to crystal; and in the midst of the throne, and round about the throne, were four living creatures, full of eyes before and behind. And the first living creature was like a lion: and the second living creature like a calf: and the third living creature, having the face, as it were, of a man: and the fourth living creature was like an eagle flying. And the four living creatures had each of them six wings; and round about and within they are full of eyes. And they rested not day and night, saying: **Holy, holy, holy, Lord God Almighty**, who was, and who is, and who is to come.
Revelation 4:1–3, 5–8

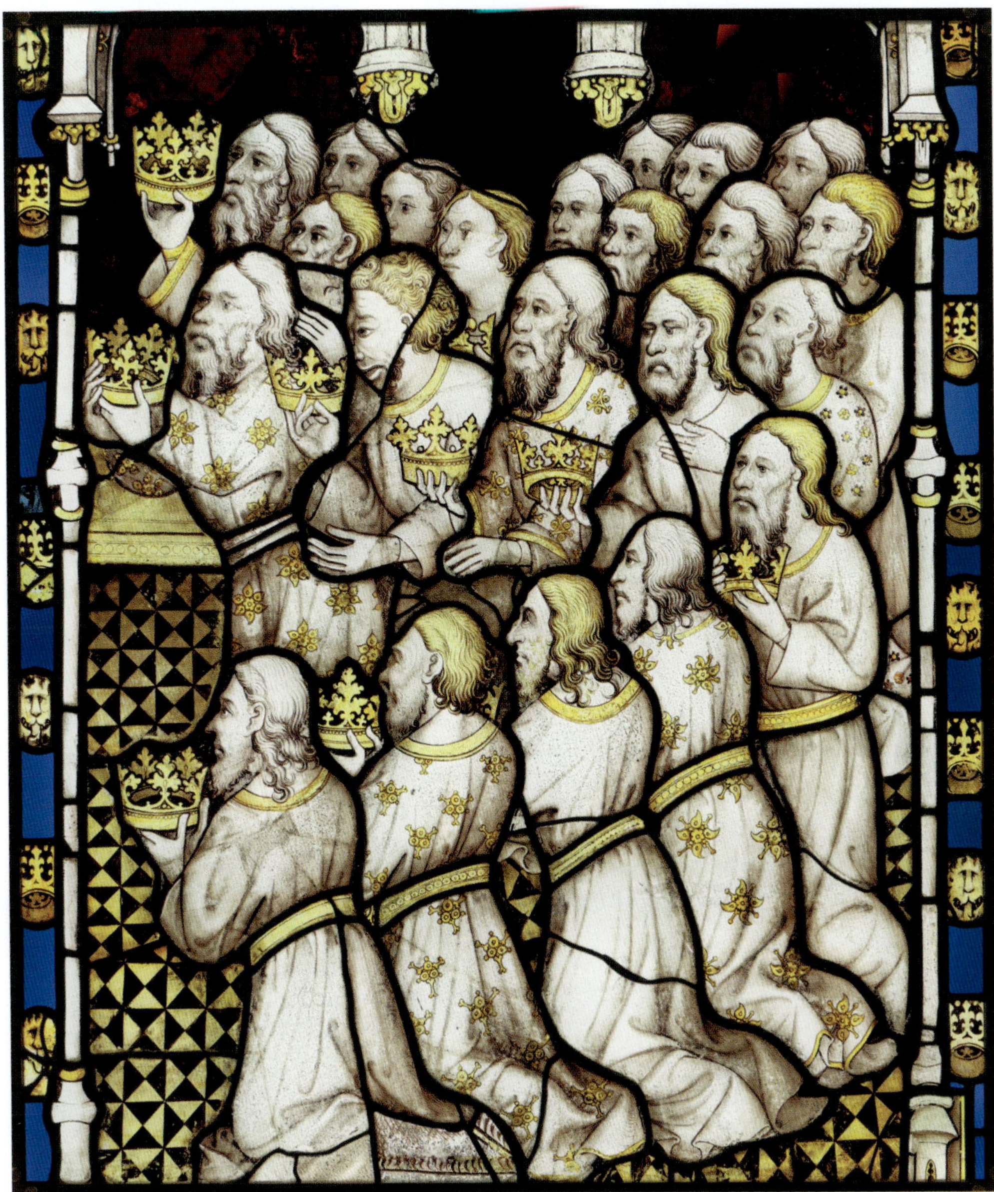

11j The Elders worship God

The four and twenty ancients fell down before him that sitteth on the throne, and adored him that liveth for ever and ever, and cast their crowns before the throne, saying: Thou art worthy, O Lord our God, to receive glory, and honour, and power: because thou hast created all things; and for thy will they were, and have been created.

Revelation 4:10–11

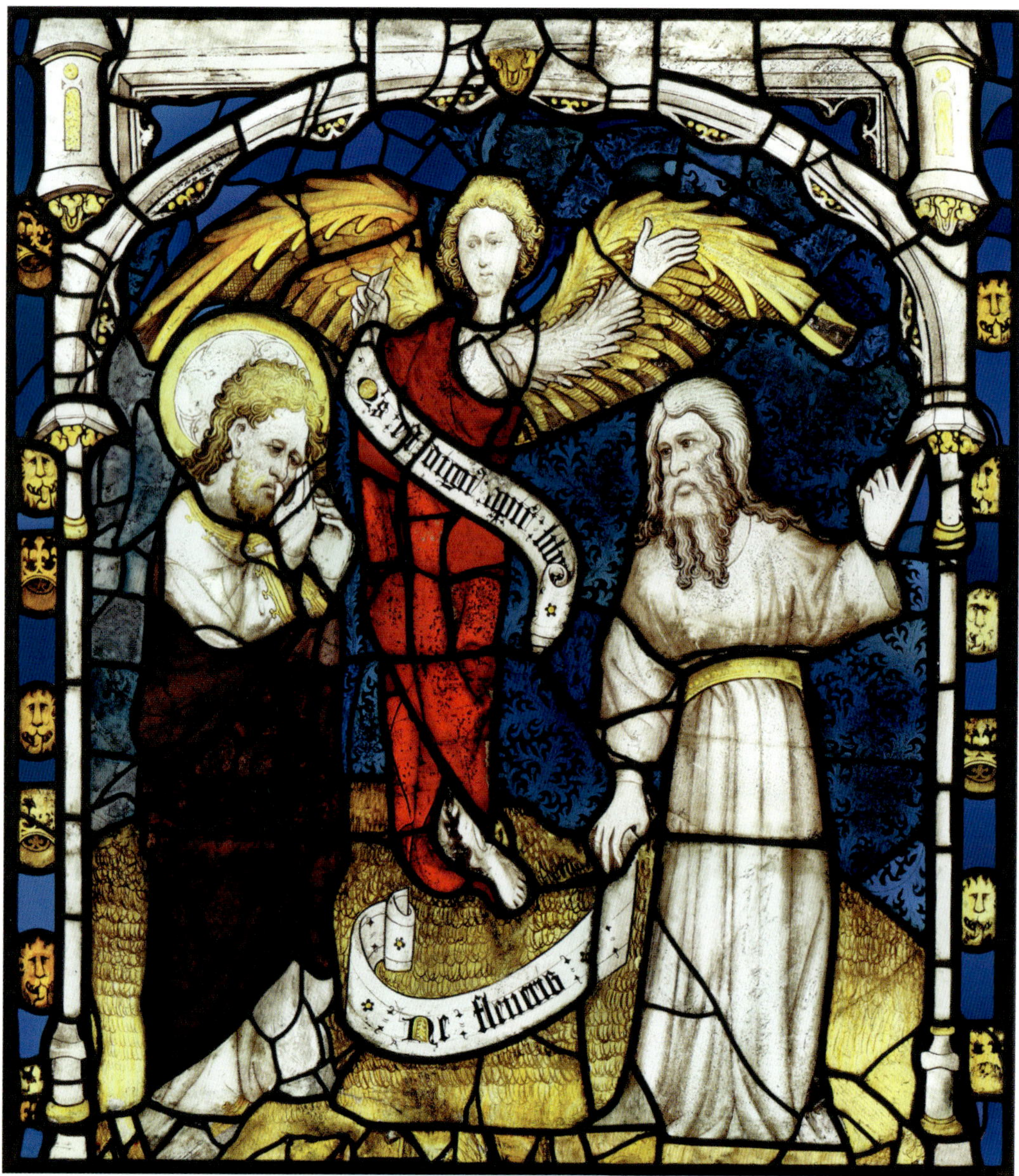

10a St John weeps

And I saw a strong angel, proclaiming with a loud voice: **Who is worthy to open the book**, and to loose the seals thereof? And no man was able, neither in heaven, nor on earth, nor under the earth, to open the book, nor to look on it. And I wept much, because no man was found worthy to open the book, nor to see it. And one of the ancients said to me: **Weep not**; behold the lion of the tribe of Juda, the root of David, hath prevailed to open the book, and to loose the seven seals thereof.
Revelation 5:2–5

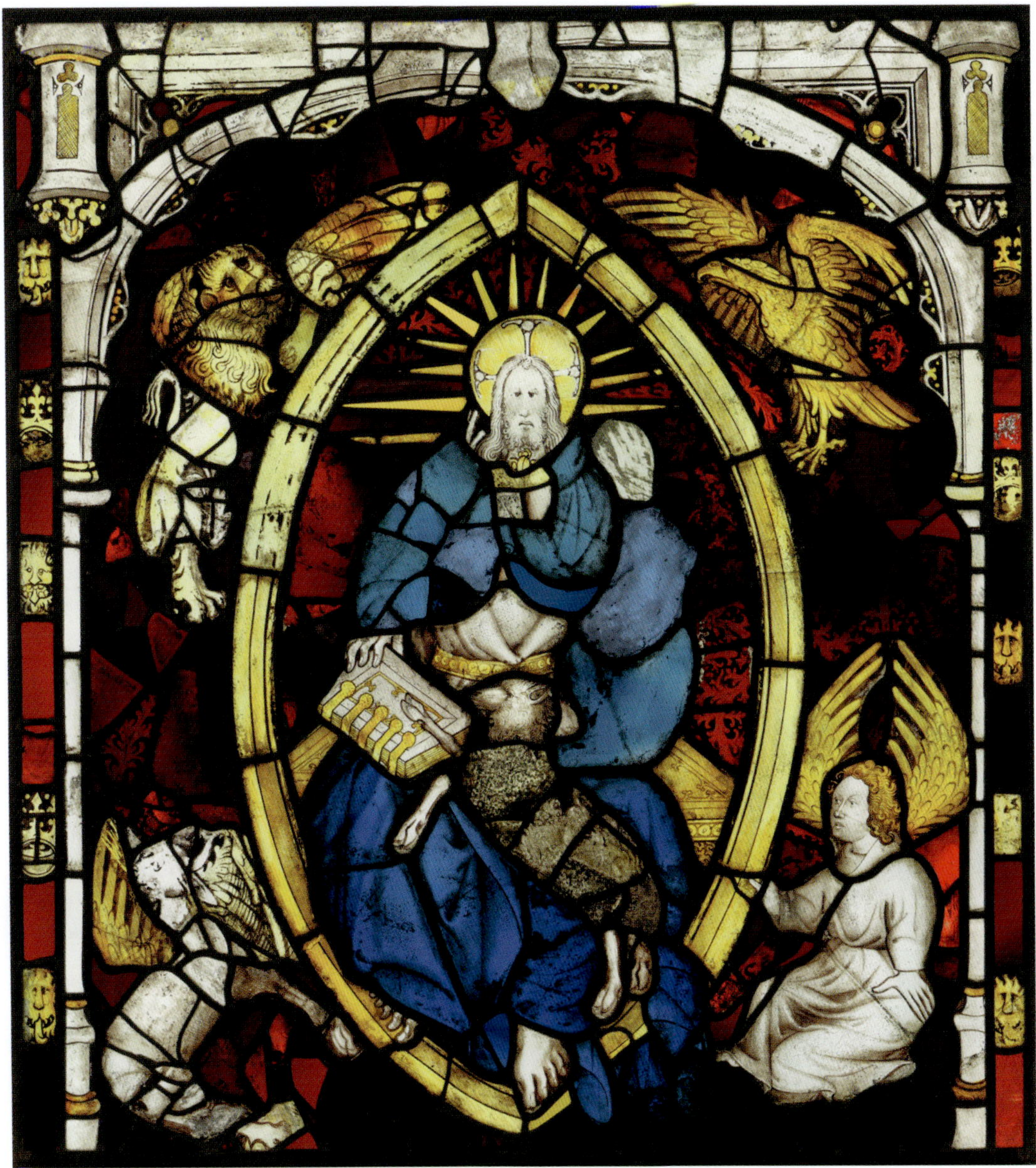

10b God in Majesty with the Lamb and the Book

And I saw: and behold in the midst of the throne and of the four living creatures, and in the midst of the ancients, a Lamb standing as it were slain, having seven horns and seven eyes: which are the seven Spirits of God, sent forth into all the earth. And he came and took the book out of the right hand of him that sat on the throne.

Revelation 5:6–7

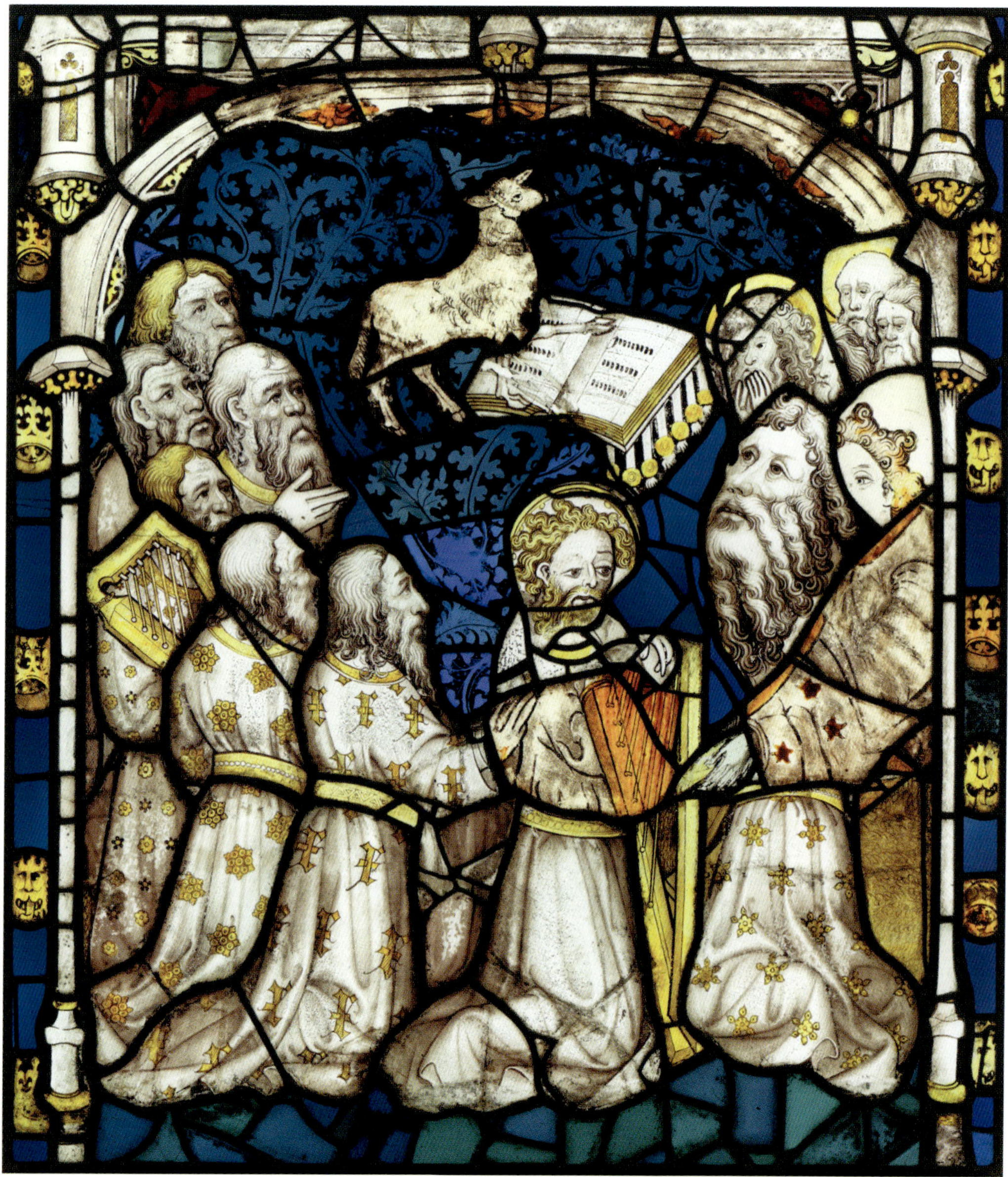

10c The Elders worship the Lamb

And when he had opened the book, the four living creatures, and the four and twenty ancients fell down before the Lamb, having every one of them harps, and golden vials full of odours, which are the prayers of saints: And they sung a new canticle, saying: Thou art worthy, O Lord, to take the book, and to open the seals thereof; because thou wast slain, and hast redeemed us to God, in thy blood, out of every tribe, and tongue, and people, and nation.
Revelation 5:8–10

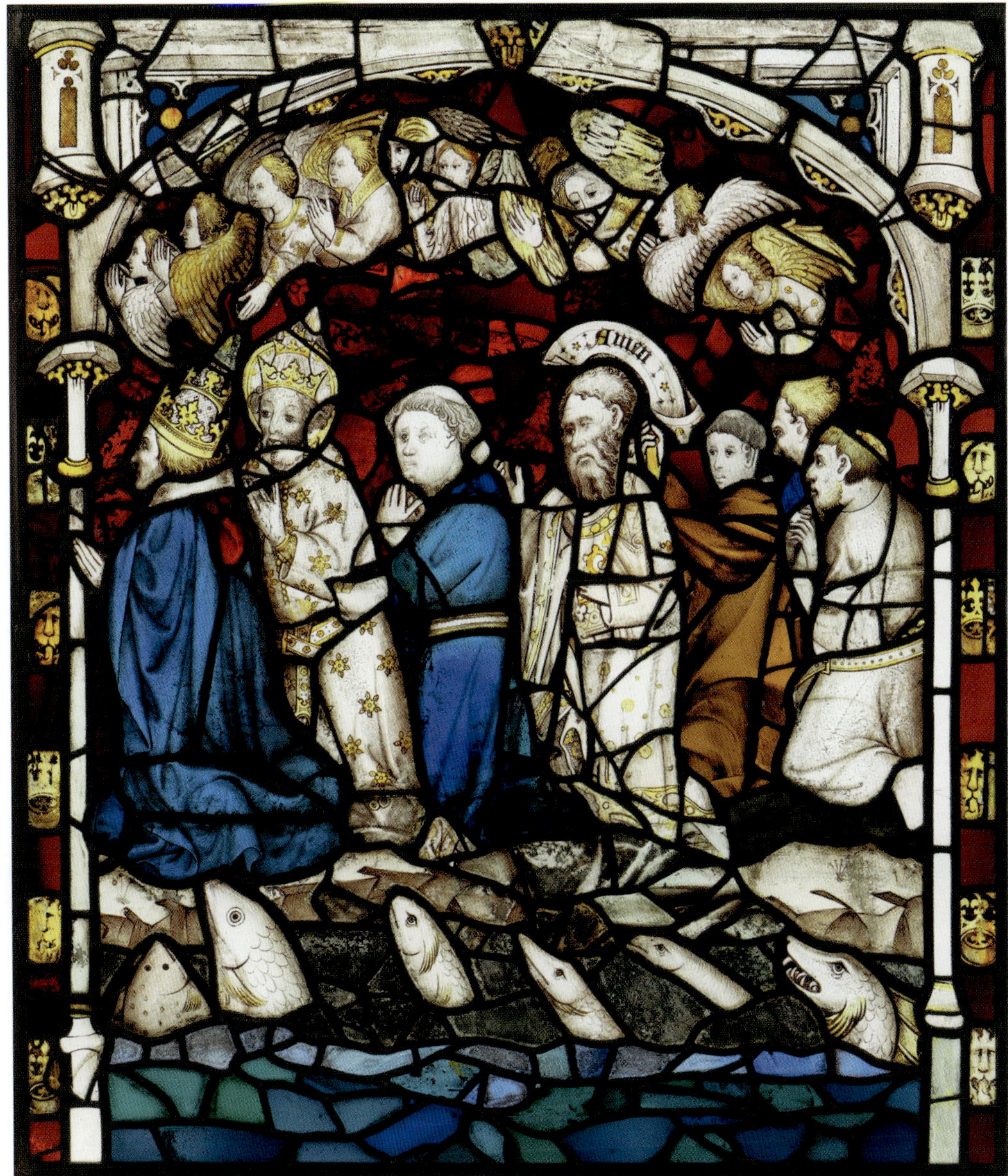

10d Creation worships the Lamb

And I beheld, and I heard the voice of many angels round about the throne, and the living creatures, and the ancients; and the number of them was thousands of thousands, Saying with a loud voice: The Lamb that was slain is worthy to receive power, and divinity, and wisdom, and strength, and honour, and glory, and benediction. And every creature, which is in heaven, and on the earth, and under the earth, and such as are in the sea, and all that are in them: I heard all saying: To him that sitteth on the throne, and to the Lamb, benediction, and honour, and glory, and power, for ever and ever. And the four living creatures said: **Amen.**
Revelation 5:11–14

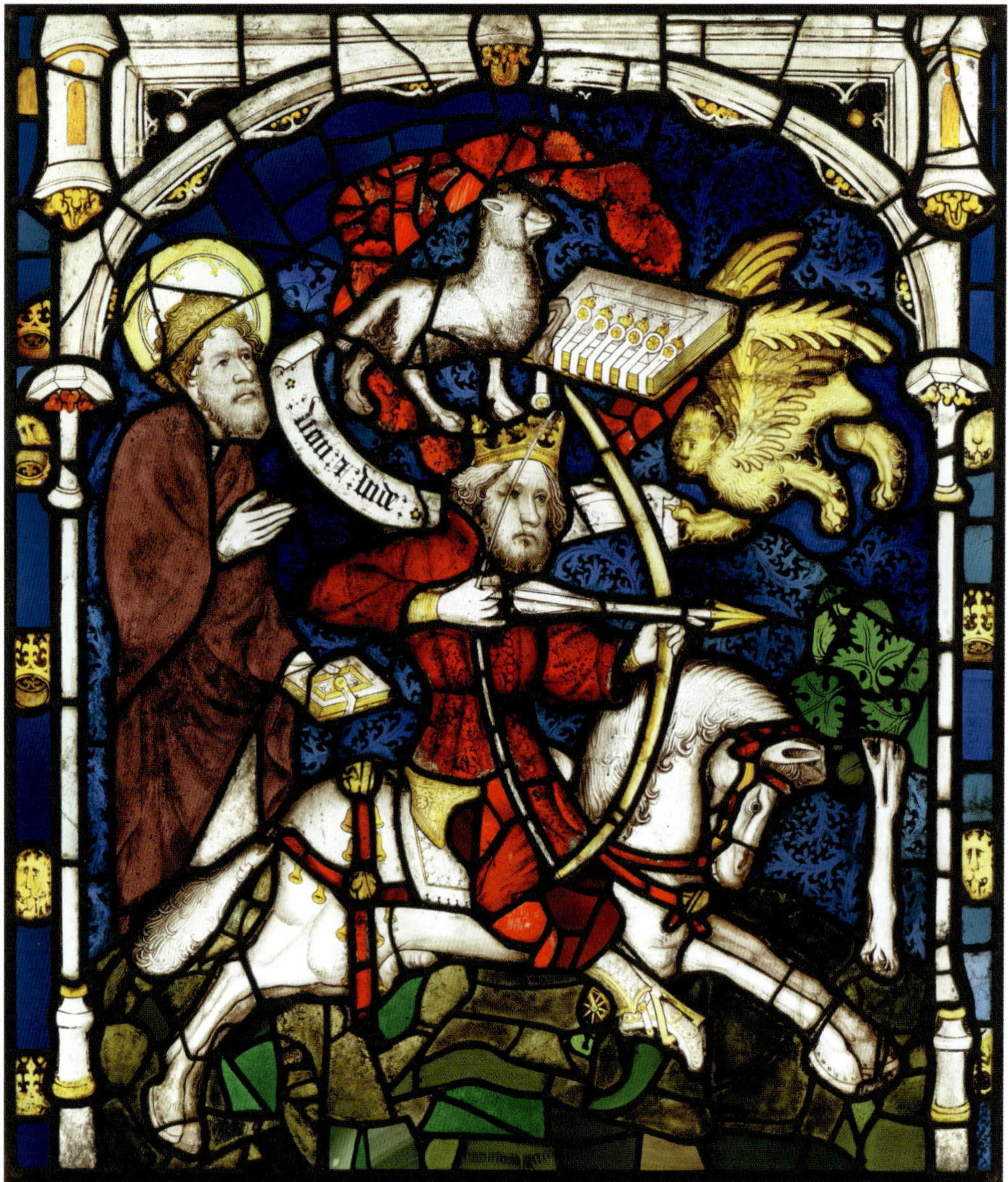

10e The Opening of the First Seal

And I saw that the Lamb had opened one of the seven seals, and I heard one of the four living creatures, as it were the voice of thunder, saying: **Come, and see**. And I saw: and behold a white horse, and he that sat on him had a bow, and there was a crown given him, and he went forth conquering that he might conquer.

Revelation 6:1–2

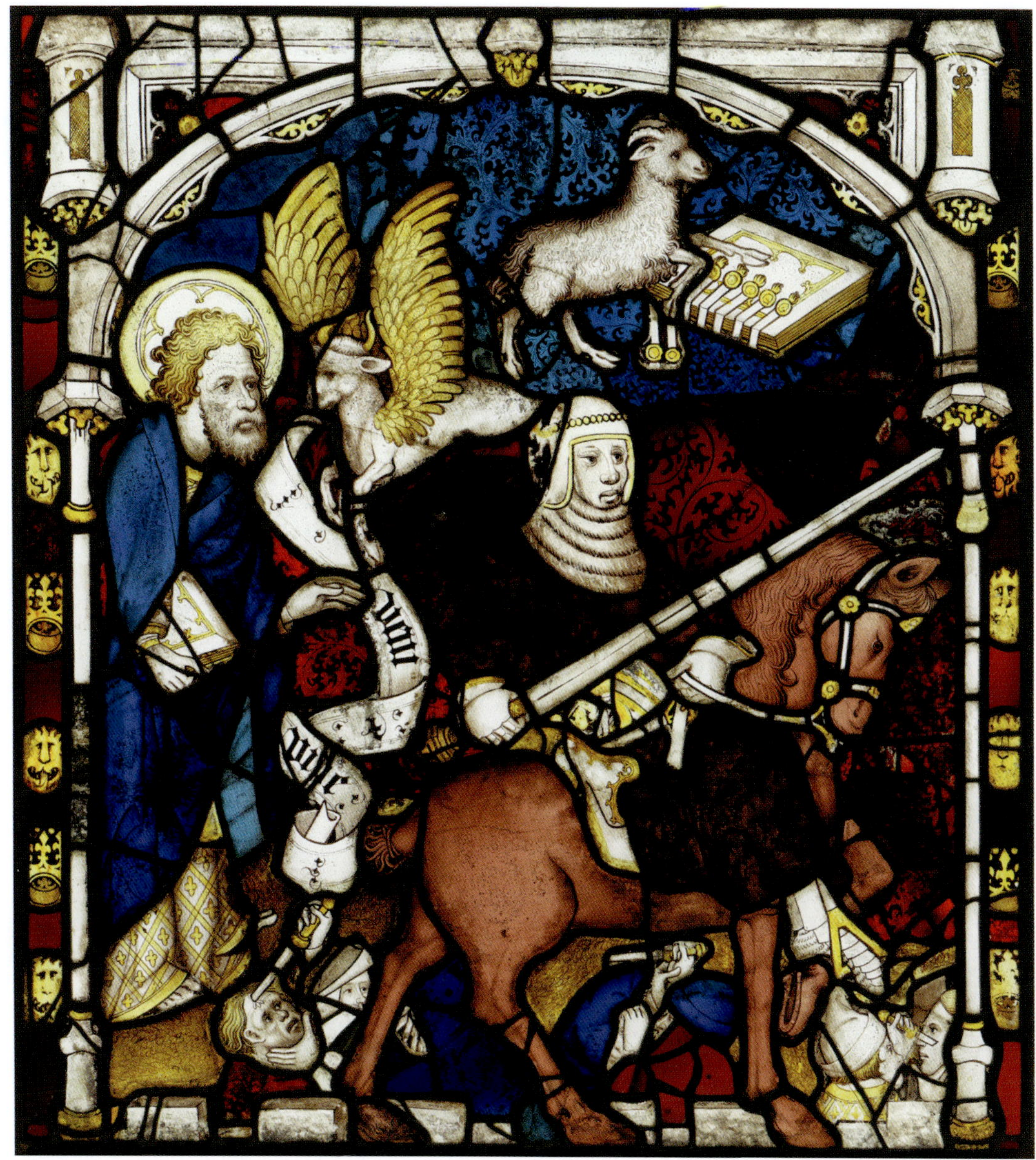

10f The Opening of the Second Seal
And when he had opened the second seal, I heard the second living creature, saying: **Come, and see**. And there went out another horse that was red: and to him that sat thereon, it was given that he should take peace from the earth, and that they should kill one another, and a great sword was given to him.
Revelation 6:3–4

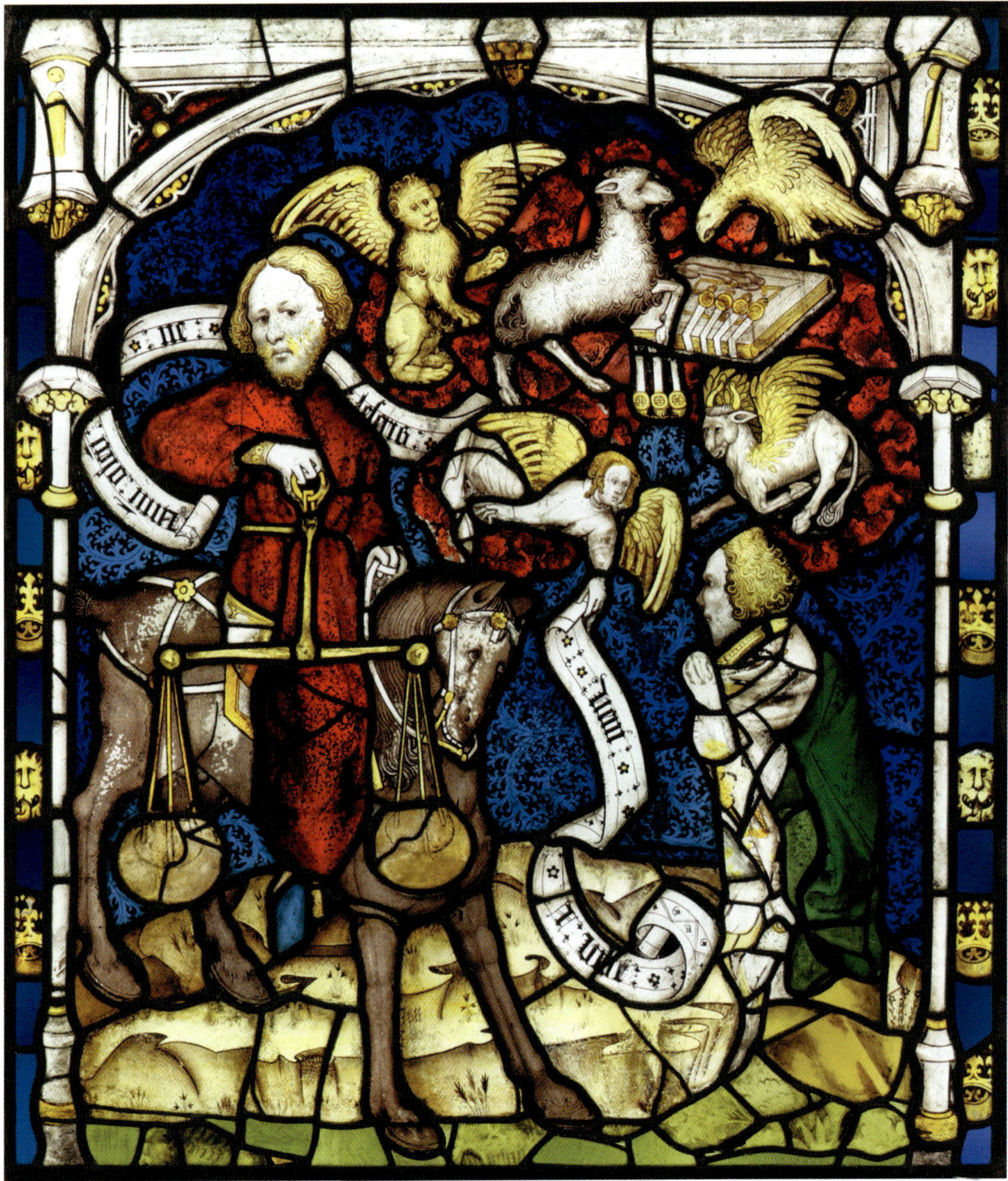

10g The Opening of the Third Seal

And when he had opened the third seal, I heard the third living creature saying: **Come, and see**. And behold a black horse, and he that sat on him had a pair of scales in his hand. And I heard as it were a voice in the midst of the four living creatures, saying: **Two pounds of wheat for a penny, and thrice two pounds of barley for a penny, and see thou hurt not the wine and the oil**.

Revelation 6:5–6

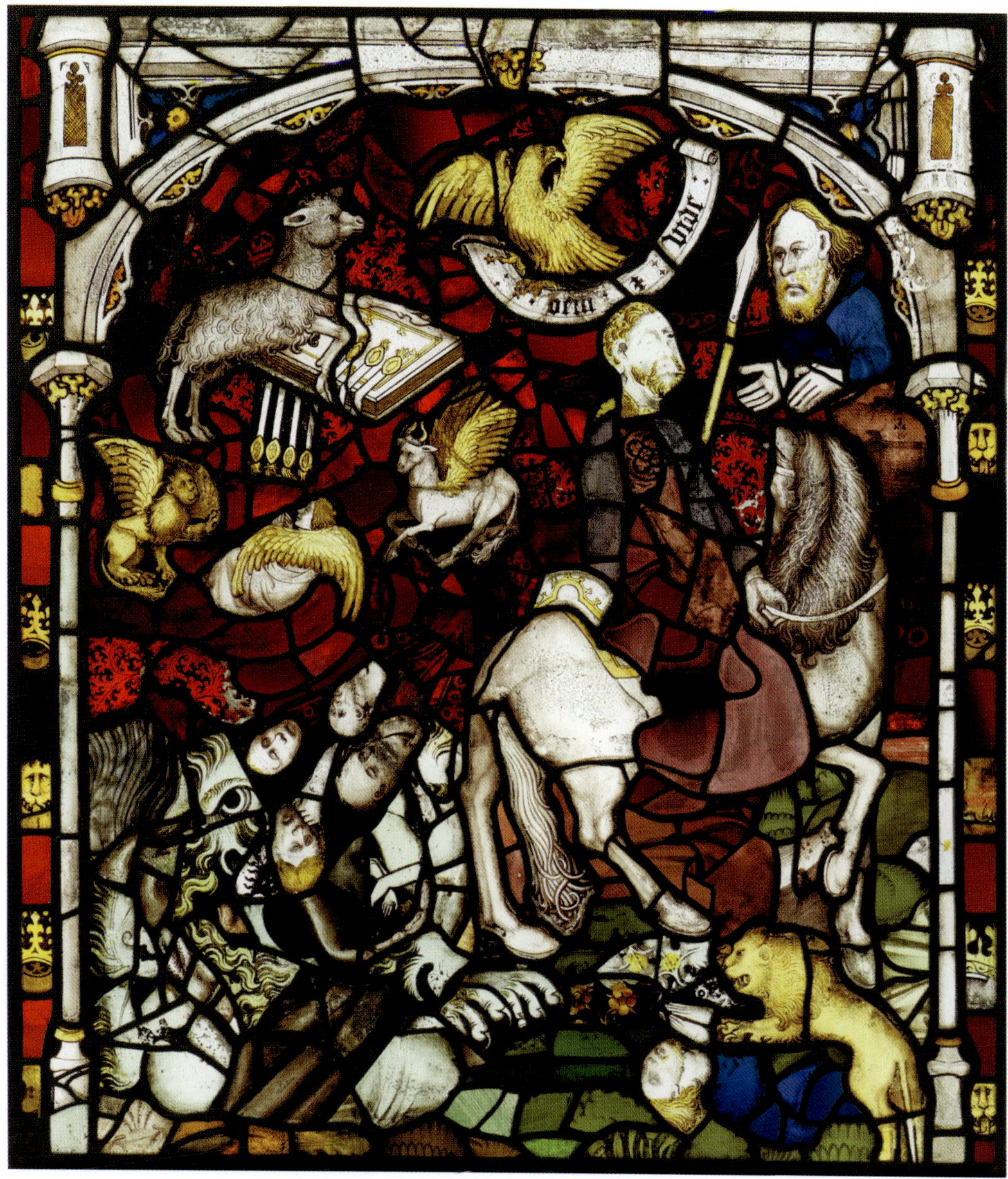

10h The Opening of the Fourth Seal

And when he had opened the fourth seal, I heard the voice of the fourth living creature, saying: Come, and see. And behold a pale horse, and he that sat upon him, his name was Death, and hell followed him. And power was given to him over the four parts of the earth, to kill with sword, with famine, and with death, and with the beasts of the earth.
Revelation 6:7–8

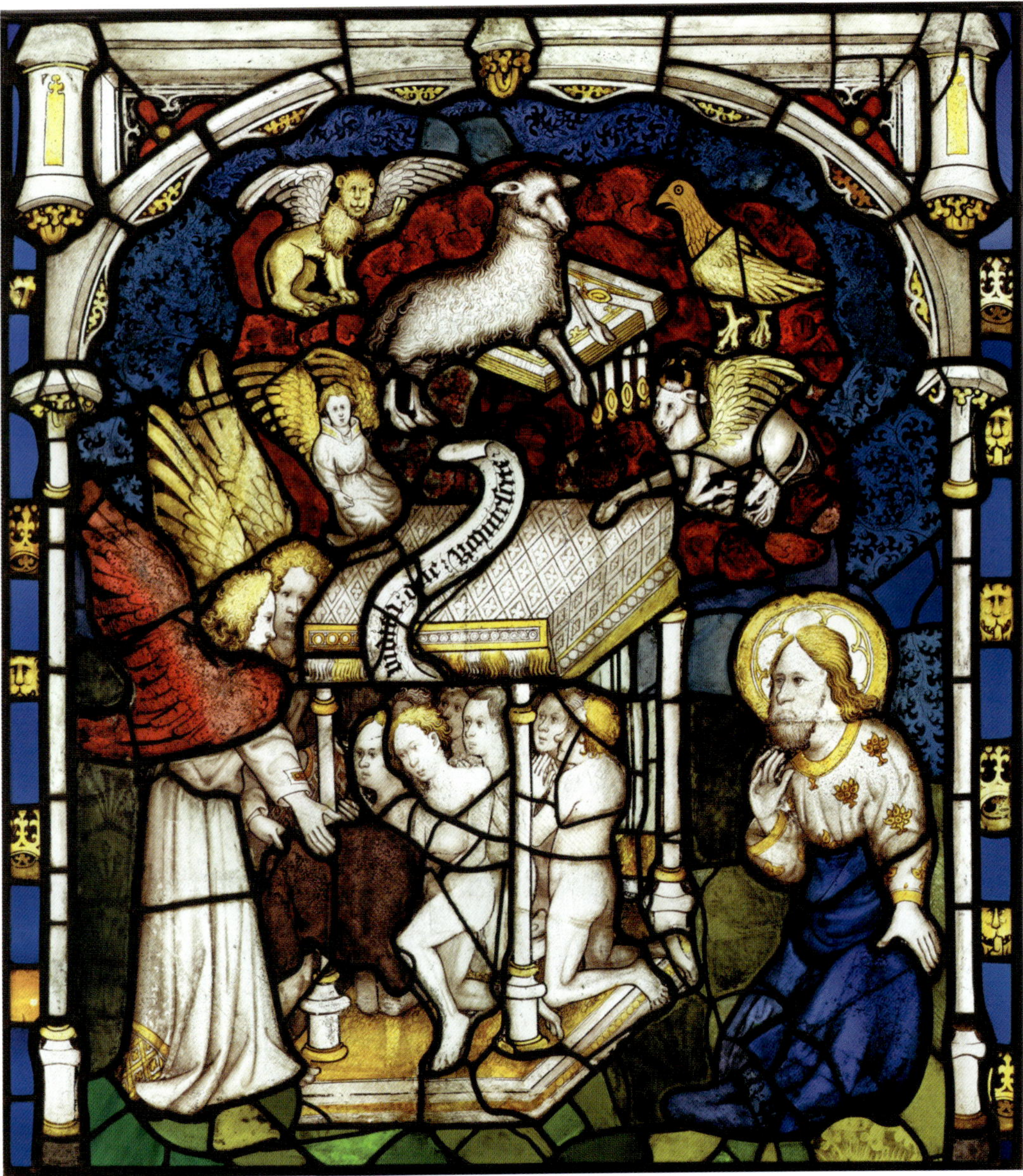

10j The Opening of the Fifth Seal
And when he had opened the fifth seal, I saw under the altar the souls of them that were slain for the word of God, and for the testimony which they held. And they cried with a loud voice, saying: How long, **O Lord** (holy and true) dost thou not judge and **revenge** our blood on them that dwell on the earth? And white robes were given to every one of them one; and it was said to them, that **they should rest** for a little time, till their fellow servants, and their brethren, who are to be slain, even as they, should be filled up.
Revelation 6:9–11

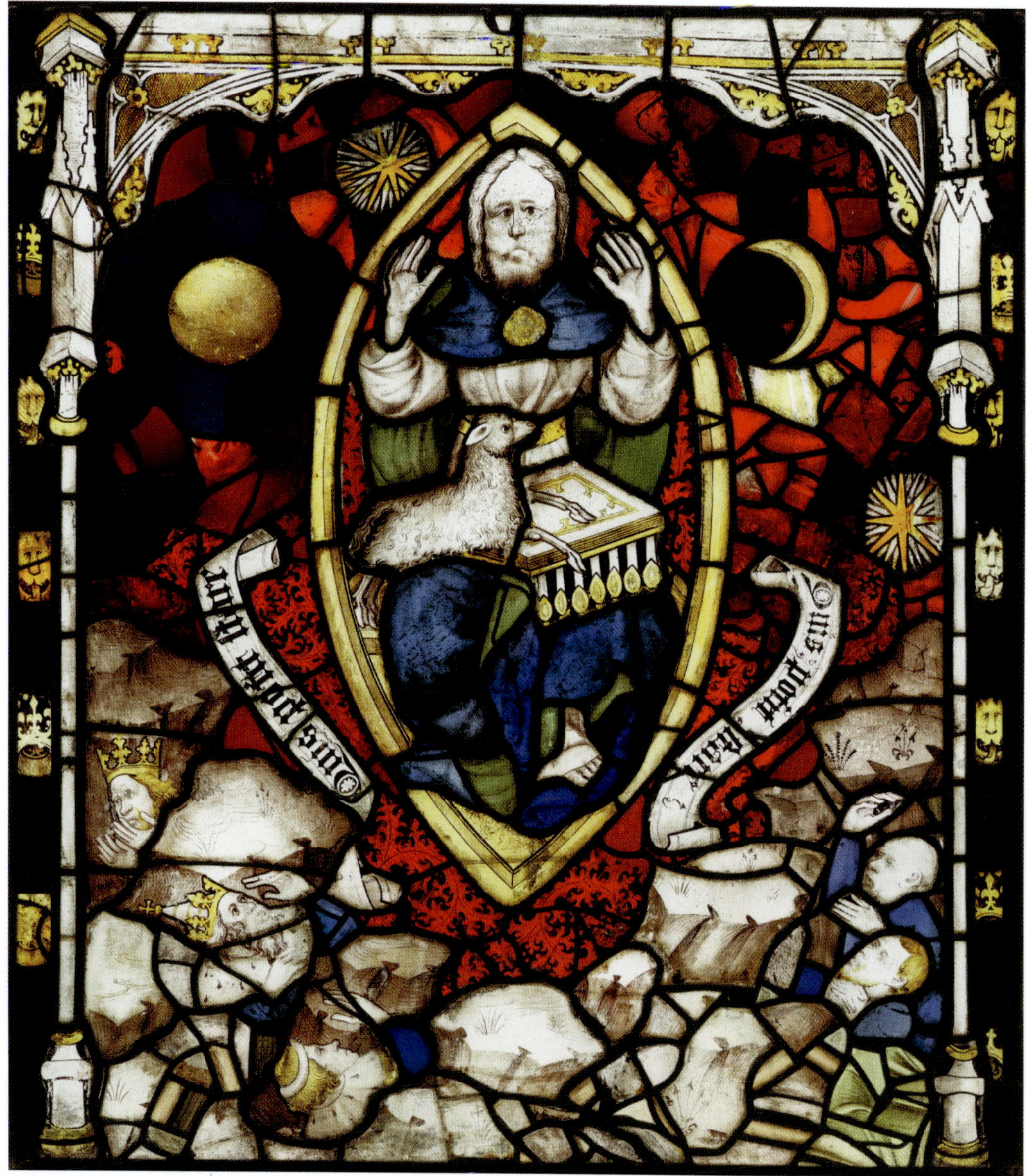

9a The Opening of the Sixth Seal

And I saw, when he had opened the sixth seal, and behold there was a great earthquake, and the sun became black as sackcloth of hair: and the whole moon became as blood: And the stars from heaven fell upon the earth ... And the kings of the earth, and the princes, and tribunes, and the rich, and the strong, and every bondman, and every freeman, hid themselves in the dens and in the rocks of mountains: And they say to the mountains and the rocks: Fall upon us, and hide us from the face of him that sitteth upon the throne and from the wrath of the Lamb: For the great day of their wrath is come, and **who shall be able to stand**?

Revelation 6:12–17

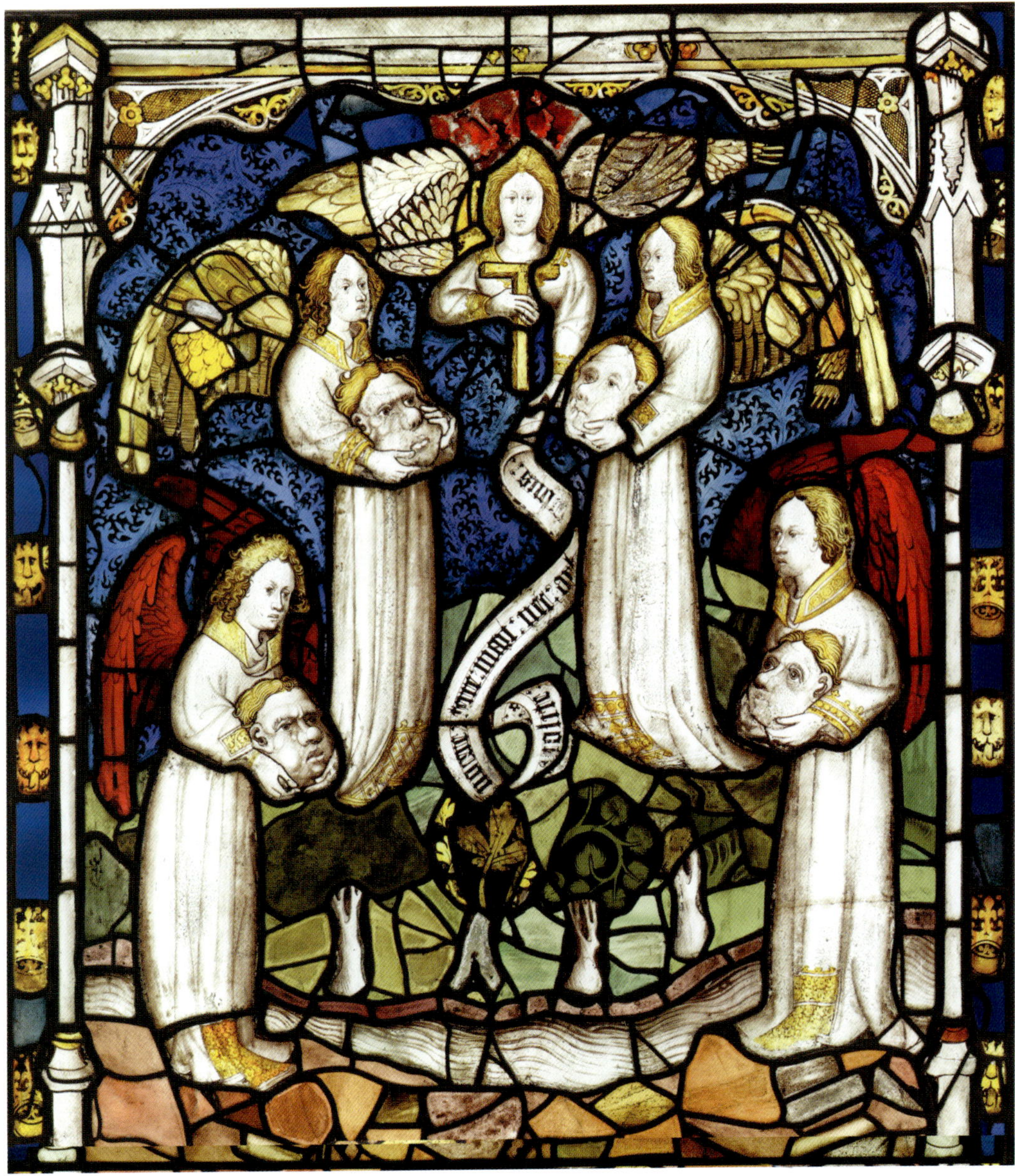

9b The Angels with the Winds and the Seal

After these things, I saw four angels standing on the four corners of the earth, holding the four winds of the earth, that they should not blow upon the earth, nor upon the sea, nor on any tree. And I saw another angel ascending from the rising of the sun, having the sign of the living God; and he cried with a loud voice to the four angels, to whom it was given to hurt the earth and the sea, Saying: **Hurt not the earth, nor the sea, nor the trees**, till we sign the servants of our God in their foreheads.

Revelation 7:1–3

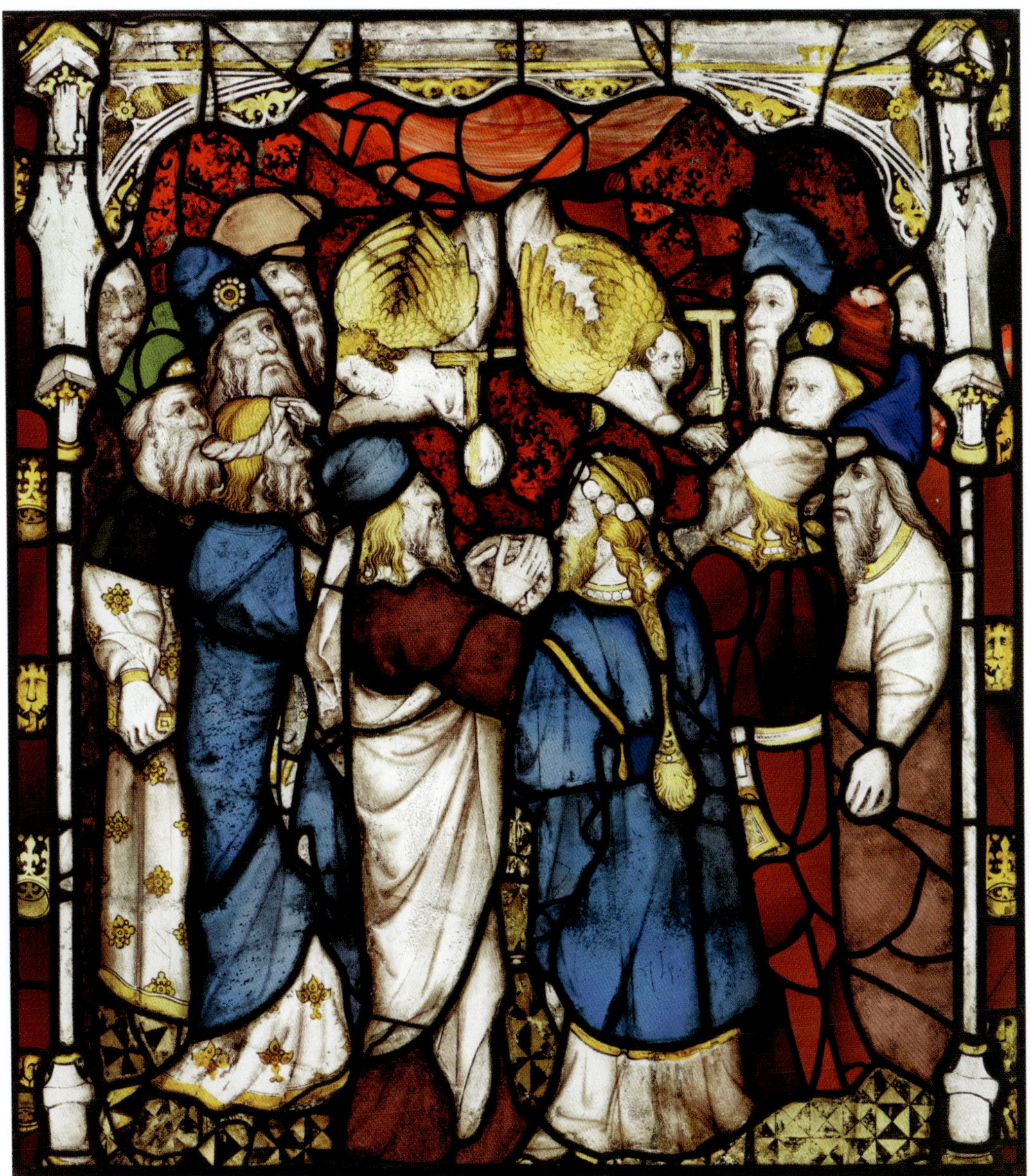

9c The Sealing of the Twelve Tribes

And I heard the number of them that were signed, an hundred forty-four thousand were signed, of every tribe of the children of Israel. Of the tribe of Juda, were twelve thousand signed ... Ruben, twelve thousand signed ... Gad, twelve thousand signed ... Aser, twelve thousand signed ... Nephthali, twelve thousand signed ... Manasses, twelve thousand signed ... Simeon, twelve thousand signed ... Levi, twelve thousand signed ... Issachar, twelve thousand signed ... Zabulon, twelve thousand signed ... Joseph, twelve thousand signed ... Benjamin, twelve thousand signed.

Revelation 7:4–8

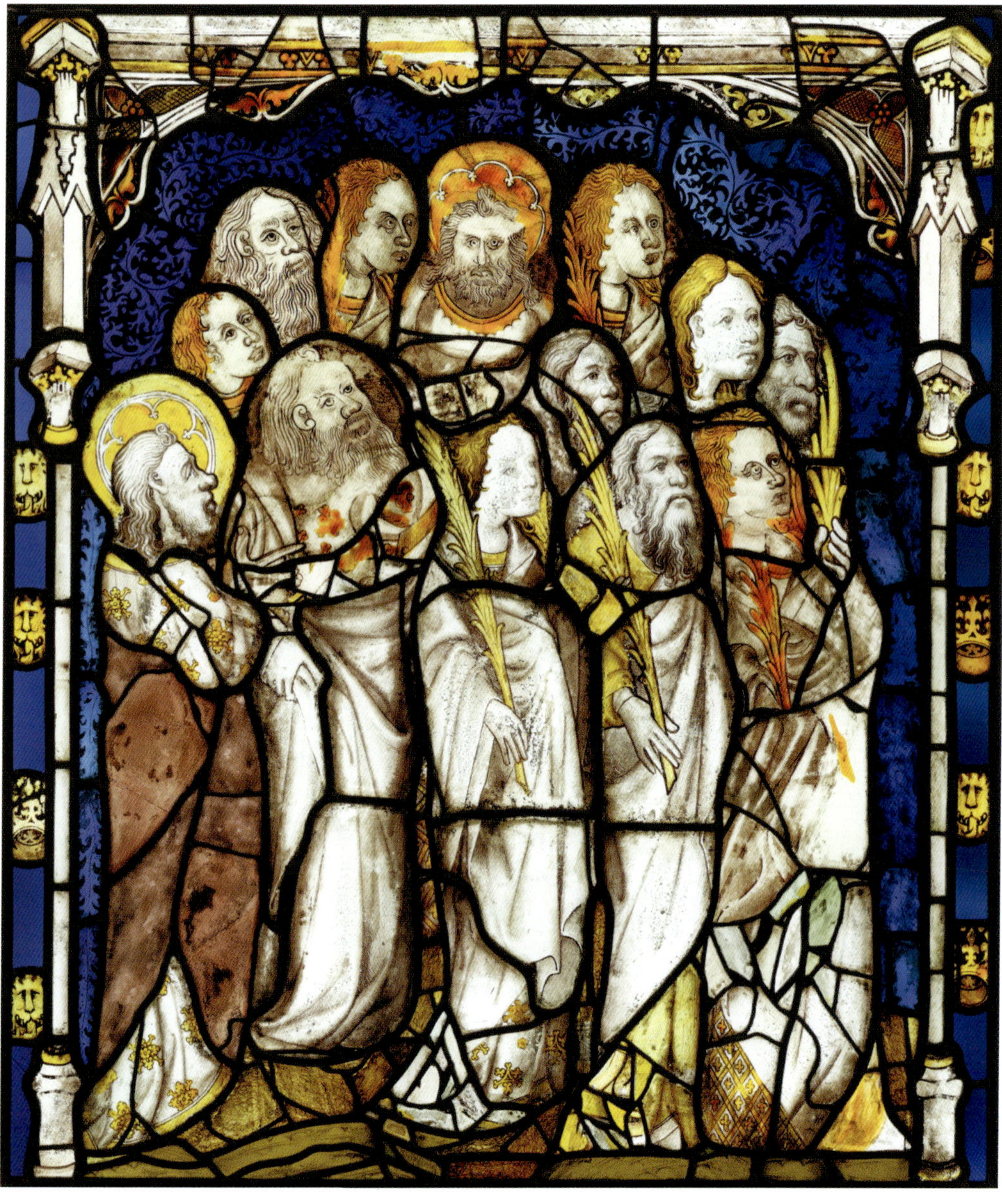

9d The Great Multitude

After this I saw a great multitude, which no man could number, of all nations, and tribes, and peoples, and tongues, standing before the throne, and in sight of the Lamb, clothed with white robes, and palms in their hands: And they cried with a loud voice, saying: Salvation to our God, who sitteth upon the throne, and to the Lamb.

Revelation 7:9–12 (with panel 9e and 9f)

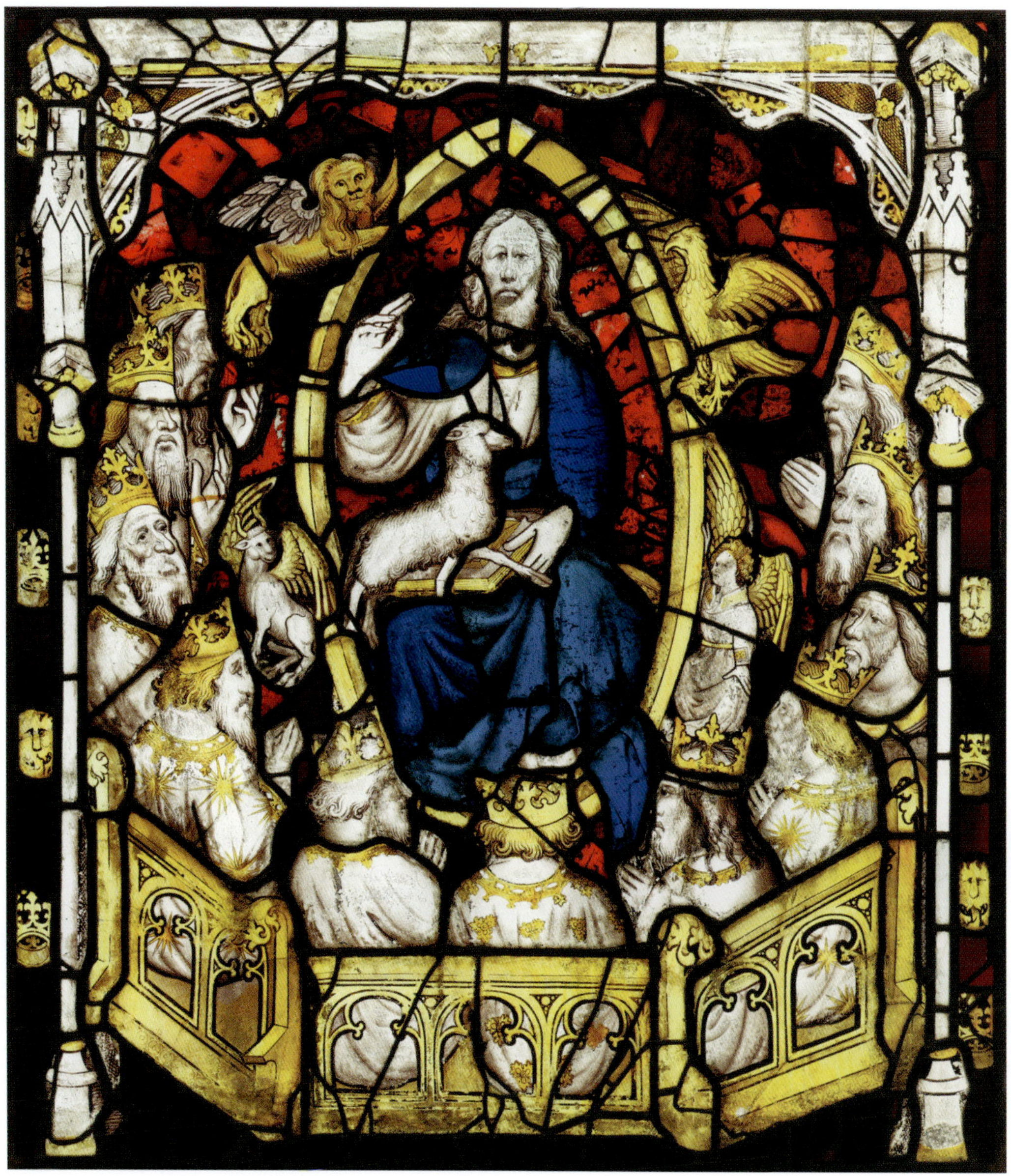

9e God and the Lamb in Majesty
... the ancients, and the four living creatures ... fell down before the throne upon their faces, and adored God, Saying: Amen. Benediction, and glory, and wisdom, and thanksgiving, honour, and power, and strength to our God for ever and ever. Amen.
Revelation 7:9–12 (with panel 9d and 9f)

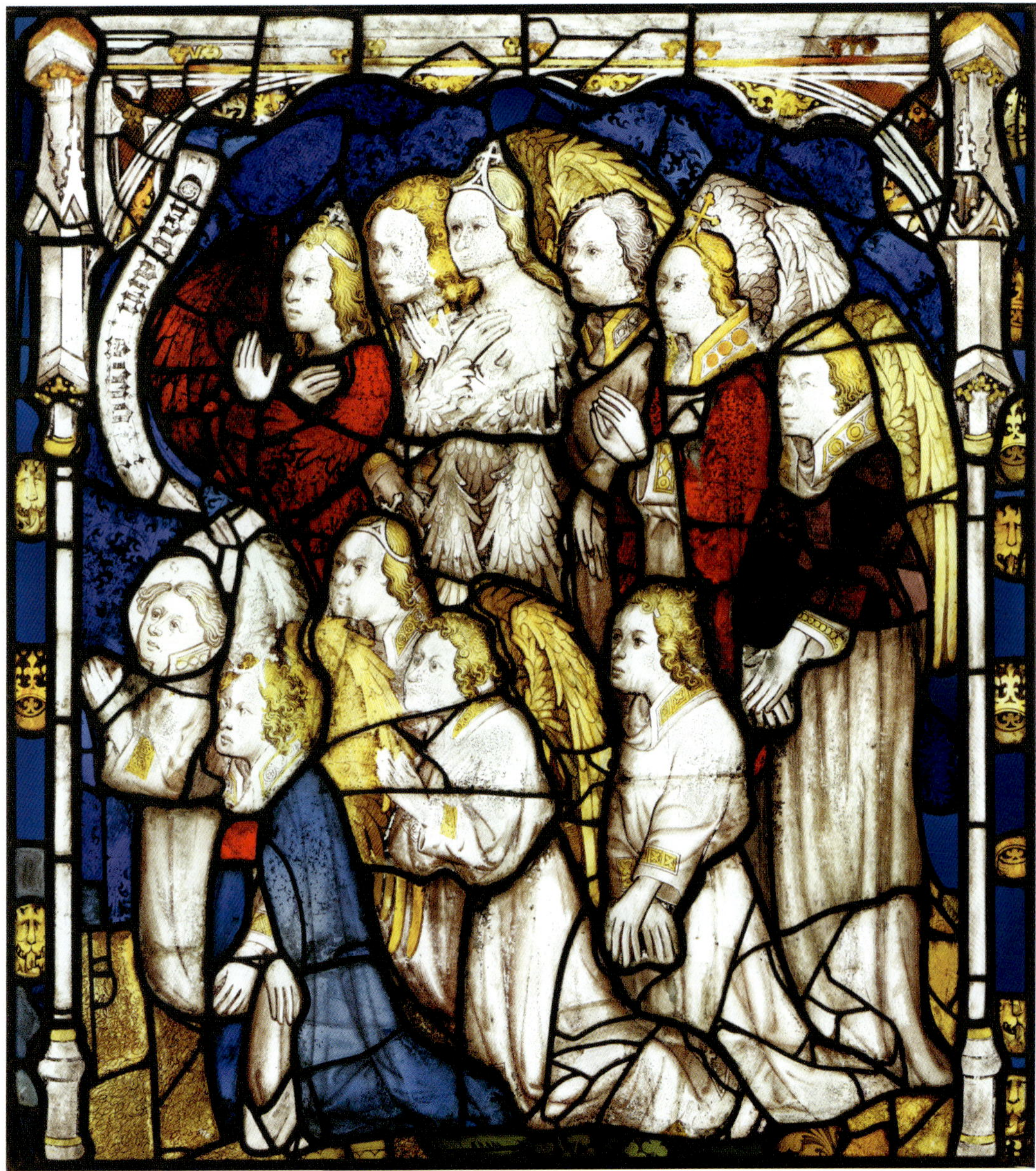

9f Angels around the Throne
... And all the angels stood round about the throne, and ... they fell down before the throne upon their faces, and adored God, Saying:
Amen. Benediction, and glory, and wisdom, and **thanksgiving**, honour, and power, and strength to our God for ever and ever. Amen.
Revelation 7:9–12 (with panel 9d and 9e)

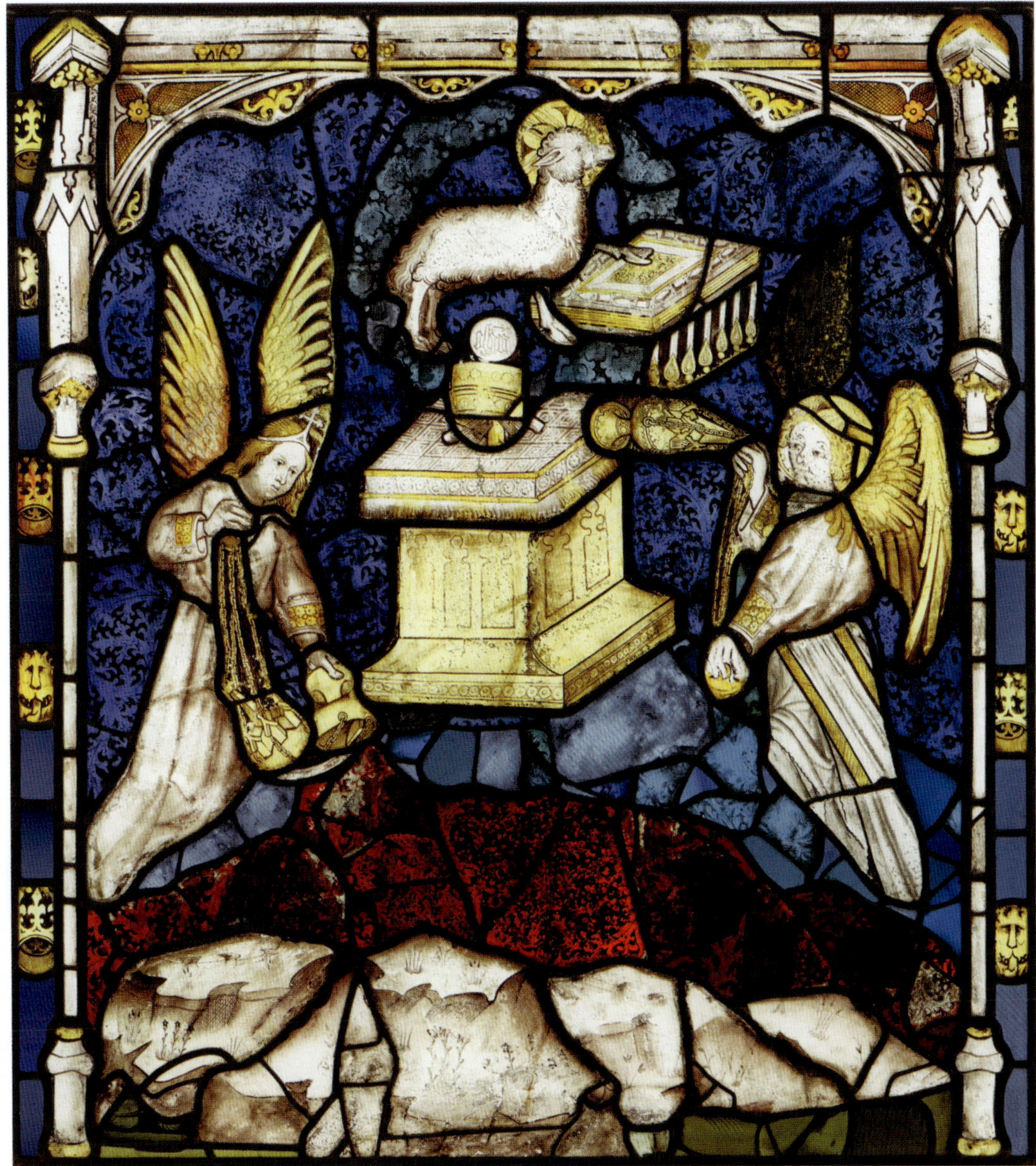

9g Angels cense the Altar

And when he had opened the seventh seal, there was silence in heaven, as it were for half an hour ... And another angel came, and stood before the altar, having a golden censer; and there was given to him much incense, that he should offer of the prayers of all saints upon the golden altar, which is before the throne of God. And the smoke of the incense of the prayers of the saints ascended up before God from the hand of the angel. And the angel took the censer, and filled it with the fire of the altar, and cast it on the earth, and there were thunders and voices and lightnings, and a great earthquake.

Revelation 8:1, 3–5

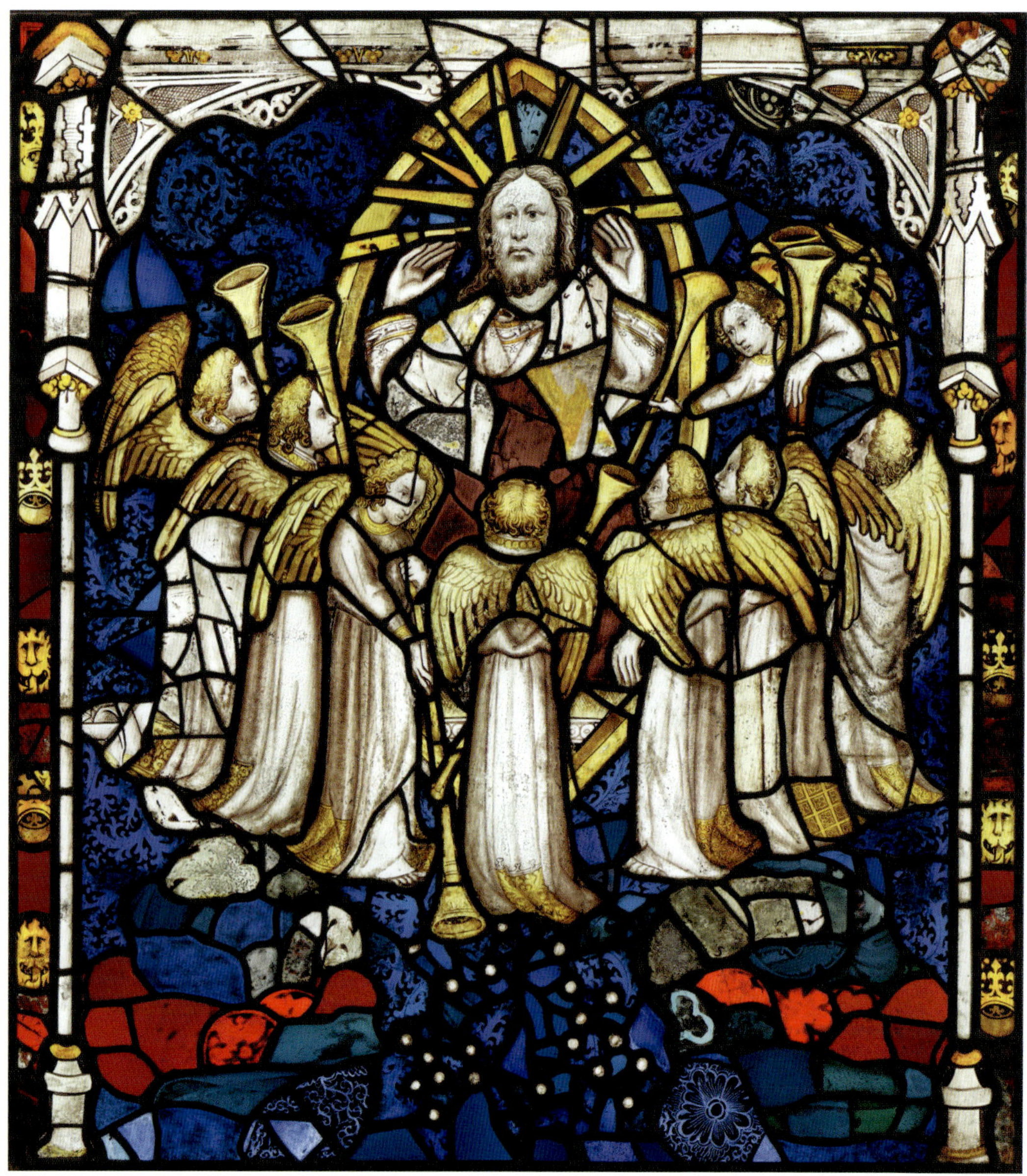

9h Seven Angels receive Seven Trumpets

And I saw seven angels standing in the presence of God; and there were given to them seven trumpets ... And the seven angels, who had the seven trumpets, prepared themselves to sound the trumpet.

Revelation 8:2 and 6

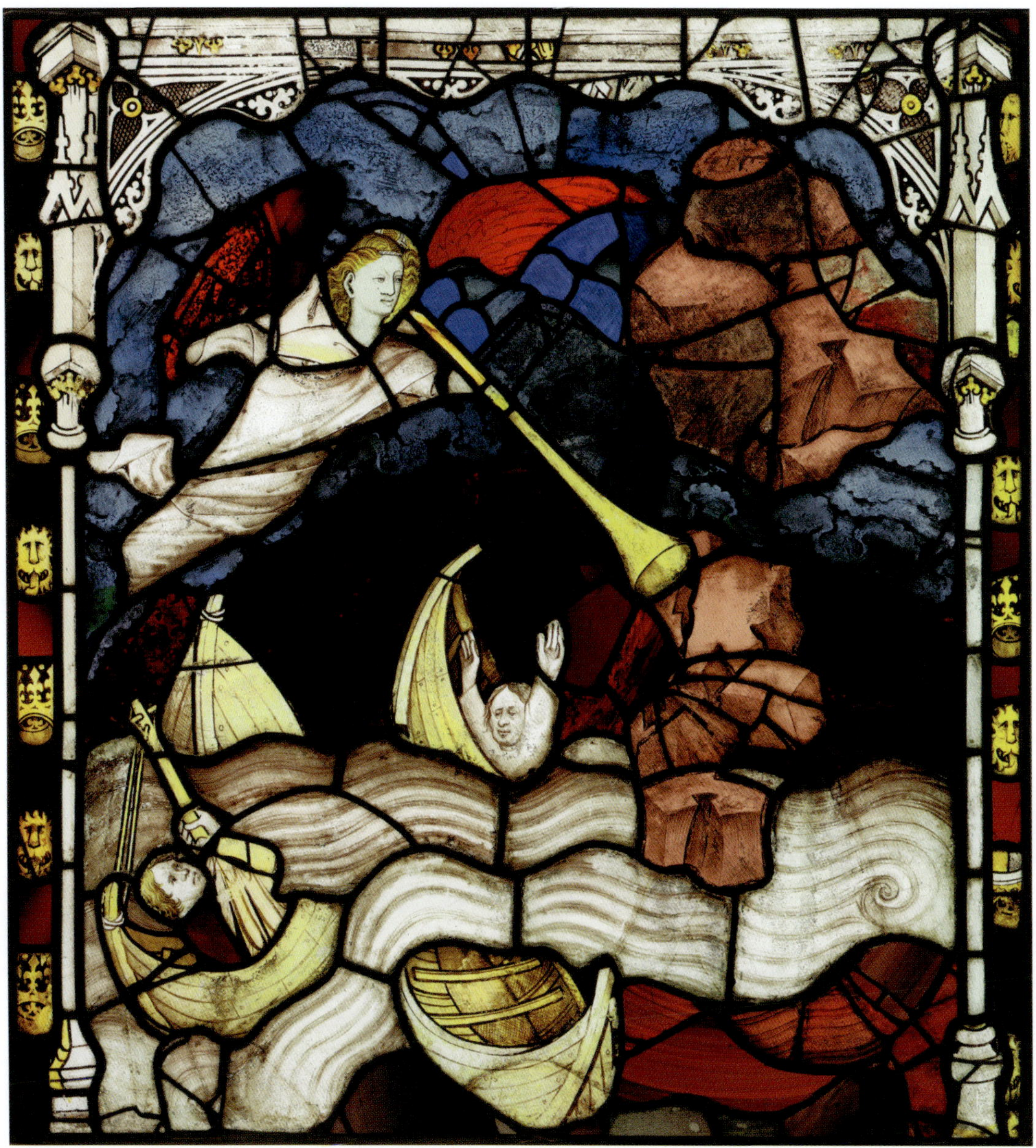

9j The Second Angel sounds the Trumpet

And the second angel sounded the trumpet: and as it were a great mountain, burning with fire, was cast into the sea, and the third part of the sea became blood: And the third part of those creatures died, which had life in the sea, and the third part of the ships was destroyed.

Revelation 8:8–9

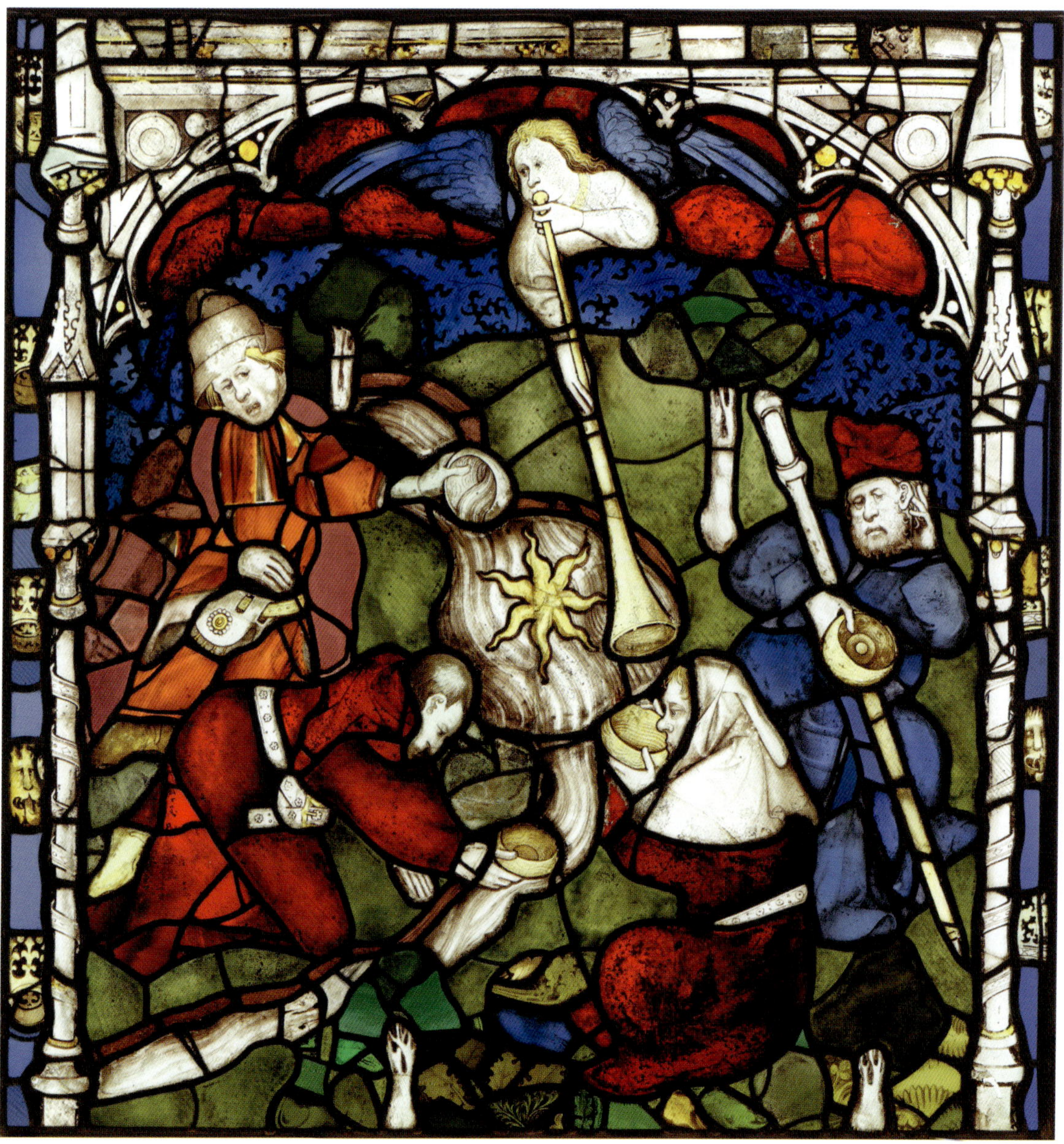

8a The Third Angel sounds the Trumpet
And the third angel sounded the trumpet, and a great star fell from heaven, burning as it were a torch, and it fell on the third part of the rivers, and upon the fountains of waters: And the name of the star is called Wormwood. And the third part of the waters became wormwood; and many men died of the waters, because they were made bitter.
Revelation 8:10–11

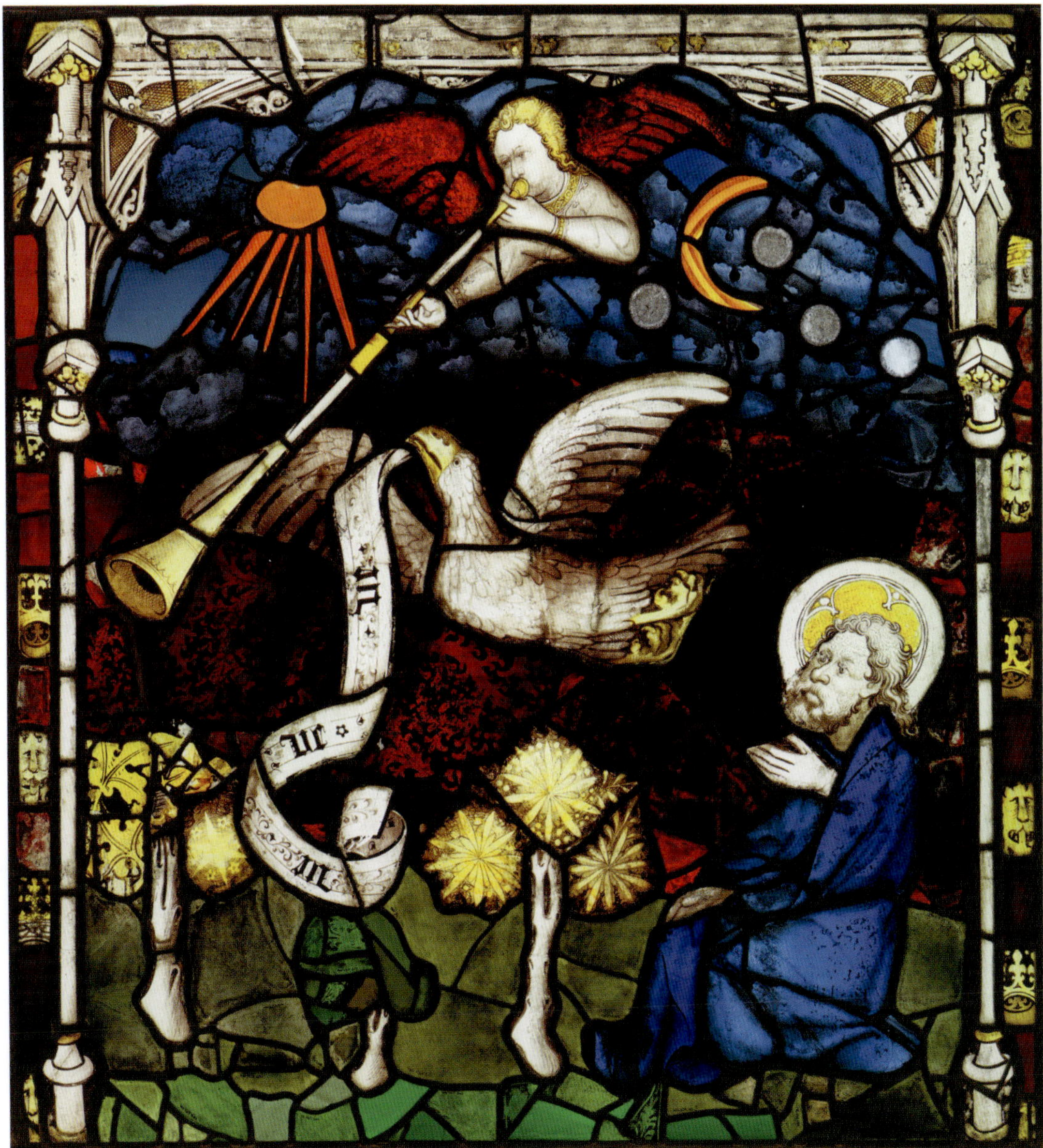

8b The Fourth Angel sounds the Trumpet
And the fourth angel sounded the trumpet, and the third part of the sun was smitten, and the third part of the moon, and the third part of the stars, so that the third part of them was darkened, and the day did not shine for a third part of it, and the night in like manner. And I beheld, and heard the voice of one eagle flying through the midst of heaven, saying with a loud voice: **Woe, woe, woe** to the inhabitants of the earth: by reason of the rest of the voices of the three angels, who are yet to sound the trumpet.
Revelation 8:12–13

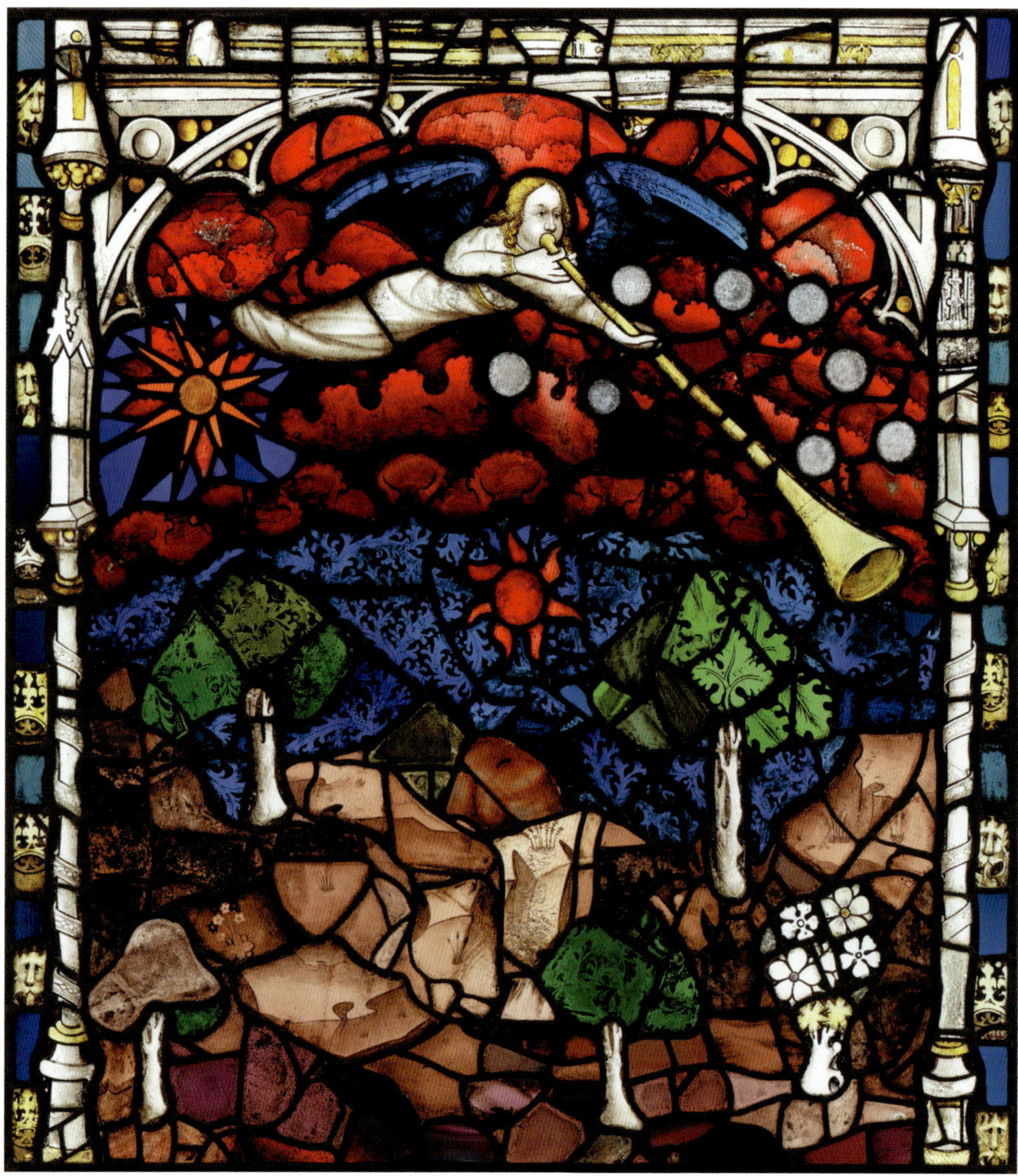

8c The First Angel sounds the Trumpet
And the first angel sounded the trumpet, and there followed hail and fire, mingled with blood, and it was cast on the earth, and the third part of the earth was burnt up, and the third part of the trees was burnt up, and all green grass was burnt up. *(This panel is out of order, see p. 27.)*
Revelation 8:7

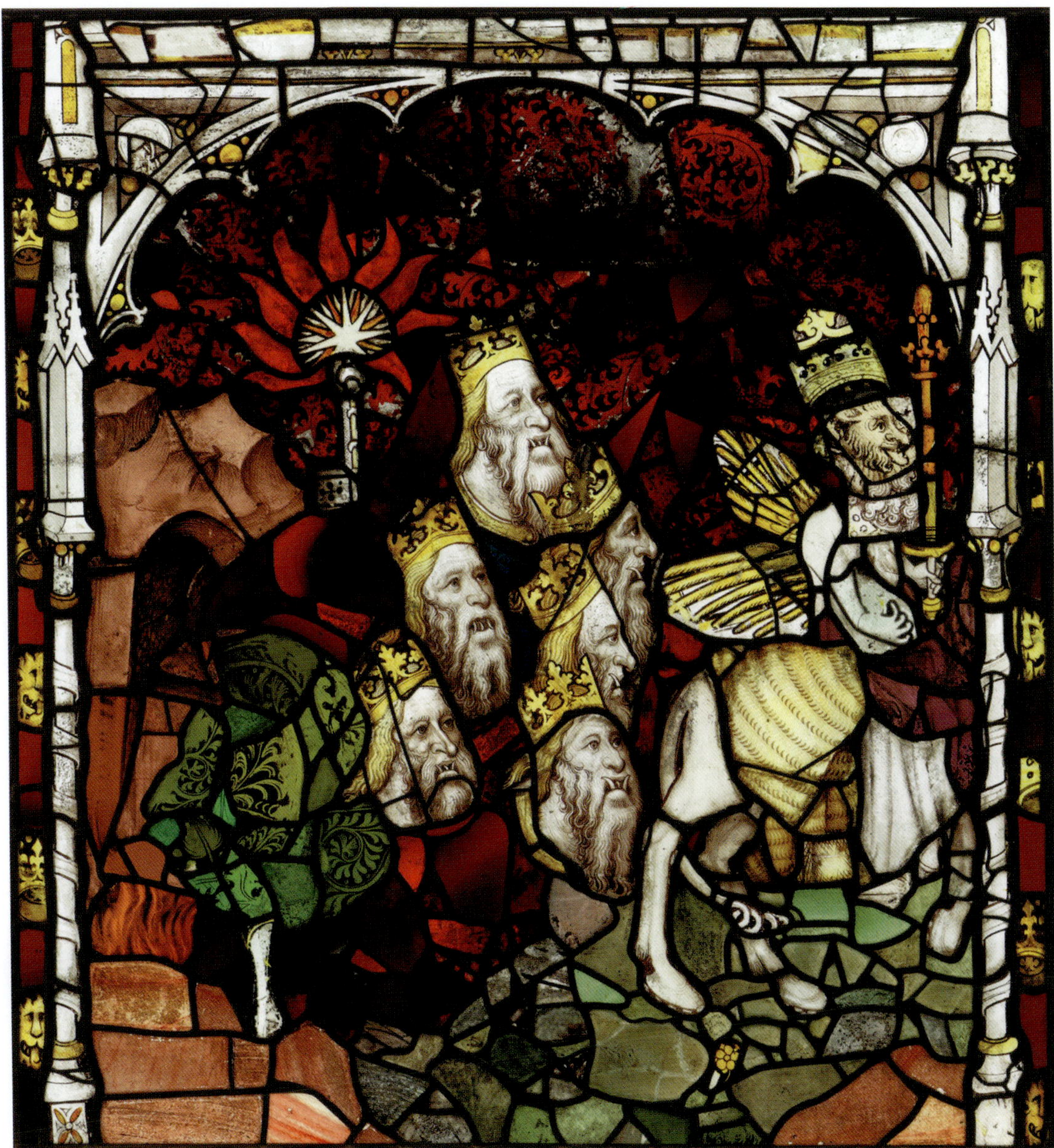

8d The Fifth Angel sounds the Trumpet

And the fifth angel sounded the trumpet, and I saw a star fall from heaven upon the earth, and there was given to him the key of the bottomless pit. And he opened the bottomless pit ... there came out locusts upon the earth. And power was given to them, as the scorpions of the earth have power: And it was commanded them that they should not hurt the grass of the earth, nor any green thing, nor any tree: but only the men who have not the sign of God on their foreheads ... And the shapes of the locusts were like unto horses prepared unto battle: and on their heads were, as it were, crowns like gold: and their faces were as the faces of men. And they had hair as the hair of women; and their teeth were as lions: And they had breastplates as breastplates of iron, and the noise of their wings was as the noise of chariots and many horses running to battle. And they had tails like to scorpions, and there were stings in their tails ... And they had over them a king, the angel of the bottomless pit; whose name in Hebrew is Abaddon, and in Greek Apollyon; in Latin Exterminans.

Revelation 9:1–11

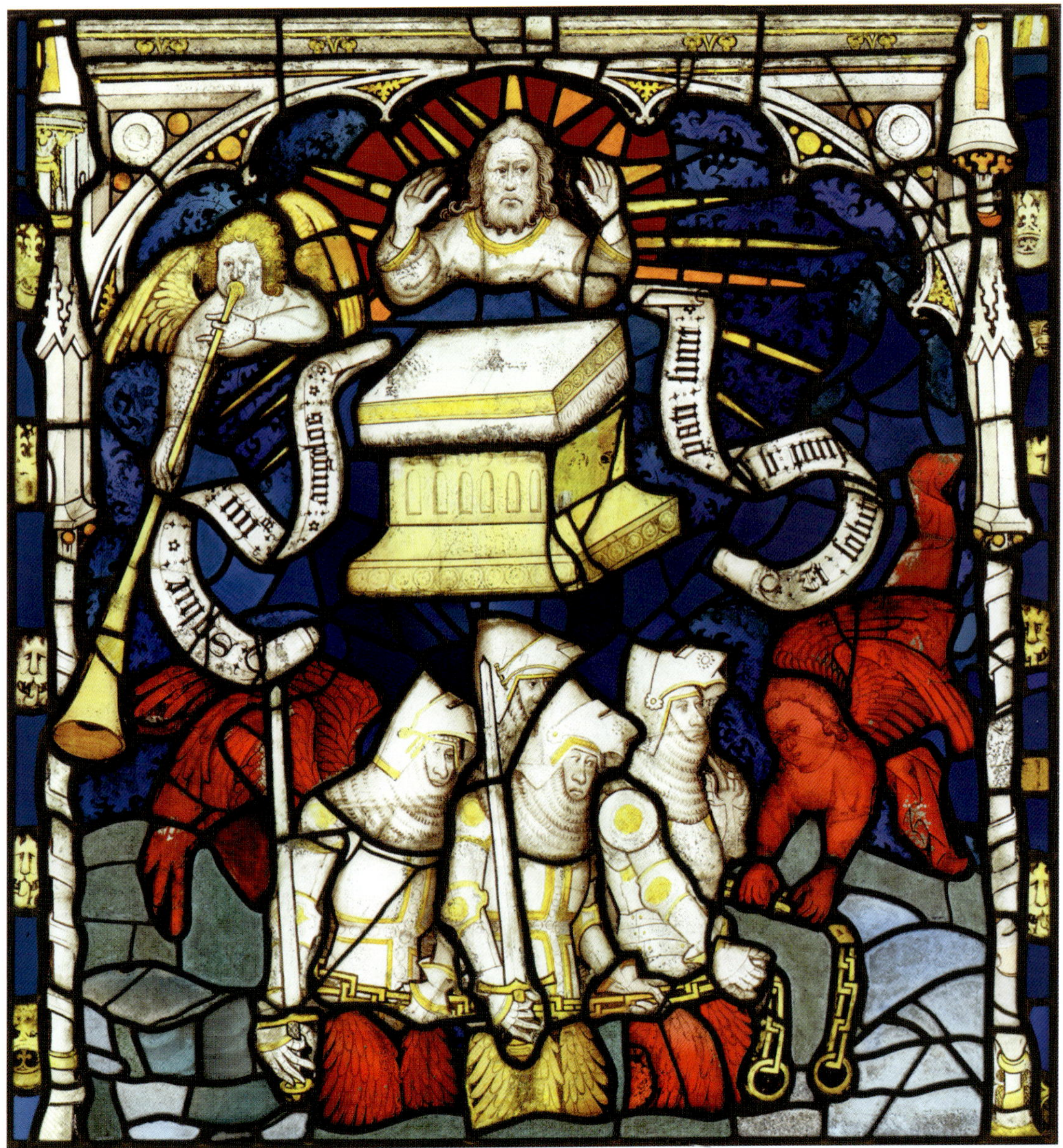

8e The Sixth Angel sounds the Trumpet

And the sixth angel sounded the trumpet: and I heard a voice from the four horns of the great altar, which is before the eyes of God, Saying to the sixth angel, who had the trumpet: **Loose the four angels**, who are bound in the great river Euphrates. **And the four angels were loosed**, who were prepared for an hour, and a day, and a month, and a year: for to kill the third part of men.
Revelation 9:13–15

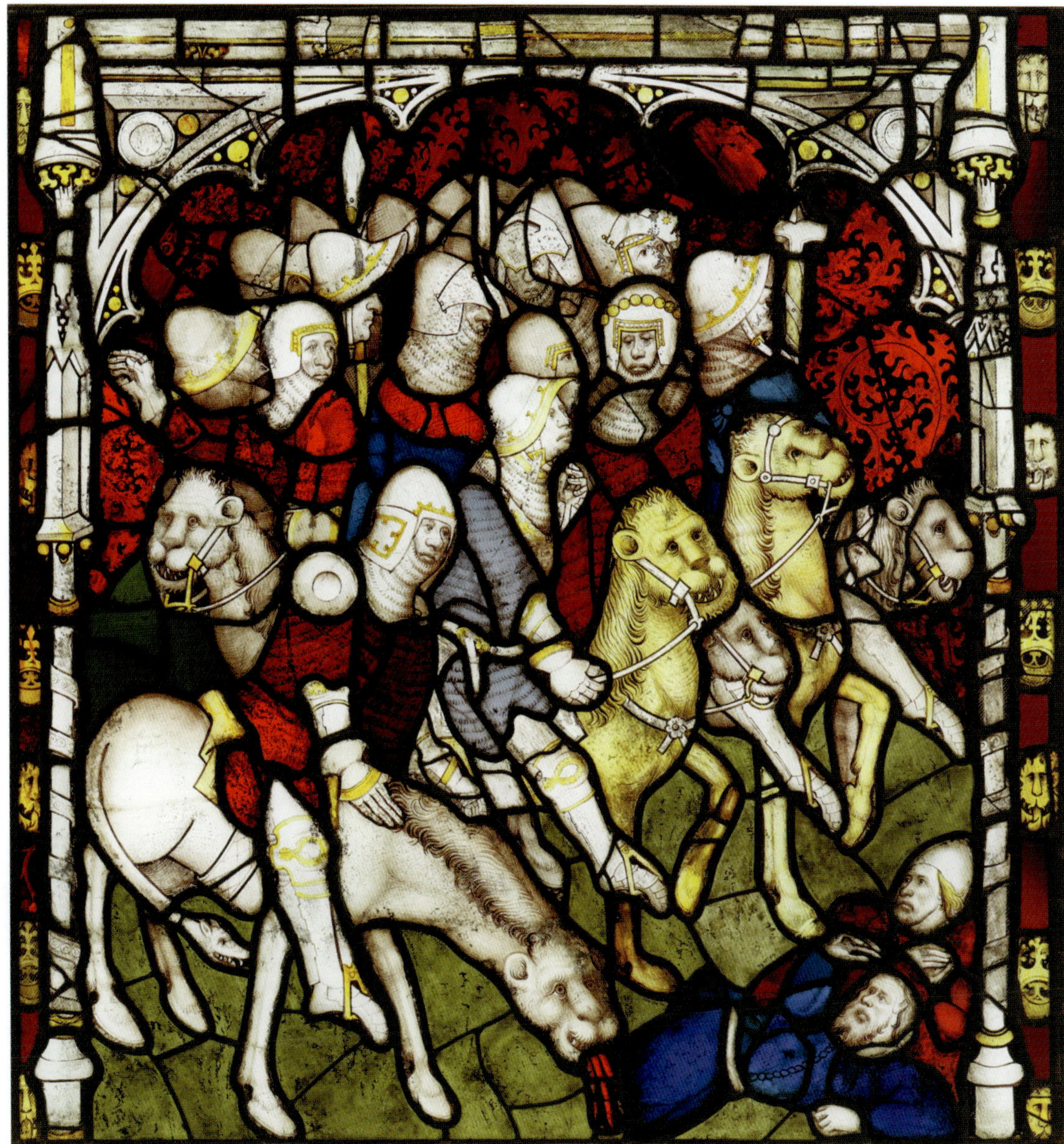

8f The Army of Horsemen

And the number of the army of horsemen was twenty thousand times ten thousand. And I heard the number of them. And thus I saw the horses in the vision: and they that sat on them, had breastplates of fire and of hyacinth and of brimstone, and the heads of the horses were as the heads of lions: and from their mouths proceeded fire, and smoke, and brimstone. And by these three plagues was slain the third part of men, by the fire and by the smoke and by the brimstone, which issued out of their mouths. For the power of the horses is in their mouths, and in their tails. For, their tails are like to serpents, and have heads: and with them they hurt.

Revelation 9:16–19

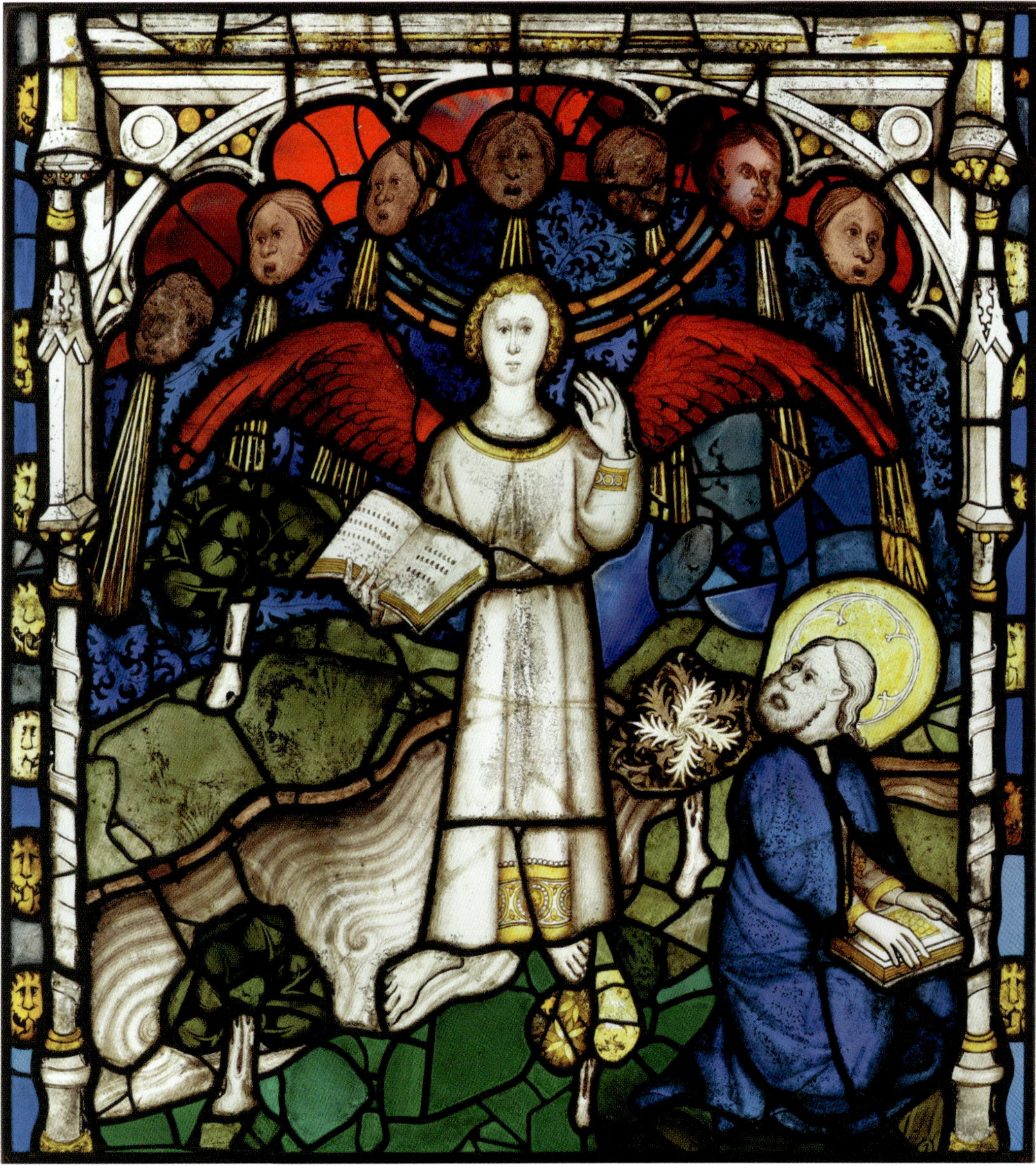

8g The Mighty Angel and the Seven Thunders

And I saw another mighty angel come down from heaven, clothed with a cloud, and a rainbow was on his head, and his face was as the sun, and his feet as pillars of fire. And he had in his hand a little book open: and he set his right foot upon the sea, and his left foot upon the earth. And he cried with a loud voice as when a lion roareth. And when he had cried, seven thunders uttered their voices. And when the seven thunders had uttered their voices, I was about to write: and I heard a voice from heaven saying to me: Seal up the things which the seven thunders have spoken; and write them not. And the angel, whom I saw standing upon the sea and upon the earth, lifted up his hand to heaven, And he swore by him that liveth for ever and ever, who created heaven, and the things which are therein; and the earth, and the things which are in it; and the sea, and the things which are therein: That time shall be no longer. But in the days of the voice of the seventh angel, when he shall begin to sound the trumpet, the mystery of God shall be finished, as he hath declared by his servants the prophets.

Revelation 10:1–7

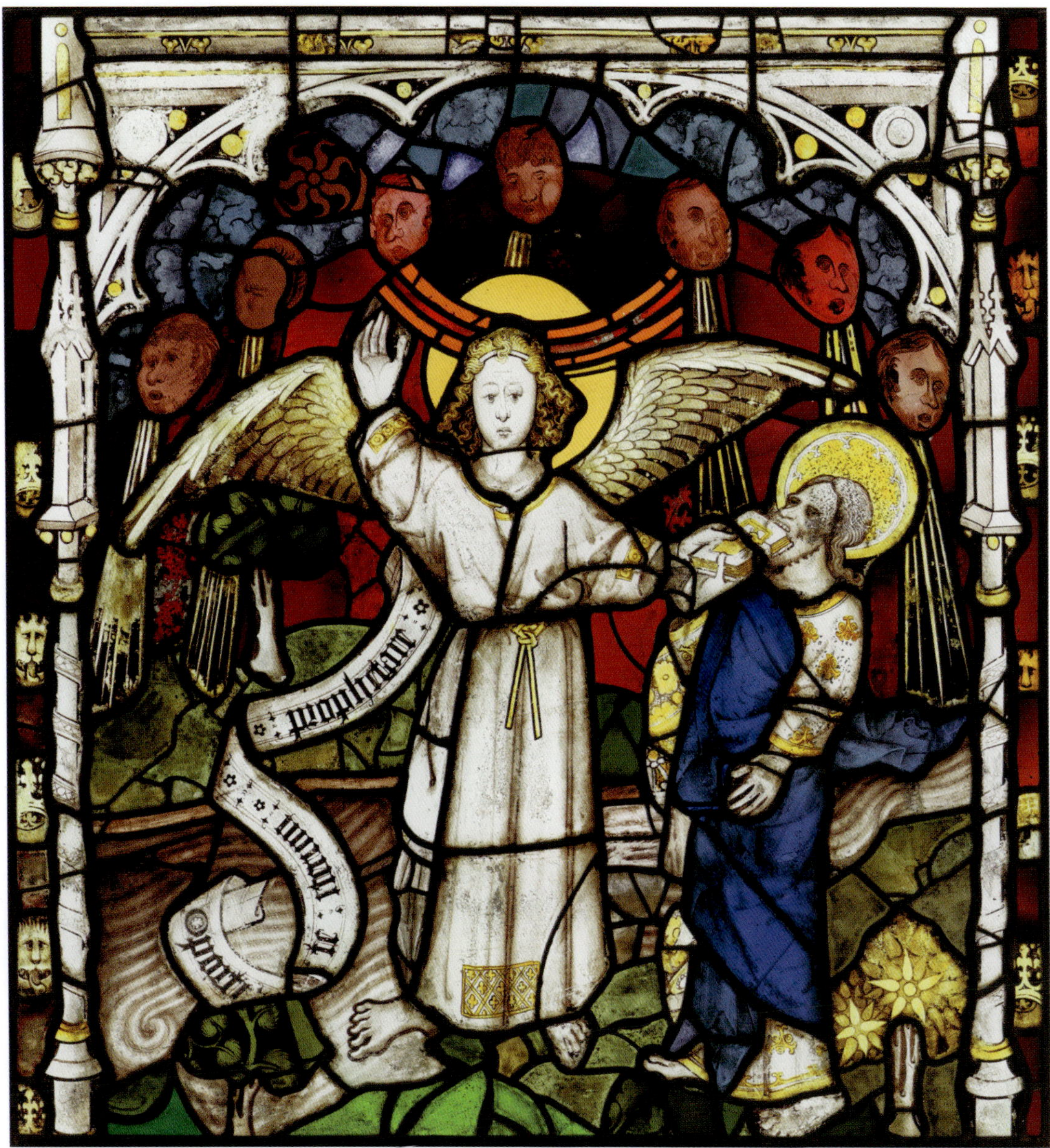

8h St John takes the Book from the Angel
And I heard a voice from heaven again speaking to me, and saying: Go, and take the book that is open, from the hand of the angel who standeth upon the sea, and upon the earth. And I went to the angel, saying unto him, that he should give me the book. And he said to me: **Take the book**, and eat it up: and it shall make thy belly bitter, but in thy mouth it shall be sweet as honey. And I took the book from the hand of the angel, and ate it up: and it was in my mouth, sweet as honey: and when I had eaten it, my belly was bitter. And he said to me: Thou must **prophesy** again to many nations, and peoples, and tongues, and kings.
Revelation 10:8–11

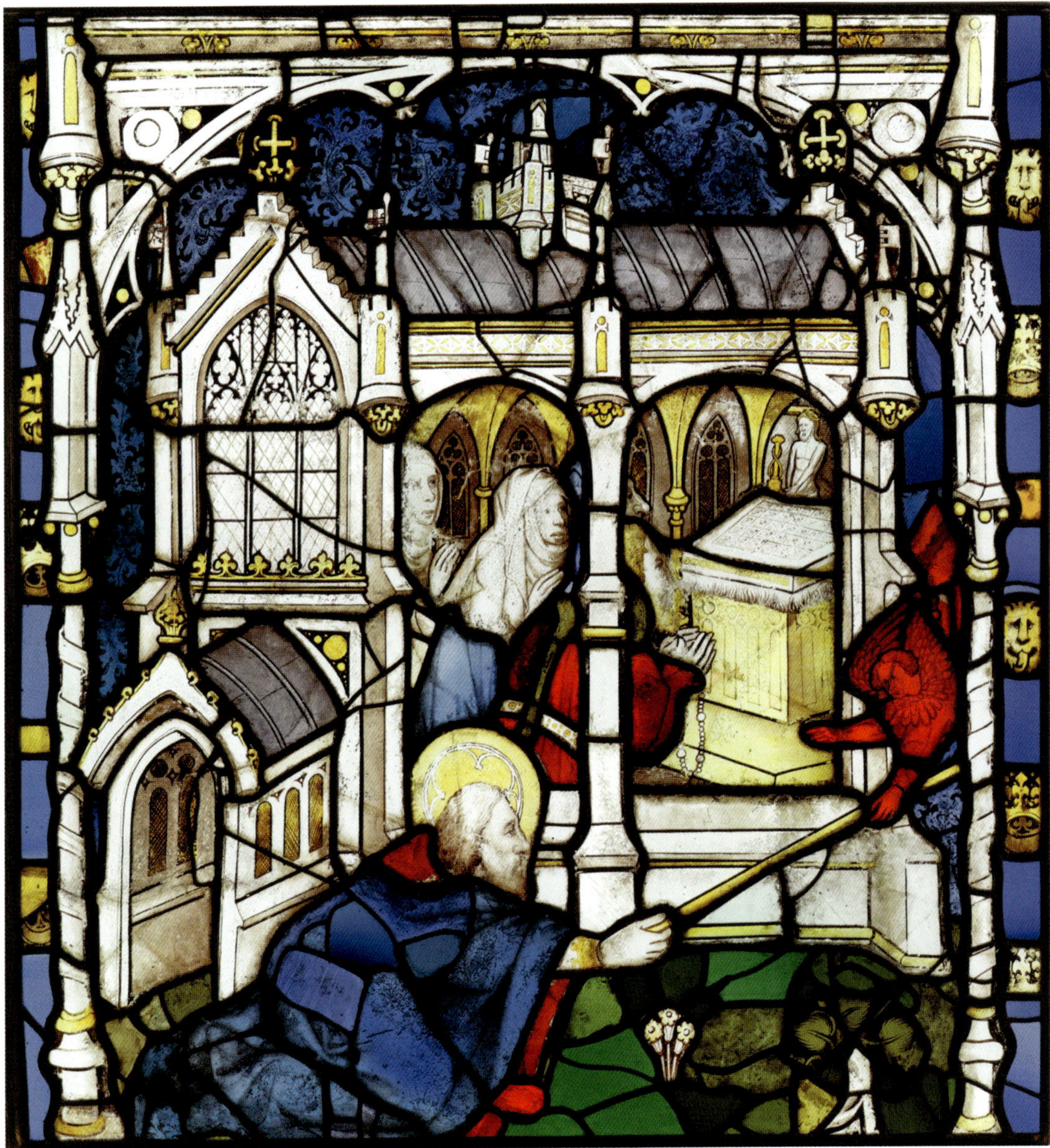

8j St John Measures the Temple
And there was given me a reed like unto a rod: and it was said to me: Arise, and measure the temple of God, and the altar and them that adore therein.
Revelation 11:1

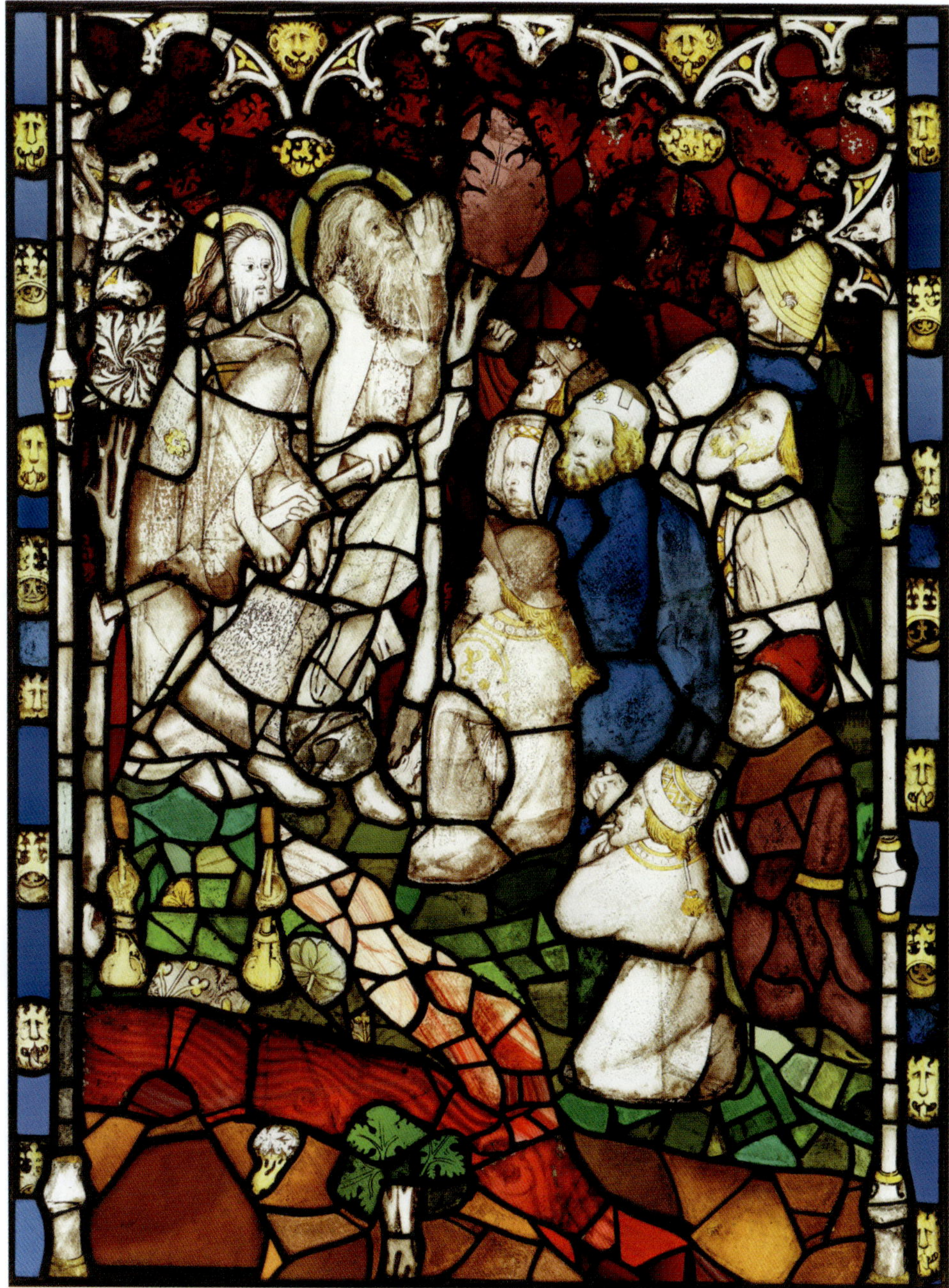

7a The Two Witnesses
And I will give unto my two witnesses, and they shall prophesy a thousand two hundred sixty days, clothed in sackcloth. These are the two olive trees, and the two candlesticks, that stand before the Lord of the earth. And if any man will hurt them, fire shall come out of their mouths, and shall devour their enemies. And if any man will hurt them, in this manner must he be slain. These have power to shut heaven, that it rain not in the days of their prophecy: and they have power over waters to turn them into blood, and to strike the earth with all plagues as often as they will.
Revelation 11:3–6

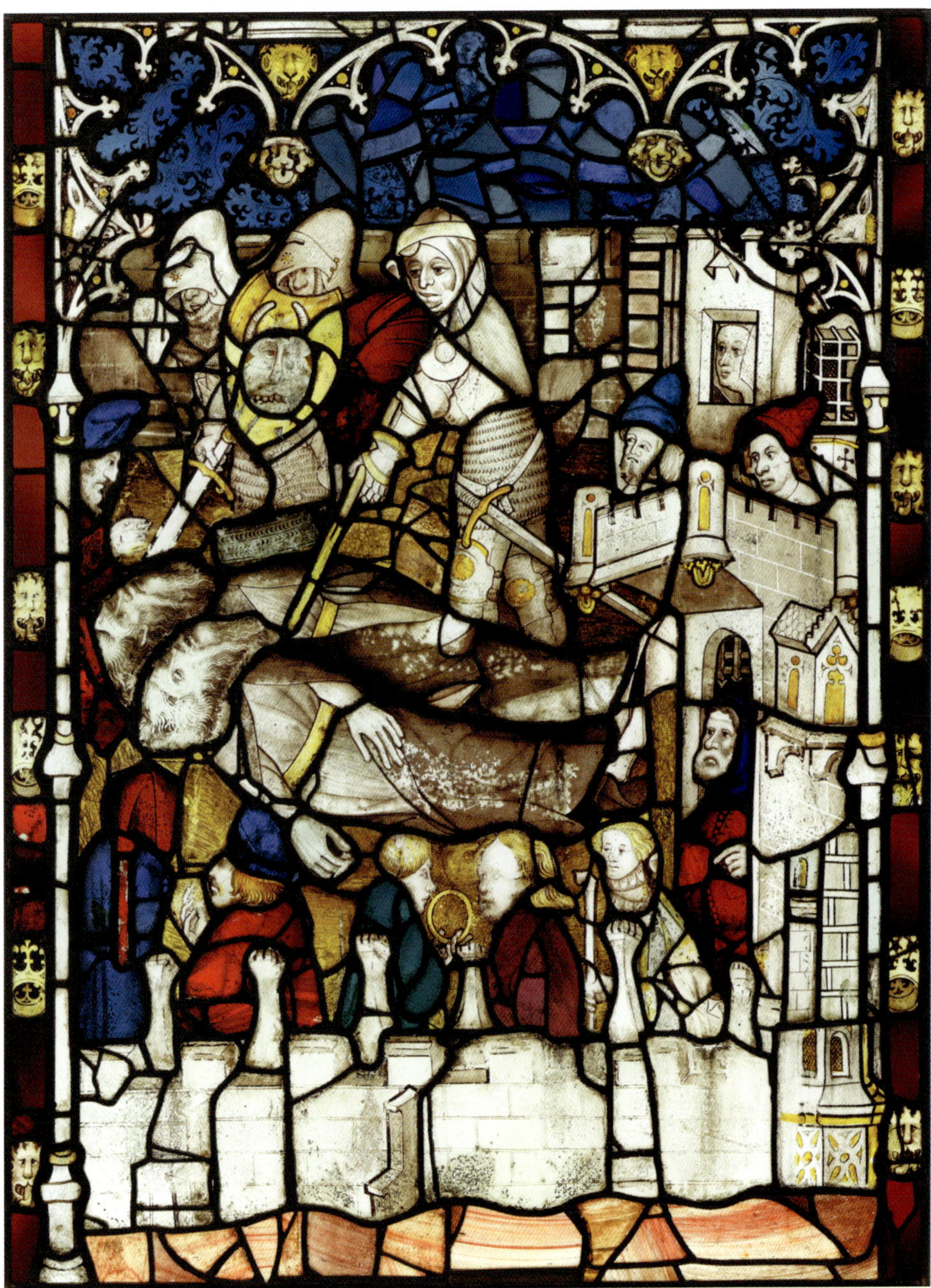

7b The Killing of the Two Witnesses

And when they shall have finished their testimony, the beast, that ascendeth out of the abyss, shall make war against them, and shall overcome them, and kill them. And their bodies shall lie in the streets of the great city, which is called spiritually, Sodom and Egypt, where their Lord also was crucified. And they of the tribes, and peoples, and tongues, and nations, shall see their bodies for three days and a half: and they shall not suffer their bodies to be laid in sepulchres. And they that dwell upon the earth shall rejoice over them, and make merry: and shall send gifts one to another, because these two prophets tormented them that dwelt upon the earth.

Revelation 11:7–10

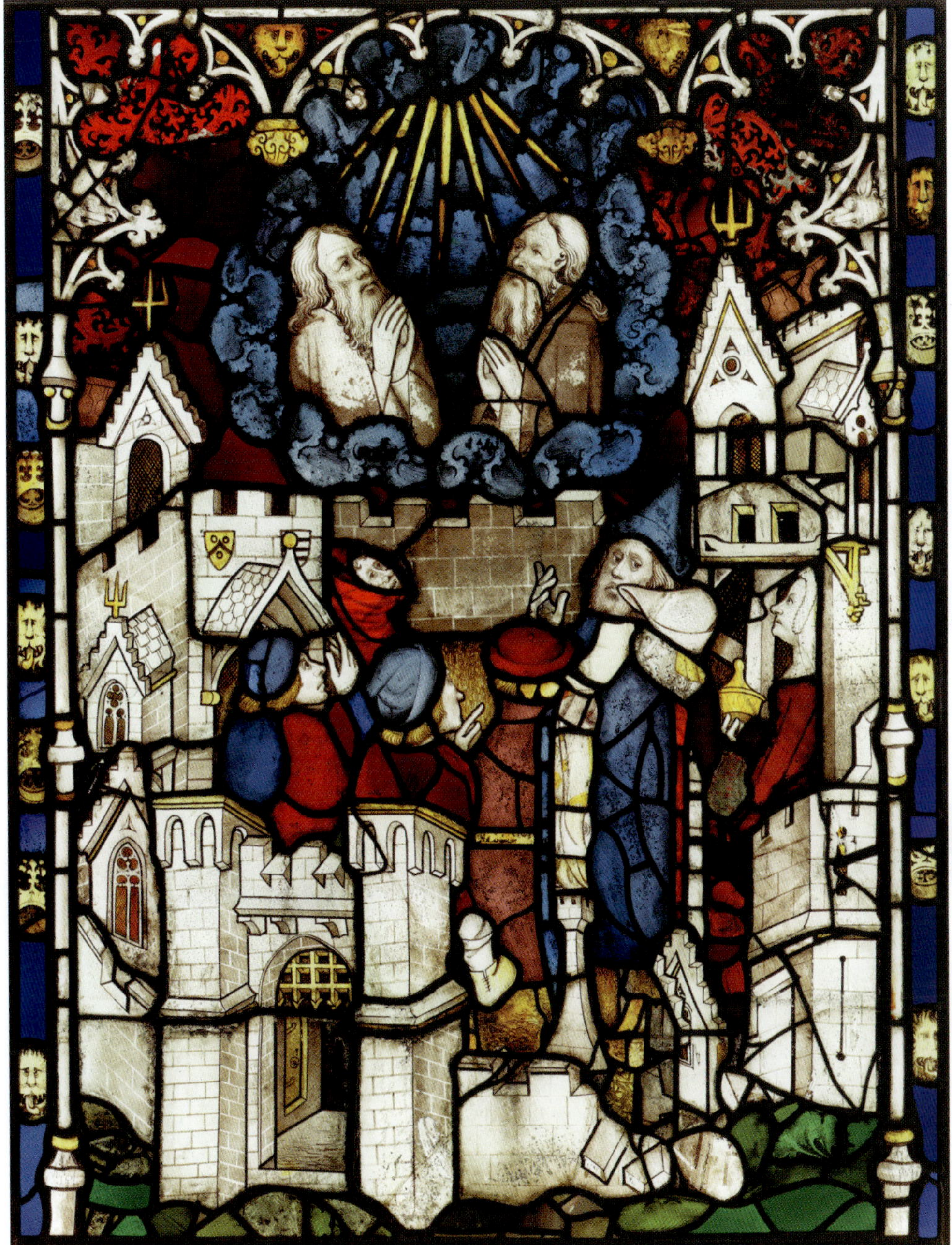

7c The Two Witnesses ascend to Heaven

And after three days and a half, the spirit of life from God entered into them. And they stood upon their feet, and great fear fell upon them that saw them. And they heard a great voice from heaven, saying to them: Come up hither. And they went up to heaven in a cloud: and their enemies saw them. And at that hour there was made a great earthquake, and the tenth part of the city fell: and there were slain in the earthquake names of men seven thousand: and the rest were cast into a fear, and gave glory to the God of heaven.
Revelation 11:11–13

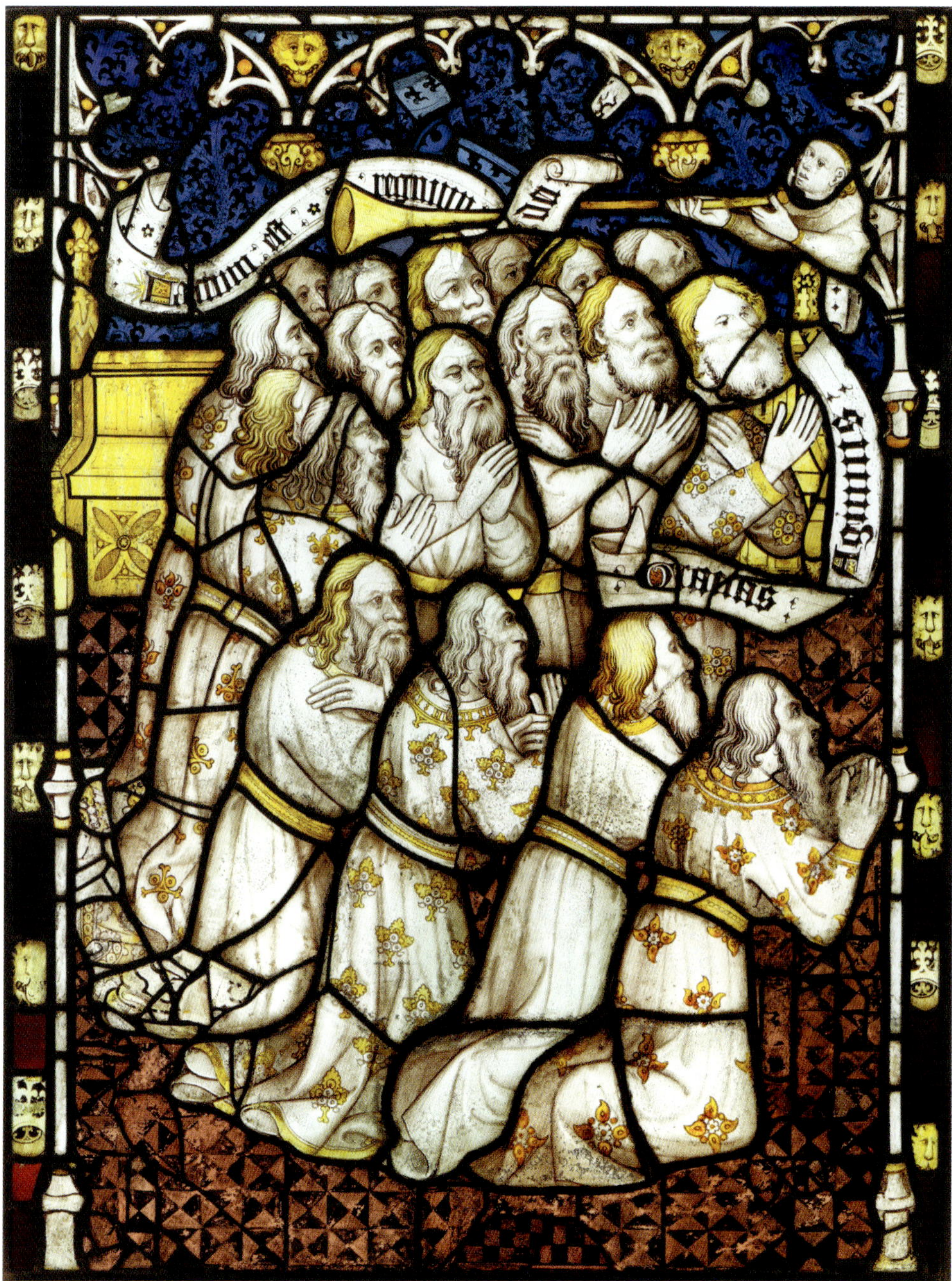

7d The Seventh Angel sounds the Trumpet

And the seventh angel sounded the trumpet: and there were great voices in heaven, saying: The kingdom of this world is become our Lord's and his Christ's, and he shall reign for ever and ever. Amen. And the four and twenty ancients, who sit on their seats in the sight of God, fell on their faces and adored God, saying: We give thee thanks, O Lord God Almighty, who art, and who wast, and who art to come: because thou hast taken to thee thy great power, and thou hast reigned.
Revelation 11:15–17

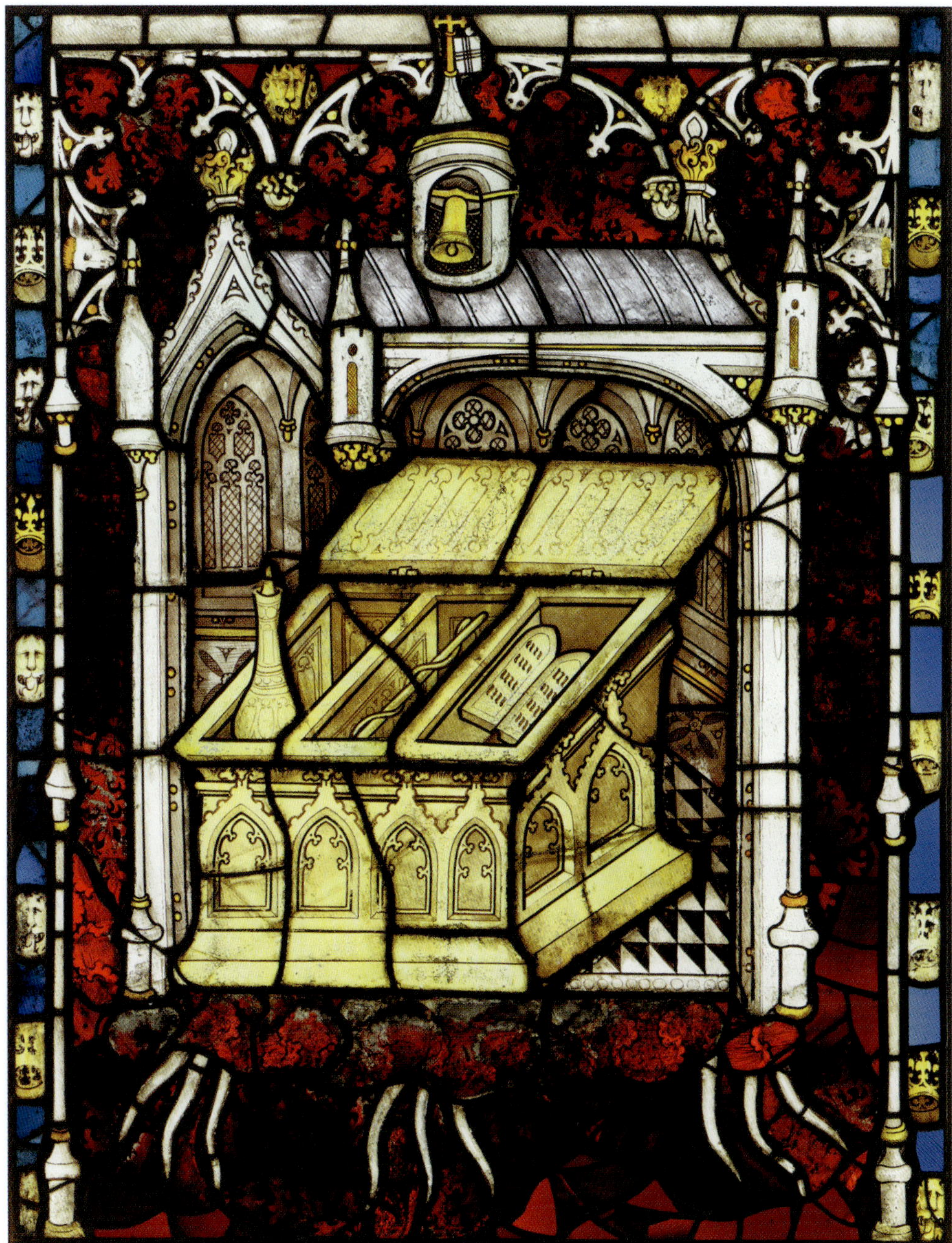

7e The Temple of God and the Ark of His Testament
And the temple of God was opened in heaven: and the ark of his testament was seen in his temple, and there were lightnings, and voices, and an earthquake, and great hail.
Revelation 11:19

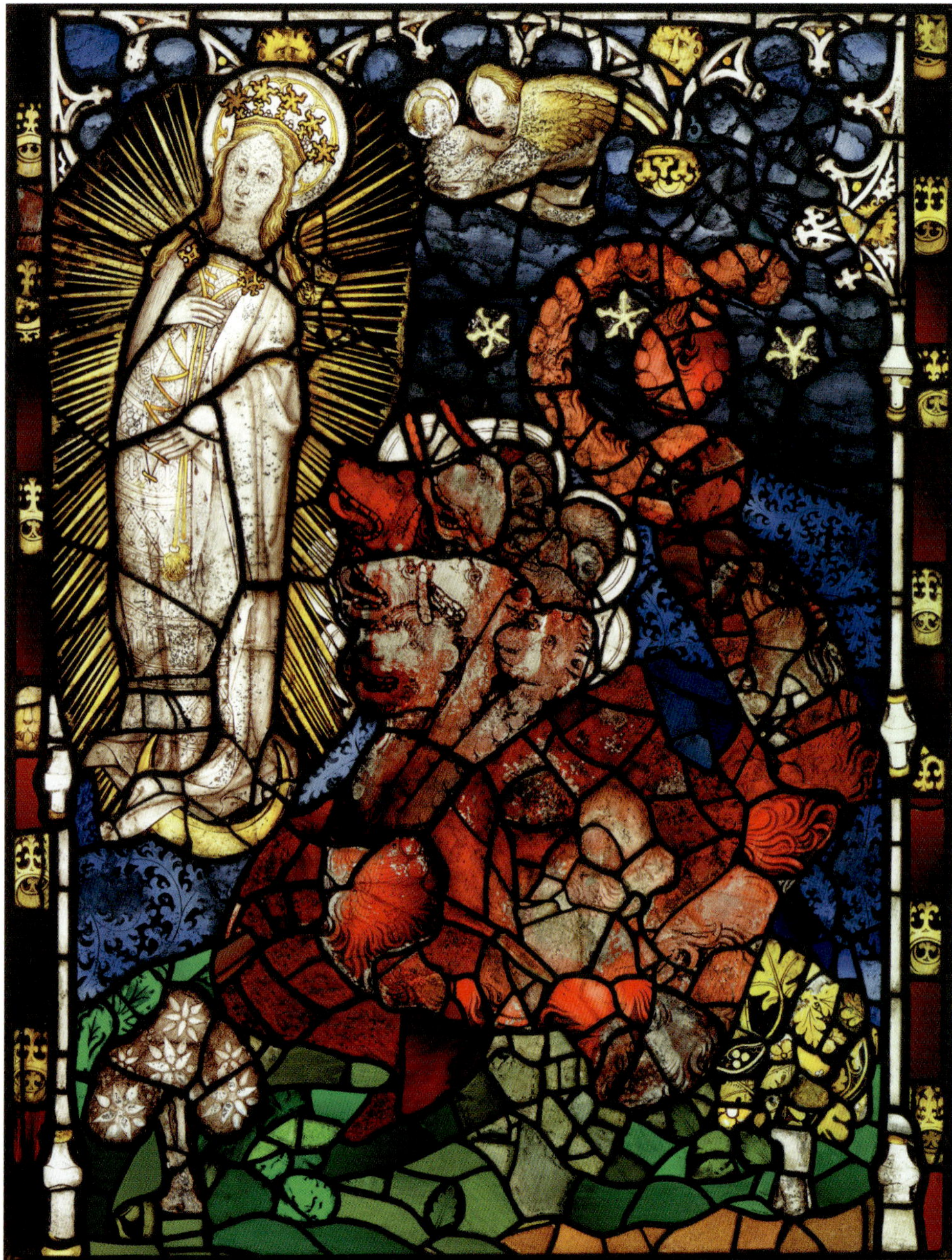

7f The Woman clothed with the Sun

And a great sign appeared in heaven: A woman clothed with the sun, and the moon under her feet, and on her head a crown of twelve stars: And being with child, she cried travailing in birth, and was in pain to be delivered. And there was seen another sign in heaven: and behold a great red dragon, having seven heads, and ten horns: and on his head seven diadems: And his tail drew the third part of the stars of heaven, and cast them to the earth: and the dragon stood before the woman who was ready to be delivered; that, when she should be delivered, he might devour her son. And she brought forth a man child, who was to rule all nations with an iron rod: and her son was taken up to God, and to his throne.

Revelation 12:1–5

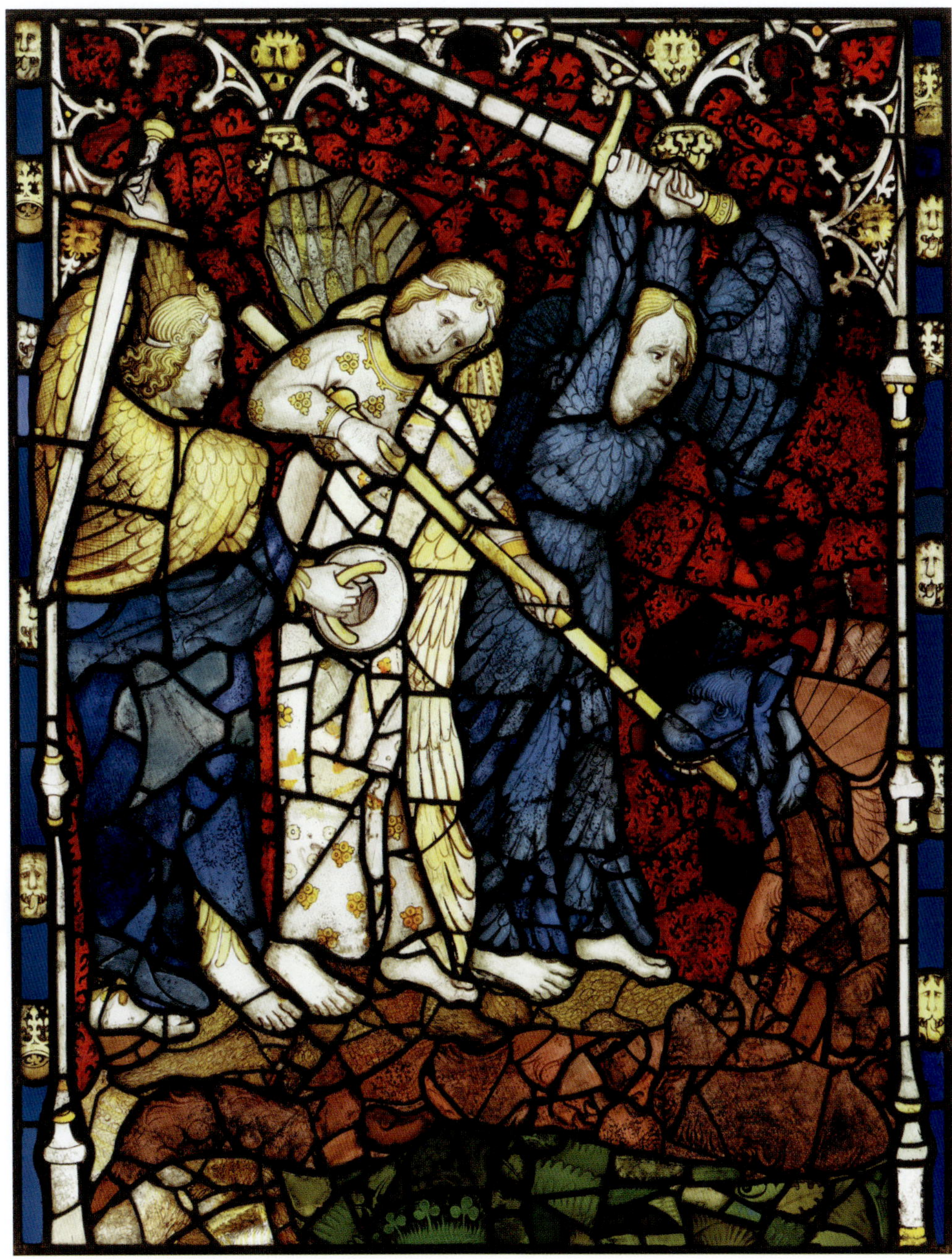

7g War in Heaven
And there was a great battle in heaven, Michael and his angels fought with the dragon, and the dragon fought and his angels: And they prevailed not, neither was their place found any more in heaven.
Revelation 12:7–8

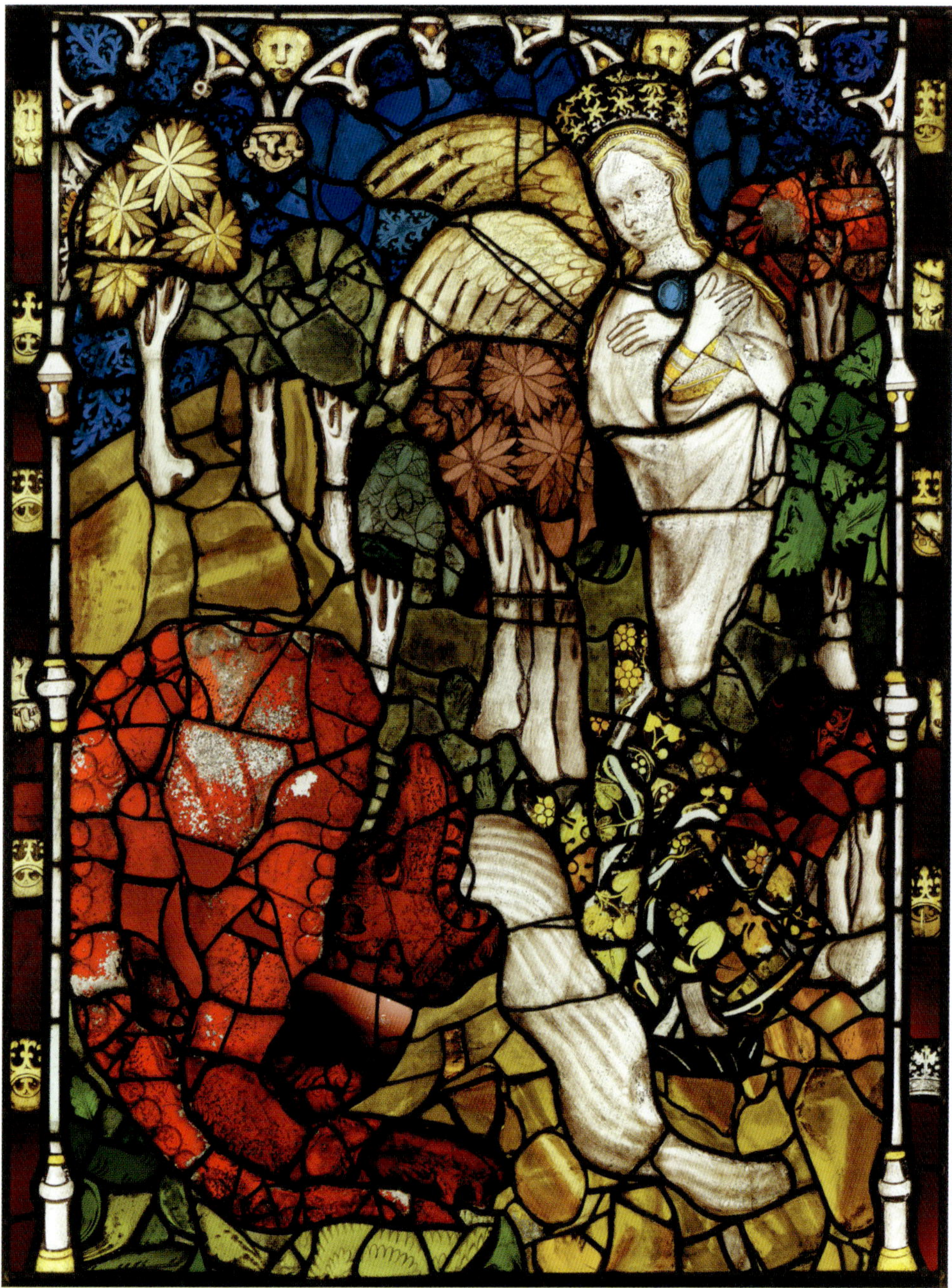

7h The Woman flees from the Dragon

And there were given to the woman two wings of a great eagle, that she might fly into the desert unto her place, where she is nourished for a time and times, and half a time, from the face of the serpent. And the serpent cast out of his mouth after the woman, water as it were a river; that he might cause her to be carried away by the river. And the earth helped the woman, and the earth opened her mouth, and swallowed up the river, which the dragon cast out of his mouth.
Revelation 12:14–16

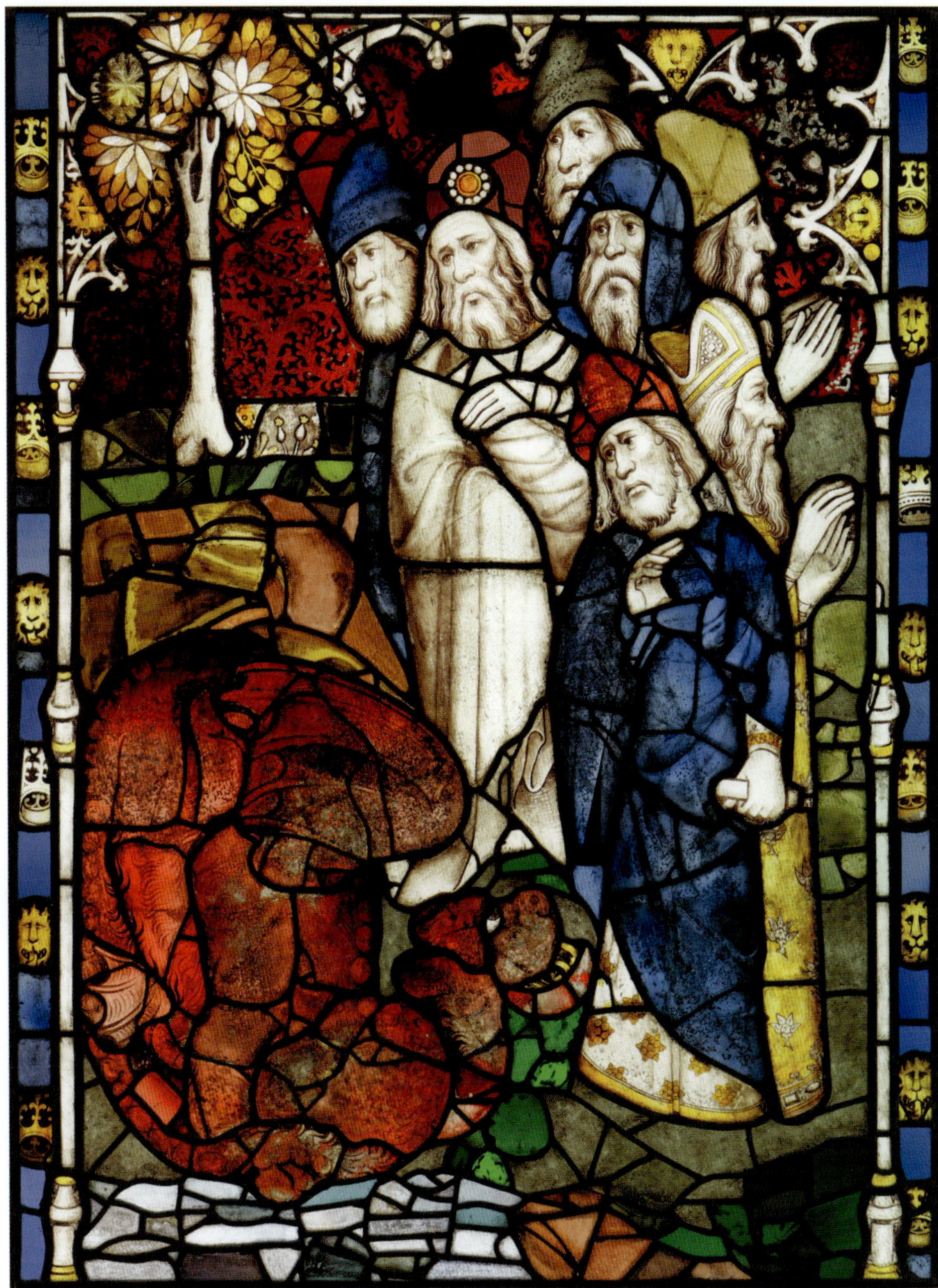

7j The Dragon makes war on the Woman's Seed
And the dragon was angry against the woman: and went to make war with the rest of her seed, who keep the commandments of God, and have the testimony of Jesus Christ.
Revelation 12:17

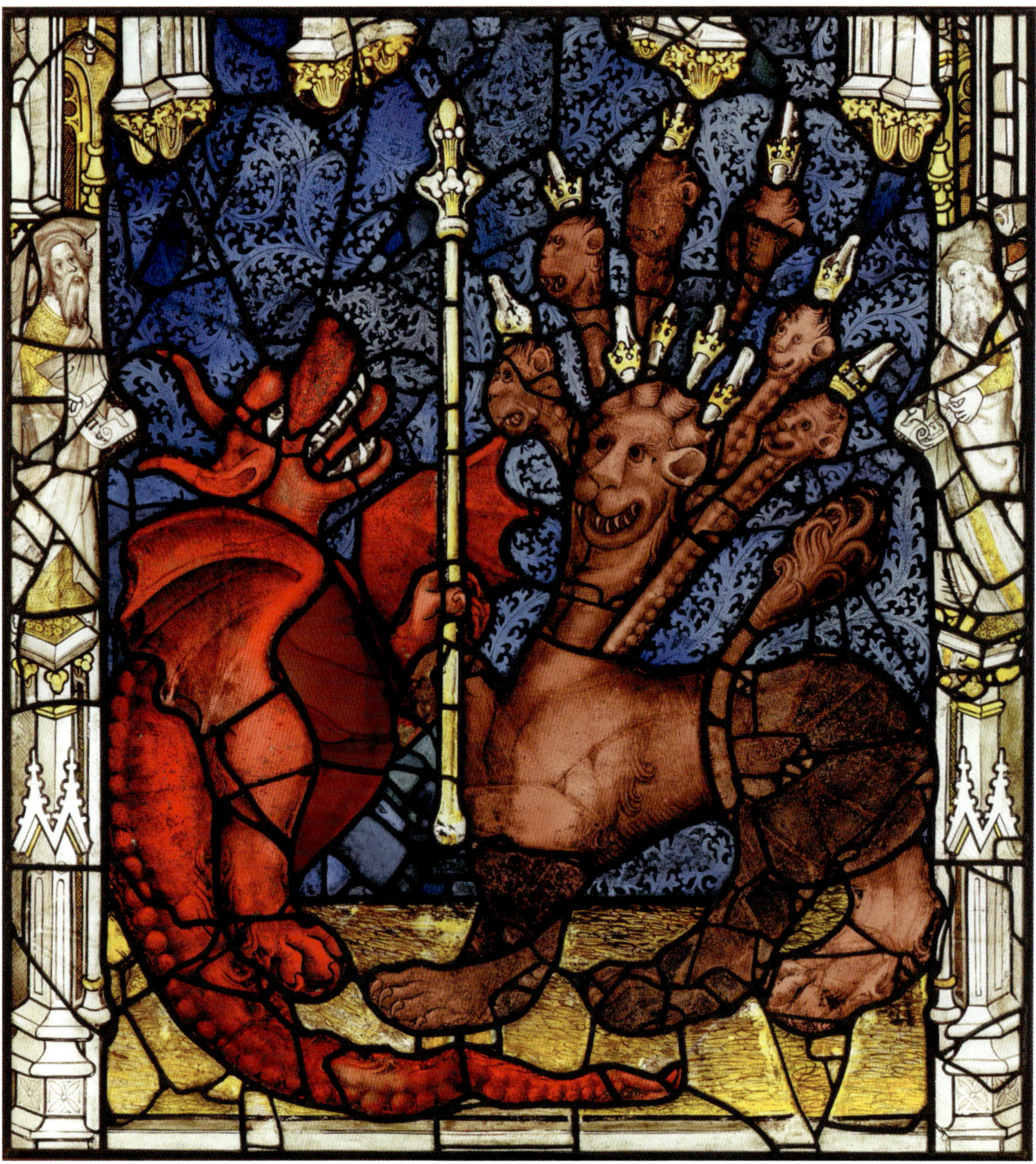

5a The Dragon gives power to the Beast

And I saw a beast coming up out of the sea, having seven heads and ten horns, and upon his horns ten diadems, and upon his heads names of blasphemy. And the beast, which I saw, was like to a leopard, and his feet were as the feet of a bear, and his mouth as the mouth of a lion. And the dragon gave him his own strength, and great power. And I saw one of his heads as it were slain to death: and his death's wound was healed. And all the earth was in admiration after the beast.

Revelation 13:1–3

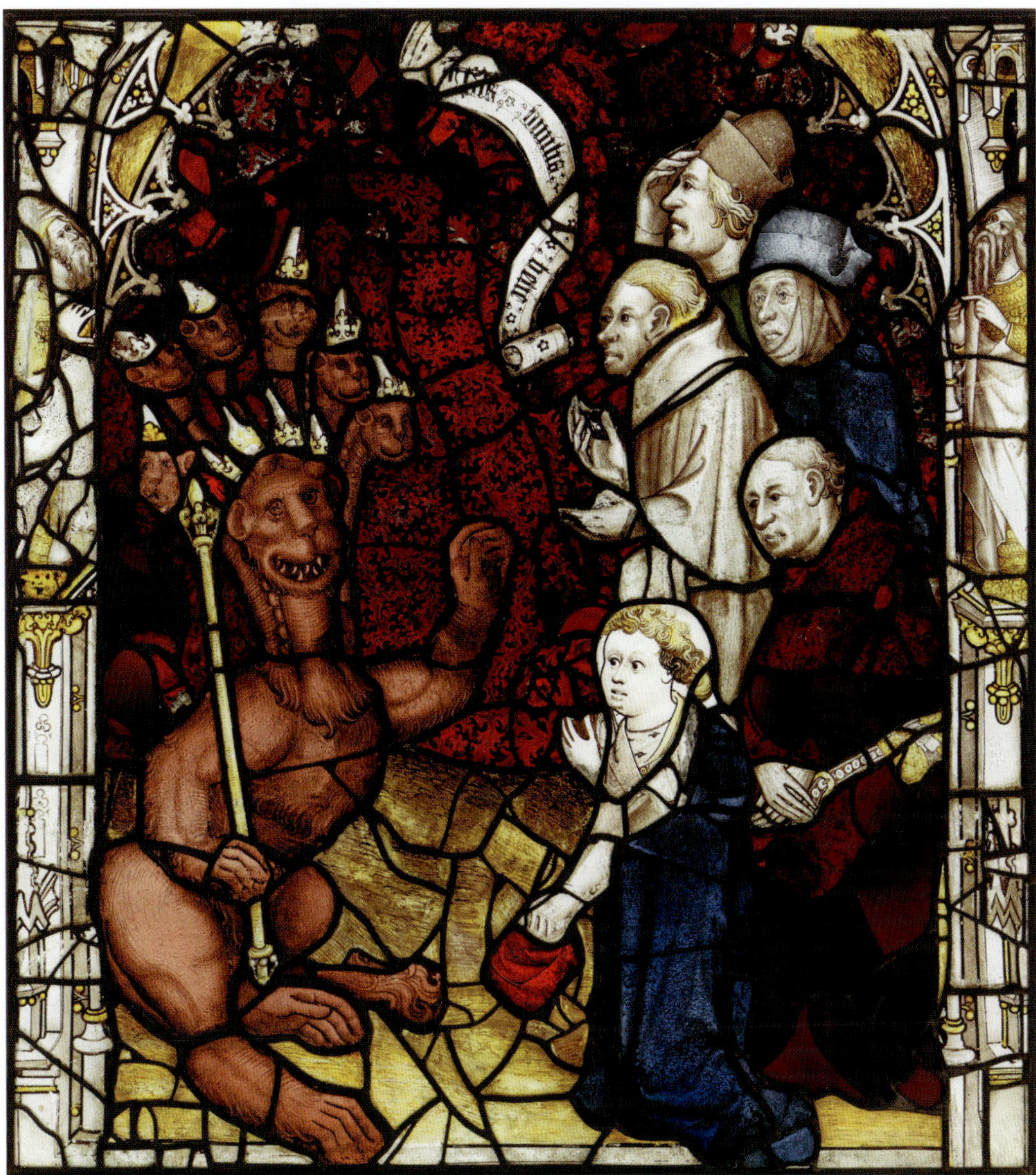

5b The Adoration of the Beast

And they adored the dragon, which gave power to the beast: and they adored the beast, saying: **Who is like to the beast?** and who shall be able to fight with him? And there was given to him a mouth speaking great things, and blasphemies: and power was given to him to do two and forty months. And he opened his mouth unto blasphemies against God, to blaspheme his name, and his tabernacle, and them that dwell in heaven.

Revelation 13:4–6

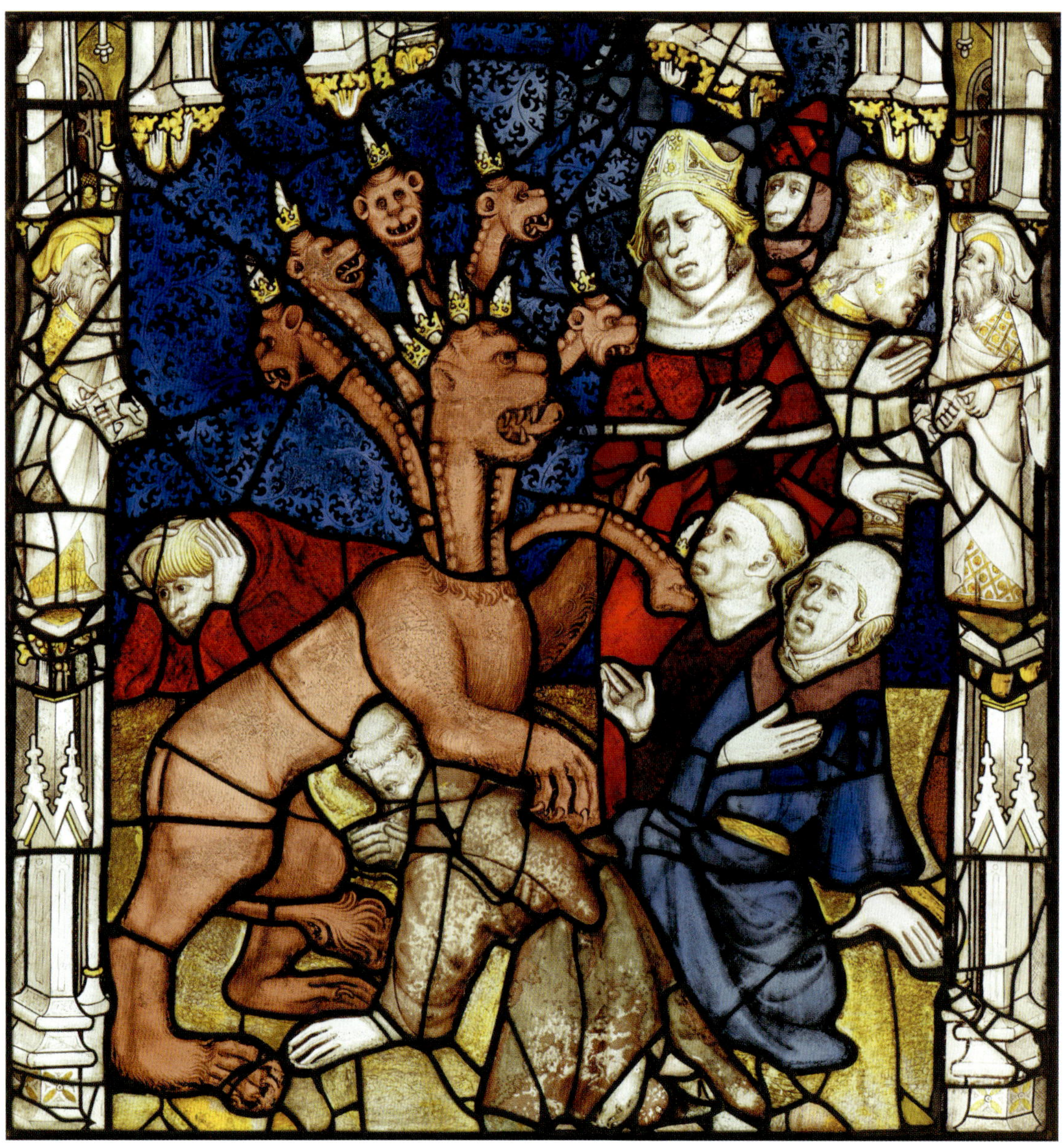

5c The Beast makes war with the Saints

And it was given unto him to make war with the saints, and to overcome them. And power was given him over every tribe, and people, and tongue, and nation.
Revelation 13:7

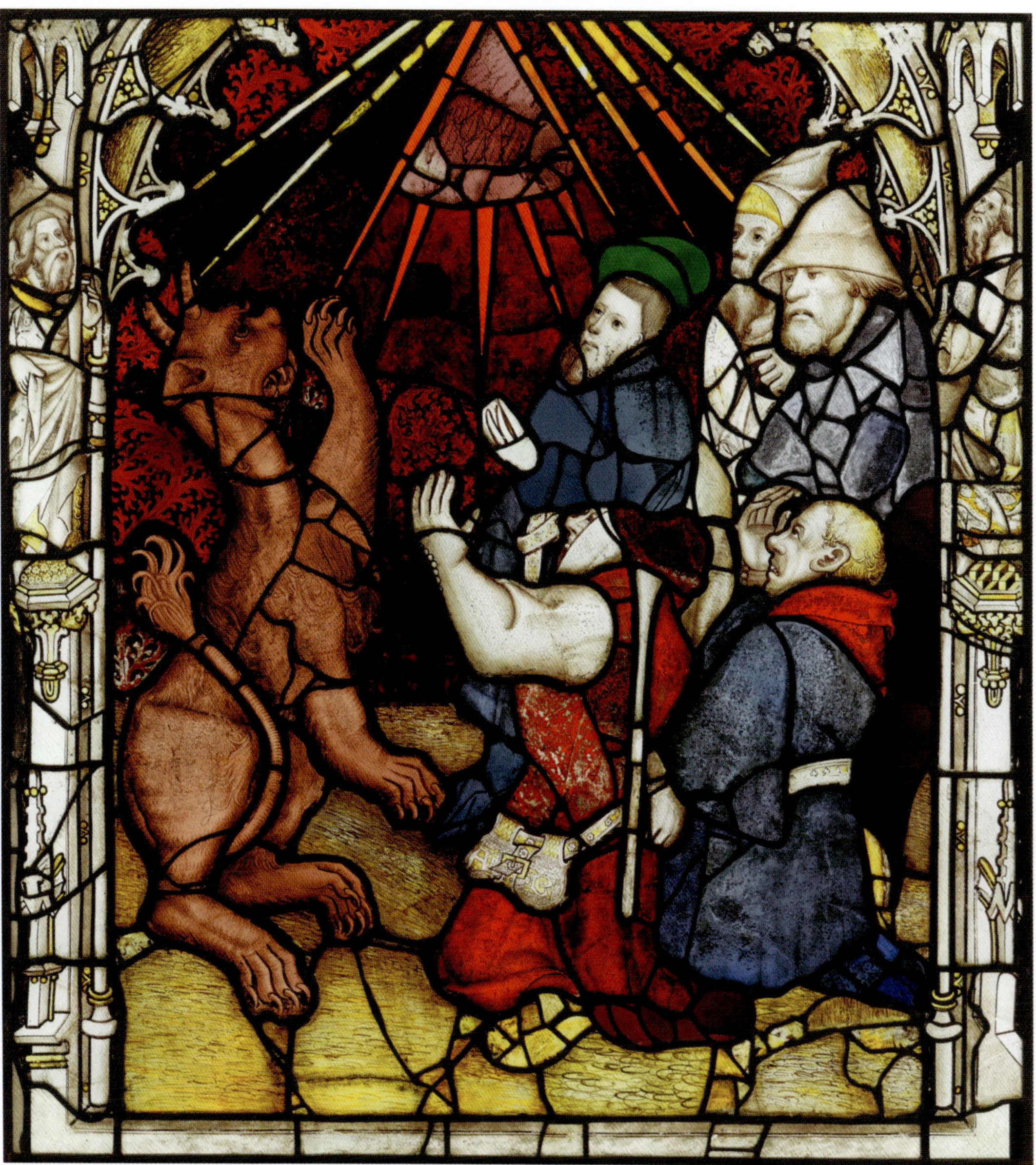

5d The Second Beast brings down fire from Heaven

And I saw another beast coming up out of the earth, and he had two horns, like a lamb, and he spoke as a dragon. And he executed all the power of the former beast in his sight; and he caused the earth, and them that dwell therein, to adore the first beast, whose wound to death was healed. And he did great signs, so that he made also fire to come down from heaven unto the earth in the sight of men. And he seduced them that dwell on the earth, for the signs, which were given him to do in the sight of the beast, saying to them that dwell on the earth, that they should make the image of the beast, which had the wound by the sword, and lived.

Revelation 13:11–14

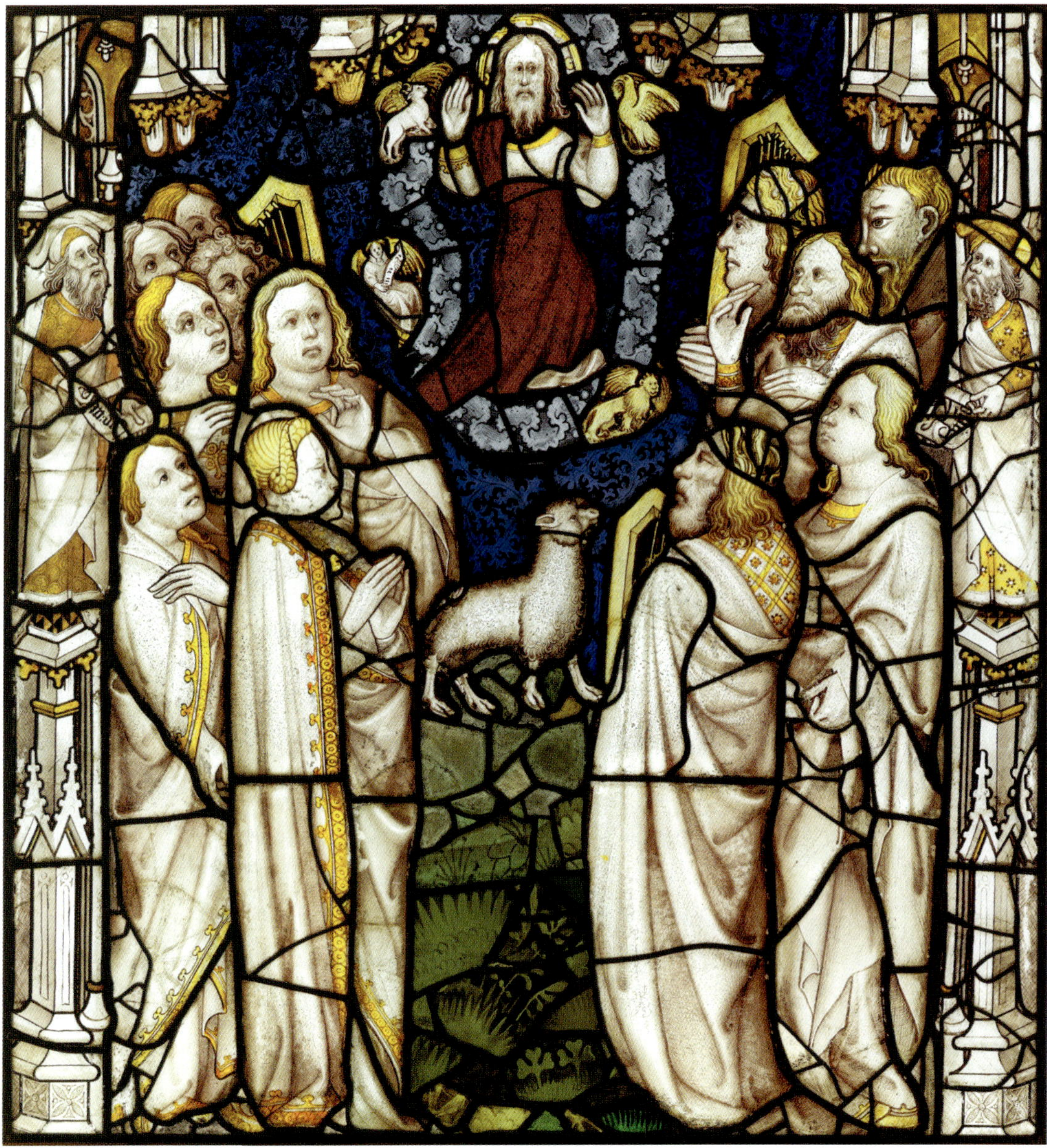

5e The Lamb on Mount Sion

And I beheld, and lo a lamb stood upon Mount Sion, and with him an hundred forty-four thousand, having his name, and the name of his Father, written on their foreheads. And I heard a voice from heaven, as the noise of many waters, and as the voice of great thunder; and the voice which I heard, was as the voice of harpers, harping on their harps. And they sung as it were a new canticle, before the throne, and before the four living creatures, and the ancients; and no man could say the canticle, but those hundred forty-four thousand, who were purchased from the earth.

Revelation 14:1–3

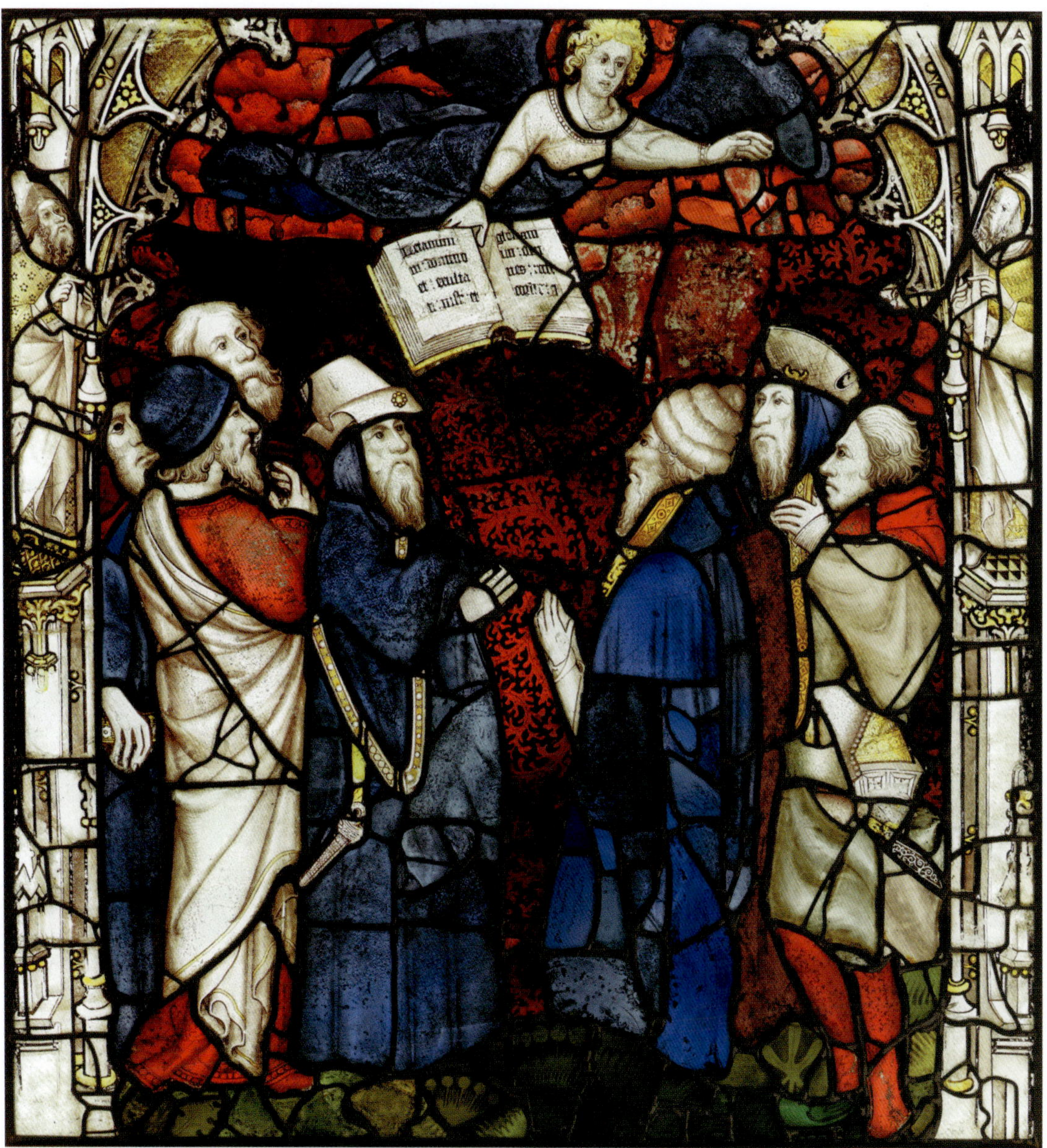

5f The Angel with the Everlasting Gospel
And I saw another angel flying through the midst of heaven, having the eternal gospel, to preach unto them that sit upon the earth, and over every nation, and tribe, and tongue, and people: Saying with a loud voice: Fear the Lord, and give him honour, because the hour of his judgment is come; and adore ye him, that made heaven and earth, the sea, and the fountains of waters.
Revelation 14:6–7

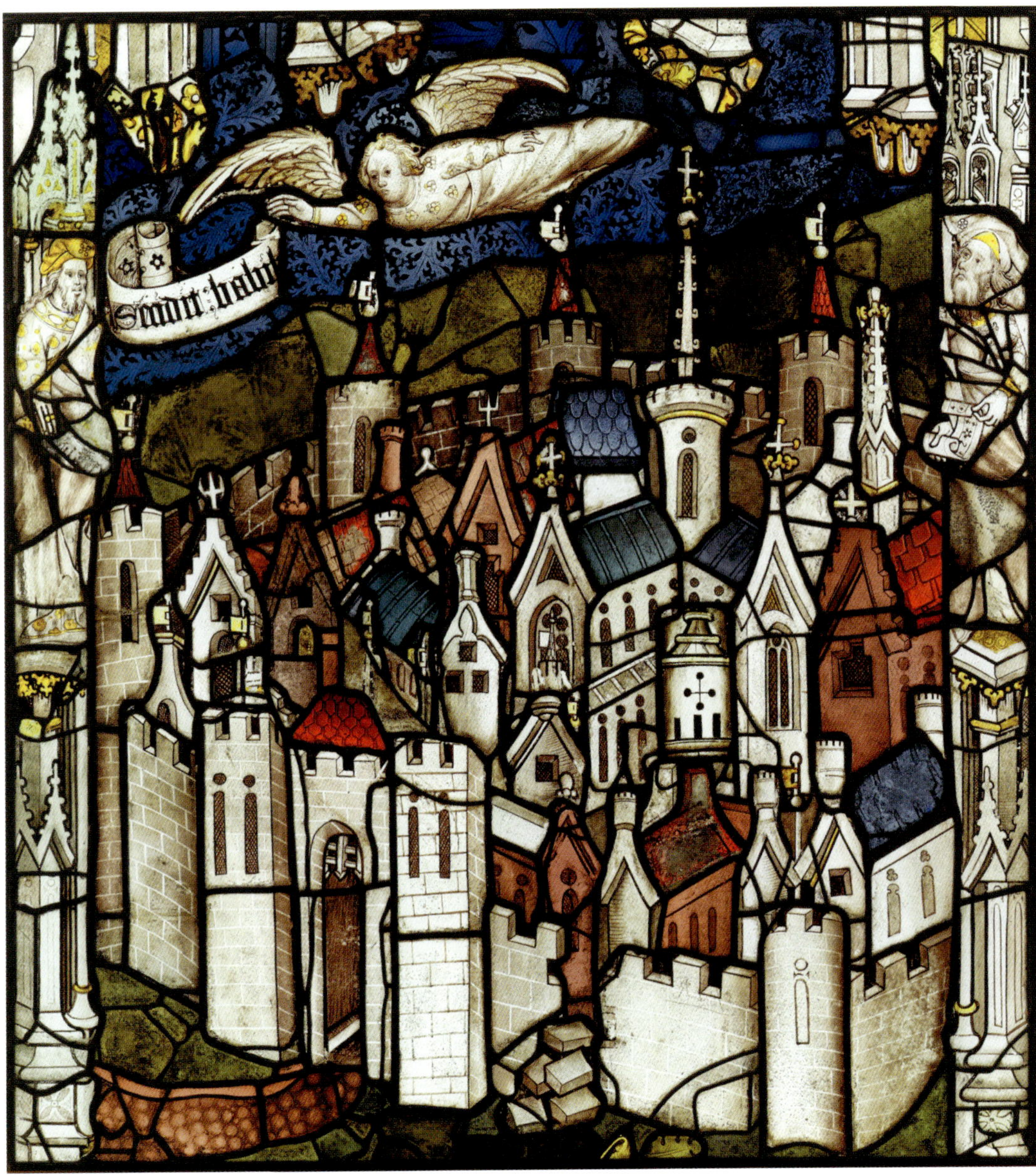

5g An Angel announces the Fall of Babylon
And another angel followed, saying: That great **Babylon is fallen**, is fallen; which made all nations to drink of the wine of the wrath of her fornication.
Revelation 14:8

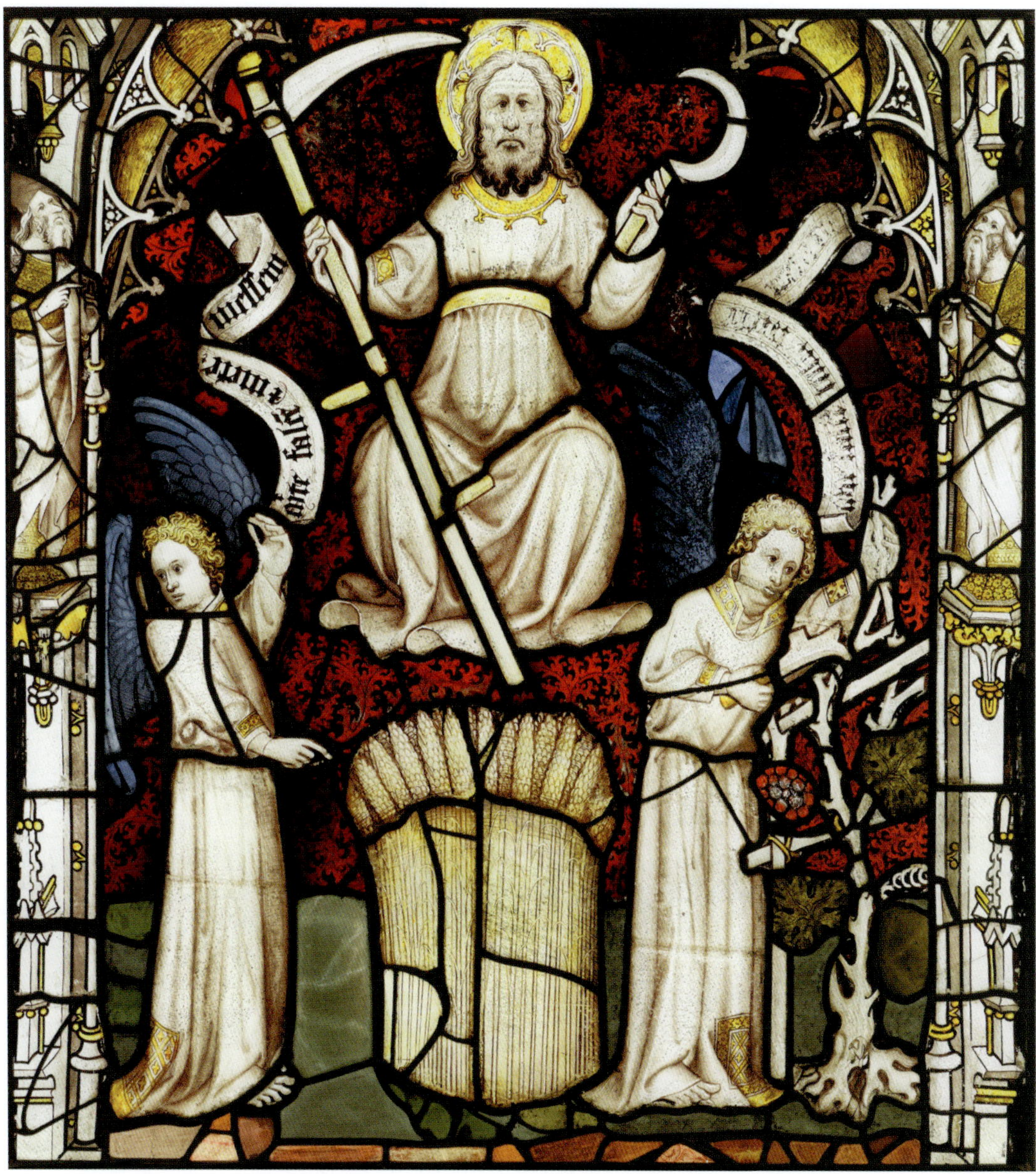

5h The Harvest of the Earth and the Vintage of the Wrath of God

And I saw, and behold a white cloud; and upon the cloud one sitting like to the Son of man, having on his head a crown of gold, and in his hand a sharp sickle. And another angel came out from the temple crying with a loud voice to him that sat upon the cloud: **Thrust in thy sickle, and reap**, because the hour is come to reap: for the harvest of the earth is ripe. And he that sat on the cloud thrust his sickle into the earth, and the earth was reaped. And another angel came out of the temple which is in heaven, he also having a sharp sickle. And another angel came out from the altar, who had power over fire; and he cried with a loud voice to him that had the sharp sickle, saying: Thrust in thy sharp sickle, and gather the clusters of the vineyard of the earth; because the grapes thereof are ripe. And the angel thrust in his sharp sickle into the earth, and gathered the vineyard of the earth, and cast it into the great press of the wrath of God.

Revelation 14:14–19

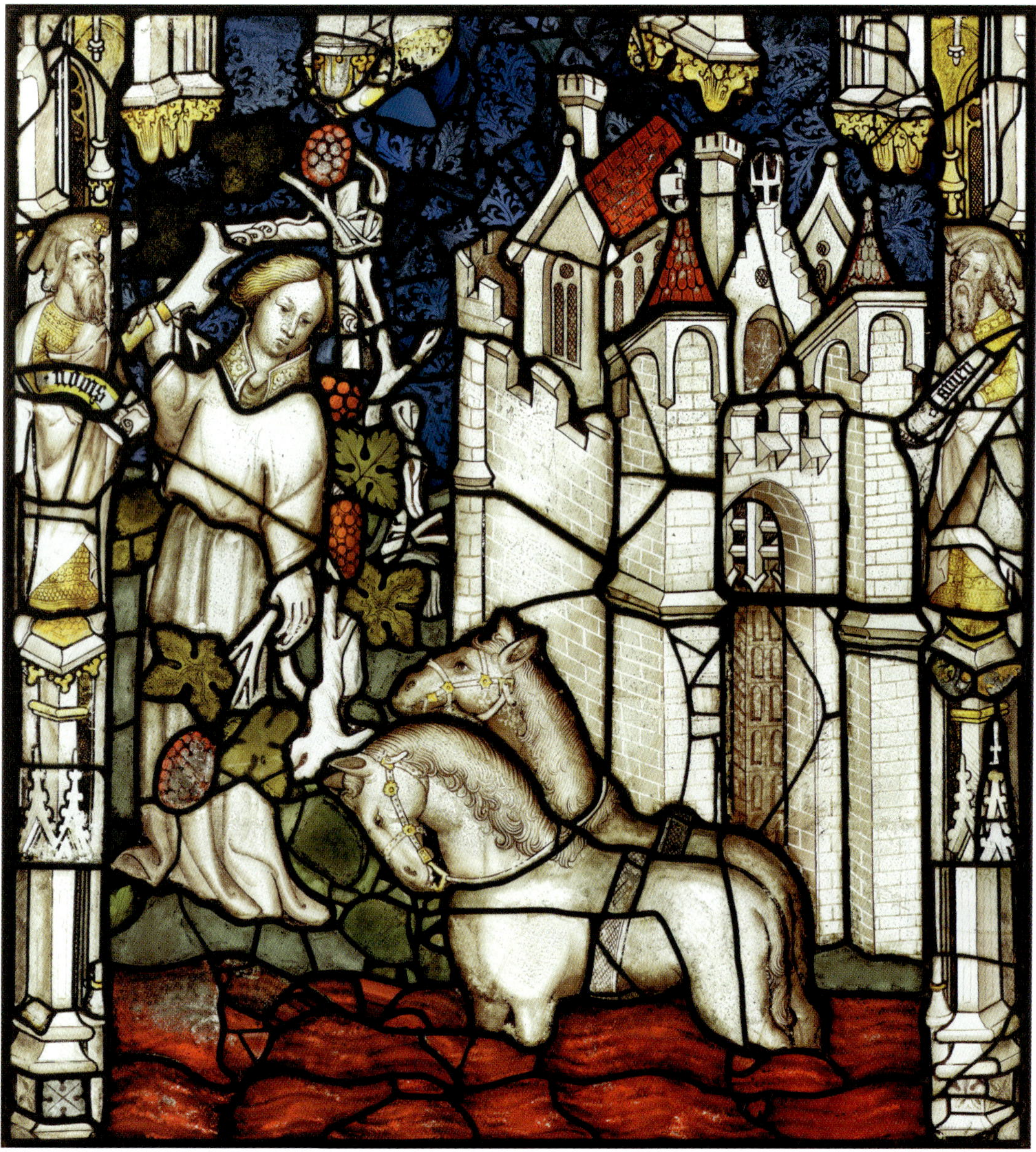

5j The Treading of the Wine Press

And the press was trodden without the city, and blood came out of the press, up to the horses' bridles, for a thousand and six hundred furlongs.
Revelation 14:20

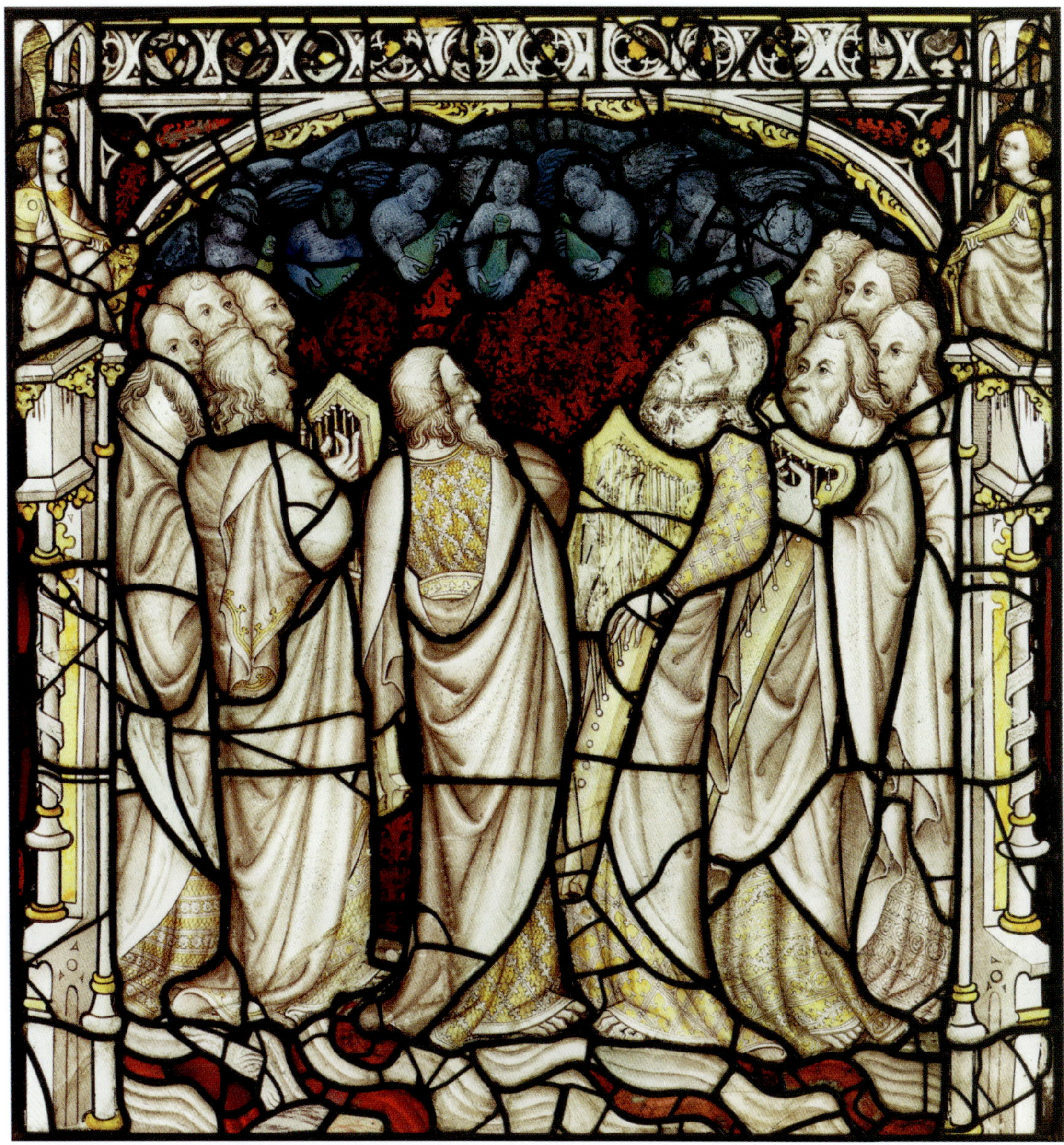

4a The Plague Angels and the Harpers

And I saw another sign in heaven, great and wonderful: seven angels having the seven last plagues. For in them is filled up the wrath of God. And I saw as it were a sea of glass mingled with fire, and them that had overcome the beast, and his image, and the number of his name, standing on the sea of glass, having the harps of God.

Revelation 15:1–2

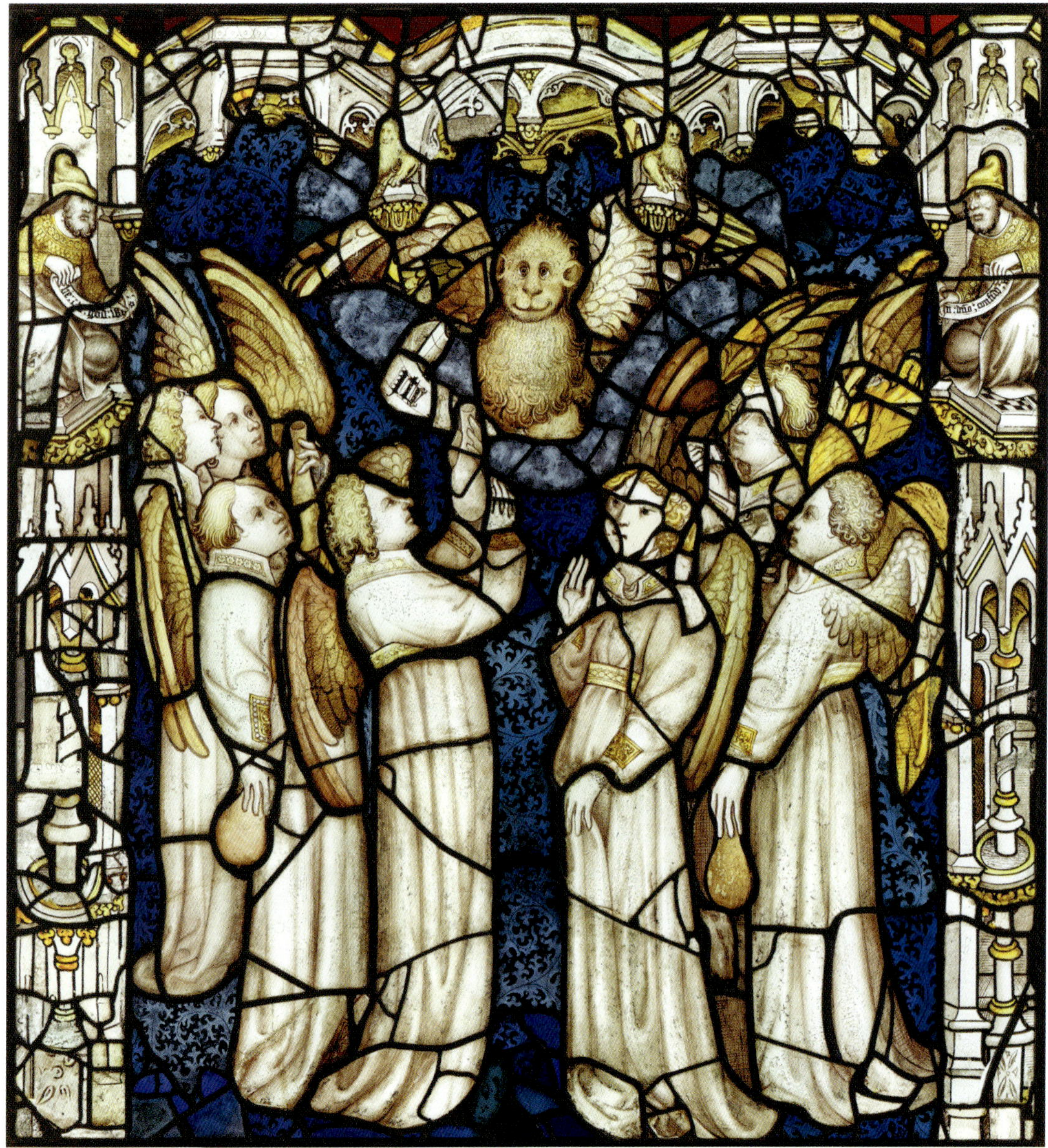

4b The Angels receive the Vials

And after these things I looked; and behold, the temple of the tabernacle of the testimony in heaven was opened: And the seven angels came out of the temple, having the seven plagues, clothed with clean and white linen, and girt about the breasts with golden girdles. And one of the four living creatures gave to the seven angels seven golden vials, full of the wrath of God, who liveth for ever and ever. And the temple was filled with smoke from the majesty of God, and from his power; and no man was able to enter into the temple, till the seven plagues of the seven angels were fulfilled. And I heard a great voice out of the temple, saying to the seven angels: Go, and pour out the seven vials of the wrath of God upon the earth.

Revelation 15:5–16:1

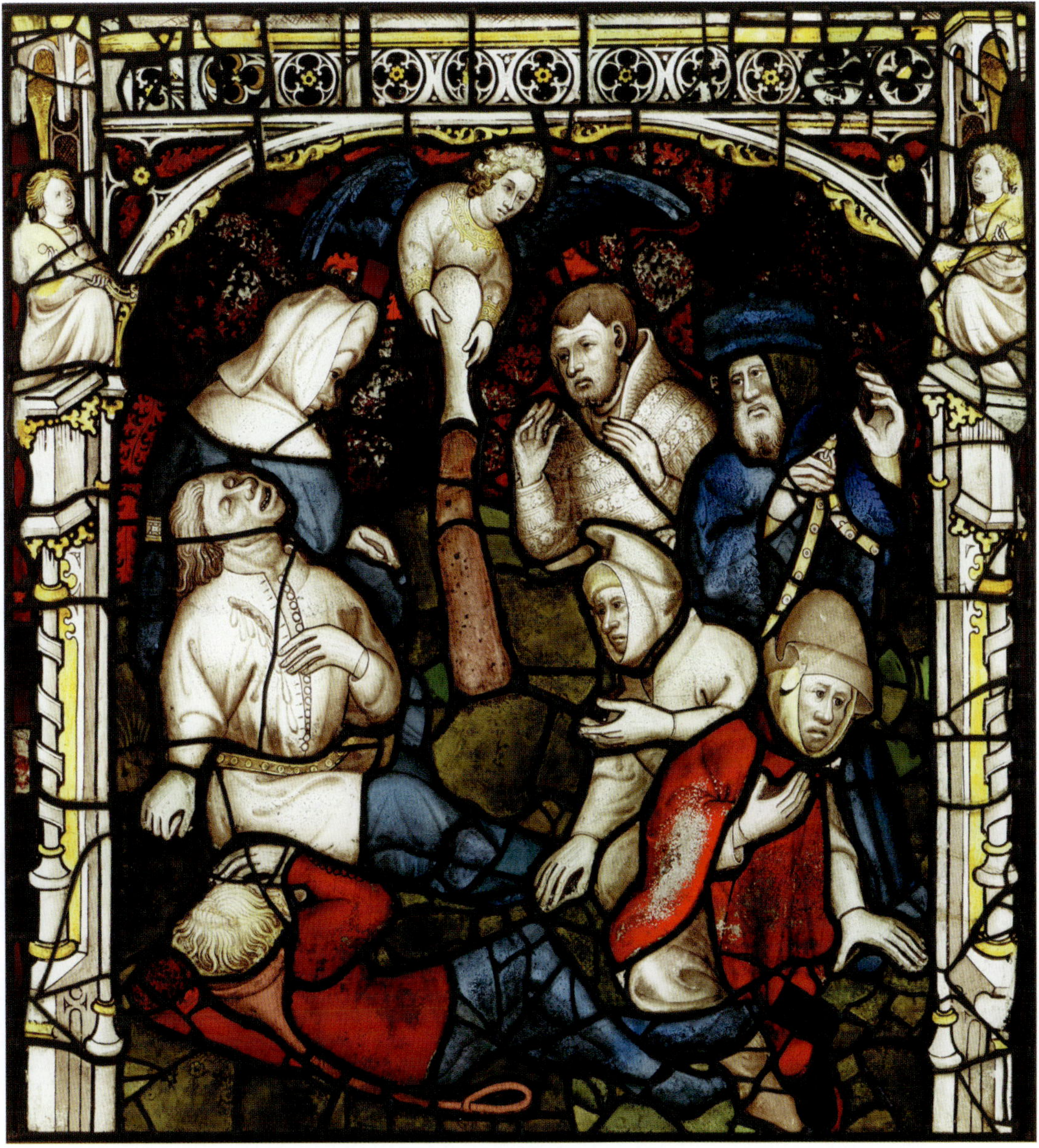

4c The First Vial

And the first went, and poured out his vial upon the earth, and there fell a sore and grievous wound upon men, who had the character of the beast; and upon them that adored the image thereof.
Revelation 16:2

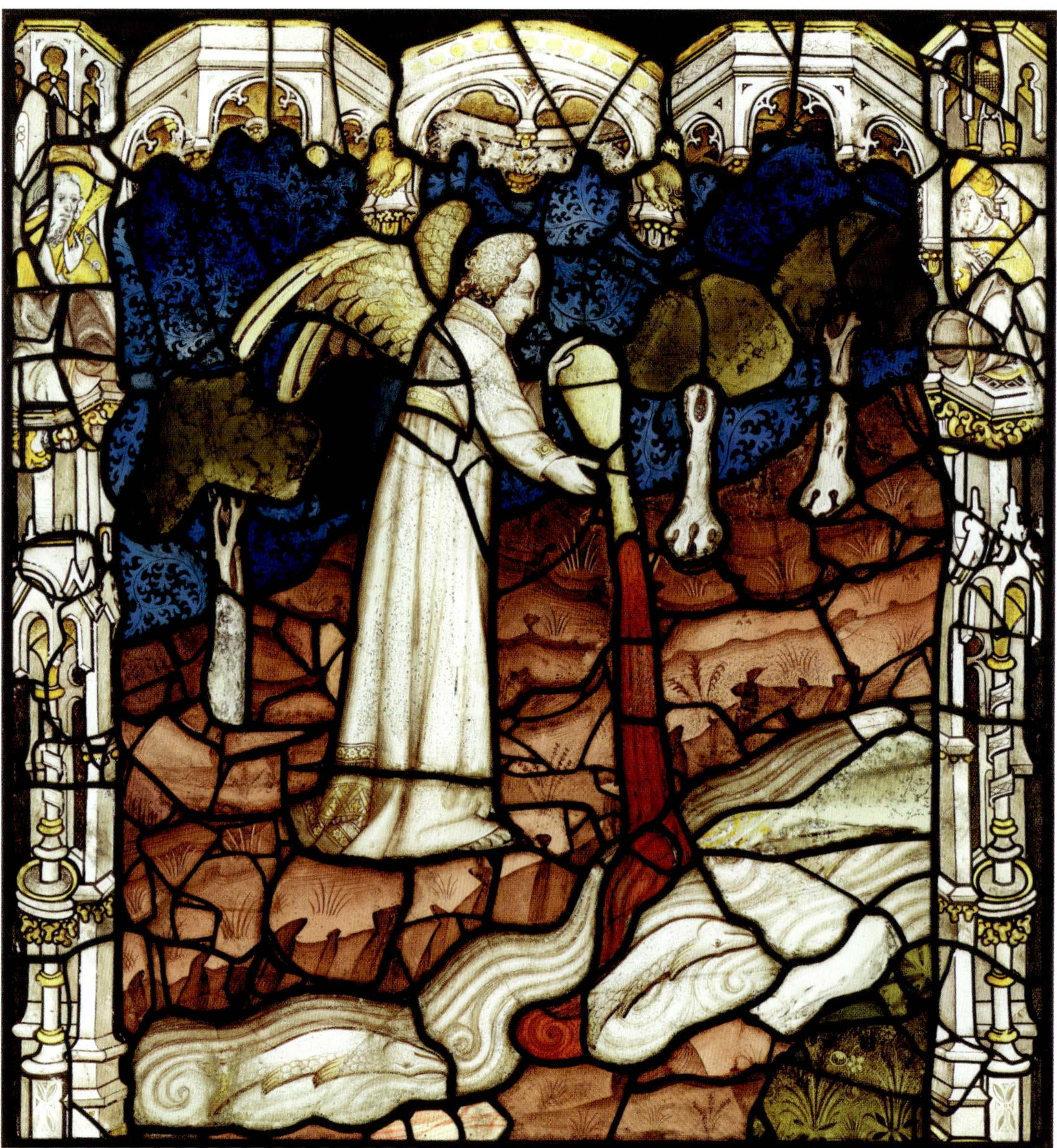

4d The Second Vial

And the second angel poured out his vial upon the sea, and there came blood as it were of a dead man; and every living soul died in the sea.

Revelation 16:3

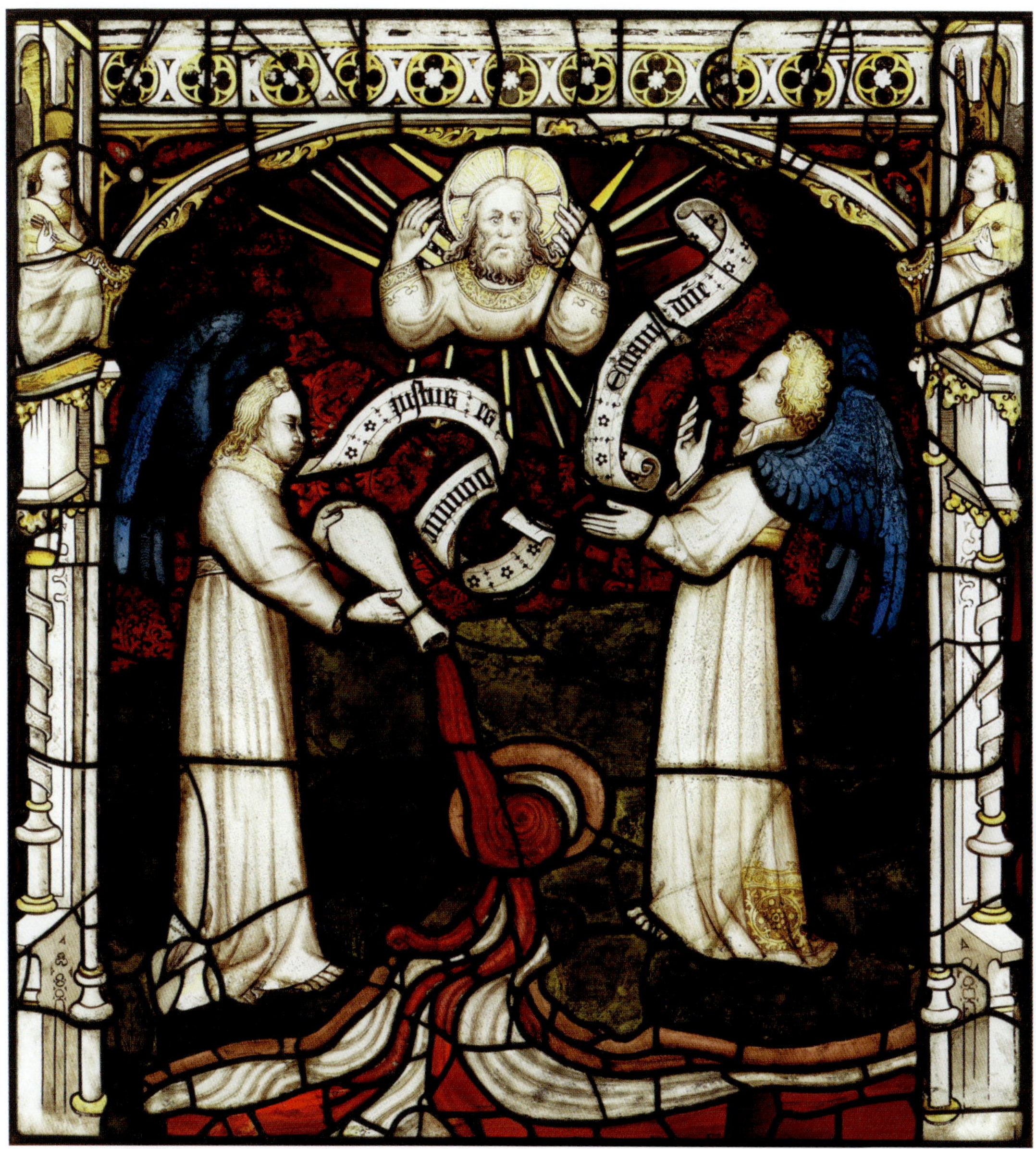

4e The Third Vial

And the third poured out his vial upon the rivers and the fountains of waters; and there was made blood. And I heard the angel of the waters saying: **Thou art just, O Lord**, who art, and who wast, the Holy One, because thou hast judged these things: For they have shed the blood of saints and prophets, and thou hast given them blood to drink; for they are worthy. And I heard another, from the altar, saying: **Yea, O Lord God Almighty**, true and just are thy judgments.
Revelation 16:4–7

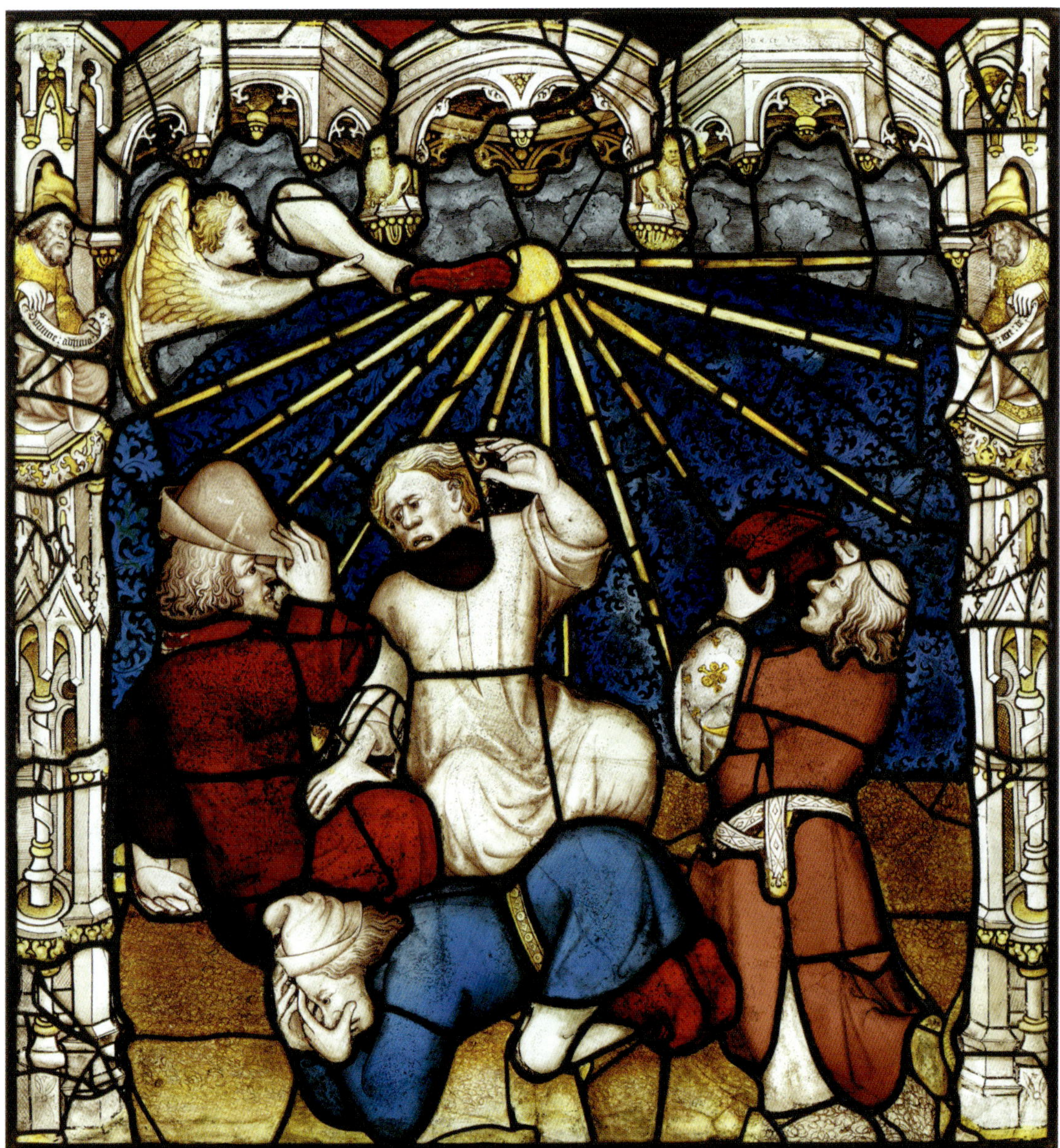

4f The Fourth Vial

And the fourth angel poured out his vial upon the sun, and it was given unto him to afflict men with heat and fire: And men were scorched with great heat, and they blasphemed the name of God, who hath power over these plagues, neither did they penance to give him glory.
Revelation 16:8–9

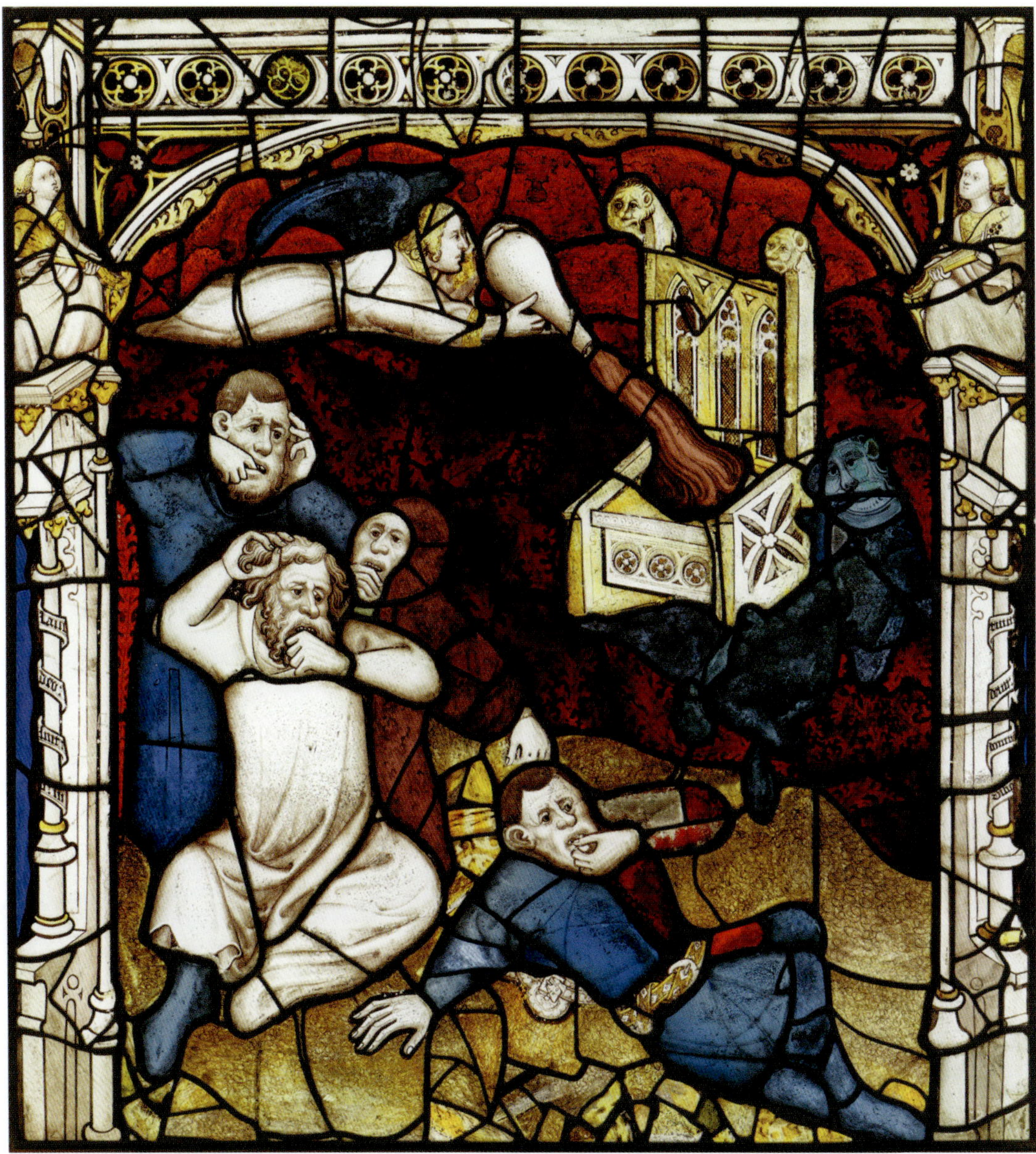

4g The Fifth Vial

And the fifth angel poured out his vial upon the seat of the beast; and his kingdom became dark, and they gnawed their tongues for pain: And they blasphemed the God of heaven, because of their pains and wounds, and did not penance for their works.

Revelation 16:10–11

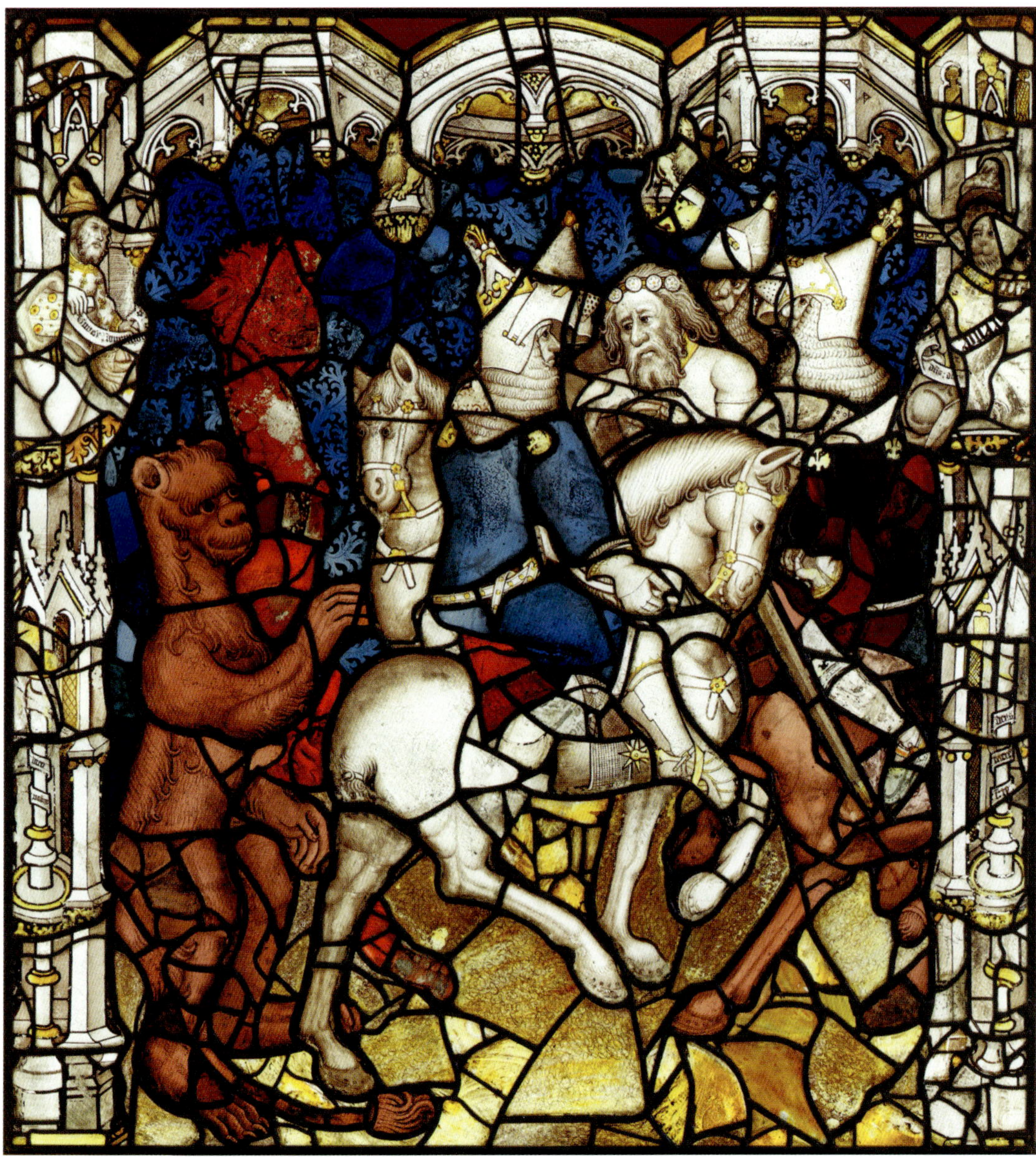

4h The Sixth Vial

And the sixth angel poured out his vial upon that great river Euphrates; and dried up the water thereof, that a way might be prepared for the kings from the rising of the sun. And I saw from the mouth of the dragon, and from the mouth of the beast, and from the mouth of the false prophet, three unclean spirits like frogs. For they are the spirits of devils working signs, and they go forth unto the kings of the whole earth, to gather them to battle against the great day of the Almighty God.

Revelation 16:12–14

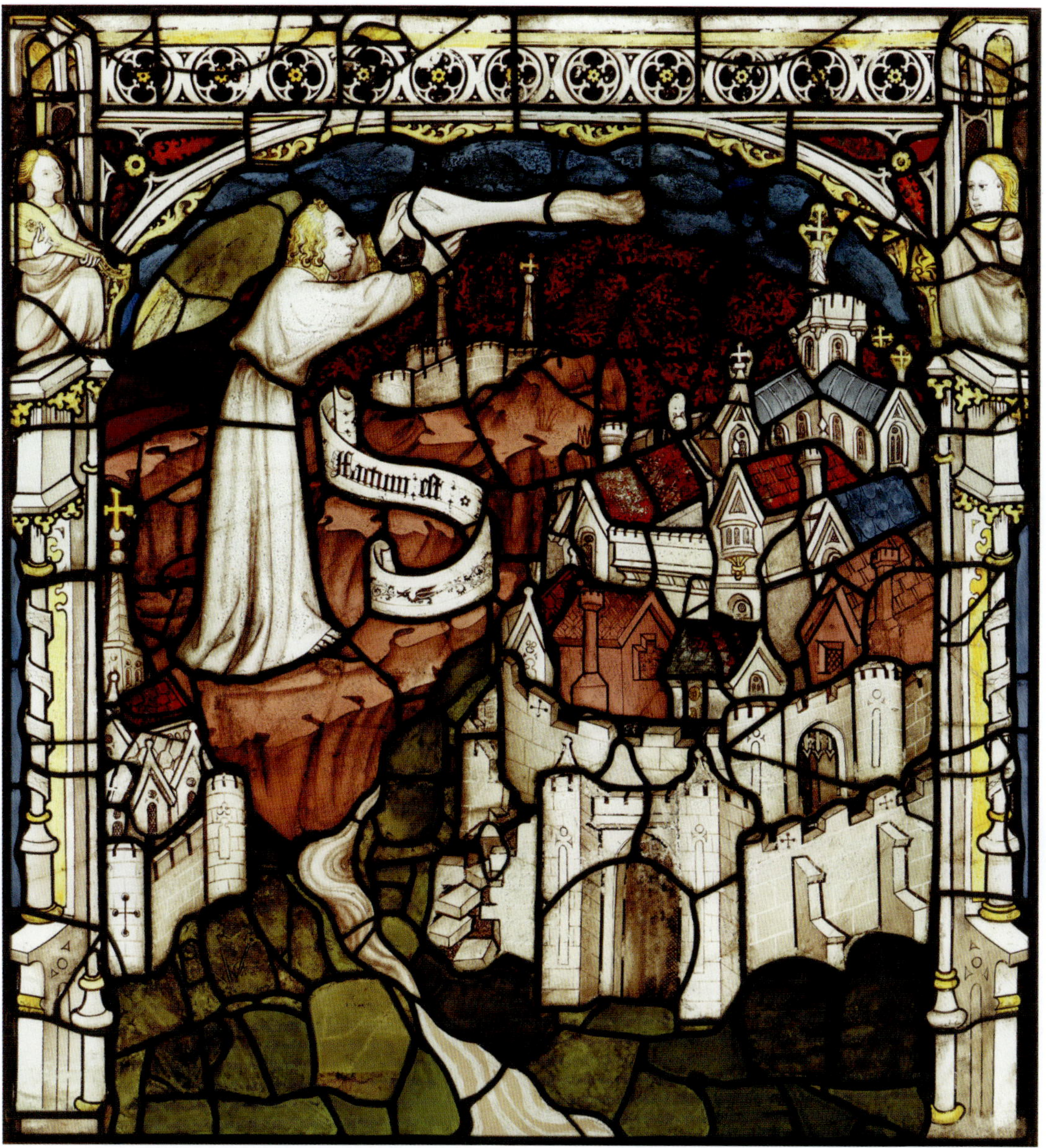

4j The Seventh Vial
And the seventh angel poured out his vial upon the air, and there came a great voice out of the temple from the throne, saying: **It is done**. And there were lightnings, and voices, and thunders, and there was a great earthquake, such a one as never had been since men were upon the earth, such an earthquake, so great. And the great city was divided into three parts; and the cities of the Gentiles fell. And great Babylon came in remembrance before God, to give her the cup of the wine of the indignation of his wrath.
Revelation 16:17–19

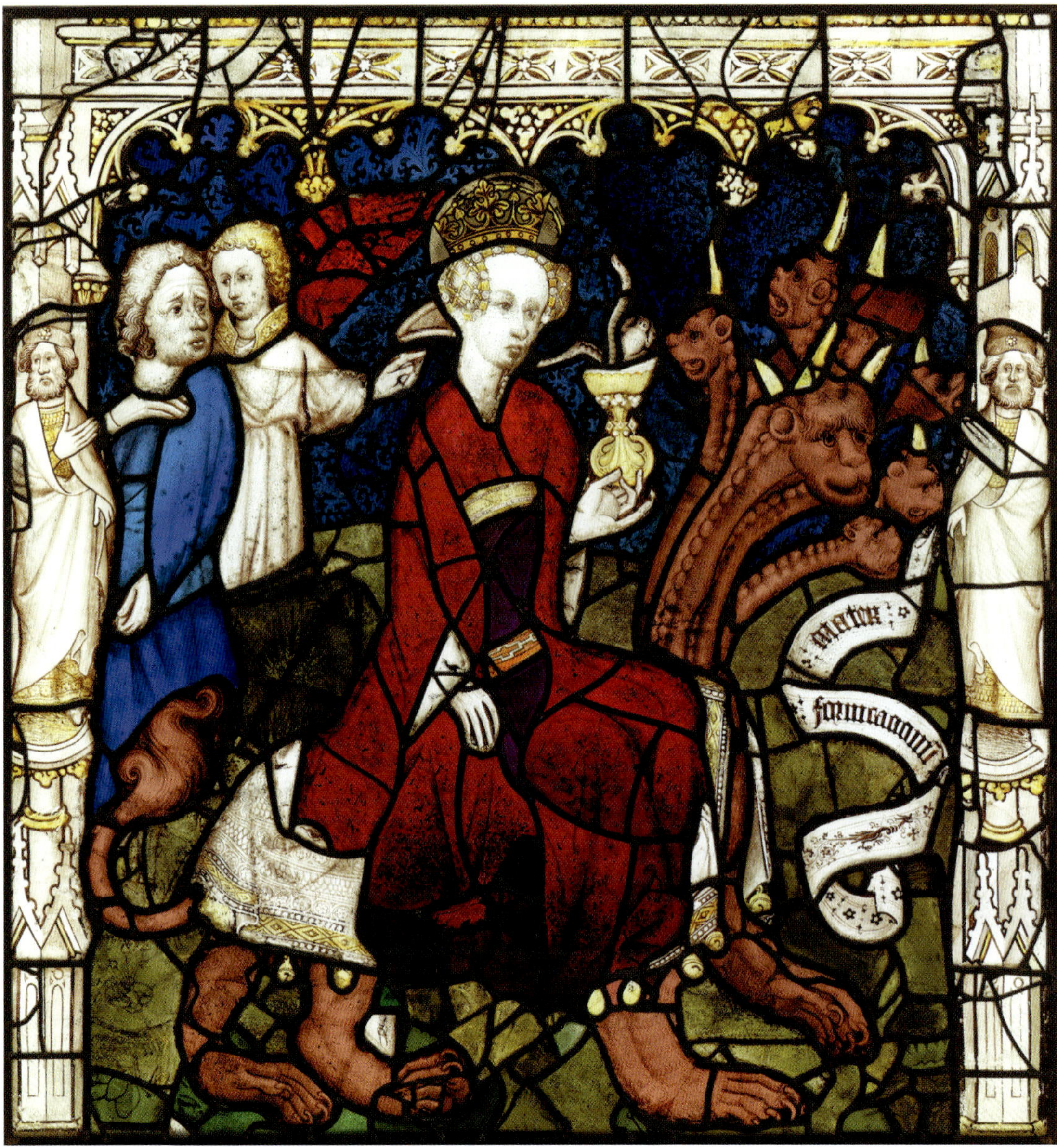

3a The Great Harlot riding the Beast

And there came one of the seven angels, who had the seven vials, and spoke with me, saying: Come, I will shew thee the condemnation of the great harlot, who sitteth upon many waters, With whom the kings of the earth have committed fornication; and they who inhabit the earth, have been made drunk with the wine of her whoredom. And he took me away in spirit into the desert. And I saw a woman sitting upon a scarlet coloured beast, full of names of blasphemy, having seven heads and ten horns. And the woman was clothed round about with purple and scarlet, and gilt with gold, and precious stones and pearls, having a golden cup in her hand, full of the abomination and filthiness of her fornication. And on her forehead a name was written: A mystery; Babylon the great, **the mother of the fornications**, and the abominations of the earth.
Revelation 17:1–5

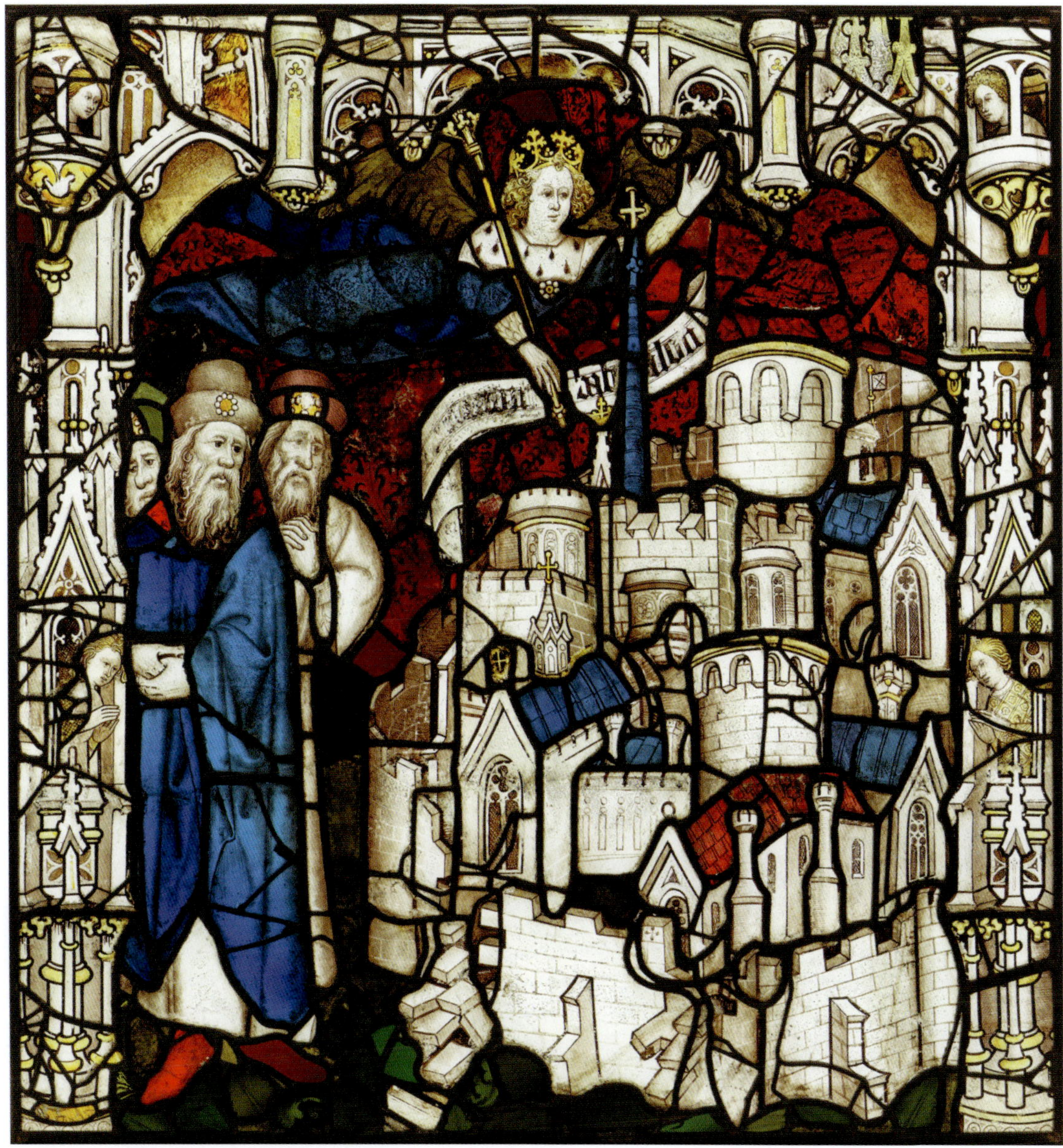

3b The Merchants mourn the Fall of Babylon

And the kings of the earth, who have committed fornication, and lived in delicacies with her, shall weep, and bewail themselves over her, when they shall see the smoke of her burning: Standing afar off for fear of her torments, saying: Alas! alas! that great city **Babylon**, that mighty city: for in one hour is thy judgment come. And the merchants of the earth shall weep, and mourn over her: for no man shall buy their merchandise any more. Merchandise of gold and silver, and precious stones; and of pearls, and fine linen, and purple, and silk, and scarlet ... The merchants of these things, who were made rich, shall stand afar off from her, for fear of her torments, weeping and mourning. And saying: Alas! alas! that great city, which was clothed with fine linen, and purple, and scarlet, and was gilt with gold, and precious stones, and pearls. For in one hour are so great riches come to nought ... Alas! alas! that great city, wherein all were made rich, that had ships at sea, by reason of her prices: for in one hour she is made desolate.

Revelation 18:9–19

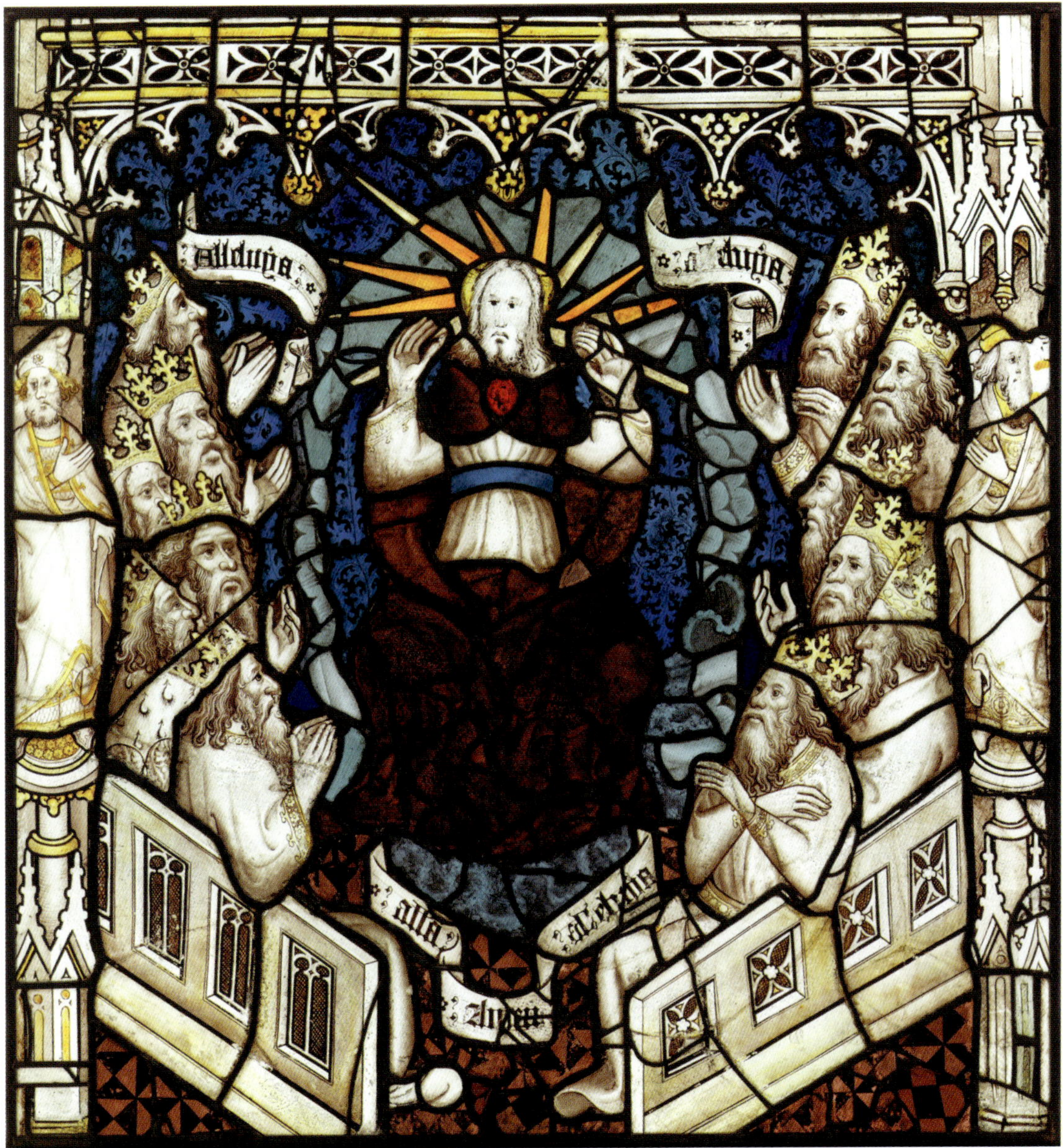

3c The Elders worship God

After these things I heard as it were the voice of much people in heaven, saying: **Alleluia**. Salvation, and glory, and power is to our God. For true and just are his judgments, who hath judged the great harlot which corrupted the earth with her fornication, and hath revenged the blood of his servants, at her hands. And again they said: **Alleluia**. And her smoke ascendeth for ever and ever. And the four and twenty ancients, and the four living creatures fell down and adored God that sitteth upon the throne, saying: **Amen; Alleluia**.

Revelation 19:1–4

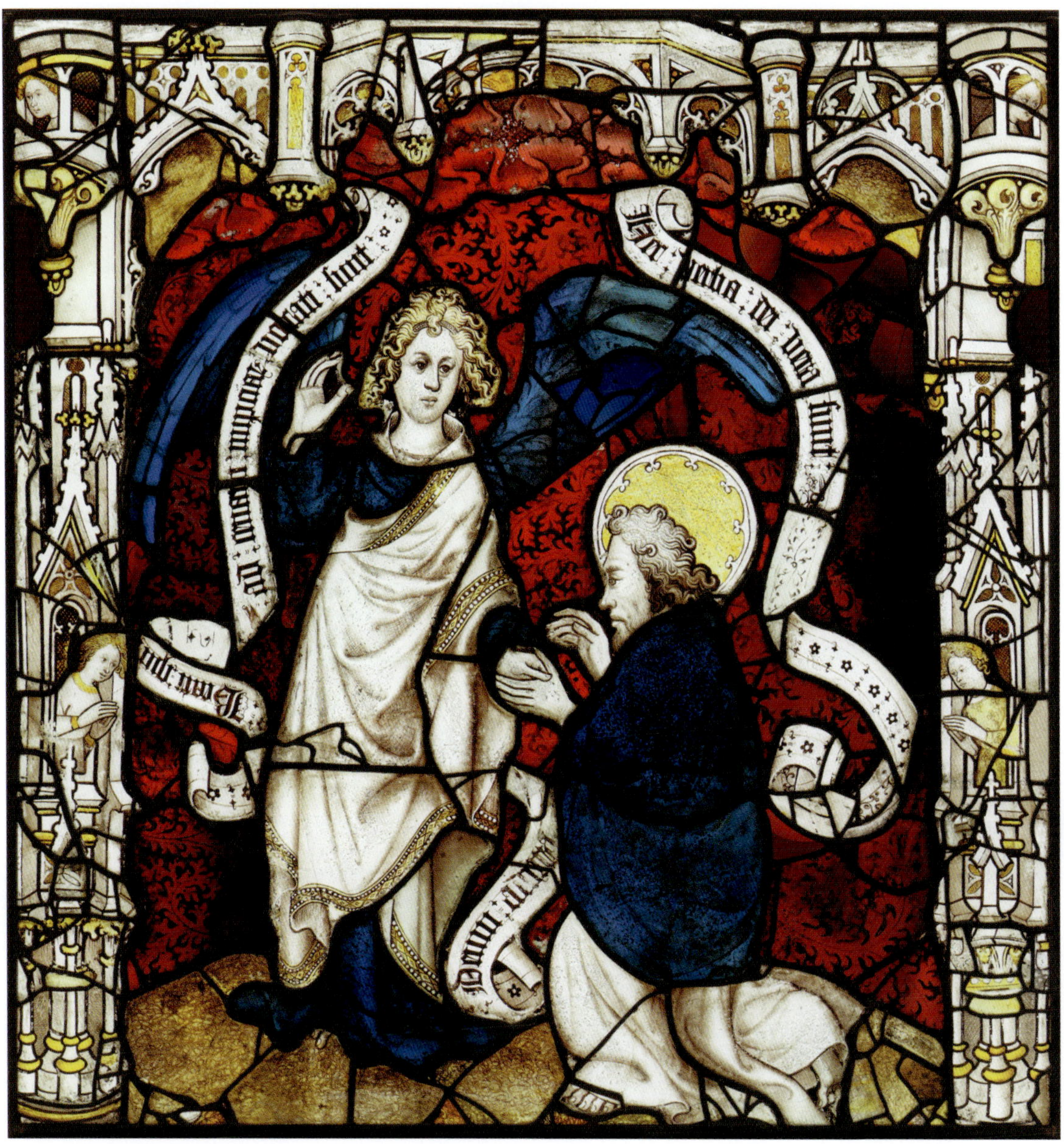

3d The Angel instructs St John to write

And he said to me: Write: **Blessed are they that are called to the marriage supper** of the Lamb. And he saith to me: **These words of God are true**. And I fell down before his feet, to adore him. And he saith to me: See thou do it not: I am thy fellow servant, and of thy brethren, who have the testimony of Jesus. **Adore God**. For the testimony of Jesus is the spirit of prophecy.
Revelation 19:9–10

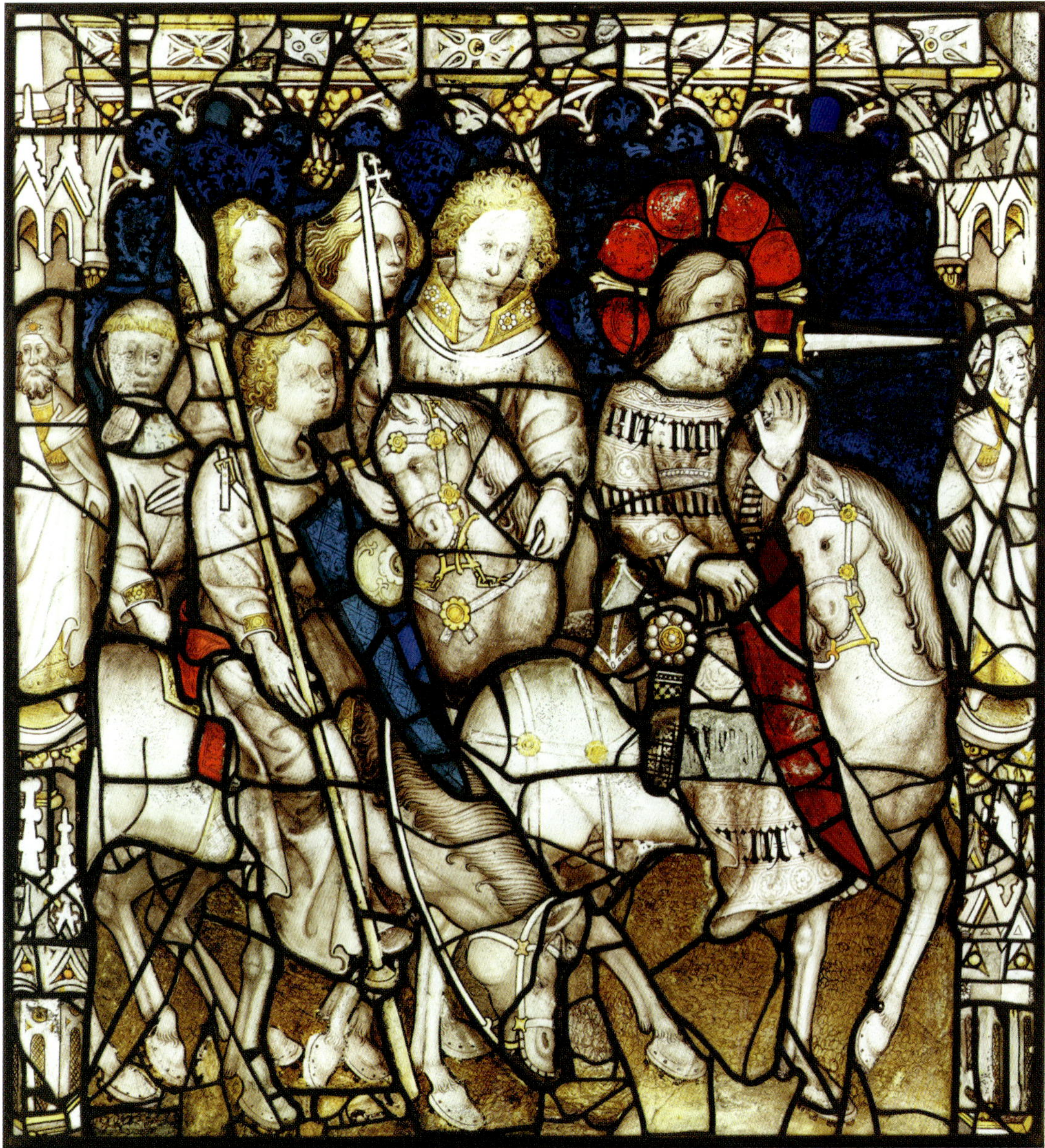

3e The King of Kings and the Armies of Heaven

And I saw heaven opened, and behold a white horse; and he that sat upon him was called faithful and true, and with justice doth he judge and fight. And his eyes were as a flame of fire, and on his head were many diadems, and he had a name written, which no man knoweth but himself. And he was clothed with a garment sprinkled with blood; and his name is called, **the Word of God**. And the armies that are in heaven followed him on white horses, clothed in fine linen, white and clean. And out of his mouth proceedeth a sharp two edged sword; that with it he may strike the nations. And he shall rule them with a rod of iron; and he treadeth the winepress of the fierceness of the wrath of God the Almighty. And he hath on his garment, and on his thigh written: **King of Kings, and Lord of Lords**.
Revelation 19:11–16

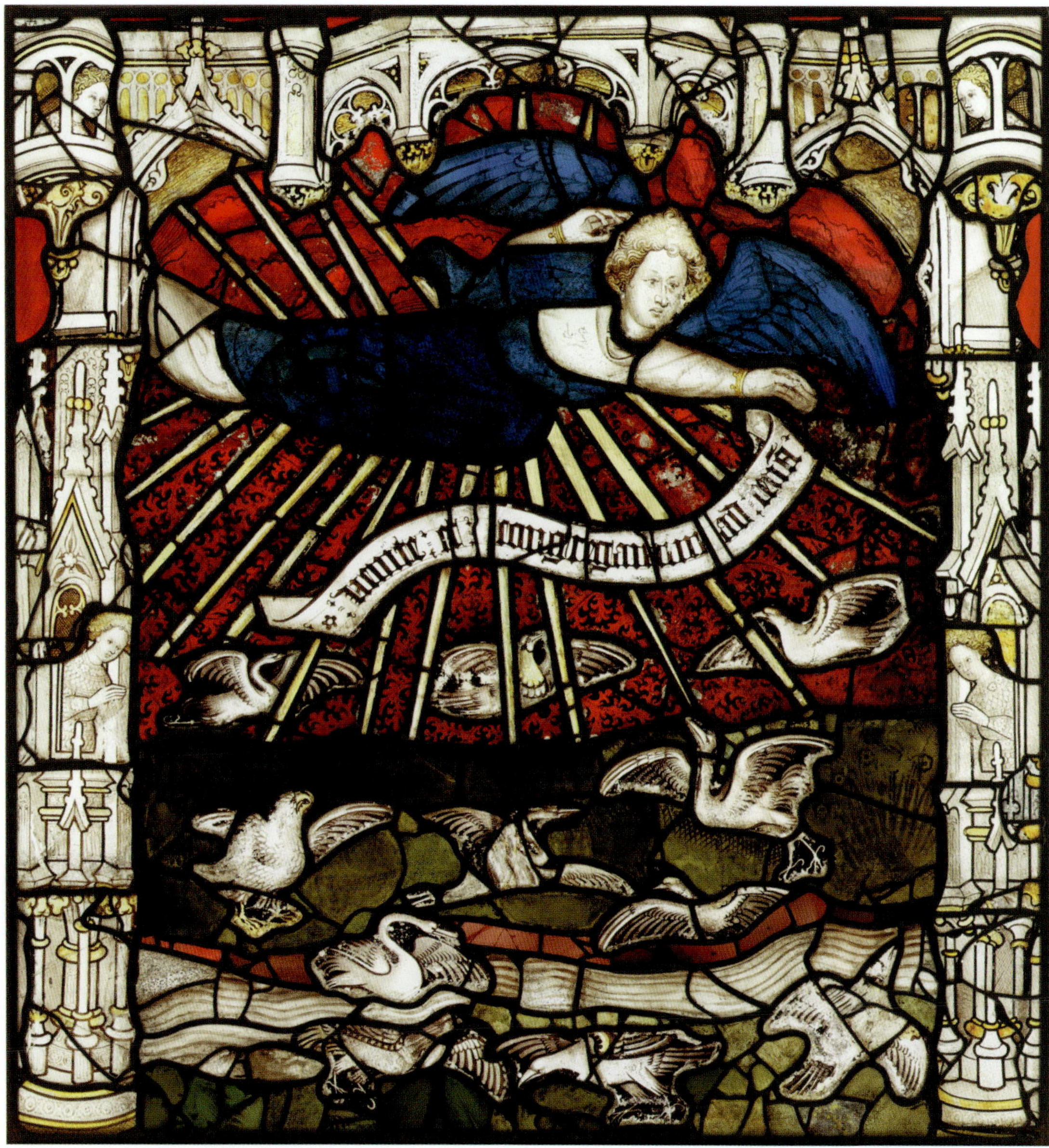

3f The Angel summons the Birds
And I saw an angel standing in the sun, and he cried with a loud voice, saying to all the birds that did fly through the midst of heaven:
Come, gather yourselves together to the great supper of God: That you may eat the flesh of kings, and the flesh of tribunes, and the flesh of mighty men, and the flesh of horses, and of them that sit on them, and the flesh of all freemen and bondmen, and of little and of great.
Revelation 19:17–18

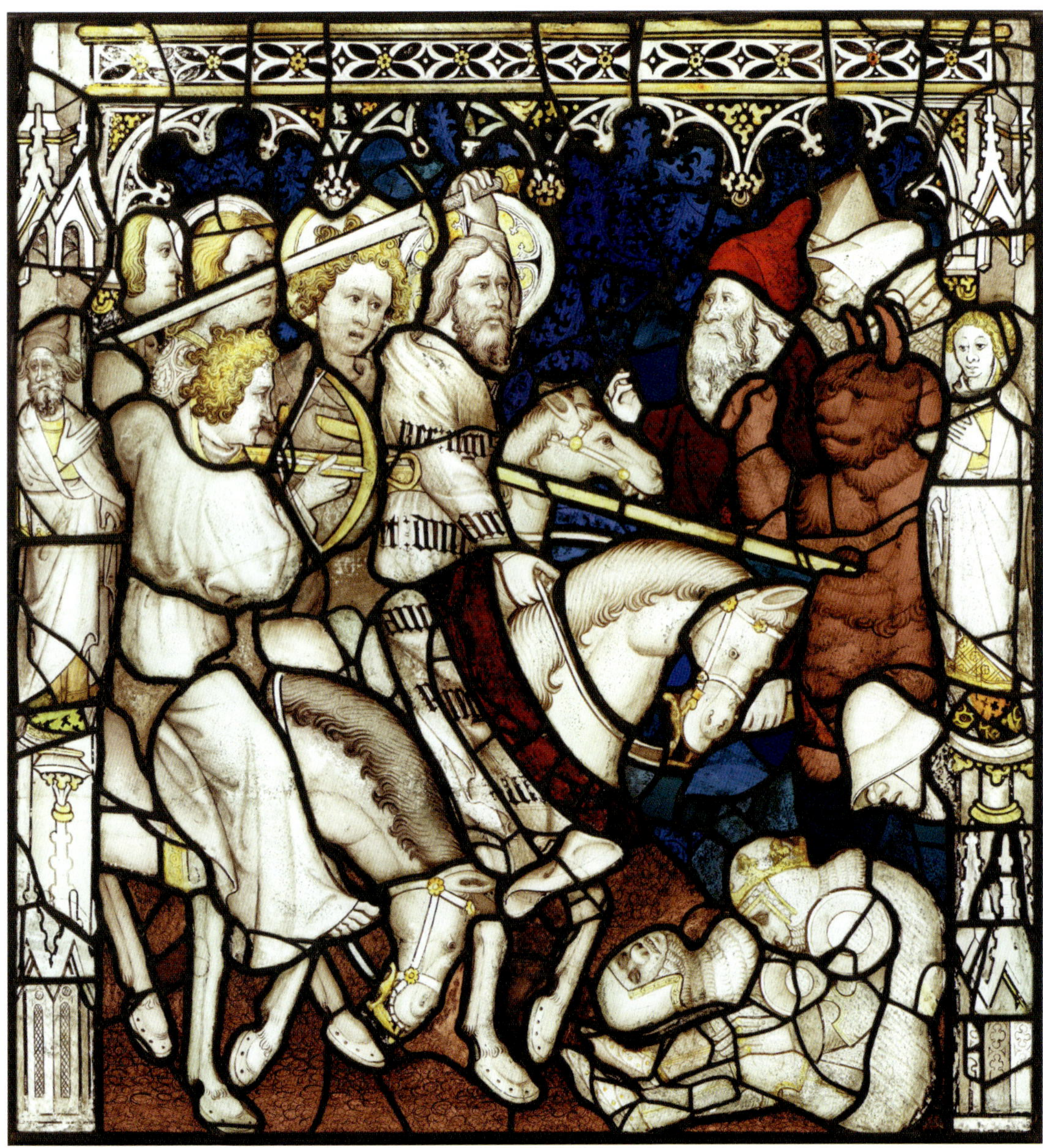

3g The King of Kings and his Armies fight the Beast
And I saw the beast, and the kings of the earth, and their armies gathered together to make war with him that sat upon the horse, and with his army.
Revelation 19:19

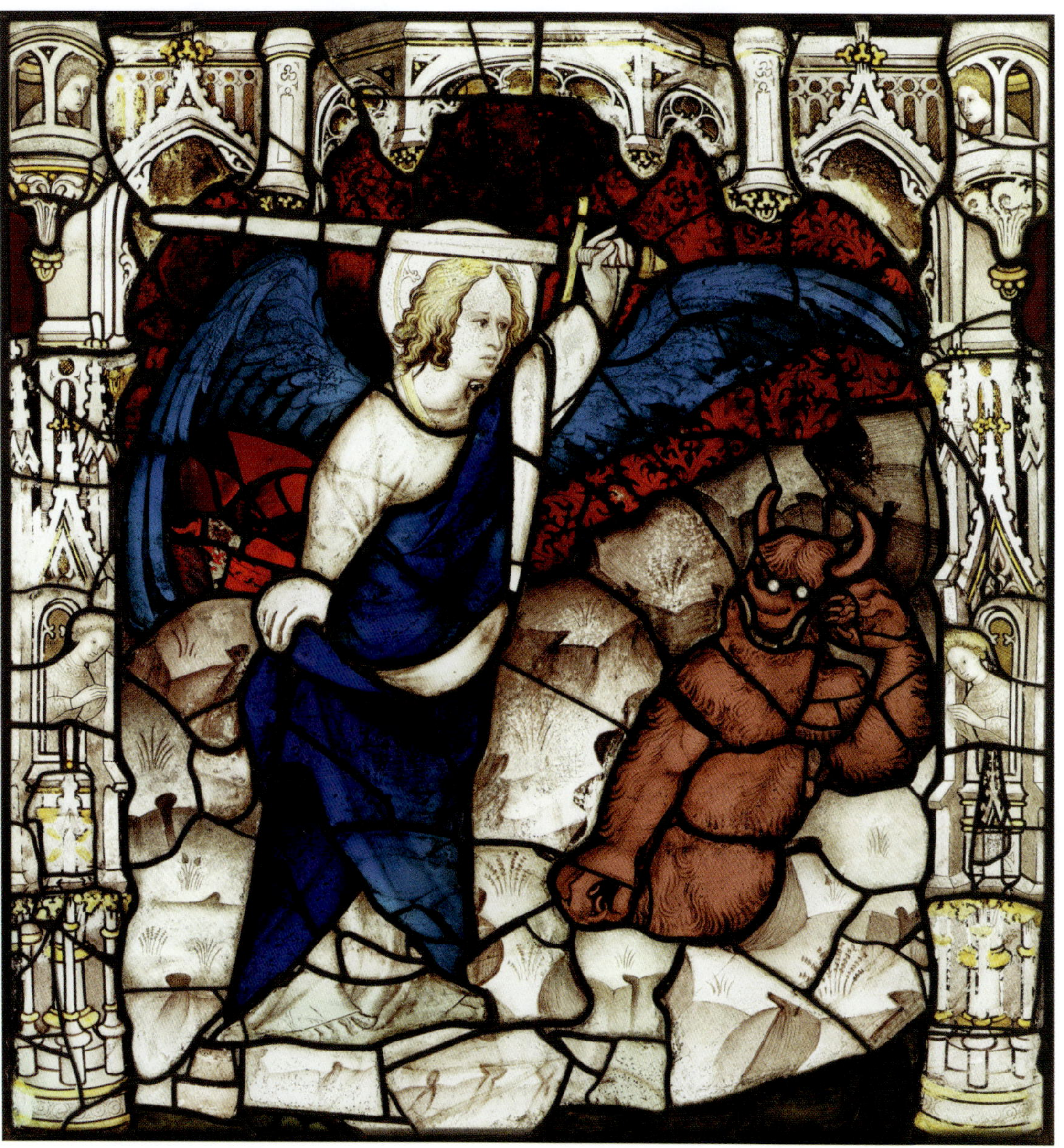

3h The Beast taken

And the beast was taken, and with him the false prophet, who wrought signs before him, wherewith he seduced them who received the character of the beast, and who adored his image. These two were cast alive into the pool of fire, burning with brimstone.
Revelation 19:20

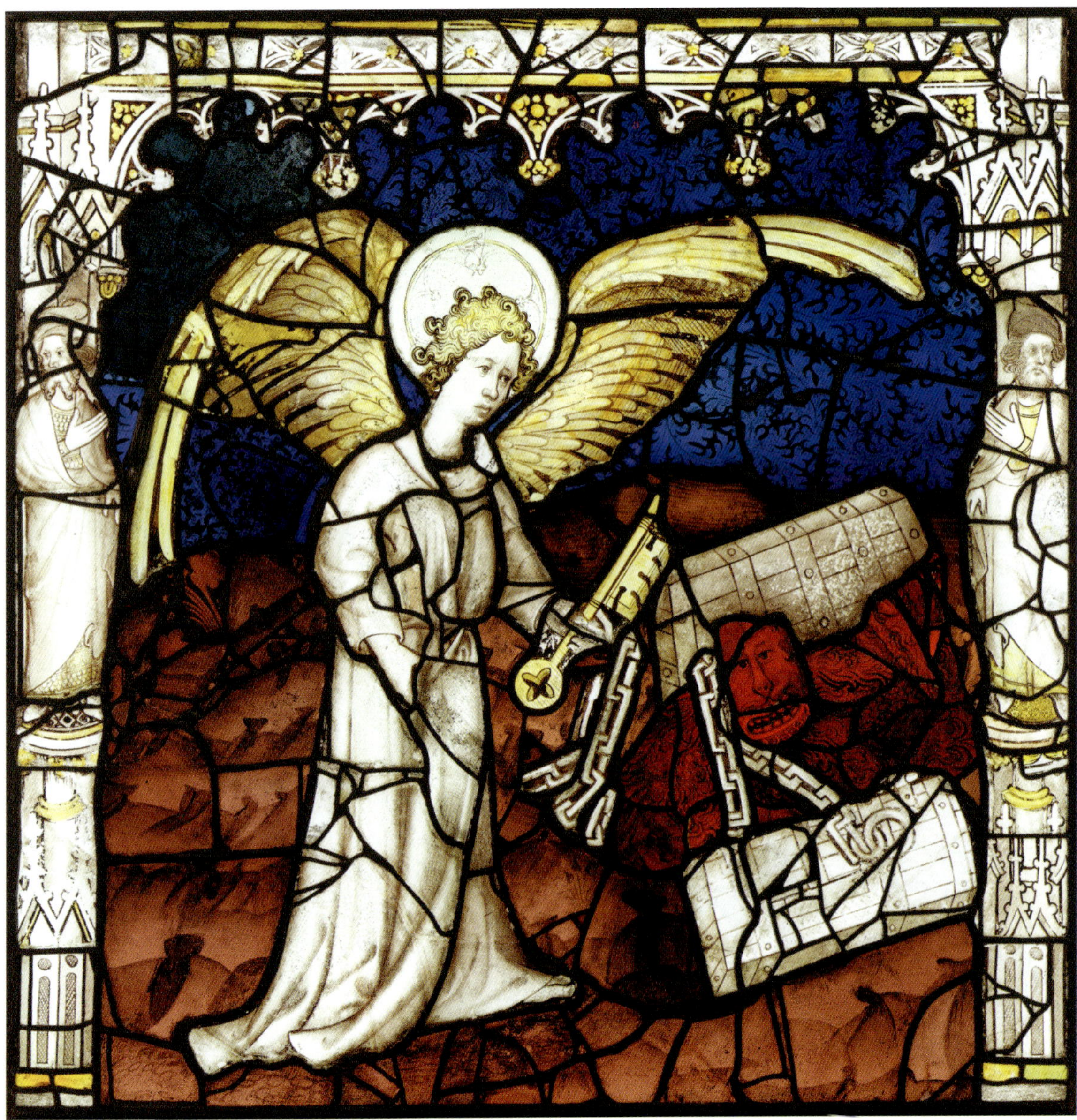

3j Satan chained in the bottomless pit
And I saw an angel coming down from heaven, having the key of the bottomless pit, and a great chain in his hand. And he laid hold on the dragon the old serpent, which is the devil and Satan, and bound him for a thousand years. And he cast him into the bottomless pit, and shut him up, and set a seal upon him, that he should no more seduce the nations, till the thousand years be finished. And after that, he must be loosed a little time.
Revelation 20:1–3

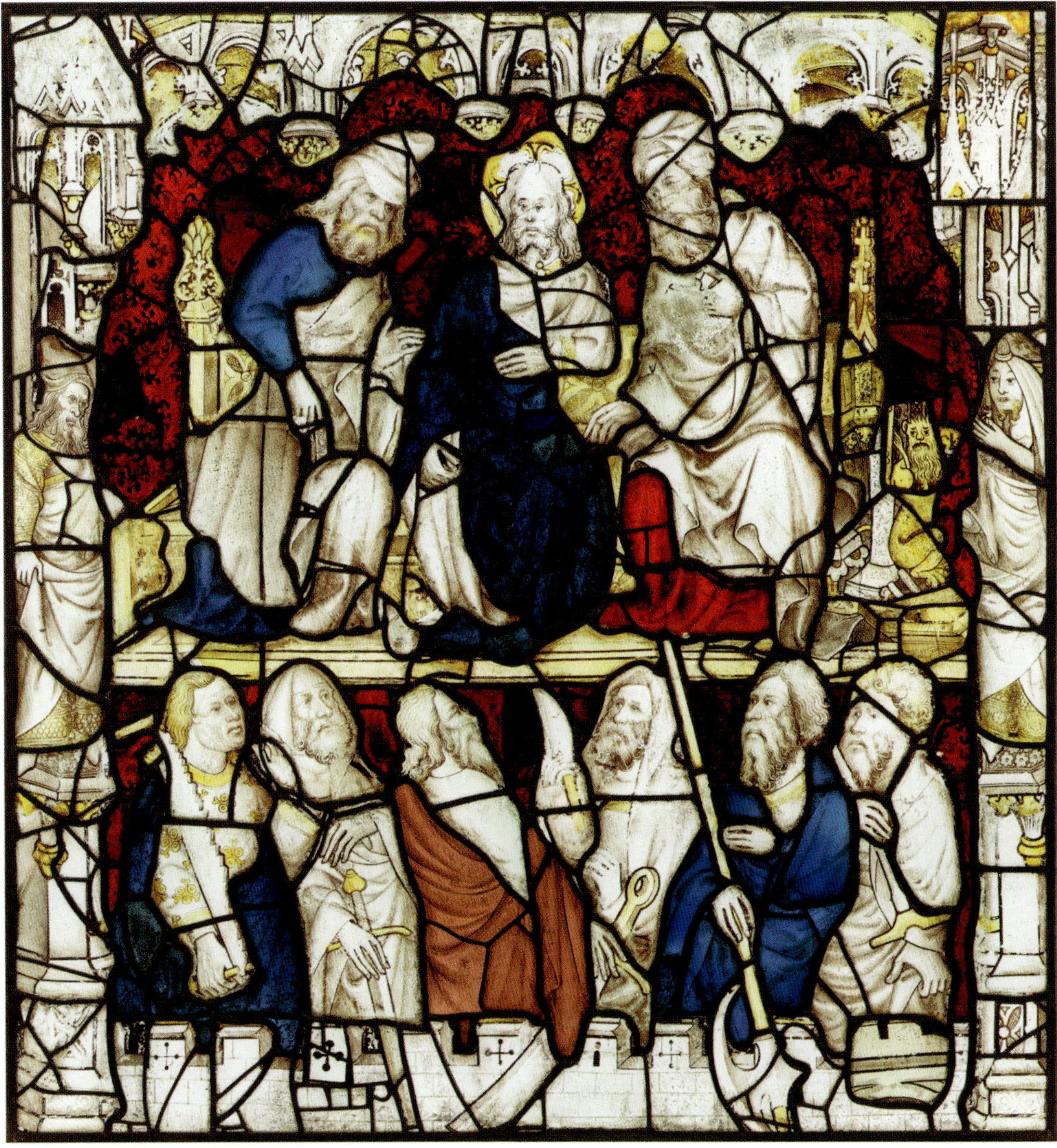

2a The Judgement for the First Resurrection
And I saw seats; and they sat upon them; and judgment was given unto them; and the souls of them that were beheaded for the testimony of Jesus, and for the word of God, and who had not adored the beast nor his image, nor received his character on their foreheads, or in their hands; and they lived and reigned with Christ a thousand years. The rest of the dead lived not, till the thousand years were finished. This is the first resurrection. Blessed and holy is he that hath part in the first resurrection. In these the second death hath no power; but they shall be priests of God and of Christ; and shall reign with him a thousand years.
Revelation 20:4–6

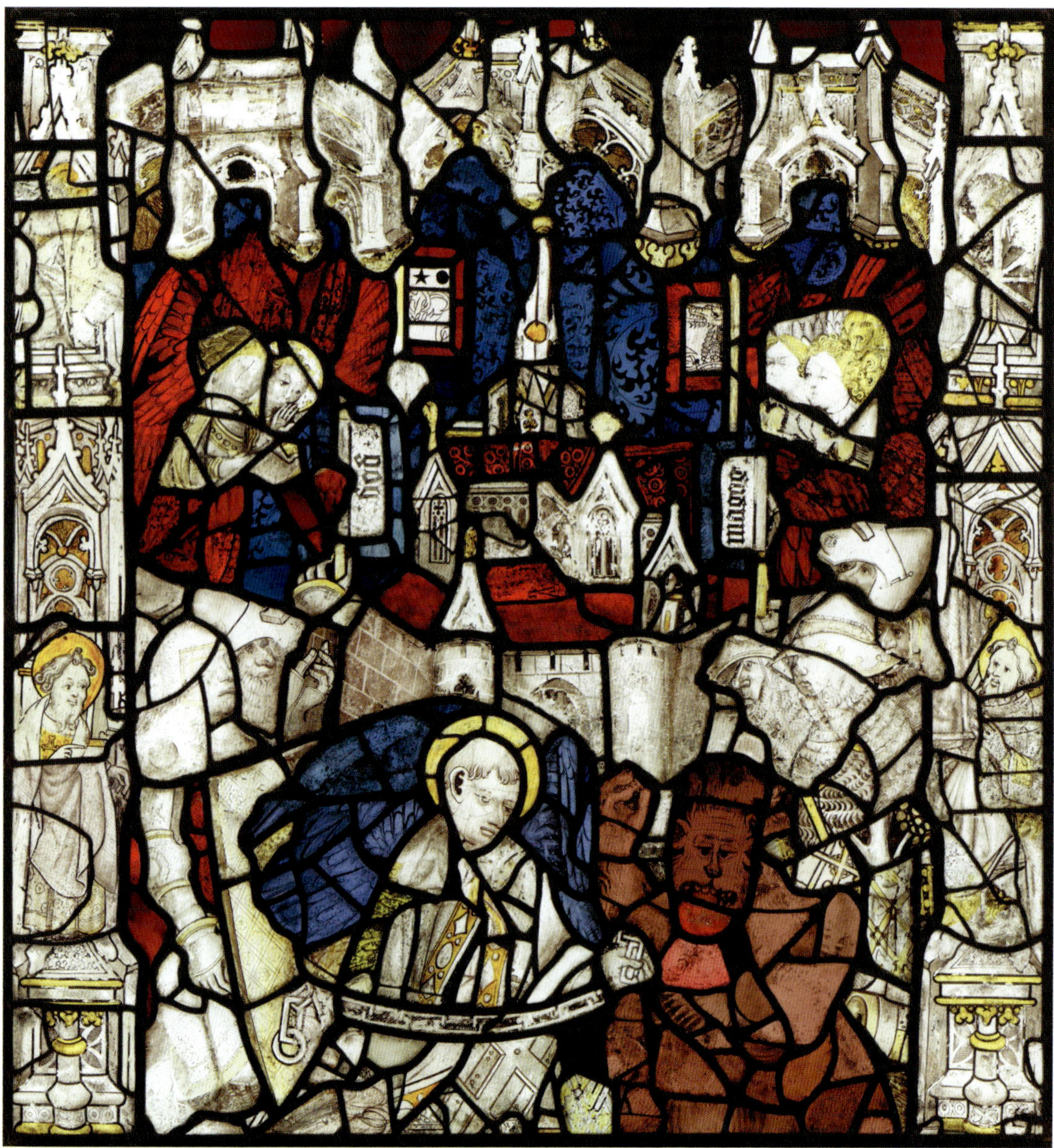

2b Satan loosed with Gog and Magog
And when the thousand years shall be finished, Satan shall be loosed out of his prison, and shall go forth, and seduce the nations, which are over the four quarters of the earth, Gog, and Magog, and shall gather them together to battle, the number of whom is as the sand of the sea. And they came upon the breadth of the earth, and encompassed the camp of the saints, and the beloved city.
Revelation 20:7–8

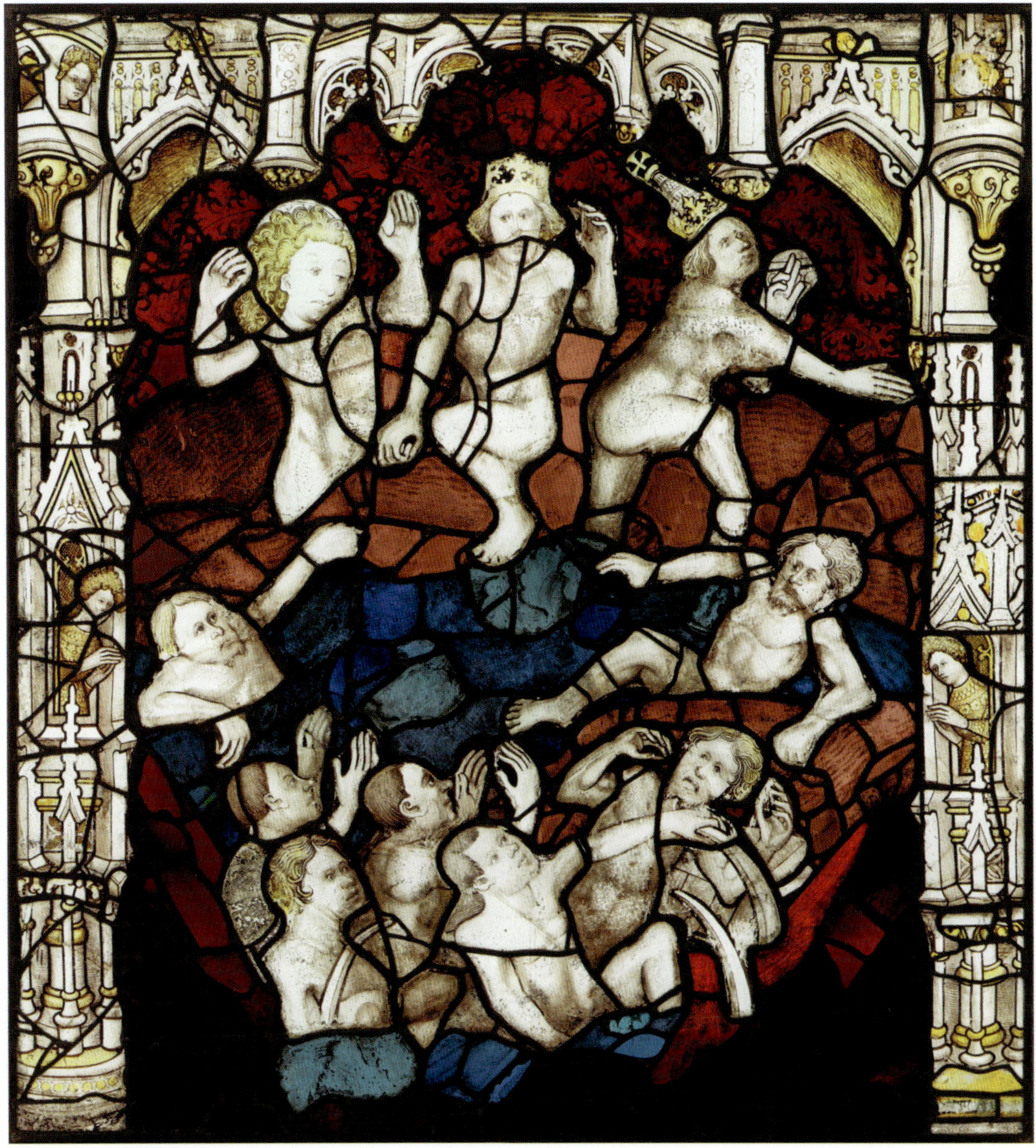

2c The Dead rising for Judgement
And I saw the dead, great and small, standing in the presence of the throne, and the books were opened; and another book was opened, which is the book of life; and the dead were judged by those things which were written in the books, according to their works. And the sea gave up the dead that were in it, and death and hell gave up their dead that were in them; and they were judged every one according to their works. And hell and death were cast into the pool of fire. This is the second death. And whosoever was not found written in the book of life, was cast into the pool of fire.
Revelation 20:12–15 (with 2d, 2e, 2f)

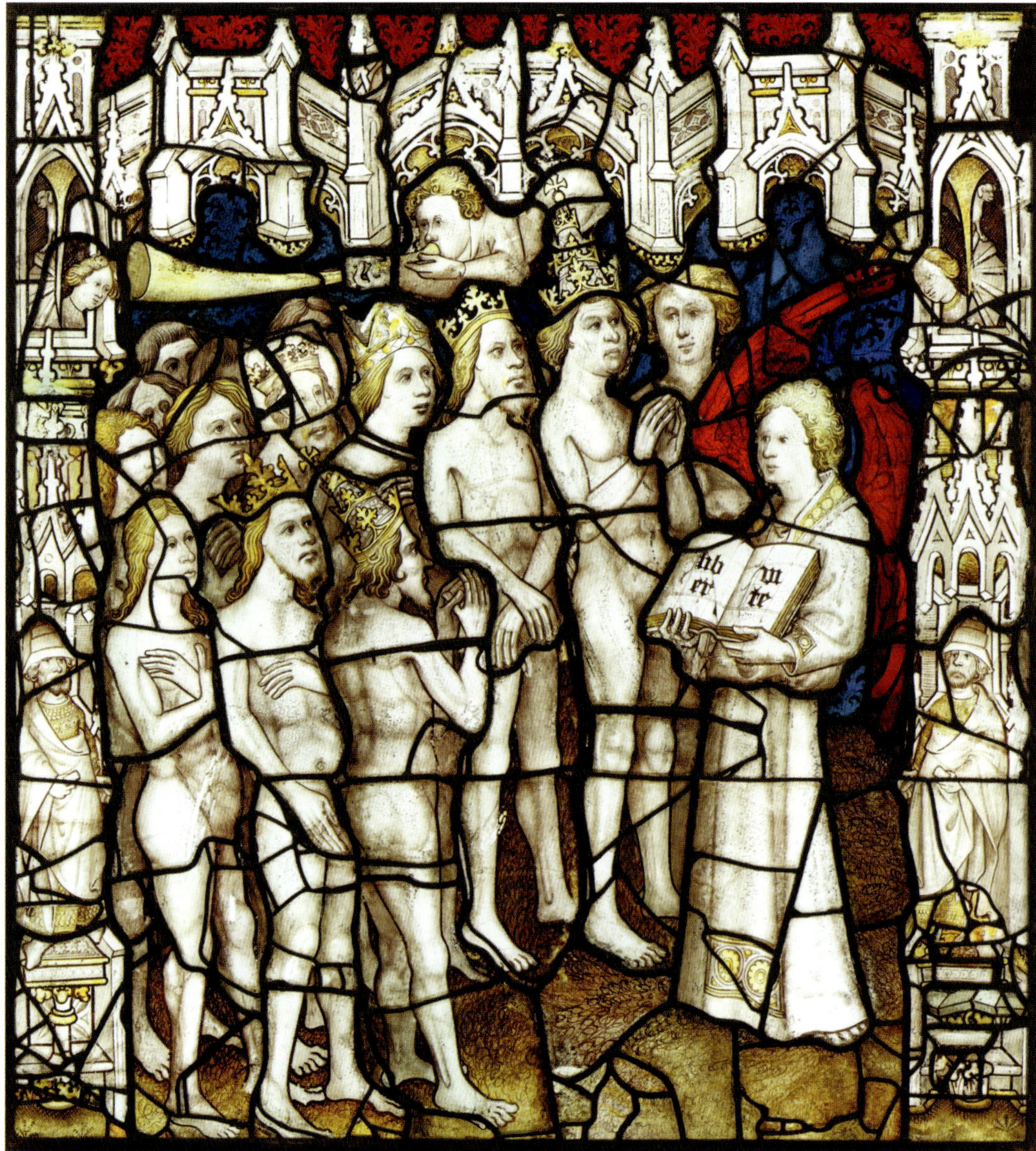

2d The Saved at the Last Judgement

And I saw the dead, great and small, standing in the presence of the throne, and the books were opened; and another book was opened, which is the book of life; and the dead were judged by those things which were written in the books, according to their works. And the sea gave up the dead that were in it, and death and hell gave up their dead that were in them; and they were judged every one according to their works. And hell and death were cast into the pool of fire. This is the second death. And whosoever was not found written in the book of life, was cast into the pool of fire.
Revelation 20:12–15 (with 2c, 2e, 2f)

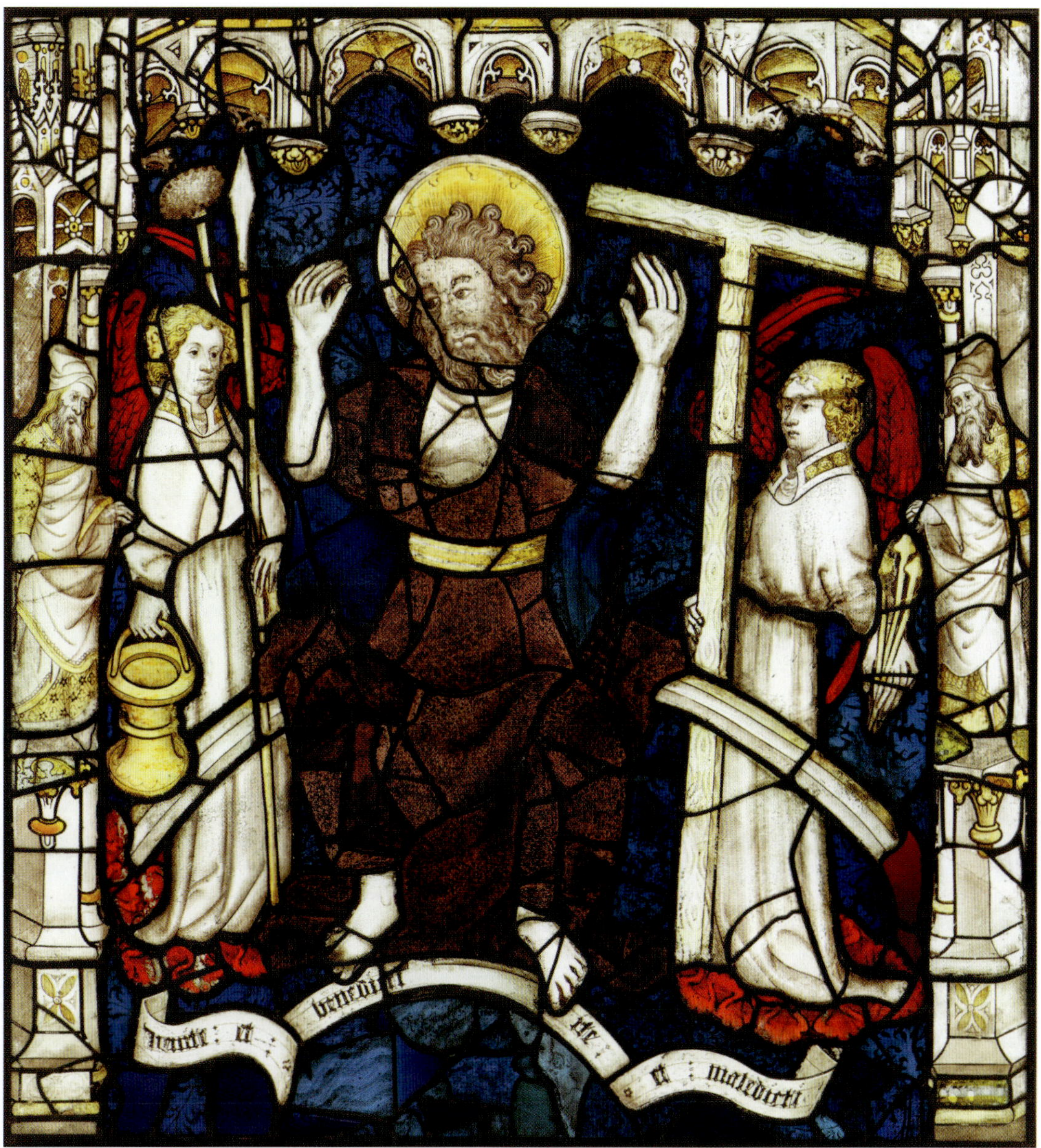

2e The Judge

And I saw a great white throne, and one sitting upon it, from whose face the earth and heaven fled away, and there was no place found for them. And I saw the dead, great and small, standing in the presence of the throne, and the books were opened; and another book was opened, which is the book of life; and the dead were judged by those things which were written in the books, according to their works. And the sea gave up the dead that were in it, and death and hell gave up their dead that were in them; and they were judged every one according to their works. And hell and death were cast into the pool of fire. This is the second death. And whosoever was not found written in the book of life, was cast into the pool of fire.
Revelation 20:11–15 (with 2c, 2d, 2f)

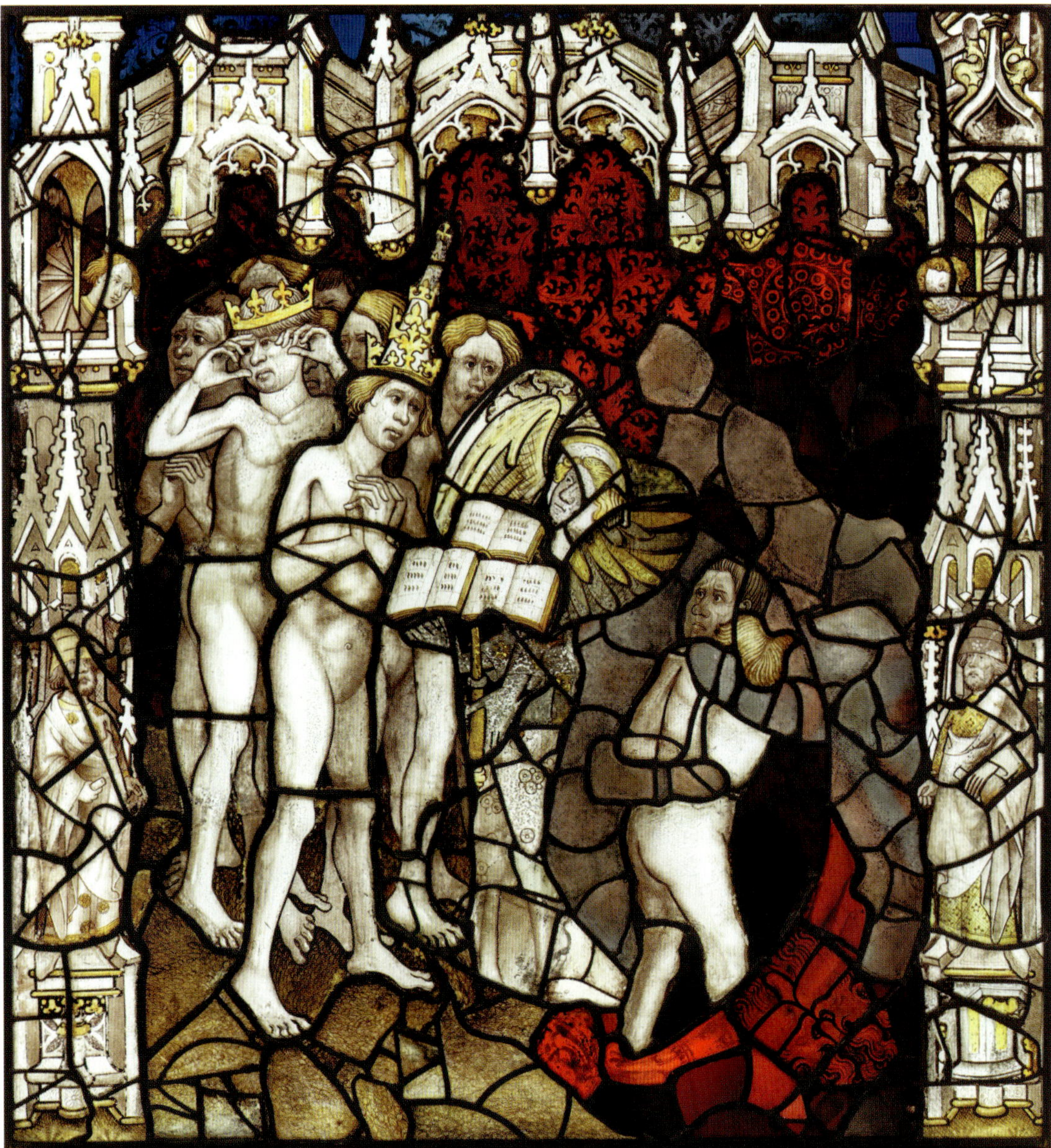

2f The Damned at the Last Judgement

And I saw the dead, great and small, standing in the presence of the throne, and the books were opened; and another book was opened, which is the book of life; and the dead were judged by those things which were written in the books, according to their works. And the sea gave up the dead that were in it, and death and hell gave up their dead that were in them; and they were judged every one according to their works. And hell and death were cast into the pool of fire. This is the second death. And whosoever was not found written in the book of life, was cast into the pool of fire.
Revelation 20:12–15 (with 2c, 2d, 2e)

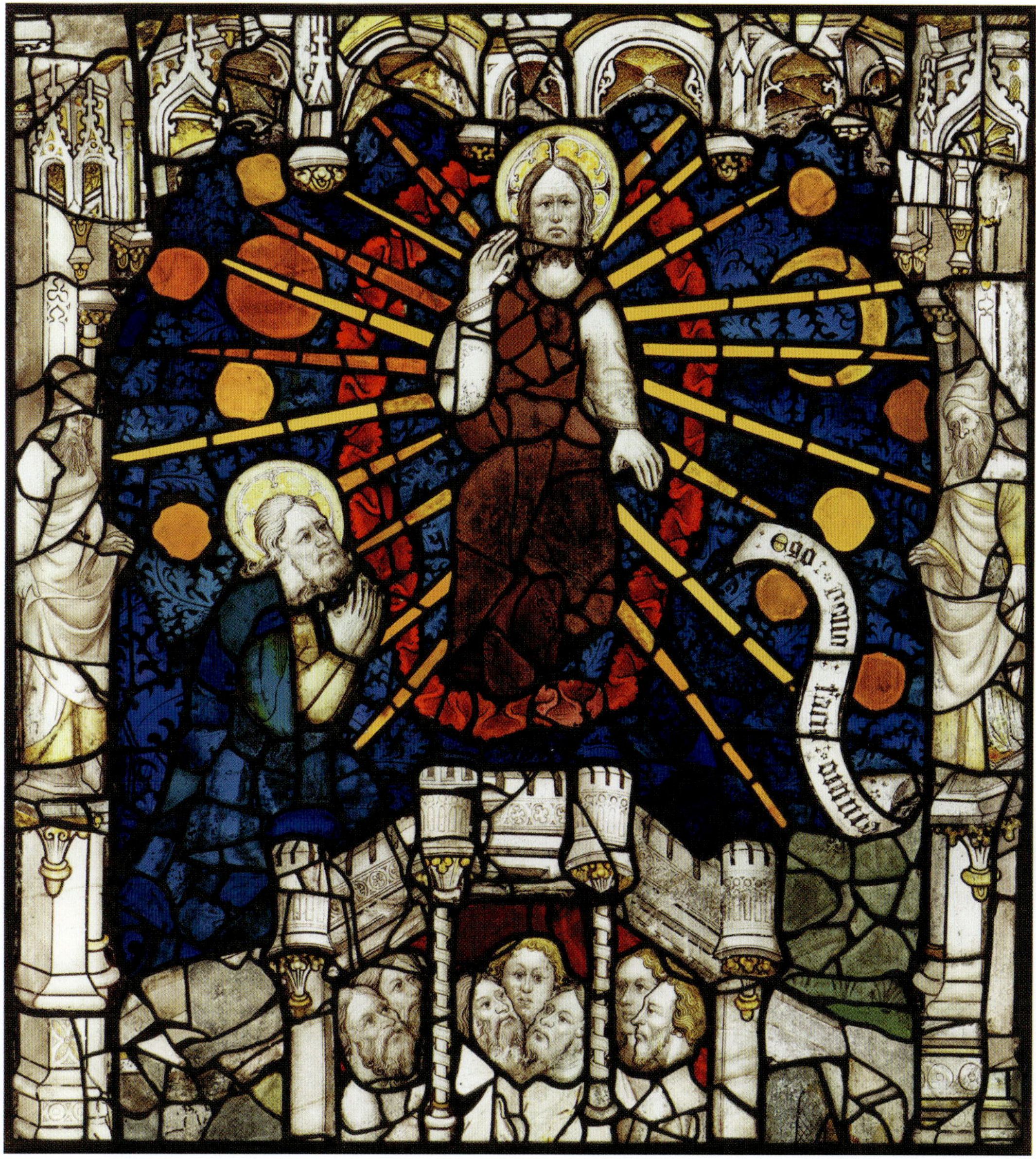

2g The New Heaven and the New Earth

And I John saw the holy city, the new Jerusalem, coming down out of heaven from God, prepared as a bride adorned for her husband. And I heard a great voice from the throne, saying: Behold the tabernacle of God with men, and he will dwell with them. And they shall be his people; and God himself with them shall be their God. And God shall wipe away all tears from their eyes: and death shall be no more, nor mourning, nor crying, nor sorrow shall be any more, for the former things are passed away. And he that sat on the throne, said: **Behold, I make all things new**. And he said to me: Write, for these words are most faithful and true.
Revelation 21:2–5

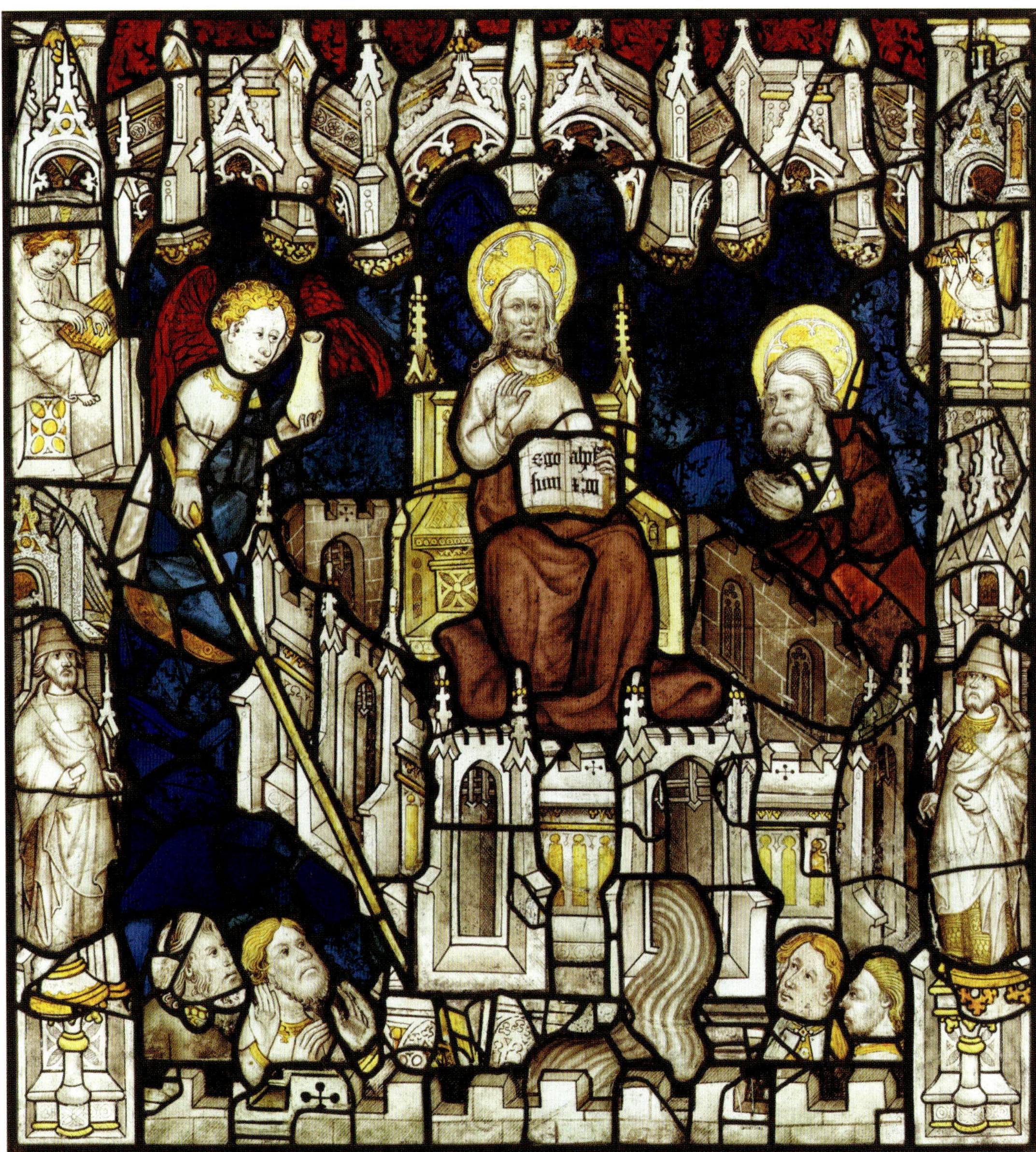

2h The New Jerusalem

And he said to me: It is done. **I am Alpha and Omega**; the beginning and the end. To him that thirsteth, I will give of the fountain of the water of life, freely ... And there came one of the seven angels, who had the vials full of the seven last plagues, and spoke with me, saying: Come, and I will shew thee the bride, the wife of the Lamb. And he took me up in spirit to a great and high mountain: and he shewed me the holy city Jerusalem coming down out of heaven from God, Having the glory of God, and the light thereof was like to a precious stone, as to the jasper stone, even as crystal. And it had a wall great and high, having twelve gates, and in the gates twelve angels, and names written thereon, which are the names of the twelve tribes of the children of Israel ... And he that spoke with me, had a measure of a reed of gold, to measure the city and the gates thereof, and the wall. And the city lieth in a foursquare, and the length thereof is as great as the breadth: and he measured the city with the golden reed for twelve thousand furlongs, and the length and the height and the breadth thereof are equal. And he measured the wall thereof an hundred and forty-four cubits, the measure of a man, which is of an angel.

Revelation 21:6, 9–17

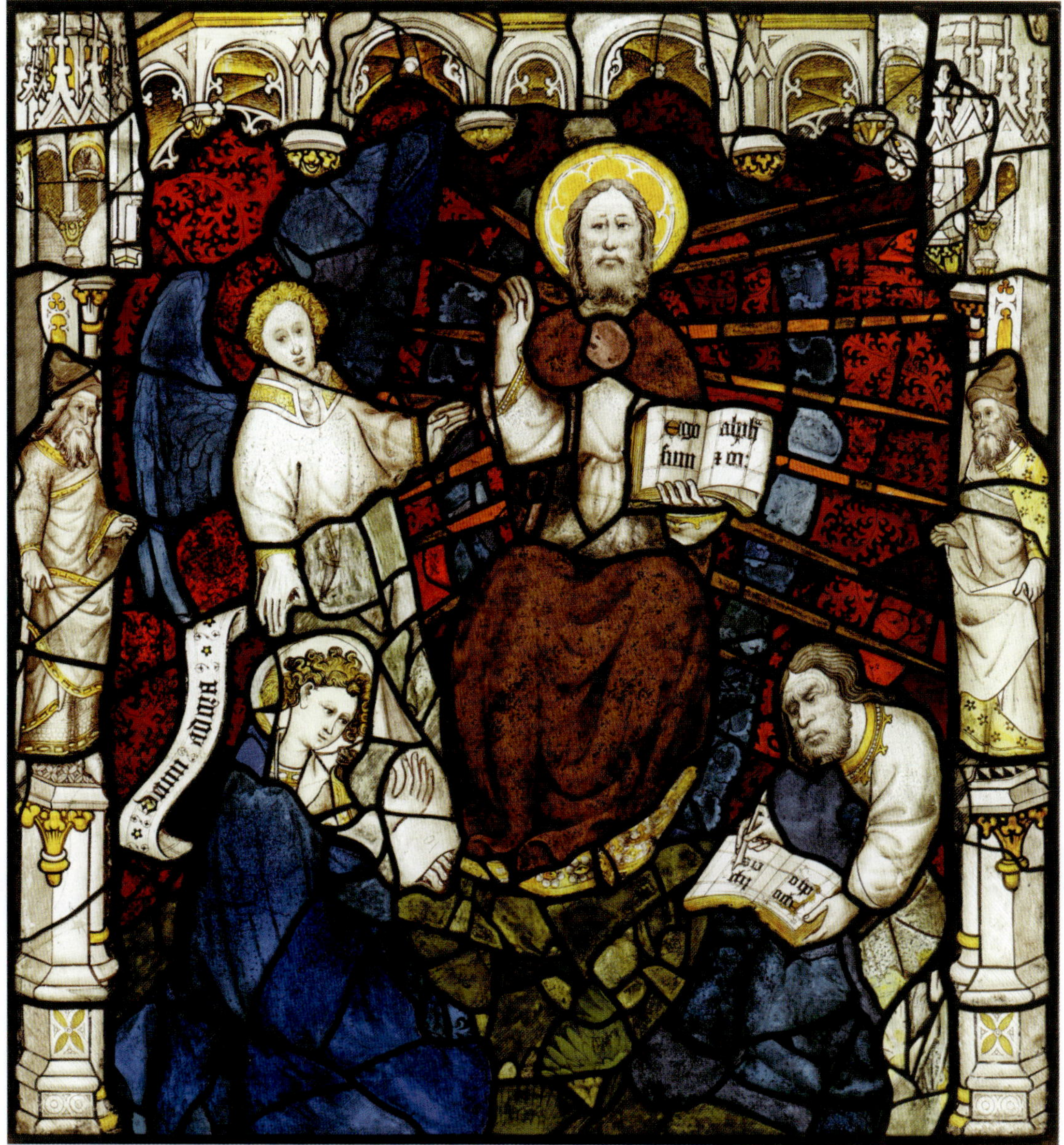

2j Christ in Majesty

And he said to me: See thou do it not: for I am thy fellow servant, and of thy brethren the prophets, and of them that keep the words of the prophecy of this book. **Adore God**. And he saith to me: Seal not the words of the prophecy of this book: for the time is at hand. He that hurteth, let him hurt still: and he that is filthy, let him be filthy still: and he that is just, let him be justified still: and he that is holy, let him be sanctified still. Behold, I come quickly; and my reward is with me, to render to every man according to his works. **I am Alpha and Omega**, the first and the last, the beginning and the end.
Revelation 22:9–13

Catalogue

Kings and Ecclesiastics

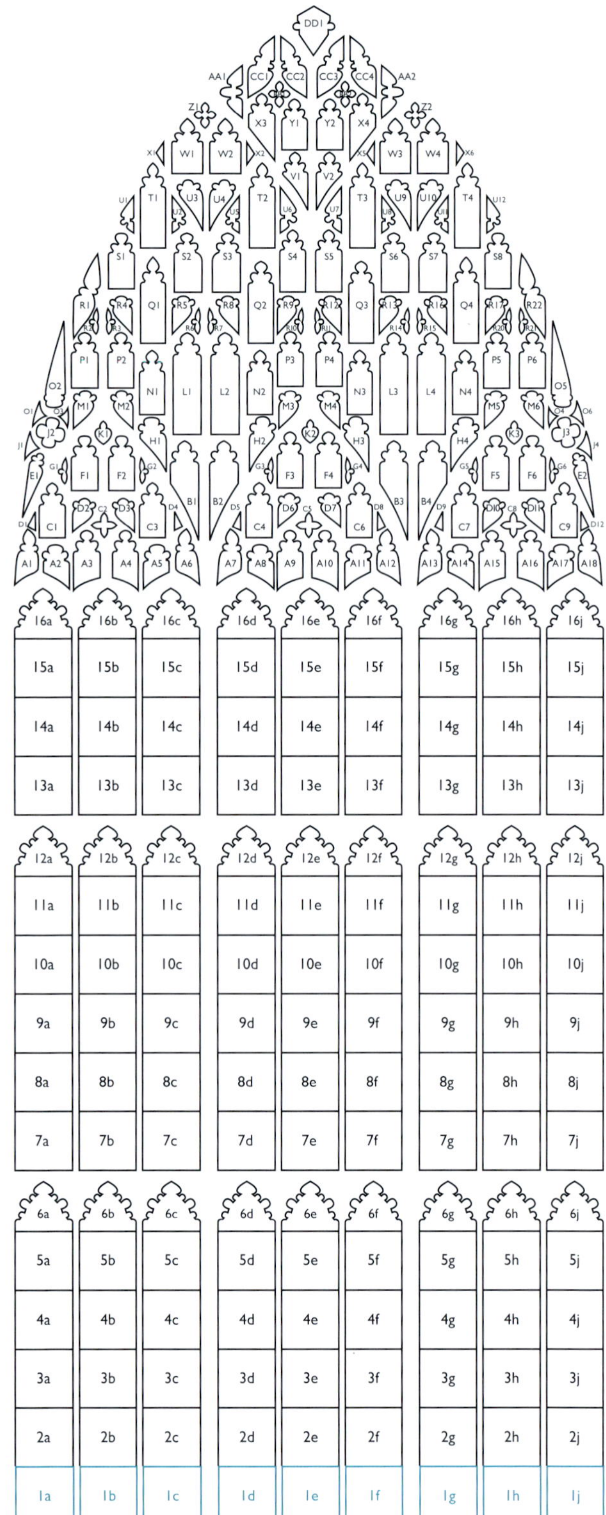

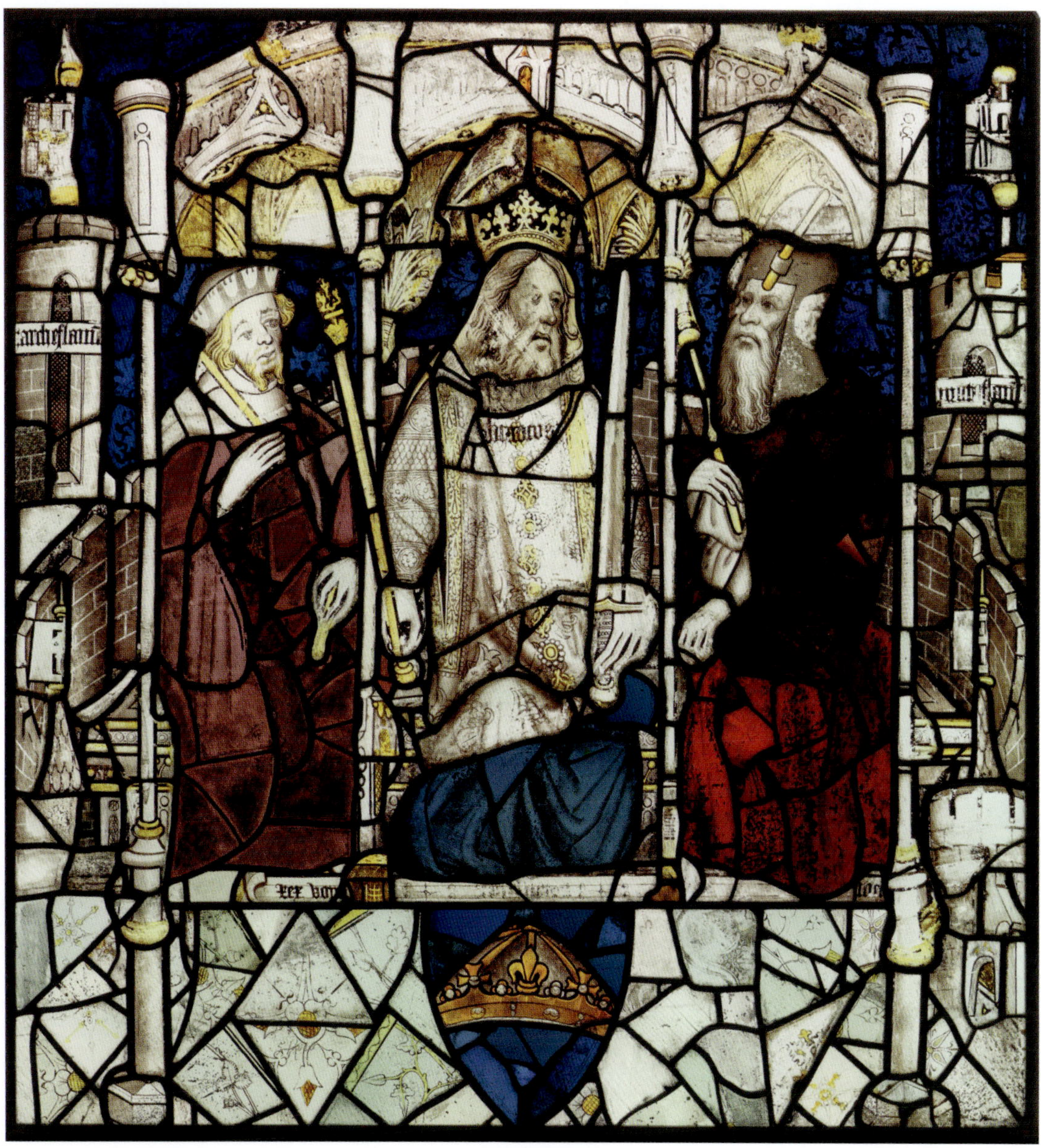

1a The Archeflamen, King Ebrauk and the Flamen, encircled by the walls of York
In the time of King David, King Ebrauk founded York, with its first Temple and its city walls. The story of the mythical King Ebrauk was made popular by Geoffrey of Monmouth's 12th-century *History of the Kings of Britain*. The arms of the city of York and Bishop Walter Skirlaw decorate pennants flying from the walls.

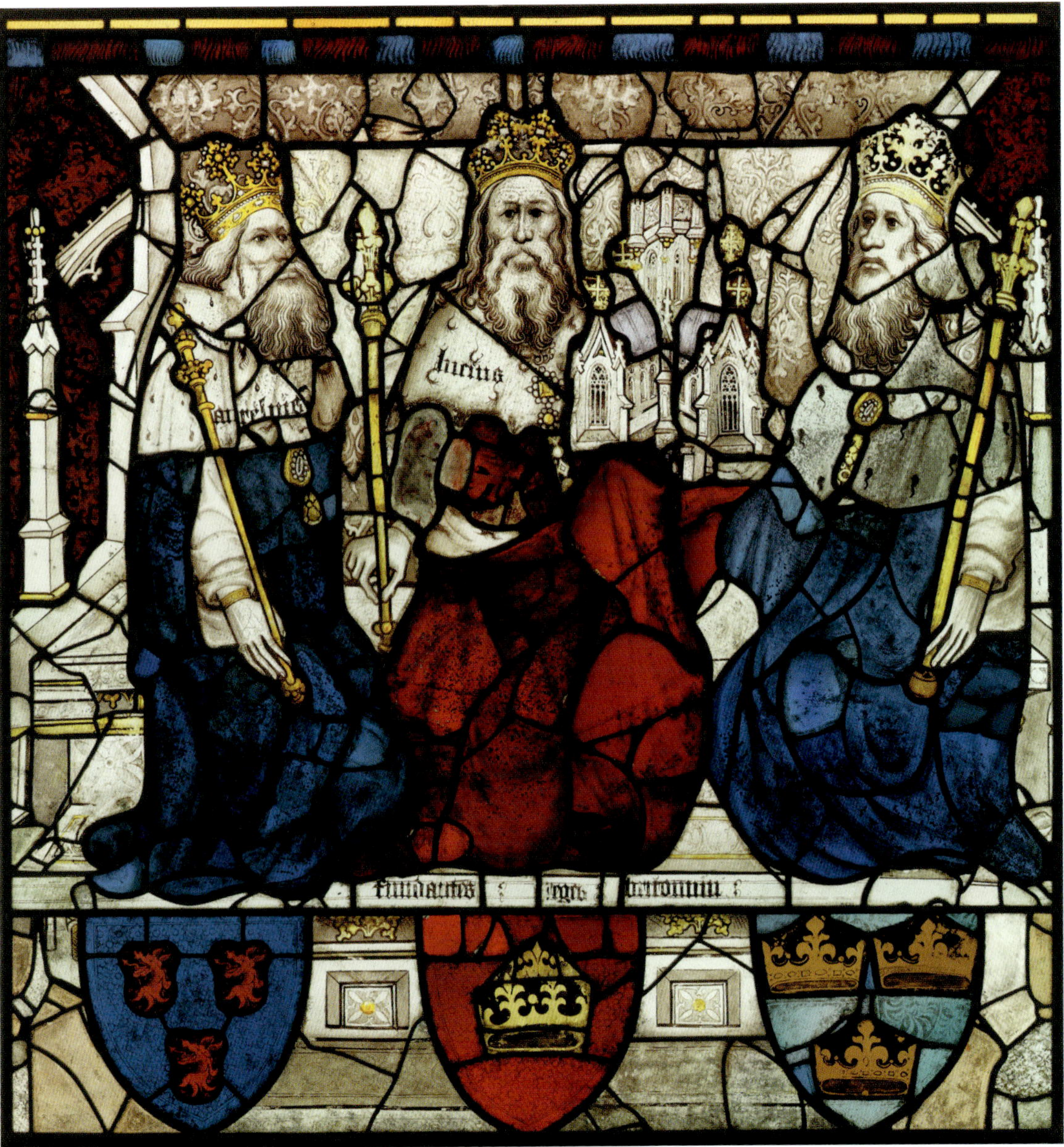

1b King Aurelius Ambrosius, King Lucius and ?King Arthur

In the second century, the British King Lucius wrote to Pope Eleutherius (1f) asking to be made a Christian. He converted the temple into the first Christian church. Bede popularised this story in his *Ecclesiastical History of the English People*. Aurelius Ambrosius, brother of Uther Pendragon, was famed as the second founder of York. King Arthur was in remembered in York as the protector of the Church.

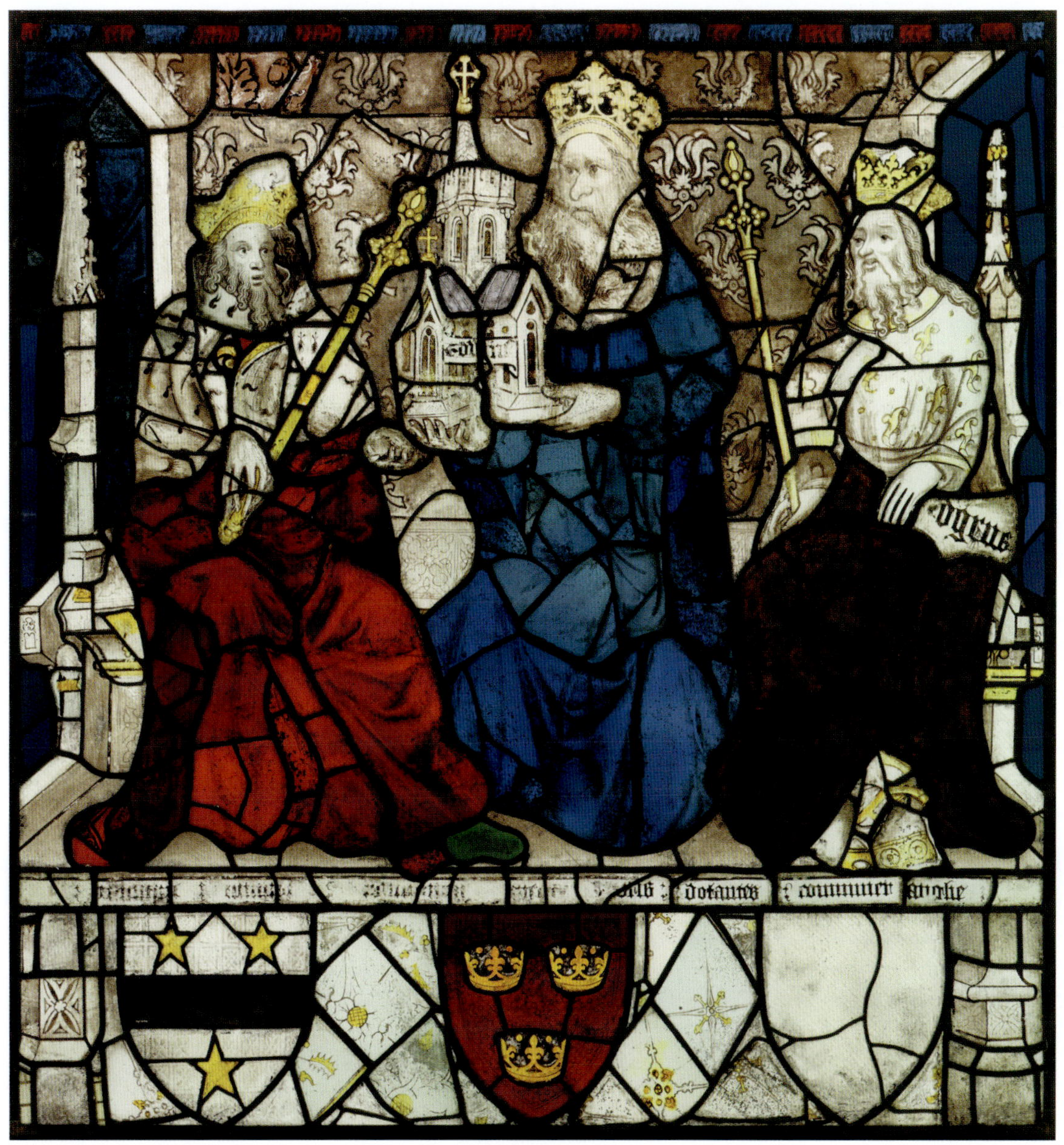

1c ?King Oswald (d.642), King Edwin (616–633) and ?King Edgar (d.975)
In 627 the Anglo-Saxon King Edwin was baptised by St Wilfrid and soon thereafter began to build a stone church. King Oswald, King of Northumbria, completed the church started by Edwin, and was martyred at the hands of the pagan Penda. The third king has long been identified as Edgar, but this identification remains tentative.

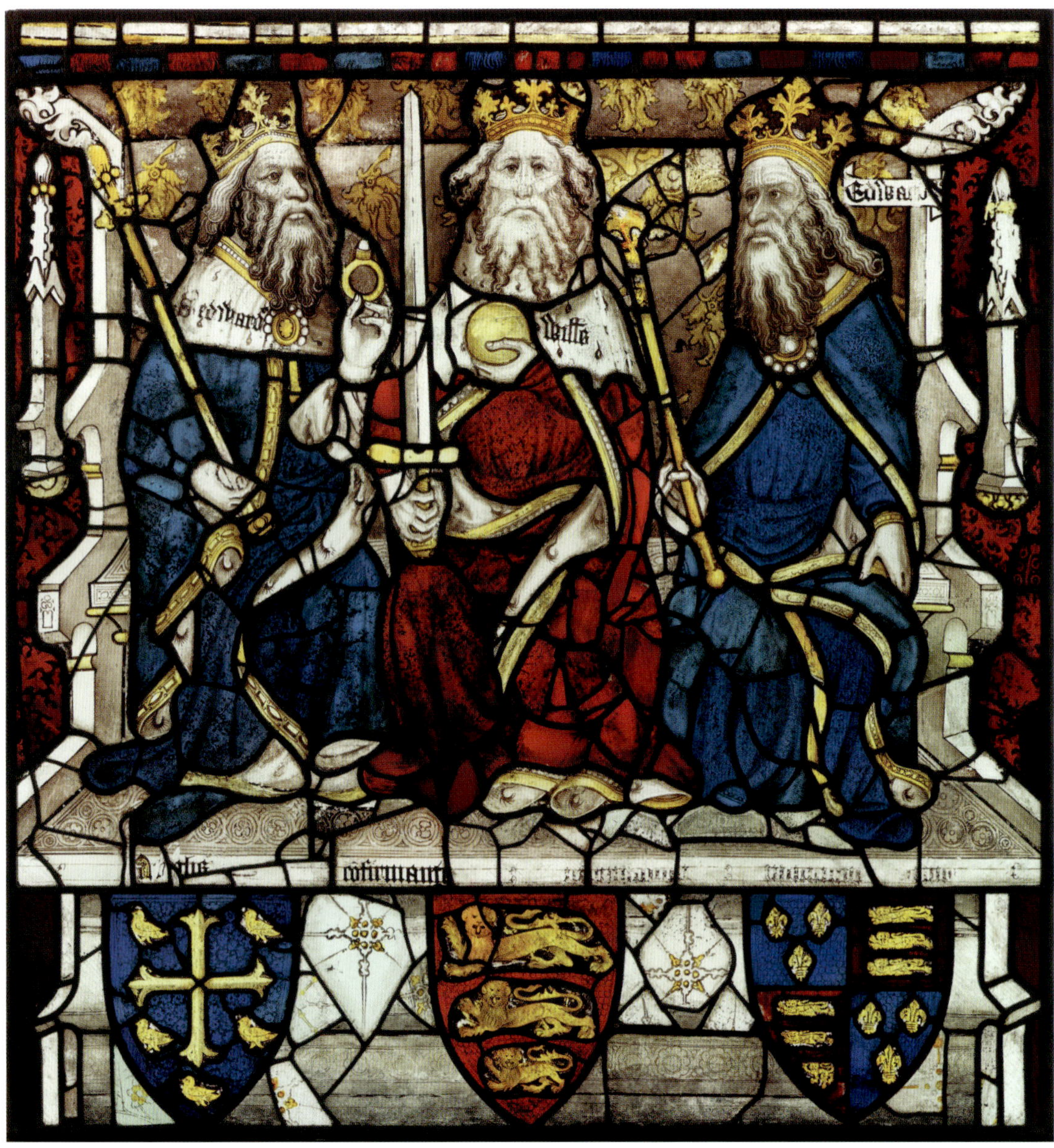

1d King Edward the Confessor (1044–1066), King William I ('The Conqueror', 1066–1087) and King Edward III (1327–1377)
The kings represent the three great royal dynasties of England, up to the beginning of the period of the choir's reconstruction. The recent deposition and death of Richard II and the rebellion of Archbishop Richard Scrope had created a period of political sensitivity which is neatly side-stepped here by the inclusion of Thorseby's great patron Edward III, grandfather of both Plantagenet King Richard II and his Lancastrian successor, Henry IV. It is actually King Henry's arms that sit beneath Edward's feet.

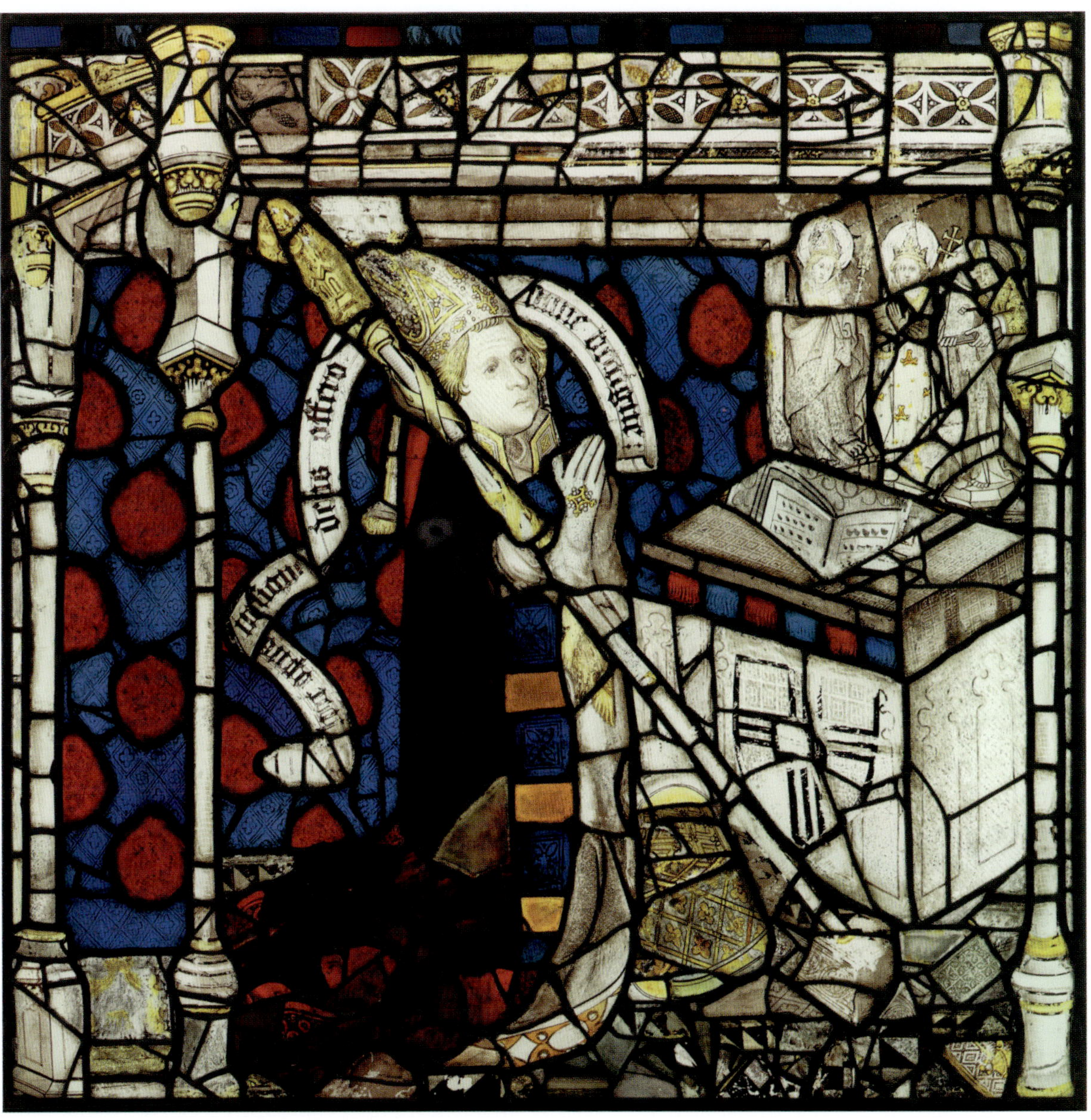

1e Bishop Walter Skirlaw (d.1406)

Bishop Skirlaw is identified by his distinctive coat of arms. He is fully vested and kneels before an altar decorated with a frontal. The reredos is now fragmentary.

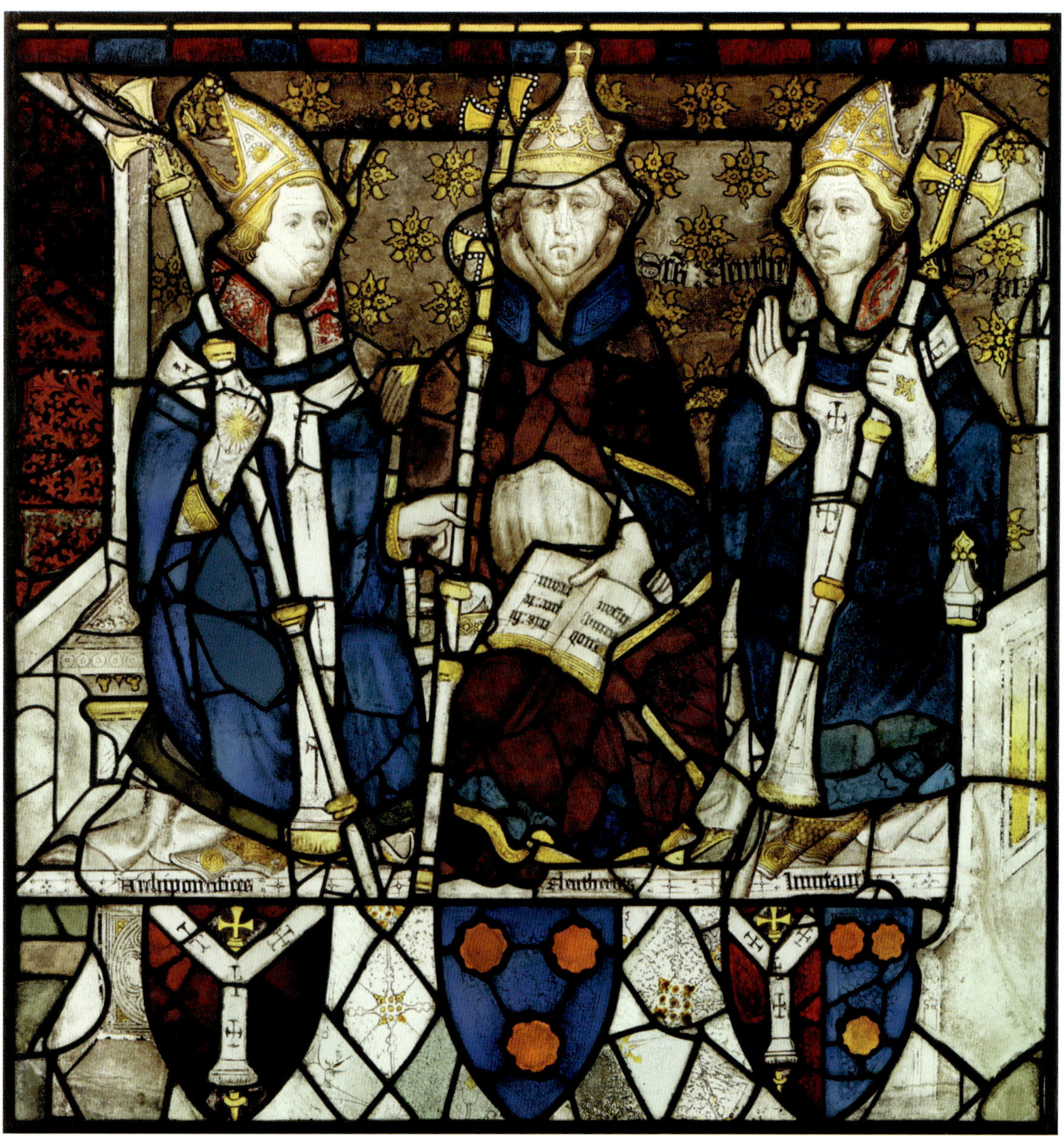

1f ?St Sampson, Pope Eleutherius (*c*.174–189) and St Pirannus

Pope Eleutherius was remembered in York for his support of King Lucius (panel 1b). He is probably accompanied by St Sampson (who would have been archbishop at the time of Aurelius Ambrosius), to whom a parish church in the city is dedicated, and Pirannus, archbishop in the time of King Arthur.

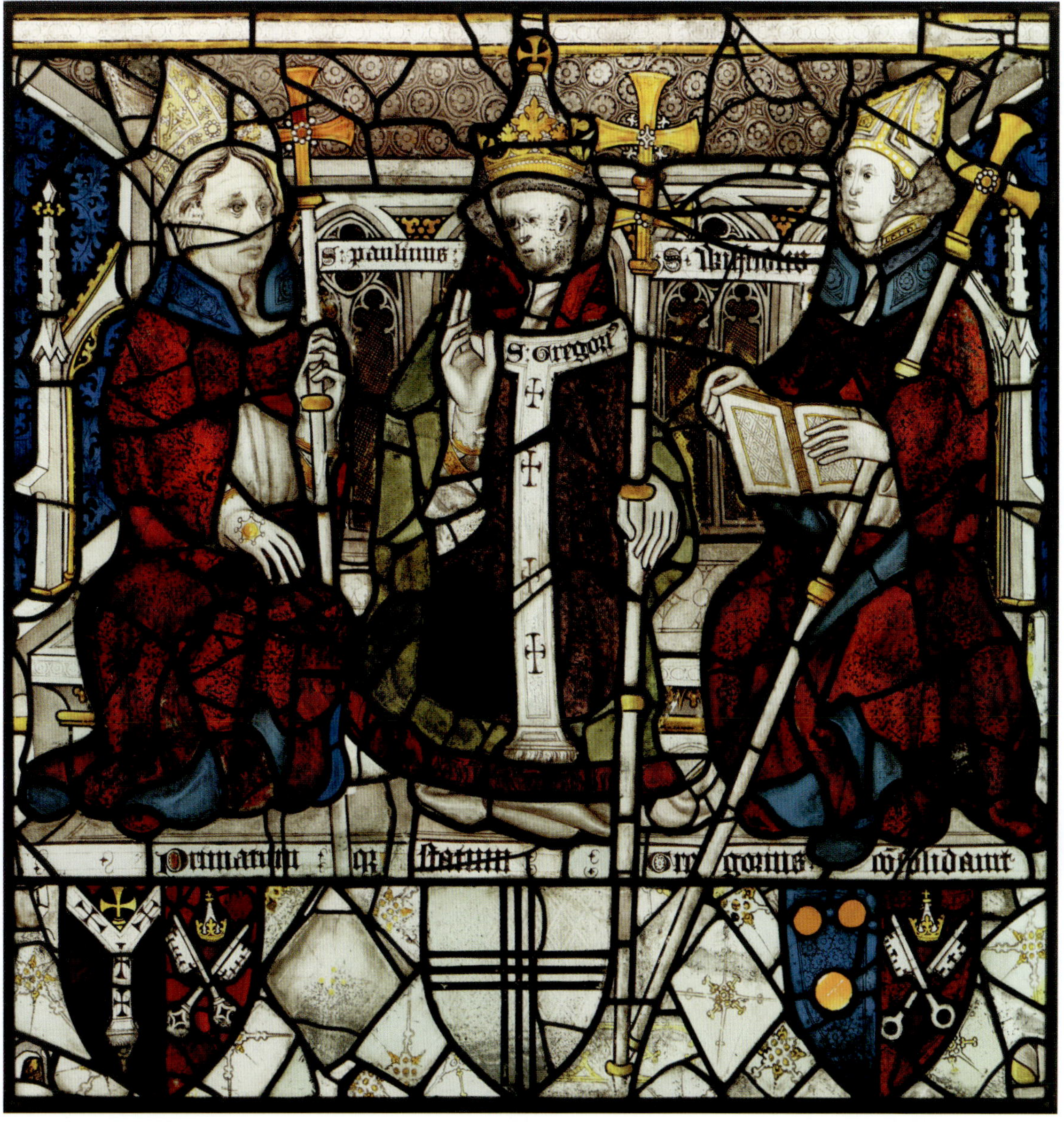

1g St Paulinus (d.644), Pope Gregory (*c*.540–604) and St Wilfrid (*c*.633–709)
Pope Gregory, apostle of the English, was famed for sending St Augustine to evangelise the Anglo-Saxons in 597. This might never have happened but for Pope Gregory's encounter with golden-haired Deiran slaves in the Roman marketplace, as recounted by Bede. Paulinus was sent in a second wave of missionaries in 601, and became the apostle of Northumbria and York's first bishop. He baptised King Edwin (panel 1c) in 627. St Wilfrid, abbot of Ripon and Hexham, and bishop of York, was the powerful advocate of the Roman observance of Easter at the Synod of Whitby in (663/4).

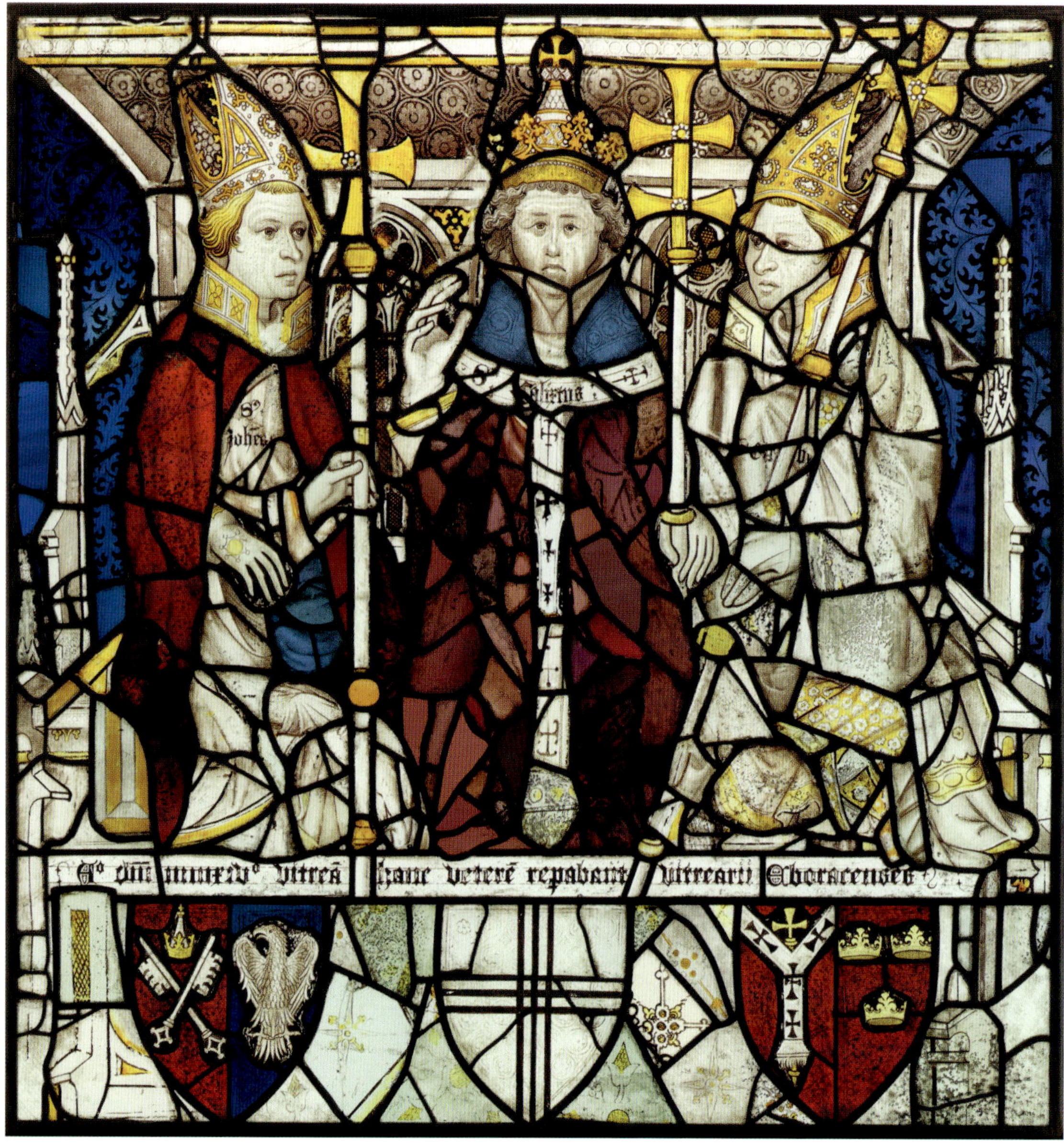

1h St John of Beverley (d.721), Pope Calixtus (1119–1124) and St Egbert (d.729)
The identity of these three figures is not in doubt as all three are labelled. St John of Beverley and St Egbert belong to the story of Christianity in the north during the Anglo-Saxon period. John succeeded Wilfrid as bishop of York and founded the monastery at Beverley. Egbert also occupied the see of York. Calixtus is chronologically the 'odd-man-out' in this panel, but was probably chosen as the Pope who consecrated Archbishop Thurstan in 1119. It was Thurstan who refused to swear an oath of obedience to Canterbury, thereby ending the primacy dispute.

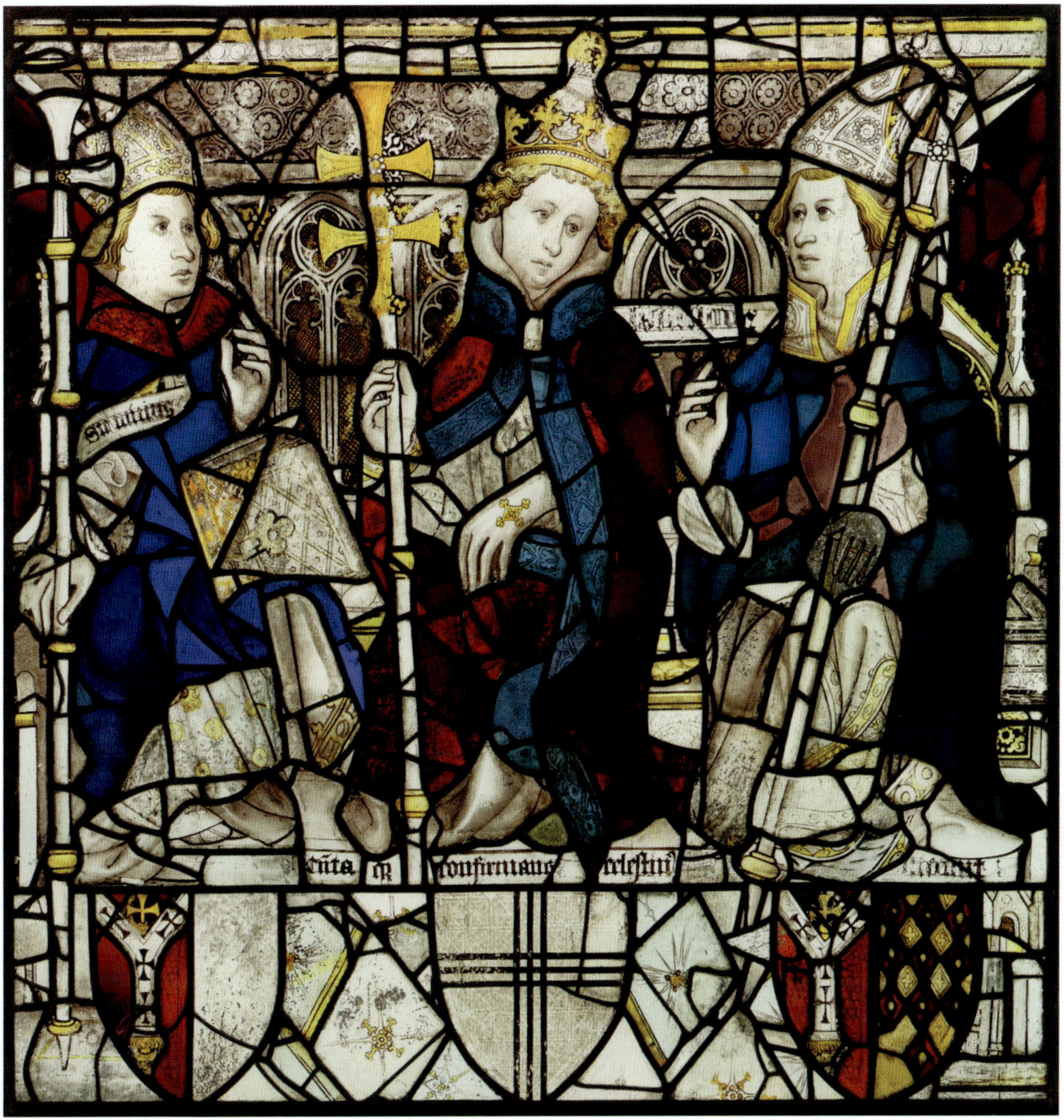

1j Unidentified Archbishop, Pope Celestine III (1191–1198) and St William (d.1154)
At the time the Great East Window was planned, St William of York, canonised in 1227, was the only one of
York's saintly archbishops to be enshrined in the Minster. He is accompanied by the Pope who reaffirmed York's
authority over the see of Durham in the late 12th century. One candidate for the left-hand episcopal figure could
be Thomas of Bayeux (d.1100), who rebuilt the Minster after a fire in 1069. Alternatively, it may be the saintly
Archbishop Thurstan (d.1140), who successfully resisted Canterbury's claim to primacy over York.

Further Reading

Acknowledgements

Benson, George, *The Ancient Painted Glass Windows in the Minster and Churches of the City of York*, Leeds: Yorkshire Philosophical Society, 1914.

Brandi, Cesare, *Theory of Restoration,* translated by Cecilia Brockwell, Rome: Istituto centrale per il restauro and Florence: Nardini, 2005.

Brown, Sarah, *'Our Magnificent Fabrick': An Architectural History of York Minster c.1220–1500,* Swindon: English Heritage, 2003.

Brown, Sarah, *Apocalypse: The Great East Window of York Minster,* London: Third Millennium Publishing, 2014.

Brown, Sarah, *Stained Glass at York Minster*, London: Scala, 2017.

Drake, Francis, *Eboracum, or The History and Antiquities of the City of York*, London, 1736.

French, Thomas, *York Minster: The Great East Window*, Corpus Vitrearum Medii Aevi (Great Britain), Summary Catalogue 2, Oxford: Oxford University Press, 1995.

French, Thomas, *York Minster: The St William Window*, Corpus Vitrearum Medii Aevi (Great Britain), Summary Catalogue 5, Oxford: Oxford University Press, 1999.

Gent, Thomas, *The Ancient and Modern History of the Famous City of York*, York, 1730.

Gent, Thomas, *The Most Delectable, Scriptural and Pious History of the Famous and Magnificent Great Eastern Window (According to Beautiful Portraiture) in St Peter's Cathedral, York*, York, 1762.

Harrison, Frederick, *The Painted Glass of York: An Account of the Medieval Stained Glass in the Minster and the Parish Churches*, London: Methuen, 1927.

Harrison, Stuart, and Norton, Christopher, *York Minster: An Illustrated Architectural History 627–c.1500,* York: Dean and Chapter of York, 2015.

Knowles, J. A., *Essays in the York School of Glass-Painting*, London: SPCK, 1936.

Milner-White, Eric, 'The Restoration of the East Window of York Minster', *Antiquaries Journal*, 30 (1950), 180–4.

Norton, Christopher, 'Richard II and York Minster', in Sarah Rees Jones (ed.) *The Government of Medieval York*, Borthwick Studies in History 3, York, 1997, 56–87.

Norton, Christopher, 'Sacred Space and Sacred History: The Glazing of the Eastern Arm of York Minster', in R. Becksmann (ed.), *Glasmalerei im Kontext- Bildprogramme und Raum Funktionen*, Nuremberg: Germanisches Nationalmuseum, 2005, 167–81.

Norton, Christopher, *St William of York*, Woodbridge: Boydell and Brewer, 2006.

Norton, Christopher, 'Richard Scrope and York Minster', in P. J. P. Goldberg (ed.), *Richard Scrope: Archbishop, Rebel, Martyr*, Donnington: Shaun Tyas, 2007, 138–213.

O'Connor, David, and Haselock, Jeremy, 'The Stained and Painted Glass', in G. E. Aylmer and R. Cant (eds.), *A History of York Minster*, Oxford: Oxford University Press, 1977, 341–64.

Online Resources

Corpus Vitrearum, *Guidelines for the Conservation and Restoration of Stained Glass*, 2nd edn, Nuremberg, 2004 http://www.cvma.ac.uk/conserv/guidelines.html.

ICOMOS, *Venice Charter*, 1964, http://www.icomos.org/en/charters-and-texts.

My greatest thanks are, as always, to my colleagues at the York Glaziers Trust, with whom I have shared the adventure of the Great East window. A particular 'thank you' to Nick Teed, Janet Parkin, Rachel Lavan and Anna Milsom, who have been involved from start to finish! Nick and Anna took all the photographs of the window used to illustrate this book and Janet undertook preparation of new art work. Working with the members of the East Window Advisory Group, Andrew Arrol, Professor Tim Ayers, Professor Richard Marks, Revd Peter Moger, Professor Christopher Norton, Dr Ivo Rauch and Dr Richard Shephard, has been a pleasure and a privilege. Laura Tempest provided research support and recorded all our deliberations and together with Nancy Georgi devised the project documentation on which future researchers will rely. Dr Joseph Spooner and Professor Nigel Morgan undertook essential preliminary research on which we could build. For practical help of every kind, and much good fellowship besides, we thank the staff of the stone yard, led by Rebecca Thompson and Alex McCallion.

The constant support of the Chapter of York and the Dean, first the Very Revd Keith Jones and more recently the Very Revd Vivienne Faull, has been crucial to our success, as has the support of the York Minster Fund, first under the direction of the Hon. Michael Benson and latterly under Neil Sanderson. Both institutions have been committed throughout to public engagement and publication of the window. For help with the latter endeavour, we thank the team at Third Millennium: Dr Joel Burden for his enthusiastic advocacy of the project, to Dr Pamela Hartshorne for her editorial guidance and to Caroline Clark and Eleanor Colussi for their patience and hard work in design and production.

Index

Subscribers

Chris Adams and Hilary Moxon
Andrew Allen
Bryan Amery
John Anderson
Mark and Clare Armour
Alan F. Bacon
Dr and Mrs A. B. Bailey
Anthony Bailey
Thomas Baldwin
Gladys Barker
Olive M. Bastow
Judith Beadle
Julian Bedford
Claire Bellis
Angela and Nicholas Bergström-Allen
Johan Bergström-Allen
Susan Waddington Binns
Richard Bossons and Rita Dawe
David and Madeline Bower
Doug Bozeman
Mary Bradshaw
John Brook
June Brooks
Elizabeth D. Brown
Professor F. M. Burdekin and Mrs J.
    Burdekin
Reverend Peter Burgess
Richard Burton
Alexander and Heidi Carberry
Ruth M. Carty
Ann Chapman
Marcus Chapman
Shirley and Malcolm Chase
David and Margaret Clegg
Richard Cockroft
Charles and Antonia Consett
Robin Cooper
Christopher John Cowles
William Crighton
Michael Crosby
Chris Curry
John David
Beryl Davy
Rosemarie de Boyer
Charles Dent
Keith Dowen
John Dyson
Helen Eaden

Richard Eales
Michael Eastwood
Kristina Echevarria
Jean Fenney
Celeste Flower
Brian Foord
Shelley Fox
Tom Gamble
Claire Gard
Ken Garland BEM
Stephen and Janet Gerrard
Noel and June Golton
Bernard Gribbin
Reverend Christine Haddon-Reece
Janet and John Haley
The Earl of Halifax
Anthony and Margaret Hammersley
Louise Hampson
Mary Harlington
Drs Peter and Elinor Harrison
Jane Hatcher
Jenifer Hawkins
Charles Hebditch
Paul Hermon
Margot Holbert
Pippa Hudson
Clare Isobel Hughes
Peter Hughes
Angus Hunter Smart
Dr Linda L. Husband
Ranall Ingalls
Elizabeth Ingram
Paula Johnson
Phyllis and Philip Johnson
John Jones
Keith Jones
Dr and Mrs Frank Kirk
Susan Lathrop Knoll
Paul Knox
Ronald Knox
Eric Lea
Chris Legard
Fr. Antony Lester, O.Carm.
Professor Roger Lewis
StClair and Françoise Logan
Fiona and Graham Long
Stephanie Luxton
Jessica L. Malay

Cai Mallett
Richard Marriott
Pamela Maryfield
Susan Mason
Dr Audrey Matheson
Sue Maxwell
Richard McDowell
Michael McNeill
Paul Medforth
Robert Middleton
David Miers
Mr and Mrs Keith Miller
Cynthia Mills
Natasha Mitchell
J. and K. Moir-Shepherd
Helena Moore
Tony and Sue Mosley
Cathy Mosscrop
John Murphy
Jill Nelson
Steve Nesom
Marie A. Newby
Anne Norton
Michael O'Donnell
Hamish Ogston
Peter Russell Owen
Michael Oxley
Susan Palmer
Roger Potts
Antony and Gillian Pritchett
Michael Pulman
Michael Rawnsley
Andrew Redhead
Petronella Ree
Adele Reynolds
Henry Robertson
David Robins
Lynda Rollason
Martin Rugg
Neil and Elizabeth Sanderson
David Scott
Colin Sherwood
Ian Simpson
Susan Smallpage
Martin W. Smith
Freda Snelson
Margot Steurbaut
Freda Stevens

Peter Stretton
Diana Terry
Rebecca and Shaun Thompson
Linda Tooley
John Townend
Geoffrey Wainwright
Lyndon Walters
Guy Stephen Ward
Angela Wheatcroft
Edward White
David Willett
Patricia Williams
Barbara Wills
Roger Willson
Roger Wood
Roger Wools
Revd Gwynne Wright
Peter and Janet Yates
York Civic Trust

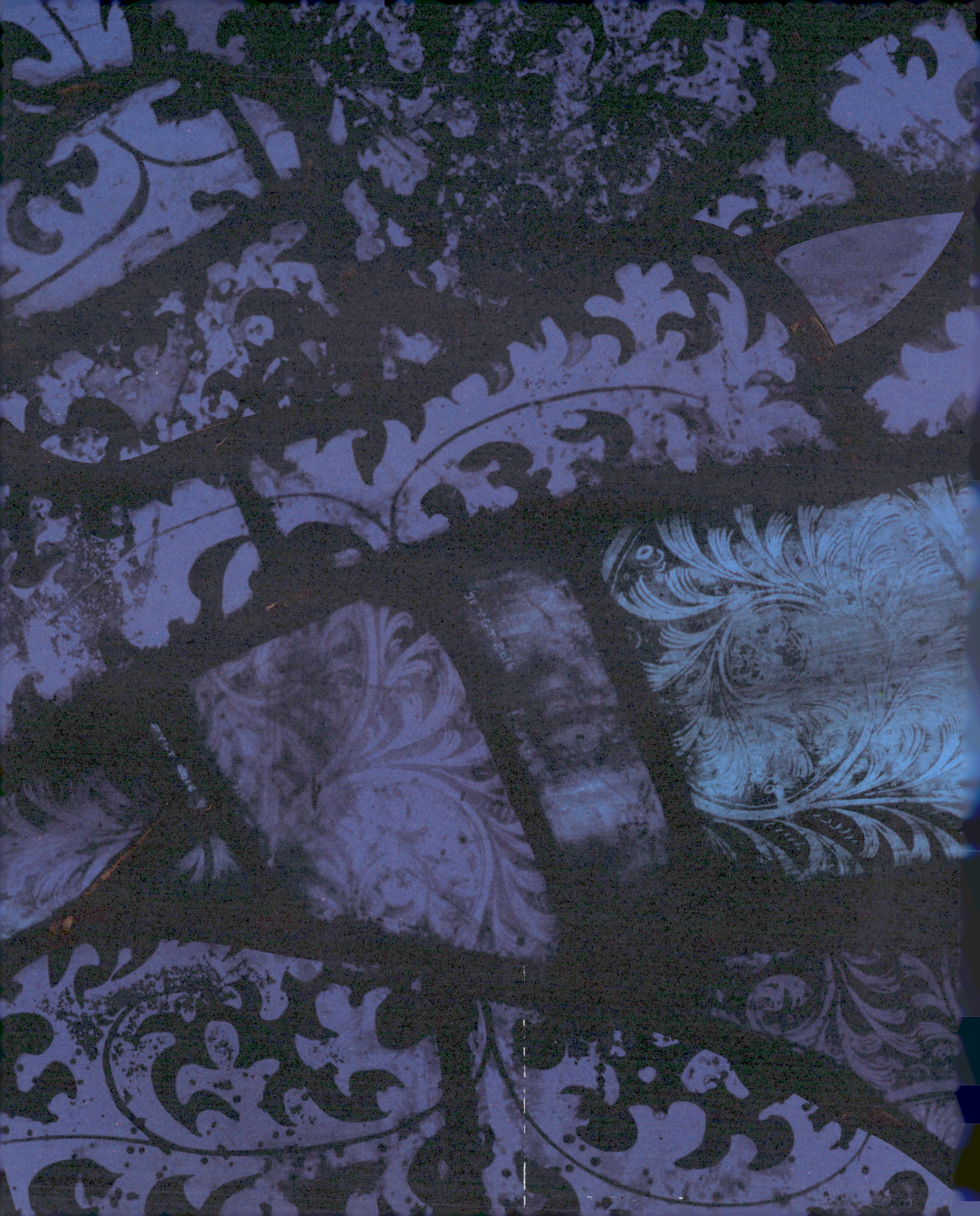